Acclaim for Suketu Mehta's

MAXIMUM CITY

An *Economist, Seattle Times,*
and *San Jose Mercury-News* Best Book of the Year

"Dazzling and absorbing. . . . Because of his zest to put every byway of the Bombay underworld on the page, his high-energy evoking of characters high and low, and the way his gaze settles on the newcomers trying to make it in the great city, Mehta's eye on Bombay reminds me of no one's so much as Balzac's on Paris."
—*Harper's*

"Sprawling, epic, vibrant—and more than a little scary—*Maximum City* does justice to its monumental subject, the city of Bombay."
—*People*

"Mehta is an urban ethnographer with an acute sensitivity to the peculiarities of his city. . . . This fidelity to his interlocutors, and to their detail and circumstance, as much as the intelligence and brightness of Mehta's own prose, makes *Maximum City* an extraordinary debut—a debut that will rival Arundhati Roy's in fiction."
—*The Nation*

"Stunning."
—*Time*

"Quite extraordinary—Mehta writes about Bombay with an unsparing ferocity born of his love, which I share, for the old pre-Mumbai city which has now been almost destroyed by corruption, gangsterism, and neo-fascist politics, its spirit surviving in tiny moments and images which he seizes upon as proof of the survival of hope. The quality of his investigative reportage, the skill with which he persuades hoodlums and murderers to open up to him, is quite amazing. It's the best book yet written about that great, ruined metropolis, my city as well as his, and it deserves to be very widely read."
—Salman Rushdie, author of *Midnight's Children* and *The Moor's Last Sigh*

"Remarkable. . . . *Maximum City* is at once paean and lament to the megalopolis that is . . . Bombay."
—*The Village Voice*

Suketu Mehta

MAXIMUM CITY

Suketu Mehta is a fiction writer and journalist based in New York. He has won the Whiting Writers Award, the O. Henry Prize, and a New York Foundation for the Arts Fellowship for his fiction. Mehta's other work has been published in *The New York Times Magazine*, *Granta*, *Harper's*, *Time*, *Condé Nast Traveler*, and *The Village Voice*, and has been featured on National Public Radio's *All Things Considered*. Mehta also cowrote *Mission Kashmir*, a Bollywood movie.

MAXIMUM CITY

MAXIMUM CITY

Bombay Lost and Found

SUKETU MEHTA

VINTAGE BOOKS

A Division of Random House, Inc.

New York

FIRST VINTAGE DEPARTURES EDITION, SEPTEMBER 2005

The Library of Congress has cataloged the Knopf edition as follows:
Mehta, Suketu.
Maximum city: Bombay lost and found / Suketu Mehta—1st ed.
p. cm.
1. Bombay (India)—Description and travel. I. Title.
DS486.B7M42 2004
954'.79205—dc22
2004048969

Vintage ISBN: 0-375-70340-3

Author photograph © Jerry Bauer
Book design by Virginia Tan
Maps by Design Temple

www.vintagebooks.com

Printed in the United States of America
10 9 8 7 6 5 4 3 2 1

For my grandparents:
Shantilal Ratanlal Mehta & Sulochanaben Shantilal Mehta
Jayantilal Manilal Parikh & Kantaben Jayantilal Parikh

As for Kabir, I went to him through the Nirgunia singers of Malwa whom I heard while lying ill in Dewas. I learnt about their capacity to create vacuum which is so crucial for a Nirgunia bhajan. They use notes in a distinctly hermit-like manner so that notes are thrown at you but you don't get hurt. They sing in loneliness. In singing Kabir my attempt is to create this essential loneliness and yet also a persisting sense of community. Kabir says it himself beautifully: I am severally alone. The total identification of the interior and the exterior is Kabir's most challenging aspect.

—KUMAR GANDHARVA

We are individually multiple.　　　　　　—KABIR MOHANTY

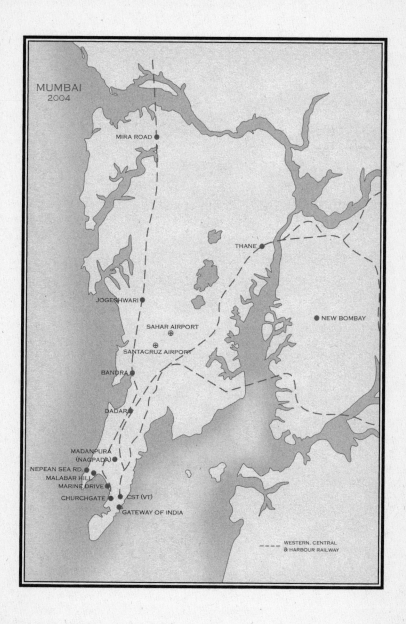

MUMBAI
2004

MIRA ROAD

THANE

JOGESHWARI

NEW BOMBAY

SAHAR AIRPORT

SANTACRUZ AIRPORT

BANDRA

DADAR

MADANPURA
(NAGPADA)
NEPEAN SEA RD.
MALABAR HILL
MARINE DRIVE
CHURCHGATE   CST (VT)
GATEWAY OF INDIA

WESTERN, CENTRAL
& HARBOUR RAILWAY

CONTENTS

PART I * POWER

Personal Geography

THERE WILL SOON BE more people living in the city of Bombay than on the continent of Australia. URBS PRIMA IN INDIS reads the plaque outside the Gateway of India. It is also the Urbs Prima in Mundis, at least in one area, the first test of the vitality of a city: the number of people living in it. With 14 million people, Bombay is the biggest city on the planet of a race of city dwellers. Bombay is the future of urban civilization on the planet. God help us.

I left Bombay in 1977 and came back twenty-one years later, when it had grown up to become Mumbai. Twenty-one years: enough time for a human being to be born, get an education, be eligible to drink, get married, drive, vote, go to war, and kill a man. In all that time, I hadn't lost my accent. I speak like a Bombay boy; it is how I am identified in Kanpur and Kansas. "Where're you from?" Searching for an answer—in Paris, in London, in Manhattan—I always fall back on "Bombay." Somewhere, buried beneath the wreck of its current condition—one of urban catastrophe—is the city that has a tight claim on my heart, a beautiful city by the sea, an island-state of hope in a very old country. I went back to look for that city with a simple question: Can you go home again? In the looking, I found the cities within me.

I AM A CITY BOY. I was born in a city in extremis, Calcutta. Then I moved to Bombay and lived there nine years. Then to New York, eight years in Jackson Heights. A year, on and off, in Paris. Five years in the East

Village. Scattered over time, another year or so in London. The only exceptions were three years in Iowa City, not a city at all, and a couple more in New Brunswick, New Jersey, college towns that prepared me for a return to the city. My two sons were born in a great city, New York. I live in cities by choice, and I'm pretty sure I will die in a city. I don't know what to do in the country, though I like it well enough on weekends.

I come from a family of mercantile wanderers. My paternal grandfather left rural Gujarat for Calcutta in the salad days of the century, to join his brother in the jewelry business. When my grandfather's brother first ventured into international territory, to Japan, in the 1930s, he had to come back and bow in apology before the caste elders, turban in his hands. But his nephews—my father and my uncle—kept moving, first to Bombay and then across the black water to Antwerp and New York, to add to what was given to them. My maternal grandfather left Gujarat for Kenya as a young man, and he now lives in London. My mother was born in Nairobi, went to college in Bombay, and now lives in New York. In my family, picking up and going to another country to live was never a matter for intense deliberation. You went where your business took you.

Once, with my grandfather, I went back to our ancestral house in Maudha, which used to be a village in Gujarat but is now a town. Sitting in the courtyard of the old house with its massive timbers, my grandfather began introducing us to the new owners, a family of Sarafs, Gujarati moneylenders, for whom Maudha was the big city. "And this is my son-in-law, who lives in Nigeria."

"Nigeria," said the Saraf, nodding.

"And this is my grandson, who is from New York."

"New York," the Saraf repeated, still nodding.

"And this is my granddaughter-in-law, who is from London."

"London."

"Now they both live in Paris."

"Paris," the Saraf dutifully recited. If at this point my grandfather had said he lived on the moon, the Saraf would, without batting an eyelid, have kept nodding and repeated, "Moon." Our dispersal was so extreme that it bordered on the farcical. But here we were, visiting the house where my grandfather grew up, still together as a family. Family was the elastic that pulled us back together, no matter how far we wandered.

* * *

IT WAS THE MUQABLA, the commercial competition, that had forced my father to leave Calcutta. It was the way jewels were bought and sold in my grandfather's business. A group of sellers would assemble at the buyer's office with the broker at an appointed time. Then the negotiations would begin. The price was not said aloud but was indicated by the number of fingers held up under a loose corner of the seller's dhoti, which would be grasped by the buyer. Part of the muqabla was loud abuse of the buyer. "Have you gone mad? Do you expect me to sell at these prices?" In a display of extreme frustration, the seller would storm out of the office, shouting loudly all the time. But he would be careful to forget his umbrella. Ten minutes later he would be back, to pick up the umbrella. By this time the buyer might have reconsidered and they might come to a conclusion, at which point the broker would say, "Then shake hands!" and there would be smiles all around. It was because of this little piece of theater that my father decided to leave the jewelry business in Calcutta. He could not stand the shouting and the abuse; he was an educated man.

My father's brother had gone to Bombay in 1966, against the will of my grandfather, who saw no reason why he should leave. But my uncle was a young man, and the twilight in Calcutta had begun. In Bombay, he went into the diamond business. Three years later, my parents were passing through Bombay, after my little sister was born in Ahmadabad. My uncle, recently married, suggested to his brother, "Why don't you stay?" So we did, four adults and two children, one a newborn, in a one-room flat, with guests always coming and going. We lived as a "joint family," sharing the flat and the expenses, and the space expanded to fit us. How can 14 million people fit onto one island? As we did in that apartment off Teen Batti.

My father and my uncle found their niche in the diamond business. We moved to a two-bedroom flat above a palace by the sea, Dariya Mahal. The palace belonged to the Maharao of Kutch. A family of Marwari industrialists bought the palace and its grounds; they chopped down the trees on the land, cleared the antiques out of the palace, and put in schoolchildren. Around the palace they built a complex of three buildings: Dariya Mahal 1 and 2, twenty-story buildings that look like open ledgers, and Dariya Mahal 3, where I grew up, the squat, stolid, twelve-story stepchild.

My uncle and my father made regular business trips to Antwerp and America. When my father asked what he could bring back from America for me, I asked him for a scratch-and-sniff T-shirt, which I'd read about in some American magazine. He came back bringing a giant bag of marsh-mallows. I ate as many as I could of the huge white cottony things, and tried to make sense of the texture, before my aunt appropriated them. After one of those trips, according to my uncle, my father had an epiphany while shaving, as often happens when you're facing yourself in a mirror without actively looking. He decided to move to America. Not for its freedom or its way of life; he moved there to make more money.

Each person's life is dominated by a central event, which shapes and distorts everything that comes after it and, in retrospect, everything that came before. For me, it was going to live in America at the age of fourteen. It's a difficult age at which to change countries. You haven't quite finished growing up where you were and you're never well in your skin in the one you're moving to. I had absolutely no idea about the country America; I had never been there. I was certainly not of a later generation of my cousins, such as Sameer, who at the age of sixteen stepped into JFK Airport fresh off the plane from Bombay wearing a Mets baseball cap and with half an American accent already in place. I traveled, in twenty-four hours, between childhood and adulthood, between innocence and knowl-edge, between predestination and chaos. Everything that has happened since, every minute and monstrous act—the way I use a fork, the way I make love, my choice of a profession and a wife—has been shaped by that central event, that fulcrum of time.

THERE WAS A STACK of *Reader's Digest*s in the back room of my grand-father's Calcutta house, dark, hot, womblike. There, in my summers, I had read true-life adventures, spy stories of the dastardly Communists, and jokes the whole family could enjoy about the antics of children and service-men. It was my introduction to America. Imagine my surprise when I got there. I was lucky, though I didn't know it then, that of all the possible cities my father could have moved us to, he chose New York. "It's just like Bombay." Thus is New York explained to people in India.

In the first year after I got to America, I sent for its previously inacces-sible treasures, the merchandise advertised on the inside covers of the

comic books. I ordered, for my friends in Bombay, the joy buzzer, the floating ghost, the hovercraft, and X-ray goggles. A brown box came in the
mail. I looked at it for a few moments before opening it; here was what
we had been denied all these years. Then the junk came spilling out. The
floating ghost was a white plastic garbage-bin liner with a stick threaded
through the top; you were supposed to hang it up and wave it around to
scare people. The X-ray goggles were a pair of plastic glasses, like the 3-D
glasses given out in science-fiction theaters, with a rough drawing of a
skeleton on both lenses. The hovercraft was a sort of red fan, attached to a
motor; when you turned it on, it really did rise over a flat surface. The joy
buzzer was a small steel device that could be worn on the inside of the palm
like a ring; you wound it up and when you shook the victim's hand a knob
was pressed and the device vibrated sharply. I looked at the mess spread out
on the floor. I had been had before in Bombay; I knew the feeling well.
Nonetheless, I sent the package to my Bombay friends, with a letter suggesting possible uses for the gags; the ghost, for instance, could be lowered
on a string to flap outside the balconies of the lower floors, possibly scaring
small children in the dark.

I knew my gifts would be welcome. Whatever their quality, they were
"imported" and therefore to be treasured. In our house in Bombay, there
used to be a showcase in the living room. It displayed imported objects
from Europe and America, the spoils of my uncle's business trips: Match-
box cars, miniature bottles of spirits, a cylinder of long matches from London shaped like a Beefeater with a furry black hat as the top, a little model
of the Eiffel Tower. There were toys, also, for the children—a battery-
powered *Apollo 11* rocket, a police cruiser with a blue revolving light, a doll
that could drink and wet her diaper—which were almost never taken out
for us. The kids in the building would assemble around the showcase and
look up at the toys inside—toys we weren't allowed to touch for fear of
breaking them.

In America, too, we had a showcase in our house. In it were kept souvenirs from India: a pair of grandparent dolls, Dada dressed in a dhoti,
Dadi in a cotton sari; a marble statue of Ganesh; a wooden mask of Hanuman; a little model of the Taj Mahal with a light that glowed from within; a
bharata natyam dancer whose head moved sideways on her neck; and a
bronze clock shaped like the official map of India with all of Kashmir
reclaimed from the Pakistanis and the Chinese. When the new baby was

born he wasn't allowed to open the showcase and play with these objects. They were too fragile; he would hurt himself. He spent his time splayed against the glass door of the showcase, staring at his heritage, like a wasp at a window.

WHEN I MOVED to New York, I missed Bombay like an organ of my body. I thought that when I left Bombay I had escaped from the worst school in the world. I was wrong. The all-boys Catholic school I went to in Queens was worse. It was in a working-class white enclave that was steadily being encroached upon by immigrants from darker countries. I was one of the first minorities to enroll, a representative of all they were trying to hold out against. Soon after I got there, a boy with curly red hair and freckles came up to my lunch table and announced, "Lincoln should never have freed the slaves." The teachers called me a pagan. My school yearbook photo shows me looking at the camera with the caption, "It's so strong I can even skip a day," referring to an advertising slogan for a brand of antiperspirant. This was how the school saw me: as a stinking heathen, emitting the foul odors of my native cooking. On the day I graduated, I walked outside the barbed-wire-topped gates, put my lips to the pavement, and kissed the ground in gratitude.

In Jackson Heights we reapproximated Bombay, my best friend Ashish and I. Ashish had also been moved from Bombay to Queens, at the age of fifteen. The happiest afternoons of that time were when we went to see Hindi movies at the Eagle Theater. With one letter changed, it had formerly been the Earle Theater, a porn house. The same screen that had been filled with monstrous penises pullulating in mutant vaginas was now displaying mythologicals of the blue-skinned god Krishna; in these films not a breast, not even a kiss was shown. Maybe the theater was being purified. But I still scanned the seats carefully before sitting down on them.

In the movies I would sometimes catch a glimpse of my building, Dariya Mahal. We spoke in Bambaiyya Hindi, Ashish and I, when we wanted to talk about other people in the subway or curse our teachers in front of them. It became a language of sabotage. It was a good language to joke in; it was a boys' language. We drank and swore in Hindi. We would walk around the streets of Jackson Heights, Ashish, his neighbor Mitthu, and I, singing Hindi movie songs from the seventies, when we had been taken away; traveling back on music, the cheapest airline. On spring nights the newly softened air carried news from home, from the past, which in Gujarati is known as "bhoot-kal"—the ghost time. A police car drew up one of those nights. Cops got out. "What're you fellas doin'?" "Nothing." Three young Gujarati men on the streets, singing suspiciously. "Don't you know you can be arrested for loitering?" It was a jailable offense: loitering in the ghost time. We moved on, waited for the cop car to go, then resumed our singing, softening the harsh Jackson Heights landscape, making it familiar, transforming it into Jaikisan Heights.

That was the true period of my exile, when I was restrained by forces greater than myself from going back. It was different from nostalgia, which is a simple desire to evade the linearity of time. I made, in the back of my school notebook, a calendar beginning early in the spring. I had been told by my father, or so I thought, that he would send me to Bombay in the summer of my junior year. Each day I crossed off the previous one and counted the remaining days like a jail sentence. I was happy toward evening because it was one less day in America and one more toward my liberation. Then, in the last week before the summer holidays, my father told me he couldn't send me to India. He'd send me the next year, after I graduated. I was lost.

I existed in New York, but I lived in India, taking little memory trains. The fields at dusk. Birds flying home overhead, your car stopping by the side of the road and you getting out. Noticing minute things again: the complexity of the gnarled peepal by the roadside, the ants making their way around it. You go to take a leak in the bushes and lift your head and see. It is warm and close and humid; you are protected once again. There are no people to be seen, not in the fields, not around the one hut you can see in the distance. Dinner is waiting in the city, at the house of your aunt, but you want to stop right here, walk across the fields by yourself, walk into the peasant's hut, ask for some water, see if you can stay in this village for a few days. A couple of flies have sprung up and are buzzing around your head; you are trying to piss and wave them away at the same time, ruining your shoes. "Bhenchod," you say.

I missed saying "bhenchod" to people who understood it. It does not mean "sister fucker." That is too literal, too crude. It is, rather, punctuation, or emphasis, as innocuous a word as "shit" or "damn." The different countries of India can be identified by the way each pronounces this word—from the Punjabi "bhaanchod" to the thin Bambaiyya "pinchud" to the Gujarati "bhenchow" to the Bhopali elaboration "bhen-ka-lowda." Parsis use it all the time, grandmothers, five-year-olds, casually and without any discernible purpose except as filler: "Here, bhenchod, get me a glass of water." "Arre, bhenchod, I went to the bhenchod bank today." As a boy, I would try consciously not to swear all day on the day of my birthday. I would take vows with the Jain kids: We will not use the B-word or the M-word.

In my first New York winter, wearing a foam jacket my parents had bought in Bombay that actually dispersed my body heat out to the atmosphere instead of preserving it, sucking in the freezing winds during my mile-long walk to school and drawing them to my body, I found I could generate warmth by screaming out this word. Walking into the wind and the snowdrifts, my head down, I would roar, *"Bhenchod! Bheyyyyyn-chod!"* The walk to school led through quiet Queens residential streets, and the good Irish, Italian, and Polish senior citizens who happened to be home in the daytime must have heard this word on very cold days, screamed out loudly by a small brown boy dressed inappropriately for the weather.

WHEN I WAS SEVENTEEN and finally went back to Bombay for a visit, three years after I'd left, the city and my friends in it had grown in wild and strange ways. They all smoked cigarettes, for one, and I did not. They drank heavily, and I did not. Nitin showed me a trick with the quickly emptied bottle of Chivas Regal I'd brought: He rubbed the bottom of it between his hands till the glass was warm and then threw a lit match down it. A pleasing blue flame shot up for an instant. He knew what to do with the bottle when it was full, and he knew what to do when it was empty.

My friends had forsaken the seaside rocks in front of our building, which a shantytown had completely taken over, for the attractions of a video-game parlor. The palace in the compound downstairs, which had become a girls' school, had sprouted an extra story. I resented this. We need to have the rooms of our childhood preserved intact, the same pictures up on the wall, the bed in the same corner, the sunlight to come in at the same angle at the same time of day. I felt this room had been let out to a boarder, and I could never move back in. I was no longer a Bombayite; from now on, my experience of the city would be as an NRI, a nonresident

Indian. But even when I was living there, there were whole worlds of the city that were as foreign to me as the ice fields of the Arctic or the deserts of Arabia.

My family tried to involve me in the diamond business. I would wake up and go with my uncle to his office. It was not a successful apprenticeship. I very quickly got bored of "assortment," the arranging of the glittery stones into different lots depending on their imperfections. I made mistakes. "You goof," my uncle's business partner said, in 1980, "like President Carter." I didn't join the business, but I kept going back and forth, spending longer and longer periods in India, up to six months at a time. It could not be called traveling; it was more like migrant work. I would get my commissions from the West—I had begun writing about India—and fulfill them in the East. I went back every four years, then every two years, then every year. In recent years, I have been going back twice a year, to write about the country. "Look at Suketu," one of my friends pointed out encouragingly to another friend, who had returned to India from the States and missed America. "He's become almost a commuter."

I ALSO CAME BACK to Bombay to marry. I had met my wife, who was born in Madras and raised in London, on an Air India plane, the perfect metaphor for a meeting of exiles: neither here nor there, happiest in transit. I was going to Bombay and Sunita to Madras. We talked about exile—and I knew at once.

My mother had come here to study at Sophia College in the fifties, all the way from Nairobi. My father would take the train from Calcutta for three days and get her at her hostel, on Marine Drive, and they would walk to Nariman Point. Then they would walk back, all the way to Chowpatty, the young suitor and his teenage fiancée, and eat chana bhaturas—chickpeas and big puris—at Cream Centre or go up to the Café Naaz and drink milkshakes. Sometimes they would go to the Jehangir Art Gallery. Thirty years later, without conscious intention, I found myself revisiting the cartography of my father's courtship with another Indian girl from abroad. We walked along the bay; we took in the pictures at the art gallery. Bombay is where my family found love. It is where my uncle, newly arrived from Calcutta, spotted my aunt at a fun fair. We came back from distant places—Nairobi, Calcutta, New York—to chase love here.

The day after my first date with Sunita, a cousin was going to Kanpur and I went to Victoria Terminus to drop him off. As the Gorakhpur Express pulled into the station, an enormous horde of migrant workers going back to their villages rushed it. The policemen beat them back with lathis. There was an immense clamor, and I stood to one side, watching, despairing. I thought of the girl I had just met, her beauty, her Englishness. She was the way I could distinguish myself from this herd, prevent myself from getting annihilated by the crowd. At that moment I realized I was in love. Being with her, with a fine woman like her, would make me an individual.

The next day, in love, I took her to Juhu Beach. The sea washed her feet and made her languorous, vulnerable. I put my arm around her, and she allowed her head to rest on my shoulder. On our third date, at the Sangam Bar overlooking the Arabian Sea—where, I found out later, my father had wooed my mother, and my uncle took my aunt—after seven bottles of London Pilsner, I proposed to Sunita. She laughed.

IN THE PLAYGROUND of New York my first son, Gautama, was always hesitant; he would look at the other children from a distance. I would watch him smiling at the other kids, rocking back and forth. Even when they returned his smile, came forward, and sought to include him in their gangs, he would run away, run to me, maintain his distance. At a very early age, too early an age, he became conscious of his difference.

I took Gautama to his first day of preschool, at the Y on 14th Street. All the two-year-olds were speaking English except my son. We had raised him speaking Gujarati at home. The teachers led the kids through a drill, telling them when to raise their hands; they sang songs. My son could not understand. I sat with him, feeling miserable. The kids in our building said about him, "He can't talk." He looked up at them hopefully, but they didn't invite him to play. When he sat in the garden downstairs, eating his khichdi—which the British had changed into kedgeree—from his little bowl, the girl living across the hall screwed up her face. "Eeeuww." This was what colonialism, fifty years after the Empire ended, had done to my son: It had rendered our language unspeakable, our food inedible.

Then our second son, Akash, was born. More and more we thought: We have to take the children home. Our children must have the experience of living in a country where everyone looks just like them. Where we can go into a restaurant in a small town in the country and all heads will not automatically turn to stare at us. In India they can grow up with confidence; they will get a sense of their unique selves, which will be welcome in the larger self. Home is not a consumable entity. You can't go home by eating certain foods, by replaying its films on your television screen. At some point you have to live there again. The dream of return had to be brought into the daylight sooner or later. But to what place would we return, my Bombay, Sunita's Madras, or someplace cheap and lovely like the Himalayas? In 1996, I had been in Bombay for two months, to write an article about the Hindu–Muslim riots. It was the longest span of time I had spent in the city since leaving, and it felt hospitable to me. Sunita could go back to school, for a master's degree. There are many Bombays; through the writing of a book, I wanted to find mine.

JUST BEFORE I LEFT New York, I walked into a magazine store where I had often browsed in the afternoon. I had never before spoken to the cashier. I picked up a magazine, took it to the counter, and realized I had forgotten my wallet. I set it down and told the cashier I would be right back. "You can give me the money later," he said, waving me on. "I know you."

I walked out of the store, exhilarated. In these last five years, I had made the East Village my home. Home is where your credit is good at the corner store. New York, under Mayor Giuliani, had experienced a rebirth. We left a safe city, where you could come out of a club at 4 a.m. and still find people on the street, couples, lovers. A city that worked, where the garbage got picked up, the fallen snow was cleared within hours, the traffic moved predictably, and subway trains were frequent and air-conditioned. There were parties at every corner.

But each time we have gotten comfortable in a place we have moved. Each time we have gotten to know a group of people, we have needed to go somewhere else to find people we didn't know. We were now going to India, not as tourists and not to visit relatives, either. Other than my uncle in Bombay and my aunts in Ahmadabad and Kanpur, I have almost no relatives left in India. They've all moved—to America, to England. India was the new world for me. And Bombay was landfall.

* * *

COMING BACK from a trip to Elephanta Island, and seeing the wedding cake of the old Taj Hotel, the imitation skyscraper of the new one, and the Gateway of India in front of them, I feel the slightest souvenir of the quickening of the heart that European travelers to India must have felt, through all those long centuries. After several months at sea, after rounding the Cape of Good Hope, after many perils and storms and illnesses, beyond this massive gate lies all of India. Here are tigers and wise men and famines. A hurried stop, a quick halt to take a bath and get a night's sleep on solid land, before the train departs early the next morning for the real India, the India of the villages. Nobody back then came to Bombay to live there forever; it was just a way station, between paradise and hell. You came to Bombay to pass through it.

It was called Heptanesia—the city of seven islands—by Ptolemy in A.D. 150. The Portuguese called it Bom Bahia, Buon Bahia, or Bombaim—Portuguese for "good bay." In 1538, they also called it Boa-Vida, the island of good life, because of its beautiful groves, its game, and its abundance of food. Another story about its name concerns the Sultan Kutb-ud-din, Mubarak Shah I, who ruled over the islands in the fourteenth century, demolished temples, and became a demon: Mumba Rakshasa. Other Hindu names for these islands were Manbai, Mambai, Mambe, Mumbadevi, Bambai, and now Mumbai. It is a city that has multiple aliases, as do gangsters and whores. Waves of rulers have owned this clump of islands: the Hindu fisherfolk, the Muslim kings, the Portuguese, the British, the Parsi and Gujarati businessmen, the sheths (joined by Sindhis, Marwaris, and Punjabis later), and now, finally, the natives again, the Maharashtrians.

If you look at Bombay from the air, if you see its location—spread your thumb and your forefinger apart at a thirty-degree angle and you'll see the shape of Bombay—you will find yourself acknowledging that it is a beautiful city: the sea on all sides, the palm trees along the shores, the light coming down from the sky and thrown back up by the sea. It has a harbor, several bays, creeks, rivers, hills. From the air, you get a sense of its possibilities. On the ground it's different. My little boy notices this. "Look," Gautama points out, as we are driving along the road from Bandra Reclamation. "On one side villages, on the other side buildings." He has identi-

'fied the slums for what they are: villages in the city. The visual shock of Bombay is the shock of this juxtaposition. And it is soon followed by violent shocks to the other four senses: the continuous din of the traffic coming in through open windows in a hot country; the stench of bombil fish drying on stilts in the open air; the inescapable humid touch of many brown bodies in the street; the searing heat of the garlic chutney on your vadapav sandwich early on your first jet-lagged morning.

From the beginnings of the city, there was a Bombay culture, unique in India. Bombay is all about transaction—dhandha. It was founded as a trading city, built at the entrance to the rest of the world, and everybody was welcome as long as they wanted to trade. Gerald Aungier, the East India Company's governor from 1672 to 1675, gave the city freedom of religion and of movement, a marked departure from the Portuguese feudal and religious policies. From then on, Bombay flourished as a free port, in every sense of the word. When the American Civil War stopped the supply of cotton to England, Bombay stepped into the breach and earned in five years, from 1861 to 1865, £81 million more than the city would normally have received for its cotton. After the opening of the Suez Canal in 1869, which cut travel time to the Empire in half, Bombay truly became the gateway to India, supplanting Calcutta as the richest city in the Indian Empire. So they came, from all over India and the world: Portuguese, Mughal, British, Gujarati, Parsi, Maratha, Sindhi, Punjabi, Bihari . . . American.

On the map of the Mumbai Metropolitan Region issued by the region's Development Authority, the land beyond the eastern boundary is marked WEST COAST OF INDIA. It is probably a cartographer's impreciseness, but the distinction is significant and valid. It was not until the late nineteenth century that Bombay started thinking of itself as an Indian city. And even now there are people who would prefer it if Bombay were a city-state, like Singapore. Oh, can you just imagine if we were like Singapore! they say. Relieved of having to bear the burden of this tiresome country, like a young couple whose bedridden aunt, whom they have been supporting and nursing for long painful years, has just died. It takes trauma to establish a city's connection with the hinterland. With the 1992–93 Hindu–Muslim riots and bomb blasts in Bombay, and the 2001 airborne demolition of the World Trade Center in New York, a certain notion of geography got altered along with the skyline: the idea that the island city could live apart

from the landmass immediately to its east—India in the case of Bombay;
the rest of the world in the case of New York. All that, we had felt, happened out there, to somebody else.

The Gateway of India, a domed arch of yellow basalt surrounded by
four turrets, was built in Bombay in 1927 to commemorate the arrival, sixteen years earlier, of the British king, George V; instead, it marked his permanent exit. In 1947, the British left their Empire under this same arch, the
last of their troops marching mournfully onto the last of their ships. Bombay, for my family too, was the threshold city; it was where we paused, for
a decade, on our journey from Calcutta to America. We sat and rested
under the arch for some time, till our ship came in. Cities are gateways: to
money, to position, to dreams and devils. A migrant from Bihar might one
day get to America; but first he needs a spell in the boot camp of the West:
Bombay, the acclimation station.

Greater Bombay's population, currently 19 million, is bigger than that
of 173 countries in the world. If it were a country by itself in 2004, it would
rank at number 54. Cities should be examined like countries. Each has a city
culture, as countries possess a national culture. There is something pecu-
liarly Bombayite about Bombayites and likewise about Delhiites or New
Yorkers or Parisians—the way the women walk, what their young people
like to do in the evenings, what their definitions of fun and horror are. The
growth of the megacity is an Asian phenomenon: Asia has eleven of the
world's fifteen biggest. Why do Asians like to live in cities? Maybe we like
people more.

India is not an overpopulated country. Its population density is lower
than that of many other countries not thought of as overpopulated. In
1999, Belgium had a population density of 130 people per square mile; the
Netherlands, 150; India, under 120. It is the cities of India that are overpopulated. Singapore has a density of 2,535 people per square mile; Berlin,
the most crowded European city, has 1,130 people per square mile. The
island city of Bombay in 1990 had a density of 17,550 people per square
mile. Some parts of central Bombay have a population density of 1 million
people per square mile. This is the highest number of individuals massed
together at any spot in the world. They are not equally dispersed across the
island. Two-thirds of the city's residents are crowded into just 5 percent of
the total area, while the richer or more rent-protected one-third monopo-
lize the remaining 95 percent.

Fifty years ago, if you wanted to see where the action was in India, you went to the villages. They contributed 71 percent of net domestic product in 1950. Today, you go to the cities, which now account for 60 percent of net domestic product. Bombay alone pays 38 percent of the nation's taxes. What makes Bombay overpopulated is the impoverishment of the country-side, so that a young man with dreams in his head will take the first train to Bombay to live on the footpath. If you fix the problems of the villages, you fix, as a happy side effect, the problems of the cities.

"Bombay is a bird of gold." A man living in a slum, without water, without toilets, was telling me why he came here, why people continue to come here. In the Bayview Bar of the Oberoi Hotel you can order a bottle of Dom Perignon for one and a half times the average annual income; this in a city where 40 percent of the houses lack safe drinking water. Another man put it differently: "Nobody starves to death in Mumbai." He was being very literal. People are still starving to death in other parts of India. In Bombay, there are several hundred slimming clinics. According to a dietician who operates one of them, fashionable models are on the verge of anorexia. This is how Bombayites know they've parted company with the rest of India. "In any class of society in Bombay," explains the dietician, "there are more people wanting to lose weight than put on weight."

Bombay is the biggest, fastest, richest city in India. It is Bombay that Krishna could have been describing in the Tenth Canto of the Bhagavad Gita, when the god manifests himself in all his fullness:

> *I am all-destroying death*
> *And the origin of things that are yet to be. . . .*
> *I am the gambling of rogues;*
> *the splendor of the splendid.*

It is a maximum city.

The Country of the No

"Can I get a gas connection?"
  "No."
  "Can I get a phone?"
  "No."

"Can I get a school for my child?"

"I'm afraid it is not possible."

"Have my parcels arrived from America?"

"I don't know."

"Can you find out?"

"No."

"Can I get a railway reservation?"

"No."

India is the Country of the No. That "no" is your test. You have to get past it. It is India's Great Wall; it keeps out foreign invaders. Pursuing it energetically and vanquishing it is your challenge. In the guru–shishya tradition, the novice is always rebuffed multiple times when he first approaches the guru. Then the guru stops saying no but doesn't say yes either; he suffers the presence of the student. When he starts acknowledging him, he assigns a series of menial tasks, meant to drive him away. Only if the disciple sticks it out through all these stages of rejection and ill treatment is he considered worthy of the sublime knowledge. India is not a tourist-friendly country. It will reveal itself to you only if you stay on, against all odds. The "no" might never become a "yes." But you will stop asking questions.

"Can I rent a flat at a price I can afford?"

"No."

Coming from New York, I am a pauper in Bombay. The going rate for a nice two-bedroom apartment in the part of South Bombay where I grew up is $3,000 a month, plus $200,000 as a deposit, interest-free and returnable in rupees. This is after the real estate prices have fallen by 40 percent. I hear a broker argue on the phone with another broker representing a flat I am to see. "But the party is *American*, holds an American passport and American visa; everything, he has. His wife is British visa. . . . What? Yes, he is originally Indian." Then he speaks apologetically to me. "It is for foreigners only." As another broker explains it, "Indians won't rent to Indians. It would be different if you were one hundred percent white-skinned." At least this is one sign that my passport changes nothing. I am one of the great brown thieving horde, no matter how far I go. In Varanasi I was refused admittance to the backpackers' inns on similar grounds: I am Indian. I might rape the white women.

The earth is round and you go all over it, but ultimately you come back to the same spot in the circle. "Look everywhere but, I guarantee you, you will be living in Dariya Mahal," my uncle predicted. It is not a flat I wanted, after the first immediate rush. The second time I came back to see it I didn't like it. But I feel as though I could never live anywhere else in Bombay. The universe is teleological. I grew up in the third building around the palace. My grandfather lived in the first. Now I have come back to live in the second, completing the trilogy. The ghost time and the present have no boundaries. Here is where I got beat up by the bully, here is where I saw my true love on Holi, here is where the men made the pyramid to get at the pot of treasure, here is where the mysterious caravan Nefertiti always parked. I am afraid that one of these days I'll meet myself, the stranger within, coming or going. The body, safely interred in the grave, will rise and, crouching, loping, come up to me from behind.

The clerk in my uncle's office, who grew up as our neighbor in Dariya Mahal 3, tells me that Dariya Mahal 2 is "cosmopolitan." This is how the real estate brokers of Nepean Sea Road describe a building that is not Gujarati-dominated. For a Gujarati, this is not a term of approval. "Cosmopolitan" means the whole world except Gujaratis and Marwaris. It includes Sindhis, Punjabis, Bengalis, Catholics, and God knows who else. Nonvegetarians. Divorcees. Growing up, I was always fascinated by the "cosmopolitan" families. I thought cosmopolitan girls more beautiful, beyond my reach. The Gujaratis I grew up among conformed to Nehru's stereotype of a "small-boned, mercantile" people. A Gujarati family's peace rests on the lack of sexual tension within it; it is an oasis from the lusts of the world. It is the most vegetarian, the least martial, of the Indian communities. But it is easygoing. "How are you?" one Gujarati asks another. "In good humor" is the standard reply, through earthquakes and bankruptcy.

We have a meeting with the owner of the flat, a Gujarati diamond merchant, to negotiate the contract. The landlord is a Palanpuri Jain and a strict vegetarian. He asks my uncle if we are too. "Arre, his wife is a Brahmin! Even more than us!" my uncle replies. And this is where we get our vegetarian discount: 20 percent off the asking rent. But in my uncle's words is evident the subtle contempt with which the Vaisyas—the merchant castes—regard the Brahmins. The Brahmins are the pantujis, the professors, the straight people. Not good in business. Eager to come home at funerals for food. Whatever the reasons for my ancestors' change of caste centuries ago—from Nagar Brahmin to Vaisya—it has served us well. Change of caste is a mechanism for evolutionary survival. Brahmins in a god-fearing age; Vaisyas in one where money is god. And we are in a naturally capitalistic city—a vaisya-nagra—one that understands the moods and movements of money.

My father has one rule for selecting a flat to live in: You should be able to change your clothes without having to draw the curtains. This simple rule, if followed, ensures two things: privacy and a sufficient flow of air and light. I forgot this dictum when putting down my deposit for the second-floor flat in Dariya Mahal. It is hemmed in by large buildings all around. People walking below or standing on their balconies in the buildings opposite can peep into every corner of my flat, watching us as we go about cooking, eating, working, sleeping. There are twenty floors in the building and ten flats on each floor. Each flat will have an average of six residents and three servants; their allocation of incidental support staff (watchmen, construction workers, sweepers) will be one per flat. That makes two thousand people in this building. Two thousand people live in the building adjoining this, and another two thousand in the one immediately behind. The school in the middle has two thousand pupils, teachers, and staff. That makes eight thousand human beings living on a few acres of land. It is the population of a small town.

The flat we have moved into was designed by a sadist, a prankster, or an idiot. The kitchen window ventilates only the refrigerator—or, rather, heats it—since there is no provision for curtains and the sun beats down on it. When I turn on the fan in the dark recesses of the kitchen, it blows out the gas flame, since the space for the range is directly underneath the fan. The only way we can get air in the living room is to open the study window, to let the sea air in. But this also brings in a sand dune's worth of thick, black, grainy dirt from outside, along with a spectacular array of filth. (We found a plastic ice-cream cone inside the bedroom once, with a film of syrup and cream still inside it.) We also receive used polyethylene milk bags, the betel-stained plastic cover of a pan, and, once, a shit-stained diaper. The air outside is a rain of thin plastic bags, which has replaced the parrots I grew up with. By five o'clock the living room is dark, since we're on such a low floor. We need the air conditioner and the lights on all the time; so our electricity bills run into monstrous figures, the necessary price of keeping the environment out.

The flat is furnished in diamond merchant luxe. Diamond merchants have a certain vision of the good life. It is not exactly vulgar, because these diamond merchants are mostly Jains: reticent, sober, vegetarian, teetotaling, and monogamous in their personal lives. They will be seen at a party, if they go to parties at all, holding glasses of Coke and wearing white shirts and dark trousers. They do not have mistresses, they stay married to their wives all their lives, and they are good to their children. But a certain extravagance might manifest itself in the furniture they choose. So the furniture in my flat erupts upon the eyes like a weather phenomenon. An enormous porcelain lamp dominates the living room, engraved with three semi-nude Greek nymphs frolicking, each one with a hand cupping one breast of the nymph immediately proximate to her, their heads shaded by a shower of illuminated crystal leaves. The glass dining table, which is interleaved with real gold ornamentation, is flanked by two more lamps, one a giant yellow pear and the other a giant pink strawberry, which, when a switch is flicked on, shine from within with fructous life. A chandelier with pink leaves looms over our heads when we sit on sofas upholstered in bright red, with golden tasseled ropes hanging from them, which my children promptly yank off. The master bedroom continues in this arboreal vein, with a pair of golden branches on the ceiling whose giant leaves shield 100-watt bulbs; vines run up and down the closet doors, painted in a vivid shade of green. Throw open a closet door and your vision will be flooded by a cascading waterfall painted on the inside. Across the giant mirror, a sun with one eye open casts its tendrils across the glass. The mirror in the other bedroom explodes in a galaxy of blue stars; glass stained with blue, red, and green waves covers the small windows. The furniture makes a terrifying din, all day and all night.

The house takes shape, slowly. The owners have not removed all their belongings. The flat's closets yield many gods, Jain and Hindu. We put them away in the drawers. We put our own up on one shelf of the study. We remove, over the objections of our landlord, the pink chandelier and the Greek lamp. He is wounded when we tell him about the lamp. "When you took down the chandelier I didn't say anything, but when you removed the statue, that I didn't like." I hasten to assure him that it is not his taste I am questioning; rather, I am protecting the masterpiece from the evil designs of my young children.

Every day the flat gets cleaned and scrubbed. We learn the caste system of the servants: the live-in maid won't clean the floors; that is for the "free servant" to do; neither of them will do the bathrooms, which are the exclusive domain of a bhangi, who does nothing else. The driver won't wash the car; that is the monopoly of the building watchman. The flat ends up swarming with servants. We wake up at six every morning to garbage, when the garbage lady comes to collect the previous day's refuse. From then on, the doorbell rings continuously all through the day: milkman, paperboy, knife sharpener, waste-paper-and-bottle buyer, massagewali, cable man. All the services of the world, brought to my door, too early in the morning.

The mountain moves, a millimeter at a time. Three-pin plugs are put in. Cable television and American-style phone lines are installed. Soon we will have curtains and then we can move about the house naked, the final test of making a place home. An account with a coconut seller has been established; he will bring fresh coconut water every morning. The elements of a luxurious life are being assembled. In the mornings we will drink coconut water and in the evenings wine. The first night I make the kitchen work I produce from it an Italian dinner: farfalle with mushrooms and sun-dried tomatoes and a salad of peppers, spring onions, tomatoes, and cucumbers. We accompany it with a white wine from the Sahyadris, a passable chardonnay. What makes the meal is the Sicilian olive oil I have brought from a pasta shop on East 10th Street, the biggest item in my luggage coming home.

FOR THE MONTH after my family arrives, I chase plumbers, electricians, and carpenters like Werther chased Lotte. The electrician attached to the building is an easygoing fellow who comes in the late afternoons, chats with me about the wiring in the flat, which he knows well from multiple previous visits, and patches up things so they work only for a little while, assuring multiple future visits. The one phone line on which I can make international calls stops working. A week ago it was the other one. Most people who can afford it have two lines, because one is always going out. Then the phone department has to be called and the workmen bribed to repair it. It is in their interest to have a lousy phone system.

As for my plumber, I want to assassinate him. He is a low, evil sort of fellow, with misshapen betel-stained teeth. He pits the occupants of the flats against one another, telling the people above and below me that I should pay to fix the numerous leaks coming into and going out of my bathrooms, then telling me I should convince *them* to pay. The geyser to heat water, the light switches, the taps, the flushes, and the drains all fail. Large drips of brown water start coming down from the ceiling. The president of the building society explains it to me: All the pipes in this building are fucked. The drainage pipes that were meant to be on the outside have been enclosed. The residents make their own alterations, and they don't let the building plumber in to fix leaks. The pipes in the building don't run straight; every time people make renovations, which is a continuous process, they get freelance plumbers to move the pipes out of the way when they're inconvenient. This blocks the natural flow of sewage and clean water, mixing them up. So if you were to follow the progress of drainwater from the twentieth floor to the first, it would make as many zigs and zags and diversions as a crazy mountain road. At each bend, a clump of dirt accumulates, which blocks the flow. The municipality enforces none of the rules about unauthorized alterations. Sewer water is constantly threatening to rise up into my bathroom, as it has in other flats in the building. The arteries of the building are clogged, sclerotic. Its skin is peeling. It is a sick building. Meanwhile, I am paying rent every month to my landlord for the privilege of fixing his flat.

We also have to learn again how to stand in line. In Bombay, people are always waiting in line: to vote, to get a flat, to get a job, to get out of the country; to make a railway reservation, make a phone call, go to the toilet. And when you get to the front of the line, you are always made conscious that you are inconveniencing all the hundreds and thousands and millions of people behind you. Hurry, hurry; get your business over with. And if you're next in line, you never stand behind the person at the head of the line; you always stand next to him, as if you were really with him, so that you can occupy the place he vacates with just one sideways step.

All this takes most of our waking time. It is a city hostile to outsiders or nostalgia-stuck returnees. We can muscle our way in with our dollars, but even when the city gives in, it resents us for making it do so. The city is groaning under the pressure of the 1 million people per square mile. It doesn't want me any more than the destitute migrant from Bihar, but it can't kick either of us out. So it makes life uncomfortable for us by guerrilla warfare, by constant low-level sniping, by creating small crises every day. All these irritations add up to a murderous rage in your mind, especially when you've come from a country where things work better, where institutions are more responsive.

Long before the millennium, Indians such as the late prime minister, Rajiv Gandhi, were talking about taking the country into the twenty-first century, as if the twentieth century could just be leapfrogged. India desires modernity; it desires computers, information technology, neural networks, video on demand. But there is no guarantee of a constant supply of electricity in most places in the country. In this as in every other area, the country is convinced it can pole-vault over the basics: develop world-class computer and management institutes without achieving basic literacy; provide advanced cardiac surgery and diagnostic imaging facilities while the most easily avoidable childhood diseases run rampant; sell washing machines that depend on a nonexistent water supply from shops that are dark most hours of the day because of power cuts; support a dozen private and public companies offering mobile phone service, while the basic land telephone network is in terrible shape; drive scores of new cars that go from 0 to 60 in ten seconds without any roads where they might do this without killing everything inside and out, man and beast.

It is an optimistic view of technological progress—that if you reach for the moon, you will somehow, automatically, span the inconvenient steps in between. India has the third largest pool of technical labor in the world, but a third of its 1 billion people can't read or write. An Indian scientist can design a supercomputer, but it won't work because the junior technician cannot maintain it properly. The country graduates the best technical brains in the world but neglects to teach my plumber how to fix a toilet so it stays fixed. It is still a Brahmin-oriented system of education; those who work with their hands have to learn for themselves. Education has to do with reading and writing, with abstractions, with higher thought.

As a result, in the Country of the No nothing is fixed the first time around. You don't just call a repairman, you begin a relationship with him. You can't bring to his attention too aggressively the fact that he is incompetent or crooked, because you will need him to set right what he has broken the first time around. Indians are craftsmen of genius, but mass production, with its attendant standardization, is not for us. All things modern in Bombay fail regularly: plumbing, telephones, the movement of huge blocks of traffic. Bombay is not the ancient Indian idea of a city. It is an imitation of a western city, maybe Chicago in the twenties. And, like all other imitations of the West here—the Hindi pop songs, the appliances, the accents people put on, the parties the rich throw—this imitation, too, is neither here nor there.

THE NEXT BIG STRUGGLE in the Country of the No is getting a gas connection. The government has a monopoly over the supply of cooking gas, which is delivered in heavy red cylinders. When I go to the designated office for Malabar Hill and ask for a cylinder, the clerk says, "No quota." The Five-Year Plans of the country have not provided for enough cooking gas for everybody.

"When will there be quota?"

"Maybe August."

This is May. We will eat sandwiches till then.

Various people advise me to try the black market. I go driving around with my aunt to try to kidnap a gas delivery man; we see one bicycling along Harkness Road. My aunt jumps out and asks him how much he will take to give me a cylinder. He explains that the cylinder is not a problem but the connector is; he promises to call after he finds a black-market connector.

My friend Manjeet tells me to take her mother to another gas office. She knows the ways of Bombay. We walk in, and I tell the clerk, "I need a gas cylinder, please." I explain the problem with the other office, their lack of quota.

"Do you know a member in the Rajya Sabha?" the clerk asks, referring to the upper house of parliament.

"No. Why should I?"

"Because if you did, it would be easy. All the Rajya Sabha MPs have a discretionary quota of gas cylinders they can award."

At this point Manjeet's mother steps in. "He has two children!" she appeals to the female bureaucrats. "Two small children! They don't even have gas to boil milk! They are crying for milk! What is he supposed to do without gas to boil milk for his two small children?"

By the next morning we have a gas cylinder in our kitchen. My friend's mother knew what had to be done to move the bureaucracy. She did not bother with official rules and procedures and forms. She appealed to the hearts of the workers in the office; they have children too. And then they volunteered the information that there was a loophole: If I ordered a commercial tank of gas, which is bigger and more expensive than the household one, I could get it immediately. No one had told me this before. But once the emotional connection was made, the rest was easy. Once the workers in the gas office were willing to pretend that my household was a business, they delivered the cylinders every couple of months efficiently, spurred on by the vision of my two little children crying for milk.

But the gas cylinder, which is supposed to last for three months, runs out in three weeks. Somewhere in the chain of supply, most of it has been siphoned off and sold on the black market. What this means to us is that it runs out the morning of the day we have invited ten people to dinner. The only way to ensure a continuous supply of cooking gas is to have two cylinders. Everyone runs a scam so they have two cylinders in their name; they transfer one from an earlier address or bribe an official to get a second one. Bombay survives on the scam; we are all complicit. A man who has made his money through a scam is more respected than a man who has made his money through hard work, because the ethic of Bombay is quick upward mobility and a scam is a shortcut. A scam shows good business sense and a quick mind. Anyone can work hard and make money. What's to admire about that? But a well-executed scam? Now, there's a thing of beauty!

Two Currencies

We debate whether to buy a car. The roads are swarming with cars now, all kinds of cars, not just the Fiat-Ambassador duopoly that reigned in the city when I left. But all those new cars have only the same old roads to use. Cars are able to go faster than ever, but traffic speeds are slower. When you get into your new Suzuki or Honda or BMW, with its fuel-injected engine raring to go, you had better tame it, for the average speed in a Bombay car journey is no more than 12 miles an hour. On Marine Drive, for example, the one road where people can really open up their cars, the average speed declined from a sedate 34 miles per hour in 1962, to 24 in 1979, and to a crawling 15 miles per hour in 1990. Marine Drive in the evenings is filled with cruising youngsters driving all the way up to Nariman Point, their radios blaring pop music out the open windows—and racing each other up and down the strip at 24, even 30, miles an hour.

One happy effect of this is that the number of traffic accidents in the city has actually decreased, from a 1991 total of 25,477 accidents with 365 deaths to 25,214 accidents with only 319 deaths in 1994. This confirms something I can see for myself in Bombay: In the mad driving, hardly anybody seems to get hurt. They aren't going fast enough to do serious damage and can brake on a dime.

Modern cities have not made their peace with the automobile. Cities are the way they are because of cars; people who drive them can live farther and farther from the center. A great city grows because of its automobiles; Bombay is now dying from them. For every flat in these three buildings there are two cars. As a result, the building staff is engaged in a constant game of musical chairs: shifting cars in and out of parking spaces. It doesn't help that the garages have been converted into general stores, doctors' offices, and copy shops. There wasn't any provision made for a shopping district when Malabar Hill exploded. The footpaths have disappeared, and young children wandering out on the roads take their lives in their hands. The terrain of my childhood was always a battle between children and cars. We played between the cars and around them. But cars have the same advantage that insects have over human intelligence: fecundity. The automobile won. No children play in the parking lot now. They're home, watching TV.

Soon after we move in, my friend Manjeet comes visiting. She needs to park her car, but I find that another car has taken my designated parking spot. I go downstairs to find Manjeet, ashen, sitting in her car, surrounded by a threatening circle of guards and servants. I remonstrate with the watchman, who points toward a man in the lobby: a very drunk man in his early forties, short but with a large mustache, who demands to know who I am. I demand to know who he is. "I am a member of the parking committee of the building!" he shouts, leaning very close to me.

Meanwhile, the circle of hoods is throwing bottle caps and little stones at my guest's car. I finally extract the name of the car owner and go up to his flat on the first floor. He is relaxing in a dhoti and seems to think he has the right to take my space because it hasn't been used in a long time. "Your flat has been closed for a year, year and a half." I get him to come downstairs to move his car; I am fuming and tell him I will call the police to haul in the drunk. "Don't do that," the man says, staring at me. He pauses, still looking at me without smiling. "You don't know his capacity."

He moves his car and I reclaim my spot. The drunk ambles around again and stands outside Manjeet's car. He is accompanied by a young man who is asking what happened. I get out of the car, take my friend, and go upstairs. Soon after, the young man comes up. "Your guest's tire has been deflated. He has taken the air out; I saw him. But don't go down now, he's still there. I'll take him upstairs, and then I'll take you to the petrol pump and we'll get air."

"I'll go downstairs and bash his brains out," I say.

"Don't do that. You have a family; you have to live here."

The drunk, the young man tells me, is a doctor. He lives on the eighth floor and is known in the building as a bad character. "Why are you moving in?" the young man asks me. "Everybody's moving out." The building is, even by Bombay standards, spectacularly badly run. I lie awake a good part of that night. Something has been brought home to me: Violence in Bombay can strike very close and at any time. And the present dispute, as usual, is about space—in this case, space for a car—the illegal usurpation of space and the defense of that usurpation through muscle power. "How long have you lived here?" the doctor had roared at me, again and again. The man on the first floor, who got used to parking his car there, asked me the same question. This is a community of insiders, people who have lived in this building for a long time; they were asking the newcomer what right he had to claim his legal privileges. And they own the guards who are supposed to enforce those privileges for me.

The wars of the twenty-first century will be fought over parking places.

OUR EARLY DAYS in Bombay are filled with battling our foreign-born children's illnesses. Gautama has had amebic dysentery for two weeks now; he keeps going all over the floor and when he takes off his T-shirt it is painful to look at him; all his ribs show. The food and the water in Bombay, India's most modern city, are contaminated with shit. Amebic dysentery is transferred through shit. We have been feeding our son shit. It could have come in the mango we gave him; it could have been in the pool we took him swimming in. It could have come from the taps in our own home, since the drainage pipes in Bombay, laid out during British times, leak into the fresh-water pipes that run right alongside. There is no defense possible. Everything is recycled in this filthy country, which poisons its children, raising them on a diet of its own shit.

In Bombay, there's always "something going around." In other countries, there is a kingdom of the sick and a kingdom of the well. Here, the two are one. We play a continuous round-robin of sickness in our family. Sunita and I both contract something the doctor calls "granular pharyngitis." If we don't want to have it, we have to stop breathing in Bombay. It's caused by pollution, which we get lots of. Even when I am not walking the streets, riding the trains, or talking to anybody, I absorb the city through my pores and inhale it into my throat, causing granules to erupt all over it. We sneeze and sniffle our way through the city. Every morning when the dust is swept a good-sized mound gathers on the broom: dirt, fibers, feathers. My children play in this dirt, breathing air that has ten times the maximum permissible levels of lead in the atmosphere, stunting their mental growth.

Visitors come and I have to strain to explain to them that it was not always thus. Bombay used to be a beautiful city, a breathable city. During a strike by the taxi and auto drivers, the air pollution comes down by a quarter from its usual level. They are marvelous January days, when everybody goes out to breathe luxuriously. It is a long time since Bombay smelled so sweet in the winter. Breathing the air in Bombay now is the equivalent of smoking two and a half packs of cigarettes a day. The sun used to set into the sea. Now it sets into the smog. The city of Bombay is divided between the air-conditioned and the non-air-conditioned parts: AC/non-AC. My nose can't handle the radical difference in the worlds of Bombay. I am continuously sneezing, I have a constantly running nose. I am advised to buy an air-conditioned car. We have no choice but to live rich, if we are to live at all.

Bombay is more expensive for us in the beginning of our stay there than later on. Newcomers find it a city without options—for housing, for education. Everything has been gobbled up by those already here. If you're going to come to Bombay, come at the bottom. There's no room at the top. Every nice place has a right to charge a newcomer's tax, which goes from the new inhabitants to the old patient ones. A city has its secrets: where you go to shop for an ice bucket, for an office chair, for a sari. Newcomers have to pay more because they don't know these places. We haggle over minuscule amounts that have no value for us: 10 rupees is only 40 cents. If we lost

40 cents in New York we would never notice it; here it becomes a matter of principle. This is because along with getting ripped off for 10 rupees comes an assumption: You are not from here, you are not Indian, so you deserve to be ripped off, to pay more than a native. So we raise our voices and demand to be charged the correct amount, the amount on the meter, because not to do so would imply acceptance of our foreign status. We are Indian, and we will pay Indian rates!

Theft is another form of the newcomers' tax. There are thieves even outside the house of God. Inside Siddhivinayak Temple, hordes of people pray earnestly for a sick relative to get better, to save their business from bankruptcy, to pass an examination. On one visit, I find that my shoes have been stolen. This God couldn't even protect my shoes; inside, people were praying to him to perform miracles. I walk out onto the filthy street in my sock feet.

A sign I see on the back of a truck says it all:

Sau me ek sau ek beimaan.
Phir bhi mera Bharat mahaan.

101 out of 100 are dishonest.
Still my India is the best.

From all around, people ask us for money. Our driver asks for money. Our maid asks for money. Friends down on their luck ask for money. Strangers ring our doorbell and ask for money. We are, in Bombay, a low-pressure system surrounded by areas of very high pressure; from all around, they zoom in on us.

This fucking city. The sea should rush in over these islands in one great tidal wave and obliterate it, cover it underwater. It should be bombed from the air. Every morning I get angry. It is the only way to get anything done; people here respond to anger, are afraid of it. In the absence of money or connections, anger will do. I begin to understand the uses of anger as theater—with taxi drivers, doormen, plumbers, government bureaucrats. Even my CD player in India responds to anger, physical violence; when a gentle press of the PLAY button fails to arouse it from its slumber, a hard smack across the side propels it into sound.

Any nostalgia I felt about my childhood has been erased. Given the chance to live again in the territory of childhood, I am coming to detest it. Why do I put myself through this? I was comfortable and happy and praised in New York; I had two places, one to live and one to work. I have given all that up for this fool's errand, looking for silhouettes in the mist of the ghost time. Now I can't wait to go back, to the place I once longed to get away from: New York. I miss cold weather and white people. I see pictures of blizzards on TV and remember the warmth inside when it's cold outside and you open the window just a crack and the air outside slices in like a solid wedge. How it reaches your nostrils and you take a deep breath. How you go outside on a bad night and the cold clears your head and makes everything better.

My father once, in New York, exasperated by my relentless demands to be sent back to finish high school in Bombay, shouted at me, "When you were there, you wanted to come here. Now that you're here, you want to go back." It was when I first realized I had a new nationality: citizen of the country of longing.

SHORTLY AFTER WE MOVE to Bombay in 1998, the country explodes five nuclear bombs, including a hydrogen bomb, and there is this great feeling of: We have shown the world, bhenchod! Meanwhile, all the economic indicators of the country plunge downward. The bad news about money hits Bombay hard. It is a population led to believe that every year they will get a little more than they had the previous year, and buy a little more: an electric toaster to begin with, a color television the next year, a fridge the year after that, a washing machine, an imported crystal chandelier for the drawing room, and finally a small car. That is usually the top of the pyramid, unless they get very lucky and are able to buy a flat. The pyramid has topped out. Those who already have a car and a flat are now thinking anxiously about their children. From the top, there is only one way to go—and it is a leap—outside the country altogether, to America, Australia, Dubai. To go from the Maruti to the Mercedes, from the blue jeans to the Armani suit, necessitates a move abroad.

After the nuclear tests, the international financial carpetbaggers start leaving Bombay, not in a group but in twos and threes. For a while, India is no longer a profit center. A city like Bombay, like New York, that is a recent creation on the planet and does not have a substantial indigenous population, is full of restless people. Those who have come here have not been at ease somewhere else. And unlike others who may have been equally uncomfortable wherever they came from, these people got up and moved. As I have discovered, having once moved, it is difficult to stop moving. So it is that the Bombayite might dream of the West, not just for the riches that lie there but also for the excitement of moving somewhere again.

Every summer, waves of Indians living overseas come back. They also send back little pictures: of their son in front of the new fifty-two-inch TV; their daughter sitting on the hood of the new minivan; the wife in the open-plan kitchen, one hand on the microwave; the whole family laughing together in the small backyard pool, their "bungalow" in the background. These pictures plant little time bombs in the minds of the siblings left behind. They hold the pictures and look around their two-room flat in Mahim and suddenly the new sofa and the two-in-one Akai stereo they have invested in with such pride look cheap and shabby in comparison. It used to be that they could reassure themselves: At least my children are growing up with Indian values. But when the children of the exiles come back, it is noticed that there isn't such a vast gulf between the Bombay kids and their cousins abroad; both wear the same football jerseys and speak in the same peculiar argot of the music video channels, an internationalized American. Often, the kids from the cold countries are interested in going to a temple; they have come back brimming with facts on Hinduism that have been taught to them in the fine schools they attend. The local kids want to take them club-hopping. When we decide to put Gautama in a Gujarati-language school, our decision is met with amazement and sometimes anger. "How could you do that to your son?" demands the lady down the hall. "You'll ruin his life." But then she reflects. "It's all right for you, you're getting out of here sooner or later. If you were living here permanently you'd put him in Cathedral."

A whole network of recently met strangers gather themselves to help us find a school for Gautama. Everyone knows a teacher or a principal or an owner at one of the few schools that has a kindergarten, and they energetically make calls on our behalf, even go personally to wheedle and convince. They paint us as innocents abroad, foreigners unsophisticated in the ways of school admissions. The fact that we need a place only for two years counts in our favor; it means that when Gautama leaves, another place will be created, to be bestowed upon someone else in exchange for a favor or a donation. Each vacant place signifies money and power. There are only seven schools in South Bombay that are considered worth sending a child to.

One of them is the Bombay International School, which has eight families living in the school building. They are long-term tenants, protected by the Rent Act. The door next to the library is someone's flat. The school is in desperate need of space for classrooms but cannot force the residents out. It inherited the tenants years ago, when it bought the building. There is no land on which to build schools; no new ones have appeared in my area since I was a child. But the population of children has exploded. There is no place for all these new learners. They have to be registered at birth. "Is it difficult, getting a place for a child in a school in Bombay?" I ask the principal.

"It's like climbing Mount Everest."

I want my son to go to a Gujarati-language school, and the only one that's any good in Bombay is New Era, a school founded by Gandhians. A trustee writes a letter for us, and after a round of begging and pleading it is done. Going to pick him up after his first day, my heart swells with gladness: I can't recognize my son. I can't pick him out from the whole crowd of brown-skinned kids in white uniforms. For the first time in his life, he's just like all the others.

But not long afterward, I become conscious of a way in which my son is not like the others. In the school bus with him coming back from New Era, little Komal tells me, in Gujarati, that her grandmother is coming to visit. She has stick-on tattoos she wants me to put on the back of her hand. Out of her schoolbag come wonderful treasures: a potato with lots of matches stuck in it, like a porcupine; outlines of drawings to be colored in; a piece of paper cut into strips and held together loosely at the top so you can fold it and something interesting will happen. She instructs me to tell Gautama's mother where to buy shoes. My son tries to talk to her, to the others on the bus, but nobody can understand his English. "But can't you speak Gujarati?" I ask him.

"I speak only a little Gujarati," he explains reasonably. "Pappa, please put me in an English-language school."

"You broke your father's heart," my uncle later tells Gautama.

*   *   *

MY SON COMES BACK from Head Start, his new English-language school, and for the first time in this country he can describe his day in detail. He painted on a piece of paper using a capsicum as a brush; then he made a house and a sun; then he played puzzles; and he ate a "square idli," which is later explained to him as a dhokla, a Gujarati snack. I listen happily. He never talked about what he did in the Gujarati school, because he never understood.

The first evening, a woman calls for Sunita. There is a birthday party for one of the students in the school that Saturday; can she and Gautama come? On the second day, Sunita meets another mother—the family has lately returned from Lagos—and makes plans to go swimming at the Breach Candy club, which used to be reserved for whites and is now open to anyone with a foreign passport. Immediately, this world takes us in. Komal's mother never fulfilled her promises to meet us; not one of the New Era mothers included us or our son in their birthday parties or sent their children over to play. We were too foreign, too "cosmopolitan." You belong to the club that takes you in, and this is ours: rich people, English-speaking people, foreign-returned people. Head Start is filled with the sons and daughters of industrialists, royal families. My son is not going to get the education I got; he is going to get, in India at least, an elite education. If we stayed here, he would go on to the "convent" schools, to Cathedral or Scottish Mission, to join the ranks of boys who looked down on my younger self. It is as difficult to move down the caste ladder as it is to move up.

At Head Start, iron-willed mothers meticulously plan their children's birthday parties. My son goes to one, in a large apartment in Cuffe Parade. The party favors are imported from Dubai. There is a professional entertainer, with a dog that has been trained to play basketball. Gautama comes home with three sets of imported crayons and coloring pens—"felt pens," as we used to call those items we craved. There might have been a hundred kids there; the hosts would have spent not less than 100,000 rupees—about $4,000—on that party. But it is a good investment in this world, in Bombay High. It is training for their children in a lifetime of parties. The question that never leaves the minds of the charmed set in Bombay, however old they are, is: Who will invite me to their party? Who will come to mine?

There is something especially frenetic about partying in a poor country. Every night there is a party, and the invitations outdo each other in inventiveness: one comes in a woolen glove, another in a shot glass, a third in a box with pasta, dried mushrooms, and Italian herbs. These are grown-up birthday parties, and the same people get invited or not invited who were invited or not invited in school. They are stocked with Bombabes: good-looking women in short skirts. I see something new this time in India: single people in their thirties, even forties, unmarried by choice. One of the rakes uses the old line to explain why he won't get married: "If you can get milk every day, why buy the cow?" The cow is a Bombabe in her thirties, a year or three away from her sell-by date. Successful at her career because she is single, desperately lonely also because of it, she is fair game for the married, the lesbian, and the fat—anybody to hold her through the endless night. But none of this vulnerability will creep into her public self. The world will never know. Married women will envy her.

Bombay is built on envy: the married envy the single, the single long to be married, the middle class envy the truly rich, the rich envy those without tax problems. The advertising billboards promote it. OWNER'S PRIDE, NEIGHBOR'S ENVY goes the slogan of a long-running TV ad, showing a green horned demon with his talons around a TV set. The third page of the *Bombay Times* and the back pages of the *Indian Express* and the columns of the Sunday edition of *Mid-Day* and the metro sections of the news-magazines are the envy pages, all designed to make the reader feel poorer, uglier, smaller, and most of all, socially outcast. So the housewife in Dadar looks up from page three at her husband sitting there in his lungi, having his hair oiled, and demands to know why he isn't being invited to any of these parties, doesn't know any of these names. Thus does a metropolis create what advertising people call "aspirational" consumers.

There is a simple truth about the society set: They hate living here but they couldn't exist anywhere else in India. "Maybe Bangalore," they say hopefully, but few of them ever move there. If they move, they go to New York or London. Better still, they bring New York and London to them, in restaurants such as Indigo, whose success is due to displacement. You walk in off the seedy Bombay street, and you're in Soho. No effort is spared to make it foreign, in the waitstaff, the food, the decor. The first world lives smack in the center of the third. I meet people in Bombay High who can tell me where to get the best chocolates in Paris but have no idea where to find good bhelpuri—the city's equivalent of New York's pizza slice—in Bombay. You would think that to go from South Bombay to the rest of the city—the area demarcated by the Mahim flyover, from the taxi zone to the auto-rickshaw zone—you would need a visa. But these people are not any less a part of the city for their determined exclusion of most of it from their lives. Bombay has always been a city of internal exiles: Parisian socialites in Colaba, London bankers in Cuffe Parade. If they ever actually made the move to the cities of their dreams, they would be adrift, valueless. Other worlds can be replicated right here, in miniature.

ONE AFTERNOON, before Sunita and the children have joined me in Bombay, I am walking on the road leading to the Strand bookstore when I see a little family: a mother with wild and ragged hair, walking with a baby boy, maybe a year old, fast asleep on her shoulder and leading by the hand another boy, maybe four or five, who is rubbing his eyes with the fist of his free hand. He is walking the way children walk when they have been walking a long time, his legs jerking outward, his head nodding in a circle, to beat the monotony, the tiredness. They are all barefoot. The mother says something gentle to the older boy, still clutching her hand. I walk past them, but then I have to stop. I stand and watch. They come up to a stall on the sidewalk, and, as I expect her to, the mother holds out her hand. The stall owner doesn't acknowledge them. Automatically I find myself opening my wallet. I look for a ten, then take out a fifty instead, and walk up to them very fast, my mind raging. I thrust the fifty into her hand—"Yes, take this"—and walk on very fast without looking back, till I get to the air-conditioned bookstore, and then I stand in a corner and shut my eyes.

The identification with my own family is so strong—a mother with two young boys—that I start constructing a past and a future for them. Probably they would have walked like that all day long, barefoot in the heat. A hundred times a day the boys would have seen their mother hold out her hand to beg. A hundred people would be watched by those clear young eyes as these strangers curse their mother, tell her to move on, or throw some change at her. And still she would carry them on her shoulder when they were tired. Sometimes she might put them down in the dirt, and then they would eat a little rice or sleep where they were from tiredness.

All day long I feel ashamed of spending money. Everything I spend that day becomes multiples of that 50-rupee note. Within twenty minutes of my giving money to the mother I have spent six times as much on books. The pizza I order in the evening is two of those fifties. The rent I will be paying per month on my flat will be two thousand times that fifty. And so on. What had my giving them 50 rupees changed? For me, it meant nothing: pocket change, less than a New York subway token. I haven't yet learnt to take the brightly colored money seriously. But it would probably be a whole day's earnings for the mother (I can't think of her as "the beggar"). Perhaps she will take her boys and her sudden good fortune and buy them a toy from the arcades under the Fort's arches. Perhaps she will buy the medicine she hasn't been able to afford for the younger child's cough. Perhaps she will take the money and give it to her man, who will buy six more bottles of country liquor. And that is the obscenity here: Our lives have two entirely separate systems of currency.

I am new in the country still. It has not hit me till now, and I feel physically exhausted. I call Sunita in London and ask her if our two children are well. I feel an intense need to hug them tight. I am still reacting to the city as a foreigner. I remember what a French friend had told me about her mother, a social worker in Paris. The first time she came to India, she stepped outside the airport with her bags to have a horde of street children come up to her, little babies being carried by only slightly older ones. Overcome by their destitution, their youth, their beauty, she opened up both her bags on the sidewalk and started handing out gifts. Within minutes her bags were picked clean. Thus unburdened, she stood up and walked forth into India.

The previous evening I had come home from the Library Bar after a small party of billionaires, people richer than any I'd ever met in New York. In the daytime I had been walking around the Bihari slums of Madanpura, scenes of fantastic deprivation. As I wake up now in this flat overlooking the sea, the children of Madanpura have long since been up in their shanties. Maybe they are working at construction sites, holding on their heads baskets of bricks weighing half again as much as themselves. Maybe they are running, fetching tea, washing vessels, servicing the desires of men. This, too, is a kind of childhood.

SLOWLY, A SYSTEM EVOLVES in the Dariya Mahal flat: a maid, a driver, and a cleaner are found and tested; bathrooms are brought to working order; communications with the outside world—newspapers, e-mail, telephones—are established. We begin to get to know the patterns of light and air, we know what time of day to draw the curtains, when to leave the windows open, and in what sequence. We still don't have many friends, but we are beginning to rely on one or two people that we will see at least once every couple of weeks. The surrounding Gujaratis make tentative attempts to reach out to me but they are unsure of how to do so, since I have left the family business and married a Madrasi.

Indian friends such as Ashish from America call me. "Can we return there too? We have been thinking for a while, but what kind of job will my wife get . . . ?" To what India do you want to return? For us, who left at the beginning of our teenage years, just after our voices broke and before we had a conception of making love or money, we kept returning to our childhoods. Then, after enough trips of enough duration, we returned to the India of our previous visits. I have another purpose for this stay: to update my India, so that my work should not be just an endless evocation of childhood, of loss, of a remembered India. I want to deal with the India of the present.

But the terrain is littered with memory mines. I step on a particular square of cement on a particular lane and look up and see a tree springing up as I saw it a quarter of a century ago. A memory explosion, an instant bridge between that precise moment and this one. As I walk around the city now, I step on little pockets of memory treasure that burst open and waft out their scents.

So I wander the streets with my laptop in a green backpack, taking rickshaws and taxis and trains whenever possible, looking for all the things that made me curious as a child. As people talk to me, my fingers dance with Miss Qwerty. But I have to pay. My currency is stories. Stories told for stories revealed—so have I heard. Stories from other worlds, carried over the waters in caravans and ships, to be exchanged for this year's harvest of stories. A hit man's story to a movie director in exchange for the movie director's story to the hit man. The film world and the underworld, the police and the press, the swamis and the sex workers, all live off stories; here in Bombay, I do too. And the city I lost is retold into existence, through the telling of its story.

Powertoni

"What does a man look like when he's on fire?" I asked Sunil.

It was December 1996, and I was sitting in a high-rise apartment in Andheri with a group of men from the Hindu nationalist Shiv Sena party. They were telling me about the riots of 1992–93, that followed the destruction of the Babri Masjid in Ayodhya.

The two other Shiv Sena men with Sunil looked at each other. Either they didn't trust me yet or they were not drunk enough on my cognac. "I wasn't there. The Sena didn't have anything to do with the rioting," one man said.

Sunil would have none of this. He put down his glass and said, "I'll tell you. I was there. A man on fire gets up, falls, runs for his life, falls, gets up, runs."

He addressed me.

"*You* couldn't bear to see it. It is horror. Oil drips from his body, his eyes become huge, huge, the white shows, white, white, you touch his arm like this"—he flicked his arm—"the white shows. It shows especially on the nose"—he rubbed his nose with two fingers as if scraping off the skin—"oil drips from him, water drips from him, white, white all over.

"Those were not days for thought," he continued. "We five people burnt one Mussulman. At four a.m. after we heard of Radhabai Chawl, a mob assembled, the likes of which I have never seen. Ladies, gents. They picked up any weapon they could. Then we marched to the Muslim side. We met a pavwallah on the highway, on a bicycle. I knew him; he used to bread every day." Sunil held up a piece of bread from the pav bhaji he w.. eating. "I set him on fire. We poured petrol on him and set him on fire. All I thought was, This is a Muslim. He was shaking. He was crying, 'I have children, I have children!' I said, 'When your Muslims were killing the Radhabai Chawl people, did you think of your children?' That day we showed them what Hindu dharma is."

The 1992–93 Riots

Ayodhya is many hundreds of miles to the north. But the rubble from its mosque, torn down in December 1992 by a Hindu mob that believed it had been constructed by the Mughal emperor Babar over the birthplace of the god Rama, swiftly provided the foundations for the walls that shot up between Hindus and Muslims in Bombay. The divided metropolis went to war with itself; a series of riots left at least fourteen hundred people dead. Four years later, I came back to write an article about it. I was planning a trip to a municipal office with a group of slum women. When I suggested the following Friday, December 6, there was a silence. The women laughed uneasily and looked away. Finally, one said, "No one will leave the house on that date."

The riots were a tragedy in three acts. First, there was a spontaneous upheaval between the largely Hindu police and Muslims. This was followed, in January 1993, by a second wave of more serious rioting—instigated by the Shiv Sena leader Bal Thackeray—in which Muslims were systematically identified and massacred, their houses and shops burnt and looted. The third stage was the revenge of the Muslims: on Friday, March 12, when every good Muslim was reading his namaaz prayers, ten powerful bombs planted by the Muslim underworld went off all over the city. One exploded in the Stock Exchange, another in the Air India building. There were bombs in cars and scooters. In all, 317 people died, many of them Muslims.

I wanted to speak to the rioters themselves, to the followers of Bal Thackeray. It was he who had formed, in 1966, a nativist political party called the Shiv Sena—Shivaji's Army—after the seventeenth-century Maharashtrian warrior king who organized a ragtag band of guerrilla fighters into a fighting force that would humble the Mughal emperor Aurangzeb and, in time, hold sway over most of central India. I wanted to find out how the business of rioting is actually planned and carried out.

One day I was at the computer office of Ashish, my old friend from Queens, talking with him about this. "I can take you to meet some Shiv Sena people who were in the riots." We turned around. A bony bespectacled man in his early twenties was smiling at us, irregular white teeth offering themselves in two crammed rows. His name was Girish Thakkar, and he was working in Ashish's office as a programmer. "Come to Jogeshwari." Most of Jogeshwari, the Hindu and especially the Muslim area, is a slum. On January 8, 1993, a Hindu family of millworkers was sleeping in a room in Radhabai Chawl, in the middle of the Muslim part of the slum. Someone locked their door from the outside; someone threw a petrol bomb in through the window. The family of six died screaming, clawing at the door to get out. One of them was a handicapped teenage girl. The flames had spread from their house to set all of Bombay on fire.

So I went with Girish one evening to Jogeshwari and sat in his family's room in the slum, talking to them about the riots. This was how I first met Sunil; he was a neighbor of theirs, sitting quietly on the one chair. Sunil was a deputy leader of the Jogeshwari shakha, or branch, of the Shiv Sena. He was favored to be pramukh, or head, of the entire shakha if the present pramukh won the legislative elections. He was in his late twenties, a short, stocky, mustached young man with a certain flair in dress and manner.

We walked outside the slum and past the highway, where there was a large circus ground for which Sunil held the parking concession. The Shiv Sena deputy invited me to piss with him. I walked with him to a patch of ground in the back, where we both unzipped. I was apprehensive. I remembered what he had said at Girish's house: "Anyone that came, the bread man, the milkman, we would check his body. If there was a difference between our bodies, we would kill him." That little flap of skin that the Muslims lacked could cost them their lives. I had an excuse at the ready for why I lacked it too: It was an infection when I was five, really, an operation, parents were much grieved. But I've atoned for it; I saved my son from the knife a day after he was born. I'll recite a sacred shloka for you.

I must have passed the test, for he introduced me to his family. When we got back the loudspeakers were playing a film song, "Neither a temple nor a mosque. . . ." His parents were there with Sunil's two-year-old daughter. He put her through her tricks, as parents and ringmasters do: "Do namaste," and she brought her palms together in front of her face. "Shake hand." And she shook my hand. One of the Sena boys carried her off to buy her a balloon.

Later, Sunil and the other two Sena boys came to drink with me in Ashish's apartment in Andheri. They looked around appreciatively. We were on the sixth floor, on a hill, and the agitated highway throbbed with traffic below us. Sunil looked out the window. "It's a good place to shoot people from," he noted, and made the rat-tat-tat motion of firing a submachine gun. I had not thought of the apartment this way. But then I was not accustomed, when I came into a new place, immediately to check out the strategic value of its location, its entrances and exits.

What sat on Sunil's mind was the thought that the handicapped girl was raped, repeatedly and in the open. There is no evidence of it; the police report makes no mention of it. Sixteen to twenty Hindu women were raped in Jogeshwari alone, said Sunil. Again, this is without foundation in the press and police reports. But that didn't matter. It was a powerful image, a catalytic image: a handicapped Hindu girl on the ground with a line of leering Muslim men waiting their turn at her while her parents matched her screams with their own as their bodies caught the flames. Many wars begin with an act of rape, real or imagined. It is always the men who are disturbed enough by the rape to go to war.

Sunil didn't use the term "riot." He used "war" instead, the English word. At J. J. Hospital, he saw scenes typical of wartime. Dead bodies all over, male and female, identified only by number tags. At Cooper Hospital, where both Hindu and Muslim rioters and victims were brought in and often lay next to one another in the same ward, fights would break out. Wounded men would rip bottles of saline out of their arms and hurl them at their enemies.

One of the men with us worked for the municipality. "These people are not Muslim, they're all Hindu!" he said. "Every one of them is a convert." Then he said they should go to Pakistan, the lot of them. The standard complaints were trotted out: They always cheered Pakistan at India–Pakistan cricket matches, the Muslim personal law allowed them to marry four wives and so they always produced ten or twelve children when Hindus stopped at two or three. In Bombay, numbers of people are important; the sense of being crowded by the Other in an already overcrowded city is very strong. "In a few years they will be more than us," the municipal employee predicted gloomily. Muslims engaged in underworld activities, he said, and they had no compunctions about killing people, while a Hindu would pause before killing and ask himself why he was doing it.

While Sunil was taking Muslim lives, he also found time to save a Muslim life. He had a friend, a Muslim woman, whom he escorted safely to her neighborhood. There he was surrounded by a group of Muslim men. He prepared to die. The girl's grandmother then came out, talked down the Muslim mob, and, hiding Sunil under her burka, spirited him out of the neighborhood. There is a peepal tree at Radhabai Chawl, said Sunil; half its leaves are black and the other half green. He knew because he took his daughter there when she was sick. She had been crying continuously, and the doctors hadn't helped. Then someone told him that the Muslims could get the evil eye out. He took her to the Radhabai Chawl area, and the Muslim holy man circled his daughter's face with the bottle of water three times. Sunil could see the water level in the bottle going down after each circle. She soon got better. "He didn't ask for money," said Sunil, of the exorcist. "Even if you go to their dargah"—shrine—"they won't ask for money. They are unselfish that way."

Sunil saw no irony in the fact that when his daughter was sick he went to the same Muslim community that he massacred and burnt during the riots. Sunil also runs the cable TV for Jogeshwari and surrounding areas. He has Muslim clients, and he often eats at their houses "to keep relations." The riots also didn't stop Sunil from doing business with the Muslims. He would go in the morning to Mohammedali Road in the central city to buy chickens from the Muslims, bring them back to Jogeshwari by twelve, and sell them to the Hindus. In the afternoons he would kill other Muslims. The chicken sellers wouldn't care that he was Hindu. Bombayites understand that business comes first. They are individually multiple.

Sunil asked me what my goals were, not just in Bombay but in the whole world. I replied that I wanted a better world for my son to grow up in. He nodded. He said he wanted the same for his daughter. "But what are your goals? What do you want to do in life?" My answers did not satisfy him. What he wanted was something beyond the happiness of his immediate family. He wanted the *nation* to be great. He bemoaned the fact that not even the Shiv Sena was beyond corruption. "In Bombay, money is God," he said in English. To him, the highest virtue was to be niswarthi, selfless. He liked to think of himself as someone who was niswarthi, who would give his life for a cause greater than himself. It was such a cause that he'd been hoping to elicit from me.

I WAS GIVEN a tour of the battlegrounds by a group of Shiv Sena men and Raghav, a private taxi operator, a short, stocky man wearing jeans labeled SAVIOUR. He was not officially a Sena member but was called by the shakha pramukh whenever there was party work to be done.

Raghav and a couple of other boys took me through passages between slums so narrow that two persons walking abreast could not pass through them. They were cautious at first. But as we passed a mosque, Raghav laughed, "This is where we shat in the masjid." Another of the men shot him a warning look. The mystery was explained later by Sunil. "My boys broke the masjid," he boasted. This was one of the high points of the war for them; the incident was recalled with glee. Sunil told me how one of them took a cylinder of cooking gas, opened the valve, lit a match, and rolled it inside the mosque. The bomber then enrolled in the police force, where he is still employed.

We were discussing all this not in some back room in whispers but in the middle of the street in the morning with hundreds of people coming and going. Raghav was completely open, neither bragging nor playing down what he did, just telling it like it happened. The Sena men, the Sainiks, were comfortable; this was their turf, the Hindu part of Jogeshwari. They pointed out the sole remaining shop owned by a Muslim: a textile shop that used to be called Ghafoor's. During the riots, some of the boys wanted to kill him but others who had grown up with him protected him, and he got away with just having his stock burnt. Now it had reopened, under the name Maharashtra Mattress. Raghav pointed to the shop next to it. "I looted the battery shop."

Raghav took me to a very large open patch of ground by the train sheds, a phantasmagoric scene with a vast garbage dump on one side with groups of people hacking at the ground with picks, a crowd of boys playing cricket, sewers running at our feet, train tracks and bogies in sheds in the middle distance, and a series of concrete tower blocks in the background. A week ago, I had been standing at the other side of this ground. A Muslim man had pointed out where I now stood, saying, "That is where the Hindus came from."

This is where Raghav and the boys caught two Muslims. They had strayed. "We burnt them. We poured kerosene on them and set them on fire," said Raghav.

"Did they scream?" I asked him.

"No, because we beat them a lot before burning them. Then their bodies lay here in the ditch, rotting, for ten days. Crows were eating them. Dogs were eating them. The police wouldn't take the bodies away, because the Jogeshwari police said it was in the Goregaon police's jurisdiction, and the Goregaon police said it was the railway police's jurisdiction."

Raghav also told me about an old Muslim man who was throwing hot water on the Sena boys. They broke down his door, dragged him out, took a neighbor's blanket, wrapped him in it, and set him on fire. "It was like a movie: silent, empty, someone burning somewhere, and us hiding, and the army. Sometimes I couldn't sleep, thinking that just as I have burnt someone, somebody could burn me."

I asked Raghav, as we were looking over the wasteland, if the Muslims they burnt would beg for their lives. "Yes, they would say, Have mercy on us. But we were filled with such hate; we had Radhabai Chawl on our minds. And even if there was one of us who said, Let him go, there would be ten others saying, No, kill him. And so we had to kill him."

"But what if he was innocent?"

Raghav looked at me. "His biggest crime was that he was Muslim."

ALL GREAT CITIES ARE SCHIZOPHRENIC, said Victor Hugo. Bombay has multiple-personality disorder. During the riots, the printing presses were running overtime. They were printing visiting cards, two sets for each person, one with a Muslim name and one with a Hindu name. When you were out in the city, if you got stopped your life depended on whether you answered to Ram or Rahim. Schizophrenia became a survival tactic.

People told people: The Muslims, angered by the destruction of the Babri Masjid, are stockpiling arms; there will be a bloodbath. The news was relayed at the panwallah's, in the commuter train, during the office tea break. In the evenings, a small convoy of cars would drive onto the beach at Shivaji Park, turn toward the wide Arabian Sea, leave their headlights on, and keep vigil all night. They were standing guard against the Iranian armada that was supposed to be just off the shores of Bombay, holds packed with all kinds of bombs and guns and missiles for the coming jihad.

After the riots, 240 NGOs united to put the city back together. Human chains of citizens were formed, stretching across the city, to demonstrate unity. Groups called Mohalla Ekta Committees were formed to bring together Hindus, Muslims, and the police, to identify fistfights before they could escalate into riots; Girish's father became a member of the Ekta Committee for Jogeshwari. There hasn't been a major riot since. But the fault lines had been set. An entire segment of the population had been made to feel like foreigners in the city in which they were born and raised.

"GO BACK TO PAKISTAN," said the Shiv Sena to the Muslims. Jalat Khan, who lives in the Muslim slums of Mahim, was in a quandary. His mother had come the other way, from Pakistan to Bombay, when she was twelve. Had I heard the news from Karachi? he asked me. "It's better here." Jalat Khan wanted me to meet his mother. I went to the back room. There was a human being lying on a low cot. It was a very old lady, covered from the neck down by thick blankets. Her hands were misshapen; she was completely paralyzed below the waist, but she had not always been like this. For eighty-six years of Roshan Jan's ninety years on earth, she had lived in peace. She remembered the British with affection. Bombay was so good in those days, she said, in the way very old people generally remember the past as being always and continuously better than the present. You could walk down the road with gold in your hands. The rice of those days smelled so good; the wheat was pure.

For eighty-six years of her life Roshan Jan could walk about her neighborhood. She would hold big feasts, slaughter two goats, cook basmati rice, and feed all who came, Hindus too. After Gandhi was assassinated, in 1948, the Muslims were scared, because people thought at first it must have been a Muslim who killed him. But nothing happened. No riots.

One night in January 1993, a group of Hindu men broke down Roshan Jan's door. One of them picked up the eighty-six-year-old woman and threw her down on the cement floor, breaking her spinal cord. Now she lay there, telling me that other Hindus, who she knew were in the riots, come to her and ask for her blessing, and she gives it to them. But she wishes they had killed her then. It would have been better.

When the retaliatory bombs were set off by the Muslims, the windows of Jalat Khan's son's school were shattered, and Jalat ran to get him out. But that didn't stop the swelling of pride he felt. "They used to curse us, tear down the burkas of our women in the trains. If the bomb blasts hadn't happened, not one of us would have survived. After the bomb blast they got a little dhilla"—a little loose, a little scared.

Durriya Padiwala, the Muslim CEO of an upholstery company, was at home when the riots broke out. She got word of the progress of the riots, across Tardeo, across Byculla, across Mohammed Ali Road. "You knew exactly when they would come to your neighborhood." In the thick of the riots, a Maharashtrian neighbor on the ground floor gave the Padiwala family shelter, and then they moved across the street to a building at the entrance of which was a Shiv Sena shakha. "We figured they wouldn't attack their own building." The building next to hers housed a wastepaper shop; it provided fine fuel for the petrol bomb that fell on it. The next day, Durriya, watching from her balcony, saw a man remove a part of the wall of the paper shop. A human arm fell out.

"The riots affected a lot of thinking, educated people. Very educated, very literate people became very anti-Muslim." Durriya—who doesn't wear a burka, or even a salwaar kameez, doesn't have hennaed hair, and doesn't look particularly Muslim—would hear comments made by people "in the strangest places. It could be in a five-star lobby. 'Oh, they deserved it, they asked for it.' " She would not counter this. "I was too scared." Durriya's business was discriminated against because it was a Muslim company. Payments would come late; bigger deposits were now required from them than from Hindu suppliers.

Three months after the riots, Durriya, working in her office, walked out to get some papers and there was a mighty blast; the ceiling collapsed in the room she'd just left. One of the bombs had gone off in her building. Her brother was working in the Stock Exchange building; when the next bomb went off in its basement, the glass of the viewing gallery shattered and fell on him, wounding him. She was not entirely displeased.

"There's no justification for the blasts," Durriya emphasized. "An eye for an eye is a terrible thing." At the same time, when the Muslims in her office traveled on the trains, they felt the Hindus were looking at them with new fear. They could raise their heads. "Their self-respect had been restored." It was the old story: the powerful wish of minorities all over the world to be the oppressor rather than the oppressed. Almost every Muslim I spoke to in Bombay agreed that the riots had devastated their sense of self-worth; they were forced to stand by helplessly as they watched their sons slaughtered, their possessions burnt before their eyes. When the bombs went off, killing and maiming people indiscriminately, the Hindus were reminded that the Muslims weren't helpless. On the trains, proving ground of dignity, they could hold their heads high again.

THE RIOTS HAD ONE CONSEQUENCE their planners couldn't have foreseen: They became a recruitment bonanza for the Muslim underworld. I met one such man, Blackeye, who became a professional hit man for the Dawood Ibrahim gang. In 1992, Blackeye, then fifteen years old, was living with his family in a large housing development named Pratiksha Nagar. One Friday, some Maharashtrian men—their neighbors, their friends—went around the complex marking the Muslim houses. They found out that there were about five thousand Muslims in the colony. The next day, a Saturday, they held a maha-aarti, a massive public puja, and the streets rang with triumphant temple bells and the blowing of conches. On Sunday morning, Blackeye was watching cartoons on television when there was a knock on the door. "We are from the government," a voice said. "Open the door. We need to see your ration card." Blackeye's father immediately slung a rod across the door, from the inside. The men started banging on the door, harder, and then broke it and stormed inside. They took the iron rod and went at his father, in front of his family. "I saw the boy who was beating my father. He was my friend. He used to come to my home to eat at Eid. He used to play cricket with me." So Blackeye folded his hands and begged. "You used to come to our house!" His friend just looked at him and told him to get out of there, because he was so small. Blackeye fled to his uncle's house, screaming for him to come help. His uncle refused; he was afraid for his own life.

Meanwhile, his mother and his sisters had locked themselves in the bedroom, clutching bottles of Tik-20, an insecticide; if the Sena men broke in, they would swallow the poison before they could be defiled. They weren't touched, but the Sena men broke everything in the house after they finished assaulting Blackeye's father. Afterward, the family abandoned the apartment and stayed in a transit camp for three days. The nearby eateries wouldn't even give them water to drink, and they lived on rotten tomatoes. But the worst was yet to come. "After the riots we had to beg," recalls Blackeye, his eyes reddening even now, years later. "We had to put our hands out—for biscuits, for clothes, from the relief agencies." He grew up, dropped out of school, joined the Muslim gang, and started killing people, including the devoutly Hindu music magnate Gulshan Kumar. "After the riots most of the boys from Pratiksha Nagar joined the Dawood gang. It was my main reason too."

The Bombay Police see Muslims as criminals, much as some American police view African Americans. A newspaper headline from December 1996 read: HOME TRUTH: MUSLIMS MORE LIKELY TO BECOME CRIMINALS THAN HINDUS. The article stated that Muslims, who comprise just under a fifth of the population of the city, were responsible for a third of its crimes, based on a survey of various police stations. The cases registered against Hindus involved accidents, fraud, and theft while the ones registered against Muslims were more violent. An inspector from Cuffe Parade station was quoted: "Muslims are caught for crimes such as extortion, rapes and murders, gang wars and organized car thefts. Hindus are mainly arrested for cheating, eve-teasing"—sexual molestation short of rape—"fraud, theft and robbery."

"The police gave us good cooperation during the riots," Sunil said to me. "Deshmukh, the Jogeshwari policeman, would say with pride, Balasaheb called me."

Between January 10 and January 18, 1993, the activist Teesta Setalvad taped conversations off the police frequency as police squads on the road coordinated activities with the control room. This is some of what went out over the airwaves:

DONGRI 1 TO CONTROL: Two military trucks have come carrying milk and other rations. They are led by Major Syed Rehmatullah. . . . A crowd has gathered. . . . Please send more men.

CONTROL: Why the fuck are you distributing milk to them landyas [circumcised pricks, i.e., Muslims]? Do you want to fuck their mothers? Over there, bhenchod mias [another term for Muslims] live.

A bit later that same day:

DONGRI 1: The people gathered to collect milk and rations have dispersed now.

CONTROL: Who has milk been distributed to? Madharchod, do you get me, do not distribute milk to landyas. Have you understood?

DONGRI 1: These two trucks . . . are military trucks, and the major's name is Syed Rehmatullah.

CONTROL: Seize that vehicle. Search the landyas. Fuck his mother, fuck the Shahi Imam.

From another location:

V.P. ROAD 1 TO CONTROL: A mob has gathered outside Maharashtra garage, Ghasgalli, Lamington Road, with the intention of setting it on fire. Send men.

CONTROL: Must be a landya's garage. Let it burn. Shit, if it belongs to a Maharashtrian, don't burn anything that belongs to a Maharashtrian. But burn everything that belongs to a mia bhenchod.

ASAD BIN SAIF, an activist in an NGO that is fighting hate in the slums, took me to Radhabai Chawl, where the Hindu family was burnt. Like everything else about the schizophrenic city, it had two names: a plaque outside identified it as GANDHI CHAWL. A women's group, Rahe-haq, had arranged a meeting for me; their office was in the very building where the atrocity had taken place.

Before the women arrived, I was sitting in the room where an entire family was burnt alive, listening to an old Muslim man tell me, "Sir, please do something to remove the hate from people's hearts, so that the Ganga and the Jamuna can flow together. You are young, do something. Some poison has entered." The room had been turned into a library and community center by Yuva, an NGO, and this man, a neighbor of the family that

was killed, was the librarian. The library's c
trunk full of books with titles that explained w
members: "Building development projects in
ties and NGOs: An action agenda for policy
Bombay—"my matrubhumi," he said, using th
land. Then he started singing, in a quavering vo
Hindustan hamara. . . ." I was unexpectedly mov
ing. This man was not cynical. He had no sense of .... was a Muslim
man working in a library in a Muslim ghetto that had no books in Urdu.
And he was singing a paean to Hindustan.

On January 17, 1993, L. K. Advani, then president of the Bharatiya
Janata Party (BJP)—the Sena's coalition partner and the instigator of the
Babri Masjid demolition—came to Gandhi Chawl to highlight this atrocity
against Hindus. Arifa Khan went to see the famed politician. He had
stepped out of his car and was looking around the slum. Arifa Khan was
suddenly moved to speak. She called out, "Why did you come here now?"
Then this short, pretty Muslim woman from the slums of Bombay said to
the man who wanted to be prime minister, "If you didn't do your kar seva,
your rath yatra, this wouldn't have happened." Advani had no answer to
Arifa's remark, which referred to his stoking of mass Hindu rage through
nationwide processions on a chariot in the weeks before the demolition. He
got back in his car, and his entourage, commandos, and cars left Jogeshwari
to its fate.

Arifa Khan, along with about twenty other Muslim women, was now
sitting in the room, which also functions as a day-care center. There was
also a Hindu couple. Then a couple of tough-looking Muslim boys dressed
in lungis joined us uninvited. Asad introduced me, and the women started
telling me about the troubles: their men shot and stabbed, by the police or
the Hindus. The azaan rang out from a nearby mosque; the women covered
their heads. The Hindus and Muslims now lived apart in the slum, out of
choice. It hurt the women I was speaking to that during the time of the curfew Hindus would not let them buy food from their areas.

Had they considered going to Pakistan? asked Asad.

"This is our watan"—homeland. "Whatever it is, it's our India." One
of the women claimed the right to live here by virtue of the fact that she
votes. "If we don't get them seats, will they get seats?"

Bombay has one and a half times the proportion of Muslim residents as

overall; Muslims in Bombay comprise more than 17 percent
population. In India as a whole, Muslims number 120 million,
ent of the general population. That makes India home to the second
gest Muslim population in the world. Half a century after Partition,
there are still more Muslims in India than in Pakistan. By choosing to stay,
they have voted with their feet. But most Hindus in the city did not believe
that Muslims were nationalistic. They believed, as Thackeray put it in his
party newspaper just after the Babri Masjid fell, "Pakistan need not cross
the border and attack India. Two hundred and fifty million Muslims in
India loyal to Pakistan will stage an armed uprising. [They are one of]
Pakistan's seven atomic bombs." Further, "A Muslim, whichever country
he belongs to, is first a Muslim. Nation is of secondary importance to him."

The Muslims of Bombay are the most diverse group of the followers of
Mohammed in the country. It's not just the division between Shia and
Sunni; there are Dawoodi Bohras, Ismailis, Deobandis, Barelvis, Memons,
Moplahs, Ahmaddiyas, and so on. The Hindutva parties spread fear of
the Muslim horde, as if it were a monolith. The truth is that many of the
groups, such as the Deobandis and Barelvis or the traditional and the
reformist Bohras, often hate each other more passionately than they do
the Hindus. But the riots united them too. The Dawoodi Bohras of Malabar
Hill discovered what they had in common with the Bihari Sunnis in the
Madanpura slums: a very public questioning of their claim to be citizens of
India. They discovered their biggest crime was that they were Muslims.

One of the angry young boys said his brother was killed in the riots
and nobody had been arrested. But when the Hindu family died, eleven
Muslims were arrested and given life sentences. A Sena corporator, an
organizer, they had heard, took the handicapped girl's corpse all around
Bombay to get the Hindus inflamed. "One woman died in Radhabai
Chawl," the angry boy said. "Fifty of our people died and nothing happened. The law is theirs; they can do what they want. If you have justice,
let it be on both sides or tell us to fight! We know how to fight." Gradually,
the boys took over the meeting; the women stopped speaking. The Hindu
couple got up and left.

After a while the boys got up to leave, but not before warning me,
"Write correct things." One of them laughed, without humor. "If you
don't write anything it'll be okay too."

After the boys left, the atmosphere lightened precipitously. The women apologized for the boys. "They are angry," one of the women said. "That's why I didn't want to bring them."

Another woman told me how much this time with me was costing her. "I am sitting here but my heart is at home. Will I get water? Will I have to wait two hours?" To get water in the slum, the women have to line up and take numbers. Each person, in groups of thirty, gets two buckets for the household's needs. Your religion determines how often you will bathe, where you will shit. "In the Hindu areas each lane has a tap, here each eight or ten lanes has one. Over there, there are toilets everywhere. In our area the toilets have been stopped for one year."

Much of the slum is a garbage dump. The sewers, which are open, run right between the houses, and children play and occasionally fall into them. They are full of a blue-black iridescent sludge. When the government sweepers come to clean the drains, they scoop it out and leave piles of it outside the latrines. I couldn't use the public toilets. I tried, once. There were two rows of toilets. Each one of them had masses of shit, overflowing out of the toilets and spread liberally all around the cubicle. For the next few hours that image and that stench stayed with me, when I ate, when I drank. It's not merely an esthetic discomfort; typhoid runs rampant through the slum and spreads through oral–fecal contact. Pools of stagnant water, which are everywhere, breed malaria. Many children also have jaundice. Animal carcasses are spread out on the counters of the butcher shops, sprinkled with flies like a moving spice. The whole slum is pervaded by a stench that I stopped noticing after a while.

They complained that neither their municipal corporator, a Muslim woman, nor their state legislator, a Shiv Sena man, listened to them. So Arifa Khan, along with a group of eight other women, started a group in the Jogeshwari slums. Rahe-haq—The Right Path—is an organization of around fifteen women, most but not all of them Muslim. They started with nine members in 1988 in response to the toilet problem. There are two million people without access to latrines in Bombay. You can see them every morning along the train tracks, trudging with a tumbler of water, looking for a vacant place to squat. It is a terrible thing, a degrading thing, for a woman to be forced to look every morning for a little privacy to go to the toilet or to clean herself while she's menstruating. No city this rich should make its women suffer this way. The women of this slum were luckier. They had toilets built by the municipality, but they were full, and the municipality wasn't doing anything about unblocking them. Every election, various leaders would come around to the slum and promise to do something about the toilets. The group of women got together and went to the municipal office. "We did bhagdaud," explained the women. This term, familiar to anybody dealing with Indian bureaucracy, means to run around, to go from one office to the next with your petition till you get what you're looking for. The women did bhagdaud, and finally some of the toilets were cleaned.

Energized by the success of their toilet struggle, the women went on to water. Water comes here for a couple of hours a day, and there is a long line of women with buckets at the municipal tap. At the time, the municipal water connections were cut back. This was done at the behest of local plumbers. They stood to make money if the municipality cut its connections, so they bribed the officials involved to do so. The plumbers charged 16,000 rupees for a half-inch pipe of water; four households might get together and pay 4,000 rupees each to buy one such connection. Tangles of pipes snake along the alleys in the slum. The women of Rahe-haq made a pani morcha, a water protest march, to the municipal office. The municipality was forced to increase the supply.

People in the slum started approaching the Committee, as the women call themselves, for other kinds of problems related to the riots. A widow who had gone mad after seeing the burnt corpse of her husband hanging from a tree was having problems getting compensation money that the government was giving to riot victims; the Committee interceded. The scope of their work became larger. Women who had been divorced by their husbands came to them; under Muslim law, a husband can part with his wife essentially by saying "I divorce you" three times. The Committee got a lawyer to provide these women with legal advice. A group of five women was set up to counsel couples between whom some shadow had entered. "We listen to both sides; we talk to orthodox people using religious arguments, then we get people back together. If the men are criminals we take them to court." The women went on to sort out problems with ration cards, and in the last local elections they supported a woman from the slum under the Janata Dal banner.

I asked the women if their husbands supported the Committee. There was a gale of laughter. "We have to hear their curses." The local branch of the Muslim League party started spreading rumors about them: They were not modest; they were dealing with men every day in their work. They accused them of being un-Islamic and finally destroyed their office.

The women set up a day-care center and ran it themselves, until the boys who had recently been sitting in the room took the center from them at knifepoint. They wanted the room to smoke charas—hashish—and ganja; after the riots, the hotheads were newly emboldened in the community. Now the women had to do with this much smaller room, this charnel house of 1993, as their day-care center. They would soon be going again to the Municipal Corporation, to press for a bigger room, with a lock. If there is hope for Bombay, it is in this group of slum women, all illiterate, and others like them. Issues of infrastructure are not abstract problems for them. Much more than the men, the women have to deal with such issues firsthand. If you want to make sure that the money you send to a poor place will be spent properly, give it to the women who live there.

I asked one of the Jogeshwari women if she wouldn't rather live in a decent apartment than the slum she lived in now, with the open gutter outside and the absence of indoor plumbing. Yes, there was a building planned nearby to resettle the slum dwellers. But people from her neighborhood wouldn't move there. "There's too much aloneness. A person can die behind the closed doors of a flat and no one will know. Here," she observed with satisfaction, "there are a lot of people."

Be it ever so humble. . . . We tend to think of a slum as an excrescence, a community of people living in perpetual misery. What we forget is that out of inhospitable surroundings, the people have formed a community, and they are as attached to its spatial geography, the social networks they have built for themselves, the village they have re-created in the midst of the city, as a Parisian might be to his quartier or as I was to Nepean Sea Road. "I like this place," said Arifa Khan of her home and her basti, her neighborhood. "This is mine. I know the people here and I like the facilities here." Any urban redevelopment plan has to take into account the curious desire of slum dwellers to live closely together. A greater horror than open gutters and filthy toilets, to the people of Jogeshwari, is the empty room in the big city.

THE SHIV SENA IS MADE UP mostly of Maharashtrian Hindus, who call themselves "sons of the soil." The Maharashtrians were people who had been born here and were not consumed by immigrant striving: a race of clerks. Their ambitions were modest, practical: a not-too-long work-day; a good lunch from the tiffin sent from home at midday; one or two trips to the cinema a week; and, for their children, a secure government job and a good marriage. They did not crave designer clothes. They did not want to eat expensive foreign food at the Taj.

I did not know many Maharashtrians when I was growing up. There was the world I lived in on Nepean Sea Road, and there was another world whose people came to wash our clothes, look at our electric meters, drive our cars, inhabit our nightmares. We lived in Bombay and never had much to do with Mumbai. Maharashtra to us was our servants, the banana lady downstairs, the textbooks we were force-fed in school. We had a term for them: ghatis—literally, the people from the ghats, or hills. It was also the word we used, generically, for "servant." I was in the fourth standard when Marathi became compulsory. How we groaned! It was a servants' lan-guage, we said. We told each other a story about its genesis. All the peoples of India had their languages, except the Maharashtrians. They went to Shiva and asked to be given a language. The god looked around, saw some pebbles, threw them in his brass pot, and shook it around. "Here's your language," he said. What did we know of the language that contains the poetry of Namdeo, Tukaram, Dilip Chitre, Namdeo Dhasal?

But all the time there was a Maharashtrian underclass, emerging, build-ing itself. And now it had gained political power, strength, and a desperate confidence. It was advancing closer and closer to the world I grew up in, the world of the rich and the named. Many of the people on Nepean Sea Road were aghast not so much that the mobs were hunting out Muslims from the tall buildings but that they had dared to come to Nepean Sea Road at all. The arrogance of ghatis demanding to see the building directories! The other Bombay now sneaks in through our streets, lives among us, doesn't like us being rude to it, occasionally beats us up. The riots of 1992 and 1993 were a milestone in the psychic life of the city, because its differ-ent worlds came together with an explosion. The monster came out of the slums.

BOTH MY GRANDFATHER in Calcutta and my uncle in Bombay shel-tered Muslims in their homes during periods of rioting and saved their lives. During the riots, my uncle also personally cooked food in a Jain temple and went, at great personal risk, to the Muslim areas to distribute it to people trapped by the curfew—five thousand packets of rice and bread and potatoes a day.

The riots taught the Muslims a lesson, said my uncle. "Even educated people like me think that with such wild people we need the Shiv Sena to battle them. The Shiv Sena are also fanatics, but we need fanatics to fight fanatics."

I had heard another version of the same theory—that the warrior Maharashtrians protected the effete business communities—from one of Sunil's friends, the municipal employee. "If we Shiv Sena people had not been here, all the Gujaratis and Marwaris in the white businesses would have been beaten, killed by the Muslims. They are not fighters," he said, with an edge of scorn. "They are after money."

My uncle looked past me, out the window at the darkening sky. He had a good Muslim friend in Calcutta, he told me, a friend who was in school with him in the tenth standard; they would then have been about fifteen. He went with this friend to see a movie, and before the main show, a newsreel came on. There was a scene with many Muslims bowing in prayer, doing their namaaz. Without thinking, my uncle said out aloud in the darkened theater, perhaps to his friend, perhaps to himself, "One bomb would take care of them."

Then my uncle realized what he had just said and remembered that the friend who was sitting next to him was also Muslim. But the friend said nothing, pretending he had not heard. "But I know he did," said my uncle, the pain evident on his face, sitting in this flat in Bombay thirty-five years later. "I was so ashamed. I have been ashamed of that all my life. Then I began to think, How did I have this hatred in me? And I realized I had been taught it since childhood. Maybe it was Partition, maybe it was their food habits—Muslims kill animals—but our parents taught us we couldn't trust them. Even my son. I tell him, 'After you're married you won't be so close to your Muslim best friend.' The events of Partition washed away the teachings of Gandhiji. Dadaji—my grandfather—and Bapuji—his brother—were staunch Gandhians except when it came to Muslims. I could never bring a Muslim friend to my home and I couldn't go to theirs."

The next day, my uncle was sitting in the room with the little shrine, doing his morning puja, as I sat with my laptop. "Don't write what I told you," he said, as I was writing it.

I asked him why.

"I've never told anyone that before."

In the act of telling, my uncle was beginning to understand for himself the origins of hate.

In the Bombay I grew up in, being Muslim or Hindu or Catholic was merely a personal eccentricity, like a hairstyle. We had a boy in our class who I realize now from his name, Arif, must have been Muslim. I remember that he was an expert in doggerel and instructed us in an obscene version of a patriotic song, "Come, children, let me teach you the story of Hindustan," in which the nationalistic exploits of the country's leaders were replaced by the sexual escapades of Bombay's movie stars. He didn't do this because he was Muslim and hence unpatriotic. He did this because he was a twelve-year-old boy.

Now it mattered. Because it mattered to Bal Thackeray.

THE SHIV SENA SHAKHA in Jogeshwari was a long hall filled with pictures of Bal Thackeray and his late wife, a bust of Shivaji, and pictures of a muscle-building competition. Every evening, Bhikhu Kamath, the shakha pramukh, sat behind a table and listened to a line of supplicants, holding a sort of durbar. There was a handicapped man come to look for work as a typist. Another man wanted an electric connection to his slum. Husbands and wives who were quarreling came to him for mediation. An ambulance was parked outside, part of a network of several hundred Sena ambulances ready to transport people from the slums to hospitals at all hours, at nominal charges.

In a city where municipal services are in a state of crisis, going through the Sena ensures access to such services. The Sena shakhas also act as a parallel government, like the party machines in American cities that helped immigrants get jobs and fixed streetlights. But the Sena likes to think of itself not so much as a political party but as a social service organization. It functions as an umbrella for a wide variety of organizations: a trade union with over 800,000 members, a students' movement, a women's wing, an employment network, a home for senior citizens, a cooperative bank, a newspaper.

Kamath was a diplomatic sort, hospitably showing me around his terrain. He had the reputation of being honest. "There are very few people like Bhikhu in the Sena," said Sunil. "He still has a black-and-white TV at home." But he could be a street thug when the occasion warranted. And through his connections in the state government, he provided political cover for Sunil. "The ministers are ours. The police are in our hands. If anything happens to me, the minister calls," boasted Sunil. He nodded. "We have powertoni."

He repeated the word a few times. Sunil had hired a Muslim boy in the Muslim locality for his cable business. "He has twelve brothers and six sisters. I give him money and his brother liquor. He will even beat up his brother for me. I hire him for powertoni." Likewise, the holy man who exorcised his daughter had powertoni. Then I realized what the word was: a contraction of *power of attorney,* the awesome ability to act on someone else's behalf or to have others do your bidding, to sign documents, release wanted criminals, cure illnesses, get people killed. *Powertoni:* a power that does not originate in yourself; a power that you are holding on somebody else's behalf. It is the only kind of power that a politician has; a power of attorney ceded to him by the voter. Democracy is about the exercise, legitimate or otherwise, of this powertoni. All over Mumbai, the Shiv Sena is the one organization that has powertoni. And the man with the greatest powertoni in Mumbai is the leader of the Shiv Sena himself, Bal Keshav Thackeray.

His monstrous ego was nurtured from infancy. Thackeray's father considered himself a social reformer and anglicized his surname after William Makepeace Thackeray, the Victorian author of *Vanity Fair.* Thackeray's mother had given birth to five girls and no sons. She prayed ardently to the family deity for a son and was blessed with Bal. He was therefore considered a navasputra, a boon directly from God. Thackeray, now in his seventies, is a cross between Pat Buchanan and Saddam Hussein. He has a cartoonist's sense of the outrageous. He loves to bait foreign journalists with his professed admiration for Adolf Hitler. Thus, in an interview for *Time* magazine at the height of the riots, when he was asked if Indian Muslims were beginning to feel like Jews in Nazi Germany, his response was, "Have they behaved like the Jews in Nazi Germany? If so, there is nothing wrong if they are treated as Jews were in Nazi Germany." A woman in the Jogeshwari slums observed, "Thackeray is more Muslim than I am." He is a man obsessed by Muslims. "He watches us, how we eat, how we pray. If his paper doesn't have the word 'Muslims' in its headline, it won't sell a single copy." The organ of his party is the newspaper *Saamna* (Confrontation), which, in Marathi and Hindi editions, distributes Thackeray's venom all over Maharashtra.

Thackeray, like anybody else in the underworld, is called by many names: the Saheb, the Supremo, the Remote Control, and, most of all, the Tiger—after the symbol of the Shiv Sena. The newspapers are full of pictures of him next to pictures of tigers. Public billboards around the city likewise display his face next to that of a real tiger. He has taken pains to be present at the inauguration of a Tiger Safari Park. He is a self-constructed mythic figure: He drinks warm beer, he smokes a pipe, he has an unusually close relationship with his daughter-in-law.

Sunil and the Sena boys described the Saheb for me. It was impossible to talk to him directly, they said; even an eloquent and fearless man like their shakha pramukh became tongue-tied in front of him, and then the Saheb would berate him. "Stand up! What's the matter, why are you dumb?" It was impossible to meet his eyes. On the other hand: "He likes it if you are direct with him. You should have the daring to ask direct questions. He doesn't like a man who says, Er . . . er. . . ."

Sunil's colleague talked with great pride about the time every year on the Saheb's birthday when they went to his bungalow and watched a long line of the city's richest and most eminent line up to pay homage. "We watched all the big people—ministers, businessmen—bow and touch his feet. All the Tata-Birlas touch his feet and then talk to him."

"Michael Jackson only meets presidents of countries. He came to meet Saheb," his friend added. The president of the giant American corporation Enron had to go to Thackeray to get a power deal cleared. When Sanjay Dutt, son of the principled MP Sunil Dutt who resigned in disgust after the riots, was newly released from jail, his first stop, even before he went home, was to go to the Saheb and touch his feet. Every time one of the corporate gods or a member of the city's film community or a politician from Delhi kowtowed before him, his boys got a thrill of pride, and their image of the Saheb as a powerful man, a man with powertoni, was reinforced.

They told me what to say if I met the Saheb. "Tell him, 'Even today, in Jogeshwari, we are ready to die for you.' Ask Saheb, 'Those people who fought for you in the riots, for Hindutva, what can your Shiv Sena do for them? Those who laid their lives down on a word from you? What can the old parents of the Pednekar brothers, who have no other children, do?' "

I felt like a go-between carrying messages from the lover to the loved one: "Tell her I am ready to die for her." But there was a hint of reproach in their questions, as if they felt their Saheb had been neglecting them, these people who had died for his love. As if the blood sacrifice their comrades had made had gone unacknowledged.

IN MARCH 1995, the Shiv Sena, the majority partner in a coalition with the BJP, came into power in Maharashtra state (the city government had already belonged to them for a decade). The government took a look at the awesome urban problems plaguing the city, the infestation of corruption at all levels of the bureaucracy and the government, the abysmal state of Hindu–Muslim relations, and took decisive action. They changed the name of the capital city to Mumbai.

Once in power, the Sena decided to go after artists, especially Muslim artists. They led the charge against M. F. Husain, India's best-known painter, for painting a nude portrait of the goddess Saraswati twenty years ago. While their government moved the courts, the Shiv Sena mouthpiece *Saamna* was busy mobilizing public opinion. *Saamna* declared that by painting the Hindu goddess nude, Husain had "displayed his innate Muslim fanaticism." Then it offered a suggestion: "If he had any guts at all he should have painted the Prophet of Islam copulating with a pig." The editor of *Saamna*, Sanjay Nirupam, an MP, asked for his pound of flesh: "Hindus, do not forget Husain's crime! He is not to be forgiven at any cost. When he returns to Mumbai he must be taken to Hutatma Chowk and be publicly flogged until he himself becomes a piece of modern art. The same fingers that have painted our Mother naked will have to be cut off." What was striking about the writer's notions of punishment was that they seem to be derived straight from Shari'a—Islamic law.

The Shiv Sena's notions of what is culturally acceptable in India show a distinct bias toward kitsch: Michael Jackson, for example. In November 1996, Thackeray announced that the first performance of the pop star in India would proceed with his blessings. This may or may not have had to do with the fact that the singer had promised to donate the profits from his concert—which eventually ran to more than a million dollars—to a Shiv

Sena—run youth employment project. The planned concert offended a number of people in the city, including Thackeray's own brother, who saw something alien in the values the singer represented. "Who is Michael Jackson and how on earth is he linked to Hindu culture, which the Shiv Sena and its boss Thackeray talk about so proudly?"

The Shiv Sena Supremo responded, "Jackson is a great artist, and we must accept him as an artist. His movements are terrific. Not many people can move that way. You will end up breaking your bones." Then the Saheb got to the heart of the matter. "And, well, what is culture? He represents certain values in America which India should not have any qualms in accepting. We would like to accept that part of America that is represented by Jackson." The pop star acknowledged Thackeray's praise by stopping off at the leader's residence on his way from the airport to his hotel and pissing in his toilet. Thackeray led photographers with pride to the sanctified bowl.

The other kind of values Thackeray likes are those of the country's industrial dynasties. Thackeray loves big business, and big business loves him. The Sena cut its teeth fighting Communists in the chawls and the factories. The Sena-controlled unions are much more dependable than the left-controlled ones. The party's money comes not from the rank and file but from the city's leading businessmen: a car dealer, an airline owner, a diamond merchant. Opposition to Thackeray comes not from the elite but from rural areas, from many middle-class Maharashtrians, and from Marathi writers. As for the courts, Thackeray is unfazed by their power. In June of 1993, the Saheb declared, "I piss on the court's judgments. Most judges are like plague-ridden rats. There must be direct action against them."

JUSTICE SRIKRISHNA WAS UNWELL. He sat in his chambers in the neo-Gothic courts complex, massaged his side, and winced. His doctor had warned him not to get too involved in his work. For almost four years now, he had been a one-man truth squad investigating the causes and responsibilities in the riots. The government had charged him with this onerous duty soon after the riots. "After hearing those poor widows and orphans . . . and then the police saying all these people spontaneously went berserk and there was no planning, no coordination? I find it difficult to swallow. After all, I am also a sensitive human being, not just a judge." But he had none of the powers of a judge, since in this matter it was only a commission of inquiry meant to come up with a report and recommendations, not a court. If he were acting as a judge, he said, he would have slapped contempt charges on the police for lying through their teeth in front of him.

I asked him when he was likely to finish. He glanced at the calendar on the wall. "Six months at the most. I'm sick of it." The Shiv Sena government suspended his work in January 1996. After a countrywide outcry, it reinstated the inquiry but hobbled Srikrishna by expanding its scope to include the bomb blasts as well. He had no power to call witnesses in the blasts, since the criminal part of that inquiry was being dealt with by a special antiterrorist court. The judge was of the sensible opinion that there should be two separate commissions of inquiry, one for the riots and one for the blasts. The whole system of commissions of inquiry was flawed, he said. The Jain Commission inquiry on the causes of the assassination of Rajiv Gandhi in 1991, for example, only began calling witnesses in 1995.

I asked Justice Srikrishna if anything good would come out of his labors. He thought a moment and then said, "If nothing else, it's an act of catharsis."

INDIA HAS NO NEED to look outside for its models of tolerance. Bombay has hundreds of very different ethnic communities, most of whom heartily dislike one another. They have been tolerating one another for centuries, until now. Each community has an intimate knowledge of the codes of the others. My grandfather did not like Muslims in general, but he knew their customs, he wore well-cut sherwanis, and he told me exemplary stories about the Mughals. When, as a little boy, I asked him why Muslims ate meat, he explained, "That is their dharma." The strictest Jains were the ministers of the Muslim Nawabs of Palanpur. They would administer their sovereign's affairs, but they would not eat in his house. Maybe this ability to live together is possible precisely because of these carefully demarcated boundaries, these notions of ritual pollution. There is no possibility of a dangerous miscegenation.

All the people at the meeting in Radhabai Chawl had told me that this kind of communal rioting was unknown in the villages of India. In the villages, people were secure in their faith; they had no need to convince themselves of their devotion by massacring infidels. As one of the hotheaded young men in Radhabai Chawl had explained, "In the village, if there are two Muslim families and there is a patel"—village headman—"the patel will take care of the Muslims. In the city, the politicians and the police harass Muslims." In the villages, they said, you live very close to your neighbors and everybody knows everybody's business and their families and predilections. There is very little mobility; you will have to live together all your lives and can't afford blood feuds with your neighbors.

Around 5 percent of Bombay's Muslims voted for the Sena in Maharashtra, in the 1995 elections, reasoning, as one Muslim put it to me, "when you give the thief the keys to the treasury he'll never steal." Very few issues affect the urban voter as much as crime. In the anonymous city, in the close quarters of the slum, the overriding interest is law and order, stability. More than water, more than housing, more than jobs, the Bombayite wants personal safety. It was in the Sena's interest to prevent riots, and Asghar Ali Engineer, who runs an institute that studies communal conflict, said that since the Sena–BJP government came to power, the incidence of communal rioting had gone down sharply. It was not that Muslims felt safe under the Sena government; as Jalat Khan put it, "They have their finger in our ass." The violence had been driven under the surface, controlled as deliberately as it was deliberately organized during the riots. Periodically, the Sena would show just what it was capable of if displeased—beating up a newspaper editor here, killing a recalcitrant tenant there. But it didn't order young men like Sunil and Raghav to go out and lay waste to whole communities. It didn't need this as long as it had the keys to the state's treasury. It was quiet in the city; but it was a quiet waiting for the storm.

Elections 1998

It is the greatest transfer of power in world history: the real devolution of power to the real majority of 1 billion people. A huge transfer had taken place when the British left India and Pakistan, but an even greater shift was to come. In fifty years, independent India has done what five thousand years of history could not do: It gave the people who are in the majority a voice in the running of the country. The Dalits (also known as untouchables), the "scheduled castes and tribes" (those specifically listed in the constitution as historically having been discriminated against), and the "other backward classes" (those not listed in the schedule but considered deserving of affirmative action) form, as a bloc, the numerical majority in the country. For thousands of years the upper castes—Hindu, Muslim, and Christian—had kept them out of power. But toward the end of the twentieth century, their time had come. For the first time in history the lower castes came into the political process and had a say in who gets to rule them. In 1997, an untouchable, K. R. Narayanan, became president. Brahmin ministers scrambled to touch his feet and ask for his blessings. A bill has come up in parliament, whose passage is inevitable, sooner or later: It will reserve one-third of the seats in the highest legislative body in the land for women, an experiment unprecedented anywhere in the world.

In the summer of 2000, the headlines in the country read 50 MILLION AT RISK OF FAMINE. The rains had failed, but there was no famine; the government machinery roused itself and sent trainloads of relief supplies all across the vast country to people who couldn't grow their own food. As late as the sixties, those headlines would have read THOUSANDS STARVE IN FAMINE. There are very few deaths from starvation in the country now. Anytime someone dies and the cause is suspected to be starvation, the newspapers cover it prominently, and the state government has to answer difficult questions in the assembly; the opposition jumps on such issues. Not least of the country's accomplishments is the abolition of famine. This view surprises the elites in Bombay, who are almost uniformly pessimistic about the future of the city.

The new leaders are extravagantly corrupt, unlike the older Oxbridge-educated ones, whose noblesse oblige and feudal wealth kept them from wholesale plunder of the public purse. And it's not just politics. Through reservations and quotas, the "backwards" are also getting their share of other government institutions such as the Indian Administrative Service. The writer U. R. Ananthamurthy tells me about a Dalit IAS officer who explained to him why he had no option but to be corrupt. He was the first one in the history of his community, he said, to matriculate and go to Delhi, fabled seat of power. Each time he returns to his village, he is expected to come back bearing the goods and spoils of office, not just for his family but for his entire impoverished community. "I am a lump of sugar," the officer said, "in an anthill."

The general election of February 1998, when I return to Bombay to

live, is a ghost election. The Election Commission has clamped down on
spending, and you would hardly know there was an election unless you
turned on the television—at least on Malabar Hill. The only poster I've
seen in my neighborhood features a Gandhi cap–wearing mustachioed
figure, the candidate of the Pajama Party, declaring, "All I want to do is to
pass motions." It is sponsored by MTV and Levi's jeans. Only they have
the money to spend on making fun of elections.

It is a contest between Sonia Gandhi, the Italian widow of Rajiv
Gandhi, and the BJP stalwart Atal Bihari Vajpayee. The chattering classes
don't like Sonia. They are patriotic and are offended by the suggestion that
we need to import our prime ministers, like two-in-one radios or designer
jeans. They do not consider Sonia Indian; she enjoys little support in Malabar Hill and Jor Bagh. Where she is accepted is in rural India. When she
gets up on the stage and begins her speeches by saying, "My husband made
my life complete," the people see before them not an Italian immigrant but
the mythic paragon of the dutiful wife, Sati Savitri. They do not see the
Italian widow of a half-Kashmiri, half-Parsi airline pilot with bad Hindi.
When a woman enters the house of her husband's family, she loses origins.
Anybody in the world can come to India and find home. Even those who
have been gone for twenty years.

WHEN I REACH the diamond merchant's office, Jayawantiben Mehta is
already sitting behind the Formica desk. Jayawantiben is a middle-aged
housewife and BJP member of parliament from the Mumbai South Constituency; her opponent is Murli Deora of the Congress, who had held this
seat for twelve years before Jayawantiben defeated him in 1996. There is a
campaign finance auction going on in the office, a tremendous haggling
over what the merchants should contribute to her campaign. Figures are
being shouted back and forth between the MP and the merchants around
her. "You gave three and three-quarter lakhs. That leaves one and a quarter more," she says. "No, no, we promised only three!" "No, no, nothing
less than five!" (One lakh is 100,000 rupees, or $4,000.) The man whose
office we are in is an official with the diamond merchants' association; he
and his father and his wife are Hindutva activists. But they are too educated
to actually run for office themselves. His wife was offered a ticket by the
BJP to contest the legislative elections. She refused: "It's a dirty business."

The official now takes a white plastic grocery bag out from under his desk and thumps it on the desk in front of Jayawantiben, who does not touch it or peer inside it. "Have someone take it to the car."

Her assistant takes out a receipt book. Jayawantiben offers them a receipt. Further negotiations ensue, what percent is to be given by check and what percent cash. Tea arrives, and as we sip it she invites me to go campaigning with her. After she leaves, I am sitting in front of the white plastic shopping bag, which is waiting to be delivered to her car. I take a quick peek. Inside are hundreds of thousands of rupees, wrapped in newspaper bundles. Printed on the front of the bag is a logo:

HALDIRAM'S SWEETS & NAMKEEN
Choice of Million

I take Jayawantiben up on her invitation and link up with her entourage one morning. I don't have far to go; she is campaigning right behind Dariya Mahal, in the hidden villages of Malabar Hill. I walk with the MP on the rocks near the sea, which is home to a large shantytown. Jayawantiben is greeted with indifference, mostly. A man laughs. "There isn't even water. They come once in five years." But in one house, a group of women come to the porch to worship the candidate. They bring out a steel plate with a coconut, a lamp, and stick of incense, do a little puja in front of her face, and then bow down to touch her feet. She blesses them. The language of the slogans being shouted by her followers changes, from Marathi to Hindi to English, as the population of the slum warrants.

The slum dwellers are pretty confident around their MP. Near the Hanging Gardens, a Gujarati lady comes out of her shack and points to a pipe in front. "The reservoir is right there"—the Malabar Hill reservoir, which supplies water to all of South Bombay—"and I have no water. I have left my job of twenty-two years because there is no water. The job begins at seven-thirty in Andheri, and I have to leave at six." She needs to be home to fill the buckets when the water tanker arrives. Jayawantiben promises to do what she can. Then the woman says, "And will you get my daughter admission?"

"Come to my office and we shall see. A convent school, a government school, a private school?"

"Walshingham. Will you get my daughter admission in Walshingham?

Just tell me." This is one of the most elite girls' schools in Bombay, the one my sisters went to. It is a pretty brazen demand the woman is making.

"Since the school is private it doesn't get government grants, but I will do what I can. That is all I can promise. I could lie and tell you I will get her admission but I don't want to do that. Come to my office and we will try."

There are other villages all around the reservoir. One of them is so beautiful it inspires one campaign worker to say to another, "You want to get a place here?" Under towering banyan trees, strewn about with blue and pink plastic bags, is the settlement, made of brick walls and corrugated roofs. Roosters and chickens run about on the grass. In the distance we can see the blue sea. Gleaming steel vessels are visible through the doorways; new ten-speed bicycles are parked out front. The inhabitants are well-dressed. The children look healthy, and there are no open gutters. But there is also a very large dead rat lying on its side on the lane; we step over it. These slums grew up after I left. They are all around me now, in every available nook and cranny, and they are here to stay; they have power and water connections. All day long, Jayawantiben goes through the fourteen slum colonies around Malabar Hill, meets people, listens to their complaints. But not once does she go into any of the posh buildings surrounding the slums.

"Why?" I ask a campaign worker.

"The rich don't come down from their buildings to vote," he responds. From the wealthy section of Malabar Hill, the legal residents of the district, the turnout is 12 percent; from the squatters in the slum colonies, for whom the issue of who comes into power means the difference between living in four walls or on the street, it's 88 percent. In the evening, I go to Bandra to meet a journalist friend. He digs out an electoral roll from 1995, when he was a poll officer. There are little red tick marks next to about half the names, grouped by the building they belong to, indicating that they've voted. He shows me the listings for the "good" buildings, the rich ones; there are only a few stray marks here and there: 20 percent, 25 percent. Then, next to "Navjivan Chawl," a slum or a group housing development, there are a whole group of tick marks; every single name in that group has been marked. This is the biggest difference between the world's two largest democracies: In India, the poor vote.

*   *   *

A MAN WHO HAS MURDERED is not entirely defined by it. After he kills a human being, a large, perhaps the largest, part of him is a murderer, and it marks him off from most of the rest of humanity who are not; but that is not all that he is. He can also be a father, a friend, a patriot, a lover. When we try to understand murder, we mistake the part for the whole; we deal only with the murderer and are inevitably left confused about how he became one, so radically different from you and me. I want to meet the other selves that form Sunil the murderer and see what became of him after the riots. So, on Election Day 1998, I decide to go back again to Jogeshwari. I phone Girish, who, thin and smiling as ever, meets me at Churchgate and takes me to his suburb.

In the Jogeshwari chowk, I meet Sunil and the boys who came to drink with me. In the year and a half since I last saw him, he's moved up in the world. Today he is wearing a crisp white shirt and black trousers and sunglasses, dangling the keys to his new motorcycle on a chain. At thirty, he has a son in addition to his daughter. Sunil is friendly as always and immediately starts introducing me around. "He came to write about the war," Sunil says. I am met with warm smiles from people who recognize me from the last time. Bhikhu Kamath, the shakha pramukh, pulls up in a rickshaw and clasps both my hands in his in greeting.

Sunil invites me to go canvassing with him for Ram Naik, the BJP–Sena candidate for parliament. "You will have to listen to some bad words." Sunil laughs. "It is the nature of canvassing." The polling area is demarcated by white lines on the road extending two hundred yards in all directions, marking the boundary within which cars and campaigning aren't allowed. Everybody wants to get me in to see the voting; the whole area bristles with men intent on assisting me. I walk back and forth in front of the school where the polling station is located. Finally, I walk up with Girish's brother Dharmendra, stand at the threshold, and watch him, with no little wistfulness. His number and name are checked off a list, an official tears off a ballot paper against a steel slide rule, and his finger is inked. He takes the seal and goes behind a chest-high cardboard barrier, marks his ballot with the seal, folds it, and finally deposits it in the slot. The city is full of people for whom it isn't this simple, people who come to the booth and look up their name and address only to find a small red mark on the list; someone has already voted in their name. Someone has stolen their right to make the only meaningful choice available in a democracy. At that point, it doesn't matter if you can prove to be who you are. You arrived second.

The campaign workers at the booths outside the polling station, who look up people's identification numbers for them and give them the registration chits, are paid by the political parties: 50 rupees if they are with the Sena–BJP and 100 rupees if they are with the Congress, plus puris, vegetables, and sheera, a sweet. Right then I know the Sena–BJP will win; you have to be paid more to support a loser. I speak to Bhatia, a Congress worker. He isn't very committed, even though he's been a Congress activist since childhood. He offers me a novel reason why people should vote for his party, the incumbents: "The Congress has already eaten. Its stomach is full. The Sena hasn't eaten. Everybody's a thief, but the Congress won't eat any more."

I WANT TO KNOW more about Sunil's life, so I take him and Girish to lunch at a plush restaurant in Lokhandwala. It is lit by candles—"to save electricity," opines Girish. Girish wants to put across the fact that he's not impressed and abuses the waiters every chance he gets. "The food took too long."

"Girish is a big man now," I say.

"He has the power of athanni now," Sunil agrees. He has powermoni.

Girish graduated from Ismail Yusuf College with a BA in Economics in '91. The world was not impressed. "I realized there I should have gone to a better college." Then he studied computers in private classes and became a sub-broker during the time of the stock market boom in the early nineties. Everybody made money. Girish wallowed in luxury; he could afford to drink fruit juice every day. "Even if we liked banana juice, we would pick the more expensive ones." After the bomb blasts of 1993, the boom ended. Girish has since worked for a variety of software companies, going back and forth between jobs and his own business ventures.

"Money is God," says Sunil. He has been to fancier places than this one. He once went to the Taj Hotel for a meal. He still keeps the bill. It came to 2,400 rupees; he shows it to skeptics in Jogeshwari. The people I meet who are seeking position or money in Bombay often use this one hotel, this one citadel of Empire, as a mark or measure of their progress upward through the strata of Bombay. The Taj was born out of a slight; because a man was turned away from a fancy hotel. When the prominent

Parsi industrialist Jamshetji Tata was refused entrance into Watson's Hotel in the nineteenth century because he was a native, he swore revenge and built the massive Taj in 1903, which outshone Watson's in every department. It is less a hotel than a proving ground for the ego. The Taj lobby and its adjoining toilets are where you test your self-worth; theoretically, anyone can come in out of the heat and sit in the plush lobby, on the ornate sofas, amid the billionaire Arabs and the society ladies, or relieve themselves in the gleaming toilets. But you need that inner confidence to project to the numerous gatekeepers, to the toilet attendants; you need first to convince yourself that you belong there, in order to convince others that you do. And then you realize that the most forbidding gatekeeper is within you.

Sunil grew up in the slums, very far from the Taj. When he was eight, in the second standard, both his parents were seriously ill. His father worked the night shift in the Premier Automobiles factory and didn't bring home a lot. He developed an ulcer, then appendicitis, and at the same time his mother had what Sunil calls "a ball in her stomach." They were in and out of the hospital for three years; his father was declared to be in the "last stage." At home, there was only Sunil and his slightly older sister; there was no earning member, and the relatives didn't help out much; if the parents died, his uncle stood to gain some three lakhs. The food at Cooper Hospital was very bad, so most of the patients had their meals brought by relatives from home. Sunil would run out of school when it finished at twelve-thirty, take the 253 bus, and go home. There, his sister would be waiting with the tiffin; she went to school at seven in the morning, then came home and cooked lunch. Sunil would dash to the hospital with the food, for he had to be there before two o'clock, when visiting hours were over. Often, he couldn't make it in time, and the doorman would tell him he couldn't go in till four, when visiting hours resumed. He would beg and plead, pointing out that his parents were upstairs, right above them on the second floor, hungry, waiting. The guard was inflexible; Sunil was only a little kid, without money. So the boy would sit by the door for two hours with the rapidly cooling lunch and watch as a procession of people who bribed the guard with a few rupees were let in. "I didn't have ten or twenty rupees, so I sat there thinking: If I can't do this, take my father his tiffin, then I can't live. If one has to live, one should live in a proper way. Then I realized that a man has to make money anyhow in Bombay—through the underworld or anything—and that even murder is all right."

Seventy-five percent of the country is below the age of twenty-five. Sunil is representative of this group—a generation that expects something better than their parents had. If they don't get it, they will be angry. And no family, no country, can withstand the anger of its young.

It is an exact and precise hell, the life of an unemployed young man in India. For eighteen years you have been brought up as a son; you have been given the best of what your family can afford. In the household, you eat first, then your father, then your mother, then your sister. If there is only so much money in the household, your father will do with half his cigarettes, your mother won't buy her new sari, and your sister will stay home, but you will be sent to school. So when you reach the age of eighteen, you have your worshipful family's expectations at your back. You dare not turn around. You know what is expected of you; you have been witness to all the petty humiliations they have suffered to get you to this place. You now need to deliver. Your sister is getting married, your mother is sick, and your father will retire next year. It's up to you; you carry a heavy burden of guilt from your childhood for having heedlessly taken the best of everything. So when you go out with your matriculation certificate or your BA and find there are no jobs—the big companies have stopped hiring or are leaving the city altogether, and the small companies will hire only relatives of people already working there, and your family is from Raigad or Bihar and has no influence here—you will look for other ways of making money. You will look for other ways of assuring your family that their investment wasn't lost. You can take beatings, you can take rejection, but you can't face your family if you don't do your duty as the son. Go out in the morning and come back at night; or go out at night and come back in the daytime if you have to, but take care of the family. You owe it to them; it is your dharma.

In his teenage years, Sunil started hanging around the Maya Dolas gang, doing errands for them, bringing them cold drinks and food, watching and learning how men make money in Bombay. He took the tenth-standard examinations and failed. He tried again and passed. When it came time to take the exams for the twelfth standard, Sunil was wiser. Studying, trying, and trying again till you succeeded was fools' work. He hired a stand-in to take the exams for him, with a forged hall ticket. He got 67 percent, First Class. After his schooling was over, Sunil joined the Shiv Sena. When he had needed transfusions, the Sena boys gave blood for him. This act touched him deeply—they are, literally, his blood brothers.

These days, his position has changed; he is no longer a tapori, a street punk. His cable business is expanding, and he has also started a small factory making pens, a mango-trading operation, and, with the purchase of a van, a tourist business. The police use Sunil's good offices to put an end to minor disputes; when a group of boys was bent on breaking a rickshaw, Sunil offered them free entry to the circus if they behaved themselves. Sunil has a stack of business cards in his front pocket; prominent among them is a card issued by the Government of Maharashtra which confers on him the title Special Executive Officer. "With this card I can do anything in Bombay. I have the power of a judge," says Sunil proudly, although he is just a glorified notary. When a political party comes to power, one of the ways it rewards its cadres is to issue such cards, making hundreds of people Special Executive Magistrates and Special Executive Officers. It often becomes an embarrassment, because a large percentage of those honored in this way have extensive criminal records. Legally, it confers almost no power on Sunil. But the card gives him status, legitimacy; when he flashes it around, few people think to ask him what it means, since it bears the seal of the government of Maharashtra.

The treatment he gets at hospitals has also changed. His father had to have another operation recently; his left testicle was removed. Sunil could afford to pay 15,000 rupees for the procedure, at Hinduja Hospital, one of the city's best, with five-star facilities. And they didn't make him wait by the door. "Now I can cross the door of any hospital—Hinduja, whatever. I can talk to Balasaheb Thackeray, and he will phone the hospital, and they will fear him."

Sunil is very pleased when his daughter calls him on his mobile phone, less because of the sound of his little girl's voice than because of the opportunity it affords him to show off his pricey gadget. He hands me the phone so I can talk to Guddi. She is in an English-language school, St. Xavier's. The admission was arranged by the minister who bailed him out during the riots. In return, Sunil arranges to round up the boys for the minister "when they are needed to burn a train or break a car."

But Sunil is still trying to understand the ways of St. Xavier's. One Parents' Day, Sunil went with Guddi to the elite school. There was a stall with books from Japan; his daughter put one into her bag. The teacher said something in English that Sunil didn't understand and asked him to sign something. The teacher was smiling, patting Guddi on the head and saying "good parents." "I also felt good," Sunil recalls, so he signed. He went home with his daughter clutching the book. The next day a deliveryman knocked at their door and deposited an entire set of encyclopedias in the middle of their shack. Sunil found he had just bought it, for 4,500 rupees— over $1,100.

Sunil met his wife while playing the contact sport of kabbadi for the school. They knew each other for almost a decade before he decided to marry her. She is of his caste, although from a poorer family, so his parents objected. "My wife is not so good in looks," he says. But she recently stood as an independent for the city council and came within eighty votes of winning. The BJP and Sena had made an adjustment, put up a joint candidate against her. I ask Sunil if there was pressure on him, as a Sena man, to withdraw his wife's candidacy. "It's democracy in the household. It's my wife's decision; what can I do?" The Sena, in the next election, will have to give her a ticket or pay large sums to buy her off and make her withdraw. This election was just an "apprenticeship." Even now, if there is a dispute among the ladies of the area, they come to Sunil's wife. At twenty-three, she was the youngest candidate in the election, and there is to be another election in three years. Sunil told her, in his English: "Try to again and again, but don't cry."

Sunil knows firsthand about the virtues of political participation. He went shopping with his wife two days ago, for his son's birthday, and as they were standing with their shopping bags at the rickshaw stand, they saw a pregnant lady arguing with a rickshaw driver. The driver was refusing to take the lady to an unsafe area of Jogeshwari near Radhabai Chawl. Sunil's wife stopped a police constable, pointing out that there was a pregnant lady trying to get a rickshaw. The constable ignored her. When Sunil's wife came back to him, he told her to go back to the cop and say, "I stood for the elections and I got eight hundred and seventy votes, and I can shut down this rickshaw stand." Thus the lady was seated in the rickshaw and the cop was reported to his superior officer. "I made my wife realize what kind of power she has," Sunil says.

As he walks me to a rickshaw, he points out a plot of ground where he expects a circus will be coming, from which, since he holds the parking concession, he'll be making extra income. He makes 50,000 rupees a month from his cable business, and another 25,000 or so from his other activities, legal and illegal.

"Seventy-five thousand," I calculate. "That's more than what some executives make."

"That's why I like myself so much," he responds.

SUNIL WILL INHERIT BOMBAY, I now see. The consequences of his burning the bread seller alive: When the Sena government came in two years later, he got appointed a Special Executive Officer; he became, officially, a person in whom public trust is reposed. He has energy; he gets to work by 10 a.m., roams far and wide over Bombay, from Jogeshwari to Dahisar, and beyond to Goa and Raigad, and still gets home late at night to be with his daughter. He is not afraid of getting his feet dirty in politics; in fact, he participates with zest and puts his wife up for elections as well. He is idealistic about the nation and utterly pragmatic about the opportunities for personal enrichment that politics offers. Sunil, in fact, can be held up as an exemplar of the capitalist success story.

The new inheritors of the country—and of the city—are very different from the ones who took over from the British, who had studied at Cambridge and the Inner Temple and come back. They are badly educated, unscrupulous, lacking a metropolitan sensibility—buffoons and small-time thugs, often—but, above all, representative. The fact that a murderer like Sunil could become successful in Bombay through engagement in local politics is both a triumph and a failure of democracy. Not all politicians are as compromised as he is, but the ones that aren't have to rely on people like Sunil to get elected. Most of the Bombay politicians need to mobilize huge sums of money for campaign expenditures. The salaries they get, the money their party officially sanctions for campaign funds, are a pittance, so they have to look elsewhere.

This shift is happening all around me. The Bombay I have grown up in is suffering from a profound sadness: the sadness of lost ownership, the transfer of the keys to the city. No longer is the political life of the city controlled by the Parsis, the Gujaratis, the Punjabis, the Marwaris. This passage was marked by the candidacy of Naval Tata in 1971. The powerful industrialist ran as an independent from the Mumbai South constituency, the richest and smallest in the country, and still he lost. In India, unlike in

America, fabulous wealth by itself can't buy you an election. Just about the only way the upper class will get into politics now is by being nominated to the upper house of parliament.

Among the former owners, there is a sense that the barbarians have been let into the city gates and are sleeping on the footpath outside their palaces. There is resentment that Bombay has to deal with the country's detritus. The only consolation is that the huddled masses are also the talent pool for South Bombay's maids, drivers, peons. That is part of the attraction of living here: You can find a maid and pay her a monthly salary smaller than the cost of breakfast at the Taj Hotel. Politics, too, has become yet another of those menial tasks that is assigned to servants or subordinates, something you drop as soon as you acquire the financial means to do so, like cleaning the toilet, doing the accounts, answering the phone, or standing in line at a government office. "Send your man," I am told again and again, when I need service for my mobile phone or money picked up from the bank. "I have no man," I respond. "I'm my own man." They do not understand. In business, in politics, in government, those who can afford it never go in person. They send their man.

But it is also these rich who create wealth, who create the conditions that will allow the mother on the streets to find a home for her children. They must be allowed their penthouses, their brandy, so the poor may be allowed their simple clean room, their rice and dal. In the post-Marxist age, we can no longer believe that redistribution solves anything, that making the rich poorer will make the poor richer. It is the death not just of ideology but of ideas. Nothing in the national debate has any strong conviction. On the right, a vague belief in foreign investment; on the left, a vague and poorly articulated fear of it. The left is apologetic about being left. Who can defend the work habits of the employees of nationalized banks? After fifty years of experiments in socialism, who can argue with a straight face that central planning is the answer to poverty? One slogan that has been conspicuously absent from the electioneering this year has been GARIBI HATAO. "Remove Poverty." It's as if there is a tacit acknowledgment on all sides that the poverty is insurmountable, so we'll move on and tackle something else, corruption or multinationals or whether we should have a temple or mosque in Ayodhya.

The cities of India are going through a transition similar to what American cities went through at the turn of the twentieth century, when the political machines of the Democratic party dominated, bringing new immigrants jobs and political power while breaking a few heads along the way. Eventually, as in the American cities, there will be reform movements, reform candidates, to clean out the muck. In Bombay, this has not yet happened. "The dregs at the bottom have become the scum at the top," Gerson da Cunha, a civic activist and figurehead of the old guard, tells me. When people in South Bombay mourn the loss of the "gracious" city, what they are really mourning is the loss of their own consequence in the city's affairs. It was never a gracious city for those who had to live under the shadow of their mansions; it was actively pestilential. It will take them a few generations, the new owners, to learn how to run their house and keep it clean and safe. But how can we begrudge them that when we, who had been the owners for such a long time and had still botched it, handed it over in such terrible disrepair?

I ASK SUNIL to take me to his slums. He and two of his Sena friends have set up three rooms on railway property. We walk through a pitch-dark alley till we get to a patch of ground with newly demolished huts set amid concrete housing for low-level railway workers. Just past this is a larger plot of land, meant to be a dumping ground for the railways. I can see the lights of a suburban train go by on the far side. We walk on wooden boards bridging open sewers and stand at the edge of the dumping ground; it is sopping wet from the rain, and my feet, shod in sandals, are covered in mud and God knows what else. "There"—Sunil points—"those three rooms with the oil lamps." That's his property. "We have captured the land."

Currently, it is occupied by laborers to whom Sunil has given the huts for free, so that tenure may be established over the land. They have been demolished twice by the railways. Each time, they have been reconstructed. They are built against the wall of a factory. Two sticks of bamboo in front support sheets of cardboard, and lots of black tarpaulin is draped over the whole structure. The cost of the material, which Sunil gets from Goregaon: 1,500 rupees. The time it takes to rebuild the shack after a demolition: an hour or two. "If you give it three kicks the whole thing will fall down," says Sunil. If they are demolished a third time, he is determined to build them again, and this time he says he will erect brick structures.

Above is a wire stretching between buildings, over poles. "All that is

my cable," says Sunil. He walks me to the other side of the plot. A wall
demarcates a construction site where housing for railway officers is to be
built. We are now standing on a new road that will link the officers' housing. This is the reason he might hit the jackpot, Sunil says. If there is a road
there will be shops, and shops can be demolished innumerable times, and
each time they will be re-erected. There is already a water tap in the back of
the factory. Electricity is more of a problem, since if Sunil's laborers tap
into the electric wire around here, their legitimate neighbors, the railway
workers, will get accused of stealing it, and there will be tension. So the
shacks are lit by lanterns. The right of the slum dwellers to live here is protected by Sunil and his friends. "We are the bhais"—the dons—"of the
area. So nobody will trouble them." They pay nothing in rent, and when
Sunil decides to build a permanent structure, they will be paid 5,000 rupees
to vacate. We go back through the funereal dark. Shapes of people walk
past us in the half-light. If someone from the Sena is elected to the legislative council, says Sunil, he will be able to convert the shack into a brick
house and he won't be bothered. Then the illegal slum will be made permanent and legal. But even if the land were to be sold now, he stands to make
a profit of ten to twelve lakhs.

The last of the demolitions happened after the 1998 general election.
The railway police, under the jurisdiction of the local BJP member of parliament, demolished nine different hutments put up by Sunil on railway
land, along with some fifty others. Sunil went to the house of the member
of parliament and spoke to his daughter, to tell her father to get the police
to stop demolishing the shacks. "You don't know what I'll do," he told the
daughter.

"What can you do?" she asked, keeping him waiting in the anteroom.

Did she know what would happen if, in the next election, the voting
stopped in a station for three or four hours? The Jogeshwari station under
Sunil's domain voted in large numbers for the Sena–BJP alliance. He had
several boys, he told the minister's daughter, who would create a riot and
stop the voting for four hours. His boys would go to jail for a few months,
but did she know how many votes her father would lose in that one station
during the time it was closed?

"There was a silence," Sunil recalls. "She said, 'Come inside.' I said,
'From now on, the decision to demolish or not is yours.' " He is confident
of the outcome. "Now they won't demolish."

I have to visit G. R. Khairnar, known as the Demolition Man, to fully grasp Sunil's potential as a slumlord. "I have demolished two hundred and eighty-five thousand structures during my entire career of twenty years," says Khairnar, a deputy municipal commissioner who has earned the ire of the Sena and all the other political parties. He tells me about the demolition process. There are twenty-three municipal wards. Each ward has a special squad to detect illegal constructions, which "are put up in connivance with municipal staff or police." The squad is supposed to give a seven-day legal notice asking for documentation that the structure is legal. If the license isn't provided, the demolition is supposed to go ahead. But "the staff is under great fear." And there is the money; "if the notice is issued, the entire file will be sold for a lakh or two to the party concerned." An employee can make more in bribes on a single building than the amount he earns in his entire career in the municipal corporation.

Khairnar won't demolish a building if a portion of it is occupied. He realizes the consequences of his work, as he prowls about the city with his wrecking crew. Many of the people living in the hutments are very poor and have nothing to lose by fighting the wreckers. They throw stones; sometimes they burn their own huts. Before he demolishes a hut, his orders are to remove the cooking utensils inside. He describes his work like a movie: "The scene is the woman is wearing a dirty half-sari. She doesn't even have drinking water; how is she supposed to wash it? The children are without clothes. I enter the hut and there are hardly any utensils inside. The corporation comes in like devils and demolishes their hut."

Once he was demolishing a hut in the big slum of Dharavi. The woman whose house he was about to destroy stood up in front of Khairnar, lifted her small baby by the legs, swung the child around her head, and was about to dash it against the ground. "We caught her just in time."

Even after he clears a slum colony, it will promptly be rebuilt with substandard material in the same place. "Settlement colonies cannot really be destroyed. They will reappear." He was once determined to clear a section of footpath in Mahim of the slums built on top of it. Every time he would knock them down and leave, they would be rebuilt in hours. "We used to clear them twice, three times a day. They would keep reappearing. They would run away behind the railway tracks and come back after we left." Each time Khairnar demolished a hut, it cost the municipality around 1,000 rupees. There were eighteen hundred huts in that area. The numbers were always against the Demolition Man.

Khairnar has been a ward officer since 1976. In 1985, when the Sena controlled the municipal corporation, the Saheb summoned Khairnar to Matoshree, the Thackeray mansion. The stepson of the chief minister had put up an illegal hotel, which Khairnar was about to demolish. Thackeray, according to Khairnar, asked him to desist; Khairnar went ahead and did his duty anyway. Eleven days later, as he parked his car in his office compound, two shots rang out, hitting a bystander standing next to him, and a third shot went clean through Khairnar's leg.

He returned to work and took on the godfather of Bombay himself, Dawood Ibrahim, who owned an illegal building, Mehejebin, under his wife's name. The day before the demolition, the police roamed through the building with dogs to check for explosives. The next day, Khairnar went in with an army of four hundred policemen, including paramilitaries from the Border Security Force, and destroyed the building with a three-ton wrecking ball. From 1992 onward, he demolished twenty-nine more buildings belonging to Dawood. His own officers, threatened by the don, begged him to back off, and the contractor that provided wrecking equipment withdrew from the contract.

Khairnar became a hero in the press. But the municipal commissioner told him he was getting a lot of pressure from above to rein Demolition Man in. When the commissioner tried to stop him by appointing a high-level committee to oversee the demolitions so he didn't have control anymore, Khairnar decided to expose the politicians. He started making fiery speeches, wild allegations, in public meetings that were called by the city's good and great, who saw in him a savior against corrupt politicians. The municipal commissioner asked Khairnar to desist from his denunciations and finally, in 1994, suspended him on the basis of insubordination. For a few years, Khairnar sat in his official bungalow, beneath a bust of Vivekananda, without any work to do and plenty of time to talk. He started an NGO for prostitutes; he raided brothels and "rescued" underage girls. In 2000, he was returned to service and went energetically back to the demolitions and the front pages of the newspapers, a hero once again of the middle class, those who already had homes.

*   *   *

IT IS FIVE YEARS after the riots, and the entire city braces itself for the autopsy: the release of the Srikrishna Commission Report. "Here swords are being sharpened," says a young man in the Muslim district of Madanpura, on the night before the report is to come out. Paramilitary forces have been put on alert. The Sena government can't delay any longer; Justice Srikrishna has invited activist groups to sue him, making him a party to the petition demanding his report's release.

When the report comes out, it is much more than the mere act of catharsis the judge hoped for. The Srikrishna Commission Report does Bombay proud. It is a detailed study of the riots and places blame where it belongs: on Thackeray and on the city police.

> The Shiv Sena pramukh Bal Thackeray, like a veteran general, commanded his loyal Shiv Sainiks to retaliate by organized attacks against Muslims. . . . The attacks on Muslims by the Shiv Sainiks were mounted with military precision, with lists of establishments and voters' lists in hand.

The Sena government officially rejects the report, accusing the judge of being biased against the Hindus. But this most learned judge is a Sanskrit scholar; nobody is fooled. Justice Srikrishna is a devout Hindu, much more so than Bal Thackeray.

In his report, Judge Srikrishna names thirty-one policemen who committed atrocities—who shot people dead or actively directed the Sena mobs. But in the end, nothing that the good judge has written will ever directly cost any individual a single minute's time behind bars. According to the terms of the act under which the commission was formed, none of the testimony given before the commission can be used to prosecute anybody. So, after five hundred depositions and close to ten thousand pages of recorded testimony, if a single one of the policemen or political leaders or street thugs who participated in the riots has to be prosecuted, the work that the Srikrishna Commission did has to begin over, in a court of law. The same witnesses must testify again, getting lawyers to represent them, filing affidavits on their behalf, and then going to the magistrate's court, to the sessions court, to the high court, to the Supreme Court. If a policeman is to be prosecuted, the government's sanction has to be obtained because he is a public servant; the magistrate has to be convinced that what he did was not done in the line of duty. All that can be done with the report is that Justice Srikrishna's conclusions can be shown to the magistrate. For many of the poorer victims, it is enough that the judge has listened to them, acknowledged that some wrong was done them. That's how little they expect of the justice system.

In response to the Srikrishna Commission Report, the *Times of India* prints an editorial titled "The Healing Touch," which calls for healing but not for justice. A *Times* reporter tells me that instructions have been issued to all the paper's reporters to soft-pedal stories on the report; all articles dealing with it—even profiles of the judge—have to be personally cleared through the resident editor. The argument advanced by management is that running anything too supportive of the report will provoke rioting by the Muslims. At this time, the paper has just one Muslim reporter on its entire Bombay staff.

A few weeks after the Srikrishna Commission Report comes out, I go back to Jogeshwari on the night of Ganapati Visarjan, when idols of Ganesha are immersed into the water all around the city. There is a mob on the chowk; two floats on trucks are advancing very slowly onto the crossroads. One procession is led by Amol, a long-haired man of impressive size whom I had met when I was investigating the riots. He has the reputation of being an uncontrollable hothead. Only his neighbor Raju, Girish's sister, can pacify him when he's on a rampage; he considers her his own sister. Sunil, who is Amol's partner in activities legal and illegal, tells me that Amol is unmanageable when drunk. "He's done three murders." Sunil touches his nose with his forefinger, to indicate that they were Muslims. "There was a man on a scooter. He poured petrol on him and burnt him alive." But the same Hindu man also regularly travels for two days to get to Ajmer Sharif in Rajasthan, to pray at the tomb of a Muslim saint. His facial hair is visible proof of his allegiance to the saint; he has let his beard grow for eight months now and has stopped smoking and drinking, in pursuance of a vow he made at the shrine. On an auspicious day, he will go to Ajmer, cut off his beard, and offer it to the Sufi saint.

Amol's procession features men dressed as Shivaji, Saibaba of Shirdi, and Lokmanya Tilak standing on top of the truck. All around them and swarming over the truck are about fifty other boys and men; three of them on top have caps and bandannas on their heads with the colors of the Union

Jack, like early videos of the Spice Girls. The floats creep toward the mosque on the main road leading toward the station. "We'll take an hour going to the masjid, and then to pass in front of the masjid it will take three hours. Fifty feet after we pass the masjid almost everybody will go home," Amol tells me.

As we approach the mosque, the procession slows almost to a halt. The drummers are in a frenzy, and the entire crowd is dancing with abandon. It helps that many of the boys have bottles of liquor in their pockets. Although there is a small contingent of women in the back (one young woman is waving a large saffron flag, the Sena banner), the men are all dancing with men. One boy has his legs between another's; as they dance, the one bends backward and the other bends over him, wriggling, humping. A child has his hand over his face; then he too begins jerking automatically to the drumbeats. Clouds of red gulal powder are thrown over the dancers. Then the explosions begin. Atom bombs. Looms. All the firecrackers the crowd has are let off in front of the mosque, and the air is thick with the smell of explosive, the stench from the open gutters, and, most of all, human sweat. It is an act of God that the fireworks don't set people on fire, set off in the middle of the dense mob as they are. Then Amol gets on top of the truck, grabs the mike, and shouts out slogans in praise of Hindu kings and the Hindu country:

"Chattrapati Shivaji Maharaj ki jai!"

The crowd responds with vigor.

"Bharat Mata ki jai!"

Saffron flags are waved in wide arcs on tall poles.

"Jai Bhavani! Jai Shivaji!" This is the Sena slogan.

Amol gets down from the truck, but the slogans are still ringing out. The other two icons—Saibaba and Tilak—are forgotten in front of the mosque. Only Shivaji the warrior is invoked. A few Muslims are watching silently, from behind the ranks of policemen lining the road. It is an infernal din. As the drums pound, as the fireworks burst, as the flags wave, as the bullhorns blare, I realize what this is: It is a victory march.

Ganesha is an unlikely god for such provocation. In the Hindu legends, he is a pleasure-loving gourmand, not an angry god bent on slaughter. But in the Jogeshwari float, he is sitting on a throne; instead of the mouse that is his usual mascot, the throne is flanked by four ferocious plaster lions. From the back of the truck people are handing out prasad—coconut pieces—and little plastic bags of sheera. At the end of the block, true to Amol's prediction, the crowd disperses, and the trucks speed on toward the swift sea to immerse their idols. The strutting past the masjid was the high point, the purpose, of the Ganapati procession: to show the Muslims that the Sena had won. This is where most riots in the country begin, in these aggressively public celebrations of a tribal, exclusive God rubbed in the face of those who would follow his rivals.

The amplified notes of the namaaz now begin coming out of the mosque. The police security cover has been excellent. Dhawle, the senior inspector and the man in charge of the Jogeshwari police station, is sitting down on a chair outside the police post, enjoying the cooling evening. The cops moved us on past the masjid in record time. A horde of plainclothesmen were constantly pushing us forward, urging the truck on. Uniformed cops were massed on both sides of the road, not allowing anybody to get too close to the building. Over the open gutters stood Muslim volunteers, a human guard against an unwary reveler falling into them in the dark.

It was not always this fraught. Before the 1993 riots, Arfin Banu, a member of the Mohalla Ekta Committee, remembers that the procession would stop making noise and bursting crackers on the block in front of the masjid and pass by quickly and silently, in deference to Muslim sentiments. This noisy display had only started in the years after the riots; some years it got very bad. Stones were thrown at the procession by the Muslims, and the possibility of a new riot was always looming. The police guard was much stronger in former years, as was the crowd. Amol would get up on top of the truck and whip the crowd up with his slogans; this year the police requested that he get down from the truck before it passed in front of the masjid, and he obeyed. So, provocative as tonight's procession was— the invoking of Hindu warriors, the bursting of explosive crackers, the profane dancing—it was, in the Bombay of today, a best-case scenario. Nobody shouted invectives against the Muslims, no pigs were flung at the mosque, and four Muslim men came forward to dance with Amol and his friends, the Hindus who had slaughtered their families five years ago.

The taxi driver carrying me home has a little shrine of Saibaba of Shirdi enclosed in an illuminated arch, next to a verse from the Koran in Arabic script. "What is that?" I ask, pointing, as I'm about to leave the cab.

"This?" he asks, touching the arch. He thinks I want to ask about the colored lights.

"That." I point to the Arabic text.

"This is Muslim."

"And you have Saibaba also?"

"Yes." He has turned around. He is smiling. I am joyous. There is still hope.

I GO TO VISIT Amol in his family's room in the slum. He comes out of his bath, clad only in his towel, broad-chested, brawny-armed. He works in the big dairy on the highway. His sister-in-law brings me a cup of hot sugared milk. It is rich thick buffalo milk, and I find it difficult to swallow. There is a large black speck on the milk and a solidified lump on the inside of the cup. But it is hospitality, and so I drink it. Amol asks if I would like to stay for dinner. I decline. The sister-in-law laughs and says to him in Marathi, "He saw the room and got frightened."

It is an even tinier room than his neighbor Girish's, but with the requisite array of electronics: a fridge, a TV, a phone. There is a stair leading to another room upstairs. An adorable seven-month old, Amol's niece, crawls about on the ground, reaches for a whiskey bottle filled with water, can't hold it, and starts crying. Soon enough, she is picked up. Here there is no aloneness. Amol can sleep through babies crying and TVs blaring. These days he roams about at night and sleeps in the day; he has got a friend to take over his duties at the dairy for him, and he gives him his salary. This leaves the night free for strife.

Amol, like Sunil, thrives on strife; they cannot imagine a world without it. They owe their positions, the respect they are accorded, and the living they make to strife. Alliances must shift constantly to ensure that strife continues, so the definitions of friend, enemy, and human being are relative terms. Theirs is a constant scrambling for place on a ladder of allegiances: who is in whose group, who will be given a ticket for the legislative elections, who gets what cut of the constant flow of payments—to unions, to the police, to the government, to your enemies in return for not extracting vengeance.

The Bombay word for strife is lafda (which can also mean an affair or romantic entanglement). People flock wherever there is a lafda; you'll notice a large group of men, watching intently, unblinking, as near as possible to the lafda, so as not to miss a single second of it. "In Bombay there must be ten to fifteen lafdas a day," Amol guesses. The foot soldiers of the lafda are the taporis: the street punks. The bhais—dons—and the netas—politicians—need a constant pool of taporis to maintain their positions. Amol is at heart a tapori: too passionate to be a shooter, too undiplomatic to be a neta, too stupid to be a bhai. He gets drunk and fights with his bare hands or with readily available weapons: glass jars from a roadside shop, swords, pieces of train track. He has a loyal following among the taporis, but he can never reach the heights that Sunil has. Sunil would never get hurt in a lafda. Amol leads out in front, but the back is where the real action is; in the back, smarter people are plotting the next move. When the time came to choose a divisional leader for the party, the shakha pramukh, Bhikhu Kamath put forward Sunil's name. Angered, Amol entered the next legislative election as an independent. Sunil got Amol's campaign workers drunk, and Amol lost out to the BJP–Sena combine.

Sunil, says Amol to me over dinner at a nearby restaurant, has a politician's mind. "Even today he thinks he is an MLA," a member of the legislative assembly. These are not words of praise from Amol, who is essentially a foot soldier, though he is a Brahmin and Sunil is a Maratha. But then, in today's Bombay, it is the Marathas who are ruling, not the Brahmin Peshwas of old. Sunil generally decides how the spoils from their various illegal ventures are split and settles the ratio to his advantage. Amol is aware that Sunil cheats him. At some point, their rivalry will boil over into blood. But still, Amol feels obliged to beat up anyone who insults Sunil. "I believe Sunil is superior to me. He is the big man in my group."

Amol has lost faith in the Saheb. "I used to respect Balasaheb more than God. Now he is sitting in Matoshree with a girl in one hand and a drink in the other, while we are getting beat up in jail. I am going to remove Balasaheb's picture from my wall and put up my own. What the Congress didn't eat in forty years the Sena ate in three." He has noticed that big companies are leaving Bombay; he has seen the jobs cut down in his own area. Men such as Amol are not dreaming of moving to Malabar Hill. Their dreams are more limited in scale. Amol has marked out the small open space in front of his house; he would like to expand the house there, build a balcony. Pleasure is taken at the beer bar. They are not especially devout, although they will follow the rituals readily enough. Most of them are loyal to the concept of the Indian nation, but they won't go into the army.

Amol is thoughtful. He is eating his food with a fork and spoon. His head lowered, he says, "There are very dangerous days ahead."

"Why?"

"People don't have jobs. The boys have no work, nothing to do all day. And everything's expensive. Now if a young man wants to go to a ladies' bar and have a couple of drinks, he won't have money to give to his people at home. You can get boys used to going to ladies' bars, to the lifestyle, and then they'll do anything for money."

"What will be the effect of this?" I ask Amol.

"Murders will cost two hundred rupees."

"How can a man kill?" I ask Amol. "How can he bring himself to do it?"

"You are a writer. After drinking you will say to yourself, now I must write a story. If you are a dancer, after drinking you will feel like dancing. If you are a killer, after drinking you will think, Now I must kill somebody." Amol flexes his arms. It's what you do; it's in your nature.

To keep from losing his boys to the underworld gangs, Bal Thackeray has constantly to channel their violent energy. He has to invent new enemies. The easiest to attack are people in the arts, ill understood by the Sena's rabble. In 1998, the Sena storms onto the stage at a concert by Ghulam Ali, the Pakistani ghazal maestro. "We can also sing," they proclaim. And they have their boys recite "Jai Maharashtra." The Saheb's diktat comes down: No Pakistani entertainers can stage a concert in their city, no Pakistani sportsmen can play. The gentry of Mumbai suffers the shutting down of the concert without a peep. The police commissioner tells the newspapers that no crime has been committed, as the organizers have not registered a complaint. After all, this is the city where murderers walk free in the streets and sit in the highest legislative chambers of the city. They have powertoni.

The Saheb also strongly objects to an art film made by a Canadian-Indian filmmaker, *Fire*, which shows a love affair between two sisters-in-law in New Delhi. "Has lesbianism spread like an epidemic that it should be portrayed as a guideline to unhappy wives not to depend on their hus-

bands?" he demands. Indian society could not tolerate the "so-called pro-
gressive culture of the West where they marry in the morning and take
divorce in the evening." Accordingly, his thugs destroy theaters showing
the film, and it is taken off screens throughout the country. There are the
usual editorials against Thackeray—in the English newspapers. Sunil and
Amol and the boys in the Sena do not read the English newspapers.

But in January 1999, the Sena makes a big mistake: It takes on Sachin
Tendulkar, the country's most idolized cricketer. A mob of Sainiks storms
into the offices of the Board of Cricket Control of India, angered by the
board's invitation to the Pakistani cricket team to tour India. They destroy
the office, including the World Cup that had been brought home to India in
1983. Tendulkar is put under police protection, and the party's leaders
speedily distance themselves from the incident. By this point it has just
become mob frenzy; the tiger Thackeray rides is now out of his control.
This latest foray is not about a particular leader or even ideology; it is all
about power and about feeding the imagination of Thackeray's hordes.
The vandals are young men, who, after working twelve-hour days as peons
in some office where they endure humiliation and even a slap or two from
men who are richer and less Maharashtrian than they are, take the train
home. Inside the train, they bathe in perspiration; the air is fetid with sweat
and farts. When they get home to the slum, their mothers and their fathers
and their grandmothers will ask them what income they have brought
home. Such a man lives with a constant sense of his own powerlessness,
except when he is part of a mob, part of a contingent of seventy patriots
fighting for the country's honor, walking unmolested into movie theaters,
posh apartments, and the offices of the cricket lords of the country, smash-
ing trophies, beating up important people who drive fine cars. All the
accumulated insults, rebukes, and disappointments of life in a decaying
megalopolis come out in a cathartic release of anger. It's okay to be angry
in a crowd; the crowd feeds on your anger, digests it, nourishes your rage as
your rage nourishes it. All of a sudden you feel powerful. You can take on
anybody. It is not their city anymore, it is your city.

You own this city by right of your anger.

I GO TO A FRIEND's apartment in a high-rise in Lokhandwala that he
has given me a key for, with Sunil and Girish. It is still raining in Novem-

ber, and there is a spectacular lightning display in the sky over Bombay. We drink whiskey on the balcony. Sunil takes off his shirt and sits in the armchair in his undershirt. He keeps looking at his new watch, not so much to check the time as to admire the timepiece. I notice, not for the first time, his sense of well-being whenever I take him to a high floor of a building. Most people from his chawl never go above the second floor.

"There is a lot of struggle ahead in Bombay," says Sunil. After ten years, Sunil plans to shift out of Bombay to Raigad, for the sake of his children. He has heard that children have been kidnapped for their kidneys. A barometer of the city's fortunes is the alcoholic strength of the liquor it imbibes. "Prices are very high, so man will struggle a lot, and from that tension he will drink a lot. The boys from the share market are drinking sixers." A sixer is just one step above country liquor. It costs 5 rupees a bottle.

It starts raining heavily, out of season. "Because of our sins," reasons Sunil. "Even God doesn't accept Bombay. God made the world, but he doesn't accept Bombay." And Sunil certainly knows about sin. On Wednesday, Friday, and Sunday, Sunil will broadcast a pornographic film on his cable network. The requests for porn often come from his female subscribers. When he goes to I.C. College, the women tell him, "Sunil-bhai, you are not taking care of us." That is the code. Early on the evening that he decides to "take care" of his subscribers, a little symbol, a star, for example, is displayed on a corner of the screen, or a message scrolls with a time across the bottom all evening—"BBC channel is changed"—and the initiates understand that a blue movie will show on a particular channel at a particular time. Such a film is shown on the nights that the people of Bombay drink: not on Tuesday, because that is the night for the worship of Ganapati; not on Thursday, for that is for Saibaba; not, usually, on Saturday, because many people observe it as Hanuman's day; and not on Monday, "when people don't drink so much because they've been drunk all weekend." Wednesdays, Fridays, and Sundays are drinkers' nights, blue-film nights, in Sunil's Bombay. The latter is best enjoyed after an evening of the former.

Sunil has rich pickings among the housewives along his cable route. "Who is allowed to enter the house? The milkman brings his milk and goes away; the ironing man takes the clothes and goes away. But I am allowed to enter the house, even the bedroom, and stay and fix things." He has fucked a total of thirteen women on his route "whom I have liked—I have chosen." Among these, he has his preferences. "I must have Gujarati ladies. Their men only do it once a week."

"I am playing the game of five women in my neighborhood," boasts Sunil. Sex and death are very close in Bombay. "Playing the game" can mean killing a person or screwing a woman. "How often does a married man give it to his wife? Twice, thrice a week? Woman wants it. Woman must have it." He never makes the first move; he never puts his hands anywhere. "I don't want to ruin my business. The women call me up, saying there is a fault in my cable. They touch me, they sit next to me, but I will let a couple of days go by." He will take any age; he has fucked a fifty-three-year-old housewife. One day, says Sunil, he will take us to the village of the Aghoris, outside Bombay. The Aghoris have a special, extremely athletic technique of fucking: The man makes the girl clasp a tree, then raises the girl's leg and puts it on his shoulder. "I can't do this kind of shot, but I have fucked an Aghori girl. Waheguru!"

Sunil and Girish speak with admiration and laughter about the exploits of a young man in their slum named Santosh. "He is a real madharchod. He's a very bad man." Santosh had declared that he considered the wife of his neighbor Raj his sister; she ties a rakhi, a sacred thread, on his wrist every year. He was allowed complete access to Raj's house and was fucking their daughter—"his niece," Sunil points out. But one day he discovered that a doctor in the lane was fucking the mother. So he demanded sexual rights to the mother also, or he would blow the whistle about her relationship with the doctor. As a result, Santosh starts his morning by strolling into Raj's house at eleven in the morning and fucking the woman he calls his sister. Then he goes with his own mother to the temple at two and prays for an hour. He comes back from the temple, goes to the gymnasium, hangs out with the boys, and then goes back to Raj's house to wait for the daughter to come back from school, at five-thirty. When she shuts the window to change her clothes, he "gets in one shot" and leaves at five-forty-five.

Then there was the bhaiyyani next door, who Santosh started fucking two days after she got her first period and has been fucking steadily for five years, with the threat: "If you don't allow me to fuck you I'll kill you." He climbs into her window when her drunk father is away, or passed out, and rapes her. There is nothing gentle about sexuality in the slum; it is furtive and feral. Once, a group of boys was spying on a couple asleep near the door of their room; the man had a hand on one of his wife's breasts. Santosh reached in through the opening for the letterbox and started squeezing the wife's other breast; she slept on, thinking that her husband was squeezing both. When she felt the extra pressure on one, she woke up and screamed but was too afraid to tell her husband what had happened. Much of what a woman in the slum puts up with she endures silently, because, as Sunil points out, "How can she tell the world what has been done to her?" They go after women who are vulnerable: the very young, the children or wives of drunkards, or women not right in the head. When their men discover what's being done to them, they too most often keep it quiet. Who would want the world to know? What does it say about their manliness, that they were unable to protect their women?

I ask them if Santosh is good-looking, to be able to fuck so many women. No, they say, he walks with a limp, he's "seventh-standard fail," and he works as a watchman, but he has a way with words. His technique is to go to the woman's house every day and sit for hours and talk: talk to the husband, talk to the woman, talk to the daughter, ingratiate himself with the household and then get what he wants. "When I see him relaxing at my house, I get worried," admits Sunil.

In the end, all would be well for Sunil and his party. "The Sena's future is good. This is Bombay," Sunil says. Then he remembers and corrects himself. "This is Mumbai." Suddenly, fireworks from some wedding go off in an explosion of color in the sky outside, followed by long white forks of lightning. All of a sudden his city is revealed anew to Sunil: He is looking down from a great height, maybe for the first time in his life, at the dazzling and sodden mess below. Slurring drunk, he observes, "This is a unique world."

IT IS GETTING increasingly difficult for me to work at home, with two active little children, so my uncle helps me find a furnished flat in Bandra that I can use as an office. When I move in, I notice a familiar picture hung on a wall, of the great freedom fighter Tilak. It seems to be a charcoal etching, but there is something odd about it. I go closer.

"It's embroidered in human hair," the doctor who owns the flat says with pride. "He was my late husband's ancestor. You can keep the picture here."

I decline her offer, with thanks.

The apartment is in the commercial heart of Bandra: Elco Arcade on Hill Road. The scene downstairs is a gluttonous chaos; the best street food in the western suburbs is reputed to be sold here. Women shop in the arcade on the ground floor and emerge from their strenuous bargaining to refresh themselves with a pani-puri and a kulfi falooda. Thursday evenings, the Sai temple downstairs bursts into robust, tuneless song, for there is pav bhaji—fried bread and vegetables—for prasad afterward. The food stalls outside are demolished by the authorities just before the elections; afterward, they reappear in massed ranks, thicker than ever before. But when I turn the key in my door and step inside, I am in a serene world: two rooms and kitchen, and a balcony with a spreading old tree just outside.

Sunil and Amol both come to drink with me one night in my office at Elco Arcade. Amol is on the wagon. That means he won't drink whiskey. I offer him a glass of wine, which doesn't qualify as alcohol. He sips delicately from the wineglass, holding it daintily between his fingers. It is an incongruous sight, the big bearded man sipping wine as if he were at a gallery opening or a ladies' tea.

They look around the office appreciatively. Amol owns a flat in Nalasopara. Sunil owns a flat in Dahisar. Neither one of them is considering moving their families out from the slum to the flat. I ask them why.

"You can give me a house anywhere—Nepean Sea Road, Bandra—but I won't leave Jogeshwari," says Amol.

"Our minds are like children," explains Sunil. "Our minds won't accept living anywhere else, just like your children won't accept living in a slum. My children can knock on the neighbor's house at one a.m. and get food. If they don't like their mother's rice and dal they can go to the neighbors; a child come to your house to eat is like God come to eat. They can eat anywhere in the chawl. But if *your* children were to knock on the neighbor's flat at one a.m. you would give them two slaps. 'Not good!' you would say to them. You don't want your neighbor to think you can't afford food for your children."

"In chawls we get all facilities," adds Amol. "All facilities" is a term used in the real estate advertisements to describe such things as indoor plumbing, a lift, a modern kitchen. But a different definition applies to what a facility is in the slum. "When you come back from work you can stand on the road with the boys and discuss. In the chawl, we can say to our neighbors that we have to go to hospital and they will come instantly."

I ask them why there is more unity, more fellow feeling, in the chawl.

Common toilets, explains Sunil. "When you go to the toilet, you have to see everyone's face. You say 'Hi, hello, haven't seen you for two days.' Then there is water. The women fill buckets with water together at the tap, and they converse: 'My grandfather is ill.' 'I have one son in the village; he is an alcoholic.' " In a block of flats, on the other hand, the toilets are all separate. "In a flat, the talk is about the neighbor's AC; he has just installed a new one in the bedroom. Or the neighbor has installed marble. In the chawl, at the water tap, the talk is about that mother-in-law who is angry at her daughter-in-law for cooking food for six people when there are only five in the house. In a flat," concludes Sunil, "the talk is on a high level."

Why don't they sell their houses and live comfortably in the village?

Sunil explains why. "In the village, the doors shut at nine."

"At eight," says Amol. "Seven."

A little later, Amol comes back from using the toilet. "Isn't there water to put in the toilet?" he asks me.

I look up at him, puzzled. "Just use the flush." But Sunil understands. He gets up and goes with him and shows him what the flush is. He teaches him; he presses the lever and water comes out of the tank above the toilet. It doesn't have to be poured in from a bucket.

Sunil, comfortable in his business and in his position in Bombay, now wants stability. He is now against more riots. "The ordinary man just wants to eat and then go to sleep at the end of the day. If he participates in a riot it is to make money." During the Kargil conflict, the Indian government banned Pakistan TV from the country's cable networks. For all his patriotism, Sunil opposed this decision. Why should he be prevented from broadcasting Pakistan TV, he asks, if the customer accepts it? "The thing that someone pays for, you should give them." Here again, his business instincts are winning over his distaste for Muslims, over his political convictions. The color of someone's money is becoming more important than that of the religious flag he carries in a procession. Bombay is seducing him away from hate, through the even more powerful attraction of greed.

But Amol is closer to the ground in Bombay. "Riots can happen any time," he says. "They could happen tonight."

The liquor has aroused a powerful hunger. We leave the office and take a rickshaw to a restaurant. Amol looks up from his butter chicken and suddenly asks me, "Do you have water twenty-four hours?" He must be still thinking about my flush.

I nod. He can't figure out how. There must be a tank on top of the building, Sunil speculates.

After a while, he asks me again, "You will sleep alone tonight?"

At first I think he's tactfully asking me if I've got a girl coming up after they leave. But when I emphasize that I am, indeed, sleeping all alone, he declares, "I've never slept alone in all my life. I need other people in the room." The big tapori is wondering how I can sleep alone, without my mother, without my wife, without babies in the room. He wouldn't be able to; the lord of lafda is scared of the dark.

THERE IS ANOTHER GENERAL ELECTION the very next year, 1999, and Jogeshwari is bustling again on Election Day. It's been drizzling, but there are crowds at every corner, and campaign workers at the party booths are making out little voter slips for people. Bhikhu asks Sunil and Amol to do a get-out-the-vote round, and we go into the lanes of the slum. Sunil knows every resident by name. He and Amol greet the Gujaratis in Gujarati—"Kem cho!"—the bhaiyyas in Hindi, and their people in Marathi. People are urged to vote for a particular political party not by name but by the symbol—"Vote for the bow"—a necessity in a country where a third of the population is illiterate. There is a strange silence in all the slum rooms, and I realize it's because none of the televisions are on, with the exception of one or two playing Doordarshan, the government broadcaster. Sunil has turned off his cable network for Election Day. "Sunil, put the cable back on!" an old man pleads. "After you vote," he responds.

When we get back to the chowk, a senior Sena worker is talking with Amol about the next round of the voter drive, in the afternoon, after lunch. By that time, the Sena's polling agent inside the booth will have a list by name of exactly who has voted and who has not. "Four or five guys won't do, we need a *mob*," says Amol to the Sena official, using the English word. "Wait, I'll bring my mob," the official assures him. The mob will then go back to each house that shows up on the list as having one or more residents who haven't voted, and demand that they do. "It is to create an atmosphere," explains Amol.

Among the candidates Sunil is friendly with is the Congress Party candidate from a nearby constituency, Mama, who is a cable businessman and leading gangster in the Chotta Rajan syndicate. Mama is all of thirty years old; he was born in Bombay. His father came here from the caste-ridden north sixty years ago. He comes from a backward caste, but Bombay liberated his family. "In the village, all the lower castes used to look up to the upper castes, be their servants. Here, they are the bosses." They have come forward in the city, through politics.

Mama points out the advantages of backing him to his contributors. "Give five lakhs," he says to a potential donor in the construction business. "And I'll get your five lakhs back to you within five days of getting elected. I'll pass one toilet block." The contract to build it would go to the donor. Sunil chortles that Mama's main campaign promise to his constituency is: "If you elect me, you'll be free from goondas." As the boss of the thugs, he is running a sort of protection racket for the entire constituency. Since the police have failed so miserably at curbing extortion, the public might as well elect the extortionist himself to guarantee protection. It is the same survival tactic that led 5 percent of the city's Muslims to vote for their blood enemy, the Sena, in the 1995 election.

Meanwhile, from Malabar Hill, a friend in the fashion industry calls me on my mobile with a question. He has decided to vote for the first time in his life today. "I'm in your old neighborhood," he says. He is entering Walshingham House School, where the voting station is located. "There are two boxes in front of me. One says Lok Sabha, one says Vidhan Sabha. Which is the Center and which is the State?" he asks me, referring in the first instance to the national elections.

Nobody in Jogeshwari would need to ask such a question. I ask Mama whose city he thinks Bombay is: that of the rich on Malabar Hill, or of the backward castes who are emerging now?

He laughs. "Bombay is the vadapav eaters' city; otherwise it is nobody's city."

The country has gone through three general elections in as many years. It is an agonized, continuous reaffirmation of loyalty to the democratic process; again and again, the country has to prove itself a democracy. The patience of the people amazes me. Year after year, with no real choices ahead of them, the country still trudges dutifully to the polls. In 1991, 57 percent of the electorate voted; in 1996, 58 percent; and in 1998, 62 percent of the 600 million voters of India exercised their right to vote. There is no good reason for the 1999 election, since after enormous expense and months of campaigning in the heat, the government in Delhi remains pretty much what it was before the election. People had been expecting a mass boycott this time; although the turnout diminishes slightly, people still stand in long lines in the heat in front of the polling stations. It is perhaps a national version of dharma. People do not ask why they are voting; they just know it is their duty to do so.

In Maharashtra, the Sena–BJP alliance, which has been in power in the state since 1995, loses the state elections in 1999. They had promised to build 4 million houses for people in the slums and ended up building fewer than four thousand.

The Saheb

"When are you going to meet Bal Thackeray?" people keep wanting to know.

"On my way to the airport," I reply. I don't want to stick around in Bombay if I somehow annoy the Saheb during an interview. So it is not until a month before I am to move back to New York, after my bags are packed, my ticket bought, that I finally meet Thackeray. A Marathi newspaper editor, who knows him well, takes me to meet the Supremo on a June evening in 2000.

There is a mass of security guards outside the bungalow. He has a small army guarding him: a total of 179 police officers, including a battalion of 154 constables, 19 subinspectors, 3 police inspectors, and 3 assistant commissioners of police. The state government, Sena or Congress, gives him police vehicles and a bulletproof automobile to travel in; his mansion in Bandra is fortified and guarded round the clock at state expense. The Tiger roars only from behind the safety of his guards.

The bungalow is one of many in a government project for artists—Kalanagar—toward the rear of a quiet lane in Bandra. It is painted in white and built in the standard Bombay glossy style, calculated to give an impression of opulence grander than the physical space it occupies. The Thackerays are from a lower-middle-class background; they have no idea how to spend all the money they've made. They buy big cars, like Pajeros, unsuitable for Bombay roads. The mansion, the editor tells me, is filled with stacks of rupees.

A metal detector is run over my person, my bag is examined, and we are shown to a hall filled with huge pictures of Shivaji. There are many chairs facing a door. All the people seated on the chairs are staring at the door, willing it to open. Barely have we taken our seat than the door opens just for us, and we are shown into a small receiving room ahead of all the others. This room is filled with many large pictures of Thackeray's deceased wife. Her death left him adrift. Then his daughter-in-law became close to him; she had recently been asked to leave the bungalow, at the insistence of Uddhav, one of his sons. There are also a couple of plaques, a small white one on the coffee table—I LIKE PEOPLE WHO CAN GET THE THINGS DONE!—and a bigger one, in gold and red lettering, NO ADMISSION FOR "NO."

A couple of minutes after we enter the receiving room, the Saheb comes in. "Jai Maharashtra," he says, and the editor returns his salutation. Then I shake the hand of the one man most directly responsible for ruining the city I grew up in.

He sits in an armchair next to an end table, on which is a statue of a Masai warrior carrying a spear and shield.

I start. "I am writing a book about Bombay—"

"Mumbai," he corrects me.

"Mumbai," I agree.

He speaks to me in fractured English. He is a thin, bony man of average height, with a thick suspiciously jet-black crop of hair, wearing very large square spectacles. He is clad in a cream silk kurta and lungi, with matching sandals. Periodically he reaches up under his kurta and a ripping sound comes forth; he is loosening the Velcro attachments of a girdle, worn for a back problem. Around 1990, Thackeray had a religious reawakening. He shed his western clothes and started wearing a kurta and lungi, usually saffron. He also started wearing rudraksha malas, long strings of beads, around his neck.

The air-conditioning is kept low for his comfort, and sweat pools in the channel between my lip and my nose. The tea, as in other Sena offices, is vigorous; it can incite insurrection. Thackeray drinks from a glass of milky gray broth. He lights a cigar, holding it in a cigar holder. I remark that

they're Cohibas. He asks if anybody smokes in the United States. I tell him
that Cuban cigars are embargoed there.

Why? he asks. I try explaining the embargo. He digests the informa-
tion. He is intrigued. "Now if American girl might have married to a
Cuban boy, then what they do? They are living there for years, then what?
They ask them to part?"

People can come, but not their products, I explain.

"That's a good one," he comments. "Good idea." I am afraid of what I
might have set in motion.

The Saheb gives me a little story about his childhood. His father was a
teacher—"he was a social reformist, he was a writer, he was everything."
His mother wanted Bal to be a government servant, at that time a prestigious occupation, but his father said, "My son will never be a clerk. I want
him to be an artist." And his father's word was the law in the household:
"When Father's order came, we wet our pants." He bought his son a
bulbul-tara, a stringed musical instrument played with both hands. Bal
proved to be an inept musician. "I tried and tried. One this, this hand
would work and the other would stop working; if the other would work,
then this one here would totally—" His father got furious and pressed his
son's hand hard into the strings, pushed down till it started bleeding. "I
started crying, and my father said, 'Get out from here! This sala will not
learn.' "

Around this time, World War II broke out. Bal would look at Ban-
bury's cartoons on the front page of the *Times of India,* and his father
would watch him. He instructed his son to make sketches every day, which
he would inspect in the evenings. Along the way, Bal got a sense of
the larger political struggles around the city, whose rule was in dispute
between the Gujaratis and the Maharashtrians. The Maharashtrians wanted
their own state, with Bombay as its capital. Bal would listen as his father
held meetings of the Samyukta Maharashtra movement in their house in
Dadar and started his career as a cartoonist at the *Free Press Journal.* In
1960 he launched his own cartoon weekly, which turned into a forum for
the Sons of the Soil, the term for the Maharashtrian movement. (Actually,
the soil in Bombay, much of it between the original seven islands, was filled
in by the British.)

In the battle for Bombay, the Maharashtrians won out over the
Gujaratis; in 1960, they got their state and the city. But still Bal's readers

were complaining, writing him letters. "We got Maharashtra, we got Mumbai, but what about our jobs?" One of them gave him a telephone directory to see for himself. "And to my surprise my goodness it was full of South Indian executives, and you find out there are more pages for Patels. And lot of Shahs." And that was how he started his movement: as an employment organization. It was a war fought over the right to be a typist. They finally managed to get up to 80 percent of jobs reserved for Maharashtrians, but they were always the lowest 80 percent: stenographers and clerks. "That will not give you justice. Unless you come in power it will not be done," he realized. And so, in 1966, Thackeray reluctantly formed a political party, holding his nose. All political parties are responsible for the mess that the city is in today, Thackeray says, "including my Shiv Sena party also." That is due to the lamentable need to garner votes, which disgusts him. "For the sake of votes you are going to ruin the country and the city? Is it?"

Even after the Sena entered politics, its focus on reservations for Maharashtrians was not lost. In 1998, the Maharashtra government turned down an affiliate of the Wharton School that wanted to set up in New Bombay, because the school refused to reserve 10 percent of the seats for Maharashtrian students. Bangalore and Hyderabad promptly jumped in with offers that included no such strings, and Bombay lost the school, which could have been the linchpin of revival in New Bombay.

The editor had told me how startled he was to find out, in a meeting with Thackeray, that the Saheb lacked a basic knowledge of the geography of the state of Maharashtra. The Sena is essentially a Bombay-based party where Maharashtrians are rapidly disappearing. Bombay itself can no longer be called a Maharashtrian city. The Maratha population of the city was 51 percent at the time of the Samyukta Maharashtra movement. The people employed in the mills were mostly Maharashtrian; with the decline of the mills, they had to leave Bombay to find jobs. Maharashtrians now comprise only 42 percent of the city's residents; 19 percent are Gujarati, and the rest are Muslim, North Indian, Sindhi, South Indian, Christian, Sikh, Parsi, and everybody else. As of July 2000, all of the MPs that the Sena has nominated to the Rajya Sabha, the upper house of parliament, are non-Maharashtrians: Gujaratis, Bengalis, Parsis, North Indians. The Sena is trying to expand its base, to include Hindus generally, because it knows it can no longer stay in power just on the basis of the Maharashtrian vote.

I ask Thackeray if Mumbai is still a Maharashtrian city. He responds immediately and aggressively. "One thing. Nobody can dare separate Mumbai from Maharashtra. We still have that fighting spirit. As long as Shiv Sena is guaranteed forever nobody will do it." It is obvious I have touched a nerve. Much of this struggle is over a question of place: Who has the right to live in Bombay? The Shiv Sena is primarily a party of exclusion. It sought from the beginning to say, This or that group does not belong here. It was the Gujaratis first, then the South Indians, then the Communists, then the Dalits, and now the Muslims. Bombay is, like any other Indian city, full of people in search of answers to the question "Who am I?" and who believe that the answer, when they find it, will allow them also to answer the other question: "Who is not I?" People like Thackeray approach the question backward. If they answer the question "Who is not I?" they will, by a process of elimination, find the answer to "Who am I?"

The editor leaves, and I am alone with the Saheb. Why do people keep coming to Bombay? I ask.

"Here crime has a good scope," he answers. "You can earn without doing anything. It can be pickpocketing. Good scope in railways." Extortion is also a growth industry in Bombay. "Telephone somebody. 'I want so much I am coming, my man will be there.' " And out of sheer fear they will pay up. Here is a novel answer to what attracts migrants to Bombay: Crime is good business here. It has a measure of truth to it. The ratio of police to criminals, he points out, is very low. "This menace"—he pronounces it *menaas*—"is increasing, this hutment-dweller menaas. You can play hide-and-seek with the police. Once you do something, even a murder, even a murder, you just simply murder anybody and just walk away, just walk. And go into the zopadpatti." As had his men, Sunil and the others, during the riots: murdered and walked away into the zopadpatti—the slums.

He tells me what can save Bombay. "Migration has to be controlled. The Bangladesh Muslims to be driven out, not only out from Mumbai but outside the country, back to Bangladesh. Find out who are the miscreants, mischief-mongers as far as ISI"—the Pakistani intelligence service—"is concerned. Hang them. Don't send them back. Hang them. These are my straight policies." He speaks admiringly of the strict policies of the Americans when anyone applies for a visa, and contrasts it with the ease of obtaining an "emigrant permit" to come to India. Thackeray says there needs to be a visa system to enter Bombay. Many of the people living in Malabar Hill, who would not otherwise support him, agree with this.

He hates the term "India," which he attributes to "Pandit Jawaharlal Nehru, him and sheer love for Muslims after the partition. They were calling it India, hence we are Indians. I hate that." Hindustan, he insists, is the original and proper name for the country. "Begins with Sindhu River. Sindh. Sindh and Sindhu Sindh." Sindh, now a province in Pakistan.

He says that an article of the constitution defines us all as Hindustanis: "Nineteen-a. The funniest thing: They only take advantage of first line, what about other lines, a b c d e f g h? There again it is very clearly stated that even though people migrate from one state to another state they should see one thing: that they should not disturb peace of the locals there. Why don't you also take that? Why show me only first lines and not other lines?"

It might be because there is no such line in the constitution. Actually, it is articles 19d and e that he might be referring to, the ones that give all Indians the right to move freely and reside anywhere in the territory of India; 19a grants citizens freedom of speech and expression, which Thackeray might be less well acquainted with. He has invented his own constitution. Which one of his boys is going to take the trouble to look up the written document to verify his confident pronouncements? It is the world's longest constitution, and probably the least read. People make of it what they will.

Outsiders would desist from crowding into Mumbai if they were taken care of in their home states, he says. "What is their chief minister doing there, with a red light on his car and big bungalow and expenditure? He should make provision for them." Again, Mumbai's mess is the fault of politicians. "Cosmopolitan city is not only Mumbai but every city. Bangalore is cosmopolitan, Calcutta is cosmopolitan. It has its own limitations because of amenities. The rains we don't know what is going to happen. The rains they come and they go. It is something like that fairy song, you know, that children sing: 'Rain rain go away, come again another day' and all that it happens like this."

I begin to entertain the suspicion that he is not all there.

I ask him what accounts for his charisma.

"If you have a flower in your hand and it has a typical fragrance, how can you say that where is the fragrance, where does it come from? A fragrance cannot be seen; a charisma cannot be explained. I don't know whether I have it or not. Whoever it may be, if anyone has that charisma. I don't know whether it is charisma or Karishma. If it is Karishma it goes to

Kapoor—" referring to the sexy actress. He laughs at his little pun. "So, charisma is better."

I ask him how he thinks he will be remembered, about his place in history.

He doesn't mind if he doesn't get remembered, he says. "I play with my grandchildren, that's all." He won't write his autobiography; he won't contest any election. "That's my decision." His not entering politics directly is essential to establishing his image among the Sena boys. The Tiger is above politics but controls politicians at his will; he has publicly boasted that he controls his chief ministers by remote control. "I hate politics. I am not a politician, I am a political cartoonist."

He reminisces about his life as a cartoonist and the Mumbai of old. "When I was in *Free Press Journal* . . . population was there of course. But some glamour was there, some thrill was there. But slowly slowly slowly slowly, when more and more people started pouring it become very difficult. I remember during that time—it was somewhere in 'forty-two, 'forty-four—the municipal people used to come whenever we used to complain there are rats, big rats. So they used to come with those hose pipes and there were hydrants on the roads. They'll fit that hose pipe to the hydrant and you put that huge hose into the hole, that rathole, and the others will keep watch with those big rods in their hands—lakdi—and naturally the water goes according to their things you know, the holes inside, under center their thing. Then they will come out from some other hole. When water is coming from this side, they will take shelter from other side. The moment they used to come out, they will beat. At least six to ten–twelve rats were killed. Now water scarcity is so much you can't afford to have that. But actually, in my backyard, when I was staying there in Dadar, the connection was given to hydrant, hydrant, from hydrant, immediately terrific force with the gust. It was somewhere in 'forty-four, 'forty-five, 'forty-six. But now you don't see hydrants because it is being misused. The hutment people. They will keep it open and if they fail to put it back, water will go on coming out, actually, with a big flow."

I am unprepared for this aperçu. "Is there a serious rat problem?" I inquire.

"Rats are bound to be there," the Saheb responds, now looking at things from a more charitable perspective. "If not the BMC, the rats clean some of the portion of the debris. Yes. Some eatables are there." He stops here, having delivered his soliloquy, and leaves me to make what I will of it.

A visitor is announced, the film producer Vijay Anand. He whispers confidentially, "His sons are actually behind bars." Actually, it is Anand's nephews. "When this man comes he becomes my devotee." The Saheb laughs.

The nephews have been accused of murdering their father's longtime mistress. But when Anand comes in, he does not immediately talk about the sons. He starts with a different kind of problem. Anand owns a theater. His assistant went to record some music using the sound equipment at the studio of another producer, Vinayak Raut, and the equipment broke down. Raut kidnapped the assistant, has held him since the afternoon of the previous day, and has now sent a letter demanding 35,000 rupees in damages. Anand shows the Saheb the letter. Raut has further informed Anand that he has worked on the Saheb's security detail, that he has collected "vasuli" for the Saheb, and he is now collecting the same extortion payments for the Saheb's own thuggish nephew, Raj Thackeray.

The Saheb gets on the phone. He remembers every detail of Anand's convoluted story and relates it to his aide. "I want to see this Raut at twelve tomorrow. I am going to appoint him head of extortion." Here is the all-powerful leader, righting wrongs with an order and a witticism. The problem will be fixed. He will get the things done.

Thackeray takes special pride in the fact that movie stars, directors, producers—"they all come here. They are all my good friends. They admire me. They have respect for me. I help them also. I solve their problems. That's true." The editor had told me that Thackeray didn't give a damn about politicians from Delhi; if Vajpayee came to see him, he would not be overwhelmed. But if Amitabh Bacchan came to see him, he would make time and would be filled with pride. It is a typical Bombayite's sense of priorities: entertainment first, politics second. When the film star Sanjay Dutt was jailed for eighteen months for his involvement in the bomb blasts, only the Saheb had the power to get him released on bail. Thackeray tells me that his great rival Sunil Dutt came to his house when his son was in jail. "He wept, he did an aarti around my wife." Eight or nine producers were sitting in the anteroom, waiting for an audience, while

Dutt circled Thackeray's wife with a lamp. All their projects with Sanjay were on the line, and they stood to lose crores. Thackeray's government let him out on bail.

I ask him if he thought Sanjay was guilty.

"They find one spring of a dismantled AK-420, and you are going to run a case against him?" He thinks that Sharad Pawar, then the chief minister, had fixed Sanjay because he was competing against his father for the Congress presidency. But if the court eventually finds him guilty, "hang him." It is a phrase the Saheb often uses, an all-purpose solution for Bangladeshi Muslims and Sanjay Dutt alike. This leader doesn't waste time on theory or process; he advocates direct immediate action: Hang them. A leader whom a young man, with little education but a lot of anger, can understand, can worship.

Thackeray's strongest support has at all times in his career come from sixteen- to thirty-year-olds. "Young blood, young men, youngsters without jobs are like dry gunpowder. It will explode any day." As they get into their thirties, they start getting respectable or lose the zeal for strife. Curiously, for a man whose support is supposed to come from the young, he goes on, "That generation. They don't have any culture or sanskar. Sanskar has no English alternative or word." The closest is "values." The Saheb is particular about his cultural tastes; Hindi movies and Michael Jackson are okay, but the city's celebration of Valentine's Day makes him furious. "Valentine's Day. I am going to ban it next year. See. They dare not. I'll tear their cards. What is Valentine's? Ridiculous! These college boys living on their pocket money given them by their fathers. I don't know it is white money or black. Enjoying life with girls and the girls are also like that. This what you call Coke generation Pepsi generation. Yes. With"—he gestures with disgust at his leg—"jeans on."

Sure enough, the next year on February 14, as he promised me, the Saheb bans Valentine's Day. The call goes out to his Sainiks, who ransack shops selling Valentine's Day cards and disrupt restaurants advertising Valentine's Day dinners. Newspapers as far as Turkey, South Africa, and Australia prominently cover his fulminations.

But he has mellowed; he is a tired, aging fascist. Now, after an outrageous statement, there is a gentle laugh, which robs the pronouncement of its "menaas." At times, joking about the movie people, smoking his cigar, he seems almost avuncular. It is difficult to connect the man sitting before me with the homicidal fury he unleashed in people like Sunil only a few years ago. But then, he is seventy-three. "I can remote control on government," he tells me, "but not on my age."

His fire reappears when he reverts back to his favorite targets. "The Bangladesh Muslims, they have come here. I don't know who is their godfather mother in Hindustan." He tells me about a recent bomb blast in Delhi, in which fifteen or twenty people were injured and the police arrested a Muslim man for the bombing. When the news of the arrest spread in the Muslim neighborhood, the call came from the mosque loudspeaker to attack, and a Muslim mob fifteen hundred men strong, according to Thackeray, invaded the police station and released the bomber. "We should tolerate this nonsense?" the Saheb thunders. "Who are you? What right do you have? You go back to your Bangladesh. This is very sad and bad."

Could this kind of incident happen in Mumbai?

"That way they have a check as far as Shiv Sena is concerned," he says with pride. No communal riot has happened since the Sena came to power, he points out.

"What is your explanation for why the Bombay riots happened in 'ninety-two and 'ninety-three?" I ask.

"Babri Masjid," he answers. "No Muslim here knows where is Lucknow, where is Babri Masjid." Neither, evidently, does Thackeray; the Babri Masjid is located in Ayodhya, hundreds of miles from Lucknow. The mosque was not a working mosque, he says; but there is a Ram Mandir underneath, where Hindu prayers have been offered. Then the mosque was demolished, and the Muslims in Mumbai took to the streets. "Then to save your secular face, dirty face, you say they were not local Muslims, they were outside Muslims, they came from Bihar and Uttar Pradesh, but how dare they come here? And inspire, instigated the locals. That is shot dead then, must be. There was a retaliation from Shiv Sena. If my boys would have not come on the streets I'm sure Hindus would have been slaughtered."

They retaliated, he says, with "whatever means we had at that time. The stone—it can be stones or tube lights or iron bars. They had some ammunition, the pistols. But even then . . . they would have massacred Hindus. You ask any community, Gujaratis, these these these, they said yes, because of Balasaheb our life was saved." As, indeed, my uncle had said.

"And then they elected you?"

"No. Once you are saved, you are saved. Then hell with you. We don't bargain, don't expect them to do. It is our bounded duty to save everybody's life then." The Sena would do the unpleasant work that my Gujaratis are too cowardly to do; they would fight the battle of Panipat against the Afghans all over again. After taking Bombay from us during the Samyukta Maharashtra movement—when they walked the streets looking for Gujaratis to beat up, shouting, "Kem chhe? Saru chhe! Danda leke maru chhe!"—they would now magnanimously protect us against the Muslim hordes.

He warns the Muslims. "Don't make us suspicious. You be free and frank. Every time you can't say, 'Islam is in danger.' Why we should worry about Islam because ours is not a Islamic country." He will oppose the Muslims if "their body is here and their heart is for Pakistan; I will be the first man to tell them get out." Their status in India is questionable to begin with. "What is this Muslim community? After the partition, they should have gone back!"

"Do you feel there will be another riot in Bombay? Is there social pressure bubbling?" I ask him.

"I am not an astrologer, neither a palmist nor a foreteller, but I can tell you this thing—my prophecy you call it or intuition you call it. If the Vajpayee government falls, there is going to be chaos and we'll be heading toward civil war. A civil war, mind you this." He is speaking very calmly, not raising his voice, not making a threat; just telling me what will happen, sure in his knowledge. "And then you will know what I have preached, what I have said. I touch wood I don't want that come true, but it will come true. The Muslims will come out. It is not just restricted to Mumbai. All over the country. It will be a civil war in the country itself."

What would the Sena do in a civil war?

"By any means we'll fight. By any means we'll fight. We'll have to fight. Retaliation is our birthright. Retaliation is our birthright."

I remind him about what he has told me: This time the Muslims are armed.

"Let us see, let us see. Let the time come. Let the time come."

THE MARATHI EDITOR later tells me he was one of a group of journalists speaking to the Saheb when the leader declared that he could see the future. He had "hallucinations," he remembers. "Of bloodshed. Blood across his eyes," and the editor draws a palm across his eyes, wiping away a sea of blood.

Thackeray has never read a book, the editor tells me. Indeed, I don't spot a single book in what I see of Thackeray's bungalow. His points of reference are movies and cartoons. He gets into trouble with writers—with Pu La Deshpande, when he compares him, punning on his name, to a falling bridge; with the All-India Marathi Litterateurs' Conference, when he withdraws their pathetic subsidy and jeers at them as "bulls on sale"— but he likes and is liked by people in the movie business, his natural kin. He feels comfortable with images and with action, but not with ideas. His conversation is studded with references to Hindi movies and such things as children's nursery rhymes. His answers, at times, don't seem to flow from my questions; they are not responses to them so much as they are stray thoughts that have been generated deep within his brain and are given free rein to surface at that particular moment.

What the editor had pointed out, and what strikes me now, is the mismatch of scale: this small-minded man controlling this very big city. "He lacks what George Bush called 'the vision thing,' " the editor had observed. The Saheb's solutions to the enormous problems of the city are precise and petty. There should be water in the hydrants so rats can be flushed out. Valentine's Day should be banned so our youth stays pure. There is no overall explanation for what ails the city, beyond general complaints about excess migration and Muslims. There is no understanding of historical process, of the vast and delicate gears and sprockets that power the city's massive economic engine. All he is concerned about is that his people are not getting rich; his solution is to demand, with the threat of mob violence, that a percentage of the jobs simply be set aside for them.

His approach is ad hoc, an immediate, forceful response to the present. Even Hindutva, which is getting developed into a full-fledged theory of race, has been borrowed from the Hindu nationalists of the RSS and the BJP. There is no connection made between two or three events, no theory, grand or minor, that he can use to explain what connects them.

In 1984, Thackeray invited a veteran Communist leader, S. A. Dange, to address a Sena meeting. Although Dange was a bitter enemy of the Sena, the men had respect for each other because they both saw themselves fighting for labor rights and had participated in the Samyukta Maharashtra movement. Dange got up and told the Sena what he thought of them: "The Shiv Sena does not have a theory, and it is impossible for an organization to survive sans a theory."

The next day, Thackeray responded. "He merely displayed arrogance by suggesting that the Shiv Sena didn't have a theory and said an organization can't survive without a theory. Then how has our organization survived for the last eighteen years?" Then he added, knife blade plunging for the final thrust, deadly because so true for the old Communist, "And how is it that, despite a theory, your organization is finished?"

The Sena had survived, flourished, because of a lack of theory. It adapted itself to changing theories; it was vaguely capitalist now, but at one point in the early 1980s Thackeray had been entranced with "practical socialism." The Sena had always hitched a ride aboard the theory of the day: anticommunism, fascism, socialism, anti-immigrant, and, now, anti-Muslim, pro-Hindu. The organization did not need a theory. It was all about praxis. Thackeray likes people who can get the things done.

I too have felt that craving for action. At night, after a hard day slogging in the turbulent city, full of anger and frustration over its bureaucratic delays, its political gridlock, I soothe myself to sleep by giving myself dictatorial powers: to abolish the Rent Act; to ban cars from the central city; to fill the judgeships on the high court and eliminate the backlog at a stroke. I am moving the city government to New Bombay, the state government to Pune. I am tearing up the mills and building parks and schools but most of all creating housing: thousands and thousands of six-story blocks, each six sharing a little play space for the children. A vast Levittown with minor variations in pattern, cheap and fast. All those who are here already shall be housed. The rest can't come in just now; I am making some space. I would need to consult no legislature to implement my sweeping plans; no consensus would need to be formed, because I know best. Enough talk; I would now act. It helps me sleep.

THE NEW CONGRESS GOVERNMENT that comes to power in Maharashtra in 2000 does so partly on the strength of its promises to implement the findings of the Srikrishna Commission Report. It lied. "More than four years after the publication of the Commission's report in 1998, no significant steps have been taken by the Government of Maharashtra to implement its recommendations," Amnesty International reported.

The commission had named thirty-one police officers for killing innocent people, acting in a communal manner, being negligent, or rioting themselves. Seventeen were formally charged in 2001, but as of 2003, none of the policemen had been put on trial. Ten of them were actually promoted. The majority of the rioters were charged under the Terrorist and Disruptive Activities Prevention Act, usually preceded in the press by the adjective "draconian." A total of 2,267 cases were lodged; 60 percent of them were closed by the police for want of evidence, under the "true but undetected" category; 894 cases were charge-sheeted. By March 1998, 853 were pending, 42 went to trial, 30 resulted in acquittals, 3 were dismissed, and a grand total of 8 resulted in convictions—for 1,400 murders. The masterminds of the bomb blasts were arrested or fled abroad, because the city's best detectives were put on the case; the masterminds of the riots, which killed many more people, got to be the government of Maharashtra and members of parliament. "Ten years of impunity for those responsible for the Mumbai riots send a deeply disturbing message to the nation and shatter public confidence in justice," Amnesty concluded.

The Sena government had gotten rid of thirteen of the fourteen cases pending against Bal Thackeray's role in the 1992 riots. The new Congress government revives the remaining case, which holds him accountable for inciting communal passions during the riots through his *Saamna* editorials. It was the least of his sins and would have brought the civil libertarians rushing to his defense in a country such as the United States. Thackeray has never been arrested. The new deputy chief minister, Chaggan Bhujbal, who earlier defected from the Sena to the Congress, has always wanted to arrest his former mentor, even if it is for one hour. He declares he will implement at least one of the recommendations of the Srikrishna Commission Report and arrest the Saheb.

"This has never happened and is not possible in future . . . If I go behind the bars they [those who arrest me] will not be able to roam freely," the Sena chief thunders while addressing the annual Dussehra rally at Shivaji Park. If he is arrested, Thackeray declares in *Saamna*, "Not only Maharashtra, [but] India could burn. This is a call for religious riots and everybody should prepare for the consequences." Sanjay Nirupam, a Shiv

Sena MP, sees opportunity if his leader is arrested. "After the 'ninety-three riots we won thirty out of thirty-four seats in the election," he points out to me. "If this is a democracy, the people have spoken. Another riot is to our political advantage."

The Sena leaders have gone underground in anticipation of the arrest. Sunil has received his orders and is in hiding. He calls me periodically. None of the Jogeshwari boys sleeps at home these days; they are constantly on the move, constantly alert. They are highly mobile, in cells of fifteen or twenty people, in small cars and motorcycles. Their orders are to target state and central government property: buses, trains, offices. It might get down to religion, and then Sunil thinks the Hindus will unite. "When it comes to religion you forget that you are a Gujarati or a bhaiyya. You are all Hindus, against Muslims. And this time we will drive them out of Bombay." All over the city, the Sena is preparing for the next war.

One Saturday night I get a call from Sunil; he is closing down the city with his boys. At the nightly meeting of the shakha, the report is that the Saheb will be arrested early the next day. In the background I can hear the angry roaring of the Tiger's troops. I sense a new vigor in Sunil. It is like the old days.

The next day, Sunil keeps calling on my cell phone to keep me apprised of his activities, as he goes about stopping trains. Sunil's boys are sent to Goregaon; the Goregaon shakha sends Sainiks to Jogeshwari. This way, they aren't recognized by their local police, who are alternately their friends and jailers. At one point, a force of two hundred policemen stands by as Sunil's boys enforce the strike. The police make ineffective noises, like taking down names and threatening to make arrests. Sunil's squad stops a bus and the driver tells all his passengers to disembark. Then the squad destroys the bus. They go into large glass-fronted shops and point out to the owner how much damage he would incur if he kept the shop open and a stone were to come hurling through his precious glass. He pulls down the shutters. Seven to eight hundred Sainiks fan out across Jogeshwari, stopping the trains and forcing taxis and rickshaws off the roads. They march into the bus depot; the manager himself offers to pull his buses off the streets so they won't be damaged. The city is effectively shut down.

What finally occurs is not civil war but farce. The Saheb declares he will voluntarily present himself in front of the court. He does so—escorted by an army of five hundred policemen, which maintains the facade of an arrest for Bhujbal—and the magistrate dismisses the case, saying it should have been prosecuted within three years of the offense. Thackeray is in and out of court in under forty-five minutes. Bombay starts breathing again.

But the view from Cuffe Parade is different. The new Miss Universe is returning triumphant to the country. During this time, "all Bombay cares about," declares the socialite columnist Shobha De, "is who's coming to Lara Datta's homecoming."

THE IMPULSE TO GENOCIDE springs from the desire for cleanliness, for a clean homogeneity, because it is well known that chaos and disorder result from a messy mix, from heterogeneity. Iqbal and Jinnah split from India because they wanted to create a pure nation, the Land of the Pure. The ethos—that much-abused word—of India is against such homogeneity. But a fair-minded person can look around Bombay and see that it really is too crowded. Somebody needs to go. But who? Well, you start with the poorest. Or the newest. Or the one farthest away from yourself, however you define yourself. Immigrants hope, ultimately, to be in a position where they have the right to keep out new immigrants, to tell the next person to get off the train in your city that he must go back, he can't stay. That's when you know you're truly native.

The 1992–93 riots were a double disaster for Bombay: They made the city much worse for the people already living here, and they did not make it less attractive for all the new people from upcountry wanting to come and join them. The next civil disturbance will be no different. It will be a worse city, but it will not lose people for being a worse city. It will not even slow down in accumulating new people.

In the new century, the Sena is experiencing troubles. They are not able to respond with vigor when the Muslim underworld goes about picking off their pramukhs. Some are killed, some are threatened. In Jogeshwari, Bhikhu Kamath gets a letter, in "Muslim language," as Sunil describes it, telling him he's next, because he has killed Muslims in the riots. Chotta Shakeel, the operational commander of the Muslim gangs, is doing what the government has failed to do. He is extracting revenge for the riots. And he is going after the right people too: the guilty people, such as ex-mayor Milind Vaidya, who was named in the Srikrishna Commission Report. Shakeel is consulting the report; he is the executive to Srikrishna's judiciary.

The Sena leaders do the worst thing you can do if you are to have the respect of the taporis: They plead for police protection. The shakha pramukhs and their deputies surround themselves with bodyguards. The Tiger squeals loudly when his security is reduced from 179 bodyguards to 149; after the killings of the pramukhs, it is raised again. The Tiger is losing his teeth. He has heart trouble, and there is a succession struggle in the offing between his son and his nephew. Power has made the senior leadership fat, rich, and soft. They can't do anything too outrageous because their people are cabinet ministers in Delhi. The BJP has acted as a moderating influence on the street army. Under the leadership of Thackeray's son Uddhav, the Sena is at risk of turning into just another regional party, a party of politicians. Things get heated within the Sena; the Tiger accuses his men of having become a "pensioners' organization."

There needs to be a new outlet for the rage of the young and the poor. The gangs will provide that if the Sena can't. The Sena needs to keep pace with the buildup of their anger; it is unable to corral it, stoke it, absorb it. The wave of young men in the eighties and early nineties who fought the Sena's street battles, like Sunil, have been rewarded and have become successful bourgeois businessmen and Special Executive Officers; they are strutting around, putting their children in English schools. The boys that have come after them are finding it harder to get by. If the Sena doesn't tap their anger, some other force will; and this time it may not be a political party. It may not be a religion, it may not even be a gang. It may just be an explosion of formless free-floating urban anger generated in young men without ideology, without faith. Young men in transit within their own city, within their individually multiple selves.

Mumbai

THE HISTORY OF EACH CITY is marked by a catalytic event, just as each life has a central event around which it is organized. For New York, it is now the September 11, 2001, attacks on the World Trade Center. For the Bombay of my time, it is the riots and the blasts of 1993. Bombay was spared the horrors of Partition in 1947. The only event related to war I remember growing up was during the war of 1971 over Bangladesh: A civilian aircraft blundered over the city by mistake one night, the air-raid sirens went off, the antiaircraft tracers started streaking from Raj Bhavan, the governor's residence nearby, and my father put us all under mattresses. In school we practiced hiding under the desks if a bomb were to fall on us.

But there was an earlier trauma in the psychic life of the city, which marked the before and after for old-timers: the explosion on the *Fort Stikine*, on April 14, 1944.

The *Fort Stikine* was a ship supposedly carrying bales of cotton and, like the hundred-odd boats that were then as now waiting in the harbor to get a berth in port, was anchored offshore. The intense pressure that cotton bales are stored under, along with the temperature on that very hot day, caused the cotton bales to catch fire. This by itself would not have been very serious, at least not to people who were not on the ship. But the *Fort Stikine* had a secret cargo. It was carrying explosives—this was wartime—and it was also carrying a secret cargo of gold and silver, worth £2 million, brought from London to stabilize the sagging Indian rupee. Then the fire department did the worst thing they possibly could; they towed the burning ship into the harbor rather than scuttling it in the bay. At a quarter to four, there was a terrific bang, a pall of smoke, and the windows of houses in the Fort area rattled. Twenty-five minutes later, there was another explosion, and the windowpanes shattered. The ammunition had caught fire, and the ship exploded at dockside, which was then full of dock laborers and firefighters. Two hundred ninety-eight people died immediately.

Then the rain started.

The sky over Bombay was filled with gold and silver, masonry, bricks, steel girders, and human limbs and torsos, flying through the air as far as Crawford Market. A jeweler was sitting in his office in Jhaveri Bazaar when a bar of solid gold crashed through the roof and arrived in front of him. A steel girder flew through the air and crashed through the roof of Victoria Terminus, the main train station. A plate of iron landed on a horse and neatly decapitated the animal. Stray limbs and fragments of bodies were blown all over the docks. Bombay had never, till then, seen any wartime action. It was as if the city had been bombed.

The disaster of the *Fort Stikine* is with us still. Bars of gold from the ship were being found as late as the 1970s, during dredging operations at the docks. But there was a mountain of more base debris from the explosion, and the British municipal authorities chose to create land out of it. They started filling in the Back Bay, where the mangroves used to be, in what is now Nariman Point, leading in time to the worst-planned office district in modern India, the prime villain in the condition of modern Bombay.

At the entrance to Cama Chamber, Building Number 23, hangs this prominent notice:

ATTENTION
This building is unsafe and likely to collapse. Persons entering the property do so at their own risk. The owner of the property will not be liable for any damage to life and property.
Owners

If you go up the narrow wooden steps, you can see the signboards of the offices in the unsafe building. They are law firms, accountants, merchant bankers. The offices themselves are sleek, modern, air-conditioned, with computers blinking and flashing. Only the building's public areas are decrepit. Gaping holes mark the first floor where windows should be. The same notice is posted by the owners on the first floor. They are getting, by force of law, almost nothing in rent for their land. So they will put nothing into repairs of the building; all they can do is put up these cautionary signs, which they hope will frighten away the clients of the businesses within.

When World War II ended, another catastrophe struck Bombay in the form of the Bombay Rents, Hotel Rates, and Lodging House Rates Control Act of 1947—popularly known as the Rent Act. Bombay is still recovering from that legislative blast. Enacted in 1948, the act froze the rents on all buildings leased at the time at their 1940 levels. In the case of other buildings, the courts were empowered to affix a "standard rent," which, once determined, could never be raised. The act also provided for transfer of the right to lease the property at the fixed rent to the legal heirs of the tenant. As long as the tenant kept paying the rent, he could not be evicted; he would not need to renew his lease. This was originally intended as an emergency wartime measure, a five-year provision to protect tenants from inflation and speculation after World War II. Bombay was full of troops early in the war. Accommodations were at a premium; Bombay was bustling. And the newcomers were rich; those who owned property in the city were not blind to this fact. So they hiked rents to whatever the market would bear. Outsiders who came in—Indians—found themselves frozen out of the city. The short-term visitors during the war were in danger of dispossessing the old-timers: thus the Rent Act.

But the act, once enacted, proved politically impossible to repeal, since there will always be more tenants than landlords. There are 2.5 million tenants in Bombay, the most powerful political lobby in the city. All the political parties are unified in warlike support of the tenants; the Rent Act has been extended more than twenty times. The tenants have proposed a solution to the landlords: sell their rented properties en masse to the tenants living in them, for a hundred times the fixed rent on each property. This would end the rent disputes once and for all, because the tenants would become owners. It would also mean that properties in the poshest areas of the city would be given over for an amount that would not buy a slum room on the open market. The landlords can do nothing but refuse to repair their properties. So there's no possibility of the housing stock of the island city improving or expanding anytime soon, and more of the island city falls down every year. There are twenty thousand buildings that are officially classified as dilapidated and need to be renovated by the public agencies; fewer than a thousand a year are actually improved.

The relative income levels of landlord and tenant make no difference as far as the law is concerned. The provisions of the Rent Act also apply to commercial buildings, benefiting multinational corporations and large government enterprises, which pay a pittance for their offices. Some of the richest people in the city live in rent-controlled bungalows all around Malabar Hill, inherited from their grandparents and great-grandparents. The reason Bombay is choking is the Rent Act. It hits the newcomer, the young, and the poor; it's the reason lovers in Bombay can't find a place to be alone. Those who come in from outside can't find a room to rent because the middle class and the rich already have a lock on all the best properties. It is the most extreme version of a Newcomers' Tax. But it doesn't keep the newcomers out; it merely condemns them to live squalidly.

In the 1930s, Bombay was full of signs saying FLATS TO LET. Very few people bought flats then; there were no mortgages. To buy a flat with a mortgage is still relatively rare in Bombay. Most people buy the property outright, with a fixed "white-black" percentage: the amount on which taxes have been paid is given in the form of a check; and shopping bags full of cash for the other color. After the Rent Act came in, the "pugree," or key money, system started. A tenant would be bribed by the owner to vacate a rent-controlled flat; in effect, he'd be paying the tenant a sizable sum for his own property. Once a criminal offense, the practice is so prevalent that in 1999 the state was forced to legalize it. The court battles over the Rent Act take on the dimensions of a war. While the state was recently considering revising the act, the head of the Property Owners' Association had to stay home for a month under armed guard. There will never be a solution to the rent mess because then all the professional activists would be out of business, one of them tells me.

Either you believe in individual property rights or you don't; either a citizen can never have any permanent claim to a piece of land or he can, and if he does it should be backed up by the full weight of the law. An owner of a flat should have the right to repossess it after the lease expires. If a piece of land has been set aside for use as a public park, the municipality should have the right to demolish any structure that invades the park. But in 1979 the government of India removed from the constitution the right to property as a "fundamental right," along with the right to be compensated when the state expropriates property. In India, the framework of existing laws—the Rent Act; the Urban Land Ceiling Act, which essentially transfers ownership of large tracts of land in Bombay to the state—creates a situation of continuous doubt in the mind of the property owner: Does this land really belong to me? This is the question that keeps 60 percent of the people homeless. Builders don't build anywhere near the amount of new housing needed because at any moment they could be told, This land doesn't belong to you.

The Greater Bombay region has an annual deficit of 45,000 houses a year. The amount of new construction every year comes up to less than half the number needed. Thus these 45,000 households every year add to the ranks of the slums. In the words of the planners, their shelter needs "are satisfied in the informal market." This slum population doubles every decade. There are also 400,000 *empty* residences in the city, empty because the owners are afraid of losing them to tenants if they rent them out. Assuming each apartment can house a family of five people, on average, that's 2 million people—one-fourth of the homeless—who could immediately find shelter if the laws were to be amended.

But the anxiety of the tenants can also be understood. The greatest fear of the Bombayite is to end up on the footpath. In New York I volunteered for an organization for the homeless, and over three years I got to know them. Homelessness is a condition; the material fact of not having a home of one's own invades one's consciousness till it becomes a person's entire self-definition. Before you are an out-of-work clerk or your father's son or your wife's husband or a Bombayite or a human being, you are homeless. There isn't that much difference, really, between living in a shack built of rags or on the footpath over which it perches. If anything, the air is better in the open, although during the rains the illusion of a barrier between you and the water goes a long way in comforting you. As very young boys we used to make these little huts in the construction ground behind the building I lived in on Ridge Road; put up three walls and a roof with any odd building material, cardboard, rags, bricks. Then we would cluster inside it, five or six little boys, while the older children mocked us. "This is Suketu, architect. And that's Dilip, engineer." The world felt different, safer, inside the little shack. In school we would likewise demarcate territory on the two-person benches we occupied. Even as children in Bombay, we were constantly trying to claim space. The important thing was not to get crowded off the space you happened to possess at the moment. The moment you left, it was up for grabs.

The Rent Act leads to peculiar constructions of "home," unique to Bombay. Each April 1, a parade of taxis and tempos will take the residents of the F. D. Petit Parsi Sanitarium at Kemps Corner to the Bhabha Sanitarium at Bandra. Four months later, they will all move to the Jehangir Bagh Sanitarium in Juhu. Four months after that, they will all come back to Kemps Corner. The mass migrations back and forth to the same place, often the same room, happen because the Parsi Panchayat, which owns the sanatoria, knows that tenants who are allowed to stay on become de facto owners. So they keep their tenants constantly on the move, even as they provide them shelter. Some of the families have been doing this merry-go-round for over half a century. Every time they move, they must reapply, coming up with a health certificate, to prove they need the salubrious quarters of a sanatorium. They are allowed to keep their bags and some furniture—but not a refrigerator. Installing a fridge is claiming home, so the residents must subsist on powdered milk.

Another cancerous outgrowth of the Bombay Rent Act is the "paying guest." In looking for an office, I am referred to the "PG rooms," which are rooms in someone else's flat. The city has a whole tribe of "paying guests," usually young professionals from other cities, suffering the daily humiliations imposed on them by their landlords—what time you can come in and who you can bring with you, how much ice you're entitled to from the fridge, how loud you can play your music. There are three personal gods that every Hindu is supposed to revere: mother, father, guest. There is no category for "paying guest."

The Rent Act was an institutionalized expropriation of private property. Democracies have a weakness: If a bad law has enough money or people behind it, it stays on the books. This allows the perpetual continuation of the most absurd, unreasonable practices. In America I can walk into a gun show and buy a handgun for less than the price of a good dinner for two, even if I am insane or a convicted criminal. In Bombay I can walk into a flat I've rented for a year and stay there for the rest of my life, pass it on to my sons after me, and defy the lawful proprietor's efforts to get my ass off his property. In both instances, I have the law behind me.

The city is full of people claiming what's not theirs. Tenants claim ownership by virtue of having squatted on the property. Millworkers demand that mills be kept open at a loss to provide them with employment. Slum dwellers demand water and power connections for illegal constructions on public land. Government employees demand the right to keep working long past when they're needed, at taxpayer expense. Commuters demand further subsidies for train fares, which are already the lowest in the world. Moviegoers demand that the government freeze ticket prices. The Indian government has long believed in the unreality of supply and demand; what you pay for an item, for a food or for a service, has no relation to what it costs the producer.

ON A VISIT to the caves of Elephanta Island, I come out to a courtyard just off the main cave. From here, I can look at two sets of pillars: on my right, the pillars commissioned by the Rashtrakuta kings in the eighth century; in front of me, the new pillars built by the Archaeological Survey of India. In one panoramic sweep you can see the whole decline of culture in India. The original pillars, built a thousand years ago, are delicately fluted and in proportion, curving gently outward like an infant's belly. The ASI pillars are stolid blocks of stone, each unmatched in shape and color and size with the others; at a glance you can tell they are wonky. They are devoid of ornamentation, which is probably just as well, since God knows what monstrosities their house sculptors would carve on the pillars if they were allowed to. What we could do so exquisitely in this country a thousand years ago we can't even attempt today. We were making some of the greatest art of the ancient world. Shattered by invasion and colonialism and an uneasy accommodation with modernity, we now can't construct five pillars of equal proportions.

We built the Konarak Temple, Hampi, the Taj Mahal. Then what happened? The quality of architecture in Bombay demonstrates the devolution of the species: What is being built today is worse than what was built fifty years ago, which is worse than what was built a century ago. The public buildings of British Bombay, in the third decade of the Victorian era, took their cue from Gothic church architecture. "It's got nothing to do with propagating Christianity," a historian had pointed out to me. "It's a sample of what they thought of as fine design and good taste." The colonnaded arcades of the stately Victorian buildings of the Fort area pullulate with the traffic of an illegal, immovable, and necessary oriental bazaar. The railway terminus and university and court buildings of the Fort area are either lovable or Gothic follies, depending on your taste, but you can look at them and feel something. There are no modern buildings in Bombay that make you feel anything.

This, then, is the geography of my childhood: tower blocks of a bastardized Bauhaus design, dwarfing and shadowing the red-roofed bungalows of the earlier rich. In front of my uncle's building is a monstrous skyscraper, its skeleton having been completed over a decade ago, lying vacant. Several of these buildings dot the city. The flats have been bought for huge sums; they are empty because they violated municipal height limits. The builders knew they were violating the limits and built them anyway, figuring the first priority was to put up the concrete reality and deal with the extraneous issues—municipal clearances, legal papers, bribes—later. But the municipal corporation put its foot down and either demolished some buildings or prevented further construction. The fate of the surviving buildings then entered the courts, where they have settled in for a prolonged spell.

The country's oldest buildings are still around. The walls of the five-thousand-year-old public buildings of Mohenjo-Daro are still standing. Not so buildings made in the 1970s. All day long, all around my flat, there is construction; gangs of men and women with hammers and picks, chipping away at the older bungalows and buildings in bits, here and there, not quite destroying but gnawing like an army of mice, then erecting awful structures much less durable than what was there before. There is no professional body that certifies civil engineers in India; they are badly trained. The sand used in the concrete comes from the creeks around Bombay, which contains salt, silt, and shit, so new buildings look weather-beaten, moth-eaten. Many of the newer buildings have one whole side covered in brown cloth, their windows blocked for a year, and scaffolding erected while workers inject granite into the spiderweb of fissures in the building's walls, shoring them up. Just when the residents are able to open their windows on one side, work begins on the next side. This can go on for years.

* * *

RAHUL MEHROTRA, whose architectural projects—particularly the combination of low- and high-tech material in his buildings—are praised by
critics, is in his tenth year of working in Bombay. More than half of his
work, the unpaid part, is an urban planning institute in Bombay. He talks to
anyone who'll listen—governments, journalists, Rotarians—about what
needs to be done in Bombay. "If you say it long enough, it might become
the truth." He is speaking to me in his new office in Tardeo, furnished in
the uncompromisingly modernist style that is his trademark. Pictures of
his kids break the rigor. "We have a special problem as planners in Bombay," says Rahul. "If we make the city nice, with good roads, trains, and
accommodation—if we make the city a nicer place to live—it attracts more
people from the outside." I see; then the city's screwed up again, from too
many people. It's like building roads. The more roads you build, the greater
the number of new cars that will rush in to use those roads, and then
they're jammed again. "Planning in India has to take into account the whole
country, the rest of the cities." Unless entry to Bombay is restricted—the
Shiv Sena's plan—it's an exercise in futility to make this a more livable
city. The crowd of bhaiyyas on the Gorakhpur Express will continue to
swell, all the more so if they think they can get off the train and be housed
by the government. Bombay's fate is solidly, inextricably, linked to India's
fate, much as the city would like to pretend otherwise.

Rahul traces the deterioration of Bombay to the late sixties. In 1964, a
commission headed by the architect Charles Correa—Rahul's father-in-
law—proposed New Bombay, a "magnet city" for Bombay, a pressure
valve. It would be located right across the bay, just to the east of the island
city. It would be a planned city; the government would own all the land,
and it would have unlimited scope for expansion, because it had all India as
its backyard.

But in the late sixties, the state government backed out of a commitment to move its offices from the Nariman Point Reclamation, on the
southern tip of the island, to New Bombay. Private businesses followed
suit. "They let Nariman Point go. It was a complete slap in the face of New
Bombay. The hubris of money and the nexus between politicians and
builders had reached a point where the city's concern was not primary."
Rahul identifies the five builders who, along with the V. P. Naik government, ruined Bombay: the Makers, the Rahejas, the Dalamals, the
Mittals, and the Tulsianis. Their names are immortalized on the office com-

plexes they constructed in Nariman Point, which, in the original development plan, had been designated for educational and mixed-use residential
housing.

If the builders hadn't violated the development plan, all the offices they
put up in Nariman Point would have gone up in New Bombay, and that
momentum and that energy would have driven the new city into being. It
would have reoriented the commuting axis of Bombay for the better. Bombay grew along a north-south axis; people live in the north and commute,
in inhumanly packed trains, to the south. Its future depends on the axis
being reoriented in an east-west direction. Metropolitan Bombay is the
largest urban area in India: 32 percent live in the island city, 42 percent in
the northern suburbs, and 18 percent in New Bombay. But 72 percent of the
jobs are in the island city, where too much of the commuting traffic heads
each day.

The reason the builders took over Nariman Point instead of New
Bombay was simple: "The greater you skew demand and supply, the higher
prices rise. The five boys must have met and had tea and decided among
themselves to corner it all in a smaller plan." Now New Bombay is that
melancholy creation, a dormitory town.

Rahul spreads out a map of Bombay and points to another solution. He
has just drawn up a new plan to develop the eastern waterfront of the
island, huge tracts of land now held by the Bombay Port Trust. This looking east puts him squarely at odds with the prevailing vision in Bombay,
which is directed west, "where the sunset is beautiful and the breeze is better," explains Rahul. By opening up the eastern waterfront, "you could
visually link the city to New Bombay; you could stand at Ballard Estate and
see New Bombay." But there is stiff resistance from the Bombay Port
Trust. "They're beginning to behave like builders."

There is land, thousands of miles of land, to the east. But the east is not
good enough for Bombay. It is determined to claim the west, all the way
until it reaches Arabia. In Bombay, we grew up looking west, because the
sea was the only direction in which the eye could roam free. If people go
out on a terrace or balcony of a Bombay apartment, and they have a 360-
degree view, their eyes will automatically move toward the west, the direction of the possible.

My science tutor in the ninth standard once looked out the window of
Dariya Mahal and said to me, "All those buildings in front of us"—Dariya

Mahal 1 and 2—"are going to presently fall into the sea." I was alarmed; my grandfather and the girl I was in love with lived in those buildings. But they were not going to stay upright for long, my tutor predicted, because they were built on land reclaimed from the sea: "re-claimed," as if we had a legitimate claim on it in the first place.

Once Bombay was composed of seven hilly islands, which were leveled, and the soil dumped into the sea, to make one big island; as the city lost height, it gained area. The history of the construction of Bombay consists of a struggle against the sea, a child standing by the ocean and throwing pebbles into the water—as did I on the rocks behind Dariya Mahal, filling in the pools: an atavistic urge to construct land, to conquer water.

The architect Hafeez Contractor, who makes blocks of flats in the shapes of seashells, mushrooms, and in one case, a phallus, has the ear of the civic authorities and now wants to "reclaim" yet more land from the western sea: 486 acres more. But the sea continually challenges the claim's validity. Water takes its revenge on our buildings; it corrodes the exteriors, makes the potato chips and the pappadams soggy, enters our walls, and leaks through our ceilings. Every monsoon is an assault on Bombay. The furious rain is a severe, pitiless arbiter of basic engineering principles. What the municipality can't do, the rain does: It demolishes unsound structures. The sea and the rain are joined by the sewage, human waste, all around us. All around where I sleep, in my rooms, there is water finding its way through my shell, invading my dry space through a dozen leaks, one drip at a time. There is water everywhere, except in my taps.

At the age of fourteen I had experienced a miracle. I turned on a tap, and clean water came gushing out. This was in the kitchen of my father's studio apartment in Jackson Heights. It had never happened to me before. In Bombay the tap, when it worked, was always the first step of a process. The water came out in raw form; things had to be done to it. First it was filtered through a thin cloth to remove visible heavy dirt. It was further filtered in a large white receptacle with candle filters. Then it might be boiled, especially in the rainy season. Finally it would be put in empty whiskey bottles and chilled in the refrigerator or, in my grandparents' house, in the big clay pots that cooled it and gave it a delicious sweet taste. It took a long time, at least twenty-four hours, between the time the water came out of the tap and the time it could enter my mouth. I had grown up drinking stale water.

Bombay depends on the hinterland for this most basic resource. It is the only city in India in which water has to be brought in from lakes as distant as sixty miles away. The reason for this was the great plague of 1896. Until the middle of the nineteenth century, the city depended on well water and tanks. After the plague, the city closed the wells and tanks. The municipal corporation now treats and supplies some 800 million gallons a day. This is only 70 percent of the total water demand. Those whose demand goes unsatisfied live mostly in the slums. They have to steal the water they need, from pipelines passing their land on the way to customers whom the municipality deems legitimate users of water. Up to a third of the corporation's water is stolen by the poor. There are periodic riots over water, even in middle-class areas such as Bhayander. The residents of this suburb, housewives and accountants alike, recently went out into the streets and burnt trains because there was no water in their taps. The police teargassed them.

The architectural profession, says Rahul, has failed to get ordinary citizens excited about urban planning, to show them how all these issues are interconnected. Rahul dismisses as a "nonstarter" the main architecture school in Bombay, J.J., and no urban planning course is taught anywhere. Young people are not coming to him to work with him in his institute. So how, I ask him, would he save the city?

His answer is disarmingly simple: by opening up more space. There are two ways for a crowded city to sustain itself, by creating new land or by thinking up new uses for existing land. New Bombay is an example of the first kind of approach, in which agricultural land is improved with adequate water supply, sewage, and transportation services to create new extensions to the city. The second approach, which Rahul implies has been insufficiently investigated, is to take existing serviced land, such as the Parel mill areas or the areas around the docks, and convert them to new uses, more suited to today's needs. These are huge industrial blocks of land, and Rahul would compensate for deficiencies in the existing structure of the city by building schools, hospitals, auditoriums, parks. Another large block of already serviced urban land is owned by the railways: the vast tracts on either side of the tracks. As it is, railway land gets converted for de facto public use anyway, when the slums—Sunil's railway shanties, for example—advance upon it.

The notion of what is a luxury and what is a basic need has been upended in Bombay. Every slum I see in Jogeshwari has a television; antennas sprout in silver branches above the shanties. Many in the middle-class slum have motorcycles, even cars. People in Bombay eat relatively well, too, even the slum dwellers. The real luxuries are running water, clean bathrooms, and transport and housing fit for human beings. It doesn't matter how much money you have. If you live in the suburbs, you'll either curse in your car, as you drive for two hours each way toward the center, or asphyxiate in the train compartments, even the first-class ones. The greatest luxury of all is solitude. A city this densely packed affords no privacy. Those without a room of their own don't have space to be alone, to defecate or write poetry or make love. A good city ought to have that; it ought to have parks or beaches where young people can kiss without being overwhelmed by the crowd.

The approach being tried now by the government planners is that of a "polynucleated city," which would spread its commercial districts beyond South Bombay to places like the Bandra–Kurla complex, Andheri, Oshiwara. But the greatest possibility for opening up land in Bombay is the mill areas, four-hundred-odd acres of prime Bombay land occupied by fifty-two mills, very few of them running. The mill areas are now dotted with very thin, brightly colored, very high postmodern buildings, out of context and ill at ease among the two- and three-story chawls, with banana trees in front of them, narrow roads, and vast undulating waves of factory roofs. Most of them are luxury residential flats. Where millions once worked, thousands now live. Going up into one building to look at a flat, I notice the same mediocre imagination at work: the cramped rooms and unnaturally large windows, completely unsuited for a country in which the sun is the enemy for much of the day.

The workers want the mills to be reopened, modernized; they don't think Bombay's days as an industrial center are over. The government drew up a plan for the mills: turn a third into low-income housing and housing for laid-off millworkers; allow the owners to sell a third as residential or commercial space, with part of the proceeds to be used for modernizing the mills; and turn a third over to the municipal corporation for public use. There are forty thousand workers still on the payroll of the mills. The owners are trying to wait out the workers, waiting for them to die or retire. Land was given to the owners by the government, say the workers, to create employment, so it is not theirs to decide to dispose of.

The millworkers who have accepted voluntary retirement take their one or two lakhs, run through the money quickly, and end up as rickshaw wallahs or drunks or in the underworld. It is, along with the Rent Act, the most potent issue in Bombay's politics and the saddest: How do you provide a measure of justice to those who built the city, once the city has no further use for them?

Then there are a series of smaller steps that Rahul sees as possible: "the micro level." Private companies could be convinced to invest in the beautification of the city they do business in. The municipality and its citizens could communicate better through instruments like the Citizen's Charter, which specifies what people have a right to expect from their local government. What Rahul wants, above all, is a "holistic" plan. The current plans are far from holistic. Flyovers, for example: The Sena built fifty-five of them, to solve the traffic problems of the city. A flyover is just a little vehicular bridge over a traffic signal, but it sounds so grand: "Fly over!" It is debatable whether the bridges make traffic any better. Most of them are in the suburbs; the central city has no new roads. As far as I can see, the flyovers just get you to your traffic jam faster.

The city cannot govern itself. It cannot change swiftly enough. The city was built on cloth; time moved on and it has to be rebuilt on something else: information. The city's older folk had difficulty reconciling themselves to the idea of a whole city, 5 million jobs, built on top of something so abstract as information: not even pieces of paper you can hold but evanescent flashes of light on a screen. The representatives of the millworkers stranded in the nineteenth century led protest marches against the new economy. The city could survive and flourish if its managers were able to convince the residents to move from things they can hold with their hands—cloth, leather, cars—to things that can be held only in the mind—cinematic images, the pyramids of ownership in unseen enterprises around the world. The city has to change. It can no longer manufacture product with its hands. It now has to sell brainpower: ideas, data, dreams. And to achieve the latter its physical structure has to change. The places where people work have to become offices instead of factories.

When Rahul recently went back to Cambridge, where he'd studied at Harvard, he found that nothing had changed in the decade he'd been away. When he came back to Bombay after four weeks, he found he couldn't recognize the pavement outside his house; they had dug it up and done new things to it. The physical landscape of the city is in perpetual motion.

Rahul is trying to keep a measure of continuity. He is active in a number of initiatives for preservation of historic districts and their revival. "We are asking, What are the contemporary engines to revive each area? An art district around Kala Ghoda. A banking district around Fort; a tourist district around the Taj Hotel." So he is partly responsible for one of the most beautiful evenings I experience in Bombay, a Hindustani vocal concert around the twelfth-century temple tank in Banganga, restored by Rahul's institute with funding from an international bank. But as soon as I walk out of the concert the stench hits me, from the slums all outside Banganga. It had been a rich man's beauty; two international banks have subsidized the beautification of Banganga and that concert. It was beautiful because the messy poor and their children had been kept out. I had seen this in Paris, which was also beautiful because the poor had been kept out of the city, shunted to the banlieu. Then there was New York, which, when I got there in 1977, was like any American city, an orphanage, an almshouse. Bombay is both, the beautiful parts and the ugly parts, fighting block by block, to the death, for victory.

Every morning, out of the window of my study, I see men easing themselves on the rocks by the sea. Twice a day, when the tide washes out, an awful stench rises from these rocks and sweeps over the half-million-dollar flats to the east. Prahlad Kakkar, an ad filmmaker, has made a film called *Bumbay,* a film about shitting in the metropolis. He used hidden videocameras to film people shitting, in toilets all over the island city. But that was only half the story, he told me. "Half the population doesn't have a toilet to shit in, so they shit outside. That's five million people. If they shit half a kilo each, that's two and a half million kilos of shit each and every day. The real story is what you don't see in the film. There are no shots of women shitting. They have to shit between two and five each morning, because it's the only time they get privacy." Kakkar discovered this window into the bowel movements of Bombayites through his driver, who took a shit whenever and wherever Kakkar got out for an appointment. When Kakkar came back, he would invariably be kept waiting outside the car for the driver, who would run back, apologizing, "Saab, I had to shit." The driver, Rasool Mian, knew where to go in any given place in the city;

he had scoped out all the best places, a location scout of the digestive system.

The World Bank recently flew in a group of experts to solve Bombay's sanitation crisis. The beneficiaries of the bank's projects are now referred to not as poor people but as "clients." But in this case, it was not individual human beings but the state—the Government of Maharashtra—that was the client. The bank's solution was to propose building 100,000 public toilets. It was an absurd idea. I have seen public latrines in the slums. None of them work. People defecate all around the toilets, because the pits have been clogged for months or years. To build 100,000 public toilets is to multiply this problem hundredfold. Indians do not have the same kind of civic sense as, say, Scandinavians. The boundary of the space you keep clean is marked at the end of the space you call your own. The flats in my building are spotlessly clean inside; they are swept and mopped every day, or twice every day. The public spaces—hallways, stairs, lobby, the building compound—are stained with betel spit; the ground is littered with congealed wet garbage, plastic bags, and dirt of human and animal origin. It is the same all over Bombay, in rich and poor areas alike.

This absence of civic sense is something that everyone from the British to the Hindu nationalists of the RSS have drawn attention to, the national defect in the Indian character. It is seen in Panchratna, the citadel of the diamond trade. The offices inside are swank; the public spaces are gutters. The owners of the offices on the first through the sixth floors have stopped paying their bills for central AC, which run up to fifty lakhs. So the building cuts off the air-conditioning. The offices with windows install window air conditioners, and they are fine. But the windowless offices have to install split cooling units; the intake is from outside the building but the exhaust ducts let out into the corridor. So people walking along the corridors, waiting for the lifts, are subjected to powerful jets of hot used air in the airless spaces. You can sweat out half your body weight waiting for the lifts. And it is a fire hazard: all those hot duct pipes snaking their way through electrical wiring in the ceilings. My uncle, who has an office in Panchratna, has to threaten to file public interest litigation to get them to remove the pipes. Most buildings in Bombay have great difficulty raising funds for renovation, because it is a joint effort and the benefit is shared—and diluted—among many people.

The government can't make the physical city a better place, but it can call it by a different name. The city is in the grip of a mass renaming frenzy. Over 50 road-renaming proposals are put before the municipal corporation each month. Between April 1996 and August 1997, the civic administration approved 123 such proposals. The roads committee of the municipal corporation spends 90 percent of its time renaming, receiving money from influential local residents in return for naming a street or chowk after their relatives. It's a perverse way to honor your ancestors, with bribery. There are only so many roads in the city that can be renamed. But there are still a host of fathers, leaders, and patrons who need their names attached to the roads. The city is running out of roads to rename. Then the politicians realized that every two roads make an intersection. A crossroads—a chowk—auspicious for temples and Irani restaurants, can have its own name. How should the city celebrate the fact that Shankar-Jaikishen, the music composers, used to drink coffee every morning at the Gaylord restaurant? Should the crossing nearest the Gaylord be renamed after them? No, it has already been given the name Ahilyabai Holkar Chowk. So an intersection two crossings away is given the name Shankar-Jaikishen Chowk.

As a result, it becomes impossible to look to official maps and road signs for municipal directions. In yet another manifestation of schizophrenia, there evolves, on road maps, in people's memories, and on postcards, an official city and an unofficial city. The names of the real city are, like the sacred Vedas, orally transmitted. Many of the neighborhoods of Bombay are named after the trees and groves that flourished there. The kambal-grove gave its name to Cumballa Hill; an acacia—babul—grove to Babulnath; a plantation of bhendi, or umbrella trees, to Bhendi Bazaar; a tamarind tree to Tamarind Lane. Tad palms below the kambala trees gave the name to Tardeo; Vad trees to Worli. A tamarind (chinch) valley became Chinchpokli. The trees no longer exist, but their names still remain, pleasantly evocative until you realize what has been lost.

A name is such that if you grow up with it you get attached to it, whatever its origins. I grew up on Nepean Sea Road, which is now Lady Laxmibai Jagmohandas Marg. I have no idea who Sir Ernest Nepean was nor do I know who Lady Laxmibai Jagmohandas was, but I am attached to the original name and see no reason why it should change. The name has acquired a resonance, over time, distinct from its origin; as rue Pascal or West 4th Street or Maiden Lane might have for someone who has grown up

in those cities. I got used to the sound of it. It is incorporated into my
address, into my dream life. I can come back to Nepean Sea Road; if some
municipal functionary bent on exacting revenge on history changes it to
Lady Laxmibai Jagmohandas Marg, he is doing a disservice to my memory.

Name-changing is in vogue all over India nowadays: Madras has been
renamed Chennai; Calcutta, that British-made city, has changed its name to
Kolkata. A BJP member of parliament has demanded that India's name be
changed to Bharat. This is a process not just of decolonization but of de-
Islamicization. The idea is to go back not just to a past but to an idealized
past, in all cases a Hindu past. But to change a name, for a person or a road
or a city, there had better be a very good reason. And there was no good
reason to change the name of Bombay. It is nonsense to say that Mumbai
was the original name. Bombay was created by the Portuguese and the
British from a cluster of malarial islands, and to them should go the bap-
tismal rights. The Gujaratis and Maharashtrians always called it Mumbai when speaking Gujarati or Marathi, and Bombay when speaking
English. There was no need to choose. In 1995, the Sena demanded that we
choose, in all our languages, Mumbai. This is how the ghatis took revenge
on us. They renamed everything after their politicians, and finally they
renamed even the city. If they couldn't afford to live on our roads, they
could at least occupy the road signs.

Number Two
After Scotland Yard

AJAY LAL IS A COP with a dream. It is a dream of the last gesture he will make as a police officer. It is not about arresting the godfather Dawood Ibrahim, or accepting a medal, or setting his troops on fire with an inspiring speech. It is a dream of micturition. "I would go to police headquarters and stand in front of it and abuse all my corrupt seniors, reveal everything. Then I would pee in their direction and turn around and leave the force."

It would be a sensational ending to his career, a cathartic ending, a blockbuster ending: the celebrated detective, before quitting the force, walks up to headquarters on one bright morning. He unzips and waves his penis at the building. In his other hand is a bullhorn. He raises it to his lips. "Fuck you, Mhatre. One crore from Shakeel. Fuck you, Shaikh. Thirty lakhs from Abu Salem. Fuck you, Gonsalves. Ten lakhs and a flat from Rajan. Fuck you, Chaturvedi. Three whores from Dawood. Fuck you, fuck you, fuck you, gentlemen." And then he pees; he has been drinking coffee all morning and he lets it out in a giant stream, right in the middle of the plaza, right in the middle of the by-now-large circle of his juniors and passersby and crime journalists and photographers, then zips up as his agitated seniors rush out of the building, picks his teeth, turns his back to them, and walks off into the sunrise.

Ajay Lal: The Blasts and the Gangwar

I meet Ajay, who is best known for rapidly solving the case of the 1993 bomb blasts, when he comes with his wife, Ritu, to my friend Vidhu Vinod

Chopra's house for dinner one evening. Vinod, a film director, has asked him over because he wants Ajay, his good friend, to read the script for *Mission Kashmir* and offer expert guidance, especially about a scene in which a police inspector interrogates a militant. Ajay Lal has the look of an intelligent boxer. His hair is cut short, more like an army man than a police officer. He has a cleft chin and is a star athlete on the force. Unlike other cops I've met, Ajay is sophisticated, well-spoken, well-dressed. He could be an executive or, with his towering good looks, a movie star. Smita Thackeray, the daughter-in-law and companion of Bal Thackeray, has been calling Ajay at home.

"All women like Ajay," his wife says, sighing.

Sitting at ease in Vinod's living room, Ajay instructs us in methods of police interrogation. First of all, he points out, it is not always done in the police station. During his investigation of the bomb blasts of 1993, the interrogation was carried out in the compound of the special reserve force. Sometimes, lacking a safe house, he has to conduct the interrogation in a moving car with darkened windows, barking questions from the front seat as his men slap the suspect around in the back.

If Ajay has the time, the suspect is deprived of sleep for a whole week. Usually, neither party has such luxury. So another method is to take two ends of an old-style telephone wire and apply it to the arms or the genitals; a portable dynamo is whirled, and a powerful electric current is generated. Sometimes, he takes the suspect to a creek and ties a heavy stone to his legs. Then one of his men gets behind, puts his arms under the suspect's, and takes him into the water, where the weight of the stone pulls him downward. All that's keeping him up is the cop; the cop is his savior, his last hope. The suspect is dunked a few times in the water; gasping, screaming, he comes up out of the water and tells Ajay what he wants to know.

"Fear of death is the most effective. During the bomb blasts I just took a few of the suspects to Borivali National Park and fired a few bullets past their ears." But with many of these suspects, ordinary violence wouldn't work. There had to be special methods. "Those who have no fear of death also have no fear of physical pain. For them we threaten their family. I tell them I'll plant some evidence on their mother or their brother and arrest them. That usually works."

When Ajay's boys make an arrest, they tell him, "Saab, we would like you to frighten him a little." So as they are bringing the prisoner into

Ajay's imposing office, they say, "The Saab will finish you; it is not in our hands now. You are a dead duck." It would be best, they suggest to the suspect, if they intercede on his behalf, make a good report to the Saab, so that he is spared the very worst of the torments ahead of him in the long night. In short, summarizes Ajay, "That very old technique: the hard and soft approach."

One last method: Give the suspect one kilo—more than two pounds—of jalebis. Then you don't give him water. This sounds like an unusually enticing form of torture, I say.

"Have you ever had sweets and not had water? If you have one kilo of sweets you must have water." A man will do anything for water after so many sweets.

A FEW WEEKS LATER, Ajay Lal pulls a thick leather-bound ledger from a drawer in his office. They are his notes of the bomb-blasts investigation, kept every day for years. It is also the story of the beginning of the gangwar.

Organized crime in the city of Bombay is controlled by two exiles, or nonresident Indians (NRIs). One is in Karachi and one in Malaysia—or Bangkok, or Luxembourg, depending on which night you ask. The gangwar is the fallout from the bomb blasts of 1993, during which a series of bombs planted by the Muslim criminal syndicate headed by Dawood Ibrahim—the D-Company—killed 317 people in the city, in revenge for the anti-Muslim pogroms of a few months earlier. After the blasts, Dawood's main lieutenant, a Hindu named Chotta Rajan, broke with him and formed his own gang, the Nana Company, so-called because Rajan is nana, elder brother, to his troops. He swore to eliminate all those involved in the bombings. The two dons—bhais, in Bombay—control their organizations from outside the country, and they have been at war ever since.

In Bombay, a gang war—gengwar, as it is pronounced with the Bambaiyya inflection—doesn't just mean a fight between two gangs. Run together, the words are another term for the underworld in its entirety, in its complexity. People identify themselves by it—"We are the folk of the gangwar"—as opposed to petty criminals, robbers, rapists, pickpockets. It is a permanent state of being. Underworld is also an expansive term and has mystique, power. But it is the wrong word to use for organized crime in

Bombay, since it implies something hidden, something beneath. In Bombay, the underworld is an overworld; it is somehow suspended *above* this world and can come down and strike any time it chooses. The hit men refer to the operational centers of the gangs—Karachi, Dubai, Malaysia—as upar, "above," and Bombay as neeche, "below." There can be nothing under "below."

Dawood Ibrahim Kaskar was born in Ratnagiri, on the Konkan coast, in 1955, one of ten children of a police constable in the Crime Branch, Ibrahim Kaskar, who was known for his brutality. Once a group of boys robbed a bank, but they made a mistake of going to a Muslim saint's tomb and garlanding it with 100-rupee notes, and giving away money to the fakirs. The police found out that four boys had been throwing money around at the tomb and caught them. The commissioner ordered the money to be recovered at any cost, and two boys were killed while being beaten by Ibrahim Kaskar's squad.

Dawood started out as a small-time hood in Nagpada, in central Bombay. At that time the city was dominated by Haji Mastan, a gold smuggler who started his career when somebody gave him a sackful of gold coins for safekeeping. He helped the poor and drifted off into politics and social service. Mastan was replaced by the Pathan gang, immigrants from Afghanistan led by Karim Lala. Dawood's steady rise as a smuggler brought him into conflict with two of the Pathan gang's chiefs, Amirzada and Alamzeb Pathan. One of Dawood's brothers, Sabir, was killed by the Pathans in 1981. Dawood swore revenge and had Amirzada shot and killed in the sessions court as he was being led to the witness box. In 1984, hounded by the police, he moved out of the country to Dubai, where he had powerful contacts in the gold smuggling business. He took advantage of the fact that gold, the supply of which was controlled by the Indian government, cost much more than in the Middle East. At the height of the business, in 1991, some two hundred tons of gold were being smuggled into the country every year. But in 1992, gold imports were liberalized and prices decreased substantially. Dawood turned to extortion, real estate, and film financing.

In 1989, he was joined in Dubai by his top lieutenant in Bombay, the thirty-one-year-old Chotta Shakeel—also a Nagpada boy—who had jumped bail. Shakeel's place at the head of the gang in Bombay was taken by a small-time black marketeer of cinema tickets, Rajendra Sadashiv Nilkhalje. He was born in 1960 and was known as Chotta Rajan—Small

Rajan—to distinguish him from his mentor, Bada Rajan. (Chotta Shakeel is so called because he is—well, short.) Chotta Rajan made his mark first by avenging the murder of his mentor. He gave a country-made pistol to a tea boy and told him to go to a cricket match where Bada Rajan's assassin was sitting. The boy killed the hit man in front of hundreds of spectators, then ran three and a half miles to safety. Chotta Rajan earned Dawood's respect after that, by arranging the killings of several important members of the Pathan gang.

Dubai suited Dawood; he re-created Bombay in lavish parties, flying in scores of the city's top film stars and cricketers as guests, and took a film starlet, Mandakini, as his mistress. His empire in the country he had exiled himself from grew, and it would have been a comfortable existence. Then came the riots. Then came the blasts.

AJAY WAS A BRIGHT YOUNG OFFICER who'd grown up in Bandra, unlike many of the other Indian Police Service officers in the city. At the time he was deputy commissioner of police for Traffic, stationed at Mahim. His duties dealt with easing congestion on the Bombay roads, possibly an even more difficult job than fighting the gangwar. On the afternoon of March 12, 1993, a bomb went off outside the Sena headquarters at Dadar on the premises of a petrol pump, and the party's senior politicians rushed to the spot. They were highly nervous, and they asked Ajay to check the place to see if there were any more bombs inside. Ajay went inside with a stick and prodded the corners. There was nothing there. Within fifteen or twenty minutes, however, the next bomb blew up at the nearby Plaza Cinema, in a parked car. Ajay realized what was happening and was the first officer to alert the Control Room; he told them to block all the airports and railway stations. "This is a chain. It is done to start communal riots."

A total of ten powerful RDX bombs exploded all over the city; three more, in the crowded inner city, failed to go off. The targets were the most prominent buildings in Bombay: the Air India building, the Stock Exchange, the Centaur Hotel, the headquarters of the Shiv Sena. In one day, 257 people died and 713 were injured. At the international airport, hand grenades were lobbed from the access road toward parked aircraft, but they couldn't reach the planes. Late that night, Police Commissioner A. S. Samra visited the sites. All this was on March 12. Two days later, Ajay got a message on the police radio that a scooter had been found abandoned at the Dadar railway station. He went there with bomb experts, who defused the bomb in it.

The commissioner told Ajay to take charge of the investigation. For two days, the police had made no headway in trying to find out who was responsible. On the night of the fourteenth, Ajay called twenty of the best police detectives he knew in the city. They gathered in a command room at 11:30 p.m., and the process of putting information together began; five hours later, on the morning of the fifteenth, Ajay arrested the first suspect.

A Maruti van had been found abandoned near the Siemens office at Worli; Ajay remembers the license plate, MFC 1972, six years later. Detonators had been found in the vehicle, but the policemen who spotted the car had not given it much attention, believing it had been abandoned just before a police checkpoint. Ajay thought the car should be investigated thoroughly, and he asked to see its papers. They showed that the car belonged to a smuggler named Mushtaq "Tiger" Memon, who had a house in Mahim behind the shrine. The police team investigated the house in Mahim but found nothing except the key to a scooter, marked with its manufacturer's name, BAJAJ. Something clicked. Ajay remembered the scooter that had been abandoned at Dadar, the one with the bomb in it. He asked one of his officers to go to Matunga Police Station, where the scooter had been taken, and try the key. It fit the scooter.

It turned out that the man assigned to take the bomb-laden scooter to its designated station had heard a blast while driving, and, thinking the vehicle between his legs would also explode, had pulled off the road, abandoned the scooter, and run off. His cowardice led to Ajay's most important clue. Now he had Memon's house searched intensively. They found a pair of chappals—sandals—with a sticky black claylike powder on them. They didn't know it then, but the powder was RDX, "black soap." In the garages of Memon's building, they found more packages of black soap, with wrappers bearing Karachi markings. "Now we were certain the scooter, the Maruti, and this house were connected."

Memon was not in the house, but people in the area told Ajay that a young man in Andheri named Manager took care of his affairs. Ajay told the team to go to his house and pick him up. "Our chaps picked up his father, mother, uncle, aunt, and Manager and brought them to the police station. Manager said, 'I've left Memon's employ; I am not working for him.' And he cursed me, mother-sister curses. I could tell he was lying. I told him, 'You are lying. If you lie I will have to trouble your mother and father and arrest them also.' He didn't give a damn. All the time his uncle and aunt kept calling him, 'Son, son.' He was responding more to them than to his parents, so I told the uncle and aunt, 'I will arrest you.' One of my officers slapped the uncle, and Manager flinched. He said, 'Please don't do anything to my uncle and aunt. They have adopted me since birth.' I said okay, and he gave me the whole thing."

The bombmakers had been filling the trunks of cars in Memon's garages with the black soap. Three ships had left Dubai early in 1993. At Karachi they were loaded with RDX and weapons. The hand grenades bore the marking ARGES, an Austrian company that had licensed a Pakistani firm to make the grenades. One of the ships came to Mhasla and two went farther south in Gujarat. Customs officials along the coast were bribed to look the other way. Different groups smuggled the weapons in trucks into Bombay. Some groups were trained to connect the detonators and set the electronic timers, which bore different colors, depending on the duration: red for fifteen minutes, yellow for an hour, and green for two hours. Other squads of Muslim boys were armed with AK-56s and ready to defend Muslims in case communal riots broke out.

Tiger Memon had left on the morning of the twelfth. He embraced his men and said, "You are all soldiers. Leave the city. There will be riots." The bombs had been set off by Muslim gangsters in the hope that the city would explode again. It had done so just a month earlier, in riots aimed at the Muslims that left thousands dead and wounded, for the first time in the city's history. The blasts were in revenge, and as an incitement to more riots. The whole operation had been planned at a meeting in Dubai organized by gang lord Dawood Ibrahim. All the participants had taken an oath of secrecy on the Koran.

A total of 168 people were arrested for the Bombay blasts. Of these, Ajay or his deputies were responsible for 160, including the most celebrated arrest, that of the actor Sanjay Dutt. "I interrogated each and every one of these hundred-sixty-odd guys. I know the connections between these people." For this work, Ajay received the Police Medal for Meritorious Service from the President of India. He got it out of turn. The medal is normally awarded to an officer with at least fifteen years' service; Ajay had only thirteen.

Unlike the riot cases—where there was no effort by the Sena government to prosecute the murderers from their own party named in the Srikrishna Commission Report—the state government went after the (mostly Muslim) bomb-blast plotters with a vengeance. In the end, charge sheets were drawn up against 189 people; 44 were absconding. Ajay's team seized 2,074 kilograms—almost two and a half tons—of RDX, 980 kilograms—over a ton—of gelatine, 63 AK-56 assault rifles, 10 9mm Tokarev pistols, 13 9mm magazines, 1,100 electric detonators, 230 AK-56 magazines, 38,917 AK-56 rounds, and 482 Arges hand grenades. These were not weapons for an underworld skirmish. These were armaments for civil war.

But civil war didn't happen this time; the Hindus' hatred of the Muslims had been spent in the riots four months ago. The city recovered quickly after the blasts. The Stock Exchange, which had been bombed, reopened two days later, using the old manual trading because the computers had been destroyed, and its index actually gained 10 percent in the next two days. Just to show them.

ISHAQ, A YOUNG MUSLIM ENTREPRENEUR to whom Girish the computer programmer introduced me, knew about the bomb blasts before they happened. One evening outside the Maratha Mandir cinema, Ishaq casually comes out with it. He's talking of his days running with the gangs in the Madanpura district, now called mini-Pakistan. The local bhai, Tajul, would give him and his friends 15,000 rupees a day without much trouble. Ishaq never spent it; he considered it haraam—profane. But he did the work.

"What kind of work?"

"Picking someone up. Giving a couple of slaps to someone. I used to go around with a Mauser in my belt. During the bomb blasts I had six AK-56s. Tajul came to me the night before the blasts and told me to hide the guns, hand grenades, and RDX. Thirty-six kilos [eighty pounds] of RDX. It was in a green box with a white skull on it. There was a whole gunnysack full of grenades, this big"—he cups his hand so—"with pins. Tajul gave me one half of a ten-rupee note. I buried the stuff in some loose earth and threw chili water on it and water mixed with mint over it, so that the dogs couldn't sniff the RDX if they came. My father abused me the whole night. He said, 'Do you know what will happen if they find out?' The next day the men came—big men with crew cuts. They had the second half of the ten-rupee note. I checked the number and gave them the stuff. Tajul had told me two hours before the blasts: 'Tell your family not to move out of Madanpura today, on any account.' So we stayed in. And then we heard a huge explosion and saw smoke coming out of the Stock Exchange building. We went to J.J. Hospital. There were stacks of corpses, twenty to twenty-five bodies on each stack."

In comprehending what the bombs he helped store did, Ishaq's mind starts playing tricks, as he thinks of the scene at the hospital. "There must have been ten thousand corpses at least."

Neither Tajul nor Ishaq was caught, even though Tajul had a very big part in the conspiracy. Ishaq still has some AK-56 bullets; he stole them from the shipment to keep as souvenirs. But he didn't want to keep the assault rifles. He touches his earlobes, shuddering at the memory. "I gave them back in three days."

THE BOMB BLASTS CHANGED BOMBAY. Until then, terrorism usually meant Sikh terrorism, linked to the troubles in Punjab. The Bombay underworld was completely secular until then. After the blasts, it became communalized, says Ajay. "There is a challenge before the police today. Hindu leaders who led rampaging mobs during the riots are targeted by Muslim gangs; Hindu gangs have targeted the bomb blasts' accused out on bail." Although there are Hindus in Dawood's gang and Muslims in the Rajan Company, "they are of local compulsions," he says, private needs. One crucial difference between the Muslim and the Hindu gangs explains why the former are more powerful. "The Dawood group probably doesn't have to pay for weapons; Chotta Rajan does." The Muslim gangs operate with arms provided by Pakistan. The normal strategy of the ISI, the Pakistani intelligence service, was to smuggle sleepers into Bombay and let them stay for years at a stretch, working unobtrusively as mechanics or factory workers, and then activating them as necessary, to plant a bomb or kill a politician. But during the blasts, the Pakistanis, working through the newly aggrieved Muslim underworld, whose families had suffered during the riots, didn't have to go through the lengthy gestation period. In addition to men, the gangs also provided the ISI with their smuggling networks and safe houses.

After the blasts, Ajay was asked to give presentations to the U.S.

ambassador and to Interpol on the Pakistani involvement in the bombings. Ajay had interrogated the bombers and seen passports, four of them, with exit stamps from Bombay and Dubai and a missing period in the dates of fifteen days. This was the time, they told Ajay, when they were taken to Islamabad and then driven north to the border between Afghanistan and Pakistan. There they stayed in camps and underwent a rigorous program of anti-Indian indoctrination; an incendiary tape of the riots in Surat after the Babri Masjid fell was shown, and the boys were told, "This is what is happening to our sisters and mothers in India." The training was along military lines; they were taught the use of sophisticated arms and explosive devices. Then they were sent back to extract vengeance.

In 1994, Chotta Rajan made his break with his Muslim boss, Dawood—he fled Dubai for Kuala Lumpur, taking a chunk of the gang's top Hindus away with him. He announced publicly that he did so because he could not work with a traitor to the nation, and he swore to eliminate the bombers himself. Dawood and Shakeel sent out a group of men to kill Rajan, and Rajan sent hit squads to Karachi, where the D-Company was now headquartered, to kill Dawood. On the ground in Bombay, meanwhile, hundreds of people started dying every year in police shootouts, gunfights between rival gangs, and extortion-related killings.

The break, according to Dawood, had nothing to do with the blasts; it was a personal falling out over a commissioned killing, a vendetta between him and Rajan that piled up bodies in Bombay, Dubai, Kathmandu, and Bangkok; an international Ping-Pong game of murder. The boys on the ground kill each other over control of the numerous lucrative rackets in Bombay, and they kill each other because their dons want to kill each other. Each member of the other gang killed, no matter how minor, is a body blow scored by one don on the person of the other. The D-Company has about eight hundred shooters, and the Nana Company between four and five hundred.

Dawood and his gang moved from Dubai to Karachi in the mid-nineties because the ruling Maktoum family was under pressure from the Indian government to extradite him. The gang's activities are run by Chotta Shakeel from Pakistan. Dawood's hand is now seen in every bad thing that happens in India, from bombs to murders to corruption; and his wealth is depicted in fantastic terms. "He is probably richer than Bill Gates and the Sultan of Brunei," one journalistic profile begins. The same profile features Dawood himself complaining, "The government of India wants to blame me for every calamity that has befallen them, even to the extent of the death of a dog. Thank God I was not around in 1947; otherwise they would have accused me of having partitioned India."

Bollywood—the Bombay film industry—Partition, and the gangwar share a common theme, a common formula: the breakup of the family. The families of the exiled dons are still in Bombay, forever sundered from them. Dawood's sister and other family members still live in Bombay, unmolested. "The police know not to bother Dawood's home people. You can kill his men—that is a give-and-take barter system," one of his lieutenants tells me. "But if they bother his home people he will bother them." The enforced separation leads to maudlin moments, filmi moments. In a newspaper interview, Rajan says, "Oh, I miss my kids enormously. But I am constantly on the phone with them. Sometimes, it's through videoconferencing. In fact, when they celebrate their birthday parties, I keep the phone on continuously throughout the entire length of the party. Almost as if I am participating in the fun—joking, singing, and talking to them."

Chotta Rajan is referred to contemptuously as the "bhangi" by Shakeel and his troops. Rajan sometimes gets drunk and calls up Shakeel: "I'm going to kill you." "You know where I live, you know my address," responds Shakeel. "Why don't you come and get me if you have the guts? Give me your address and I'll come and finish you." They ate from the same plate, they were both the favorite sons of Dawood. There is a photo of Dawood at Rajan's wedding; Rajan's wife, Sujata, tied a rakhi around Dawood's wrist and made him her brother. And then Rajan betrayed him. It is a fight between estranged brothers.

There is also a third and smaller gang, led by Arun Gawli, an ex-Dawood man. Gawli floats in and out of jail, holding court from his fortress in Dagdi Chawl. He commands total loyalty in his neighborhood. Parents in the vast apartment complex of Dagdi Chawl instruct their sons, when they come of age, to go work for Gawli. The Gawli gang is also known as the chaddi company, because of their predilection for wearing shorts. They drink country liquor and eat vadapav sandwiches, so their needs are inexpensively fulfilled. But the Dawood people have more refined tastes. "They need to go to beer bars with lights," a senior Dawood operative explains. The chaddi gang is mostly staffed with laid-off millworkers; they might be selling vegetables at Dadar market when they get a call to leave their vegetable stall for half an hour and go knock somebody off. The D-Company shooters speak admiringly of the Gawli gang: "They have the most daring shooters. But then Gawli went into politics and fucked his company." He started thinking of himself as a social servant. In 1997, Gawli floated a political party that, when it became a threat to the Sena, led Thackeray to bring the police down hard on Gawli. When he is in jail, Gawli's wife, Asha, runs the company, but as a D-Company man explains to me, "Only a man can run a gangwar."

Organized crime in Bombay is unique. "All our killings, our terrorist activities, are ordered from abroad," says Ajay, speaking about why the Bombay Police aren't able to put a definitive stop to the underworld. "We arrest the shooters, the people who did the job. If we are lucky, we are able to get the people who provided the weapons. But we only have the hands and feet here. The brains are outside the country." The gang lords—who travel under different passports all around the world, from Buenos Aires to Bangkok—move their troops around on the ground through satellite phones. "They really burn up those phone lines."

The revenues of the Bombay gangs come from protection rackets, extortion, money laundering, gambling, bootlegging, film financing, up-scale prostitution, and drugs. Lately, the Bombay gangs have been net-working with terrorist outfits from around the subcontinent, such as the Liberation Tigers of Tamil Eelam in Sri Lanka, the United Liberation Front of Assam, and the People's War Group in Andhra Pradesh. These outfits sell weapons to the gangs, and the gangs act as their financiers. "I have names of Dawood gang members in Guwahati," in distant Assam, says Ajay.

The revenues from prostitution and bootlegging are used to look after the rank and file, for the gang lawyers' fees, and for salaries paid to families while their men are in jail, Ajay tells me. The revenues from extortion pay-ments are split. For every 100,000 rupees extorted by the gangs, 60,000 go to the boss abroad and 40,000 are kept in the kitty to be distributed to the troops on the ground. The money goes abroad through the hawala net-works, a paperless money-laundering system in which a bag of rupees given to a shopkeeper or diamond merchant in Bombay transforms itself quickly and efficiently into an envelope full of dollars in Dubai.

The gangs are in the process of going "white," forming companies that run hotels, resorts, and department stores, even banks. The entertainment industry is particularly loved by gangsters: Chotta Rajan is heavily invested in Bombay's cable networks. They also deal in overseas rights for films and traveling stage shows and control much of the music industry, because banks generally won't finance entertainment ventures—the accounting controls are close to nonexistent.

Contrary to the public proclamations of the dons, they are involved, inevitably, in drugs. But they are afraid of the American and British authorities, who go after drug traffickers with a special vengeance, so they never talk about this part of their business and keep it on a relatively low scale. The barbiturate Mandrax is the only drug that is produced extensively in India, where many loss-making pharmaceutical units manufacture the tablets. The price of one tablet of Mandrax, which includes the costs of manufacturing, bribes, and transport to Mauritius—close to the shores of South Africa, which is its eventual destination—is 99 paise, or 2½ cents. The moment it reaches South Africa, that tablet's value is $2.50, a hundred-fold increase. One container holds up to two tons of these tablets. "If you have one container reaching the shores of South Africa, you're made for life," observes Ajay.

The boys don't refer to the organizations they work for as gangs, they call them companies, and there is indeed something corporate about the organization. Within the structure of the gang, there is a minute specialization of labor. There are people responsible for giving out salaries every month, just like in a company. There are others in charge of supplying weapons, and a separate group responsible for storing weapons. There are special cells that are in charge of threatening witnesses. They haunt the courtrooms and make sure that, in cases involving the gang, hostile witnesses are turned to their favor. There are doctors, lawyers, sympathizers, foot soldiers, scouts, and people who run safe houses. Then there is the elaborate support structure for members of the gang in jail. To avoid gang warfare inside the jails, the government has earmarked specific jails for different gangs: The Gawli gang is spread out over the Yerawada and Amravati jails; the Rajan gang is in Arthur Road; and the D-Company is put up in the Byculla, Thane, and Nashik jails. Near the Nashik jail, the D-Company has purchased a number of flats and auto-rickshaws and hired cooks and delivery boys. Chefs in the flats prepare breakfast, lunch, and dinner, and delivery boys hop into the rickshaws and deliver hot meals to the jailbirds. It is a thoroughly planned, thoroughly efficient catering system. The man lucky enough to be arrested after a hit looks forward to a spell inside, with all his needs taken care of in style. And there is also a strange kind of competitive generosity behind bars. During the Ganesh festival, Arun Gawli sent a box of sweets to the D-Company jailbirds in Thane, one of them had told me. "The D-Company boss said 'Accha! Is that so?' and sent a huge plate full of halva back to Gawli."

As in sports and entertainment, the gangs hire scouts. The scouts are everywhere, finding out who is successful in the city and the precise measure of their success and reporting back to the gangs. A substantial portion of the eventual payment is sent back to the scouts. The gangs, like Ajay, live on information. They are hungry, ravenous, for information, constantly sniffing for it in the newspapers, in pan shops, in executive suites, in politicians' chambers, on the Internet.

The gangs flourish because they form a parallel justice system in a country with the world's largest backlog of court cases. Indicative of this judicial paralysis is the fact that, as of 2003, a decade after the Bombay blasts, the trial of the plotters is still dragging on. "The criminal justice system has totally collapsed," says Ajay. "This is the reason why the underworld thrives. A dispute over a flat, which takes twenty years in court, is taken care of in a week or a month by the underworld. You work out the economics."

Politicians will come and go, the city will boom and bust, but the gangwar will never end. The culture of the gangwar is intrinsic to the culture of the city. Madanpura, Nagpada, Agripada, Byculla, Dongri, Bhendi Bazaar, Dagdi Chawl: The heart of Bombay is the heart of the gangwar.

I AM HAVING DINNER with a friend of my uncle, a Polish jeweler from America. The jeweler has been coming to Bombay for twenty-five years. On every trip he's seen the city improving. But four years ago, the curve started dropping. It is more polluted, he says. There is a dust storm that evening and he can't breathe. And then there is the steadily increasing violence. He has been reading in the papers about the gang shootouts, which have even made the *New York Times;* his wife in Connecticut wants him to come back at once. The world has discovered that Bombay has a gangster problem.

"Would you feel safe walking down this road? Could I walk here?" the jeweler asks, as we are driving from the Taj to the Oberoi (there should be a special air-conditioned causeway or ropeway connecting the two hotels, the traffic between them is so intensive and exclusive). It is around eleven, and there isn't anybody on the poorly lit sidewalk.

"Yes, I would," says my uncle.

Bombay is still a city where I can travel about pretty much anywhere at all hours of the day or night. Muggings are virtually unknown. Women aren't molested like they are in Delhi. A Parsi woman at a society party tells me about an incident when she was traveling on the highway with her family. Their car broke down in front of a slum colony, and she and her husband got out. People came up out of the slum. She got scared; she was wearing a miniskirt. They came closer and told her to get back inside. She felt the car moving; the slum dwellers were trying unsuccessfully to push it into starting. Meanwhile, friends in the car ahead had come back. The slum dwellers told them to leave the car there overnight. She was sure the car would be stripped by the next day, but they had no choice. When they came back, the car was untouched; the slum colony had deputed a couple of people to watch over it, all night long.

Bombay's menace is not street crime. It's bigger and more organized than that.

My uncle shows me the invitations that he's been getting from his fellow diamond merchants for the December wedding season. They are the usual lavish cards, each costing 50 or 100 rupees, each one a small chapbook decorated with little Ganeshas, wrapped in silk, containing individual cards for the different modules that make up such a wedding: Hasta-Milap (the religious ceremony), Dandiya-Raas (the dance), Bollywood Nite, Gala Dinner. He opens one. The main venue is written on a patch of paper that has been pasted over the main card, like an afterthought. It is at a small hall I haven't heard of. My uncle peels back the patch: Underneath is the original venue, the Racecourse. The wedding has been moved so as not to attract attention from the gangs. Another wedding, in the family of a movie financier, features an elaborate card but again a humble venue: the lawn of the financier's own apartment building. At a previous wedding in the family, a roster of Bollywood stars came to dance like performing monkeys; this one will be a small family affair. A wedding caterer of my uncle's acquaintance was asked by the gangs for his client list for the coming season. "I had no choice. I had to hand over the list," the caterer said. How does the underworld get information on who has money? It is through all the intermediaries: the contractors, the domestics, the interior designers.

The *Bombay Times* features a story on marriages being toned down because of the possibility of extortion. The byline is Staff Reporter. At the end of the story, a line states, *All names changed on request.* Anonymity has now become a survival tactic.

The stories build, carried aloft from person to person on the collective fear of rich people in a poor country. A family has dinner at a five-star restaurant and is presented with the bill. It is in five figures, and they protest. The waiter tells them the bill includes payment for the dinner of the six men sitting over there in the corner. They have a choice: They can either foot this bill or say good-bye to the new Ford car they drove to the hotel in.

Another of my cousin's friends is approached for money. "You have bought a new flat and sold the old one for eight lakhs. Give us one."

My cousin advises his friend, "For peace of mind you should just give them the lakh."

"They don't want one lakh," the friend says, "they want one crore." (One crore is a hundred lakhs.) When the caller from Karachi calls again to demand the money, the friend's father asks for the extortionist's fax number. He then faxes the caller his income-tax returns for the past four years, which demonstrate that he is making no money at all. It is like applying for financial aid at an American college. Poverty is a virtue.

The city's great and good are panicked. They struggle to imagine just how abysmally low the value of human life has sunk. The gossip columnist Shobha De puts it into the proper perspective. "Today, a supari [contract] killing costs anything between an entirely affordable five to ten thousand rupees, from a high of five to ten lakhs a few years ago," she explains to readers of her column. "Unemployed youths are ready to kill for the price of a Gossard brassiere. Isn't that something? A statistic worth thinking about." So the rich are forced into humiliating changes of lifestyle. Another Shobha De column narrates the plight of a young lady in South Bombay.

The same girl has taken to wearing fake jewellery—plastic baubles and silver junk. "I get the feeling I'm being followed, maybe this sounds paranoid. But my fear is real. I get back pretty late from parties. It's a long drive home. What would I do if armed gang-sters decide to rob me of my Cartier and Bulgari stuff on Marine Drive? I've even switched cars. I keep the Mercedes at home and take a Maruti."

The gangsters have the same effect on Bombay society that the Bolshe-viks had on the Russian nobility. What all the protest marches by the left couldn't do, a few phone calls from the bhais have managed: They have forced the Bombay rich to stop flaunting their wealth.

In business, so entrenched has extortion become that the Bombay High Court recently ruled that extortion payments are tax deductible as a legiti-mate business expense. Extortion is a form of tax. Since there is a parallel justice system, there have to be parallel taxes. It used to be that there was only one gang—Dawood's. But now that there are multiple gangs operat-ing, as soon as the businessman pays one, all the others line up for their payments, so he finds himself paying four or five gangs at once. He might even be paying freelance extortionists, people who pose no real threat. The implicit or explicit tradeoff in the protection racket—you give me money, I give you protection from myself and others—no longer applies. The gangs are powerless to afford protection against the others. It is less a pro-tection racket now and more like a simple mugging: You give me your money or I'll kill you.

"Extortion and kidnapping are the crimes of the future." says Ajay, because the net investment is 1 rupee, the price of a phone call. He recently arrested two MBA students who were extorting the professor who had been teaching them about entrepreneurship. "I said, You fellows are crazy. They said, We have more brains than the others." Kidnapping, too, thrives on fear. One Dawood-affiliated gangster has a sideline in kidnapping. He takes his victims to a room in the suburbs, blindfolds them, and throws live snakes at them.

In 1999, Ajay has a new posting, as Additional Commissioner of Police, Northwest Region, which puts him in an area that covers half of Bombay, from Bandra to Dahisar, but is the site of three-quarters of its crime. He is now chief of thirty-one out of the seventy-two police stations in Mumbai and has ten thousand men working for him. In this appointment, he has superseded six officers with seniority over him, because of a dramatic increase in extortion-related crimes in the city. "They expect me to come in with a magic wand and solve the problems," Ajay says. The newspapers advertise him as a knight on a white charger; they speak of his work in the bomb-blasts investigation and tout him as the one man who can fix Bombay's current crime problem. I am interested to see if he will succeed. On a pleasant evening, I suggest to Vinod, the movie director, that we go for a walk and meet Ajay in his office down the road. Anu, his wife and a film journalist, says she wants to come too.

Ajay's new office has a nice view of the sea. As we come in, a police inspector and his informant enter and brief Ajay about a recent shootout. "Who were on the team that is playing the game of the blasts suspects?" asks Ajay.

They say that in the shootout, "the fielding had been in place for four days." Team, fielding, playing the game: They might be talking about a cricket match. And, actually, the thrill of belonging to a gang is not unlike the thrill of playing on a team. The captain has to be the smartest, he has to be the brain. He has to arrange the fielding, the batting order; he has to rest some players and test the newcomers.

The inspector and the informant tell him they will be able to produce the key player in not less than six days. Ajay urges them to do it sooner and tells the informant that he'll take care of the cases against him. All evening long, informants come to him and huddle over his desk, in low urgent voices, as he nods and takes notes in his ledger; all evening long, he barks and growls, threatening mutilation, castration, death, and the execution of loved ones, in his ceaseless quest for information. All evening long, he listens to the multiple whisperings of the heated city, developing contacts, developing sources.

Ajay defines the essence of how to conduct an interrogation: "You have a little information, and you must let him think you have more." The suspect will also try to string Ajay along, revealing a little at a time, until he can get to the safety of the courts. Ajay squeezes; then he squeezes a little more. "First comes the sugar-cane juice, then the lemon juice," he explains, turning a crank in the air. But it's not a simple matter of physical force. "Everyone cannot just be beaten black and blue. Knowledge is power." He might start the session with the briefest of hints that he knows everything but is waiting for the suspect to confess voluntarily. "Sometimes on this they start. Sometimes they take your measure: How much do you really know?" So the interrogation is a game, in which the players are constantly trying to read each other's minds. And not all the power is with the policeman holding the stick, the electric wire.

Ajay's mobile rings. Khan, one of his top informants, is waiting to speak to him. The door opens, and a very thin man in his twenties comes in and huddles over the desk with Ajay.

After he leaves, Ajay tells us that Khan is a burglar and a ladies' man. His trade name is Chikna. He is sleeping with the wives of four or five top gangsters. "I'm jealous of him," says Ajay. But Khan's days are numbered. Ajay found this out when Khan was first brought in on burglary charges. Ajay's men beat him up, not stopping until Khan began vomiting blood all over the floor. At this point the burglar informed his tormentors that he had full-blown AIDS, and they reported this to Ajay. "The first thing I told my men to do was to clean up all the blood and pour Dettol over the floor." Then he talked to the burglar and found out that he could be turned into an informant.

Why would he do that? I asked. Was it for money?

Ajay shakes his head. "Proximity to me." He comes into the commissioner's office whenever he wants, moves around in his car. "It makes him feel powerful." Ajay is good to his informant. "In the last six months of his life I'll make him feel like a king." He has given Khan a mobile phone and Ajay's personal mobile number, on which the burglar can call the ACP day and night. What about his burglaries, I ask Ajay. Is he still continuing them?

"I've allowed him one or two." But he's locked him up for two others that involved gunplay, once for six months and once for eight. This also made the gangs feel sure that Khan wasn't a police informant.

Tonight he has come with some interesting information. One of the gangsters whose wives he has been sleeping with will come to visit the wife tonight, at her home. Ajay picks up the phone and asks, "What happened to that auto-rickshaw we confiscated? Is it still in working order?" The plan is to have Khan pose as an auto-rickshaw driver and park in front of the wife's house. Ajay's men will be around in plainclothes, as hawkers or passersby. When the gangster arrives to visit his wife, Khan will identify him to the cops. If he doesn't arrive tonight, the burglar knows he'll go to church on Sunday, and Ajay's men will be waiting outside the church.

"What will you do with the gangster?" I ask Ajay.

He looks at me, at Vinod, at Anu, and then back at me, and there is a slight smile playing about his mouth. "Do I have an option?"

Anu asks if Khan could have transmitted AIDS to the gangster through his wife.

Vinod is excited about this as a plot point for a movie: a police agent who kills off gangsters by sleeping with their wives and infecting them with HIV. Ajay shoots this down immediately. "The gestation period is too long: six years. They can do lots of damage in six years."

Next follows a meeting of Ajay's station chiefs, sleek, fat, sly fellows who are lords of their turf. I can see why Ajay refers to them, after they leave, as bandicoots. Then a policeman comes in and tells him they caught a car with counterfeit money in it. Ajay asks him, "How much did they have?"

"Four lakhs."

"What did they say?"

"They're not saying anything."

"Bring them in."

Ajay tells us to sit in the back of the room, on a small sofa. The door opens, and two men are led in by three plainclothes policemen.

Almost immediately the beating starts. "Tell the Saab who gave you the money!" screams one of the cops.

"I don't know, sir."

He is slapped hard across the face. This man is a fat Sindhi bourgeois. The taller, thinner man says he's his cousin and drove the car. Both speak English, and are well dressed. They are uncomfortably familiar. A little more money, a little more education, and they would be People Like Us. Four and a half lakhs in counterfeit 500-rupee notes are brought out of a bag and put on Ajay's desk, neat green bundles of untruth. A few more slaps follow. "Who gave you the money?"

"I don't know, sir. Someone called and asked me to pick up the bag."

"Some stranger called and asked you to pick up four lakhs?" shouts Ajay. "You think we were born yesterday! Take off their clothes."

The other policemen remove the men's belts and hit them viciously with them. Anu is cringing; Vinod is holding her hand.

The fat man volunteers a little information. He had met the man who arranged the deal through his "keep," as Ajay refers to her, a beer bar dancer in Mira Road.

"What's his name?"

"I don't know, sir."

"Bring in the electric wire and the strap," Ajay commands a constable.

The constable comes back with a thick leather strap, about six inches wide, attached to a wooden handle. One of the cops takes it and brings it savagely down across the fat man's face. The sound of leather hitting bare human flesh is impossible to describe unless you've heard it. The man screams. The cop brings it down again. Meanwhile, the cousin is getting blows in his back with the other policeman's elbow. Both men are bending, cringing, to avoid the blows, with the strap, the belts, and the policemen's bare hands, which are landing all over their faces and bodies. The strap across the fat man's face causes the most pain, and he is bent nearly double trying to ward off the blows. The thin man has a spot of blood on his forehead, or maybe a tikka from the temple; I can't tell. Vinod is murmuring something over and over to his wife, holding her hands very tightly in his.

"Do you have any children?" Ajay asks the fat man.

"One."

"How old?"

"Five years."

"Bring in his wife and children. We'll beat his children in front of him if he doesn't talk."

"No, sir! I'll tell you everything. I've told you everything."

The three policemen attack the men randomly. The thin man takes it without crying; once the policeman near him, much shorter than him, hits him in the eye with his belt. The thin man barely flinches, as if a fly had landed there. "Tell the Saab what you told me," the short policeman commands.

"It's not anything," the thin man protests.

The cop flies at his face with the belt. "Tell him!"

"Sir, my parents came over from Pakistan in 'forty-seven, when Partition happened."

The short policeman looks at Ajay eagerly, perhaps hoping to be rewarded for having extracted an important bit of information crucial to

establishing the Sindhi's double loyalties. Ajay is unimpressed. Several million people in India, including the deputy prime minister, would be traitors
by this standard.

"Take them to the room and put the electric wire down there." Ajay
addresses the fat man. "You won't be able to do your work by your
mistress."

More information comes out: The fat man took 450,000 rupees from a
Pakistani agent and gave 325,000 rupees in genuine Indian currency in
exchange. As they are being beaten, they address their tormentors as "sir."
Thus we addressed our teachers in school; thus do Vinod's film crew
address him. Not once do they fly out; not once do they scream an
obscenity at the people who are slapping them with open palms across their
faces. For the first time, I am hearing Ajay curse. "I'll shove it so hard up
your ass that everything will come out of your mouth." But he is holding
himself back. The men are not being electrocuted in their genitals, not yet,
not in this room, because there is a woman present.

"Take them both to Sanjay Gandhi National Park and shoot them. Put
a revolver next to him and a chopper next to the other one. We'll say they
tried to escape in their car."

The men are led out by the three policemen and the three of us move to
the front of the office. Vinod, who has witnessed such scenes before, is
laughing about how affected Anu is. He had kept asking her if she wanted
to leave. But she had her eyes wide open and could not tear herself away in
spite of her shock. "I've never seen anybody being beaten. I can't wait to
go home and hug my child."

"This is nothing," says Ajay. "This is Walt Disney."

"The real beating is still to come," says Vinod knowledgeably.
"They'll be taken somewhere."

Ajay smiles. "To the Resort."

I had an idea of "the real beating" from speaking to Blackeye, the
young D-Company hit man, who had been arrested earlier for the murder
of a music producer. The policemen stripped him and put him facedown on
a small bench in the interrogation room. They tied his hands to the bench.
The officer put on gloves. He took a small bottle containing a particular
kind of acid; one drop on human skin will eat through it like Drano down
a bathroom drain. The gloved hands spread his buttocks. "They put it in

my godown," Blackeye told me. "They stretched my godown and put the whole bottle in my godown." More than a year later, every time he shits, a little bit of flesh comes out.

The counterfeiters wouldn't be shot; they're small time. And their kids and wives wouldn't be beaten. Unlike others in the force, Ajay is not a sadist; his bark is much worse than his bite. His technique is to extract the maximum amount of information with the minimum of physical pain. But the dancer in Mira Road, the fat man's mistress whose name he gave up first, would be brought in that night. They would press her for more names. The mistress is always given up first.

The dancer later leads them to the entire ring. Ajay arrests a total of seven people and recovers $100,000 worth of Indian currency. He finds out that the Dawood gang is involved, under the guidance of the Pakistanis. Their aim is to flood the country with forged notes. The beating of the men revealed the chain of distribution: the fake Indian currency was manufactured outside Islamabad in the Pakistani government printing press, whose plates turned out hundreds of thousands of pictures with the portrait of Mahatma Gandhi, and was sent to Kathmandu, where it was picked up and sent by rail or road all over India. Once in the country, it was exchanged for smaller amounts of genuine currency or mixed with real notes and spent in the bazaar, or thrown on the dancing girls in beer bars. This is a new kind of cross-border aggression: economic sabotage. Bombay, as the financial capital of the country, is particularly vulnerable. There is already a rumor going around that the Reserve Bank of India will stop accepting 500-rupee notes. Some shopkeepers have already stopped accepting them, leading to fights between them and their customers. In Kathmandu the previous year I was told by my hotel that it wouldn't take 500-rupee Indian notes for this very reason—that so many of them were counterfeit.

"There's a whole world around us that we know nothing about," says Anu, walking back to her house from Ajay's office. "I just want to watch my Hindi films and be safe." All of a sudden, she's conscious of some subterranean stream of homicidal violence five minutes down the road from her plant-filled house, some deep river of pain on whose banks she lives.

At the story session for *Mission Kashmir* immediately afterward in

Vinod's house, Vinod is explaining a scene to Hrithik Roshan, the hero. "And then you'll have thirty bullets going in your back, and you'll fall like this." He falls flat on the ground, a movie director's idea of death.

"Fantastic!" says the star.

AJAY IS A BANDRA BOY, a star batsman in his schooldays. He joined the Indian Police Service in 1981, after he graduated from Bombay University with an honors degree in history and political science. He worked in various ranks all around the state and city. Through the years, Ajay got to know the precise details of every racket in the city, big or small. He tells me, for example, that the franchise to make big chalk pictures of Jesus Christ on the footpath, on which passersby throw coins, is sold for 75,000 rupees for six months by the toughs who control that section.

After his work in the blasts investigation, Ajay was promoted to deputy commissioner in the Crime Branch, where for four years he was responsible for tracking terrorist and gang activity in the entire city of Mumbai. Then, in 1996, he made a bad career decision: He raided the house of Jaidev Thackeray. Jaidev is Bal's son. The old man got on the phone and had Ajay transferred to the State Police for his audacity. There Ajay remained, dealing with tribal crime in the rural areas, until 1998, when the authorities decided that the nuisance of Ajay's incorruptibility was outweighed by his expertise in fighting the gangwar, and brought him back into the City Police.

Ajay has one abiding hatred: the movie industry. His father was a movie producer who died of powerlessness. At one time his father signed Rajesh Khanna for a movie. After getting the superstar's dates, he rented a studio for a week and constructed an elaborate set for a song sequence. The actor didn't show up on Monday, then he didn't show up the next day. The set was ready; the crew and the producer were waiting. Every day meant a huge expense. Khanna didn't show up all that week, and by Saturday the entire set had to be demolished, a fantasy that would remain a fantasy. On that Saturday, Ajay's father had his first stroke.

Sometime later he signed up another actor, Vinod Khanna, and again took a set of dates from him. On the day of shooting, the star was untraceable. He had become a follower of Rajneesh and had disappeared into the guru's ashram in Pune. The star's secretaries didn't know how to get hold of him. Once again the producer saw his money disappearing before his eyes. He had his second stroke then.

"I was very fond of my father," Ajay says. "I used to wake up at three-thirty in the morning, and my father wouldn't be in his bed. I would walk to the garden and see him sitting outside, smoking. When I went up to him and asked what the matter was, he said, 'I've borrowed money at thirty-six percent interest. What will I do?' He had lost twenty-five lakhs. I hate the film line; it's a dirty business. I swore that when I grew up I would be a man in a position of power over these people who ruined my father." So he became a police officer, rather than a lawyer or a doctor or a businessman; rather than a movie producer. "In the uniform there is power."

In his current position as ACP, Northwest Region, he has suzerainty over Bandra and Juhu, the Beverly Hills of Bombay, where the stars live and work. They make a beeline for Ajay's office every time they get a menacing phone call from the underworld, including the actors who caused his father to die a slow death. "They came to me to say they were very good friends of my father. I told them what my father told me and how my family felt about them." They sat in front of him, squirming. "I had half a mind to throw them out. But then there's the reputation of the department." So he helps them out, makes the calls that need to be made, and rounds up the extortionists that need to be rounded up, so the stars can sleep easy. But there's one difference between Ajay and his father. Today, it's Ajay who gives the stars his dates.

WHEN AJAY AND HIS WIFE, Ritu, come to our flat for dinner, I offer him a drink, but Ajay is that rarity in Bombay: a cop who doesn't drink. "I saw so much liquor in my house, growing up. I didn't like my father drinking. A person loses control when he drinks. I don't like to drink or smoke. Never." He repeats the word, I suspect, for himself: "Never."

He is also a rarity in another way: He doesn't take bribes. He says he must be the only government official in India who pays his own phone bills for his private line: 2,000 rupees a month. For not taking bribes, and for being from a well-off family, Ajay says he has very little in common with the rest of his colleagues. "Most of the people in the force are jealous. The rest, maybe the seniors, are frightened of me." As a result, he never socializes with other policemen.

For ten days before Diwali, the senior police officers' quarters in Worli see a procession of men bearing baskets of expensive fruits and sweet-meats, gifts for the officers. Ritu summarily refuses all such gifts—a bottle of champagne from a movie director, for example. The other officers, especially Ajay's superiors, are concerned about how Ajay's honesty reflects on their own acceptance of gifts, so they give him some fatherly advice. "You have to be practical."

"Have the gangs ever tried to buy you?" I ask Ajay.

"After the blasts I was offered fifty lakhs by my senior officer not to assault someone. He said, 'Don't beat this fellow up, he's very connected. I know of someone who's ready to give fifty lakhs. I'm not telling you to do anything illegal; I'm telling you not to beat him up.' I said, 'Sir, I've trained under you. If you weren't my senior officer I would assault *you*.' My problem is I get very emotional about my honesty."

Ajay's monthly salary, as an IPS officer, is just under 20,000 rupees. A skilled secretary in a multinational corporation makes more than that. "That needs to be revised," I tell him.

"It was revised. Until last year it was seven thousand."

"Seven thousand a month?"

"I began in 1981 at seven hundred and fifty rupees"—$75 at the time—"a month, as Assistant Commissioner of Police." Ritu, who comes from a rich family in Delhi, was aghast when she saw the quarters they would live in. There was no furniture. Although Ajay doesn't drink, he loves meat, the rarer the better. In his parents' home he ate only meat for his meals. When he began in the police force, he couldn't afford to buy meat for a year. When he was posted to a district, he made up for what he couldn't buy in the marketplace by going hunting for boar. On the walls of his quarters now are a tiger's head and a deer's head.

Ajay wants to go abroad to study terrorism. The Bombay Police's knowledge of the international linkages between criminal syndicates and terror groups is, he says, cursory and scattershot. No police force can fight the demon of organized crime alone; if its head is cut off in Bombay it grows a new one in Delhi or in Dubai. But strict limits on contacts with foreigners are imposed on police officers in India. The only place where Ajay could hope to make such contacts is outside the country, on a study leave from the force. He wants to see how other democracies fight the enemy within.

In 1999, Bombay emerged as the nerve center for the hijacking of an Indian Airlines plane by Kashmiri separatists. The fake passports of some of the hijackers were made here. From the plane sitting on the runway in Kandahar, Afghanistan, the hijackers would get regular updates by phone from a part of their group, which was based in Jogeshwari and monitoring what the Indian media were saying about the incident. In fact, the relatives of the hijacked were getting hysterical in front of the cameras of the world. The pressure was very high on the Indian government to give in to the terrorists, which it eventually did. Among the jihadis released as part of the deal was Sheikh Omar, who, three years later, murdered the journalist Danny Pearl. The accomplices of the hijackers, when caught, also had lists of Hindu political leaders targeted for assassination.

Ajay foresees a global linkage of the Muslim militant organizations— in Afghanistan, in Chechnya—with the Muslim criminal gangs in Bombay and in Russia. "For them, Mumbai is very important. If India has to be hit financially, crippling Mumbai is a must. They want to create fear and panic in the city." He knows for a fact that Dawood and his chief lieutenant, Chotta Shakeel, had a meeting with Osama bin Laden outside Kabul in August 1999. They discussed the purchase of weapons and ways they could work together. As Kamal, the paymaster of the D-Company in Bombay, explained to me, "The Muslim community doesn't take Osama bin Laden as a terrorist, he is taken as a messiah. He is not selfish at all. He is the second richest man in Saudi; he is an economy unto himself. Muslims admire that he left this lavish lifestyle to live as a gypsy. So a lot of people are following him."

Ajay has a sense of vast foreign networks always watching the police lines for gaps to start trouble in his beloved city. The total amount of RDX that blew up on March 12, 1993, was only 16 kilos, 350 pounds. But Ajay seized much more than that: almost two and a half tons. And that's not the half of it. "The entire consignment that came in before the blasts has not been recovered," says Ajay. "It's still sitting around somewhere."

"The next riot will be very mighty," a shooter of the D-Company had predicted. He compared it to a fire. "Any wind can blow it from here to there, anybody can set it off for the smallest of reasons. Everywhere there will be a conflagration." And this time, unlike the last, the Muslims will be armed and ready.

A few years ago, Ajay received a call from an official in Delhi. South

Africa needed police officers from third-world countries to retrain its police services, and Ajay had been nominated for a two-year posting in Johannesburg. Johannesburg "is the drug capital of the world," says Ajay. He thought about it that night and made up his mind to go. In the morning he consulted two former police commissioners who thought highly of him. Both advised against it. Ajay is on the hit list of the underworld gangs. "They have set you up to be killed there," the men said. Ajay passed on the opportunity, but thinking back on it now, he says it was "a tactical mistake."

Ritu read history at Oxford. She had applied to study at Cambridge, and they offered her a lectureship with a sizable stipend attached to it. She turned it down to marry Ajay. But she hasn't been able to pursue her career. She wants to go to America, where she will be able to study again. Every time they pass by the airport road, Ajay's ten-year-old son asks, "Pappa, can we take that road?" He knows that abroad is the only place his father can truly relax. As soon as the plane leaves the ground in Bombay, all the stress disappears. "It's like an on/off switch," Ajay says.

"He never takes his kids to the zoo," complains Mrs. Lal.

"Every day I am in a zoo," responds Mr. Lal.

In every conversation with me Ritu has brought up the fact that she gave up her career immediately after getting married. She insists it was the right decision, to raise two children, to be a good wife to Ajay. And by dint of being Ajay's wife, she has to endure pressures that would drive another woman to break down. "After the bomb blasts I would get calls in the middle of the night: 'We know you have a son who goes to Cathedral.' " The callers would demand that Ajay back off. The sons, Rahul and Ravin, are under twenty-four-hour armed guard. After the blasts, there was one day when gangsters were waiting with grenades to throw at the car taking Rahul to school, as it passed under the Marine Drive flyover, a road where it has to slow down. At the last minute Ajay found out about the plot, and the car took a different route.

When their sons go to school, armed policemen stand outside their class. Rahul, the older son, doesn't like the constables always being with him. "It curtails his freedom," notes Ajay. "He can't go down to play like the other kids." Once, when Rahul was in the second standard, Ritu picked up the phone, and the caller told her he'd put a bomb in her son's classroom. She called Ajay, frantic, but could not get through to him. Two minutes later, the security officer assigned to her son called up to confirm the threat, saying the school was being evacuated. Ritu rushed downstairs, jumped into the car, and drove to the school in a panic, running all the red lights, her heart in her mouth, as she imagined what was happening to her son. She found him safe and sound outside the school and brought him home. This happened several times. Ajay says the bomb squad was regularly dispatched to his son's school.

All this explains the anger I see in him during his interrogations. "If the family is tense and frightened, automatically I get tense." Aside from Shrikant Bapat, the commissioner at the time of the riots and the one named in the Srikrishna Commission Report for allowing the rioters a free hand, Ajay is the only officer of the Mumbai Police who has been provided such extraordinary security, because his family lives under an extraordinary threat. But Ajay can carry on because he has a good woman by his side. "Ritu's accepted it amazingly well," he tells me later. "She's been very strong. She's never told me, Don't do this. Never." So now he wants to go abroad, for two or three years, to escape the attentions of the gangs and let his guard down a bit. "Out of sight, out of mind, hopefully."

As Ajay and Ritu leave the flat and walk downstairs, I look out of the kitchen window. A white Ambassador with a police light on it pulls up, Ajay and Ritu get in, other men run about, some get into the Ambassador with him. Behind them, a jeep pulls out, full of policemen with long guns, and the convoy leaves in the quiet night. The cars had pulled up to the entrance before my guests reached the ground floor; there must have been guards outside my door, or in the lobby, waiting all evening for my dinner party to finish. We had never been so secure—or so unsafe.

THE BOMBAY POLICE was established by the British. The most famous police chief of British times, the one who modernized the force, was Charles Forjett, an Anglo-Indian. He set the tradition of policing the city with an iron hand, and also of being hated for what he did at the behest of its citizens. He considered that his foremost duty was "to crush evil in the bud." Ajay could be his reincarnation; when I ask him what drives him, he responds simply, "The fight against evil."

During the 1857 mutiny, Commissioner Forjett traveled incognito around the city, arresting on the spot anyone whom he overheard praising the actions of the mutineers. He erected a gibbet in the compound of the

Police Office, summoned the chief citizens whom he knew to be disaffected, and pointed to the gibbet. Two of the mutineers were chained to cannons on the Maidan, the public was invited to watch, and the cannons were fired. The Maidan was filled with an odor of burnt flesh.

Bombay's businessmen gave Forjett a sum of £1,300 in 1859 and, after he retired to England in 1864, another £1,500, "in token of their strong gratitude for one whose almost despotic powers and zealous energy had so quelled the explosive forces of native society that they seem to have become permanently subdued." But the Empire was not so generous; he was a half-breed. According to a later British history of the force, "Forjett is said to have regarded himself as slighted by Government in not having received from them any decoration. It certainly seems curious that so admirable a public servant should not have been rewarded with a Knighthood or admitted to one of the orders of chivalry." Forjett's pension was paid in rupees. After the decline in the exchange rate, he asked for it to be paid in pounds; his request was not honored. He died in England at the age of eighty, in a house in Buckinghamshire, which in his bitterness he named not after any of the British governors he had served but after Sir Cowasji Jehangir, a Parsi notable from Bombay. A native.

A century and a half after Forjett professionalized the force, the Mumbai Police is still fairly considered the best in India, with the best detectives. Ajay remembers taking a team of New York City policemen around the Dharavi slums. "They were amazed." He points to the city's massive population, the difficulties of tracking a constant stream of migrants and their crimes. "In every case you are waving a magic wand and detecting them. I don't see any city in the world which has got such a wide range of crimes as ours." Ajay wonders what fabulous facilities the American police might enjoy. "If it's like the movies, they have a gym, a shower room."

Ajay once had an argument with the editor of the *Bombay Times*, who was comparing the Bombay Police unfavorably with Scotland Yard. Ajay responded that statistics would show that almost all the cases given to the Bombay cops were solved. How come there were so many cases? the editor asked. It's because there are so many complaints. In Ajay's current posting, he spends the day dealing with sixty to seventy visitors, members of the public asking for his help with everything from extortion calls to a woman wanting Ajay to bring her runaway husband back to her. "Eighty percent of the people who come to me say, 'Get him out of my flat,' or, 'That fellow's trying to get me out of my flat,' " Ajay tells me. "And if I help the man get someone out of his flat, the one I get out will say, 'The police have been paid off.' " The fallout from the Rent Act takes up most of Ajay's time. What really stands between him and his kids' right to time with their father and his wife's right to time with her husband is the Rent Act, not the gangwar.

The root of the problem is that there are simply not enough policemen for this exploding city. In 1951, four years after independence and a halcyon time for Bombay, there were 4.3 policemen per thousand people. By 1998, when I moved back, this ratio had been halved; there were now only 2.6 per thousand. As a result, points out Ajay, the force is grossly overworked. "Practically everybody here from the commissioner on down works fourteen to fifteen hours a day. A constable has a twelve-hour shift, eight to eight. But he may go home at ten or eleven. There's no overtime." A constable takes home a salary of 4,000 rupees a month, less than what I am paying my driver. Police housing can accommodate only about 60 percent of the force; 40 percent live in slums. More than ten thousand police constables are waiting for government quarters, which they only qualify for after ten years of service. "So the constable goes to the slumlord, and he tells him, 'You are charging others twenty-five thousand for a hut; you give it to me for twenty thousand and take the money in phased payment, installments.' Do you expect such a guy to take action against slumlords? He will say, 'What has the department done for me?' " And it's not as if sustained devotion to duty can bring a constable hope of giving his children a better life. Under the rules of the Bombay Police, a constable can rise no higher than the rank of an assistant inspector of police. It is no wonder that the father of Dawood Ibrahim was a constable in the employ of the Bombay Police. His example notwithstanding, the strength of Muslims in the force, which is under 5 percent, needs to be increased, says Ajay.

The weapons and the laboratories available to the Bombay Police are antiquated. The Dawood gang gets its weapons from the bazaars on the Pakistan–Afghanistan border: AK-47s, hand grenades. Some of the automatic rifles are even equipped with silencers. At the beginning of the twenty-first century, sections of the Bombay Police are still armed with .303 rifles used in World War II. "After the army got modernized," Ajay explains, "their old weapons were handed over to the police. There was a shortage of revolvers and pistols." When Ajay got off duty as a junior police officer, he had to hand his weapon to the officer relieving him. So if a constable is faced with a professional hit man firing his Mauser, he has to stop, unstrap his mighty musket from his shoulder, load the bullet, raise it to his shoulder, line up the target through the sight mounted on the barrel, and wing him. By this time the hit man will be in Dubai.

And it's not as if the police are adequately trained, even when they are properly equipped, as Ajay explains with a story. One day in the late eighties, when he was posted to the northeast region of Bombay, he got a call from one of the officers under his command that an elephant had gone berserk. He asked the officer to get a veterinarian. A little while later, the officer called again: The elephant was running amok, uprooting things. Ajay went to the scene of the beast's rampages. By the time he got there, the vet had arrived and had tranquilized the elephant, who was now being transferred onto a truck with the aid of a crane. As he was showing Ajay around, the police officer added sheepishly, "Sir, I had to fire a round." Ajay informed the veterinarian and asked him to check the elephant for a bullet. That night, the vet called Ajay: He couldn't find the bullet. Ajay told the vet to check again. "I said, an elephant's skin is very thick, search with a fine-tooth comb, and you'll find the bullet." Very late that night the vet called back; there was no bullet in the elephant's hide.

The next morning Ajay went back to the site and checked for himself, accompanied by the police officer who had fired. Ajay then found the bullet, embedded in the door of a doctor's dispensary that had been behind the beast. "He had missed."

I look up from my notes. "How close was the officer to the elephant?"

"He had fired from ten feet away."

Even if a suspect is arrested and his weapon found, the whole support structure Ajay has to rely on to secure a conviction, everything from the forensics laboratories to information technology to the public prosecutors, is substandard. "It's very easy for people abroad to talk about human rights. In New York or the UK, a confession made before a police officer is admissible. Here it is not. We are given the worst lawyers, the ones who are not good at private practice. The gangs have the best." In the age of the market economy, globalization, and multinationals, "the police is a nonprofit institution. Why should they put money into it?"

So the police take shortcuts to solving crimes. Maharashtra had the highest number of custodial deaths in the whole country in 1997: 200, a

500 percent increase from the previous year's total of 30. Two hundred people tortured to death in police custody! The record outstrips that of many military dictatorships around the world. According to a police report of the causes of 155 custodial deaths in Maharashtra in the 1980s, only 15 were due to "police action." The rest had causes ranging from "fell from bed" to "fell on others."

Most people in this part of the world, rich or poor, give the police station a wide berth. A friend tells me his accountant has stolen forty-five lakhs and run off to the south, where he is hiding. My friend files a complaint with the police, who arrest the accountant's sister. She is not involved in the crime, but they keep her in custody for twenty days, hoping it will put pressure on her brother to surrender. When my friend goes to the station, the police officer in charge tells her she's in the lockup and invites him to "Do what you want with her." My friend fears for her safety and sends a man from his office to sit at the station day and night, guarding her from the officers of the law.

My uncle castigates me for having sent Sunita to pick up some forms from Special Branch, the agency responsible for registering foreigners. "You can't send ladies to the police station." And sure enough, she is harassed. She hears the inspectors making lewd comments about her in Marathi. The officer in charge tells my wife he can send her and my children to court if he so wishes. I should just have dropped Ajay's name; the forms would have been delivered to my door. But it was still early in our return home; we still labored under the propriety that we had learnt in the West. This changed as we got used to the Country of the No.

I get a taste of Ajay's power when my sister and her fiancé fly in from San Francisco. I am sitting in his office and I tell him I have to leave to fetch them. Ajay makes a call to the inspector in charge of the airport. I go to the airport police station. "Lal Saab's guest. Arrange the courtesy for him," the desk inspector orders. A plainclothes officer escorts me into the restricted area of the airport, all the way to the escalator coming down from the arrival gate, where I greet my astonished sister. I take them to the front of the immigration line—oh, the joy of skipping that endless line!—and go right through customs. The assistant commissioner of customs shakes my hand and asks feebly, "Anything to declare?" "Nothing," I say, leading my sister and her fiancé past the helpless men in white. They don't have anything that is liable for duty, but there is power in knowing that we could have brought in computers, munitions, liquor, and heroin if we had wanted to. So often, coming into this airport, I have felt completely helpless. Now I have police swarming around me; I walk past closed doors, past men with guns. The normal rules don't apply to me.

I could get used to this.

BY NINE O'CLOCK these days, when the air-raid siren goes off, it is already steaming. All those who can have fled. Only those who have had a bad year—the failed students, the failed businessmen—are left behind to suffer summer in the city, to take the trains, to walk the melting streets. Each year it gets hotter. The sun rises late but makes up for it with its vigor. All winter long it has gathered strength; now it is loaded for bear.

I get to Ajay's office one evening at seven. He is running a fever and has switched off the AC; the office smells of stale sweat. It is infested with mosquitoes, which feast on my blood. Ajay has recently arrested several members of a gang who worked at a shoe factory in Dharavi, earning between 800 and 1,500 rupees a month for their work there. It's a miserable life for the millions of young men who work in the factories of the city. They labor in dark, hot rooms, where they can never stand up straight, for fear of getting nicked by the whirling blades of ceiling fans jury-rigged from the tin ceilings. They are mostly from Bihar or Uttar Pradesh, and they work fourteen hours a day, every day, in silence, hands moving in automatic gestures. If there is an urgent order, they'll work all day and all night. Most employers here pay their employees by the piece: Making a wallet, for example, earns them between 14 and 25 rupees. They start working as young as eight and can't work past twenty, because their hands are no longer quick, their eyes not so bright. "They have no friends' circle, no nothing. In their life, they have no program for the future," one of the workshop owners had explained to me. Their transcendence is the last show at Maratha Mandir on Sunday evening or a trip to the crowded beach at Juhu to marvel at the freedom of the sea. In the afternoon, the factory workers eat straight from a pot, sitting on their haunches. When they finish working, they lie down on the same patch of ground on which they've been sitting for fourteen hours, in rooms where they might be able to see a little bit of sky and a luxury high-rise on the not-too-distant horizon.

Ajay tells me how these men can be drawn into a gang. A person from their village who is already in the gang would take them to the beer bars; there, the newcomers would see their village man throw money at the dancing girls. They would see that the girls came over to him, touched him, went out with him for the night. "To the guy from the village, the beer-bar girls are like Madhuri Dixit," notes Ajay. They would think, This man came to Bombay just six months before me, how is he living so well? He is wearing good clothes, moving around in a car. So they would be drawn in, given the gun already cocked, told to go up to the target and pull the trigger and run; that's all there is to it. A shooter's average age is anything between eighteen and twenty-six ("Anything above that, you're organizing it," says Ajay). That is, if he lives that long. The shooters don't look anything like their movie counterparts. "A shooter's appearance has to be absolutely nondescript. That will afford him the ability to melt into the crowd. Ultimately it just takes a little pressure of the finger to pull the trigger, not physical strength. Ultimately it takes the ability not to feel remorse when they shoot a man and see blood."

The first interrogation of the evening begins. Two plainclothes police officers and a plainclothes constable come in, bringing a veiled figure. The officers tell Ajay that the suspect is a shooter in the gang that killed a mob lawyer. When the veil is removed, it discloses a puny man, scarcely five feet tall, so scrawny you wouldn't look at him twice in the street. As the towel is removed, he brings his palms together in a hesitant namaste.

Ajay presses him for details. "When did you get the order for the work?"

"Eleven . . . before eleven. It was before eleven, early in the morning, that bhai called me to do the work."

"Do the bhais ever wake up before eleven?" Ajay demands angrily, catching the lie. "Bhais never wake up before eleven!"

After the suspect and the plainclothes policemen leave, Ajay tells me he's almost sure the man didn't do it. He's being paid to take the fall for someone else the gang wants to protect. "But I suspect that officer is mixed up in it"—indicating the chair to my left, where the big policeman was sitting.

I am astonished. Ajay is referring to a police officer nominally under his own command.

"He's a mole." Ajay might have to interrogate him himself, if he doesn't get the information by the next morning.

The new political structure doesn't want Ajay in Bandra. He doesn't expect to last in his office past September. Ajay's boss, the police commissioner, is about to be replaced, and he does not know whether the new man is someone he can trust. When he does not know whether his chiefs themselves are beholden to the gangs, he has to operate in secrecy from his superiors. If he lets them know who he's going after, and if the suspect happens to be from the gang that the superior is allied with, the gang will be tipped off. So Ajay has to hide what he's doing, both from the bandicoots in charge of the stations and from the politically savvy men above him.

For the last couple of years, and especially since his posting to Bandra, Ajay has been unable to sleep at night. He tosses and turns, thinking of his various operations, anticipating the gangsters' next move. "When I get up in the morning, I think I don't want to go to the office. I think I would like to get sick. I'm burning out." On the rare Sunday that he doesn't go to his office, he starts getting panicky by evening, thinking he's losing control of his region.

The previous morning, his wife said to him, "Your son needs you." Ajay points to the newspapers on his desk. In one of them is the news that Rahul has scored a winning goal for his school hockey team, which he captains. His son hasn't read the report. Ajay won't get home in time to congratulate his son, so he calls Ritu to do so. "When I leave early in the morning he's sleeping, and when I get back late at night he's sleeping. I haven't seen my son at all."

An unmarked Maruti Omni pulls up outside the station, and some men are led out with their heads covered. A detective comes into Ajay's office escorting Akbar, a thirty-one-year-old rickshaw wallah from Andhra, a shooter who is suspected of killing several members of the D-Company. Akbar has studied up to the third standard at the Jogeshwari municipal school. He is wearing a dirty white shirt with a green alligator on it. He seems a bit slow; he holds his head and scratches it when attempting to dig up a name. "What was his name . . . ?"—slowly moving his fingers through his hair—"What was his name . . . ?" But he is avoiding nothing. Without being prompted, he comes out with the fact that he fired the bullets. He used to own a rickshaw, which he sold to raise money for his sister's wedding. Then he drove a rented one. The policemen slap him around a little, but it's really not necessary. He talks readily about his works. First was a man at a motor training school. His accomplice had fired two rounds at him, and he had fired once.

"How did you learn to fire a gun?" asks Ajay.

"He gave me the gun and told me to press a button. The bullets were already filled." Akbar's main concern seems to be to protect his brother, who figured marginally in the job, having picked up some of the gang's money on his way home from the station.

"I'll drag your whole family in," promises Ajay. "How much money did you get?"

"I got fifteen hundred rupees to shoot the bullet." Then there was the work of a D-Company member whom he had shot two bullets into at a traffic light, as the victim frantically attempted to hide in the back of his jeep. "I got a net of thirty-five hundred rupees." For three murders, total.

"What did you do with the money?"

"I gave it to my family, to my wife and kids. I have two kids, one six years and the other six months."

"So you've destroyed your kids' lives!" Then Ajay puts to him a question I had been asking a lot in Bombay: "Don't you feel anything about taking a life?"

Akbar replies, "After the bullet fires I just don't know where it goes. I hit him from very close." He shows how, stretching out his arm; he had hit him at arm's length. "If I had to shoot from afar I couldn't do it."

The detective turns to Ajay. "This is a demon. He should be finished off."

After the man is led out, Ajay tells me his gang is behind the biggest shootouts of the past couple of weeks. They work for the Rajan gang and have, unluckily for them, been caught with five guns that ballistics confirmed were used in the shootouts. "Fifteen hundred rupees," Ajay repeats. That's what Akbar was paid to pump two rounds into a living human being. And now he will spend at least ten years of his unfortunate life paying for it behind bars, for the sake of $35 to give to his wife and children.

"What's the lowest price for a life you've seen in Bombay?" I ask Ajay.

He thinks for a while. Then he tells me about the ragpicker.

In 1995, several pieces of a body were found in the municipal dump in Deonar. An informant tipped Ajay off on the murderer: He was a sixteen-year-old boy, a ragpicker, who lived in a shack on the dump. The boy was brought in for interrogation and confessed. He had been approached by a boarder staying with a couple. The husband of the couple was working the night shift in the Mazagaon docks and had taken in the boarder. It is unwise for married men to work the night shift, and the inevitable happened: love bloomed between the boarder and the wife. The husband was the thorn. He suspected his wife and beat her. One day the wife cooked drugged food for the husband; he ate it and fell asleep. The boarder and the ragpicker then smashed in his head with a rock and transported the body to the Deonar dump. There, the ragpicker spent two hours cutting the body into many pieces, and distributing them around the dump. The wife filed a missing person complaint.

Ajay asked the boy how much money he'd been paid for all that work: killing the husband, transporting his body, sawing away at it, walking around with the bloody head and torso and limbs looking for strategic spots to dump them.

"Fifty," said the boy.

"Fifty thousand?"

"No. Fifty rupees."

It was the month of May. In June the rains would come. The ragpicker needed 50 rupees to buy a gunnysack to put on the roof of his shack so his home wouldn't get flooded in the rain. So he killed a man for a sum of money that would not buy a cup of coffee at a good hotel in the city.

After the interrogation, I invite Ajay to dinner at my house. Ajay asks if we can write a book together; he trusts me. He has never been in the slightest doubt that I am writing a book; when he has people beaten in his office, he can see me on the sofa in the back of the room, scribbling away in my notebook, noting each slap, writing down the exact wording of each death threat. Isn't he afraid he'll get into trouble after this gets published? All I have told him by way of reassurance is that the names in my book will be changed. Perhaps he lets me sit there because he needs someone to stand witness, to keep a record of these melancholy evenings of his life. Or perhaps he is simply past caring.

Encounter

On the threshold of sleep and waking one morning, I have a dream. My eyes haven fallen on a document on Ajay's desk. It is about me. He is out of the room, so I filch it. They have been monitoring my movements, tapping my phone. He is leading the surveillance operation on me. There is a plan drawn up to eliminate me; the special squad has been named. I run, take a rickshaw. I have to get myself and my family out of Bombay. When he comes back to his desk he is going to notice the missing document and throw all his men on my track. They are going to encounter me.

It is an innocuous word, "encounter," suggesting a chance meeting while strolling in the park. But in Bombay it has come to mean murder by the state without benefit of trial, an extrajudicial killing. It occurs when the police arrest and interrogate a suspect and then take him to a public place and shoot him dead. The explanation they give out to the press is that they "encountered" a dreaded gangster, asked him to surrender, found themselves fired upon, and fired back in retaliation, killing him. The gangwar boys have shortened the word still further. "He has been 'countered,' " they will say.

Naeem Husain, the crime reporter for one of the leading Bombay dailies, is to meet with Assistant Police Inspector Vijay Salaskar, the top "encounter specialist" of the Bombay Police. He takes me along. Salaskar's office is in a little hut all the way in the back of Nagpada Police Station. We wait for him to come back from headquarters.

As we are waiting, I hear an agonized screaming. The office across the corridor, which has been open, now has its doors closed and a man is howling inside.

"Interrogation?" I ask a senior inspector.

He smiles, nods. Nobody else looks up from their tea, their newspaper.

Just as Salaskar is about to come into the office, two boxes of milk sweets come in, and I am offered pedas from a huge box. Before realizing what I am celebrating, I have eaten one. Salaskar has just been acquitted in the Sada Pawale encounter case. The gangster had set out to get away from Bombay. He asked his sister and his brothers to travel with him in the car. The car was stopped at a junction by Salaskar and his men, and the family was made to get out. The sister knew what was coming; she put her body around her brother's and said, "Don't shoot him." The police separated them and shot him at the junction, in front of his family. Five of them testified about the encounter. The police put a constable in Pawale's home and attached a loudspeaker to the phone, so that every incoming call rang around the house. They told the sister, Do you want to lose your youngest brother also? The Aguiar Commission, investigating the incident, held that the encounter was fake, but the high court had just cleared Salaskar because all the witnesses, including the victim's brother, sister, and sister-in-law, had suddenly recanted their testimony. Four sets of fresh testimonies appeared in court: We didn't say what we said, we didn't see what we saw.

All the time I am in Salaskar's office, top policemen come in and shake his hand and tell him, "Congratulations." One of them says in Marathi that starting tomorrow he should resume the killings "with full force." Salaskar receives their greetings with a smile. He seems curiously gentle for Bombay's top encounter cop; he has the demeanor of a middle-class Maharashtrian engineer. But he has almost single-handedly wiped out the Gawli gang, killed five of their top shooters. This is why, says Husain, "Salaskar allegedly has links to Shakeel." Every senior police officer has these alleged links, even Ajay. The gangs watch the records of individual policemen jealously. Is he shooting more men of the D-Company? Then he must be a Chotta Rajan man. Is he killing off the Gawli boys? Then he must be a Sena man. These rumors attach themselves to a person, and they are hard to shake. The only way to clear your name is to kill some people of the gang you allegedly have links to. Salaskar, when Husain asks him if he has specially targeted the Gawli gang, protests that he has killed Shakeel men too.

Husain asks him how many encounters he's been involved in and what kind of gun he uses.

The cop thinks. "Deaths . . . twenty."

Salaskar brings a black leather pouch out of a cupboard, unzips it—and then I'm holding it in my hands. It is a six-shooter, with a brown handle and a steel barrel. It bears the logo TITAN TIGER, and, below it, .38 and the provenance: MIAMI, FL. On the handle is engraved a bearded Norse god. It looks like a prop in a Hollywood movie of the 1950s. I stare down the barrel.

I ask Salaskar if he has ever felt bad after an encounter, after taking a human life.

"They are not humans," he replies immediately. "They are animals. Waste." To take a human life, you first of all have to deny that the victim is human. You have to reclassify him.

Husain asks if he has ever been in any kind of personal danger during an encounter. Never, he says. The trick is to fire on the targets "before retaliatory fire." He says that he or his men get very close to the target before firing. He is not a good marksman, he admits, but then he has never had to fire from a distance of more than twenty-five feet.

As Judge Aguiar wrote in his report on the recent encounter:

> It is amazing that despite Sada Pawale having fired from a sophisticated weapon, namely, an AK-56 which is capable of firing 600 rounds per minute and having an effective range of 300 meters, neither API Salaskar nor PSI Desai, or any of the police officers, suffered any bullet injury. . . . The police officers must surely bear a charmed life.

The gangs will never go after the policemen, says Salaskar, not even after a constable. "What you saw in *Satya*"—referring to a scene in a gangster movie in which a police commissioner is shot dead by the gangs—"only happens in the movies." He doesn't feel personally threatened. "I am fair. I know where the criminals' families are, but I never touch them."

Husain asks Salaskar about his family. He has a ten-year-old daughter. "Do you want your children to join the police force?"

The cop shakes his head emphatically: no.

The parade of felicitators continues all through our conversation. The screaming in the next room also continues. Nothing can be heard of the screaming man's interrogators; there are no shouts, nothing but the steady, full-throated screaming. Then I hear a series of thwacks, some instrument hitting something soft. Nobody is taking any notice except me. A senior inspector says they will have to get everybody on the team that did the encounter together and celebrate. Salaskar will now have whatever strictures that remained on his behavior lifted. The Titan Tiger is ready to take its twenty-first life.

"Does it have a safety catch?" Husain asks, turning the gun over in his hands.

"No safety catch."

Husain tells me later about seeing a man begging for his life shot dead by the police. "It's wrong to call it an encounter. It was cold-blooded murder." He was taken to the spot ahead of time by the police. He was shown his place to stand and watch. Don't move from here, he was told. You could get hit by a bullet. "What chutiapanthi"—bullshit—Husain says to me.

He describes what he saw. It was 11:30 p.m. Six policemen came in two gypsy vans to the spot. The man knew what was coming. He was groveling, pleading for his life. "I have children, sir, please spare me. I'll do anything, I'll become an informer, anything." As he was begging, the police raised their guns and began firing, different shots from different angles, according to a prearranged plan. One policeman would stand at a particular spot and fire two shots, another at a different spot; it was agreed that about six or seven rounds in all would be fired upon the begging man. As they fired, they were cursing vigorously at him, but there was no regret or rationalization on the faces of the cops that Husain saw. After the man hit the ground, they brought out a revolver, holding it with a handkerchief, put it in the dead man's hand, and made the corpse's hand squeeze off two shots. Whatever public there was at the spot had long since fled after hearing the police's first shots. The cops waited for forty-five minutes, till there were no more signs of life in the body, then took it to a hospital. "I couldn't sleep till 3 a.m. that night, and I couldn't eat for three days," Husain recalls. "I had seen someone begging for his life. I saw blood squirting out of his head." It changed his relationship with the cops. "I hate them. Bombay cops are the worst." Husain is probably the city's best crime reporter, and he works for a major newspaper. He has never written about that incident. He now realizes that everything the press reports about police encounters is nonsense; he is a glorified stenographer. "We are the munshis of the police."

The police, the newspapers, and the courts all keep up the fiction of the encounter killing. They know the script—the gangsters are always supposed to have fired first, and the police fire only in self-defense—and they never bother to ask questions, just as they never bother to ask logical questions about the plots of Hindi movies. If you were to believe the press reports of encounters, you would think that all gangsters are astoundingly bad shots. The police, on the other hand, get their man every time.

In America they call it the thin blue line, the cops who (dressed in blue) separate us, society—men and women who work in jobs in offices and come home and sleep and go to work the next day—from the bad guys, the people who are constantly peering into our brightly lit living rooms from the road below. In Bombay it would be the thin khaki line. But the line here is fuzzy. It is not discernibly a part of us, and it is not clear who is being protected from whom. It is a ragged, childlike slash with a piece of heavy chalk. At times it is fat and sturdy; other times it is so faint it has all but disappeared. *They* are constantly watching for such gaps, such breaches, into which they can slip, like otters into water on a dark night.

Among the public, there is a steadily increasing tolerance for violence. In October 1998, the Mumbai Police formed six secret Special Teams "whose sole brief was to gun down gangsters," according to a report Husain wrote in his newspaper. The police had killed ten people in encounters in the nine months before setting up the Special Teams. In the five months after the teams were formed, the police shot dead fifty-three alleged gangsters in forty-three encounters. One of the death squads was headed by Salaskar, another by Ajay. The teams were not limited by jurisdiction; they could roam far and wide over the city, picking off targets as they chose. When an encounter occurred, it was officially credited to the nearest police station. This did not make the front page in Husain's newspaper; no other paper followed up on Husain's exclusive. There was no reaction from the public, no outrage that the police had decided to turn executioners.

When you live in a world of fear, you give unlimited power to the state. "What about the human rights of the innocent businessmen killed by the criminals?" demands a trader at a large public meeting of traders and state government officials, called to discuss the widespread extortion threats that the businessmen have been receiving. A few of them have been shot dead for not paying. The speeches at the meeting are a curious mixture of fawning obeisance and veiled threat. The favorite comparison of the Bombay Police is with Scotland Yard. "Best in the world after Scotland Yard" was something I'd grown up with, probably a misquote of some survey carried out in the West. And the people on the other side of the law repeated the phrase as if it were established fact. Amol the street ruffian, who has been suspended between two tires hanging in midair and beaten by the police, said to me with no little pride, "After Scotland, our Bombay Police are number two." Now it has changed, as at the traders' meeting, to "Better even than Scotland police." But the traders are upset. They are threatening to stop paying sales taxes, which are collected by the state government.

In the meantime, the city goes about its business, convinced of its own menace. The newspaper headlines, the movies, suit gangsters and cops both: the gangsters because it increases their stature in society—after all, they live on fear, fear is their sugar solution—and the cops because the public now grants them the highest power, the power to take a life without a trial. I get the sense of a city straining to imagine itself more violent than it actually is.

ONE EVENING, on the way home to Nepean Sea Road, I get a ride in the commissioner's car. I tell Ajay about my meeting with Salaskar. "They're exterminators," he says of Salaskar and other encounter specialists like Pradeep Sharma and Pradeep Sawant. "Good police work involves picking up a little clue and building it and staying with it till you crack the whole puzzle." He elaborates on the encounter specialists. "They're contract killers. They get orders from one faction to shoot members of the other gang." He has heard reports that Gawli himself ordered some members of his gang killed, men who could become potential rivals. For this reason, the moment Salaskar or Pradeep Sharma does an encounter, "immediately a big question mark is put. He cannot do all and sundry which he probably did a couple of years back."

Although Ajay is a leader of one of the six Special Teams, he does not have a reputation as an encounter specialist. But he uses the fear that Salaskar and Sharma and Sawant evoke to good effect in his own investigations. When Ajay threatens the men he's interrogating with encounters, they believe him. Every single time I've seen him interrogating suspects in his office, he's threatened to kill them without benefit of a trial. Ajay keeps tight control over who his people shoot. He doesn't give his lower ranks the discretion, the license to kill. "I have told my entire people, no encounters without telling the DCP and myself. Unless we give the green signal, no. We have done twenty-three in our region in the time I have come." It hasn't even been a year.

How does he deal with the responsibility? He sees the decisions he makes, whether to take a man's life or spare it, as courageous ones. "It is a thin line. It requires moral fiber on the part of the police officer to decide on encounters."

I ask Ajay if he has ever killed anybody with his own hands.

"During the riots one has opened fire," he says carefully. "There were four incidents. Six people died. It was a mob situation. I was DCP Traffic. When Mahim went out of control, the commissioner asked me to take care of Mahim, and so I went to Mahim."

But Ajay also sees the reasons why encounters are so prevalent. "The judicial system is so tilted in favor of the accused that he is not at all afraid. It's very frustrating for the police. Someone is arrested in a murder case, the case comes up in four years, the witness is threatened and turns hostile, and you know the man is going back to kill again. He is operating with absolute impunity, and the courts are giving him bail." This agreed with my own experience. All the hit men I had spoken to, men who had murdered many people, had been in and out of jail on murder charges. The only fear they had was of the encounter.

When Ajay catches a gangster and releases him into the judicial system, the chances of securing a conviction are, at the best of times, 10 percent. The conviction rate for criminal offenses, which was 18 to 25 percent a decade earlier, fell to an all-time low of 4 percent in 2000. But before the case comes up for trial, it lolls around for several years in the courts. This is the only time that a criminal might see the inside of a jail—but only if he is too poor to make bail or afford a good lawyer. Seventy-three percent of the country's jail population is on trial or waiting for a trial; only a quarter of them are actually serving out a sentence. Each year, forty thousand new cases are filed in Bombay.

The country's criminal laws need a total overhaul, says Ajay. The pillar of the justice system today is still the Indian Penal Code, which dates from 1861—almost 150 years ago—and the Criminal Procedure Code is 50 years old. The facilities Ajay has access to need to be modernized, as do the personnel. The force has a lie detector today but no personnel trained to operate it. It owns a voice identification system, but the results are not admissible in a court of law as evidence. The public prosecutors who argue the state's cases are at the bottom of the ladder in terms of quality—they are the ones who cannot get jobs in the private sector—and they are pitted against the finest legal minds defending the gangsters.

But it's not just the criminal laws that need to be revamped. This becomes apparent to me one evening when I have dinner with a cousin from Surat. He is a small businessman and appears troubled; I know he has been having money worries. I tell him about my book, that I am meeting gangsters. He listens closely, then asks me for my help. He has given nine lakhs to a business associate, partly in cash, partly in shares, to invest. The associate, in turn, gave the money to a builder in Bombay, who put the money in real estate and has declined to return it. It has been a year and nine months since my cousin last saw the money. The builder simply refuses to give it back; he is thriving. My cousin wants to know if I will ask the gangs to help him get the money back.

"Why don't you file suit against the builder?" I ask him.

My cousin looks at me. "If I file a suit now, my four-year-old son's son will see the verdict."

He is desperate. He hasn't told his father about the nine lakhs, and his business is failing. It's a huge amount for him; one night, driven by business worries, he had paced up and down in his house, a bottle of sleeping pills in his hand, as he thought about ending his worries once and for all. The sight of his sleeping wife and child kept him from swallowing the pills.

I tell him I can introduce him to someone.

Then he thinks. "We should be very sure of who we go to. Because the builder too will have his contacts. And his contacts shouldn't be greater than our contacts. We should go to the Supreme Court."

The judicial system of the country he is in provides him absolutely no recourse in recovering money that is rightfully his. He has to turn to the alternative judiciary. Their justice will be swift and sure, but the court fees are high. "What the courts don't do, we do," Mama, a top member of the Chotta Rajan gang, had told me. The gangs thrive in Bombay first and foremost because the judiciary doesn't. "Backlog and delay plague a wide variety of legal systems," in various countries, the authors of a 1998 study of the Indian civil justice system, published in the *New York University Journal of International Law and Politics,* concede. "Nowhere, however, does backlog and delay appear to be more accentuated than in modern-day India." The total backlog of cases in the Indian courts at the close of the twentieth century stood at 25 million cases at least, one lawsuit for every forty men, women, eunuchs, and children in the country.

The judge/population ratio in the United States is 107 judges per million people; in India it is 13 judges per million. Forty percent of the judgeships in the Bombay High Court are vacant; each judge has over three thousand cases pending. Qualified lawyers do not want to be behind the bench, because the pay is too low compared to what they can earn in private practice. There are no costs associated with filing lawsuits; so the overwhelming majority are frivolous. Adjournments are too readily given. In 1996, hearings of interim—not final—appeals were proceeding with appeals filed only in 1984. Disposal of suits proceeds at the rate of half of fresh filings each year. This means that every year the Bombay High Court adds as many new cases to the backlog as it resolves.

At the current rate, it will take 350 years to end the backlog.

The tackling of evidence in a civil case averages five years. For many cases, final appeals take over twenty years to be decided; many cases languishing in the courts today were originally filed in the early 1950s. So if my family had been sued or had sued somebody when I left Bombay as a child, the matter would only now be close to being settled. Unless we had gone to someone like Mama. "If someone is sitting on your property, whatever is pending for ten or twenty years in the courts, we goondas will resolve in ten days. Whatever the police, the politicians, the courts can't do, we goondas do. When people are tired of the courts, when they are ruined, when they are looking for a way out, they come to us and say, 'Do something.' What you have forgotten is yours, we will restore to you."

At a party in Cuffe Parade, I meet a woman who is in the middle of a property dispute with her landlord: She's an educated woman who travels abroad extensively. She has engaged a consultant to help her get back a large amount of money from the landlord. "We'll have his daughter abducted," the consultant tells her. She is taken aback. Will it be that easy? "If I have my back to the wall I'm not sure I wouldn't do that."

You have to break the law to survive. I break the law often and casually. I dislike giving bribes, I dislike buying movie tickets in the black. But since the legal option is so ridiculously arduous—in getting a driver's license, in buying a movie ticket—I take the easy way out. If the whole country collectively takes the easy way out, an alternate system is established whose rules are more or less known to all, whose rates are fixed. The "parallel economy," a traveling partner of the official economy, is always there, just turn your head a little to the left or right and you'll see it. To survive in Bombay, you have to know its habits. If you have a child, you have to know how much "donation" to give to the school to get admission. If you have a traffic accident, you have to know how much to give to the cops to dispose of the matter and how much to give to the father of the child you've run over to stop the mob from lynching you. If you're a tenant, you have to know how much to demand in key money from the landlord to move out. The parallel economy is fed on a diet of judicial rot. The system of justice, supreme legacy of the British, is in tatters, starved by a succession of governments afraid of its power over them. It was a judge in the

Allahabad High Court who nullified Indira Gandhi's election victory in 1975; she promptly suspended the constitution. It was another judge who finally had the courage to name Thackeray as the agent behind the Bombay riots. But politicians have power too. They have the power to impoverish judges, to not name new ones when a vacancy on the bench comes up. So the parallel economy lives, fat, rich, and happy, because human beings need a system of exchange, to trade their labor for the goods and services of this world.

"It is a good city for gangwar," observes Mama. Like an area of low pressure in the atmosphere, the underworld enters the areas that the state has withdrawn from: the judiciary, personal protection, the channeling of capital. The men in the gangwar see themselves as hardworking men. As Chotta Shakeel explained it to a journalist friend of mine, "There are blue-collar workers and white-collar workers. We are black-collar workers."

TANUJA CHANDRA, the movie director who is a mutual friend of Ajay's and mine, calls up shortly after Ajay has left on a holiday to England. A senior police officer has told her producer and mentor Mahesh Bhatt that the Central Bureau of Investigation is tapping Ajay's phone because they suspect he has dealings with members of the underworld: financial dealings. Tanuja is very disturbed and asks me if I think there's any truth to this. His lifestyle is not commensurate with his salary: his trips abroad, the appliances in his house, the Guy Laroche watch he wears. Mahesh tells me that Ajay has been very jumpy of late and doesn't want to talk on the phone. "Who knows human motives?" he speculates. He remembers the policeman telling him that if Mahesh ever needs it, Ajay can intervene personally with the gang lords: "He'll talk to the guys and exchange a favor."

I ask Ajay directly about this. "In eighteen years of service I haven't taken a glass of water from anybody," he declares. He had long ago made a career decision. "In the long run, it pays to be clean." His money comes from college friends who, he says, have invested wisely on his behalf. But there are people in the police force out to get him. They plant stories about him. "Only Ritu and my mother and my sister have stood by me." Ajay and his family have just come out of a departmental inquiry instigated against him, on allegations of corruption, that dragged on for four years. Ritu had to account for every rupee she spent during those years, down to where she got the money for the washing machine. Finally, Ajay was cleared of all charges.

So Ajay, like Commissioner Forjett a century ago, is bitter. He has the bitterness of someone from a good family who has taken a job he has given his life to and feels he is not being rewarded for his sacrifice. "This morning when I was driving to the office I was seeing in Shivaji Park a father teaching his son how to play football. I was thinking I was such a good sportsman but I have never had time to teach my son how to play football or basketball. Yesterday my son had a football match in school. All the parents went. I couldn't go. I feel I am doing gross injustice to my family."

I ask Ajay about what he sees as his future. "I know the department. The authorities are going to use me. Apart from going abroad there is nothing else. There is nothing here."

I help Ajay prepare his résumé and send it sailing into the ocean of the Internet. Bruce Hoffman of the Rand Institute, the world's leading authority on terrorism, writes back. He invites Ajay to come to Washington for a research stint. He will be able to work with the best minds on the subject, and the force would profit greatly by his knowledge once he returns. But Ajay can't get a letter of permission from the Commissioner of Police. It would have to go through the Indian Police Service and then the Ministry of External Affairs. The commissioner is suspicious of Hoffman. "This is how the CIA recruits people," he tells Ajay. "They give them scholarships to go abroad." Ajay tells his boss about the prestige of Rand. The commissioner counters with another argument: "He said the battle is only half over, how can you leave now? I felt like saying I've been fighting the battle for so many years." But Ajay does not say this to his superior officer, and so he continues in Bombay, ready to join battle with the newest crop of the underworld.

AFTER THE NEW CONGRESS GOVERNMENT assumes power in Maharashtra in 1999, Ajay is kicked upstairs; he is made Commissioner of Railway Police. The most skilled detective in the city has now been put to work chasing ticketless travelers. Ajay is hurt that "there was no hue and cry over my transfer" on the part of all the people he had protected in his region. But as Commissioner of Railways, Ajay Lal is a relaxed man. He can now go to a movie with Ritu, "to a three o'clock show!" In his new posting he chases pickpockets, thieves who administer stupefying drugs to travelers and rob them of their possessions, and chain snatchers. In the first week after taking up his post, he asks for the files of the previous five years and pores over them. He notices a pattern with train robbers on the long-distance routes: Most of the robberies are committed between Santacruz and Khar. He figures out that this is where the long-distance trains intersect with local trains: The robbers do their work, leap out of the trains, and climb directly aboard the locals. So Ajay stations some of his men at those points and immediately catches a gang of robbers. It is not big-news work, but for the first time in many years he has time to spend with his family. His son loves it. Ajay is now able to attend Rahul's football game on Sundays.

Ajay asks me what Vinod is filming these days; a visiting friend from the police force would like to see a movie shoot. I look up the schedule for *Mission Kashmir*. On the day Ajay's friend is in town, Vinod is due to shoot a scene where a police officer is getting information from captured militants. "It might be interesting for your friend, as a police officer, to watch this interrogation scene," I say.

"And who plays the policeman, Sanjay Dutt?"

I pause, realizing the multiple ironies—Ajay himself had sent Sanjay Dutt to jail for a year and a half for his role in the bomb blasts—and laugh.

"He would be better at advising the person being interrogated on how to act," Dutt's real-life tormentor notes.

Sanjay Dutt later tells me that he became good friends with the other men accused in the bomb blasts. One of them was someone who called himself the Nawab of Tonk, Salim Durrani, "an educated man," as Sanjay repeatedly refers to him. The Nawab wrote and smuggled a pamphlet out to Sanjay, "Voices," about the tortures the police purportedly inflicted upon those accused in the blasts. Sanjay describes its contents. "They made a daughter-in-law suck her father-in-law's cock. He committed suicide afterward."

The suspects had sent the document to the UN and the press, hoping to draw attention to the state of human rights in Bombay. I look for the document a long time, and finally a human rights lawyer sends it to me when I am in America for a short trip. It is a badly typed bundle of sheets with the title "VOICES—From the Draconian Dungeons." I read it, horrified, in a quiet old farmhouse in New Hampshire, the fall unfurling all around me. Many of the interrogations that the document describes were conducted by

Ajay or in his presence. The document claims systematic torture, not just of the suspects but also of their wives, mothers, and infant children. There is a particular focus, with wounded relish, on sexual torture of the women. "A beautiful newly married convent-educated girl was stripped and her naked body was placed on ice slab while the drunk policemen violated her naked body. Her body was inflicted with cigarette burns." And, "Najma was forced to fondle with her father's penis and eat up his shit too.. . . . Young naked Manzoor Ahmed was forced to insert his penis into the mouth of Zaibunnisa Kazi, a woman of his mother's age. . . . Sons-in-law were forced to undress their mothers-in-law." Much of the document reads like a penny-dreadful novel. "Urine and feces were parts of the food, spitting into mouth and even spitting by especially bought lepers were just for the fun of it and heartily enjoyed by the police. Even Satan might have shuddered to his inmost at this sadistic savagery."

Parts of "Voices" are true; the difficulty is in knowing which parts. The basic facts of the story of Rakesh Khurana are true. Khurana owned a restaurant and a laundry in Bandra and had a peripheral connection with Piloo Khan, a drug smuggler. One night shortly after the blasts, when Khurana was having dinner with his family, the police came and asked him to come to the station for an inquiry. He told them he would come in later, and they left. All that evening, he seemed very troubled. Then he went into the station, came back, and drove his wife and son and daughter to a cul-de-sac in Juhu. As his wife attempted to shield the little children with her arms, he shot them all dead and then shot himself. What had the police said to him that so troubled Khurana? Here is the gray world between fact and hearsay. The "Voices" document claims that Khurana murdered his family after he saw what the police officer at the station, Maneckshaw, was doing to the wife of a blasts' accused in front of Khurana at the station. "If you fail to find out Piloo Khan by tomorrow, I will call your wife and order my constables to rape her," the document quotes Maneckshaw as saying.

At least one part of the document is demonstrably true. In March 2000, the National Human Rights Commission ordered the Maharashtra government to pay five lakhs' compensation to the family of Iqbal Haspatel for doing what it did to them over a fortnight in April 1993. Haspatel was a sixty-year-old weaver who lived with his extended family in Alibag, outside Bombay. A consignment of the arms and explosives used in the blasts had been smuggled in on the beaches of Alibag, and the local police were hot on the trail. When they burst in through the door of Haspatel's house, they saw a suspicious cylinder in a showcase in the living room. The police officers decided it was a "rocket projectile," arrested the entire family, and paraded them around the mosque, asking Muslims why they had nurtured "a serpent like him." At the police station, they stripped Haspatel, his son, and his cousin in front of his wife, daughters, and daughter-in-law. When the women covered their eyes, the police struck their arms with nightsticks, ordering them to look. As the naked father tried to hide his privates from his daughters and daughter-in-law, he was kicked in the spine; he crashed headfirst into a table. The women were kicked and hit with a leather belt. Then the officers of the law took Haspatel's twenty-five-year-old son, tied his arms and legs, hung him on a rod suspended between two desks, and played football with his body, kicking it with such force that it rotated clear around the rod. His father, watching this, prayed that his son would die. His son came near enough to it; he often lost consciousness and developed convulsions by the end of six days of this game. The family was kept in the police lockup for a fortnight.

Meanwhile, another of Haspatel's relatives found out what was happening. He led the police to a textile factory, where an engineer pointed out to the sleuths another cylinder that was exactly the same as the "rocket projectile." It was a textile spindle. The family was allowed to go back home, where they found out that the police had destroyed all the furniture in the house and stolen much of the removable property. There was the usual inquiry. None of the Haspatel family's tormentors were ever arrested, even though the whole incident was amply documented. One of the policemen who could not tell the difference between a rocket and a piece of textile machinery has been posted to the Intelligence Bureau.

When I get back to India I ask Ajay about the "Voices" document. He says that most of it is fiction and points out logical inconsistencies within the document. After his work in the blasts, there were forty-seven petitions in court against Ajay from the suspects, alleging torture. None of them came to anything.

What do I do with Ajay? He is a brutal interrogator; this I have seen for myself. But Ajay had become a friend of sorts. "We'll miss you, Suketu!" he said with genuine feeling, when I was about to leave for America. "We got used to having you around."

What is in dispute is the extent to which he will torture people. What would be reassuring to believe is that he will only beat men that he knows are criminals, and that he will only beat them with a strap or have his men give them electric shocks—pain that will not permanently harm them but will act as that necessary spur, in the absence of a functioning judiciary, for them to give out information that will save lives, information that will prevent bombs from being planted that will blow up completely innocent people not connected to the gangwar in any way. It is evident that Ajay does not enjoy the torture part of his work. I have never seen him physically hit anyone, only direct others to do so. He is also unaffiliated with any political party, gang, or religion; I have never heard Ajay mention God, not even once.

I am told by the human rights activist Javed Anand that Ajay has gone after the Sena thugs as few other officers dare to. And the journalist Jyoti Punwani also tells me that Ajay's deposition before the Srikrishna Commission, investigating the riots, was much better than the lies the other policemen spouted. Even Sanjay Dutt says he is a good officer. And among the common people of his district, Ajay is a hero. He is one of the few senior police officers who sticks up for people without money; that is because he is one of the few police officers who doesn't take money to do his job. The newspapers are filled with grateful statements about Ajay from Bandra residents fighting slum lords and builders.

On the sliding scale of the Bombay Police, Ajay Lal is a good cop. Ajay will not shoot people wholesale. He hates the "exterminators" like Salaskar and Sharma and Sawant, not because death is a violation of human rights but, rather, bad police work. "It's no light thing, to take a human life," he says about the encounter specialists. "It requires a special kind of psychology." What kind of psychology does it take to electrocute a human being's genitals, when that person is incapable of fighting back? Ajay is convinced he is in a fight against evil. He sees himself as providing the same kind of protection to the weak as the Sena thought they were offering during the riots. Ajay and the Sena boys will become evil themselves in order to fight evil. In doing so, they are protecting the good doctors, traders, and professors of the city who, burdened by their consciences, are too weak to become evil to fight evil. When the call comes in from Karachi, threatening their children, their wives, they want Ajay to do whatever he has to. They don't mind if he hurts the gangsters' wives, *their* children.

Ajay admits that the constant threats to kill his wife or blow up his sons' school have affected him. "I would have left long back. But the department protects me. If I leave the department, where is the protection?" His sons would go to school unguarded. There would be no armed policemen outside his door. "So I'm now in this Catch-22 situation: I'm neither here nor there. I want to leave but I can't leave." He can never leave the police force while he is living in Bombay; not for lucre, not out of disgust. The work that put the President's Medal on his uniform also ensured that the uniform would never come off.

Last year, a top industrialist offered Ajay a way out. He asked Ajay to be head of security for his company. The package included a salary of three lakhs a month, plus a flat and a car in Bandra; his phone bills would be paid; plus one holiday abroad each year for the family, with first-class airfare, plus free education for his children—all if he would quit the force and be on their board of directors. He heard later from a mutual friend that they would have gone up to five lakhs a month, twenty-five times his current salary. He turned them down. I asked him why. "Right now I can make them wait. I made them wait half an hour for me out there. If I work for them they'll make me wait three hours." He won't be anyone's Gurkha. Besides, on his current salary, supplemented by the smart investments his friends have made for him, "we have established a lifestyle. We have what we need, and more won't make a difference. I don't mind these cars and everything being taken away."

"Do you want Rahul to be a police officer?" I ask.

"No. Never." He wants his son to get an MBA or become a doctor. He wouldn't mind if he went into the civil service or the foreign service, but not the IPS. "I know what price I have had to pay. If I could do it again," says the winner of the President's Medal for Meritorious Service for his work in detecting the Bombay blasts, "I would have called in sick on the day they assigned me the bomb-blasts case."

So why doesn't he do something else? Start a business, for example?

And then Ajay admits it. After all the tortured explanations of study abroad and threats to his life and redeeming of parental honor, he finally spells out his doom, gives me the inescapable "The End" of his story: "If you ask me, I don't think I can do anything else but this. I can't do anything else but be a cop."

Black-Collar Workers

THE SLAUGHTER WILL CONTINUE for three days. Thousands of goats and cattle have been brought to Madanpura, in central Bombay, for the Bakri Id festival. Girish has been invited for the feast by his good friend and occasional business partner Ishaq, another young entrepreneur, and Girish and I set out in a taxi. The streetscape as you approach Madanpura becomes heterogeneous, kaleidoscopic. A sign just before the overpass at Bombay Central heralds DR. GANJAWALA, ANESTHETIST. On the main street of Madanpura, you see a bonesetter next to a hotel next to a chemist next to an eatery making kababs on coals next to Ishaq's STD booth, where people can make long-distance calls. There are thousands of small workshops here making blow lamps, belt buckles, textile machinery parts, and a myriad of small but essential items that keep Bombay's economy humming. The roads are in danger of being overwhelmed from the Bihari slums spilling out over the sidewalks on either side. The back alleys have lots of mosques, one for each sect. There are boundaries everyone knows that separate the Muslim and Hindu areas. Before the riots, there were many Hindus in the Muslim area and vice versa. After 1993, the minority community on each side started selling out and leaving. The segregation is almost complete. "Mini-Pakistan," people in the city call Madanpura.

Sitting in the rough but air-conditioned office of Ishaq's stove-parts factory, his cousin Shahbuddin, a movie-star-handsome doctor in his twenties, explains to me the meaning of Id-ul-Adha. "When Allah mia called upon Ibrahim to sacrifice his son, Ibrahim took him to the mountain. He closed his eyes, raised the sword, and when he was ready to bring it down, he saw a goat standing in his son's place. The festival means that you have to sacrifice something to God that is dear to you."

We go outside.

A young bull is led to an open space in front of the factories. It belongs to a pipe fitter who is extra grateful to God this year; for he has narrowly escaped extortion by a gang. They phoned him and then came to his factory, looking for him. He wasn't there then, but the gang told his workers they would shoot him if he didn't pay two lakhs. The pipe fitter called Ishaq. Ishaq and his men waited for the gang, armed with iron rods. But the gangsters didn't show up, and the pipe fitter bought a bull for 20,000 rupees and is about to give a public demonstration of his thanks to God.

The children are brought out. "The children should see," says Dr. Shahbuddin. The animal is toppled to the ground and its head yanked back, its legs tied up. A one-year-old child is placed on the bull, then lifted up again. The imam asks in whose name the sacrifice is to be offered and is given a piece of paper. He reads seven names aloud and says a prayer. Then a man, not a professional butcher, draws a knife across the beast's neck. I am watching from the ladder leading to Ishaq's office, so I have a vantage point as the throat opens up, the blood gushes out, and the suddenly white arteries quiver madly. There is involuntary movement all over the animal's body; the head is jerking, the feet are twitching. "The meat will keep trembling at home," one of the men says to another. The muscle movements might continue for over an hour, during which time the meat will be dressed and put on the table, ready to be cooked. On the kitchen counter it may suddenly spasm, especially the outer muscles.

In the broad street behind the factory, the road is sloppy with blood. I see another bullock being dragged by a gang of men. A rope has been dragged through its nostrils, and they are trying to topple it over. They tie up its front and rear feet and push. The beast goes over, but somehow it struggles and gets up again. With a jerk, the bull is splayed out again. One of the men holds its mouth closed. Another comes up with a foot-long sharpened blade. The spectators crowd around; it is still early on the first day. There are lots of very young children. The bull struggles a bit, there is a deep rumble from the depths of its being, and then the blade is drawn with one swift motion across a vein. A torrent of blood gushes out, they pull its head and body in opposite directions, and the whole neck is open to the street, blood streaming out in bucketfuls, all over the clothes of the professionals. The fresh blood has an unreal color about it, as if it is paint; it is not the deep red of a few moments later but a light, bright pinkish-red. A bucket of water is brought and splashed into the bull's exposed throat, to keep the blood from clotting. The head and the body struggle separately. They leave it there for a few moments for the blood to drain out, then commence cutting the carcass. When a sack in its stomach is cut, it releases gobs of warm dung, mixing with the blood and the entrails. Next to it, another bull's carcass, its skin cut away, suddenly releases a stream of yellow liquid; fifteen minutes after it has lost its head, the torso is pissing.

As the fur and the skin and the flesh are cut away in layers, the animals' bodies reveal treasures in multiple vivid colors: the brownish-red of the liver; the elegant white-and-red stripes of the inside of the rib cage; the brown, white, black of the fur; the crystal of the eyes; the pure cream of the intestines, unfurled. I see the marvelous arrangement of the cow's body within and without, the complex cornucopia of its insides, the fine differentiation of the organs, each admirably suited to its purpose. All this had been working in tandem a minute before, and now each part is freed from the yoke of the mind and acts independently, twitching, pissing, growing, hardening. Now they will go their separate ways. After one cow is slaughtered, the children pull at the white fat inside its body; it stretches like an elastic sheet. A man pokes the open eye of the dead animal; its mouth suddenly opens in reflex, showing a line of teeth. The man repeats his gesture; the mouth opens again.

One thing surprises me: Of the thousands of animals, live and dead, in these streets, there is no sound. No bleating of the terrified goats, no bellowing of the cattle. The killing takes place right next to the live beasts; a massive bullock goes on chewing grass while another is brought to its side right next to it. Similarly with the goats. Don't the animals sense something, the stink of slaughter all around them? Aside from a slight trembling that I see in one goat, and a curious silence, there is no reaction. They look, if anything, depressed. One bull allows itself to be brought to its side and lies there waiting for the knife with its eyes open. When the blade is drawn across its throat, it doesn't even struggle.

Grinning children run barefoot through the streets deep with blood, holding the freshly cut heads, all the eyes open. There are groups of municipal garbage collectors who take away the waste entrails, the dung-filled stomach sacs. Huge dumps are filled with these carcasses. A man stands inside a municipal garbage container, cutting a big animal's insides, disposing of the remains right inside the container around his feet. Cats and dogs are having a feast on the leftovers. At the corner there are the knife sellers, and a man on a bicycle with a knife-sharpening wheel attached. As he pedals, the wheel spins; as he holds the blade at an angle to the wheel, a stream of sparks flows in one direction.

The Muslims of this area are sensualists. On festival days and at weddings, the older folks take a napkin, anoint it with attar, put a pellet of opium on the tip, and stick it inside their ear. Then they can be high all evening. On the streets outside, the children of the Bihari slums, dressed in their best—like one little boy in a brown suit with a black bow tie stitched on—are being given rides in small hand-turned Ferris wheels. Men are playing games on the sidewalk. A ring is tossed over a group of toys and gadgets; if your ring lands and completely encircles, say, a deck of playing cards, the deck is yours. The narrow streets are slippery with blood and shit, the filthiest time of the year in the filthiest part of the city. On the road leading to the factory I notice a dead squashed rat, covered with flies. An open manhole reveals huge red cockroaches ringing the tunnel. The animal hides are stacked and put in front of mosques, for charity. Men walk about with reddened shirts; they look as if they've been playing Holi.

According to the laws, cattle are supposed to be slaughtered only in the Deonar abattoir. A truckful of policemen looks on as the bulls are slaughtered in front of their eyes. The cattle that I see are all bullocks, though the doctor says that, since the cow is cheaper and more delicate, they prefer that meat, and some are smuggled in against the laws and slaughtered here. "It is against the feelings of the other community," he says. "If they find out, in one hour there would be a riot."

There is none of the usual western avoidance of the fact of death behind the dressed-up food on the plate; the animal is brought in live, and you see the before and after. You see exactly which part of the animal's insides a cut of meat comes from. You see the beast struggle to stay upright as it's brought down; you see its eyes open wide as the men sit on its body; you see the desperate gasping and trembling of the body after the blood has left it. Before this, I have seen killing only on the Discovery Channel. But now here it is: in full view, in the open street, in the broad day. When I see my first cow slaughtered I feel sick inside; I want to go and stop it. I have been a vegetarian for some eleven years now. But I cannot tear myself away. I climb over a handcart, to get a better view. I look at my blue denim shirt as the man hacks at the bull's carcass with an ax. A bright red droplet of blood has landed on the blue and stands there, solid. I am afraid to touch it. After a while it turns black, and then it is harmless, just another black speck.

The freshly killed meat is supposed to taste better than the flesh killed in distant countries, many months or years ago. Hunters must get this charge, but it is nothing like this; the rifle confers the privilege of distance. This is the most direct form of hunting, where you plunge the knife straight into the neck of the struggling animal and rip its body apart with your own hands. The men are all eager, happy to participate in the killing and the carving up. The laborers in Ishaq's factory are in a good mood. This is the beginning of a three-day holiday, a holiday in the city, for there isn't enough time to go back to the village. All day long, there is just the killing and the feasting. All the poor will be fed, and fed well, on fresh meat; three-fourths will be distributed to them. The bullock meat is tough, and most of it is made into seekh kababs and mincemeat. The goat meat is more tender. The chickens in their cages in the market are safe for the next few days.

It is hot, baking hot, and the meat lies in the open streets. After the carcasses are cut, they are left on the street or in the gutters where they have fallen. Then they are dragged over the surface of the road on their way to people's homes or to the Gulf countries, where a lot of the meat is exported. I don't see a freezer anywhere. By midmorning, a lot of this will be in people's stomachs, the one animal going into the other. In the workshop, I see a man wring out a long tube from a goat's inside; a shower of hard black droplets of dung falls out into a bucket. Then he chops up the edible parts of the goat and throws them into the same bucket, where they mix again with the dung.

There will be feasting for three continuous days. "In the evening of the third day," says the doctor, "we go out to a hotel and eat vegetarian food."

Inside his factory, Ishaq shows off his pet goat. He is feeding the goat mutton. He laughs. "It will eat anything." Its diet over the last year included tea and cigarettes. He has developed feelings for the goat. On the day after tomorrow he will slaughter it.

I see children leading baby goats—kids—through the lanes, petting them, feeding them lettuce leaves. A worker in Ishaq's factory, dressed in white just before he steps into the washing pit to kill a goat whose horns have been painted green, says these animals are lucky, because they are being killed for religion—"they are happy"—whereas all the others are killed just for food. That's why they aren't making any sounds, he says. He goes into the pit and hacks at the goat's throat, and the blood pours out on his white clothes, making him red all over.

In his village, the doctor says, he has killed goats dear to him. "It is best to sacrifice a goat that you have raised from infancy, that you have developed love for." At the moment of sacrifice, he says, the religious sentiment overpowers the reluctance to kill the one you love. "Not what they do here: buy the animal the day before, that they don't even know, so the only sacrifice is of your money. All this blood you see today—Allah doesn't like that." They are eating mutton right now, Shahbuddin and Ishaq, dipping chunks of pav into the meat. It is liver. Some people prize the liver, others the heart, others the thick soup that is made of cattle hooves, which is supposed to give strength to the eater; the doctor prefers the muscle of a cow's udder.

Shahbuddin says, "If animals could speak a human language, then very few would be cut." He is trying to defend the practice. He believes he has a soft heart, he says, and so these things affect him. But his religion believes that every single thing on earth was created by Allah for the enjoyment of man, and so if animals weren't meant to be slaughtered and eaten, what are they here for? "If someone can prove to me that animals aren't created for the use of human beings, I'll give it up." He asks me: Some people believe it's okay to kill a chicken but not a goat. Why is that? I answer that it's because the goat has a greater capacity for pain. But to an ant, responds Shahbuddin, its pain is as great and its life has the same value as that of an elephant. "But you may ask me why I won't eat meat that's not halal. You may say that the meat is the same; what's the difference if one has a prayer said over it?" He is willing to admit doubt into his belief system. At any rate, he is thinking about the slaughter going on outside, and ever so gently he is addressing my unasked questions.

Mohsin: The D-Company

Ishaq and Shahbuddin—whose clinic is just down the road from Ishaq's shop—are originally from Azamgarh, in Uttar Pradesh, which is famous for its criminals, such as the D-Company lieutenant Abu Salem, who was born there. I am talking to them about an article on Azamgarh that appeared recently in the paper. It mentioned its reputation as the money-laundering capital of India. "We ourselves did it!" chorus Shahbuddin and Ishaq. Shahbuddin's grandfather was a big hawala operator. Money would be given to him in rupees; he would phone Saudi Arabia and, through a code, instruct the operator there to disburse a sum of rials to the receiving party. "In any crime anywhere in the world, if investigated thoroughly, the name of Azamgarh will come in somewhere," declares the doctor. In Azamgarh, says Ishaq, the panwallahs do a side trade in guns. You can buy an AK-47, smuggled from Nepal, from a pan stand for 65,000 rupees. "Why do people keep AK-47s?" I ask him.

"Just. As a hobby," he explains.

Madanpura, too, is famous for its gangs. "They've distributed the business," notes Dr. Shahbuddin. "Someone is in property, someone in killing, someone in kidnapping." The kids around here will murder for 5,000 rupees. They do it out of poverty, but they take the money and flaunt it in the beer bars, throwing it at the girls. After the murder there's no life left for them. They are hunted by the police. They might even be hunted by the very people who have commissioned the murder.

"Any man who is doing these inhuman things is deceiving himself," Asad bin Saif of the peace group had told me about the Hindus of the Sena who had killed during the riots. It was interesting how he had put it: "deceiving himself" rather than "deceiving God" or "deceiving humanity." There is a gulf between the human heart and murder, and I was intent on seeing the bridges men build for themselves over that gulf. I had met the rioters and the encounter specialists, and I now sought out the professional murderers of the gangwar, men who deceive themselves every day of their lives.

ONE AFTERNOON, I sit down in a dhaba, a cheap eatery, in Madanpura and order Pepsis for myself, Ishaq, and Anees, a fair-complexioned, enthusiastic young man who grew up with Ishaq. Anees tells me about the war in the underworld that has so far, in 1998, officially claimed two hundred lives. He is "company touch"—not officially in the D-Company but associated with them, available for small works. He has a friend who is a shooter in the Dawood gang, a professional murderer. I ask Anees if I might meet him. He agrees but says it will have to be in a public place, which he will not tell me about beforehand.

A couple of days later I am met in Ishaq's shop and walked into the Venus Café, below the Maratha Mandir cinema hall. It is a modern, brightly lit place, open to the street, filled with couples waiting for their movie to start. With Anees this time is a small thin man with a mustache, whose name is given to me as Mohsin. Anees leans forward. "He's done two murders."

"Seven and a half!" Mohsin immediately says, offended. "Seven and a half!"

"Seven and a half." Anees corrects himself.

We order coffee and juice. There is a party of young English girls at a booth behind us, travelers from the station next door. They may be waiting for a night train out of Bombay. They are not molested in this café, or even commented upon. This is not Delhi. Behind us Ishaq and another boy sit on the single bench, facing our backs, like the coachmen on the back of a carriage.

Mohsin is another of Ishaq's childhood friends. Ishaq has seen him after a decade, and later tells me, "We used to mock him when he was a kid." He could be anybody, the lift man, the peon in my uncle's office, any one of the people walking on the sidewalk as I pass in my car. But he has a murderer's eyes, dark, glinting. He meets my eyes, and if I lower them to look at my notebook to write something he touches my hand lightly with his. I have to look him in the eyes.

Of the seven and a half "open" cases against him—the ones the police have registered—six and a half were done on behalf of the gang, and one was a freelance job. His first murder was in 1991—he stabbed a man fourteen times, but the victim lived. That was the half murder. The next one was a liquor seller, Philips Daruwala, and that was the first proper murder. After that, there were five more that the police know about. "The ones that are not open only I know." If he is caught, he says, "at least ten to fifteen murders will be charged to my name." When he kills, he likes to take "a big wicket"—someone whose death will frighten ten others.

His own company is arranged in groups of cells. One person doesn't know what the other is doing; it's all organized from Dubai. His weekly expenses are 20,000 rupees: 10,000 goes to his mobile phone bills, 5,000 for himself—mostly for charas—and the rest is given to his family. When he is in need of a big sum, he will take on a supari, a contract killing, which will bring in two lakhs: half in advance, half on performance. If the man to be killed is a non-Muslim, he will kill him right away. But if he is Muslim, Mohsin will find out if the matter is correct, if the man is in the wrong; if not, he will walk away from the contract, giving up the second half of the money.

"I'm doing this for Islam," Mohsin explains. "During the riots, it was a matter of our izzat"—honor. If there had been no Hindu–Muslim issue, there would be no gangwar. After the blasts, he points out, Chotta Rajan had said that anyone who escaped the law wouldn't escape him. "I am not a literate man. If I had a brain I wouldn't be doing all these things. In jail they did readings of the Koran, which is where I learnt everything." He is not afraid of death, because if he dies he will become close to Allah; he will become a shaheed. "I had dreams, but now they're broken. I've left everything up to Allah Malik. Everyone has to die. I have gone to kill so many people and they've lived, maybe I'll live too."

The party of English girls behind us suddenly bursts out into "Happy Birthday to You!"

After the meeting in the café we walk about a bit through the streets of Madanpura. There is plenty of light from all the shops, but it is a tinny kind of light, like the music coming out of the radios. Outside the Bihari slums, a class of Muslim kids on the footpath, all loudly and enthusiastically reciting their multiplication tables, is being led by a young teacher marking time with a stick. Mohsin has now relaxed a bit and tells me he is to get married on the sixteenth of this month. At first the girl's parents were reluctant, but since everybody in the neighborhood seems to be enlisting in the gangwar, they've given their consent, saying, "If it's in the girl's fate to marry him, she will do so."

We agree to meet again, for a longer period, someplace more private.

AFTER LUNCHTIME a few days later, seven of us walk into the lobby of a small hotel in Byculla. Ishaq, Shahbuddin, Girish, and I get into the elevator, along with Mohsin, Anees, and another young man, even thinner than Mohsin, who seems to be his apprentice. In the beginning, I am faintly irritated by Ishaq and Shahbuddin's presence; I think they have come there for the food and drink I order up to the room I have rented for the day. Then I understand. They are standing guarantee for me, as well as making sure I won't get shot dead.

The hotel is owned by a retired Pathan gangster who used to be Dawood Ibrahim's mentor, they tell me. Every street in this part of central Bombay is mythic for the underworld. In the modern air-conditioned room, Mohsin takes off his shoes and sits comfortably on the bed. He is dressed in a lightweight shirt and black jeans. The others arrange themselves on the sofa and around Mohsin on the bed. Girish shouldn't be here; he's supposed to be meeting with a sales prospect in Andheri. But this is more important than business. It is why Girish will always be a bad businessman. He finds his own city too fascinating.

I take a chair opposite Mohsin and start up my laptop. I am careful to refer to these guys in the formal "aap" rather than the familiar "tu," which everybody in Bombay uses. It confirms my outsider status and also gives them a certain measure of respect from a man of the other Bombay.

Trust is very important, says Mohsin, looking at me. "The Muslim boys are trustworthy, but they are also the greatest traitors. When you come into this line, you have to have trust. I have come here"—he means this hotel room—"on trust. I have come here because of my friend," and he indicates Ishaq. "Otherwise, if I were to see anybody else with a computer, I'd take it and tell him to fuck off."

I tell him that I am also here on trust, that I realize he can take my computer at any time. I have to let him have that at the very beginning, acknowledge that in this room at this time in the city of Bombay, it is he who has the power, and I, the nonresident Indian from Malabar Hill, am inferior to him in the order of things. He does not need to exercise his power, but he does need it to be recognized, to be put into words.

Mohsin started out working with a smuggler in Andheri, gold biscuits mostly, when he was a teenager—he is twenty-eight now. When his pockets started getting pleasantly filled, he began visiting the beer bars. When the government liberalized gold imports, the biscuit business crashed, and Mohsin went to Baroda and robbed a bank. He was arrested. "They put big photos of us in the paper," he says with pride. He got out on 15,000 rupees' bail, but the money from the robbery was confiscated. In jail, a friend had given him a phone number. "He said, talk to Shakeel Bhai." And thus, five years ago, Mohsin came into the D-Company. Now he still does a little gold business, but mostly he's into extortion and ransom. The Company is a sort of tax collector. "All in the film industry give money to Shakeel. The Company takes money from all: builder, director, financier. If the call comes from Dubai, it doesn't matter who you put in between—a minister or whoever—but you have to pay."

Mohsin explains the benefits of being in the Company very simply: "If someone shoots me, at least one lakh will come to my home. If I am hit by a taxi, nothing will come to my home." A friend of his, Afzal, was killed by the police. When his sister was married six months later, Shakeel sent three lakhs to her. When Mohsin came out of jail, his mother had died and his brother was to get married. The bhai sent him 50,000 rupees for the wedding and told him, "If you want more, call."

"I only have to open my mouth to get money," Mohsin says with confidence. "If I want a car for a while it is arranged." Because the gangwar is a paying proposition, there is a glut of shooters in Bombay; the Biharis have come in and are driving down the rates. "They've fucked our mothers. Now everyone wants to join the Company."

Anees, unlike the others, has a notion of the economic injustice of the way the gangs are organized. "In Dubai the sheths get crores for work they pay one lakh to the boy here to do."

Mohsin has three enemies: Chotta Rajan's men, the police, and the informants. If the gangwar men can kidnap an informer, they torture him before killing him. Otherwise they shoot him where they find him. Nowadays the police are giving informants powerful guns to protect themselves. Mohsin had been "given the work of"—told to kill—Husain Vastara, an informant in the bomb blasts and close to Ajay Lal, my policeman friend. Vastara was extremely cautious and rarely ventured out of his lair in Pydhonie. Some of the newer police commandos are only now starting to wear bulletproof vests as they go into the gangwar, says Mohsin. Husain Vastara was a gangster who wore a bulletproof vest.

Mohsin is a seasoned shooter, and he has developed a maxim for his work: "You should know a man's hobbies if you want to kill him." A man can stop work, but he cannot stop pursuing his hobbies. Vastara had a great love of cricket; he went out to watch a match. His bodyguards were drinking tea as Mohsin drove up on his motorcycle. "I went up and shot at him.

My equipment locked. He had a look of great fear. His face had the look of death." Mohsin turned around and sped off on his motorcycle; he had not been recognized. The bad gun had saved Vastara's life for the moment.

Mohsin's immediate boss is Mohammed Ali, a Hindu who converted to Islam so as to improve his career prospects in the D-Company. "He runs Bombay for Chotta Shakeel." The next day Mohsin and Mohammed Ali, who is related to Vastara, went to Vastara's office and sat down to chat. Vastara brought out a gun. "He was moving his pistol around, aiming first at one of us, then the other." His arm swept in a wide arc, like a pendulum, stopping in front of one face, pausing, then moving back to the other face. The two were frightened. After they left the office, they called Vastara from a pay phone. Vastara said to Mohsin, "I know you two came to shoot me." Mohsin hung up the phone and said to Mohammed Ali, "Let's run."

They hid out in a social club in Grant Road, the Dana Club, and played cards. The phone rang; it was for them. When they picked up the instrument they heard Vastara's voice. "It's not good to play cards so much," Vastara told them. Now they were really scared. How did he know where they were? They phoned Shakeel and asked him what to do. "Who else knew where you were?" the bhai asked. Stanley knew. Stanley was the lead shooter of their cell. Shakeel called Stanley and asked him how Vastara could have known that Moshin and Mohammed Ali were playing cards in the club. There was something off about the way Stanley answered the bhai's questions; it was not right. So Shakeel called Mohsin back and said, "Shoot him." They went looking for Stanley and found him, standing on the road.

"First shot I hit him, *dhadam!* He held up his hand to stop the bullet when the gun came up. The first shot was on his heart—the second on the other side—the third in the neck—the fourth in the stomach. Mohammed Ali held up his head by the hair and emptied his gun into his head. Then we walked away. All the people had run away while we were shooting. This was in Narialwadi, five minutes from here. We walked to Rani Bagh and took the bus to Wadala. Then we came back at night and had a good dinner in Bhendi Bazaar. We ate quail. Then we played carom. We forgot we had done any work."

This was two years ago. Mohammed Ali got caught for the murder, but not Mohsin. When Mohsin read about Ali's arrest in the paper, he knew that he too would be caught before long. Mohammed Ali gave up Mohsin's name. "I have no enmity toward him; he was beaten." And Vastara? "He's still there. But when the Company wants some work to be done, it will be done, if not today, then tomorrow." And sure enough, a few months later, Vastara was shot dead by another D-Company hit man as he was coming out of his mistress's building. Shakeel had found out another of his hobbies.

Mohsin explains his work technique. "Most of the time we shoot for the head, the head shot. Then there is no tension about whether he'll live or die." Except once, when he shot a man near Bombay Central. "I put the gun to his head and fired. The bullet glanced off his forehead and he lived. Now what can I do? My job is to shoot and kill. I try to kill. What can I do if the bullet slips?" He likes to take his time. "If I can kill him at leisure I will do so. If I have to kill and run, then only the Man Upstairs knows whether he'll live or die."

Mohsin uses a .38, with anywhere between seven and nine rounds. For those who can't afford the imported guns, there is the katta, the country-made gun, used to shoot deer. "The hole it makes in the front is very small, but in the back it is huge. The bullet spins as it enters the flesh. After you fire two or three bullets from it, you have to let it cool down. If you fire it more than that, your hand blows off." When Mohsin doesn't or can't use a gun, he uses a razor or a chopper. For the half murder in 1991, Mohsin used a khanjar, a short dagger. I ask him if he needs strength to use a knife to stab through muscle and bone. "Have you ever cut a watermelon?" Mohsin asks of me. "It's the same. A man's flesh is so delicate."

The second man on the bike, the assistant in a shooting, is called "number-kari." Chotta Shakeel pioneered the use of motorbikes to execute gangwar hits; now all the companies use them. "We stop the bike and do it. The motor is racing. The man shoots and gets on. A third man is always standing by, silent. If he is needed he will come; otherwise, the public doesn't know about him. If he is needed, he starts shooting and the public thinks we are everywhere." Unlike hit men in more advanced countries, Mohsin never has to worry about disposal of the bodies. He just leaves them where they fall and zooms away on the bike.

WHEN HE WENT TO kill Philips Daruwala, Mohsin had typhoid. When you have a fever, he notes, your mind operates on another level, and then to have to go out and kill someone can be a special experience. It was Ramadan, and he had to do the work alone. Daruwala was a man of some style, wearing safari suits and black sunglasses, and he had a Doberman who was constantly with him. During the riots he had given money and arms to the Hindus. The order came down to do the work on him. Even though Mohsin was sick, he had to do it, the work was very important. When Mohsin rose from his sickbed and went to Daruwala's liquor shop, he found uniformed policemen sitting with him. Mohsin went away and came back in the evening. There were still men around Daruwala, but they were in plainclothes. Mohsin didn't know that they were also policemen from the Crime Branch, come to collect their bribes as they did every Saturday. He followed Daruwala as he left the dog and his visitors to take a leak inside a country liquor bar next door. As he was pissing, Mohsin came up behind him in the bathroom and raised his hand with the gun. It would have been an easy shot, but Mohsin was suddenly struck with a scruple: A man, he thought, should not be shot while he was pissing. He would wait for him to finish.

Daruwala zipped up and turned around and saw the gun staring him in the face. "His face was death." But Mohsin's weapon locked. "I was also frightened. I should have shot him in the back the first time." He reloaded, fired again, and shot him in the head. Daruwala stumbled out onto the road and fell. "Then I loaded again—*dhadam*, *dhadam*—fired twice, and left."

Daruwala's men ran after Mohsin; he fired once at them, and they fled. But then the Crime Branch cops got into their car and went after him. As he was being chased, Mohsin raised his hand with the gun in their direction. The driver swerved and turned, and Mohsin jumped into a passing taxi. When he got home, his fever was raging. "I put my blanket on and went to sleep."

Mohsin was not arrested for Daruwala's murder, but he has been for others. If the cops find Mohsin, they'll ring up Shakeel and ask how much he's willing to pay to get his shooter released. If the negotiations fail, the police will torture him. He tells me what has been done to him. The police handcuffed his hands behind his legs, inserted a stick in between his knees, and balanced the stick on the backs of two chairs, so he was hanging in the air like a pig on a poke. Then they lined up on either side of him and took their shots at him as he swung back and forth. His eyelids were propped open all night with matchsticks. Then there was a portable generator; clamps were attached to his fingers, earlobes, and genitals, a wheel was turned, emitting sparks, and his skinny body trembled and jumped as the twelve-volt electric shocks coursed through it. "Doing that causes an effect on the mind," Anees explains.

Once, in the station, the cops tied one end of a pair of handcuffs to Mohsin's foot and hung him upside down from the ceiling. This was supposed to be only a temporary measure. But there was a procession outside, protesting something or other, and the cops had to go deal with it. "I hung like that for four hours. My entire leg was swollen. I forgot I had a foot."

He holds up his hand, spreading out his palm, showing us the effect of the police's attentions to it. "Not one finger is straight." Dr. Shahbuddin looks at it with professional interest.

The police will have a good amount to drink while they're beating their prisoners. When someone is being beaten, everyone in the police station clusters around. "It's like when a goat is being killed, how people come around to see." In the interrogations, the police try to scare the captives. One trick they use with simple men is to bring out a lemon and a knife. Then they tell the suspect, We will cut a lemon on your head and it will affect your brain, and you will tell us everything. This works with the superstitious; as they see the cop approach their skull with the lemon and begin to cut it over them, the juice spurting out over their exposed head, they might babble out everything. But not Mohsin. "I said, Then why beat me? Just cut the lemon." Then they really got angry. He cursed them. He had already appeared in court, so he couldn't be killed in an encounter, he informed his tormentors. This is one of the rules governing encounters, recognized and followed by cops and criminals alike. If a judge is aware that a man is alive and in police custody, he stays alive.

Mohsin has three men left in his group within the larger gang. The other five have been shot dead by the police in encounters. According to Mohsin, it had been ordered by the state government that whoever has two cases against him should be shot in an encounter. By this standard, Mohsin is five and a half cases overdue. The weapon the cops leave by the side of the encounter victim is an indication of his status. With a junior person in the gangwar, they'll leave a "sixer." For a person of more importance, they'll leave a Mauser. For the big guys, the real bhais, it'll be a submachine gun, an AK-47 or AK-56.

Two waiters come into the room bearing trays of sandwiches. We stop talking till they leave.

Mohsin is now a year out of jail, where he spent three very comfortable years. "I was stoned throughout." There were separate quarters for the gangwar boys. He enjoyed charas and Phensydril, a potent cough syrup. The Company sent him 7,000 rupees a month for his expenses in jail, and a further 10,000 to his family. The jail had all the facilities for the Company men, including TV and a carom board, around which the stoned gangsters whiled away their time. Twice a day, their tiffin came from the Company. They could get girls, booze; all it took was to pay the "customs"—bribe the guards. Those who have nobody in Bombay to give them money for their expenses in jail resort to another means of income: "They sell their behinds."

In jail, the people who had been in the business of girls and brown sugar—heroin—are beaten up and money extorted from them. The brown sugar is sold out of sacks behind V.T. Station by the Africans between four and five in the morning. The police are afraid of the brown-sugar people. They throw their own shit at the cops; they cut themselves with blades before a court appearance and tell the judge the police did it. In 1993, there was a riot in Nashik jail, where Mohsin was lodged at the time. Indians are fed first in the jail, then the foreigners. An African threw hot dal on a guard's face, and there was a riot. The jail guards hit the black men with their iron-tipped bamboo sticks, to no effect. Then one African swung at a guard, and the guard was immediately knocked out. The riot was out of control; the guards had lost power. So they opened the gate of the gang-sters from Bombay and let them loose in the African cells. The Bombay wallahs rushed in with homemade knives and started slashing the Africans left and right. "The matter was finished. Two Negroes were killed. No records were kept of the crime. In jail there is wild justice."

Mohsin is about to get married. After his wedding, he might do some "good work," as opposed to the kind he's doing now: "Some factory, something. I can live under another name somewhere else." And he can always flee the country. After a big work, a valuable shooter will go from Bombay to Dubai and thence to Karachi. They have connections with the police at the Bombay airport.

At this point, Girish decides to try his hand at reforming the hit man. "You are getting married. Now at least stop."

Mohsin is not swayed by his plea. "I have to earn my expenses for the wedding." His fiancée has said the same thing to him: Leave all this. And Mohsin put forward a challenge to her: "If you have the power, make me leave all this." It is a love marriage; the girl is his cousin. After the wedding he has to go to Surat to avenge an assault on one of his men, Yasin. He was in the middle of drinking a sip of water, and his enemies had come at him with a sword; "his head opened up, all his teeth came into his hands." He was left for dead, and now Mohsin has to go to Surat. It is a matter of personal honor, not a Company matter. "My izzat is there."

"He will not improve," predicts Anees, in front of Mohsin.

I hear water running in the bathroom behind me. The doctor is taking a shower. He had been sitting quietly on the sofa, through all the talk of torture and murder, staring with purpose at the bathroom. I remember what he once told me about water in Madanpura, explaining why he doesn't like living in Bombay. "Every morning I have to decide; if I bathe, there won't be enough water left to drink in the evening." When confronted with a bathroom that has running water, and hot water at that, he has decided to make the most of it. He takes his time in the shower and comes out glowing.

Mohsin and Anees speak of the criminal associations of their community with pride, the pride of an oppressed minority that fights back and dares to venture in the illicit "outline" trades. "The outline people are mostly Mussulmans, because today the most money trouble is felt by young Muslims. Mussulmans are in beer bars, gangwar. . . . Mussulmans are not less in anything." Anees points out that for the whole month of Ramadan, the beer bars are closed or half empty—during that month, they won't even swallow their spit—and then "on Eid, the beer bars are houseful with Mussulmans."

These criminal associations do not go unnoticed by the Bombay Police, of whom only 5 percent are Muslim. "Very bad curses they say to us," Anees tells me. "They call us traitors to the nation, betrayers." But they were born here. If there is trouble, asks Mohsin, where are they going to run? He is ready to fight for the country. He sees his work in the underworld as "not a matter of the nation but a matter of the qaum," of the universal nation of Islam. The riots, and the political party that instigated them, are always on Mohsin's mind. He refers to Thackeray as "the main wicket." The D-Company is watching the goings-on around the Babri

Masjid very closely. If there is more trouble over the mosque it won't be
like last time; this time they are prepared and will respond instantly. Many
people in far places will die. The gangs have stockpiled equipment. "We
have a rocket launcher, but we haven't used it." Stinger missiles from the
Afghan war have been distributed over the subcontinent, held in reserve
for the next big riot.

The group discusses the previous night, when the police had called
a few of the Madanpura boys to the meeting of the Ekta Committee,
designed to prevent Hindu–Muslim riots. There was a lafda, a strike; the
boys had noticed a lot of police running around but they didn't go. The
tension is building every day. Mohsin speaks with fear of the times ahead.
"What we can't imagine will happen." The next affair, Mohsin says, will
happen all over the world, a global war of Islam against its enemies. They
have numbers and geography on their side. "Muslims are everywhere.
Hindus are only in India," he points out. They are on the right side of
history.

One of the Muslim men agrees, telling me, "If you really want to see
the mujahideen, you have to go to Palestine. There, even nine-year-old
boys carry AK-47s." He recites the international rosary of the jihad: Palestine, Afghanistan, Kashmir, Bosnia. I have heard this before, in a mosque in
Brooklyn, in the imam's sermon: the careful perusal of every Islamic struggle worldwide, the bugles of distant battles, a sense of a global wrong.
These are the street skirmishes in the larger worldwide war, a war that has
been going on for centuries, beginning in an obscure hot place among people convinced that there was a good and there was an evil, and evil had
to be fought and good defended. The lives of the young Muslims in the
gangwar are given meaning by this fight, not to convert the kafirs—the
infidels—but to protect their own honor. It is a sentiment that has been
transmitted, nearly intact, across enemy lines to Sunil and the Sena boys,
who think of themselves as all that stands between the Islamic hordes and
us. "All you Marwaris, Gujaratis, you people living in Malabar Hill, if
it weren't for us you would have been finished off long ago." Both sides
see what is happening in Bombay today as only the latest in a long series of
historic battles. Bombay is where worlds collide; it is their Tours, their
Kosovo, their Panipat. Here the line will be drawn, in this Hindu nation
ringed by Islamic countries.

The TV is on in the hotel room and is showing a gangster movie,

Parinda. The movie was directed by Vidhu Vinod Chopra, whom I had not yet met. A man is being killed in a hair oil factory. "This shot is very good," says Mohsin. They all watch the screen with interest. "Look how his blood mixes with the oil." The police are interrogating the murderer. "Where did that man go?" they ask. Answers the killer, "He is in the Worli gutter." Ever since this movie, "He is in the Worli gutter" has become underworld slang for "He has been killed."

My technique for getting the gangwar boys to tell me their stories is simple: I am going to put their lives in the movies. This is no lie on my part; I am in touch with directors who want me to work with them on films about the underworld. It is up to me to get the stories. Can an outlaw life be made legitimate if turned into art, into myth?

The boys tell me that, for authenticity in my picture, my characters must use the proper bhai language. There is one word for work, sex, and death in the Bombay underworld: kaam. "Uska kaam kiya" can mean "I killed him," "I fucked her," or "I worked for him."

Over time, the necessity of hiding their activities from the police has led the underworld to develop an entire numerology of slang. Each number from 1 to 40 has an equivalent in bhai language. For example, a girl or "item" is, in this argot, chabbis (26). Her boyfriend is her chhava. A girl is also paaya, paneri, or chawal: rice, which can be of different qualities, as in "This is basmati chawal." She dances in "school"—a beer bar. Nalli jhatakna refers to the male orgasm. Screwing is atkana.

A gun, not surprisingly, is known by many names: samaan (equipment), bartan (vessel), mithai (sweet), baja (musical instrument), dhatu (metal), chappal (sandal), sixer, chakri. Very often, it is called a ghoda (horse); it is as dear and crucial to a shooter as a horse to a medieval warrior. A submachine gun or, as Mohsin refers to it, a "gun machine," is also called a guitar, spray, or jhadu, for its sweeping disposal of targets. A small gun is called, endearingly, amma; the bullets, her offspring, bacche. A bullet is also called tablet, capsule, or dana (grain). A hand grenade is a potato, stone, or pomegranate. A sword is lambi—the tall one.

One euphemism for a killing is "outdoor shooting," as in a movie. The sheth tells his boys, "Wet his head" or "Total him." For a hit in which the body should disappear: "Uska potla kar de" or "Parcel kar de," as in "Parcel him out of this world." Another version of the same order is "Kamti kar do"—minus him, or lessen him. The term supari became associated with contract killing from the tradition of giving pan and supari at festive occasions such as weddings. Before the shooter is sent out on a mission, he is often given a bit of betel nut for good luck.

To have sex with a girl—bajaana—is to play with her. It could also be thokna (hitting) or gaadi chalana (driving a car). Sex and death are never far apart; a gun can also be called a gaadi. Shot lena could mean firing a gun or fucking. Girls, as well as drugs, generically, are maal—cargo—and charas is kala sona—black gold. The police are thola; a police van, a dabba.

Many of the terms are borrowed from cricket, as I have seen in Ajay's interrogation sessions: The lookouts are called fielding; they watch for the police while the shooters "play the game" of the victim or "take a wicket." The gang lords love cricket; they spend a lot of time watching it and bring cricketers over to the countries where they are hiding. They love the game so much that they absolutely must know who will win before it is played; they regularly bribe players to throw the matches. And they make large sums betting against them.

Information is tichki, or a light flick of the fingers, as in, "I'm going to do so-and-so's work. Give me a tichki on him." Money is number, as in "What number came up for you?" Money can also be message, as in "Your message has come for ten"—10,000 rupees have arrived for you. The underworld speaks of money in modest, reductive ways; one lakh is often referred to as one rupya. To raise money by stealing is to "fund."

When a shooter goes overseas, whether it is to Dubai, Malaysia, or Toronto, he goes upar—up—to the gaon—the village. Once you leave Bombay, the rest of the world is a village.

Downstairs, the middle-class Bohra Muslims of Byculla are coming and going; a wedding is in progress. We leave the hotel and get into my car. As we are driving through the central city, Anees points out a beer bar, the Gold Mine. "Two murders happened in it. It's owned by a Shetty. He had two bodyguards. The Company asked him for money, and he didn't pay it. One day he walked into his bar and found the head of his bodyguard on a table."

I drop them off in Kamathipura and they wander off into Fifth Lane. "Now we'll just smoke charas," says Mohsin, who gave up alcohol five years ago, but has been a charasi since the age of fifteen. "There is no difficulty, only profit. The high cools down my mind. I have a hot mind." The hashish will make them hungry and horny; they'll eat sweets and go to the whores after smoking it, so they are able to stay hard longer. "You see how our life is. We wake up at one p.m., sleep at any time." They are happy about the lack of structure in their lives; always under the looming shadow of death, their freedom. They spend their days and, more important, their nights wandering, free-floating through the charms of the city, from the kabab joints and carom clubs of Madanpura to the charas dens and brothels of Kamathipura, where their anger can be stripped off. At any point in the day or night, there are these boys clustered around central Bombay, ever on the lookout for profitable strife. They watch the streets the way stockbrokers watch their computer screens, or grain merchants watch the onset of the monsoon, looking for the slightest change in the market, the slightest sign of excitement.

After the meeting in the hotel I go to a dinner party in Worli. There are about seven or eight couples in the apartment. It is a long high-ceilinged room with abstract art on the walls—all deformed dark faces—and a few carefully selected pieces of antique furniture. I could be in Soho. The owner has come back to Bombay after a decade in California; most of the other guests have also done spells in America: at the Wharton School or at Harvard. There is a sizable contingent from the Doon School in the Himalayas. The talk in the room is of babies, of the terrible state of the economy, old school stories. We drink the host's French wine and listen to Eartha Kitt and Annie Lennox on his sleek stereo. A woman comes in, pale white and with blond hair. From a distance, I think she is American. Then I hear her accent: pure Bombay. She has done something to her hair, she has done something to her skin, and she has been able to afford to keep it out of the sun.

I make the mistake of telling one person about my day and soon the room is abuzz; everyone wants to hear about my afternoon with the hit men. The people at this party are as fascinated by my account of Madanpura as, a couple of nights ago, Ishaq and Girish and Shahbuddin were fascinated by my account of a party of industrialists at the Library Bar: "What are they like? How do they talk? How do they dress?" I am angry with myself for shooting my mouth off, at my own need to talk with someone about the stories I have been hearing all day. I have not yet developed a stomach for them; I cannot keep them within myself and write them out the next morning. As it turns out, there is some benefit to sharing the stories with this odd group. Slowly, from the investment bankers, the industrialists, their own stories start coming out. No one will admit to being directly targeted or to giving in to the gangs' demands, but they refer to a relative or a friend of a friend who has paid up. Mohsin and his company are not so far away from this room; when I look out the window at the quiet Worli road, I notice clusters of men desultorily standing about, perhaps watching the people moving about through this brightly lit room. They can see us better than we can see them.

The man who gives me a ride home, an investment banker, asks me where in Bombay he can buy a gun. He says he once fired a gun on his brother-in-law's farm. "It was the greatest high of my life."

A FEW MONTHS LATER, Anees fills me in on what happened to Mohsin. He didn't get married; a couple of days after our meeting, the Crime Branch arrested him, stuffed his ears with cotton, blindfolded him, and took him away to an unknown place for three days. They beat him and asked two things of him: that he become an informer and that he kill men the police consider their enemies. "He would rather die than become an informer," Anees says. So the police phoned Shakeel, who paid three lakhs for his life. They released him, and he fled north. From Surat, Mohsin sent Anees a newspaper article about a murder with his photo in it. "Congratulate me," he said to Anees on the phone. True to his vow, he had murdered the man who had tried to kill his friend Yasin. He had closed the "open" work he had told me about.

Satish: The Dal Badlu

I am in the hot airless outer office of Phone-in Services, to get a meeting with the don Chotta Shakeel. Yet another of Girish's vast circle of college friends, Kamal, has the power to get me such an appointment. Kamal is the paymaster for the shooters; when they need money, or if they're killed or in jail and their families need money, he's the one who takes care of them. Several of the top figures on the most wanted list call him "bhai." Kamal has a slightly vulpine face and takes care to dress well and speak English well. He has a college degree and a natural entrepreneurial talent and he runs a series of white businesses for the Dawood company. He was directly involved in the underworld, known and feared, until three years ago. The Madanpura boys—Anees, Mohsin—used to fetch tea and cold drinks for him. "If I entered the room, they would not have the right to sit down in my presence. They would keep standing."

Phone-in Services is a suburban shopping service and the most above-board of Kamal's enterprises.

> With Phone-in Services, the harried commuter returning home to Mira Road after a long train journey just has to make one phone call and his dinner will be brought to his table from the restaurant of his choice, his television will be picked up from the repair shop so he can watch his favorite program that night, and his office clothes for the next morning will be delivered freshly laundered to his doorstep.

On its letterhead, Phone-in Services lists a Hindu at the top. He owns only 15 percent of the company, but the real owner, Kamal, formerly known as Shahid, cannot be named. Girish's friend inhabits a succession of names as others do business offices, to be discarded when the costs associated with the name become too heavy, when the name has built up too much bad will. Kamal is inside his office now with a couple he is advising, in his capacity as bhai. A girl has run away from Aurangabad to be with her lover, and the parents want to get her back. Kamal is mediating. Presently, he emerges and goes to the STD shop around the corner to make a call to Chotta Shakeel on my behalf.

The don asks, "Do you know him? Is he a friend of yours?"

"He isn't a friend, but he's the good friend of a good friend."

"Find out about him. I need to talk to him first."

BACK IN HIS OFFICE, Kamal proposes that I write the real story of the gangwar in a movie script, unlike any other movie made before: "No fairy tales." He will give me all the help I need in the research. I can go to Dubai and spend fifteen days watching the operational command structure of the gang. I can see how much they miss Bombay. They are miserable there; there is no life outside work for them. In their free time, they go to the

Pizza Hut and drink juice or go shopping for Hindi movies to watch. All the time, they keep wondering what their families are doing at home, what a brother might be doing on a particular festival. When Kamal spent a couple of weeks in Dubai with Chotta Shakeel, he noticed that the tape of the song "I Love My India" had been worn out from playing.

I should do this script, says Kamal, because then the government will know the real situation of the gangwar and will have better strategies to fight the gangs. It will be a service to the country, says the gang comptroller. If the government wants to stop extortion, it should allow smuggling to be profitable again. "It should put restrictions again on gold, imported watches, electronic items. You can never finish the underworld." The gangs will sometimes fight each other just to keep their names in the papers, he says. Otherwise, ordinary people will not fear them. "It's like stocking their shop with goods. Fear is what they stock their shop with."

Before going out for a hit, some shooters tie a piece of thread from Ajmer Sharif on each other's wrists, like a rakhi, says Kamal. "All the underworld people are godfearing. They are constantly conscious that they are sinning, and so they have to respect God for their survival." God is the biggest bhai. Kamal's office has verses from the Koran all over the walls, on the desk. He does namaaz five times a day. Like many of the gangwar people, Kamal ties one or more green bands—called a taveez—around his arm and a few around his chest. When Girish visits Kamal's office there is a constant religious discussion going on, between Kamal, his staff, and his visitors. The business at hand is put aside to discuss the Upanishads and the Koran, comparing and contrasting Hinduism, Islam, and Christianity without demeaning any of them, exalting all. It is getting a bit too much for Girish.

There is a new air conditioner in Kamal's office but also a lot of mosquitoes. Girish tries to kill one and claps his hands in the air. He examines his palms; they are clean. "You have no scope in the underworld," remarks Kamal. "You can't even kill a mosquito."

Girish has been sick from the bad air of Bombay. In the evenings he can't breathe. He has been trying a variety of traditional doctors: ayurvedics, homeopaths, hakims, and most recently, on Kamal's recommendation, a woman in Mira Road who sees djinns. People come and ask their djinn, through the woman: My parents in America, how is their health? And the djinn answers, cheaper and more reliable than a telephone call.

Kamal regularly visits the medium to get news of his D-Company associates in Dubai. In these days when the police have every gangster's phone tapped, the djinn network, operating securely in the otherworld, is invaluable to the underworld.

One of the men sitting in Kamal's office is named Zameer. He is in his mid-twenties, under five feet tall and very thin, with a small mustache. He commutes seven hours a day for Kamal, overseeing one of his construction projects in Daman. Zameer tells me that the stewards, dancers, and owners of the beer bars are the main information networks for the gangs. Also, barbers. Zameer seems to know a lot about the underworld.

The phone call with Shakeel I have been waiting for doesn't happen immediately, but Kamal does me a greater favor: He sends me a top shooter of his company, a man who is "absconding from Bandra to Borivali," the territory throughout which the police are after him, where he is in maximum danger. He can meet me south of Bandra or north of Borivali. Kamal has told the hit man that I am writing a movie script about the underworld.

WE MEET THEM at the long-distance bus stand in Bhayander, on the municipal limits of Bombay, on a July afternoon. I am with my friend Vikram, who is writing a novel about the underworld and who has asked to come along. We go inside a small café by the bus stand and find Zameer, eating his lunch of methi parathas. He indicates another man constantly on the phone at the booth outside. "That's him."

When Zameer has finished eating, we go outside to meet the occupant of the phone booth. He is a stocky man in his mid-twenties, wearing a checked shirt and jeans, a sacred thread on his wrist, and a ring. He is good-looking, with intelligent eyes and a slight beard—stubble, actually. He is introduced to me with one name and later, as I am trusted more, with another name; still later, in Dubai, I am told a third name. I am going to give him a name that is none of these: Satish.

We take a Garuda, a sort of elongated rickshaw that seats eight people in the back on two opposing benches and three or four in the front, depending on the driver's tolerance, and head for a hotel. There is light traffic on the road. But Satish wants the Garuda to go faster. He sees an obstruction ahead, a vehicle or a person or an animal. I can't see it from where I am sitting but I hear him tell the driver, "Blow him away from the road, no fear."

We get down at a billboard that says MAXWELL RESORT. It advertises a swimming pool, and there are pictures, mysteriously, of a helicopter and a kangaroo. From the road we walk up about a mile to the hotel. The road is along the ridge of a hill; on our left are old bungalows with Catholic names on the doorposts and a few shrines to Jesus. On our right we can see the white sea, past paddy fields ripe green in the rains. The whole landscape is softened by the monsoon mist, and we don't mind the mile-long uphill walk.

As we enter the hotel, one mystery is solved: sheltered in a summer-house past the entrance are a toy helicopter and a kangaroo, with slots for money at the side; they are children's rides. When they are fed with money they move in various ways. We go inside the hotel and bargain with the owner. As I am negotiating the rate, a couple of employees of the hotel come up to the owner.

"The police are here. They say they have a warrant for you."

The owner, a small man with a large mustache, nods slowly. "The police are here? Tell them their father's sitting here." The police never come inside.

We go up to the room, which costs me 500 rupees. It is completely functional, with a bed and a few plastic chairs. I open my backpack and take out my computer, and Satish tells me about his first murder.

The bhai of the company he was in then, Chotta Rajan, had sent two "mithais"—sweetmeats, guns—for Satish and a Sikh friend of his. At first they would just play with the guns, threatening people with them but not using them. One day Satish's girl took him to a temple and tied the sacred red thread around his right wrist. As she was doing this, she told him, "Do no evil." The next day, the instructions came from the bhai: They were to kill a Muslim man involved in the bomb blasts. The target was in his thirties and had left the gangs behind; he was now devout and went regularly to the mosque.

When Satish went to kill the bomb-blasts man, "I saw fire and fear in his eyes." As he brought up his right hand, he remembered the thread on it and his girl's words. So "I fired with my left hand, but it was hard, and it missed. It hit his leg. He ran. I felt a little pity. He didn't have a big role in it. If I had five minutes with him he might have touched my feet. I could not kill him; I became double-minded. He ran inside his home, and I didn't fire on him for fear of hitting his children." Then, enchanted by the sound of the firing, Satish continued shooting into the air, walking some distance and firing, the public running all around him.

The calls from above got more insistent. The blasts suspect had to be killed. So the setting was arranged again. Four people, including Satish, waited for him at a bus station in a congested area. They all had sophisticated weapons: a 9mm, a Mauser, a .38 bore, and a semiautomatic. They set up their coordinates on their cell phones. At the bus station, one of the group sat next to the target. The others looked around for exit routes. They had their equipment hidden in plastic shopping bags. When everything was in place, "We signaled our friend next to him. He did a brain shot. We did the confirmation firing on him. Everybody ran; the public also got hurt. I stood for about a minute, looking at all the blood. The flesh was falling from his brain. The blood was boiling, like when you see water boiling on the gas."

It was his first murder. "Thus the work started."

We speak in Hindi and also in English. Satish is an intelligent man, and he has a way of focusing on you completely when he speaks; he meets your eyes and puts forward his point of view forcefully and articulately, without expecting you to agree or sympathize with him. He had studied for a chemistry degree up to the second year of college; one more and he would have had a BSc.

When Satish was seven years old, in 1981, in the third standard, he saw his mother burning alive in front of him. I ask how this affected him.

"The next day I was eating chocolates."

The police said his father, an income-tax officer, had killed his mother. His father maintained that it was a suicide. He was suspended from his job at the income tax department, jailed, tried, and sentenced to life. Years later, he was acquitted on appeal by the high court.

Meanwhile, Satish went to an English-language school in Andheri. He was a good student, in the top ten in his class. But "the situation was not good at home." He found friends in school, tough guys. He started getting into trouble; he once urinated on the blackboard and was suspended. "The people at home found out what we were up to and told us with emotion to stop." When he talks, Satish often uses the first-person plural to refer to himself, not so much like royalty as like someone who seeks anonymity or evades responsibility by being part of a group.

The need for money to take out girls became pressing. Satish and his friends snatched chains, stole cars, beat people up and took their money. Sometimes there was a problem; sometimes *they* would get beaten up in a fight. "We wouldn't have been if we had a revolver. We went to the movies and thought we should have a ghoda." A friend from Uttar Pradesh had been involved in a fight; Satish and his mates stabbed his opponents. But the opposite side was in touch with the gangs, and so the friend from UP bought a country-made revolver. This was Satish's first ghoda. "We kept watching ourselves in the mirror. We felt very good. We roamed around with it." And a wish grew steadily in him: "We wanted to fire the gun." Satish marks his life not by the people he meets but by the particular gun he used at the time. For each stage of his adult life, he remembers the gun in his waistband like other men remember the woman they were with.

Satish went on to college but sold guns and bombs for use in the 1993 riots. One of Satish's group was arrested by Salaskar, the encounter specialist I had met, and they found eighteen imported pistols with the group. The police came looking for Satish at his father's house. Not finding him there, they put a gun to his father's head and asked for his son's whereabouts. His father pleaded for his son's life, and gave money to the inspector, asking him not to kill the boy.

Satish was held by the police for an inquiry, to see if he was involved with the bomb blasts. In front of him, they beat his accomplice, putting the wire on him. That night, Satish was informed, he would be beaten too. He stayed in his cell, greatly afraid of the beating to come. Then he remembered that a Muslim friend had given him a powerful mantra. When the officer came to beat him, Satish pretended to be asleep and chanted the mantra furiously to himself. The officer stood over him, looked at the sleeping boy, and then walked away. "To this day I believe in the mantra," says Satish.

The police didn't find a link between Satish and the bomb blasts, so they let him go. As he walked up to his building, late at night, he saw the lights on in his family's flat. When he opened the door, he saw his father, brother, and sister, sitting up. "I had no mother, of course." For the first time in his life, he saw his father crying. "He said, 'I thought you would study, be a doctor.' " Stricken with guilt, Satish went to his ancestral village in Maharashtra. His grandfather was extremely strict with him and made him work in the fields. He pushed the plow with his shoulders and didn't have enough to eat. When he was sick his grandfather begrudged him medicine. Meanwhile, his brother, who had been put into a hostel, sent a letter to Satish saying he was very sick and needed to see him. But when Satish asked a cousin for money to go to the hostel to see his sick brother, the cousin refused. "I felt very bad," recalls Satish. "When I did bad work, I had lots of money; now that I was doing honest work, I had no money." He ran away to Bombay.

In Bombay he found a job with a flight services company, where there was a lot of smuggling. With his first paycheck, Satish bought his father a watch. "Even today I feel his happiness," he remembers. There was a dispute in his job, and he next joined a courier firm owned by another cousin. He had to transport parcels into Bombay on the trains. Just before the octroi, or excise tax, station, at the Bombay border, he had to throw the load out of the running train, follow it with his body, and then smuggle the load past the tax collector. One day he made a mistake; he asked a man next to him to push out the load and it fell under the train. The parcel, consisting of imported saris and machinery, was ruined, and his cousin refused to pay him for delivering it. Satish left that job too.

After this, an old friend contacted Satish. The friend had been in jail, where he had come into contact with the gangs. Along with the friend, Satish enlisted in the Rajan Company. That's when Chotta Rajan gave him the job to kill the man involved in the bomb blasts. After that first murder, there were others. Rajan had a dispute with a movie producer over a picture he had financed. The producer thought he was untouchable; he was protected by thirty or forty boys at all times. He was sitting in his office one day, surrounded by his guards, when Satish set fire to his bungalow nearby. The boys ran to the bungalow to put the fire out, and Satish went into the office. The producer was on the phone, sitting amid some visitors. "We cursed him and put a bullet in his chest. The rest didn't even speak. We came out and fled in a car."

All this was in the early nineties, during the troubles in Punjab. A Sikh friend who was with the terrorists was asked by them to bring in some good shooters from Bombay. A policeman was to be hit. Satish went with four others, shot the policeman, and got caught. He was in the Patiala jail for four months. It was a huge jail, filled with terrorists. Many of them were highly intelligent; one had a PhD, and Satish's cellmate was an assistant collector's son. He was supposed to be in solitary confinement, but "we had two thousand rupees and we were connected." There were three other men in the next cell. Through the walls, they played antakshari, the game of Hindi film songs, where each person starts a song beginning with the syllable that the last one has ended on. The jail resounded with the full-throated voices of terrorists singing love songs.

One of Satish's tasks was to clean the gallows. The gallows consisted of a platform, over which there was the rope, and an underground room below, where the body on the rope dropped. Satish had to clean the top platform, where flocks of parrots flew over the gallows and speckled it with their shit. But the real cleaning job was in the underground room. According to Satish, people watching the platform could not imagine the sufferings of the hanged when they dropped underground. The room was spattered with feces and tongues. As the condemned hung writhing from the rope, they shit their pants and bit down on their tongues.

After they got out of jail, Satish and his companions were on good terms with the Punjab policemen; one of them had even helped Satish obtain his release, because Satish was the son of a senior government official, however disgraced. They became, in a way, friends. Now, when the Punjab police come to Bombay, they are met at the station in a car by Satish and his boys and taken to 007, a brothel in Kamathipura. Satish knows the menu by heart. "For one hundred fifty rupees you can get a good-looking girl, one that could be a college-going girl. For one hour it costs three hundred, and for the whole night, seven hundred fifty." By taking them to the brothel, Satish is only returning a favor. He tells me a story about the Punjabi policemen's hospitality.

One day, in Punjab, Satish was invited to one of his policeman friends' homes. There was a lavish dinner with the man's family. "He knew I liked to fuck." So after dinner he told Satish to get on the back seat of his Bullet motorcycle, and they roared off into the countryside. They stopped outside a house, and the policeman knocked on the door. A man opened it and the officer put a gun to his head. Behind the man stood his wife. "He told me to take the wife into the next room and fuck her." So Satish did: "I quickly took my shot." Then the police officer had his turn, with Satish sitting at the edge of the bed, watching. "He fucked her very hard, and watching him, I was on standby again, and I got on her again. She was crying, 'No, no!'" But the police officer told her to cooperate. "He said, 'This is our guest.'" The husband and their young daughter were in the next room. "The husband had a gun held to his head by some constables. In

Punjab the police can do what they want." I ask Satish if he'd raped the daughter as well. He hadn't. She was only eighteen, and, he said, "I felt bad about doing her."

Satish tries to rationalize it. "The woman must be having an affair with someone, and they thought, If she can do it with someone else, why not with us?"

As I am listening to this, I have to pause. With an effort, I keep what I am feeling to myself. I ask Satish if he feels fear when he is shooting.

The sound of the bullet banishes fear, he replies. "After the first bullet comes out, everything becomes clear. Then the fun comes." Different shooters have different ways of dealing with their work. Afterward, some drink. Some get stoned. Some celebrate in the ladies' bars. After Satish murders somebody, he eats a huge strictly vegetarian meal. He is a tee-totaler and a nonsmoker, and he doesn't do drugs. He goes straight home, has a bath—"I always have a bath"—does a puja to Hanuman, and sits down to eat a nonviolent repast. He won't even eat eggs. It began when he left jail; the experience had roused a great anger in him. "I felt then that I should kill every day." He had been a confirmed meat-eater, even eating meat for breakfast. Then one day he gave it up, all at once. "Now that I'm a vegetarian my mind stays calm, I don't get angry, and I can give attention to my work."

After the post-murder meal, he sleeps soundly and for a long time. "Some people feel other things," he allows. He has a shooter friend who had been having a problem with the aftereffects of the murders he'd done. "When he killed a man, that man's soul came and sat on his chest." The soul would try to extract his heart from his body. The shooter couldn't sleep at night. Then a magician advised him on how to trick the soul. "He told him to turn on his side when he sleeps, so the soul can't grab his heart." So now the shooter sleeps on his side, and if he sees the soul coming into the room he curls up into a fetal position to protect his heart.

Some of the shooters have become psychos. Satish knows one who is the only child of a doctor and was himself a medical student. Whenever he had a problem at home, he would run away and do something psychotic. He was always high. He had one eccentricity: After he killed someone, he would take out the brain and, with a sword, make a mince out of it. Satish chops up the air very fine with his hand, demonstrating.

"What is he doing now?" I ask.

"He has resumed his medical studies."

Shooters, maintains Satish, are very sensitive and take things easily to heart. This causes him difficulties in romance. "When I love a girl, I don't know how to express it. When I love a girl I love her a lot and she starts avoiding me. If she even talks to another boy I will kill him. Then I think I should kill the girl too. I haven't killed one yet, but I feel one will die by my hand." Maybe he developed this attitude through watching movies, he speculates.

On the other hand, the girls that the shooters go out with know they are in the gangs and know the risks. Some of them are with the shooters for the food and drink, others for sympathy. "The dancers and whores understand us more. They love us more. They understand the situation. Here, it is kill or be killed. They are also like that. They don't have the power of guns; they are searching for a shoulder." If the shooters are broke or wanted by the police, they can always find a place to hide out in the homes of the dancers. "It feels like home. They love us. The time passes by."

There was one woman Satish was very serious about, a doctor who came from a family of doctors from Delhi. They had met in college; he double-dated her along with his Sikh friend, who was also seeing a doctor. "It was expensive. They were of a high status, and you needed good money. We would go to the Taj and sit, to the Leela and sit." He was with her for almost two years. "I was satisfied mentally, sexually, everything." She tried to reform him. Satish was a science student in college. "She wanted me to be in her line. She wanted me to be a pathologist." But they broke up before their second anniversary. His mind started playing "psycho-tricks" on him. "I started thinking she had affairs with other people in her group, other doctors. I used to curse her, beat her. She would say, Beat me, but don't curse me with such bad words." But she was very serious about him and very ambitious about her career. Satish saw the end coming. "I felt I was going very deep into this. I felt that if I were caught, she and her family would be dishonored, so I broke it off."

Later, he tried to get back with her, but she avoided him. "A few days ago I went to kill someone early in the morning. I didn't find him. I was waiting outside a hotel in Dahisar when she came there to visit a relative. She saw me, but she didn't say anything. After that I called her many times. My friends would beat me, but still I kept calling."

After the Rajan Company, Satish and his group did some work for the

Manchekar Company. The Manchekar Company specialized in the powder business—drugs—and they also preyed on doctors in Kalyan and Dombivali. The Manchekar Company was a poor one; it was known as the gang of the scheduled castes and scheduled tribes, but it always paid its shooters on time. Satish smuggled guns for them. When he wants to get guns, he will travel to Nepal or to UP. He tells me about a trip to UP: "There I murdered." The countryside is in a constant state of caste warfare, and the young people have no other profession but politics. A person's honor is in his rifle. Homemade bombs are available for 1½ rupees. "The people who make them have rotted their insides from handling them." He was visiting a local member of parliament, who was supplying them with ammunition. Satish had a proposal for the MP: If he did some work for Satish's group in Bombay, Satish and his boys would do work for them in UP. One morning as Satish was shitting in a field behind the village he heard gunshots. There was a fight between the Thakurs and the Brahmins. Satish went with sixty armed men into the village of the Brahmins. The whole village fled. One person was killed and many hurt. "We felt we were an army, we had so many weapons."

Satish had a decent record in the Rajan Company. He has two murders on his official record, four or five attempts, and a few other murders that are not on his record. Satish has now been in the D-Company—or "Mucchad Company," as he refers to Dawood and his mustache—for only a couple of months. During this time he has already carried out two assignments. He switched because of the money he is given in this company and because of the good quality of the ammunition they provide. "A shooter has two weaknesses: girls and guns. When the bullet fires, there is a great happiness and everything opens up. When a man dies I feel even greater happiness."

I ask Satish if the people he kills beg for their lives. "Some of them do, so you should kill them immediately and not wait for them to talk."

AS WE FINISH for the day and walk out of the hotel, Satish says, "I like such places." It is quiet in the evening, and the air is cool. "It is like the village, and my mind is at ease. But after a few days of this I start getting restless." As we are waiting for a Garuda, Satish asks, "What's that in the middle of the road?" It is some distance off, an animal slinking along the road. At first I think it might be a mongoose creeping along, but then Satish observes, "It's a cat that got hit by that car." A white Maruti has just sped by. The cat is not crying at all. It attempts to pick itself up and crawl to the side of the road. It is a curious form of locomotion; it gets up with half of its body, then falls and slithers frantically about, like some elongated worm, this way and that.

"Now what would you do with that cat?" Satish asks us. "You can do one of two things: You can put it in the middle of the road so that its pain is shortened, or you can pick it up and put it on the side. What would you do?"

"If I had an instrument to kill it, I'd do so," says Vikram, the novelist.

The cat crawls to the side; then it crawls back toward the middle. "The cat thought the same thing," notes Satish. "Could you kill a cat?"

"I don't know. I've gone hunting a couple of times," Vikram replies.

"That thrashing about of the cat is what the children of the middle class of Bombay are doing. We"—he means the shooters—"give them mukti." Liberate them. The Garuda pulls ahead, leaving the cat still slithering about, waiting to be delivered by the next car or bus.

Presently, Satish launches into a soliloquy on God. "God is like smelling money that you've earned. There is no smell, really, but you have felt him. We are all part of God's game." Even God has a game: In the underworld sense, to "play someone's game" is to kill them. The biggest game is God's. Satish tells me I am researching the wrong subject. I should be doing spiritual research, like our ancients, the jnanis. "They knew everything. They never talked, they just laughed."

I ask him if he has done a lot of spiritual research. "I don't do research. I go within myself. Everything is in me. You want to know when I reach the deepest meditation? It's when I'm in the toilet. It's a very creative time for me. I plan everything, all my work, in the toilet."

We drive past a police checkpoint. The cops are checking cars for couples looking to neck on the deserted beaches. They wave me and the gangsters on. When we get to the Surahi restaurant, there is a party of drunk cops there too, all the way in the back. They are arguing. One of them wants another to have one more peg. A third lets out a huge belch. One of them takes off his shirt and stands up. As they leave, I see him with a new shirt, the label still sticking out over the back. "They must have collected today," says Satish, clearly disgusted. The gangsters refer to the police as gande log, "dirty folk."

A FEW DAYS LATER, Zameer arranges a second meeting with Satish, on a Friday. Of the first meeting, he says, "That was just the trailer." For the main feature, Zameer will be bringing Satish and another hit man to meet me. Vikram can't make it; he is being interviewed on a television program in Delhi. So I go alone, the second time, to meet the gangsters.

When Zameer comes to pick me up in a rickshaw, I try to make conversation. But he isn't talking. He is tense about something, and I am conscious of being alone. On the road up to the hotel we start seeing his boys: two, four, eight of them. There is an army coming up to the hotel. Why? Zameer isn't offering to give any of them a ride. I ask him if he has ever gone abroad. He hasn't so far, but in a week he is going to Dubai. Why? I know that, after a big hit, the shooters are generally sent out of the country for a spell. Who is Zameer going to kill now?

I ask Zameer if it is absolutely safe, my going in there alone. Zameer replies that since he is taking me in, it's probably okay. "But in this line, things change in five minutes," he says. "If I get a call from above saying 'Eliminate Suketu,' I'll do it, even if I'm your greatest friend. Because if I don't do it, I'll get killed myself."

As I'm registering in the hotel, Zameer says that only four people will be in the room. What were all those boys coming up for, then? "They've come for swimming," he explains. We wait silently in the room. Through the window we can see trees. The room this time has the same kind of bed, a steel wardrobe, a desk, and a couple of chairs. It is bare, functional, perfect for sex or death. You bring yourself to such a room and decorate it with yourself. The only excess is yourself.

Satish has shaved today and is wearing jeans, and a shirt with broad red and white stripes. With him is a tall well-built young Sikh man named Mickey. I take out my computer and Mickey sits on a chair by the bed. He has on a tight blue T-shirt that shows off his muscles. He wears a neatly trimmed mustache and beard and constantly runs his hands through his short hair, perhaps feeling for the turban he has given up.

Mickey now stands, pulls up his T-shirt, and takes a gun out from under the waistband of his jeans. He hands it over to Satish. Satish holds it, looks at it closely, and turns to me.

He puts the gun in my hand.

I feel its weight and heft and turn it over. It is a 9mm Mauser, gray, with the steel showing where all the marking has been removed. The scratches give the impression that the gun has been well used. It feels very big in my hand. Satish shows me the clip. Mickey points out that it can hold ten bullets, but they generally put in only seven because the spring in the mechanism gets damaged if it's full. It can empty in ten seconds. Satish takes out the bullets and shows them to me. They are copper bullets with a steel core, and each one bears the markings KF for Kanpur Factory, the government ordnance factory. The gun costs between two and a half and three lakhs on the street, and each bullet sells for between 70 and 180 rupees. They are proud of the gun; they speak of it like a prodigal child. "In a man it will make such a big hole," says Mickey. He should know. He'd made these holes in six men by the time he was in his early twenties.

Mickey is fond of listening to the Backstreet Boys—and to the sound of a Mauser. "There is something in that sound. My brother's friend heard me test it, and he said, 'Look at my arm, the hair is standing on end.'" Mickey urges me to try it. "Even if you fire two or three rounds you will get confidence. Its sound has that quality. The more it fires, the more your confidence will open up." An AK-47 and more sophisticated weapons don't have the quality of that voice, he says, like someone comparing classical singers. The Sound is used to convince extortion targets; Mickey plays it like a record for businessmen he visits on the bhai's errands. "Sometimes he needs to hear the Sound. Sometimes I need to run a bullet through his hands or his legs." Upon hearing it, the businessman suddenly becomes subordinate to Mickey. In normal circumstances, the hit men, like the Sena boys, are spectacularly powerless in the big city. They make themselves powerful by killing; they imbibe their victims' power.

"We are anti-alchemists," says Satish. "Whatever we touch turns to iron."

Satish is aiming the gun, practicing; taking the clip out and pulling the trigger, putting the clip back in without the bullets and aiming it, taking the clip out again, loading the bullets and waving the gun around the room, pointing it at Zameer and smiling, making a soft sound with his mouth: *"Phroo!"*—it sounds like a raspberry—as he blows him away.

Mickey was the Sikh friend who had taken Satish to Punjab to kill a police officer. Five of them went from Bombay, got a Maruti car, took the weapons—each of them was given a pistol—and did the work. They were chased. They threw away their guns, climbed on top of a freight train, and then ran into a forest, full of very old rare trees. The police closed in on them, shining flashlights through the forest. The sound of the police came from all directions in the cold fog, and the hit men decided to walk in a group toward one of the police parties. The police stood them in a line in a clearing, and they knew they were going to be shot. Just at that time, another of the squads pursuing them arrived and began quarreling with the first one, saying they wanted to interrogate the captured boys. There was a dispute over which one of the squads would get credit for the catch. The second squad finally took them away, alive. "We used to take God's name a lot," says Mickey. "Maybe that's why we lived." Satish is raising the gun, aiming it, pulling on the trigger.

The interrogation in Punjab began. The police made cuts into the sides of Satish's groin, and he shows us how: one diagonal cut, sloping toward the penis, left, and one on the right, in the crevices just below his balls. They then took hot chili powder and rubbed it into the bleeding incisions.

Mickey tells me about the roller. He was stretched out, and a large rolling pin was placed over his body. Two big cops got on it, one on each side, and rolled it over his body with all their weight. It caused Mickey to call out loud to his entire family, including his grandparents. "After you torture a person like that you had better kill him," suggests Mickey. "Because if you release him, nothing on your earth has the power to scare him anymore."

They were briefly jailed, but the judge in their case had been fixed and they went back to Bombay. After their exploits in Punjab, the group found themselves being ardently wooed by all the gangs. They started doing free-lance work for political parties—their "independent business"—which they define as "taking the air out of opposition parties." For one general election they were hired by a Congress legislator fighting for a seat against a BJP man who was a rich smuggler and landing agent at the airport. The BJP candidate had police security, but Satish and Mickey managed to get it removed long enough to go into his office, beat up his boys, and go at him with swords. They would have killed him, but he was rescued in time. The BJP man was connected to the home minister; public demonstrations were held, demanding the arrest of his assailants. But Satish and Mickey also knew the minister; they had had a photograph taken with him. Besides, they had no particular enmity toward the BJP. Their last contract was with the BJP and, before that, with the RPI, the Republican Party of India. "We don't support parties, we support the individual," Mickey says. They have no interest in politics; they don't go to party rallies. "The member tells us he has a difficulty with a particular man. We try to make him understand," explains Satish.

"Some people understand immediately," adds Mickey. "Others after going home. Others after hearing a firecracker. We make them understand as each can." But there is one politician whom they sincerely admire. "If we were to choose one man to support for the country," says Satish, "we would support Atal Bihari Vajpayee. He is a genuine person. If he can bring about a revolution we will support him. He is a bachelor. He has made politics his mistress. There is no scam in which his name figures. All parties respect him." What impresses them most about Vajpayee is his decision to test the nuclear bomb. "Now the whole world looks at India. There is now a power," exults Mickey.

"He took the decision to go to war over Kargil," points out Satish. "No other PM would have been able to do this." They admire his ability to make powerful decisions, warlike decisions. "Nowadays who remembers Gandhiji?" asks Satish. But he still uses the respectful suffix.

For all their fighting on the side of the terrorists in Punjab, for all Satish's work on behalf of the Pakistan-based bhai, both of them insist that they are not against the nation. "Patriotism and the gangwar are completely different," says Satish. In fact, the two of them had been discussing the conflict in Kargil the previous day. They decided that if they got the chance, they would go to Kargil and fight for India. If the bhais actually tell them to do antinational work, they will quit the D-Company, maintains Satish. His greatest wish is to kill those who planned the bomb blasts. "They did wrong things." He doesn't want to kill the blast participants still left on the ground in Bombay—"They were pawns; they just stored the weapons in their homes"—no, not them. "I want to kill Tiger Memon. I want to kill Dawood. I want to kill Chotta Shakeel." He is talking about the leaders of the D-Company. Satish is sitting here and announcing, in the presence of Zameer and Mickey and myself, that he wants to kill the bhai of his own gang. (Later, Zameer tells me he appreciates the fact that Satish said out loud he wants to kill Shakeel, whom Zameer works for. "He doesn't have one thing in his heart and another on his tongue.")

I ask about the structure of their lives, their daily routine.

"We mostly go to sleep late," answers Satish. "We watch TV till two. We wake up and have breakfast and do our puja by noon. Most of the time is spent on the phone. We go after flesh; mostly, college girls. We wear good clothes, have cars and mobiles. Sixty to seventy percent of the girls get seduced this way. With fifteen percent we speak English well. With the others we give money. That's it: one hundred percent," says Satish, totaling up. But the girls also try to make suckers out of them. He points to me. "Gentlemen like you can't seduce girls like we can. With us, if we give her chocolates once, we want to screw her on the second date."

Then Mickey says—and I don't know whether he is being serious or mocking—"We believe in pure Indian principles. First the wedding night, then the children, then the home." Maybe Mickey's desire for doing things the Indian way comes from some heartbreak, for he adds, "We believe that a woman will always go to someone better, someone with better clothes. She will leave you for someone better."

"A mother's love is pure," continues Satish, who has known so little of it. "She doesn't think, 'This boy failed in school, he is not my son, that one came first in his class, he *is* my son.' A wife or a girlfriend's love can never be that pure." He has noticed a fact about love that he wants to call to my attention. "The day we do something very bad, we get a lot of love at home. When the police come and tell the people at home that they're going to bring their son's corpse home, they hug us then, they say, 'Son, we love you.' If I think about that love, I won't be able to do any crime. I won't even be able to tell a lie." So he takes pains to avoid thinking about it.

"Mostly I am not attracted to anything," Mickey explains. "I think about a person only as long as he is with me. When he goes a little away, I go very far away from him. Like our leader: I don't think of him at all. I can even kill him. Even girls; I have affairs at the most for four or five days with them. Even my family: When I am away from them I don't think too much about them."

Why did their parents give birth to them? Satish wonders. "They must be regretting it."

When a man touches his killer's feet and begs for his life, saying, "Please don't kill me. I have young children," it is the worst argument he can offer. Thinking the killer will let you off because you have kids assumes that you can locate a hidden source of sympathy in your killer based on something shared, something in common. But very few killers are fathers. Very few of them have had good experiences with their own fathers. So that bond between father and child, which for you and me is the most convincing argument against your death—don't kill me because it will break that sacred bond—means nothing to them. It is a bond, in fact, that the hit men have consciously been trying to break all their lives. As far as they're concerned, ridding your children of a father is the greatest favor they can do them.

Suddenly, Satish declares, "There is no meaning in this kind of research that you're doing. There is no ending to this." He repeats his advice: "If you did spiritual research instead, you might even find God."

"Every man has the same story," says Mickey, in agreement that my research is a waste of time.

"If four criminals die, eight more will be born," says Satish. "There wasn't so much crime before. Now there is only one business left: the Bullet business. All this is God's game; we have to play it. Our existence has absolutely no meaning. Whatever our story is, it is finished."

"We could die two hours from now," says Mickey. But he is prepared for it. "We have seen everything there is to be seen."

AT THIS TIME, Satish and Mickey are hiding out north of Dahisar. I later ask Zameer why they won't be caught here. He explains it is because of politics among the police stations and zones. If a particular crime has been committed in a particular area, the prestige of that area's police station is at stake in capturing the perpetrator. The other stations or zones will not cooperate willingly with them; and the original station does not like to ask the others for information on the man they are in search of. It's the difference between food cooked at home and food asked for from someone else, explains Zameer. The police force is ridden by political factions, and no one follows these political struggles more closely than the folk of the gang-war. They know the names of all of the encounter specialists, and each has a mythology built up around him similar to the kind built up around the top hit men. At the slightest prodding, they can tell you about the exploits of Vijay Salaskar, Pradeep Sharma, Pradeep Sawant. "Sunil Mane is in good form nowadays," says Mickey, as if speaking about a cricket player. They speak of the police shooters with no less respect than they speak of the star gang shooters.

But the shooters of the Bombay gangs are getting restive. They are getting killed in multiple encounters. The bhais forbid them from hitting back. Satish declares, "We are ready to kill the cops. But the people on top are afraid of enmity with the police, because then the police will wipe out that company." Instead, the bhais tell the police to kill the shooters when necessary; they inform on their own men. Satish wants to hit back at the police. "If two–four cops were hit, the encounters would stop. Right now everything—politics, the gangwar—is running on the backs of the shooters. The day the shooters feel that the people on top are not supporting them . . ." There is a kind of class consciousness developing among the shooters.

The Company tries to take care of shooters on the run like Satish. They are rotated around a series of safe houses, in good buildings around the city, and they are given mobile phones and, occasionally, cars. "I am at a place right now where I don't have to shift every night, but the boys with me have to shift every night or every week," says Satish. He is in a curious position. By now he has been in three companies, and they know he has no permanent allegiances. He is not working for his faith, as the Muslims in the Company profess to, or for the nation, as the Hindus in the Rajan Company claim. He is in it strictly for the gold. At the moment, he needs to raise money for the wedding of a friend's sister; the friend had been jailed after a botched job. He has no love for Rajan or for Dawood. "There is no loyalty," he says. "There is no trust."

I remember what Kamal had told me about the dal badlus, the men who change loyalty from one gang to another. This usually happens after a disagreement with the bhai. It could happen emotionally, "such as when the bhai shoots your brother." When he sends out feelers to the rival gang that he wants to change parties, the second bhai will tell him, "Give us a gift," and the dal badlu will shoot a member of the first gang, perhaps the leader, as an offering. But he is always mistrusted by the gang he goes to; he is always the first to be given up to the police. "Such a man is killed after he's used."

Satish, all of twenty-five years old, can never leave the gangwar. "Now there is no use in getting out. Now there are opposite people"—the many enemies he has made in the opposition. He remembers that the first man he had murdered, the Muslim blasts' suspect, had "improved." He had left the gangwar. "He had a wife, two kids. He got traced." Satish often thinks about his own death. "I have seen so many deaths. When I am killed I will die quickly, there will be no trouble. I want only this: Of the people who kill me, I want one of them to die by my hand."

Before he goes out on a job, Satish blesses himself ceremoniously. "I give myself blessings. I don't take anybody else's blessing. For all good and evil, I give myself blessings, because I alone am responsible for everything in this world. I don't believe in good or evil; I believe in karma." Then, turning to me, Satish asks, "Do you believe in sin and virtue?"

I say that I do.

"Only weak persons believe in sin and virtue. My father works a lot, suffers in the trains. Now there is me. I don't work a lot. I sit, I get a phone call, I go and put a bullet in someone and get a lakh of rupees. It is no big thing for me, but my father won't be able to do that work. So he will give his fear a name: sin. He will call it principles or whatever."

He tells me a story about his cousin, a civil engineer. He was much loved at home and now earns several thousand rupees a month working for a builder. "I never got that pampering at home. I earn a lot of money. Who is more successful, I can't say. His progress is slow and steady, mine is all at once, but there is no use." He envies his cousin, envies him his respectability—the families must be comparing the two of them constantly—but has a measure of contempt for him. "He would never have thought of anything outside of his life." One day, when they were both children, they had a big fight. The cousin was living next to an automobile factory that made the omnipresent little Fiat cars. Satish and his cousin were talking about cars, as little boys do. Satish was speaking about the fancy cars he had heard about: Toyota, Mercedes. He told his cousin that the Mercedes was the most expensive car in the world. His cousin, seeing the Fiats roll out every day next to his house, insisted that the Fiat was the most expensive car in the world. "I felt like breaking his head," recalls Satish. "He is, bhenchod, a frog in a well."

He asks me about my education. I tell him I have a master's degree. "I think I also have a master's degree," he says. "Because I am in this line I think very fast. My confidence level has been raised; it is flying. If you have to shoot a man standing in the midst of ten people, you need confidence. If

I apply myself to math or science or business I will get very good results because of my confidence. I am at an advanced stage of confidence." Satish thinks that if he were to go into business in Bombay, he would do well there too. "You know why? Nobody will be able to extort me. In Bombay, to be a capable businessman, you have to be in touch with the underworld."

But Satish's mind has not been at ease for a while now. He has not been able to meditate. He used to be able to meditate for hours at a time. Bombay makes him uneasy. "In Bombay there is something in the air. In Bombay you see death all the time." Even on the trains. "Have you traveled on the Virar train? Just traveling on it will make you strong. I feel more tension hanging from the Virar train than from a shooting."

A few days ago he had been on one of those trains. It was packed in the way only a Bombay train can be, and Satish was crushed against a Gujarati man standing with his wife and children and brother. Satish asked him politely to move a little, give him a little space. The Gujarati got agitated. "Don't be a wiseass!" he shouted at Satish. His brother grabbed Satish's neck, and Satish kicked out and hit the man's son by mistake. He felt bad about hitting the little boy. The Gujarati was showing off in front of his wife and children and brother, cursing the lone Maharashtrian man. He shook his umbrella at Satish, intending to swat him with it. Satish had one hand on his gun. "I asked myself, should I, shouldn't I?" He appealed to the man's wife: "Aunty, please make him understand." The Gujarati raised his umbrella; Satish felt his gun. But what if the man told the crowd that Satish had touched his wife? The crowd could do anything to him. So he let his challenge go and took a backward leap off the train. "But I will meet him again, I'm sure of it." He is laughing as he mimes the Gujarati waving his umbrella, not knowing how close he was to death. A gangster must not be offended, however inconsequentially. A slight which for normal people would be merely annoying, soon forgotten, is for someone like Satish a huge ego wound. That sense of being slighted can lead to homicide. There is no proportionality to his response. A hit man's character is defined above all by narcissism, that complex mix of egotism and self-hatred.

There is something in the Bombay air that agitates him, Satish repeats. "My mind has not been stable for a while. Something is always going on, even in sleep." When he eats, he feels very hot all over, and thinks, Ma ki chud, I want to kill someone. Satish turns to me. He asks, "Have you ever fired a gun?"

"No."

"Do you have a desire to?"

I smile.

"I liked your partner's answer." Satish turns to Mickey and tells him what Vikram had said at our last meeting. "A cat was dying in the middle of the road. When I asked him what should be done with the cat, he answered that if he had some instrument he would kill it with his hands. It appeared to me a very straightforward answer." But I am different. "You are not a gentleman!" Satish says. "You are worse than criminals."

"Why?"

"The more educated you are, the more criminal you are. You become heartless, self-centered. You use the power of your money to give people trouble."

"What *is* a gentleman?" Mickey wonders. "I don't know."

"A gentleman is one who kills his heart's every desire, who doesn't have guts," says Satish. "I used to get only ten rupees a day pocket money to go to college. My father told me that in his day he used to walk to his college. But I stole and went in a rickshaw with my girl. I wasn't afraid, and so I got laid."

Then, holding the gun in his hand, Satish asks me point-blank, "Are you afraid of death?"

My answer is crucial. My answer must be exactly right.

He is loading the gun. "What do you think will happen to you after you die?"

I look up from my computer. I reply that my religion tells me we will all reach moksha and unite with God.

"It's not so easy, that you die and immediately get moksha," Satish notes.

"I know," I say. "It takes millions of lifetimes. With all the sins I've committed in this life, I'll probably be reborn an ant."

They laugh and the tension breaks. I start breathing again.

Satish takes off his jeans and goes swimming in his trunks in the hotel pool while I continue talking to Mickey. Mickey badly wants to get out of Bombay, he tells me. He asks me how he can get to Canada or America or Germany. "Will you take me with you? You only need to take me as far as the airport there; then I'll manage." He has studied computers at an institute. He has relatives abroad. He should get out of Bombay while he is still alive. Besides, he says, the chances of a new riot in Bombay are high. "This one will be preplanned. It will be very bad."

Satish has finished his swim and comes back in his towel and is listening. "Muslims have accumulated a lot of arms. The countries next door have armed them." He puts on strings of prayer beads around his neck. "What will Hindus bring to the fight, cannons?"

During the 1993 riots, Satish and his friends had taken advantage of the unrest to loot timber ships and cloth shops. But he had also saved the life of a Muslim friend; given him a Hindu identity and a name, Amar, and hidden him. "We wanted to rob, not kill. My friends were killing women. I didn't like that." He blames Thackeray squarely for the riots and says that the Srikrishna Commission Report, which the Sena detests, is a "perfect report." This is an unusual opinion for a devout Hindu, especially a Maharashtrian, but then Satish is not the usual Hindu. The members of Satish's group are all intensely religious, but they all belong to different religions; they could be an advertisement for communal harmony. There is Satish himself; there is Mickey, who is Sikh; and Zameer, who is Muslim. "We had Catholics too. But they get diverted too easily by girlfriends; they don't have much hunger for money."

Satish gets on the floor now, puts a pink towel over his head like a scarf or a veil, and begins praying, with the gun at his right on the bed. He recites Sanskrit verses by heart, rapidly and loudly, rocking a little back and forth, holding his hands up heavenward, palms open. The room is filled with the strange sight of this half-naked man praying in an ancient language next to his gun, as I continue talking to his companion and typing on my laptop. He prays for about fifteen minutes. Then he stands up, bows, touches his forehead to the floor, and rises again. When he sits back on the bed the first thing he does is to pick up his gun and touch it to his forehead. "This is God!" he exclaims, in English.

"What can give life, what can take life, can only be God," observes Mickey.

"I think you are a very big criminal," Satish tells me suddenly. "Have you ever killed anybody?"

"No."

"Ever gotten anybody killed?"

"No."

"The line of his head is very big," he says to Mickey, indicating my palm. He has read my palm from across the room. The line indicates that I am a very big criminal.

As it gets dark, they are getting increasingly edgy. They have been using my mobile all afternoon and evening. They have been making calls, and my number has been registered in the memory of the mobiles of their contacts. Another thought makes my blood run cold: They can get the phone numbers of my home and those of all my friends from the mobile's memory. All they need to do is press the number sign and '1'. A number will come up, and the display will ask them: HOME? If they respond to its invitation and press YES, they will be speaking to my wife.

I shut down my computer and end the session. Mickey puts the gun back under his waistband, and I walk out of that room feeling light, so light.

In the rickshaw going back, we pass two men by the road. One of them is holding an air rifle, the other a flashlight, and both are pointed up at the trees. The first man fires the rifle. A bird falls down, fluttering. It is the same road where we saw the dying cat the last time we were here.

Once we reach the town, we stroll past the police station. The Sikh is swaggering, running his hand through his hair. He and I and all of us are conscious of the piece under his waistband. We walk across the tracks at Bhayander. With the train looming down on us, Satish asks me, "Do you know a man who can answer my questions? I have a lot of questions. Do you know a man who knows the answers to everything?"

"What kind of questions?"

"On philosophy, on the nation. *You* can't answer my questions. You only keep listening. Either you don't have the capacity to answer my questions—I'm speaking frankly—or you don't want to; you choose not to. I need someone to answer my questions. That's why I stopped meditation, why I just finish my puja anyhow, very quickly." We come up to the restaurant, the same one we had eaten at before. "I am very uneasy because of my questions. I don't get satisfaction from my work. It's like I'm having sex but not getting the orgasm."

In the restaurant I decide to tackle it head on. "Give me one or two of your questions."

The hit man smiles and leans forward across the table. "What is God? Does he have a beginning or an end?"

I tell him what my grandfather told me—that according to the Gita, God is "anant, akhand, anari" and I explain the meaning of the words: unending, inseparable, unborn.

Once, he tells me, when the police were closing in on his group and they were all under imminent threat of being shot dead in an encounter, "We sat in one room and talked of God constantly. We discussed God like others discuss girls; we talked about whether he has a beginning or an end, how he could come from nothing. Then we gave up, because we decided that research into God would make us unhappy. So we just started reciting the name of God."

I point out they had begun with Jnana Yoga, approaching God through knowledge, and moved on to Bhakti Yoga, through devotion. It's in the Gita.

Next question: "What is right and what is wrong?"

I tell him I can't answer this question for him. Most people are taught about right and wrong by their parents or by their religions. But these rules are funny, I acknowledge; people will tell you that it's wrong to kill but they'll say it's right to kill for your country. So I tell him that since the questions came from inside him, the answers will also come from inside him.

The questions torment him, he says. They frighten him, they make him uneasy. He asks the next one: "Why do we respect boundaries? Why do we call [the country] Bharat Ma? Why do we sing these patriotic songs?"

I answer that I don't know why either. Since I moved to America, I have never believed in boundaries or patriotism. Two Punjabis across the border have much more in common with each other than a Punjabi and an Arunachali. These boundaries are British-made boundaries.

Then Zameer speaks up. He disagrees with me, politely. He postulates an example. If you have a house, it is necessary to divide your property from your neighbor's property by means of a boundary, otherwise he will swallow what is yours. Pakistan might swallow Kashmir.

Satish wants to know when the answers to his questions will come. They are affecting his mind.

"Have you ever thought of suicide?" I ask.

"When I'm uneasy, I want to kill someone else, not myself. Maybe I'm not brave enough." He asks me about a Muslim gangster I had told him about meeting, who said he fought for his faith. "What did you say to him? Did you try to improve him?"

"Who am I to improve him?"

He likes this answer very much. "For the first time in two days you've spoken frankly."

Satish thinks of his vegetarianism as a first step in his own improvement. Then he might give up girls, then he might give up everything. But he wants to know why his desire keeps increasing. First he was content with one–two shots each time he was with a girl. "Now it's up to five, six, seven. Why is that?"

I tell him that desire is nature's way of furthering the species. But he says he wants to eliminate his desires one by one. "We can't tolerate defeat. We must always have victory. When we go to do our work we cannot lose."

"What if you go to kill someone and the opposite party has a gun and kills you? Is that defeat?"

The Sikh, Mickey, answers this one. "The man who gets killed will not admit to a defeat. But five others will say he lost."

I tell them about the Gita again, about its lesson that it's enough to do your dharma.

"Truly, the Gita reduces all tension," says Satish. He feels lighter now that he knows that the answers are within him. He invites me to go on holiday with them to Mahabaleshwar. Then they are on to planning their next operation, in Chembur. There is hurried whispering with Zameer, and then they are both gone, in separate directions.

Zameer now gives me the real names of the two men. And then comes the greatest surprise: Mickey, says Zameer, is actually a shooter for the Rajan Company, sworn enemy of Satish's company. When Satish left the Rajan gang, Mickey stayed. He had come there today to warn Satish that one of the bomb-blasts people associated with the D-Company was about to be hit and to give Satish the name so the target could be warned and flee. This he did because they were friends, and also because Mickey felt some compassion for the target; he was just a nobody who had stored some ammunition. Zameer observes, "There is honor even among thieves." He leans back and lights a cigarette. "Now for the first time today I can relax. I was really afraid about what they were going to do with that bartan. I was going nineteen–twenty, up and down." Zameer had jumped to get a rick-shaw when we left the hotel. He was afraid the shooters would fire the gun on the road if we walked down. They had been raring to go all afternoon and evening; they had asked him if they could fire it in the bathroom. In that hotel room, Zameer says, Satish was holding the bullets up to his nose and smelling them.

THAT MORNING, before going to meet the shooters the second time, I had written down in my computer the name of God and then backspaced over it, so that his name would be woven invisibly into the screen, would form a foundation or wash for all the accounts of murder and assault that I would be writing that day. I don't like Satish and I don't like Mickey. If the police or another gangster shoot them dead—*when* the police or another gangster shoot them dead—I will feel no regret. I will not feel that the earth is a poorer place for their passing.

And yet, and yet . . . at the time I am sitting with them, when my eyes are anxiously following the gun as it goes from hand to hand, the clip as the bullets are removed and reloaded, the angle of the gun as it is aimed, and the finger put on the trigger—they are doing it so fast, like three-card-monte artists, might they not make a mistake and have one bullet left when they think they've emptied the chamber?—that time in the room when I am with these men who think good and evil, sin and virtue are for the common people, for frogs in the well, is there not an exhilaration in me? Why am I not tired of listening to them? Why do the nine hours pass by effort-lessly, as with a new lover?

The day after my second meeting with Satish, and the day after that, I walk about in the world of the mundane in a daze. I go with Sunita into the city to meet an old friend, to take in a movie, to have dinner. But the rest of the world seems trivial. Their conversations revolve around trivialities: careers, taxes, shopping. Nobody in that Bombay talks about God, or sin and virtue, or death except when it is imminent, looming over a near rela-tive, and then it is dealt with in a quick, frightened fashion, as if to get it out of the way as quickly as possible. But I have been immersed in extended contemplation of those questions with people who have to face them every hour of every day, and it has been exhilarating. The last time I can recall exploring those topics in such depth was with my grandfather, as he lay dying in my uncle's house in Bombay. But I was not as close to death then as I was in that hotel room.

Now, ordinary conversations bore me. "How much more do you need?" my wife, my friends keep asking me, concerned about my safety. They are asking the question based on the wrong premise. They think I keep meeting the gangsters for material for my book.

Chotta Shakeel: The Don in Exile

A few weeks later, Kamal tells me that Zameer has gone to the Gulf. "He has gone to the bhai log."

"When will he be back?"

"He won't. You have met a future don. You know that shooter you met? He is controlled by Zameer. Zameer reports directly to Shakeel. You will be reading his name in the headlines in a few days." I think of that small intelligent man. He hadn't said much during my conversations with Satish, but it was obvious that the shooter was taking orders from him. Now, on Zameer's orders, Satish had killed a Muslim man named Salim, a former colleague of theirs who had switched to the Chotta Rajan gang. Kamal tells me that because Zameer was with me during my meetings in the hotel, I was safe. Otherwise the shooters are a bit mad. "If you had asked the wrong question they would have shot you and then said sorry. A gun is such a thing that if it is in a eunuch's hand he will think himself a man."

I tell Kamal I still want to go to Pakistan and meet Chotta Shakeel. The modalities of my meeting are worked out: I am to go to Dubai and meet a man named Anwar, Chotta Shakeel's younger brother, whom the don has always kept out of the gangs—he runs a cargo business. He will take me to Karachi, where I will meet Shakeel, and I can talk to him as much as I like. Kamal knows Shakeel well; he has spent time with him, and he tells me about him.

Shakeel is sometimes referred to as the Sheth, or as Haji saab. He isn't much to look at, Kamal confirms. He is truly small, five feet tall and thin. Shakeel is also called paun takla by his friends, because he is three-quarters bald from the front. His father worked at the Mazagaon docks as a technician, was laid off, and then found itinerant work as a ship painter. His mother sorted grain for a living. They had five children, and all of them lived in one small room. Shakeel, the second brother, passed high school and started out repairing televisions. He began selling counterfeit watches. Then he started doing matter, or debt recovery, work and caught Dawood's eye.

Shakeel first made his name during a customs seizure of a consignment of smuggled gold. He was a junior operative back then. When the customs men from Delhi came for him, Shakeel jumped out the window into a gutter, leaving the gold behind. The agents sealed it and wrote up the quantity. Shakeel waited for them to come out of the building gate downstairs, held a gun to the first customs agent to walk through the door, and took the gold back. Then he slapped the agents and sent them off. The agents and the police sealed off the entire area of Nagpada and demanded only one man: "that shorty." Through their political connections, the gang got him out. Eventually, he fled to Dubai in 1989.

Shakeel is married and has two daughters, who are with him in Pakistan and hate being there; they curse it. But his entire extended family runs on his money. In Pakistan, Shakeel occupies himself by watching western movies all night on a huge projector screen in his house.

"What kind?" I ask.

"Shootouts."

Kamal has a good relationship with Shakeel. "He's a nice person. When he used to talk with me, he talked with respect. 'Do this, beta.' Like an elder brother." He forgives easily, unless you talk to him in anger. He has another name: Insaaf ka Tarazu, the Scales of Justice. Kamal saw why with his own eyes. An old man owed eight lakhs to someone, and the creditor had taken the matter to Shakeel's court. Kamal was playing carom in Shakeel's office when the old man was brought in, alone. The old man explained that he was in great need; his daughter had to get married. "And then Shakeel said he was not to pay one paisa; in fact, Shakeel gave the old man two lakhs."

In the absence of justice from the legal system, the bhais take on the role of judges. They stress that when they step into a dispute, they don't just take one side and extort the other side for money. If a businessman comes to the bhai to recover money from a debtor, the matter is looked into by the bhai before the debtor is approached to pay. This makes business sense for the underworld. It is much more difficult to get someone to part with money that he doesn't owe than it is to get him to pay up legitimate debts. Even the language the bhais use in settling disputes is borrowed from the courts. The sense that justice can be obtained from the under-world is so pervasive that the phenomenon has reached its logical conclu-sion: In November 1999, a senior judge in Bombay himself approached Shakeel for his assistance in recovering forty lakhs that he was owed in a "chit fund," an informal savings scheme. A mob lawyer named Shaikh arranged for the judge to speak to Shakeel, according to a transcript of the talk made public by the police:

SHAIKH: Please talk to Judge saheb, he is in the sessions court and a good man.

JUDGE: Salam aleikum!

SHAKEEL: Salam, salam, tell me.

JUDGE: I have got to recover some money from somebody. His name is —————.

SHAKEEL: Just a moment. Fayeem, give me the pen and the diary. Yes. How much?

JUDGE: Around 40 lakh. It's mine, my son's, and son-in-law's together.

SHAKEEL: What is his shop called?

JUDGE: —————.

SHAKEEL: Okay, the one in Sion?

JUDGE: Yes, yes.

SHAKEEL: I know that. I already have his matter involving two crores. But I will clear you.

[Shakeel then uses the opportunity to talk about police brutality.]

SHAKEEL: Why don't you take any action against the police for encounters?

JUDGE: The matter should come before us.

SHAKEEL: That will come. But even after Judge Aguiar's report, more encounters happened. The police just don't care for the law.

JUDGE: It is an injustice, it is an atrocity.

[Shakeel then goes on to narrate an encounter incident.]

SHAKEEL: In none of the encounters were the police hurt.

JUDGE: They should, they should [be hurt].

SHAKEEL: Now, what do I do about these officers?

JUDGE: You are a wise man.

SHAKEEL: I know I am.

It is a conversation between two judges, or between a judge and a supplicant. "I already have his matter involving two crores," the more powerful judge says, after asking his clerk to get his pen and diary. The judicial courtesies are observed: "You are a wise man." The senior judge reproves the junior one for tolerating lawlessness among the police force. But he reassures the petitioner: "I will clear you." In this particular incident, the litigation failed. The lawyer, Shaikh, was murdered by his own gang. The police had been taping Shaikh's calls and had stumbled upon the judge's conversation with Shakeel. If the lawyer's phone had not been tapped, the chances would have been better than even that the judge would have recovered his money, minus the usual legal expenses, the contingency fee. As Police Commissioner M. N. Singh said, summarizing the conversation, "A judge has lost faith in the judiciary and approaches a gangster to settle a personal matter."

KAMAL SAYS he has been telling me all about the underworld because I am in the media and he wants this message to be passed on to the government, to the society, to the system, and to the underworld: Everybody is selfish in the underworld; nobody is anybody's friend. Zameer is not Satish's friend; he uses him for his own ends. Dawood and Shakeel don't trust each other. "There is a fight between the two. It is an internal matter." Shakeel depends on Dawood's money to stay alive and, in turn, shields his don from Chotta Rajan. But Shakeel is not safe in Karachi, says Kamal. "I think in the near future the ISI people will kill Shakeel." Pakistani intelligence suspects he might be playing both sides of the fence, supplying information to Indian intelligence. The Indian government, given a choice, would support Shakeel over Dawood; Shakeel, as far as anyone knows, had no role in the bomb blasts. "He is a very communal gangster, a well-wisher of the community," admits Kamal. "But he won't do it to an innocent." It

was Dawood and Tiger Memon, also hiding in Karachi, who were involved
with the blasts. "They are guests of Pakistan, so they have to do Pakistan's
bidding." On this point the police and the mob controller agree: Dawood
now lives in Karachi as a guest and prisoner of the ISI. Ajay Lal explains,
"Dawood is his own prisoner at the moment. He can't back out. He
requires the ISI there. The moment he comes back here he'll be killed, by
his opponents or his own people."

Still, Dawood lives in style in his adopted home, collecting houses,
cars, passports, and women. He dresses in Armani suits and cruises the seas
off Karachi in a speedboat, shooting seagulls. But all his money couldn't
keep his nine-year-old daughter Mariah from dying of meningitis in Karachi in 1997. Dawood was broken by her death and stepped away from
active control of his empire, leaving it to his brother Anees and to Shakeel.
They have become rivals, and there is bound to be an internal gangwar in
the D-Company after its namesake dies.

Kamal later speaks to Shakeel about our trip to Pakistan, and the don
advises against it. The atmosphere there isn't good, he tells Kamal. "A civil
war is about to start. The agencies ask about everyone from India."
Instead, he will speak to me on the phone from Dubai, where I am stopping
on my way to America. I am equally interested in seeing how Zameer is
faring in his new home.

THEY ARE WAITING for me right outside the airport, Zameer and
another young man. Zameer smiles when he sees me; he needs a shave and
his eyes are bloodshot. It is very early in the morning; they had been waiting since five-thirty. On his mobile, the silent man with Zameer calls their
bhai for instructions, and we are told to take a taxi to a hotel.

If Bombay has a twin, it is Dubai. It is the aspirational ideal for most
of Bombay, except for the section that yearns for New York or London.
We drive through the spanking new city, and I tell Zameer that it looks
as if it were built yesterday. This is quite a change from Mira Road.
We are driving in a big American car on fast new roads past skyscrapers,
and there is not a single human being to be seen. Zameer has been in
Dubai for a month. "Do you like it here?" I ask him. He quickly shakes his
head no.

The taxi stops at the hotel, and there is some argument between the young man and the cabbie over 1 dirham. Once we get into the room, this colleague, who I ascertain in the lift is also from Bombay, suddenly bursts out with, "Those Pakistanis are real bastards."

"Why?" asks Zameer. "Was the taxidriver Pakistani?"

"Yes. Swine."

A little later, we go out for lunch to an Indian restaurant. Zameer and a college friend of Girish's, a stocky Keralite who changed his name from Sree to Shoaib after joining the D-Company, tell me about their lives in Dubai. They are subjected to daily humiliations. At the telephone office, they might be waiting in a long line of Indians and Pakistanis, and a man in Arab dress will go straight to the window and his payment will be taken first. The Arabs refer to the Indians and Pakistanis as beggars, or harami, bastards. "If someone comes from Bombay," says Shoaib, who has been living here for a few years, "we eagerly ask him, 'What's happening in Bombay?' "

Zameer tells Shoaib about how wonderful Bombay has become. "Fifty-five flyovers! You'll be able to get from Andheri to Colaba in speed limit." He has nostalgic memories of train-hopping from Mira Road to Borivali and Borivali to Andheri and Andheri to Dadar. He remembers the greenery everywhere; in Dubai there are few trees to look at. He misses his family most of all, the fact that ten people would be in tension if he was late, that apnapan, that sense of belonging. Here they have to wash their own clothes, cook their own meals, clean their own toilets. They are living in a city they detest, and survive by creating a facsimile Bombay world, through the television and through constant phone conversations with their troops on the ground in Bombay. "We have no friends among the nationals." They have, it occurs to me, no friends at all.

LATER, ZAMEER AND I WALK out into the neon Dubai night. The bars and streets of the sheikhdom are filled with prostitutes: very young Malay girls and very white Russian girls wearing tight shorts and walking with long strides down the empty boulevards. We go into a pub, where I grate-fully sip from a pint of Kilkenny beer. "I can't go back anymore. Down-stairs is finished for me," says Zameer matter-of-factly. Salim, the man he had ordered killed, was working for Chotta Rajan. He had already killed three bomb-blasts suspects and was going to kill Zameer himself; he had been scoping out Zameer's place when Zameer's boys noticed him. Zameer got the order from Shakeel. "Do him."

He set Satish on the case, who kidnapped him in a car, beat him, and put him on the phone to Zameer to decide his fate. Salim pleaded for his life. "There were waves in his voice," recalls Zameer, flattening his hand into a chop and making it tremble. He told him he was sorry and he would henceforth work only for the D-Company. Zameer was conducting this conversation while pacing up and down on the street below his apartment, on the other side of the Arabian Sea. Zameer cursed him for having killed the three bomb-blasts suspects and told him he was a traitor.

But there was a technical problem: Chotta Shakeel had given his word to the Bombay Police that not a single bullet would be fired by his gang during the elections. So Satish took a large knife and cut Salim open. "It takes huge guts to be able to do that, when blood is spouting at you," observes Zameer. He slit him so that his kidneys came out. Half an hour after he died, Satish phoned Zameer again; the work had been done. The body lay for three days, from Monday to Wednesday, on the terrace of a building in Mira Road. But Chotta Rajan, who had ordered Salim to kill Zameer, knew from Monday on that his boy was missing, so he told the police about Zameer and where to find his family. The cops were lying in wait outside his house to encounter him, but Zameer had already fled to Dubai.

Zameer's family is in tension. He hasn't spoken to them since he got here; the police might be monitoring their phone lines. They picked up his brother and tortured him till he went mute, and Zameer had to pay them 50,000 rupees through Kamal to get him released. "If they had killed him, I would do anything," the small man says with emotion. "Throw a bomb, anything." Another large sum went to release Satish's brother-in-law, who was also involved in the murder. Shakeel gave him two lakhs total for the job. This is the advantage in not doing work on a contract basis; if he had contracted to do the job for, say, one lakh (which is already a high sum, given the 5,000-rupee payments to the actual shooters), with what face would he be able to ask the bhai for more if the cost of paying off people was higher than originally thought? There is no set price when Shakeel asks him to kill someone. To Zameer according to his need, from Shakeel according to his ability. "The underworld gives, it doesn't take," he avers.

He enumerates the munificence of the company. Zameer's apartment, which he shares with Shoaib and other people, costs 35,000 dirhams a year. He has a laundry, a TV, a stereo, and the latest-model mobile phone; his phone bill to India averages 70,000 rupees a month. Also, any amount he requests for his family—the cost of a wedding, for example—is immediately sent on by Shakeel. Zameer estimates it costs eighteen lakhs a year for Shakeel to keep Zameer in Dubai. Some of the time that Zameer works— he has two hundred men under him in Bombay—he is planning the hits, the escape routes for the shooters, and how to deal with the police inquiry that will follow. He draws charts, with a pencil, to help him visualize the scene on the ground.

Zameer suggests we go to another pub for variety. We walk out into the humid street again and see pictures of girls for a ladies' bar in a hotel. We go inside and stop at the gents. I go to a urinal while he goes into a lavatory booth, as straight men do when only two of them are in a public toilet. But Zameer opens the door of his cubicle immediately and steps out. "Cockroach." I see it, the white cockroach that has scared the budding don pissless.

Upstairs in the hotel are two rooms, both with music playing. "Pakistani," says the doorman for one, trying to invite us into a room with a Pakistani ghazal singer. "Indian," says the man in front of the other, which has the dancers. Both are trying to entice us. "Come, come!" Without hesitation, Zameer walks into the Indian room, and I follow him. It is a sad excuse for a ladies' bar. The fat girls, imported from Bombay, sit on chairs onstage wearing pantsuits. There is a fog machine. Old songs are playing, the kind that NRIs are fond of: "Eena Meena Deega" and "Bole re Papeehara." It is almost empty. "In Dubai everyone knows I work for Shakeel Bhai. It is open. In Bombay there will be one or two Crime Branch people in every bar. If I were sitting like this in Bombay I would have four or five bodyguards standing behind me." Here, in this strange country, Zameer is anonymous, sad, and safe.

This is the true meaning of exile: some insurmountable force that keeps you from going back. Zameer will be shot dead on his way home from the airport if he goes back, either by the police or by the Rajan Company. So he sits at home in the evenings in a country he hates, watching endless Sony TV and Zee TV. He dreams of taking the train at Mira Road and praises the fifty-five flyovers of Bombay to his friends, in between phone calls in which he orders the destruction of the city he longs for.

After three months he can go to Karachi, which he hates even more than Dubai—in Dubai, at least, he says, the people are disciplined—or to Bangkok. Zameer is a special category of refugee: not a political refugee, not an economic refugee, but a criminal refugee.

SHOAIB KEEPS CALLING PAKISTAN from my hotel room, trying to get Shakeel on the phone. The boys refer to him with respect as "Chotte Saab." He is a namaazi, they say; he prays five times a day and never drinks, smokes, womanizes, or curses. My friend the crime reporter Naeem Husain had once argued with Chotta Shakeel. "How can you say you kill for Islam? When you shoot another Muslim, is that Islamic?"

"The prophet is dead and Allah is in heaven," Shakeel had replied. "We have to do what we can on earth."

I speak to Anwar, Shakeel's brother, once. "I hope you are experiencing no trouble in Dubai? There is nothing to worry about," he reassures me, without my asking.

At first it appears that Shakeel has gone to visit Dawood, whose mother has just died in Bombay—of natural causes. There is some tension among the fraternity in Karachi as a result, and Shoaib is uncertain about whether I'll be able to get my interview. I have bought 300 dirhams' worth of prepaid phone cards from a supermarket and fed them into Shoaib's mobile. We call again. Finally, I hear Shoaib's voice change. "Ji, bhai. Ji, bhai," he says into the phone. His face tenses up and he stands rooted to one spot in the room. The phone is handed to me, and Chotta Shakeel comes on the line.

The don brings my attention to the fact that he never gives interviews, he has no need of fame, and he is doing this only because I, a man from America, have traveled so far to talk to him. He repeats this contention several times throughout our conversation. He speaks in chaste Urdu; obviously, his years in Dubai and Pakistan have changed his Bambaiyya Hindi. Throughout, he is very respectful, relaxed, confident. He never hesitates; it is a voice used to giving orders. There is not the merest hint of anger in the don's voice, just suggestions he expects to be obeyed—"You are not to write of this"—when we discuss matters that could cause him real trouble. To difficult questions, his answers are roundabout, like those of a politician.

I ask the don whether he misses Bombay.

"There is no other city like it in the whole world. I miss my people, my land; that air, that sky; those known faces, those relatives." I sense he is straining to convey, in Urdu, his great longing in some poetic form. "It is like a dish which, once tasted, is never forgotten. I miss my whole family, but apart from that I was born there. A man never forgets where he was born. A man never forgets his childhood, his lanes, his neighborhood. A man loves this very much. To go to picnics during school . . . to see films . . . to go out with friends . . . My story is this," he says, in the manner of an actor explaining himself in a movie scene. "I read up to SSC"—eleventh standard—"and I wanted to read more. My intention was to join the military or be an officer. You know how, in school, people write on the topic 'What I Want to Be'? I had a vision of becoming a military officer, and I wrote a composition on it. I wanted to die for my country. The feeling a man has for his country—some people think about it, some people do it. I had a desire to do it, but the circumstances and conditions took such a turn that I am a lieutenant in the D-Company." He knows who to blame for his inability to serve his country. "The police people have a hand in my life being spoiled. Then I got involved in this line and the result is in front of you."

I ask him how he controls such a huge operation from so far away. I do not say "from Karachi"; his boys have already said it to me a dozen times today.

"Don't write the name of this country," he commands. "The planning and the activities are known to the boys on down, and they do the work according to their way. There is a communications link." Shakeel spends a lot of time on the phone. He expresses amazement at the Internet. "You press a button and the whole of the news is in front of you!" The don spends a couple of hours every day on the Internet, scanning the Bombay newspapers: checking the financial pages, seeing who has made a killing in the market. "The biggest source of information worldwide is the electronic media. The second is political magazines, which people like you put out." Then there is his intelligence network. "I have many contacts downstairs, who tell me what is going on all over India. The news that you don't get I get before you." The don is also a bibliophile; he is particularly partial to spy novels. He has liked reading since he was a boy. "I can read a novel in half or three-fourths of an hour."

I ask him why he is at war with Chotta Rajan. Is it, as Rajan says, because of the blasts?

"Listen closely," the don commands. "In all Bombay it is known that Chotta Rajan has not split apart because of the bomb blasts. One year before the blasts, from 1991 to '92, he got a fault in his heart and became a traitor. Three boys of his—Diwakar Chudi, Amar, Sanjay Raggad, his boys—we killed all three for being traitors to the company. The fourth was Chotta Rajan. Twelve to fifteen years Dawood raised him like a little boy. Instead of killing him, he forgave him. He had raised him like a child, and Rajan touched his feet and wept a lot, so he forgave him. He didn't do anything for the Company. After the bomb blasts, six months later, he left Dubai. He had to tell people why he broke away, so he told people it was because of the bomb blasts. He knew what the reality of the blasts was and who did it."

"So who did it?" I ask.

"You are not to talk about it now," the don suggests.

It is not true, Shakeel claims, that the people of the Muslim community go into the D-Company, and the people of the Hindu community go to Chotta Rajan or Gawli. "Many Hindu boys are with us," he says, putting the ratio as high as fifty–fifty. For Hindu festivals, the Hindu members of his company are given money. "Our motto," he declares, "is insaaniyat"— humanity.

I ask him his opinion of the police. It is not vituperative, as I have found among the shooters. "Particular officers are tied to particular gangs, but not the whole department. Some officers are good, even today. All the IPS officers—those are neutral and do good work." He allows that the police have to do their work, even if it involves killing his men. "Encounters should happen to those who pose a danger to the public, who harass the public." But they should have ethics. "They should also want that an innocent not die at their hands, because he is also someone's child, someone's breadwinner." The police have been killing innocents of late. "In some departments there are people who do things according to religion. They've been killing Muslim boys for the last four months, saying this boy belongs to the D-Company. Seventy-five percent of those boys aren't mine, and I don't know them." This is a fair estimate, according to what I've seen in Bombay. "The police bring them in and kill them, saying this man is of the D-Company, or with Chotta Shakeel." Then he adds, "Which is one and the same thing." The afterthought is significant. People have been questioning this assumption. But he is saying it confidently. Shakeel is not going to break with the D-Company, he is going to inherit it.

Since he is residing in enemy country, I ask him what he feels about the recent war in Kashmir.

"Suketubhai, war is a very bad thing these days. Because people's lives are lost, the economy gets ruined. The whole nation goes back a hundred years. Who benefited after the war? So many weapons and missiles are being made, millions of dollars. These same monies, if they are spent on the poor, then every country, not just Hindustan, would be very happy." He avers that, contrary to his reputation, he loves India and wants to die for it. "There is no doubt about this. The country in which a man is born, a man does not become a traitor to that land. A man can only give his life for his country. That is a very big medal for him. That is a very big respect. When a man wants to join the military, he doesn't want to go there to play cricket or exercise; he wants to martyr himself."

The mastermind of the largest criminal syndicate in the subcontinent now comes out with a line from JFK. "My intention is, What can I do for my country? Not, What has the country done for me?" Then he adds, "Think about that."

He is in favor of power being transferred to the younger generation, "who have a plan for the future." The politicians of today, he says, "have become so old that their only future is death, whether in a year or two or five." He speaks of them with special venom, enumerating the assorted scams and scandals they are involved in: a leather scam, a fodder scam. There is a difference between criminals and politicians, whom he compares using the standard Bombay metaphor of the movies. "The difference is that all the criminals do their work on the screen, which people can see. Politicians work behind the screen, which the public can't see. It is the same, whether you work from behind or in front of the screen. Politicians are bigger criminals than us. We fight among ourselves, but these people are ruining the whole world." It is clear which party he favors in Bombay. "Today the Shiv Sena have ruined Maharashtra. Good government has been done in the Congress rule."

I ask him if he is satisfied with the way his own life has turned out.

"A human being is incomplete. All his life, something or the other is after him. Whether a man does good work or bad, he is never satisfied with himself. What I wanted to do—become a military officer, that dream I had—was crushed from the beginning. Now what dream should I see, what wish should I have for the future?" he asks me. He reverts back to the language of Bollywood. "The way life goes, the THE END, only Allah knows."

Does he have any regrets?

"A man who does bad things can never think them good. I think that something went wrong, or I did something wrong."

I ask him how, as a man who professes to be a good Muslim, he reconciles being religious with being a murderer.

"Enmity and religion have nothing to do with each other. Both of them have their place in life. Some steps are taken for the sake of the religion. Not just mine; you do it too." The gangwar will never end. "Enemies die, but not the enmity. An enemy dies, and another is born." Then he defends himself: "My record is that I have never done anything to any innocent man. I don't kill anyone for extortion." He claims, further: "I don't ask for extortion money. I have so many businesses that I have no need." Since the whole work of extortion is done over the phone, he points out, there are many people who extort in his name. Recently, two Marwaris had been killed under his name. When the police need to close their files, they attribute all kinds of murders to him, which he has had nothing to do with. "It is not a good thing that murders happen for extortion," the don opines.

Still, he seems to have a heavy sense of his involvement in "wrong work." "What is wrong is wrong. A sin is a sin." The punishment would come after death. But "a man should be given the chance to improve. If even what he hasn't done is stuck on him, then a man can't return. His life becomes"—and he uses the English phrase—"one-way traffic."

My card runs out and the line is cut. After a minute Shoaib's phone rings and first an assistant gets on, then Shakeel. I can hear a blast of car horns in the background; perhaps he is in traffic, or the noise is coming in through an open window. He explains again that he doesn't have that much time. "But I thought, since you came from America . . ." He is reminding me again of the courtesy he is doing me. "Our true faces should come in front of the public. People have spoilt our faces." But this is true in every field: "People who love you and people who hate you." At the end, he asks me, "Now you tell me, what did you think of me?" It is a strange question. Is he anxious about my opinion, anxious to be liked, or is he trying to suss out what I will be writing about him, so it can be stopped in time? As I am talking to their boss, the boys are leaning over my computer, watching what I am typing. I have to tread carefully.

"You speak like a poet," I reply, knowing my countrymen.

The don is pleased by this response. He offers me a gift. "Any kind of work that you need from me, at any time, you call me. Leave your phone numbers with these people or contact me through them." It is an immense favor, offered to me by someone who has absolute power to grant it. I guess it is his way of keeping journalists happy. The government might give a house; companies would provide a junket; the mob boss throws in a death to my enemies. He is offering me something from the Company store. I thank him and tell him I have no such need at the present moment.

"Very few people understand me," he says, at the end of our conversation. He says it with some pride.

I say good-bye to Zameer in the lobby of the hotel. And then Zameer repeats Shakeel's offer: "Any trouble you have in Bombay. One work free. Bhai said so."

My childhood was filled not so much with violence as the constant fear of violence. I longed for a defender against the bullies in my school, in my building. Now at last I have my protectors: Ajay Lal, Kamal, Shakeel himself. They will lay waste to my enemies. The tough guys, the Lords of the Last Bench in my school, have grown up and they are my friends. I now walk around the world with a different status, a different sense of security. The don has offered me one free hit.

Later, when I repeat this story to close friends in Bombay, in New York, a wistful look comes into their eyes, and they start making lists of the people they would eliminate if they were granted such a favor. They are only half joking, and I am genuinely shocked by some of the names they give me—ex-lovers, colleagues. The women are more interested in using such a gift than the men. If men dream about killing someone, they want to do it themselves, squeezing the trigger, plunging the knife. Women need it done for them. Most of the names they have in mind are those of people they once loved greatly and now hate with equal passion. Each one of us, I am beginning to discover, has a circle of people close to us whose deaths we fantasize about.

I hold on to my favor like a rabbit's foot in my pocket; it makes me feel secure, walking around Bombay, and I am calmer with people who threaten me, more tolerant. I know what I can do if I am really provoked. That knowledge makes me magnanimous, forgiving of slights. I become a better human being because I know I can get the person of my choice murdered.

IN APRIL 2000, two shakha pramukhs are shot dead by Shakeel's men. Sunil and Amol are out on the streets, shutting down all of Jogeshwari, taking rickshaws off the road, ordering shops to pull down their shutters. The State Reserve Police is called out. The Sena goes on the warpath in the assembly. They demand the resignation of the Congress government over the issue of "breakdown of law and order in the state." The government goes all out to find the killers of the Sena pramukhs. Ajay Lal tells me why one of the shakha pramukhs was killed. "He was banging a Muslim girl," the cop says, with the glee of someone who is privy to information that is unprintable in the newspapers. "And Shakeel didn't like the kafirs messing with their girls. He said, 'Do him.'"

Girish is getting more and more frightened. He phones me one Sunday night. "You know the Sena work? It was done by our friend." Kamal had showed him two sketches of the killers, put out by the police in the newspapers. Any citizens who recognize these two men have been asked to contact the police. Girish recognized them as Satish and Mickey.

I call Kamal. He tells me that Zameer had sent out the order for the work, and Satish and Mickey had executed it. "They have become superstars." The D-Company is now extracting its revenge for the forty or fifty members of the gang that were killed by the previous Sena government. Under the aegis of the more friendly Congress government, they are going after the shakha pramukhs; and the police officers, who had been kicked around by the pramukhs, are not unsympathetic to Shakeel's boys.

Once again, I am in possession of dangerous information. I know the two assassins that the entire police force is looking for; even Ajay has misidentified the man who did the work of the shakha pramukhs as Nilesh Kokam, who was subsequently shot dead. The police, hunting high and low for Satish, had killed a number of people who had nothing to do with the shooting; in one twenty-four-hour period, four men are killed in three separate encounters. But I know their real names, what they like to eat, how they love, what their precise relationship is with God. I know who controls them in faraway countries. And I know exactly who, when tortured, will give up their hiding places.

At this point, I quit my researches into the underworld. But the gang-war will never end. Because, at its core, it is not the gangsters against the police or one gang against another. It is a young man with a Mauser against history, personal and political; it is revolution, one murder at a time.

PART II * PLEASURE

Vadapav Eaters' City

DARIYA MAHAL IS HISTORY. Would that it were rubble.

It was a necessary mistake. I didn't say good-bye to Dariya Mahal. I felt no need to be in that flat one second longer than I had to. I had forgotten, at my peril, how much I am affected by the physical space I live in. A couple of months after I find the office in Elco Arcade, I also find, through a broker, a flat to call home in Bandra. I have no personal history in Bandra; it was as remote for me when I was growing up as Patagonia. It used to be considered a suburb, populated by Catholics. The only Catholics I knew were my teachers at school, and my knowledge of their lifestyle was gleaned from the Hindi movies, where the Christian women always wore short skirts and the men always drank excessively. I liked them for this reason. As I got older, I felt more comfortable among them than the Gujaratis I grew up with, where if you went to someone's house for dinner you got very good vegetarian food but no liquor to build up an appetite with.

The new flat is the home of a famous actress who starred in some of the best films of the parallel cinema in the eighties, before her untimely death. Now her sister is renting it out. The contract negotiation couldn't be more different from the one for the Dariya Mahal flat, which was basically done over a handshake with the diamond merchant. The contract for the Bandra flat is the longest and most detailed contract I have ever signed. We begin with a premise, strongly reinforced by the broker, of mutual suspicion and distrust. Among the items enumerated by the owner, so that we cannot steal them when we leave: curtain rods, the number and type of ceiling light fittings, and a toilet paper holder. We go over every line, every word, like arms negotiators scrutinizing a ballistic missiles treaty. At the end, the owner does not shake my hand or wish me well in her home. All this for a third-floor walkup an hour distant from the city center. The Rent Act has made Bombay a city without trust.

But it's a much nicer flat, worth all the hassle in getting it. The wood furniture is as spare and elegant as that of the Dariya Mahal flat was not. This flat, too, has a view of the sea. In front of me, an ugly pink building, but beyond it, to the left, my sea. I can have the windows open and junk won't fly in. Above, the vast sky. A clean house in which the light is perfect for a portrait sitting. All afternoon the light changes, soothes. And then it rains and there is the lovely monsoon light. Living in Dariya Mahal, I forgot that Bombay, too, has light that is worthy of notice. Monday afternoon, and I see no people as I look out the window. It's India, and I don't see any people! Luxurious vista for the eyes to roam about, settling at leisure on the palm trees, the rolled-back sea at low tide, the towels hanging still from the laundry lines. But there! A servant comes to the window opposite and takes up the laundry. Well, one person is okay. For contrast.

Outside the children's bedroom is an almond tree, which surprises us of a morning with a bright red leaf among the broad green leaves; it has changed color overnight, as if painted by a practical joker.

IN BOMBAY, after the first year, our lifestyle is much like it was in the East Village. We begin making friends again, adding to our wealth. By now we have accumulated a fine collection of generous people on three continents; not so much loved ones as liked ones. Friends, separate or common to me and Sunita, drop in from out of town—Bhopal, New York, New Delhi, London—along with my sisters and cousins, and without planning it we have a party. Our friends don't mind if we wait to begin cooking until they arrive, and they don't mind chopping onions and ginger for the meal. As some of us cook in the kitchen, others sprawl around the living-room floor and balance my sons on their stomachs or construct Meccano cars with them. We offer them beer and wine, and sometimes something stronger, and food carefully cooked and casually served. Some smoke dope by the window. There might be music, and my kids dance to it. You can wander from cluster to cluster of people and join in whatever conversation is happening—about the toxic corridor in Gujarat that the friend from Greenpeace is fighting; or about photography, and Dayanita's exhibition; or whether or not the friend from Bhopal should get married to his latest girlfriend. Or you can not talk at all and put a towel on and off your head, causing Akash to go off into peals of laughter. There are people who don't like each other, people who have good reason to hate each other because they were once in love, but they are here together now by accident and have to make the best of it. After the fourth drink they find out that their differences are nonexistent. They will be rediscovered with the hangover tomorrow morning, but for now there is only the boozy fellowship. Presently, at an advanced hour, after everybody is suitably drunk, dinner will be put on the table, often in the pots in which it is cooked, and it will be hot as hell in order to get through to our taste buds, deadened by the alcohol. My sons stay awake till everyone leaves, at one in the morning, two in the morning, or till they drop. This feels familiar. This is what we like to do of an evening, wherever we are.

Other things start changing for us. We begin understanding simple things: how to negotiate with shopkeepers, taxi drivers, and relatives. Sunita's Hindi gets better, and she learns how not to get ripped off by the servants. We now know never to go to anyone's place for dinner before nine-thirty. In the first year, we would show up at eight—New York time—and sit around drinking nervously as the hostess attempted to get dressed and cook and make conversation with us all at the same time. We find out where to shop for corkscrews, bedsheets, oregano, and computers. The kids stop getting sick all the time, and when they do we don't worry so much. All the kids in Bombay are sick much of the time. It is the bad air, the bad water, the bad food—and the country still has 1 billion people. One billion thin, often sickly, but alive people, some of them magnificently alive.

Even in the Bandra flat, things break down regularly. The air conditioners all fail with unerring frequency; the one in my study periodically leaks on my head as I am writing. For the entire summer, there is no running water all day. It goes at nine-thirty in the morning and sputters back in the taps at eight-thirty in the evening. This continues into the monsoon. Outside my window, there are sheets of rain; inside, in the plush bathroom, a row of bright-colored buckets waiting under the dry taps to be replenished. But what would have upset us in the first year hardly troubles us in the second. We get up early to store the water in buckets and ration it out.

If the servant doesn't show up for a week, we clean up ourselves. If the porcelain flush tank above the toilet cracks in two, we call, with our new-found knowledge, not the plumber but the electrician, who is reliable and honest. The electrician brings in a plumber, and when he sees that the plumber is up to the usual plumber's deceptions, he kicks him out and does the job himself, patching up the tank with cement. It may not be that we get ripped off any less, but we accept it as a newcomer's tax, and we shed our American expectation of propriety in financial dealings. One night I cheat a taxi driver. He brings us home just at midnight, when the fares go up, but my watch is slow and I show him the time on it: 11:57. He takes the lower fare. I get out, and Sunita rebukes me. I realize that I have become vicious.

We learn the uses of "influence." The WIAA club, when I phone to ask for a reservation for an out-of-town visitor, says there are no rooms available. Then my uncle calls a friend, who uses his influence, and a room miraculously materializes, like the universe manifesting itself from nothing. I had forgotten the crucial difference. There's very little you can do anonymously, as a member of the vast masses. You have to go through someone. The reservations clerk needs that personal touch of a human being he recognizes. It is the same with railway reservations, theater tickets, apartments, and marriages. It has to be one person linking with another who knows another and so on till you reach your destination; the path your request takes has to go through this network. You cannot jump the chain by going directly to someone who doesn't know you, connected only by the phone line. Then it becomes just a buyer and a seller, a transaction rather than a favor. A friend went from Bombay to London and told me she was horrified that she could spend an entire day—buy tickets on the Tube, go to a play, eat—without ever needing to make a personal connection. When you want to book a hotel in Matheran or a movie ticket at Metro, you ask around: "Who has influence?" This is why people stay on in Bombay, in spite of everything. They have built a network here; they have influence.

On our Sundays in Bombay, time becomes gelid. On a Sunday morning, the smell of fish curry being stirred in family-sized pots wafts all over Khar and Bandra. The two most elusive qualities in a metropolis are intimacy and silence. Both exist here, within the Sunday afternoon. Sleep till lunch, then eat a big meal with beer, then have sex with your spouse, then sleep again. In the evening there is the walk along Carter Road or a movie for which tickets have been bought three weeks ago. Or you can walk a bit along Nariman Point, take the boy for a merry-go-round ride, look at the green-blue water studded with coconut shells, the tall buildings rising up Walkeshwar Road. If you go around Fountain or Fort you will be able to walk on the sidewalks on this day of rest; the streets will be revealed for what they really are: broad, tree-shaded, flanked by stately palaces. Sunday afternoon is what stands between the city and a general insurrection. The rest of the week people get home too late to do anything but eat and sleep, like animals, driven by animal needs. Sundays we become human again.

Gautama starts speaking Bambaiyya Hindi, that rough carpenter's language. "You're a bekaar amma," he tells his mother, when vexed. He is finding his place in the country of his bloodline. The kids of the building are playing Holi, and to my great surprise my son is laughing with them, bedecked. The parking lot downstairs has turned into a carnival. With every face multicolored, no one can see who's a servant and who's a sheth; all are drunk or stoned. You can even touch the women; on this day you can touch all the women.

In India, people are friendly to my boys. The receptionist at the airport lounge follows us about, makes us coffee, brings out cookies for the kids. She engages Gautama in conversation; they discuss the toys each of them possesses. A businessman looks up from his morning paper and speaks to Akash in Tamil. In India, my kids approach strangers with confidence; they rest their hands on our guests' knees, play with the women's dupattas. They will have to learn to put more distance between themselves and other people when we go back to America. They must learn that people don't like to be touched. Why, it's happened right here, in the first-world parts of Bombay. A friend who has lived in New York and returned is irritated by Akash because he touches things in her apartment—the music system— and climbs on her table. Then, in the taxi going home, the driver turns around and says, without preamble, "Children live under the shade of God. What adults wouldn't be able to tolerate, if they get hurt, doesn't affect little children."

The rich have the theater, parties, foreign trips. The poor have their children; they are entertained by them, they are sustained by them. When they come home off the Virar local, the children are awake, later than they really should be—they will have trouble getting up for school in the morning—but the fathers want it. They want to see their children for the half hour that tells them what they've been working for. Murderers, whores, clerks, drain cleaners, and struggling film actors alike live for the moment when they go home and their little girl comes running up to them, or wakes from deep sleep and scolds them for not coming home sooner. On holidays, they sit in the one room, watching their own children play with the neighbors' children, commenting on the habits and preferences and eccentricities of each, following their feuds like bards in medieval Italian courts. In the evening they might take the children, their own and the neighbors', to a picture, sneak in the over-five-year-old and put the child on his father's lap, eat the homemade snacks prepared by the women, and watch Amitabh Bacchan fight and dance, those creatures of light, till the child, against his will, gradually subsides, and his head drops, and the air-conditioning isn't working, and the boy is six years old, but on his father's lap he isn't heavy; he has very little weight, hardly any weight at all.

WHOSE CITY IS BOMBAY? Bombay is the vadapav eaters' city, Mama of the Rajan Company had said to me. It is the lunch of the chawl dwellers, the cart pullers, the street urchins; the clerks, the cops, and the gangsters.

I ask people sitting around my uncle's office where the best vadapav in Bombay is. They chorus in unison: "Borkar!" I set out into the afternoon heat of the central city in search of Borkar. I don't have much time; they have told me Borkar conducts his trade for only three hours a day, from four to seven, or till the vadas are gone. I walk along narrow roads dug up in the center, revealing gaping holes, past a vegetable market, past Kotachi Wadi, where some of the loveliest old houses are still inhabited by the original Catholic tenants, past the wedding-card market, past the Jain Clinic, till finally I get to Borkar. There is a small crowd of people, men to one side, women to the other, holding out money. Borkar sits on his stall, frying up a fresh batch. An old board says:

> Vadapav   —4 Rs.
> Vada   —3 Rs.
> Single Pav—1 Re.
> Prop: Borkar

I wait for him to finish frying; the dozens of people around me do the same. I am tensed, with my money at the ready. As soon as the ladle emerges from the vat of boiling oil full of vadas, beignets conjoined with wisps of yellow batter, the frenzy begins. People are thrusting their money forward, mostly 10-rupee notes; in front of the assistant is a thali full of 2-rupee coins. Nobody seems to be ordering just one. Not everybody will get their vadapav from this batch; the timid will have to keep waiting. The assistant serves the women first. The stacks of pav have been sprinkled with chutney—the top half of the inside of the bun is bathed in green chutney, the bottom with red garlic chutney—and the assistant reaches out with one hand, in one continuous arc of his arm opening the pav, scooping up two of the vadas, one in each nest of pav, and delivering it to the hungry customer. I walk away from the stall and crush the vada by pressing down on it with the pav; little cracks appear in the crispy surface, and the vada oozes out its potato-and-pea mixture. I eat. The crispy batter, the mouthful of sweet-soft pav tempering the heat of the chutney, the spices of the vada mixture—dark with garam masala and studded with whole cloves of garlic that look like cashews—get masticated into a good mouthful, a good mouth-*feel*. My stomach is getting filled, and I feel I am eating something nourishing after a long spell of sobbing. Borkar has done his dharma.

I go next to the cold-drink house at Sikkanagar, thirsty after the fire of the vadapav. There are pleasant Formica booths to sit in; the whole space has a restful, leisurely atmosphere, within which one can sip one's cold drink and watch the bustling street in peace. There is a menu of sherbets on the wall in Marathi; each is reputed to have some salubrious property. The amla essence is good for urinary problems, night blindness, and aggravation; the ginger sherbet is recommended for flatulence, bronchitis, and menstrual pain. Most of them taste great and are a quiet subversion of the worldwide dominance of cola-flavored drinks. In fact, you can launch a direct assault on Coca-Cola: You can order a masala Coke. This is the same old Coca-Cola you know, the same fizzy brown liquid, but with lemon, rock salt, pepper, and cumin added to it. When the Coke is poured into the glass, which has a couple of teaspoons of the masala waiting to attack the liquid from the bottom up, the American drink froths up in astonished anger. The waiter stands at your booth, waiting till the froth dies down, then puts in a little more of the Coke, then waits a moment more, then pours in the rest. And, lo! it has become a Hindu Coke. The alien invader has come into the country. It has been accepted into the pantheon of local drinks but has a little spice added to it, a little more zing. The cocaine is back in the Coke.

My nose is red and raw from the pollution of the central city, but I can't keep my eyes from the psychedelic chaos of the streetscape. Rows of small shops, each dedicated to furnishing the city with a microscopically precise commodity or service: wood furniture polish, typing, hair oil, fireworks, roasted chapatis, coffins, handmade footwear. These shops are run now by the fourth generation of the same family. They live upstairs in the same building, paying 15 rupees, 45 rupees, as rent. The shops are open from 11 a.m. to 9 p.m.; and the owners know where to get the best rose sherbet, the best sabudana khichdi, in that universal intimacy small traders have with street food. When out-of-town relatives come visiting, the sight-seeing doesn't go much beyond this quarter. The evening is capped off, as mine often is, with the last show at Maratha Mandir. The shopowners can never earn enough to get out of their rented accommodations, but such a possibility is unthinkable anyway. Their children will inherit this business, going strong since British times. Over patient decades, a high degree of comfort, of familiarity, has evolved.

I REDISCOVER THE IRANI RESTAURANTS, among my favorite places in Bombay to meet people or just to come in from the heat and wait. One of the lodestars of my childhood was the Café Naaz, up on Malabar Hill. It came to the city along with independence and had the finest and cheapest views of the city. I would go there every time I came back to Bombay and sit on the highest terrace (which had a 15-rupee fee added to the bill for the privilege) and, overlooking all of Chowpatty and keeping hungry crows at bay, drink my beer and catch up with friends from all countries. The avenging forces of the city government, hell-bent on destroying any vestige of beauty within the precincts of Mumbai, swooped down. The Café Naaz had been leased from the city, and there was a fight among the family members who owned it; the Municipal Corporation revoked the lease, demolished the café, and erected a water monitoring station in its place. It was too inexpensively lovely to survive in modern Mumbai.

The Iranis came to Bombay around the turn of the twentieth century. They were Zoroastrians who came from the smaller villages of Persia, such as Yezd, not from the cities, and were not well off in their home country. The Iranis were very hard workers but were persecuted for their religion in Iran. They were distinct from the Parsis, who were Iranian Zoroastrians who came to India from the eighth century onward.

The Iranis began as dealers in provisions and branched out into bakeries and eateries. They benefited from a superstition among their Hindu business competitors: It is unlucky to place a shop on a street corner. For the Iranis it was lucky; their establishments are visible on two sides and have lots of light and air because they are wide open to the intersection. They are furnished with marble-top tables and bent teakwood chairs; the walls are typically adorned with portraits of Zoroaster and full-length mirrors. Over the sink where you wash your hands in the back might be a set of instructions, which the poet Nissim Ezekiel realized form a complete poem:

> *Do not write letter*
> *Without order refreshment*
> *Do not comb*
> *Hair is spoiling floor*
> *Do not make mischiefs in cabin*
> *Our waiter is reporting*
> *Come again*
> *All are welcome whatever caste*
> *If not satisfied tell us*
> *Otherwise tell others*
> *God is great.*

An Irani serves the simplest of menus: tea, coffee, bread and butter (always Polson), salted biscuits, cakes, hard bread, buttered buns, hard-boiled eggs, buns with mincemeat, berry pilaf, and mutton biryani. Mostly the Iranis sell time and shade: A cup of tea and the table is yours for an hour while you read your newspaper or look out at the street circus. They are a whole world away, in price and atmosphere, from the Punjabi and Chinese restaurants that are now all the rage among the middle class. Your family need make no sacrifices so that you can eat here.

The clientele of the Iranis came from immigrant laborers in the city, who lived eight to a room and needed cheap basic meals—tea and brun maska, a hard bread with butter. If they couldn't afford brun maska they could have a khara biscuit. It was and remains a filler for those who can't afford anything else; the tea gives the poor energy from the many spoons of sugar in each cup. In the seventies, the South Indian Udupis started replacing the Iranis and are themselves getting replaced by beer bars. Very few of the owners' children are interested in carrying on with the Iranis; because of the community's emphasis on education, they've branched off into the professions or gone abroad. So some of the Iranis have turned into banks and department stores. Others have met change halfway, dividing their interiors into an area where beer can be consumed—the "permit room"—and another strictly for tea—the "family room."

One of those is, along with the Naaz, my favorite Irani, the Brabourne, which has been around since 1934. It used to be a stable. It is named after Lord Brabourne, the governor of Bombay at the time. Rashid Irani is one of the owners of the Brabourne. He has no family, but he does have three or four thousand books in his flat; he writes film reviews and keeps an open house for Bombay's writers, painters, and filmmakers. Rashid's Irani is one of the last four or five Iranis that hasn't gone upmarket. It serves simple fare: eggs, bread, minced beef, biscuits, tea. Twelve years ago Rashid added beer to his Irani's offerings, and now the evening hours are filled mostly with beer drinkers, some of them just waiting out the peak hours before the long commute home. "What a lovely way to wait!" exclaims Rashid.

Rashid wants to keep the Brabourne just the way it is. There is a great sense of space at the Brabourne not found in Bombay at restaurants ten times as expensive. For a couple of years in the seventies, the Brabourne experimented with a jukebox, playing Pat Boone, Elvis Presley, and Hindi film songs for 4 annas each. "We tried to get trendy." But there was a problem: the music. At the Brabourne, the waiter announces the bill to the owners instead of giving him a piece of paper. The partners, of the old generation and therefore hard of hearing, said, "What the hell, we can't hear what the waiters are saying." So they got rid of the jukebox and the Brabourne returned to its sedate self, the only noise the occasional shouts of inebriated cotton merchants discussing cricket.

The Brabourne has its set rhythms. It opens at six-thirty for people wanting their first cup of tea. Then the taxi drivers come in for their breakfast of "doll," which is the Parsi way of saying dal, eaten with pav bread. "The afternoon is colorless," as Rashid puts it. In the evening, people come for their beer. There is a huge cloth market nearby, and the cloth traders come in around seven. They talk mostly among themselves and live in the suburbs; they have a couple of beers here because they can't drink at home. At ten o'clock, Rashid pulls down the shutters. "For a bar we shut far too early," he says.

Most of the customers are of a certain age. In the mornings, from six onward, the tables are taken by the longtime regulars, mostly Parsis and Catholics. One group of four or five old Parsi men has a favorite table at the Brabourne. They get very anxious if they have to sit anywhere else. If there is just one person occupying that table, they will sit at the table next to or across from it and stare at him silently. Or they will stand around it and crowd the usurper. "It's a fetish," says Rashid. Once ensconced at their table, they will discuss issues of the day with vehemence. But the first thing they turn to is the Deaths column in the *Jam-e-Jamshed,* the community organ, the chronicler of the steady diminishment of their community.

Another old Parsi gent would come every afternoon at three o'clock. As soon as the waiters saw him sit down they would put three cups of tea in front of him. He wanted, for his own reasons, all three cups of tea simultaneously, with three pieces of brun maska. The brun maska he would dunk in just one of the cups. As soon as he got there, he always made it a point to put a 50-paise coin on the table, for the tip. Most of the Brabourne's clients, who are more affluent than he is, do not tip. But this gentleman had been cheated out of his house; all day long he sat in the fire temple down the road and lived on the alms the devout gave him. So, observes Rashid, "this man dependent on alms knew the value of both giving and receiving." The photographer Sooni Taraporevala had once taken a picture of him, as part of her series on Parsis. She made a print and gave it to him. He took a look at it and gave it back. "What for?"

A City in Heat

CITIES LIKE BOMBAY live at night. The day is a gathering-up of forces for the night. The city unfurls itself, luxuriously, after the sun sets, in the receptions, premieres, parties, and dinners of the night; in the beer bars, hotels, dance clubs, whorehouses, and alleyways. The night has no time; it is freed from the corporate rigor of the day. And the night contains sexual possibility: that man so fine in his jacket, that woman across the room lighting a cigarette.

"When the Crime Branch people catch you, they first ask who's your kept woman," says Mohsin the hit man. "Most people in this line have a mistress." Some of them end up marrying the kept woman. Only gangsters will marry them, and this is due to a common absence of honor, Mohsin says. "If I don't have izzat, what is her izzat?" The gangsters are free, like the bar-line girls, from the conventions and restraints of honor.

At this point his friend Anees, who lives on the fringes of the gangwar, tells me about the courtship of bar-line girls. "Bombay has every taste, every fetish," he begins. The city is humid with sex. At bottom are the Nepali whores, who the bhaiyyas from North India go to, paying by the half hour: 30 rupees, 50 rupees. "They are for the public. We won't even spit on them." For the gangwar boys there are only the bar dancers. There are several hundred bars in Bombay, variously called beer bars or ladies' bars or dance bars. In suburbs like Chembur and Malad there seems to be one on every block. In these bars, fully clothed young girls dance on an extravagantly decorated stage to recorded Hindi film music, and men come to watch, shower money over their heads, and fall in love. That world, which the dancers and the patrons call the bar line, is unique to Bombay, and for me it is the intersection of everything that makes the city fascinating: money, sex, love, death, and show business.

It goes this way: A gangwar boy might start becoming a regular at a bar. He might see a girl that he fancies. He might imagine himself protecting her from villains, or he pictures the girl nursing his wounds after a gunfight or an encounter. So he goes up to the girl on his way out and asks to see her after the bar closes. She smiles and asks him to come back tomorrow. He comes back the next evening and sits there and now watches only her among the dancers. She remembers him from the previous day, smiles once or twice at him, and he asks the waiter to garland her with 1,000 or 5,000 rupees. She dances a little faster for him, in his direction. He stays till the bar closes and then asks her again for her number. She asks him to come the next night; she will be waiting for him. And so he comes again and again to the bar, throwing a little more money over her head each time, till finally one night when he is least expecting it she quickly thrusts a piece of paper into his hand. On it is written the magic telephone number and her name.

The next day he gets on the phone as soon as he wakes up, eleven o'clock. There is no answer or, in the case of the more modern girls, an answering machine. All morning he calls, until finally, at one or two in the afternoon, a sleepy voice answers. "Hullo?" And so begins their relationship on the phone. In the big anonymous city, she becomes an ear for him. She listens to his problems with his wife, his parents; she understands when his work isn't going well, she worries when he doesn't eat. "Had your lunch?" she asks him.

"Yes."

"What did you have?"

"Oh, I don't know . . . a vadapav."

"You call that lunch? You just eat anything, don't even take care of yourself."

"So I'm coming over and you make me lunch," he might say at this point, trying his luck.

"Not today, my brother is coming. But soon I want to make you a meal with my own hands. I don't know why, I feel good with you. I haven't found anyone that can understand me like you. Will you come to the bar tonight? I'll be waiting for you."

And so, each afternoon, he talks to her on the phone, each evening he goes to the bar, and now when he watches her on the stage there is an intimacy between them. Of all the people in this room, of all the people in this city, she knows secrets about him. She is the only one who has asked him that day if he's eaten. He sits behind the table stacked with his money and smokes and drinks and watches her steadily, watches the way her hips rotate to the song he keeps paying 50 rupees to the waiter to play, thinks about her lying in bed talking to him, thinks about that comment she made, that she'd just come out of the bath when his call came and hadn't had time to put on any clothes.

Each day now he wants to meet her outside the bar. "Let's go to Khandala for a couple of days," he suggests.

"No. I like you a lot, but I'm not that kind of girl. I'm not like the other girls in the bar line."

He keeps coming to the bar. He keeps blowing money on her. He keeps asking her to meet him.

"Not yet, not yet," she demurs. What she doesn't say, what keeps him going, is "Not ever." By now she's the centerpiece of his fantasies; he sees the way she's looking at him in the bar, differently from the way she looks at everyone else. When she dances for other men, he knows she's only doing it for the money, but when she turns to him, when she comes in front of his table, it's quite clear she's doing it because she wants to. Didn't she say so herself, this afternoon? One evening he couldn't come to the bar—the bhai had some work for him—and she rang him early the next afternoon and was almost crying. "Where were you? I was so worried about you! Your work is so dangerous. Always, always call me if you aren't going to be coming. Otherwise the whole of last night I kept watching the door, hoping you would walk in. The other girls noticed, they kept joking with me about it: When is your chhava coming?"

SO HE ASKS HER to meet him just for a cup of coffee, and one afternoon after he's spent a lot of money the night before, after the notes showering from his hand have made her twirl in a frenzy that dazzles the entire bar, she agrees and asks him to meet her at the Heera-Panna Shopping Centre that Saturday. When he shows up, she is very happy to see him and tells him so. They stroll among the lanes of the mall, just a regular guy and his girl, just like all the other dating couples from Malabar Hill and Breach Candy, and he thinks he notices some of the men look in her direction and then look at him with envy and admiration. They walk by an electronics shop, and she squeals, turns to him, and says, "Oh, that's such a nice juicer! You know, the doctor's asked my mother to drink fresh juice every morning!" And so, gallant that he is, he will walk into the store and, without asking the price, tell the clerk, "That juicer. Pack it." They will go into other stores. "That's such a lovely shirtpiece," she says. "It would look great on my little brother." As a reward, she might lead him into a lingerie store and get the clerk to show them their most exciting underwear. She might deliberate over the purchases, holding the bra over her shirt, the g-string over her crotch, might ask him to admire the material, giggle over her naughtiness. The clerk has seen all this before, many times, and he plays his part well, showing them his most expensive wares, addressing the suitor with the respect appropriate for a big man, a ladies' man. He orders Cokes for both of them, which take some time coming, during which she keeps making more purchases, so that every time the mark makes a move to go, the clerk protests, "But the cold drinks are just coming, sir!" The clerk knows he is too embarrassed to ask the prices of the items he is buying, so they can be made up on the spot; the next day the girl will come back with her wispy purchases and bargain hard over splitting up the spoils. But in the meantime, the suitor is thinking of her in all of these items, that red lace bra, those see-through panties. He is determined that tonight he will see her in them, and then he will see her without them.

The shopping expedition might have cost him over a lakh. He will have to ask the bhai to send down some more money and, in return, he will have to kill or beat someone for the gang. On his way out, he says to her with urgency, "After you get off work tonight you're coming with me." This time he will not take no for an answer. This time she can see he intends to have his way or she will lose him. He will curse her and never come to the bar again, and neither will his money.

So she will finally say, "Okay, tonight." And after the bar closes, he will be waiting outside for her, and they might take a taxi to a good hotel— the Oberoi or the Taj or the Marine Plaza.

Or, if the girl is more imaginative, if she has a poetry about her, they will do what Anees the gangster tells me they have done with him. She will use the birds.

"You have to go to Haji Ali, to drink juice at one a.m.," he begins. Haji Ali is the tomb of a Sufi saint, and there is a causeway leading off the road to go to his tomb, on which there is always a line, Hindus and Muslims both, seeking the blessings of the saint. Every year, on a monsoon high tide, waves wash some of the worshipers from the exposed causeway. The taxi drivers touch their lips and their hearts as they drive by Haji Ali. At night it becomes a juice center. When I was growing up, I used to be taken by my parents after an evening in a restaurant to Haji Ali, where we would sit in the car and a man would bring fresh juice to our car windows. The breeze that comes in off the sea from the west cools you, and the iced juice with a little masala refreshes you and is good for your health. I did not know then what Mohsin and Anees told me, that one of the people associated with the juice stand is a brown-sugar smuggler, dealing in very large heroin shipments. To me it was just a beautiful place to drink a nonalcoholic beverage.

So at 1 a.m. the suitor will be waiting for the bar girl in a taxi at Haji Ali, anxiously scanning every person walking toward him, every car that pulls up. She might be late, he might think she's ditched him and might start cursing her, but then finally she shows and she takes his breath away, she is so beautiful. When she gets in the taxi with him she is dressed in a miniskirt, and he notices how smooth and fair her thighs are. He smells her perfume. She is wearing something that leaves her arms bare, or she is wearing a sari and a backless blouse. She is not smiling now, she is not meeting his eyes now. She is watching the sidewalk for something, till finally she sees him: a man with a couple of cages slung over his shoulder, filled with birds.

She gives the taxi driver a fifty and tells him to take a walk, go drink some juice.

She calls out to the bird seller and he comes over. His cages have tiny songbirds fluttering about inside, with beaks of different colors. The dancer asks her man to buy some of the birds—six for 500 rupees; "If you want more fun take a dozen," advises Anees—and the girl rolls up all the windows of the taxi and opens the door of the cage and all the birds fly out and fill the small dark taxi with their energy and their music. She laughs with delight and asks her man to play a game with her: Catch the birds. They reach out their hands to grab the birds, who are small and quick, and they have to wave their arms wildly about even to touch them. As the girl and her ardent suitor reach out to catch a bird, they sometimes, accidentally, can't help touching each other. This is new for the man—remember, he hasn't touched her up to this point. As a bird lands on her shoulder, he must make a grab for it, and if the bird flies off, his hand lands on her shoulder. If it should fly close to her breast, why, it is within the rules of the game that he should try his best to capture the songbird, which might just be that little bit too quick for him, and his hand, in its dart forward, might meet with something else, softer, harder. And so the whole of the tiny Fiat taxi is filled with birdsong, her giggling, his laughter, and, every now and then, a quick female gasp. And so it is that at last, at long last, the dancing girl and her patient suitor go all soft and hot in the back of the taxi, the space around them filled with fluttering and panicked songbirds.

Half an hour or an hour later, the door of the taxi opens and half a dozen or a dozen dead birds are thrown out on the road. If there are any remaining alive, they fly out over the great dark sea, free at last.

Monalisa Dances

I started going to the beer bars because I was puzzled. I couldn't figure out why men would want to spend colossal amounts of money there. On a good night a dancer in a Bombay bar can make twice as much as a high-class stripper in a New York bar. The difference is that the dancer in Bombay doesn't have to sleep with the customers, is forbidden to touch them in the bar, and wears more clothes on her body than the average Bombay secretary does on the broad public street.

One night a young man named Mustafa, who used to manage my friend Ashish's computer business, takes me to Worli. As we drive up the avenue, there are no lights outside the Carnival Bar. It is way after twelve-thirty, when the bars are supposed to be closed. But we drive slowly. A man sitting in front of the small alley asks us, "Hotel?" and we get out of the car, and other men appear and park the car opposite. We are motioned to walk inside the completely dark alley and I think we might be in the wrong place, but suddenly a small flashlight comes on at the other end and we walk toward it. A burly man salaams us and passes us on to the next torch-light. Finally we get to the back entrance of the bar. The door opens and

inside it is ablaze with light and music and flowing with liquor and filled
with people at 3 a.m., five rooms packed to the walls. There are about ten
dancers to a room, dressed only a little provocatively in full saris and tight
backless blouses. One or two of them have such young faces they must
have padded their blouses. The men in the audience, Mustafa says, are diamond merchants and bankers. I think I recognize the fat man sitting next to
us, one of my uncle's friends, and he too looks at me a second longer than
the generally accepted definition of "casually."

Mustafa worked in the stock market in the fat times. In the mid-
nineties, sub-brokers could make two lakhs a day from cheating a client,
telling him his shares were sold at a few paise lower than they really were,
pocketing the difference—and then blowing it away that night, as easily as
it came, in the beer bars. The boom went bust, but Mustafa is still here,
drinking his rum with soda and Coke.

The customers literally blow money away on the dancers: paise udana,
send money into flight. They will walk up to the dance floor and stand with
a stack of notes over the head of the favored dancer. The notes, in an expert
hand, traverse the distance between customer and dancer on air and fluff
out, forming a halo or fan around the girl, enveloping her in the supreme
grace of currency, its wealth adding immeasurably to the radiance of her
face, exalting her in this most commercial of cities, till the floor is littered
with rupee notes and the male attendants scurry around to collect them and
deposit them in the dancer's account.

The more timid admirers will give their money to a waiter, who will
shuffle it out over the dancer like a deck of cards downward from the palm,
a more precisely targeted stream of paper, easier to collect and allot to the
particular girl. Other customers like to play games. A dancer named Kajal
plays the lottery with one of her customers. He sits at the bar with ten slips
of paper, on each of which is written an amount of money. She dances and
then picks one of the slips, and the customer gives her that amount; it could
be anywhere from a few thousand up to 100,000 rupees. Another man is at
a table, singing dreamily along with the songs. There is a pile of tens in
front of him, which he holds up in the air two at a time, singing all the while
and not even looking at the girls, who dance over, pick them up quickly,
and dart away, like goldfish nibbling in quick jerks at pieces of bread you
throw into a pool.

You can also "garland" the girl of your choice, with a ring of plastic-encased 50-, 100-, or 500-rupee notes that is draped around the dancer's neck and stays on her through the entire duration of the song you have requested. If you are annoyed at her, if you have figured out that money is all she wants, you can fling a huge stack of money at her face or, most care-free or contemptuous of all, not even look at her while throwing hundreds of notes back over your shoulder in her general direction, while smiling at the audience. Then you throw your empty hands into the air: This is how little the money and the girl mean to me.

"Why are they doing this? What do these men get in return?" I ask Mustafa.

"Five minutes' attention. Even a garage mechanic can come here and get attention from these girls." This is one place where the classes meet, where the only thing important is the color of your money. Because it's not just the mechanics and the taporis; it's also the rich traders and merchants of South Bombay, who are surrounded by men during the day and by their fat wives in the evening. This might be the only place in their lives where they can look directly at beautiful young girls, young enough to be their daughters. The moment the customer walks in, he's the star in his own custom-made Hindi movie song. No matter how old or ugly or fat he is, for the two hours he's in the bar he's a movie star, he's Shahrukh Khan. The customer inhabits the song being sung; he will sing along to the music, throwing back his head, moving his arms, singing to his girl, who has assumed the female role in the duet. Moving her body in the dance motions of the original video, she is lip-synching along with the song. It is an easy deception; the movie songs are all playback anyway. So the customer, in the midst of a hundred other men just like him, can sustain an illusion of individuality.

VINOD CHOPRA, the movie director, says he wants to go to the beer bars to research a film on the city. He has never been, so I arrange, one night, to take him. Paresh, the guide Mustafa has arranged, is waiting for us around nine. He is a bar-code printer, a fat man with tobacco-stained teeth. The bar Paresh takes us to, Dilbar, is a low small room on the second floor of a building, in a lane off Grant Road. Among the dancers, there is one who has a heavier tread than the others. She is taller, thicker built, and fairer, has a pleasant face, and hardly dances. "That's Honey," Paresh says.

I first heard about Honey, the most famous dancer in all of Bombay, from Naeem Husain, the crime reporter. Husain knew Honey's great secret: "She is actually a he." Vinod and I are introduced to her, and I give her 100 rupees and tell her we are writing a movie: Could I talk to her? She is very polite, but when I say I would like to meet her outside the bar she adopts the classic Bombay strategy of the No. She says it will only be possible "next week." She doesn't want to meet now because her relatives are visiting her.

We move on to the second bar, only a couple of blocks away. "In previous days people used to come to Bombay to see the Gateway of India," says Paresh, as a door is thrown open for us by a uniformed guard. "Now they come to see Sapphire."

Sapphire! It was another world in my childhood. As I step in through the door, I am hungry, salivating for food I no longer eat: tandoori chicken. This was where my father would take us on Sundays, all through my boyhood, to feast on that most delicious red-pink flesh, so fresh I fancied I heard the clucking of the birds being slaughtered in the kitchen. GRADE 1 EATING HOUSE the sign at the entrance read, in the middle of the shopping district of Grant Road. Afterward, walking along Marine Drive, I felt free to ask my father all the questions in the world—how planes fly and why Indira Gandhi imposed the emergency—and he answered them at leisure, with patience. Sapphire was the central event of those Sunday nights.

"It's like a Hindi movie," observes Vinod. We have walked into a Bollywood song sequence. There are two rooms in the front, each with a slightly raised stage, on which colored spotlights illuminate the girls dancing to movie songs. The chiffon saris the girls are wearing could have come from a Yash Chopra film, and the backless cholis from one by Sooraj Barjatya. The dancers are all doing movements they have seen on the big screen. Then there are three more rooms in the back: the theater hall, the VIP hall, and the large mujra hall. The theater hall sports sofas, with stadium seating, so the girls don't have to bend down to talk to the customers and everybody has a clear line of sight. The VIP room is small and exclusive, and the sofas are arranged around the dance floor in a manner that permits maximum closeness to the dancers. It looks like my Dariya Mahal flat, all mirrors and gilt and European classical sculptures and frescoes. The mirrors are etched with drawings of maharajas being fed wine by nautch girls. When you sit in the mujra hall you might relax and stretch out your feet before you realize that your boots are resting on female breasts. Each table in front of you is supported by a sculpture of a woman with bare breasts holding up the glass table with her hands and knees. The clay breasts are large and pointed, like a minor range of hills. In between the halls is a makeup room for the dancers. Its mirror is lined with a row of stickers of various gods and goddesses—mainly goddesses—that the bar girls pray to.

IT WAS JAIMAN who had first pointed her out to me.

Jaiman, the first Marwari editor of Russian *Playboy* and a friend of mine from New York, had half a mind to take a girl from India back to Moscow for his magazine. He had been traveling around the country: Delhi, Rajasthan, and now Bombay. He wanted one girl, an exemplar of the sultry beauties of India, for the delectation of his Slavic readership. I had heard about Sapphire from Mustafa, and a couple of months before I went there with Vinod I had gone into the bar for the first time with Jaiman.

We had first noticed her when she danced to the Vengaboys' remake of the song "Brazil." In the middle of the more or less demure girls on the stage, there she was, the tallest, the one with the longest hair, the most dazzling smile. All the other girls blurred and faded, as in a movie when the heroine suddenly comes into sharp focus as she's walking in a crowd of people in the street.

Jaiman was totally taken with her. He thought she was the most beautiful woman he had seen in India and the only openly sexual one. "Fuck those rich Bombay girls, who needs them!" he had declared, after several nights of unsuccessful flirtation with rich Bombay girls. This girl had a way of turning her back to the audience, bending forward, and slowly rotating her buttocks that was a clear mime of sex, doggy-style. She was . . . presenting. Then she turned back to face the audience and flashed a smile, a teenager's smile. She had big bee-stung lips, a high neck, large eyes, and a snub nose. Jaiman gave her 100-rupee notes and tried to tell her above the music that he was a *Playboy* editor and could he meet her after the place closed? She asked him to come back the next day; he explained that he was leaving for Moscow the next morning. In that case, she replied, they would not be able to meet.

But she was kind enough to give him her name. I will call her Monalisa.

SAPPHIRE, THIS EVENING, is standing room only. But seats are cleared right up front for us; some customers are told to move. This time around, Monalisa is dressed in a yellow sari and choli. She comes behind where we are sitting to talk to Minesh, another friend of Mustapha's. He is a short, balding man in his early thirties, wearing glasses and a yellow shirt. She recognizes me from the last time, or pretends to, smiles, and says, "Hi!" Minesh introduces her to me, then points at my companion and asks Monalisa if she recognizes him. "Have you heard the name Vidhu Vinod Chopra?" Her mouth and her eyes open wide, as if a long-lost friend or sibling has just walked in. She changed her name so it could be the same as that of the hero in one of Vinod's films, Minesh informs us. She rushes back to the stage. During the next song, she is not dancing, she is auditioning. All the other dancers are acting out an imitation of some actress's moves. One is trying to be Madhuri, another Manisha. But Monalisa's dancing rises out of the heat of her own body; she learnt dancing by watching herself in the mirror. Vinod's eyes are on her. "If she were from Malabar Hill she'd be on top of the film world," he says, appraising her professionally.

Next to her a young girl—but they are all young—in a blue sari and blouse stands staring back at the audience, not dancing, her mouth working at something; finally, a little pink bubble appears out of it, inflates, and pops. An old white man is making a lot of noise. He holds out a 10-rupee note that the girls are reluctant to touch, but finally one ends up taking it, more out of politeness than anything else. Adrift in his former empire, he is the cheapest man in the joint.

Monalisa comes back to our table. I lean forward, 100-rupee note in my hand, and tell her I am writing a script with Vinod and would like to talk to her. She pushes away the money—the first time a bar girl has ever refused my money—writes down her number on a piece of paper, and gives it to me. Such is the magic of the movies.

*   *   *

MONALISA WALKS into the coffee shop of the Sea Princess in Juhu a few days later, and as she comes toward me every head turns to look at her, the men with lust, the women with hate. She is wearing a red Ralph Lauren tank top, jeans, and platform shoes; a lacy black bra peeps out from the straps of the top. Her chest looks tanned; actually, it has been reddened from playing Holi the previous day. Her hair is up and in a ponytail behind her head; she apologizes for it. "I've just oiled it." She has woken up only fifteen minutes ago.

She says, "There is a girl wearing brown on your right. Look at her." I casually glance to the right. "Do you see the man with her?" He is much older, plump and dark, with a mustache. They are sitting on the same side of the table, scanning the menus. "She's one of the girls. We recognized each other as soon as I came in."

She tells me about the bar she works in and its dancers. Sapphire has the best girls in the city, good sexy dancers, with good figures and height, fair, with long hair. Most of the bar-line girls come from the village; there are very few native Bombayites. They are brought into the bar line when they're thirteen or fourteen by their parents, an older sister, or an agent; by the time they're in their mid-twenties, they're too old for it. They live in the areas around Foras Road or in Congress House, where the rent for a shoddy little room is an exorbitant 10,000 rupees and the deposit seven and a half lakhs, but there is safety in numbers. Three or four girls might share a room, an air-conditioned one. They all have cell phones and some of them drive their own cars. Most of them are saving money to send to their parents in the village, to buy a house with their earnings. "Behind every earner there are fifty eaters," points out Monalisa.

The customers at Sapphire can be very young, just out of their teenage years, stealing away from home and without much money. Monalisa has no time to waste on such children. The next age group is the boys in their early to mid-twenties, "handsome, young, and good. These are the ones with whom the girls fall in love." But she can't be too public about her affection, can't advertise her fealty. "There it all runs on ego. If a girl talks too much to a client he will think, She is mine only. He will take her for granted." So when a bar girl's heart is lost to a man, she had better not, if she is smart, wear it on her sleeve.

The whole idea of the bar line, she explains, is to make the client fall in love with her and to make him think she loves him too. I ask her how she does it, how she can make a man fall so in love with her that he becomes obsessed and spends all his time and money on her.

She tells me her techniques, the courtesan's secrets. When she sees a man throwing money in the bar the first time, she gives him her full attention and smiles at him. (And there is power in Monalisa's smile. It makes you feel slightly less shoddy than you have become.) "Everyone wants me as a physical," she explains. "The first sight goes onto the body. In Sapphire, the customer looks at me physically, then looks at me dancing. They think I am very fast and hi-fi. I don't mind. What can I do?" On the phone, each day, she will draw out his problems at home. "I throw tantrums, I tell him to get me this and that, just like a spoilt child." After some connection has been established, "I tell him, 'You will only talk to me and to no other.' I take care of my customers like a wife takes care of her husband: I'm only yours. I'm only yours. I'm only yours."

Somewhere within him the mark knows that in this town nobody belongs to anybody else, but he lets himself be lulled into the pleasant illusion that Monalisa loves him so much that she is jealous when he talks to other women. The bar-line dancers' livelihoods and their safety depend on a microscopic knowledge of men: what makes them hard, what makes them soft. There is a chance that when a customer gets a girl, gets what he wants, he will stop meeting her afterward. He might then say to his friends, "I've had her, you can also have her." So a girl might sleep readily with a customer who knows what he wants and will not be budged, and each takes what they can get. But she will not sleep with a "decent" customer, one with some scruples or gentleness to him, because she can milk him for a long time. Nice guys pay more.

If Monalisa doesn't want to go to bed with a customer, she gives him exaggerated respect, becomes his friend, his sister, his daughter, till gradually he stops thinking of her in that way, in that hot way. She strokes him. "You have such a good nature." He might be hot and heavy, wanting to talk about her body; she brings it around to his heart. "When he starts taking care of me like a little girl, I know he's in love." After a while, he realizes that Monalisa cannot reciprocate his love and inevitably breaks it off himself. Or she throws herself at his mercy, a little girl lost in the big city. "However strong a man is outside, with a girl he bows down completely." This applies especially to businessmen, men who have to go into an office and be in charge of others, and thus become mature. She asks for his protection, and being a big man in Bombay he can't refuse. He adopts her. You can't fuck your adopted daughter.

If two of her regular customers turn up at Sapphire at the same time, she has to take care of them both. "I smile first at one and then at the other." Monalisa has customers from all over India and abroad: America, Dubai. She likes the out-of-town customers; they are mostly mature businessmen, and they don't constantly ask where she was the night before. She has to give them izzat, phone them once in a while, and give them her full attention when they come to Bombay. But she doesn't have to waste her time on extended phone conversations with them every day, like the Bombay customers.

There are some girls who are popular among Arabs—who pay very well—and others who are popular among Malayalis or Sikhs, whom she hates because they say dirty things to the girls. Monalisa is especially popular with western tourists who come to Sapphire, who tell her, "You are so spicy!" Unfortunately, they don't know how to spend money. They offer her $1 bills and she laughs at them.

The man most obsessed with her was a Maharashtrian cement contractor from Latur. There had been an earthquake there, and fifteen thousand people had died. He was tied to the government in some way; millions had been siphoned off from the reconstruction funds. Some of that money found its way to Monalisa. He came to Sapphire for six months, each time spending tens of thousands of rupees on her. Once he was in Hyderabad and he missed her sorely. He called her and said he needed to see her face. So he sent her a round-trip ticket to the southern city; she took the plane in the morning, met him at the airport, talked to him for half an hour, and took the same plane back to Bombay. For this one glimpse of her face he paid her 50,000 rupees.

The bar-line girls who want to make more money do private parties, which are generally held at private residences. These can be arranged in two setups: the Congress party, where you can't touch the girls, only watch them dance; and the Janata party, where the public is free to touch and fondle, a free-for-all. Some of them involve stripping on a stage, with an orchestra, singers, waitresses. One night Monalisa was paid to take part in such a show on a boat sailing from the Gateway of India. She started dancing, and the men got up and started moving with her. They were dancing very close, touching her, putting money in her cleavage, in her waistband, sticking close to her. After one song, she fled from the room to the top of the boat. There were a couple of other dancers still downstairs. She saw that one of the girls was in a separate room, and the customers were all lined up outside. In two hours the girl took on twenty men, "some doing hard, some doing light, some biting." All Monalisa got was 1,000 rupees for the one song; she is not a call girl.

Earlier, while setting up our meeting on the phone, Monalisa had told me, "I'm having an affair with Minesh. Since one year." I think of the man I had met in the bar, a dweeb or nerd, and try to picture him with the magnificent Monalisa. It doesn't work. I can't think of them together in the same frame.

"Nobody will marry me," declares Monalisa.

"Absolutely, someone will marry you," I respond.

"No, they won't. Even if love happens, how could I enter his family? What if I went somewhere with them and somebody recognized me, one of the customers from the bar? People come all the way from Rajasthan and Bangalore to see me." Besides, she says, she has no interest in getting married. "I am standing on my own feet; I am not living on anyone else. I never want to have to stretch out my hand toward my husband for five thousand rupees to go shopping." Then she reflects, "No girl my age earns this much. I earn enough. I earn with izzat." It should feel odd, hearing a woman whom most people would consider a prostitute say that she is earning with honor, but it doesn't. "All the men give me izzat," she says. Izzat is the most important concept in the bar line, more desirable than sex, more durable than love.

She loves Bombay properly. She flourishes in the city, as she could not in Delhi, as she would not in New York. Unlike the girls of Malabar Hill, where I grew up, Monalisa has no desire to go to America. "Bombay is correct." In ten years, she says, India will be as free as America. Monalisa likes the freedom money gives her. She bought a Maruti 800, banged it up, and upgraded to a Maruti Esteem. She loves to go shopping. After she finishes work in Sapphire, Monalisa roams the discos of the city, often just by herself. "I do everything. I drink, I go to discos, I play pool. Everything happens in Bombay. I can wear any kind of clothes freely. How free is the life in Bombay!" As Monalisa moves around the city, she travels on her self-confidence. In a disco, if she sees a good-looking boy with a girlfriend jealously guarding him, she'll make sure to go up to him as she's leaving the club, grab him by the collar, put her face close to him, and tell him, "You're so handsome!" She laughs. "The next time he'll come alone."

Monalisa doesn't consider herself beautiful. She thinks of herself as attractive, sexy. She volunteers her measurements: 32-28-36. She was at 1900's once, the disco in the Taj, and even the film idol Shahrukh Khan stopped and stared at her for a minute when he saw her.

I point to her neck. There is a simple black thread around it, with the knot in front. "What's that?"

"That's my mala. From Goddess Meldima of Surendranagar Temple. I believe in her very much." She keeps vows for her.

I ask her how far she's studied. She says to the tenth standard, in a Gujarati school.

"You're Gujarati?" I'm astonished.

She nods and smiles, showing uneven teeth. Her people are from Amreli, in Saurashtra. Her real name is Rupa Patel. I look at her in a whole new way. She is closer to me now. Very few of the dancing girls, but many of the customers, are Gujarati. Sometimes, one of her customers who is aware of her origins will put on the song "Dil Lagi Kudi Gujarat Di," which is a paean to a Gujarati girl, for her to dance to. Monalisa and I have another thing in common: Both of us come from families who've made their living through glittery stones. Her father and brother are diamond cutters. Monalisa herself, for a few months, worked at a diamond factory in the suburbs, cutting rough diamonds "with oiled hair and dressed in a sal-waar kameez." It was not her style. She got bored.

She went back to Amreli once. I asked her what happened. "Dogs started barking," she said.

She grew up in Bombay, in a slum in Kalina. "The one who gave birth to me put me in this line," Monalisa tells me. She doesn't say "mother," which is a term she reserves for the goddess. Her parents divorced, and her mother, a waitress in a beer bar, brought her to the bar line at the age of seventeen. She hates her mother now, moved out of her house and spent six months living on her own, and has hardly seen her for three years. But she still sends her money, sometimes. She will not talk to her father, who is in Gujarat.

Monalisa has thought about doing something other than dancing in bars: modeling, for example, but she's heard that you need someone to support you, otherwise you get exploited; they take you up to a certain point and then say, You have to sleep with me; otherwise it will all stop. "Your world is like that," she tells me.

"It's not my world!" I protest.

I take out my mobile phone and dial the number of Rustom, the fashion photographer. I first met Rustom when I was considering renting a room in his apartment for use as a study; I didn't rent the room, but I became fast friends with him, drawn by his cockeyed Parsi take on Bombay. He says he will come to watch her at the bar; then, if he likes what he sees, he'll do a shoot.

I am finished with our talk. Then I notice the marks.

She has turned over a hand to get something on the table and I notice a row of slashes going all the way up from the heel of the palm, all across her wrist and to the crook of her arm. It's the same on her other arm. I take a chance. "What are those marks?" I ask her.

"Those are cuts." She looks at the marks. "Here I had eight stitches." Then she points to a series of raised dots on her skin. "Those are cigarette burns."

I trace the cuts and the welts with my finger. "Who did this to you?"

"I did it myself."

"Why?"

"One was after I left home. The other was after my love broke." She has done this about four times, with a razor blade. Her last attempt was three months ago.

"Why?"

"I was alone. I was bored." Her veins don't supply enough blood to her palms now, because they've been cut so often. Her wrist is scarred and pitted like a dirt road. She can't lift anything heavy. One of her attempts was so serious that her hand all but fell off and had to be surgically reattached. She is twenty years old.

As we're leaving, she says she lives a five-minute walk away. "So come home sometime?" I think about what this means. Is she inviting me home for sex? No, because then she wouldn't ask me to come to her room. She would ask me to go upstairs, in the hotel we're in. This is "come home sometime" in the best Indian sense: Come home for a meal, come home as a guest.

I tell her, "You come to my home sometime too."

We walk out of the five-star hotel, and again all eyes are on her, and on me by association. She has a way of moving her head—I've seen it before, in New York, among the young girls there—a smile and a slight forward and backward nudge of the head, African in origin. She likes being looked at, likes being noticed.

RUSTOM HAS A REPUTATION in the industry. The girls love him. They sleep with him. Then they become his friends, and it shows in the pictures they allow him to take of them. He is at the age where the current generation of the models "is the last batch I can sleep with without feeling like a pedophile."

I take Rustom to Sapphire to see Monalisa. In between the other dancers, Monalisa is a lotus among lilies. In the song sequence that's being enacted here, she's the heroine and they are the chorus line. She's dressed tonight all in black: a black skirt and a black choli that covers her breasts but shows off her entire back. She dances hard, it's hard work—swooping all the way down to the ground, the two halves of her body churning at different speeds, her navel the center of gravity, her long hair flying around her. This young Gujarati girl becomes, on the dance floor, an animal with not enough space to move, and every part of her body strains against, is energized by, the restraint: her legs, her buttocks, her chest, her arms, her lips, her hair, her eyes.

Rustom watches her and the others with the eye of an experienced ad photographer. "The shampoo guys would go mad over that hair," he says about Monalisa. "She's a young Protima Bedi." But his gaze is straying to a girl in pink, behind her, who's not really dancing. She's more petite, and her chin has a dimple in it. "I could get *her* work tomorrow," says the photographer. She's what the ad guys look for, to sell to the great Indian middle class. "Sweet. Moon-faced, filmi-looking, nonthreatening. That's what works with consumer products and Hindi films. Pleasant. It's reflecting the times. Everything should be sweet and nice and happy."

Monalisa, Rustom thinks, is the more attractive of the two. But that much energy is disturbing in an advertisement intended to hawk face cream or saris. Women would not react well to someone with Monalisa's raw sexual power. "She'd be better in moving pictures," says Rustom. "How's her bod?" he asks me.

"I don't know. I didn't find out."

In the middle of her sexy dances, Monalisa pauses to pray, and the men at the tables watch her avidly. She interrupts the gyrating of her legs, the thrusting of her buttocks, the collecting of lucre, to turn her back on us all and commune with her goddess. It is a shockingly intimate activity, prayer.

Rustom looks around. "It's like a sweet version of a striptease joint." All around him are men desperate for women. The fashion photographer reflects on his profession. "I thank God I'm in this line. God is good to me." He looks upward, nods.

When Rustom drops me back in front of my building, I see a man that I'm pretty sure was in the bar this evening. He's waiting alone for the lift downstairs, clutching his mobile phone. He's middle-aged and wearing an office shirt and pants. "Now he's going to go wake up his wife and really do his duty by her, after what he's seen in Sapphire," I say.

"I'm never going to get married in my whole life," responds Rustom.

I TAKE MONALISA to Rustom's studio, so she can look at his work and be reassured that he's not a pornographer. Marika, who is at this moment the hottest model in the country, is hanging out at the studio, looking just like a regular girl in a salwaar kameez. "You were in the Bhatti video," Monalisa says in a small voice, in Hindi.

After we've looked at the photographs, as we're walking out, Monalisa says to me about the model, "She's also cut."

"What?"

"I saw, on her arms."

Rustom later confirms this. I've met Marika at least a half-dozen times, but I've never noticed the cuts. Monalisa knew within five minutes of meeting her. The bar girl noticed some tension on the model's face, noticed she was talking a little too much, laughing a little too much. So she looked at her wrists. Later I find out the model's story. She is the mistress of a married man with three children. For a year she disappeared; no one knew where she'd gone or with whom. Then she came back and retook the modeling world by storm: Her face, her light eyes, are used to move all manner of products. She is more than a mistress; she has married her lover in a secret temple ceremony. He is connected with the underworld and threatens to kill anyone who gets too close. So Marika stays true to him, out of fear or love. She will call a bunch of completely unrelated people to dinner at her place, suggest they all go to someone else's place, then get a phone call on her mobile and suddenly disappear for the rest of the night, leaving her guests shifting on their feet in a stranger's house.

Her lover will never leave his wife, so Marika marks time on her wrists. There must be a citywide sorority of these women who've slit their wrists and survived, who recognize one another automatically. A sisterhood of the slashed. The top model in India and the top bar dancer in Bombay have this in common: Their arms are marked with their anguish, like gang tattoos.

ONE AFTERNOON, Monalisa comes to the apartment in Bandra, above Elco Arcade, that I'm using as an office. She is dressed very simply, not provocatively, in a striped T-shirt and black jeans. We were going to have lunch in a restaurant but she says she's not hungry, and I'd had a sandwich earlier. We need a place to talk, so we go up to the apartment. I have to make a conscious effort to keep my hand from trembling as I put the key in the lock.

Inside, I offer to make her iced coffee, and she comes into the kitchen with me. As I put the milk in the glasses, she perches on the kitchen counter, her long legs dangling over the edge. I've had guests in the apartment before, but nobody has done that. It is an informal, spontaneous gesture, and I realize it has been a long time since I've been alone with anybody of this age. She watches me make the coffee with amusement. "You forgot the sugar," she points out, laughing. By the end of the afternoon, the sugar bowl is nearly empty; Monalisa likes her coffee sweet. The next day I notice that Monalisa washed the coffee things and put them neatly on the counter. She would not let me wash dishes or serve food; it is not something a man does.

She has brought a gift for me from a recent trip to Ahmadabad. It is a cloth file for my papers, handmade in Gujarat, where she was born. Her mother welcomed her into the world by picking her up and throwing her onto the veranda.

The One Who Gave Birth to Monalisa was raised in an orphanage. Men would come to the orphanage to select girls to marry. Monalisa's father came on such an errand, saw a pretty girl, and married her against his family's wishes. They lived in his village, with his six brothers and their wives and children. He soon started beating her, and his family beat her as well.

A year and a half after Monalisa was born, she gave birth to another child, a son. This caused jubilation in the family, since one of the brothers was childless. He spoke to Monalisa's father, who told his wife to give up her newborn son to his brother. "My mother had no say in the matter," explains Monalisa. All her life she had to live with the knowledge that her firstborn son was growing up somewhere in the village, and she had no claim on him. Monalisa hasn't seen her brother since childhood. "I wouldn't even recognize him now." But the loss was soon made up. Monalisa's mother had another boy, Viju, whom she was allowed to keep.

The family moved to Bombay. They were living in a slum, a zopadpatti. Her mother started having an affair with a man who was giving her money. When her father found out about his wife's affair, he swallowed poison. His wife took him to the hospital and nursed him. When he got better he divorced her and left for the village, taking the children. Monalisa was five at the time. Her father's family had a large house in the village, with buffaloes in the yard. She grew up playing marbles. "Even when I was a girl I would only play with the boys."

"I loved my father a lot," says Monalisa, using the past tense. When she was just a baby she had fallen so ill that her family made preparations to take her to the funeral ground. Then she sat up and said loudly, "Pappa!" All the time she was growing up, she was his princess. "If he saw a tear drop from my eyes he would say, This isn't a tear, it's a pearl; don't waste it." The women of his extended family, however, held it against Monalisa and her father that he was divorced and wouldn't take care of them. They were stingy with food; the chapatis were counted out for each person before they sat down to eat. When Monalisa was ten, he came back to Bombay, lived with his wife again, and left her again. But this time he left Monalisa and her younger brother with their mother. He then married another woman and had two children by her.

"I didn't know that my father would leave," says Monalisa. He told her he was going to the village and would come back later. "When I found out my father had another marriage, I thought, He forgot me? The one who loved me so much? I will never go to my father." Monalisa hasn't spoken to her father in ten years. He phoned Sapphire recently; she refused to come to the phone to speak to him.

Her mother found a new man to keep her, to give her a flat. Monalisa remembers him as being good to her and her brother. Then her mother left him or he left her, Monalisa can't recall. One day in the monsoons Monalisa was walking home from school along the divider on the highway, and she put her face up to the water and got thoroughly soaked, as children all over the city like to do. When her mother found out, she got furious, as parents will, but her fury extended to pulling Monalisa out of school entirely. Periodically, Monalisa's mother has attempted to finish what she started when her daughter emerged from her womb. She went at her with a wooden ladle used to beat the laundry. There were marks all over her body before she started putting them on herself. For days the girl would not be able to get up from her bed because of the beatings. If her mother thought she was flirting with boys she would beat her. If there wasn't enough salt in Monalisa's cooking she would beat her. While her mother pursued her own entertainments, Monalisa was made to do the cooking and the cleaning; she was little better than a servant. By the time she was seventeen, she was so used to her mother's beatings that she sat on the floor, smoking a cigarette, with her arms around her knees, while her mother rained blows on her. At one point she ran away from home, but the police found her and put her in a children's home. The experience there was scary; it was the only place worse than home. Most of the children came from the slums, and the young girls were supplied to politicians. Some, as young as thirteen, got pregnant.

So Monalisa, in her teens, stayed home when everybody around her was going to school and watched television when her mother was out of the house. Here she first discovered the world that was outside the slum where she lived, far beyond her savage mother, far from the father who had abandoned her. On the television screen she found a world of young people who lived only to dance. "I would watch MTV, Channel V, and get a strange feeling. All this is happening outside. I thought I should have boyfriends—not sex or anything—but I had a feeling I should be with them. I wanted to wear such clothes, shorts. I was very fond of dance. I wanted to be free."

She started sneaking out to the dance competitions in the suburbs. Growing up, Monalisa was called "horsey" or "duck" because of her long legs and her height. But this now worked to her advantage; she came in first in one of the competitions, dancing to an Ila Arun song, "Resham ka Rumaal." This brought her to the attention of the local lads. "There was a line of boys outside my building waiting to look at me." There were boys who kissed her, put her on their laps. When her mother found out, she told Monalisa she had fixed her engagement. The man was twenty-eight. Monalisa was sixteen.

Monalisa was told to go meet her fiancé for the first time at Nariman Point. She decided to come clean with him. She told the older man she had a boyfriend and begged him to tell her family that he didn't want to marry Monalisa for his own reasons. But the fiancé did not respect her confidence. He told Monalisa's mother everything. At this point the mother hit her again, savagely, and this time she was assisted by Monalisa's younger brother. But during this beating Monalisa rebelled and spoke back. "I got mad and said I'll *never* get married." That was when Monalisa's mother took her for the first time to the stage at a bar called Deepa. Since Monalisa would never get married, she would be put into the bar line.

When the first garland of 100-rupee notes was put around her neck, she started sobbing in front of the whole audience. As a Gujarati, she had been brought up to respect money; this was its shaming. But the other girls were nice to her. They showed her how to put on makeup. She soon got used to the bar line. The suburban bars operate according to different routines from the ones in town. There, a good dancer can make a "single entry"—she will be the only one onstage. A typical night for Monalisa would include two singles and six duets. In the suburban bars she had her own makeup room. She would walk into the owner's office and sit on his chair; the owners smiled, indulged her. She started out in Deepa, then went to Night Lovers, Natraj, Jharna, Ratna Park. Monalisa had a reputation as a sexy dancer from the beginning. "I danced without any fear, bindass." She also knows how to reveal herself while dancing. "To expose is an art. Open, but try to hide it." In the bar line, she is thought of as being awara—fallen.

In Jharna a man in his forties would come daily to watch her. He was experienced in the bar line and a frequent customer of the top bars, looking for very young girls that he could treat like children. Every day he would give Monalisa fifteen, twenty thousand, and then one day she met him outside the bar. She started to like him. "He was decent with me. He took care of me like a little girl." The man was a film producer named Hari Virani. His wife had jumped out the window of their sixth-floor flat, leaving him two sons, eight and ten. He started giving money to Monalisa's mother as well.

The standard euphemism for taking a girl's virginity is nath utarna. A Maharashtrian husband, before he makes love to his virgin bride on his wedding night, will tenderly take off her big golden nose ring, her nath, the first person to have the prerogative to do so. The defloration of a bar girl has its own ritual. When a bar-line girl loses her virginity, it is called sar dhakna, the veiling of the head—the first realization of shame. It is stretched out as far as possible. When a customer is desirous of deflowering a virgin dancer, as Monalisa was at the time, he will first contact her mother. He will find out what the current price is; a girl like Monalisa would have fetched at least five lakhs. If there is competition, the mother will try to get a little bidding action going, advising the customer, "Let the girl grow a little." A lot of shopping is done for the girl's family members, sometimes over years.

Hari did not want to wait that long. One night, he asked Monalisa to have dinner with him at the Sun 'n' Sand Hotel and to phone her mother and tell her that she would be late. When she got there, she found he had booked a room. He got on top of her. She was very scared and asked him to stop. "I said, get down, get down off me right now. I don't like this. But he pataoed me." Pataoed—not rape, not quite; not seduction, not quite. More like a confidence trick. When she came home, her mother took one look at her and knew she had lost her virginity. "She knew from the way I walked." She gave it away to Hari for free, she says, because she was in love with him. If he called in the middle of the night she would run to him. He talked about his whole life with her: how he would sleep on the footpaths when he was new in the city, how he rose in the film industry. He promised her a flat in Lokhandwala. He protected her, enveloped her in his power.

One day Hari paid Monalisa's mother 20,000 rupees to take her daughter to Indore, where he was writing a screenplay. The scriptwriter said to Hari, "I like this girl." First they gave her two bottles of fortified beer; it was the first time in her life that Monalisa drank. Then the scriptwriter asked her to have sex with him. Hari, watching, told him to do what he wanted with her. But by this time the drink had got to Monalisa, and she vomited. "Then naturally no one can touch me." She must have been incredibly hurt. But she had her revenge, a child's revenge: "Hari then fell in my eyes."

Within a few months, the demands for money from her mother, who sensed a mark, increased beyond all bounds. So Hari, who had a keen sense about the proper duration of an affair with a bar girl, dumped her after six months, but carefully. "He thought I loved him a lot and was scared I'd do something against him."

One morning Monalisa's mother woke her early and threw her out of the house. In her aunt's house, Monalisa had been going to the temple and giving money to the goddess, whom she considered her real mother, which upset the one who gave birth to her. Monalisa moved out, living first with her aunt and then in a rented 1,000-rupee-a-month flat in Byculla. That was the first time she tried to kill herself by cutting her wrists.

Then Samar came into her life and saved it. It was September 15, 1996, in Ratna Park; she will always remember the date. Monalisa had a friend named Adi, one of the many men she considers a brother. Over the months, I was to hear about many more of these "brothers." The relationship is a safe and efficient means of neutralizing sexual attraction and is laden with myth and meaning in India. When Monalisa tells someone she considers him a brother, not only will he stop thinking about her as a lover, he will be obligated to protect her.

Adi had stolen his father's car. He had his arm around his "item" next to him, and he took Monalisa and another young man out for a drive. Adi's friend was a handsome Muslim boy, sixteen and a half, a year younger than Monalisa, named Samar. They were out for a joyride; they might drive all the way to Lonavla. As they were driving, a car came up fast behind, overtook them, and cut them off. Adi's father emerged from the pursuing car, wrathful. He slapped his son and he slapped Samar, but he said not a word to the girls; he understood immediately that they were bar girls. Adi was dragged back home by his father, the other girl went to her home, and Monalisa and Samar turned to each other.

"We went back to my house and didn't emerge for three days. We were in the bed nonstop for two–three months. We never got tired. Every day. Two–three times a day, and then at night, after drinking. Four, six, ten times in one day. We went at it like insane people."

After three days Samar went home to get money. He came back to Monalisa, and the honeymoon continued; they spent their nights in the discos, in the pubs, just wandering around the illuminated city. He wanted to hear every detail of her life. Monalisa had stopped going to work. Samar had left his studies and his large family. Then one night—two weeks after they met—Samar took her to a bar named Sapphire. Here, she would be able to earn a lot more than what she was making at Ratna Park, he said. It was the soundest career advice anyone had ever given her.

"Even now I am very afraid of the world. If I had been alone till now I would have been ruined." But by the goddess's grace she found Samar. "I looked at Samar and found the love with him in one year that I didn't find in seventeen years."

Samar was the grandson of a man named Karim Lala, who in the seventies had been the biggest don in Bombay, leader of the Pathan gang. Samar had a way of talking, a kind of shaan, bravado. "You just see what I do in six months! I'm off to Dubai, and then you see how I make money!" he would say to Monalisa. It was a high-energy affair. "We lived like children, often fighting." Once Monalisa fought with him and walked out onto the street, wearing her skimpy little clothes. Two rickshaw drivers saw this tasty bit walking down the street and approached her. They told her to come with them, but she felt threatened and went back up and told Samar. He came down, took off his belt, and beat both rickshaw wallahs into the gutter. "He is Mohammedan. They have that anger, and they want what is theirs to stay theirs." He told her not to wear such clothes. But she was heedless. "He wanted me to dress like a Mohammedan; I said, I'm Gujarati." She didn't compromise even during the one time she met Samar's parents. It was at his sister's wedding. She was dressed in a black sari and a tiny blouse. After she passed, his father turned to Samar and asked, "Who *was* that madam?"

Monalisa met his sister, his grandmother. "He said, 'I only loved my grandmother and then you.'" But there was no way Samar's family would accept Monalisa, so Samar did what very few customers ever do: He moved out of his house and lived with her. His family hated her for this. He didn't tell them about her work. "If they had found out I was a bar-line girl, they wouldn't have let him live, so he had to lie." When he moved in with her—she bought a flat in Mira Road for them to live together—she also supported him. For Samar had no income. He was only a teenager.

One night they went to Madh Island for a rave, and they were drinking and dancing on the beach. Going back early in the morning, they passed by a lane, and Monalisa pointed down it, telling Samar, "This is my home." Her mother lived there. Samar decided he would go with her to meet her mother. When they showed up at her house, her mother threatened to call the police; Monalisa was still a minor and could be forced to go back home. Then Samar spoke up. He told her to leave Monalisa alone and to deal with him directly. For the first time in her life, Monalisa had found someone who would protect her from her mother, stand up to her bullying.

She got pregnant by Samar, more than once. She tried various home remedies: eating papayas, drinking hot pepper water with jaggery and then having very hard sex till the bleeding started. At one point she was three and a half months pregnant. She was prepared to have it, but she miscarried while dancing. "I cried a lot. I wanted the child." But after a few months of living together, Monalisa left Samar. She is frank about the cause: "Because he wasn't earning. I told Samar, I want the money that *you've* earned, not the money your father has earned." She wanted to leave the bar line, and Samar was not her exit ticket.

They still speak on the phone, but she doesn't go to meet him. Every year, a couple of months before her birthday in October, he'll ask Monalisa what she wants for a gift and save up to buy her a gold chain or locket. He asks her, "If I start earning, will you marry me?" She won't. "I can't marry Samar now because I stayed with him for one and a half years and then went with another. The thing that was his then belonged to someone else. I fell in my own eyes." She feels soiled by living in another man's house, like Sita in the Ramayana.

ONE NIGHT after Monalisa broke up with Samar, a group of boys from Hong Kong came into Sapphire. Among them was a very handsome Sindhi named Vijay. He flirted expertly with Monalisa, and she gave him her mobile number. Vijay was a dance-bar stud. He had girls in every bar: Dilbar, Pinky, Golden Goose, Carnival. Like Samar, he too had a kind of style about him; he would grab a girl's hand and flood her with his charm. He cried easily, and all the girls fell in love with him. One New Year's Eve, a friend of his was giving Monalisa a line; he presented her with a rose. Vijay took him outside and beat him till blood ran down his shirt. "Any girl will think he loves her."

And Vijay was an expert at playing games. When Monalisa phoned him, he would say he would call her back in half an hour. She would wait by the phone. Three hours would go by, then four. Then Monalisa would call him. Vijay turned the tables on the relationship between dancer and customer. He wanted to show his friends that he could get money from a bar girl. He gave nothing to Monalisa: "I never took five paise from Vijay." At the height of Monalisa's love, he told her he needed money. She promptly gave him 25,000 rupees; he never returned it. "I never asked, because I gave it to him in love," said Monalisa. "He had a mind that could get money out from anywhere." I came across many such stories, of bar girls supporting some deadbeat for years, because they had given their hearts to him. In the end, the biggest suckers—ulloos, dhoors, chutiyas—were the bar girls, and the people who made ulloos of them—lovers, parents, siblings—used the same confidence trick the dancers did: love.

Finally, Vijay left her for another dancer. Monalisa was devastated. After dancing most of the night she would spend the remainder of it at the discotheques, drinking hard. There were drugs, too; marijuana regularly and the filthiest of drugs, brown sugar, once. She would go home, cry herself to sleep, and, as soon as she woke up, have two or three beers for breakfast. Minesh, a regular customer at Sapphire, took care of her at that time; he paid her rent and gave her money to go to the discos. "He was my friend in a bad time." And he was falling for her. She took advantage of this. She would get drunk, go to his apartment, say she was feeling hot, take off all her clothes, and go to sleep on his bed. He would cover her with a sheet without touching her.

Three months before I met Monalisa, she had gone to Carnival one night. Vijay was there with his friends, and she was talking to them when Vijay introduced someone to Monalisa: his new girlfriend. Monalisa talked to her normally, but her insides were churning. The drinking helped. She went home and drank some more. The next night, she was dancing at Sapphire and not feeling very good about it. "I was afraid of the future." Abruptly, she left the bar and drove home. Minesh, who was at the bar, noticed. After a while he called her mobile. There was no answer. He called her home. No answer. So he jumped into his car and drove all the way to Juhu and rang her doorbell. When she opened the door, there was blood all over the floor; it had been three-quarters of an hour since she had begun savagely hacking at her arms with a razor blade. She was prepared to go. She had put on the song "Missing" by Everything But The Girl that she had danced to with Samar at the discotheques, the one she would request that the DJ play and call out publicly, to embarrass him, "To Monalisa with love from Samar." This song was now playing over and over again as Monalisa, drunk, weeping, slashed her arms.

Minesh asked her to hold her hands up. Her veins had come out of the flesh. He opened the top of the bottle of RC, the whiskey she'd been drinking, held it over her arms, and poured the alcohol over her open veins. "I didn't even flinch." She took out a cigarette, lit it herself, and sat smoking, as Minesh called his family doctor, who got her a room at the hospital.

The first time she tried to kill herself, she could bandage her hands herself and then go to the doctor to have a plaster cast put on. That time, and the second time she cut her wrists, there had been no need for stitches. The third time, she required eight stitches. But this time, all her veins were showing and her hands had turned black. The hospital attached a heart monitor to her. The doctor was talking to her like a child, and injecting her with something, and sewing her flesh up. Forty-five stitches were required to close the wounds. Even now, three of her fingers don't work properly. Monalisa had done a thorough job.

As she is telling me all this, she is taking puffs of her cigarette, shutting her eyes, lightly rocking and saying something to herself.

"Are you praying?" I ask her.

"I won't tell you."

Why does she do it? Why does she cut and burn herself?

"I was angry."

"Who at?"

Herself, she answers. When she gets angry at a man, "when he doesn't understand what *I* want, when he doesn't understand what *I* need, I get angry at myself. Why is the person opposite behaving like this with me when I don't take any money from him?" It is a term she often uses to describe her men: "the person opposite." Since the person opposite is treating her badly, and she can find no reason for the bad behavior, the fault must lie with her. It must be her fault that he's so selfish, so unthinking.

When Monalisa got out of the hospital, Minesh knew she would probably try to kill herself again. Although he was in love with her, he made a phone call to his rival, Samar. They knew each other; at one point, they had even considered going into business together, selling mobile phones. He told him what had happened and then discreetly left the scene. Samar immediately went to Monalisa's house. Since her arms were bandaged, he bathed her, and he cleaned the house himself—not something a Bombay boy, a don's grandson, ever does. For seven days and seven nights he stayed with her. They slept spooned together like little children; not once did they make love. But Minesh did not know this. Minesh stayed away, but he could not sleep at night. "I imagined him touching you," he told Monalisa later.

Both of them have offered to live with her. "Forget the past. Begin a new life with me." Monalisa has gradually allowed Minesh into her life, into her flat. He was with her all night once, and his father, a rich solicitor, got mad at him when he got back home. So Minesh phoned Monalisa and said that he was leaving his home and renting his own apartment, and was now free to marry her. There was just one obstruction.

"I said, 'What?' He said, 'You have to say yes.' "

But she is not attracted to him. Samar was handsome, a Pathan, with a wild anger in him. Minesh is a short Gujarati man, balding, with glasses. Next to her, he looks like a kid brother or attendant. "Minesh is a good friend; I give him izzat." A month ago Monalisa told Minesh, very gently, that she doesn't love him. That she would be leaving him today so that his life would be set tomorrow. So that he wouldn't bankrupt himself. Every month he had been blowing a lakh or more at Sapphire, plus rent for the apartment he maintained to be with her, and the clothes he bought her, and what he spent on her at the discos and the meals he bought her at five-star hotels. He wept when she told him this; he begged her not to leave him. But it had to happen sooner or later, and she told him she would still meet him, talk to him, be his friend. "But for the last month there have been no relations." So now Minesh goes with other girls and then comes home and gives Monalisa the details.

MONALISA HAS TWO LIVES. One is her life in the bar and the time she spends with her customers. Then there is the other life: her time in the discos, watching TV, sleeping all day. She never goes to bed before six in the morning. In our conversations, if I mix up the lives, she will say about her work world, "That life is completely different. That is a jooth ki duniya"— a world of lies. Once, on the phone, I tell her in English that I am going to lie down and take a nap. She asks what "nap" means. When I explain the meaning, she repeats it, making a connection. "Lie. Lie also means jooth. It also means to sleep." In Monalisa's world, to tell a lie and to lie with someone are not so far apart.

"For Muharram, the bar is very quiet," she tells me one day. "All this wrong work has stopped."

"Why? Do you think the work you do is wrong work?"

"Of course it's wrong work. Drinking in a bar is also wrong work."

I ask her if she thinks Sapphire is exploitative.

"It's okay as long as there's a limit," she responds. "It took me two years to understand this. A man comes into a bar when he is tired of his family, of taking care of his wife and children, and tired of the office. The dancers are buying the armaan of the customers. That is a very bad thing. Why can't we save our money? Why do we have bad luck? Because we buy their difficulties." She has misunderstood my question. She is telling me that Sapphire is exploitative, but of the customers. Whatever happens to her and the other dancers after that—if they should fall in love with a customer and he mistreats them—is deserved, because they have been exploiting these men's human need for comfort.

"I get very quickly attracted to a person," explains Monalisa. "I like Hari even now, because at least he took care of me for a few months." Recently, Monalisa was dancing at Razzberry when she saw a familiar face. It was Hari. She went up to him and confronted him. "Hari, you ruined my life. You taught me to drink, to smoke. Whatever I've become today is because of you." Then she stopped venting, because when she looked closely at the old man in the flashing lights of the disco, she saw that his eyes had filled up with tears.

Hari has fallen on bad times. WARRANT ISSUED AGAINST BOLLYWOOD FILM PRODUCER says a headline in the paper one morning. A nonbailable warrant has been issued against Hari Virani for failure to repay a thirty-five-lakh loan taken from a car finance company. I call Monalisa and read the item on Hari to her.

"I am happy and upset also," she says, without gloating. She's happy that he's now getting back what he did to her and to other girls, but "I'm upset that he still hasn't improved himself." His pictures have flopped, she points out, and "he has left the bar line"—as if Hari were also employed in the industry, just as Monalisa is. In Sapphire, Minesh had also put it that way: "I have been in the bar line for seven years." The bar line has a wholeness about it that can envelop even the customers, so that it becomes their primary point of identification, at least in the dark part of the twenty-four hours.

She says all of a sudden, in English, "You're my best friend!"

These days, she's my best friend too.

Monalisa asks me, "Where's your family? Do you live alone in Bombay?"

"Most of my family is in America. I have family everywhere: in America, in England, some in Bombay. My mother's family is from Kenya." I haven't told her about my wife and children. I remember that Monalisa is still under the protection of the don's grandson. She is of the shadow world; I keep my family insulated from such people. Hit men, dancing girls, rioters: As far as they are concerned, I live alone in the apartment in Elco, which is actually my office. If there is a problem later, if they decide to take a violent dislike to me or what I write about them, it is only me they can hurt.

"I never talk about my life with anybody," she says. I am listening.

RUSTOM CALLS, and we arrange for Monalisa to be photographed in his studio.

Monalisa's car is a battered Esteem. The air-conditioning is out of order, and she's driving it without a license. My seat is missing the headrest, and paint is flaking across the bumper. She's driving with her bare feet, because when she steps on the clutch her platform shoes get in the way and she can't depress it fully. I get in and notice the profuse images of the goddess. JAI SHRI MELDIMA read the Gujarati stickers. We drive into town through exhaust fumes coming in the open windows. It is powerfully hot this afternoon. But she is, as always, cheerful.

When we step out into the crowd in front of Eros Cinema, every single human being turns to look at her. I watch their faces, the men and the women; their heads swivel like spectators at a tennis game. Some are walking, distracted by their own world until Monalisa passes by them, and they suddenly do a double-take. I fancy I hear the sound of many cars braking abruptly. If there were dogs around, they would bark. She's dressed in a light-green halter top. It must be her platform shoe–raised walk, the confidence with which she holds her head. We go into a café for a quick sandwich. Here, too, everybody turns around to look, surreptitiously or involuntarily. Monalisa is amused. Even when she wears a salwaar kameez, she gets it cut revealingly. "Those who want to, can see. Those who don't, lower your eyes," she instructs all of Bombay.

In the studio, she is nervous and shy and giggly. Rustom has it all set up: two gay makeup men, two assistants, lights, umbrellas, props. Rustom tells her to take her bra off. But it's not because he wants to see her boobs; Rustom has seen enough boobs to make an entire infant nursery coo with pleasure. It is because the marks of the elastic straps show up in the pictures. It takes at least an hour—an hour and a half for the women with the slightest fat on their skin, the "pleasant" types the regional ads need—for strap marks to fade. Monalisa complies and takes off her bra under her shirt. But then Rustom makes a more daring request; he asks her to remove the black thread from her neck. She shakes her head. A little later, the makeup man also asks her to get rid of the thread, and again she refuses. She'll take off everything but Goddess Meldima's token.

Rustom turns up the music in the large lighted space and begins shooting. In front of the camera Monalisa is not a good model. An assistant blows her hair over her face with a vacuum cleaner hose, which also blows her thread over her neck and chin, making it seem as if she's being strangled or garroted. Under her black velvet top, I notice for the first time that she has a small paunch, a belly that has popped out. Her smile is crooked; her lips curl up at the extreme left of her mouth. The marks all down her arms can be seen clearly under the glare of the powerful studio lights. Rustom shouts instructions to her in English: "Play with your hair! Flip your head up!" I'm not sure she understands them fully over the music, and she is trying hard not to giggle. The music—Alanis Morissette, Phil Collins, assorted hip-hop—is not of her world, and nobody is throwing money at her. When the contact sheets come back, it is apparent that she has not tested well. Monalisa does not look like someone who could convince the great masses of Indian women to buy shampoo, refrigerators, or sanitary napkins.

A COUPLE OF MONTHS after I start meeting Monalisa, I am preoccupied for a month shifting my home and office to Bandra. I can't return Monalisa's daily phone calls. Monalisa goes crying to Minesh, who is still pursuing her. "Suketu is drifting away from me." She thinks she knows why, and she asks me when she calls one morning, "Is there anything you expect from me that I'm not giving you?"

I tell her there isn't. I have just been busy.

"Every person want me," Monalisa says, in English. It seems less a boast than a statement of fact.

She hasn't eaten much the whole of the previous day: a club sandwich at Sapphire. And now her aunt has made her a full meal. "Have you eaten?" she asks me. I'm just about to, I say. "Then come here and eat with me."

Monalisa lives on the ground floor of a middle-class building in Juhu. Her apartment has an outside room furnished with two faded sofas, which is never used except to take off your shoes. Inside is a kitchen, an Indian-style bathroom with a hole in the floor, and two bedrooms. There are no chairs in the bedrooms, so Monalisa receives her guests in bed. A television is always on and, next to it, a powerful boom box. The apartment is bereft of natural light; plaster peels from the ceilings, and the whole place badly needs a paint job. But Monalisa has her usual cheerful energy. She places the roses I have brought her on the headstand of her bed, next to a droopy stuffed toy gorilla. Her kitchen has a large shrine devoted to the goddess, with a fresh garland of white and red flowers around it. Her fridge contains only water, cheese, and one bag of vegetables. In the living bedroom there is a stack of liquor glasses but no liquor since her last suicide attempt.

What happens when you enter the apartment of a single Indian woman for the first time? She shows you photographs of her family. There are two little pictures of her kid brother Viju, a fair-skinned young boy. Monalisa loves Viju, who is seventeen, almost six feet tall, and with a good physique; she thinks he should be a model. He has left college and is in and out of work as a diamond cutter. He is aware of what Monalisa does for a living and meets her secretly on Sunday afternoons, telling his mother he is going out with his friends. He comes to her flat and watches television, and she feeds him chicken biryani. If her mother finds out, she will want to come too. Sunday is family day for the patrons of Sapphire; they spend the day in their legitimate households. Therefore, it is a day of rest for the bar girls.

Her brother is just about the only family that Monalisa keeps in touch with. Her relatives in the village, including her other brother—the one who was given up to her uncle at birth—think she's married and know nothing about what she does for a living. This is one of the reasons she stays away from her father as well: "so they don't find out." She won't go back to her village. But the bar provides its substitute family. On top of the TV is a picture of Monalisa hugging a younger girl on a beach. "That's my daughter." It is Muskan, the girl Monalisa has "adopted," in the bar-line way. Muskan is a dancer in Sapphire from Indore, and she is thirteen years old. She is one of the four remaining virgins in the bar, and the other girls treat her like a little doll. Very soon, she will sell her virginity for anywhere between two and five lakhs, maybe to Mohammed the Arab, who has been coming to Sapphire for the last five years and buying the right to deflower the youngest girls. He once told Monalisa, "You look like an ice cream."

When I am ready to eat she suggests we sit on the bed she sleeps in, and I prop myself up on her pillows and put my feet on the bed. She gets on and stretches out likewise, very close to me. I see her very long legs for the first time, in her very tight spandex shorts. She hugs a pillow and points out the bloodstains on it. "This is from when I cut myself. I haven't got it washed." Behind us is a telephone scratch pad filled with dozens of numbers, most of them beginning with 98: mobile phone numbers. Most of the men's names have only a mobile number next to them; the females have land lines. Monalisa is the kind of girl men don't give their home numbers to.

She had asked me if I liked my food spicy and I had foolishly said yes. It is the hottest food I have ever eaten in an Indian home. Baby chili potatoes, a spinach dal, chapatis, rice. In addition to this, Monalisa brings out two bottles of pickles. She spoons more chilies out of them on my plate, one green, one red. I am ravenous, and I eat—first with pleasure, then with pain; in the way, I imagine, any kind of relationship with Monalisa would be. I am not shy of spice—my kitchen cabinet in all countries always has a stash of habanero peppers—but this is beyond me. Monalisa, however, shows no signs of being on fire. "This is why they say to me, You're so spicy," she says, her long fingers mixing the rice and the dal. Talking about the food, Monalisa switches to Gujarati, the only time she uses the language common to us. Her Gujarati has a strong Kathiawari accent, but she is self-conscious about it. She prefers Hindi: Bambaiyya Hindi, filmi Hindi, tapori Hindi. Gujarati is the first language, the core language, and it is too intimate to be used between us, narrator and chronicler.

She tells me about how she discovered her own body and its pleasures. The girls in the village were no innocents; they had sex with eggplants, relations with trees. After moving to Bombay, after her menses, Monalisa found that she was "interested in myself." She remembers the first time she had a period; she was eleven or twelve. "I was sleeping. I woke up and felt very wet. I thought, What happened, who did this? I was very hot. I hated myself. I would sit the whole day: What happened to me?" Her mother, of course, had explained nothing. All she had taught her was fear. "My mother wouldn't even let me sleep with my father."

She would watch music videos on television, and they would affect her dreams. "My feeling would be completed in sleep. Then I used to get frightened, that someone was doing this to me in my sleep and impregnating me." She actually went to the doctor once, when she was sixteen and had missed her period, to check that she was not pregnant from the vision in her sleep. Even now, she says, if she hasn't had relations for a month, she will "discharge" in her sleep. "I sleep with a pillow between my thighs; even if it touches me lightly, I'll discharge." Lately, she has been finding that she can also discharge in the shower. It is an apt term, one I have not heard before in this context, like a battery stored for too long. As the electricity within builds up, discharge it or it will leak or explode.

Monalisa has a keen understanding of why sex for most middle-class Indians is such a joyless experience. "Here what happens is, the man lives with his parents. Then he goes into his family business; he can't do what he really wants to. Then he has to get married to the girl his parents choose. There is no feeling. When he wants sex, he has relations in the same mood with his wife—as a bodily need. He discharges. When he finds a new girl, he has relations the same way. He might want to do something else, but he doesn't know how. The wife also, breeding children, cooking at home, doesn't know what life is like outside. They have to give when the husband wants, not when they want. Many women don't know what discharge is. Their life is: They cook all day and watch TV at home. Even at night, in bed, all they say is, 'Your sister did this, your brother's wife did that.' " It is not a happy view of marriage. Monalisa has made the connections—why there seems to be such sexual unhappiness in the city. If all the other areas of a person's life—work, family—are circumscribed, if the pattern has been established even before they are born, then when it comes to sex it will be similarly conditioned, its positions and its techniques preordained or hastily improvised in the darkness. A man or woman with a deadened brain could not possibly realize the peaks of pleasure that Monalisa and Samar, adventurous spirits in all areas of life, climbed so readily and so often.

The college boys, said Monalisa, are better in bed. They get drunk, see adult movies, set up their own businesses, do things their own way. She likes their freedom from convention; she herself wants Rustom to take nude shots of her. As she is telling me all this, I get the feeling that the air conditioner isn't working. As she is telling me all this, she has the cushion grabbed tight between her legs.

I tell Monalisa that I am changing the names of all of the people who might get in trouble from being in my book. "What name do you want for yourself in the book?"

"Why? No, no, no!" she cries, beating her fists in the air. She wants to be known by her real name; she has nothing to hide and is quite delighted that the world should know about her life.

I insist; I tell her there is no predicting what consequences publishing these intimate details of her life might have. So she suggests one: "Finalfi."

"Finalfi? That's a dog's name."

She says she hasn't heard it before, so she likes it. It shouldn't be a very common name. Then she comes up with another suggestion: "Monalisa."

And that's how Monalisa gets her name. It fits. Beauty, mystery, and a little bit of sadness.

Later, we go to Just Around the Corner, a trendy new cafeteria that Monalisa has been curious about. I am nervous. At any moment somebody's going to recognize me and ask, "How're the kids?" Monalisa suggests that she and I go away for a few days to the seaside resort of Daman—"with two or three couples," she adds. She tells me she had missed me very much on Sunday and had gone out to catch the last show at Sterling. I don't tell her that I was there too, in the audience, with my wife. I realize the chances were very great that we would have met and I would have had to explain my wife to her. It is now too late in my friendship with Monalisa to mention my family without some explanation. Nurtured in the shade, it has acquired the status of a secret.

Instead of Daman, I take Monalisa out for dinner and a movie. At the arcade in the theater, we play video games, shooting cowboys and racing cars. She gets samosas and two containers of popcorn, and we sit in the balcony and watch *A Bug's Life*, Monalisa eating throughout the movie. She has bought lots of tokens for the video games, and after the movie we shoot some more cowboys. I try to be nineteen again, but I am always conscious of it.

After the movie we go to the Orchid, a new hotel near the airport, and wait for Minesh, who—with slow and patient wooing, after I pass up the opportunity to accompany her to Daman—is back in Monalisa's life as a lover. The hotel has a waterfall in the center of the lobby atrium, tubes of water falling from a great height. We eat and make inconsequential conversation about the World Cup. I am beginning to realize that there is very little I can communicate to her about my world; she doesn't know where France and Kenya are, has no wish ever to leave Bombay, go to the village, or go abroad. When I tell Monalisa I'm off to Delhi and might be meeting Vajpayee, she doesn't say anything.

"Atal Bihari Vajpayee. The prime minister."

"I don't know who the prime minister is these days. I only know Indira Gandhi, Rajiv Gandhi, and Mahatma Gandhi. These were the names that were taught to us." She doesn't ever read a newspaper, never watches the news on TV.

Minesh comes in, dressed in baggy shorts. He is thirty-two and looks older. He is losing his hair, and there is a curious darkness around his mouth, probably from tobacco. He went to a Gujarati school—"I am a vernacular boy." Then he got a law degree but never practiced. Instead, he started a software company which exports to the United States; the previous year he traveled there four times. Minesh is also an amateur playwright, in Gujarati, and, like many amateur playwrights, wants to start his own political party in ten years. We talk in English, about technical recruiting and costing software and taxes, with Monalisa between us. We're both hiding something: I'm hiding my family from Monalisa, Minesh is hiding Monalisa from his family. Only Monalisa's hiding nothing. She has no family to hide anything from. She is sleepy and tired. She does not belong with us, I feel; she is young and beautiful and she should be with people her own age, young men filled with the same energy and lightness, men who have different uses for her, more innocent ones, than either of us do.

AROUND THIS TIME, Dayanita Singh, a photographer friend of mine from Delhi, comes to Bombay for a shoot. She is supposed to be here only for a couple of days. Dayanita has a special rapport with sex workers and people of indefinite gender: eunuchs, prostitutes. I describe the world of the bar line to her and she wants to go immediately. She ends up staying in

Bombay for several weeks, following my friends with her camera. At Sapphire, watching the way Monalisa's face brightens up on seeing me and the extra energy that infuses her dancing when she's in front of me, Dayanita says, "I'm worried that she'll fall in love with you."

"Or vice versa."

"That's impossible," she says. Why? I am about to ask.

"How could you not fall in love with her?" she says. "I'm half in love with her already."

Monalisa introduces Dayanita and me to BK, the manager of Sapphire. He is a mild-mannered Parsi who was in the "technical line" before he started running Sapphire. I ask BK about Monalisa. "She's different from the other dancers," he says.

"In what way is she different?"

"I like her," the Parsi man explains.

BK is the most adored manager in the Bombay bars; the girls will do anything for him. Dancing all night is hard work. Before the current 12:30 p.m. curfew, they would dance till eight in the morning: from 9 p.m. to 2:30 a.m., then a short break for "supper," then again till the sun was high in the world outside. When their energy flagged, the manager would urge them to "turn the key!" And the dolls would dance.

But BK keeps his hands strictly off them. They refer to him as "BK Sir," as with a teacher. Monalisa is sensitive to a fault to the moods of her boss. Once, when she was going through a bad phase with Vijay the Sindhi, she was losing other customers over him. A faithful customer like Raj, who came to the bar with four gun-toting bodyguards behind him and spent big amounts on her, would feel slighted when he saw her mooning over Vijay the whole time. One night, Monalisa was supposed to be showing a new dancer the ropes, but instead she just stood on the stage with her, not dancing, just holding her hand. BK saw this from the back and, already irritated by Monalisa's neglect of her customers, shouted at her, "Drop her hand!" Monalisa ran home and started drinking. Weeping, drinking, she brooded over what the manager had said. Then she went back to Sapphire and showed him her arm: There were six fresh cigarette burns in the soft brown flesh. "Look what you made me do." He has never spoken harshly to her since.

Dayanita photographs Monalisa in the afternoon, in an empty hall at Sapphire. She gets her beauty. But I wonder if she gets that one look I know so well: in the middle of "Jalwa" or "Brazil," when Monalisa spins around all of a sudden, crouching low and forward, and looks at you through that mane of hair falling on both sides of her face. She is not smiling, not even attempting to please, and her eyes are looking directly at you, and her mouth is set, furious almost, in pure sexual challenge. "I'm afraid of that kind of sensuality," says Dayanita. Over time, as I get to see Monalisa's nice side, I mustn't forget this look. I mustn't forget her core, which is based on sex, on lust. That movement of her buttocks, which men look at and imagine stripping away the thin sari covering them. You won't have to move at all; she'll do it all for you.

Later, at Nariman Point, she is being shot in the midst of the Saturday evening crowds. Dayanita wants to test her, see how she takes to being photographed in public. She shows no anxiety, no shyness. And she can hear the public asking each other, "Who's that girl? Haven't I seen her somewhere?" For the first time, the audience is not saying, "There's that bar dancer." They are saying, "There's that model."

AS I AM LEAVING SAPPHIRE a few nights later—I am to meet up with Monalisa at the Marine Plaza after she takes off her makeup and changes out of her costume—the parking valets come up to me. "You are to sit in Minesh Saab's car." Presently, Monalisa's boyfriend emerges from the bar and drives me to the hotel. He has not been invited.

We take a table by the bay windows, through which we can see nothing—it's 1:30 a.m.—and arrange ourselves around it: me, Monalisa, and Minesh. Minesh has been drinking that night: six whiskeys and three shots of tequila. Without being asked, he explains why men go to bars: "False-man ego. I can command there—from Monalisa, from BK. I can't command at home. I need to command."

Minesh starts telling me his story. He speaks in English. "I started going to bars seven years ago. I know one girl in every bar. I used to be scared entering the bars. Then I was pure. Now I'm not. I'm in love with this woman. I saw a good woman, I bought her. Let's be honest: It's ego." Minesh switches to the third person to refer to himself when he talks about falling in love. "For five and a half years this man who goes into a bar and looks at Monalisa and becomes a very good friend of hers, after six and a half years this man suddenly becomes jealous of another man, and you realize he's in love." I remember that the gangsters often used the third person when talking about their killings. It is hard to take first-person responsibility for love or murder.

"That's when I realized I needed this woman," Minesh continues, speaking about how he first fell for Monalisa. "I've slept with an amazing amount of bar women—a dozen plus. If I slept with a woman I did not go back to that bar so I didn't get addicted to her. This was the one woman I slept with and went back to the bar the next day. There was a time she didn't sleep with me, but every day she slept in my house. I would drop her at a disco till six in the morning, and she would come drunk to my house. I would not sleep. I was worried that people would use her, not that they would sleep with her. If she's drunk and someone uses her it affects me."

Minesh refers to the bar line as the "industry." He and the other regular customers are as much a part of the industry as the bar dancers or owners. "All the men who go there are dissatisfied with life or have an inferiority complex. Because, if I have money, I can say to this woman to not look at any other customer. They are a service industry; they have to service me whenever I have money. She knows that the moment I am jealous that means more money."

He attributes his inferiority complex, his false-man ego, to his situation at home. "I am not satisfied at home. I want my mother to say, Son, drink your tea, but she doesn't. I want attention. When I spend money at the bar there are four hundred eyes looking at me. Today BK calls me Mineshbhai because I am one of the biggest customers at Sapphire. If I stop for a few months they'll say this guy's become a chutiya." They will understand that he has been milked dry by a bar girl. Minesh is wise to the techniques of the bar girls, their adroit manipulation of the false-man ego. For example, one customer might give a girl a gift, a T-shirt, say; the girl will turn around and give the same T-shirt to another customer, as a token of her love. The second customer will show this off. Wearing the T-shirt, he will bring his friends to the bar and brag, "She bought this for me."

Minesh is seasoned in the techniques of hooking a bar girl. It is a contest; the girls try to make chutiyas of the customers and the customers try to get the girls to sleep with them after blowing the least possible amount of money or, best of all, to fall in love with them. "If I'm smart, for ten days I'll give her money but not ask her name. On the eleventh day I'll come up with a dialogue: 'Jaan, tonight I won't get any sleep. And even if I get sleep you'll come in my dreams. And if you come in my dreams, by what name shall I call you?' " This was the line that Minesh first used with Monalisa, after many days of giving her money and not saying a single word. As he explains it, "In a bar you have to be *filmi* different." He notes that if he were to meet a girl like Monalisa in a disco, he'd have to do something else to attract her: dance well, for example. "Monalisa doesn't think so, but I dance well. You don't need good looks. Looks are deceptive, every woman knows that." It has been commented upon by her friends in the bar: this stunning young woman and her balding, bespectacled escort, several inches shorter, several years older.

"Can I be very honest?" asks Minesh. "Do you know why Monalisa slept with me the first time? She wanted to fuck up the last guy who screwed her up."

Now, Minesh hangs out with Monalisa's friends as well, such as the thirteen-year-old virgin Muskan, who, Minesh claims, is in love with him. "I am the only customer in the history of the industry who took two bar girls together to a movie."

"When you spend money on a girl and she comes to you, she's coming to your money. She's not coming to you for your conversation or your looks or your good heart," I point out to Minesh.

"But it's the power of my money. I can feel proud of how much money I have!" One of his fellow customers in the industry once gave him an accounting of his relationship with his steady girl at Sapphire. "I've spent so much on Ranjita, and I've slept with her so many times. So I've paid three thousand rupees a night. And I love her."

Minesh takes a puff on his cigarette and addresses Monalisa. "If I had spent on different women what I've spent on you, by now I would have slept with fifteen or twenty women."

Monalisa says nothing. Absolutely nothing. He could have been talking about the weather.

Minesh turns to me. "Monalisa has an *amazing* body."

I ask him how he feels when she sees other customers. Monalisa interjects, speaking more to Minesh than to me. "I can go to meet customers for coffee. It's my work."

"Go," says Minesh, tilting his head and blowing out smoke. "I trust you." He addresses me again. "I always tell her, 'I took a lot of money from you in my last birth; in this birth I'm giving it back to you.' "

I ask Minesh what the future of his relationship with Monalisa might be, and if he sees her future in the movies or as a model.

"What I've heard about the film industry and the modeling industry is that it's a bitch. They will all use you: sexually, physically, mentally. She's been ruined physically in any case by the industry. So you are scared"—now switching to the second person—"that this would happen to her and she would break. Although she's very capable to do very well in the media—modeling, film, serials—I would not let her go into it. It may be an inferiority complex to feel I would lose her. Because if it was not an inferiority complex I would not be here for seven years roaming around in the dance bars. If there was no complex, Minesh would not be here. Maybe I'm trying to lie to myself. I have zero savings."

He has just got to the core of his life, and maybe what he found there has surprised him as well. "How much money have you spent in the bars altogether?" I ask him.

"Let me not count, but huge money."

I ask for an estimate, a ballpark figure.

"Let me not count." He is pleading. He cannot face it, cannot even face the process of calculating how foolish or obsessed he's been. "Let me get on to another topic."

Monalisa takes a hairband, gathers up her hair with both hands from the back of her head, and puts it up so that it piles up high and comes down on both sides of her face. She is looking extraordinarily, heartbreakingly lovely. Fifty thousand rupees, for a glimpse of this face.

In the car, as we say good-bye, I notice Minesh's left arm. There are two deep gashes on it. "A glass window broke. It bled for three days," he says. Monalisa tells me later how it happened. He had gone to Sapphire, and she told him she would meet him later at Juhu. He went to her house; she wasn't there, so he knew she had lied. She had gone to meet another customer. He was drunk and had smoked a lot of grass, and he slashed his arm there. It bled heavily, and he wiped it with a napkin and left. When Monalisa finally got home she found the bloody napkin. The doorbell rang; Minesh said he had come back to get his napkin. She bandaged him and he slept in her bed. In the morning he went to the doctor and got eleven stitches. The top customer of the top bar dancer had joined the sorority of the slashed.

*   *   *

EVERYBODY IN MONALISA'S FAMILY has tried to kill themselves at least once. Her brother, just the previous month, took an overdose of sleeping pills because his mother was mean to him. Her father once tried to give her mother poison and then took poison himself, so that the ten-year-old Monalisa had to rush him to the doctor in the middle of the night. Her mother tried to poison herself over a lover who was bad to her. And, of course, Monalisa herself—even before her love affairs—while she was living with her mother, took medicine used to kill fleas. "Children will learn what they see their parents doing," she explains.

And now, after twelve years, Monalisa is going to meet the father who abandoned her.

She has been meeting her mother lately. They went to the Essel World theme park together and she allowed herself to call her "Mummy." Her father had phoned her mother recently, and her mother told him about their daughter. On hearing that she'd been in contact, he decided to come up to Bombay. Her mother asked Monalisa if she would see him, and Monalisa agreed. All day he'd been asking his ex-wife, using his daughter's real name, "Did Rupa call? Did Rupa call?" He hasn't even seen pictures of her.

I ask Monalisa if she's nervous. "I'm very nervous. I won't be able to say anything to him."

"You want me to come with you?"

She thinks for a quick moment and then says, "Yes. Come."

I PICK HER UP the next morning outside Minesh's building in Juhu, which is in front of an enormous red Ganesh, sprouting seven heads of the main gods—Shiva, Rama, Hanuman—and fourteen arms, all protected by the spread hood of a cobra. Monalisa walks out and turns around to say good-bye to Minesh, who is leaning out of his second-floor window, bare-chested. We take an air-conditioned taxi to Mira Road. She has just woken up and is still very sleepy; she leans her head on my shoulder and shuts her eyes. I remember, and then forget, that she has just gotten out of another man's bed without a bath; he is probably still in her.

The highway marks the progress of her life. At one end are the slums she grew up in, and she points them out along the side of the road. There in the giant Gujarati complexes in Bhayander are the places her aunt hid her when she ran away from home, hundreds of multistory buildings sprouting all over the weedy ground. There are the suburban bars she danced in, in Goregaon and Borivali, patronized by the crass Maharashtrian builders and the diffident bhaiyyas who kept cattle in pens in the middle of the city. At the other end is the flat she had once bought in Mira Road, just across from her mother's, a one-bedroom with a terrace. She sold the flat in Mira Road for four lakhs. She put one lakh into a fixed deposit account at the bank. "Then I roamed around for two–three months. I drank. It went." Her eyes roll heavenward and close.

Many girls in the bar line now live in Mira Road; the Foras Road girls are rapidly shifting to the new city. The 12:30 train to Mira Road gets filled up at Grant Road with the bar girls, shouting and talking on their mobiles. The expensive Sterling School in the suburb is filled with the children of these girls. Mira Road is an instant city, where nobody asks questions because everyone is a newcomer. As we approach Mira Road, where her father is waiting for her, she says, "Now I feel something inside," and she opens and closes her fist, like the beating of a heart. I give her a hug and hold her hand in mine.

We walk to her mother's apartment, and Monalisa sees her father sitting in an armchair in the living room, legs up, a balding man with gentle eyes, dressed in an undershirt and lungi. "Hullo, Pappa," she says, as if she's been out for a morning walk.

"Touch his feet, touch his feet!" shouts her mother from the kitchen. "It's been so long since you've met him."

She goes over to him and doesn't touch his feet. She shakes his hand. She is afraid that he might be angry; she thinks she sees anger on his face.

I come in and sit on the sofa; she sits next to me, away from her father.

"How long has it been?" asks the mother.

"Ten years," says Monalisa.

"Not that long. I used to come to your school, remember?" says the father. But she wouldn't agree to see him there.

"You've lost hair. And your stomach has grown," observes Monalisa. He smiles. He makes no remarks about his daughter's appearance.

The mother goes into the kitchen. She is still dressed in a cotton nightie, a woman in her mid-forties proud of her former good looks. The brother, Viju, enters the room, a fresh-faced, tall young man, true to his picture. He smiles often; one of his front teeth is a deep yellow and broken in half.

The father stares intently at me, without speaking, for several minutes after I sit down. The television is switched on and never shut off thereafter. We all stare at it in relief: the long-lost father, the daughter who dances in front of strangers for money, the mother who sold her daughter, the brother who recently tried to kill himself, and me. When they ask me, "What is your business?" I reply, "I'm a writer." It is an effective conversation-stopper.

The flat consists of a living room and two bedrooms, all freshly painted in pink. Like most of the flats in Mira Road, it is a flat of the striving middle class, the first step up from the slums. It is clean, and the open window brings in lots of light and air but also swarms of mosquitoes. There is a battery-powered cuckoo clock on one wall and copies of two big pictures of Viju, which I'd seen in Monalisa's house, up on the showcase. "I'm going to put up two pictures, one on this wall and one on this one," says Viju.

"Whose pictures?" asks Monalisa.

"Mine."

Monalisa quickly turns her face away.

She ignores her father and asks her brother to bring the album of her baby pictures. There she is, just any Gujarati girl in Bombay, holding her brother's hand and smiling for the camera; she could be my sister. There is not a single picture of her father. Then there are the pictures taken a couple of weeks ago when Monalisa went with Muskan and her brother and mother to Essel World and to Water Kingdom. The two bar girls are vamping outrageously for Viju's camera, undulating in matching red tank tops and tight black pants. In some of the pictures they are kissing each other; in one, the younger girl has her mouth on Monalisa's bared belly, kissing it. In others they are in swimsuits. Monalisa asks her father if he's seen these pictures; they would have been the first sight of his grown daughter. He nods yes, silently.

After a while the father goes into the bedroom. Monalisa follows him. The mother comes out and tells me, smiling, "He's crying." They are in there by themselves for about fifteen minutes. I watch the soap opera on the screen in the living room. An extended family is experiencing heated conflict.

They return to the living room, and an animated discussion begins about the brother's career. He is a ninth-standard dropout. He has a choice: go into diamond sorting, which pays more and has better prospects than cutting stones in a factory; or go to Kenya, to Nairobi, to work in his aunt's hotel. The factory work here is a dead end; he earns about what a peon in an office or a driver might make. Monalisa wants him to go to Kenya so he can learn to fend for himself.

"But I don't want to go to Kenya!" Viju protests. He is afraid of the crime there.

Monalisa starts making chapatis in the kitchen. Her fingers knead the long white-brown tube of dough, and it elongates, descends, from her palms. Then she breaks off a disk from the tube, rolls it out on the wooden platform, and throws it first in the pan and then directly on the fire, where it gathers air, swells, becomes a balloon so fluffy it might lift off, and then settles as Monalisa smears ghee over it.

The lunch is full of small courtesies done to me in the Indian way. I am invited to eat by the father, as if it were still his house, and I sit on the floor in front of my plate. The food is less spicy than at Monalisa's house: chapatis, potato-and-eggplant curry, dal, rice, and long green not-very-hot fried chilies. There is a pile of chapatis in front of me. As I eat, the mother comes out of the kitchen with a hot chapati and directs Monalisa, "Take the cold one from him." Monalisa reaches over to my plate, takes the one made earlier, and replaces it with the hot chapati. Then she eats the cold one.

The mother apologizes to me that she hasn't made anything special. "I didn't know a man was coming. When Monalisa told me she was bringing a friend, I thought it was a girl, or I would have made undhiyu."

As we eat, the family berates Viju for not going to work that day. "He has no excuse," says the father. "There's a toilet next to the factory!"

"But when I'm feeling like that how can I work?"

"He's having loose motions," Monalisa explains to me. "But that's no reason not to go to work."

The brother appeals to me. "How can you work when you're like that?"

The mother wants him to eat something. "Eat some rice and yogurt.

Your stomach is empty." He doesn't want to, but the mother forces it on him. He sits down and eats with us, with his troubled bowels.

After the meal the father belches and washes his hands in his plate, with water from his water glass, as they do in the village. He tells me to do the same, and I do, running my fingers quickly under the stream of cold water, which falls into my saucer of dal and turns it a murky yellow. "You're Gujarati," he says approvingly. "He's still Gujarati," agrees Monalisa. She herself washes her hands in the basin in the kitchen. The father takes his seat and reads the Gujarati paper, his lips moving silently as he does so. He is clearly at home; there is absolutely no indication that this is a divorced couple. "We have five houses in the village," says the mother. "Bungalows. One is of my mister, the others belong to his brothers."

After lunch, Monalisa and her brother are stretched out on the floor, leaning their heads on bolsters and horsing around. He tickles her; she yanks at his hair. "They're very close," the mother says. "They would fight and tell me tales about the other one, and when I would beat him, she would stand in a corner and cry. When I beat her, he would cry. She's very strong, and he's not. When Viju would get beaten up by the boys in the building, Rupa would go down and give them two punches, these big strong boys, and they would all run. But Viju's very delicate. Even if I give him a little pinch on his skin he cries loudly and says I've hit him too hard. In the night sometimes I take his hair while he's sleeping and tie it in two tails on either side of his head." She puts her hair up over her temples with both hands, like a devil's horns. "We used to dress him up in frocks like a girl."

The brother is smiling widely.

"He used to wet his bed till four years ago. We all slept together, and when I woke up my nightie would be soaking wet. And Rupa's hair would be completely wet. That's why it's so long and beautiful. It's her conditioner. When people ask Rupa, What's the secret of your hair? she should say, It's my brother's piss." She laughs loudly, while her son desperately tries to shush her. But then he realizes she is not going to stop, and, trying with all his life to catch up in the joke—to demonstrate to me that he too thinks it's funny—he says, "Maybe I should bottle it and sell it."

Then the mother and the brother describe Monalisa's impressive appetite to me. The mother enumerates all the things she needs to eat throughout the day: so many parathas for breakfast, so much for lunch, and two dinners. "Two pav bhajis and twelve to sixteen pav," says Viju.

Monalisa laughs along. "In the children's home I would be weeping, but I would still be eating. I would weep and eat, weep and eat."

Something hidden and savage is being played out in this family for me, the lone member of the audience. I say I will be going, but the mother is adamant that Monalisa leave with me, even though Monalisa is stretching out for a nap. The beer-bar waitress is all smiles and laughter with me and asks me to visit them again. I am from America; I am probably rich; Monalisa must go home with me.

ON THE TRAIN GOING BACK she is quiet. We stand near the open door to catch the breeze. She tells me that when she went into the bedroom, her father had put both of his hands up to the face of his lost daughter and burst into tears. He said he missed her. "Did he say he was sorry for having left you?" I ask.

She shakes her head no.

He left her because she had asked him, he had told her. When she was ten, she saw that her mother had kept another man, and her father was having an affair with another woman, so she told him to go away from there. "And he always obeyed whatever I said, even as a child," she explains to me and to herself.

He had asked her to keep just one secret: not to tell her mother that he has three cars in the village. It would not go over well that his second wife was having a better life than his first. "Even now, my father loves my mother," Monalisa tells me, and smiles. "Otherwise why would he talk to her? It feels good to me for some time when I see them together."

She had put her head in his lap and talked to him. She told him everything about her line of work. He had asked her to get married. "Girls in this line can never get married," she had replied. She asked him to come to her house when he came back to Bombay, and she would cook him a meal with her own hands. I ask her if she had cried. "I didn't cry."

"Why not?"

"Tears didn't come. They'll come when I'm alone. I cry when I'm alone and I'm listening to songs. As soon as the song begins, I start to cry."

I realize why there are so few tears in that family. If Monalisa—if her mother, if her brother—were to allow herself to cry every time she felt the weight of pain or heightened emotion, she would be all dried out from the crying. She would be weeping her blood out. So when she met the father who had abandoned her half a lifetime ago, she could watch him cry and yet hold herself in check. No, that's not right; she was not holding herself in check. It was nothing so willed as all that. By the age of twenty, it just came naturally to Miss Monalisa Patel, when she encountered a situation of great pain. She stayed strong. She did it like a pro.

OVER TIME, I started liking Sapphire. I liked the happiness there. Here were people who came after a hard day in a brutal city, and there was music they liked, and booze, and lights, and pretty girls dancing. The girls were enjoying themselves too, making money, being fawned over. There was a kind of beery fraternity among the spectators. Men came with their friends, and, their commercial instincts deadened or diminished by happiness, threw on the girls the contents of their wallets that they worked so hard to accumulate: Look, this is how little they mean to me, these brightly colored pieces of paper. Men came here to debase money.

Whenever Monalisa sees me coming in with my friends, her face lights up. We walk easily past the guards and doors into the VIP room, armed with the magic key of her name. She speaks to the waiter, and seats are cleared for us while everyone else is kept standing. Monalisa has the songs I like played for me, and she dances to them in front of me, forgoing many thousands of rupees that other men are offering her to dance for them. And all the assembled gangsters, policemen, businessmen, sheiks, and tourists crane their necks to see who this dignitary is for whom the RESERVED signs are taken off the best tables. And what does she get for doing this for me, keeping my izzat?

In love, as Monalisa knows so well, the most potent weapon you have is your ear.

Monalisa had been explaining the difference between sex, love, and friendship to Dayanita, when they were alone. "What is sex? Sex is nothing. What you need is someone who will be there all night, whose breathing you can hear all night, who you can still see in your bed in the morning after you've had sex with him. A person with whom you have relations lasts for six months or a year; a friend you can have for life. Among guys I have only one friend, Suketu. It's pure friendship. There is no love in it."

"What about Minesh?"

"That began in friendship, but then love came in. It's strange." She was talking about love as if it were a pollutant.

I am explaining all this to a friend, a poet. "Monalisa is a specialist in making men fall in love with her. I'm following her life. Since January I've been meeting her or speaking to her on the phone almost every single day."

"Oh, so she's succeeded."

"In what?" I ask, before I realize.

"Every person want me," Monalisa had said. People in Bombay think I want her too, and when they see how I am received at the bar, they infer that she has given in to my want. I know what color and type of underwear she wears. I know how she likes to make love. I know when she is sad, when she is suicidal, when she is exuberant. What is sex after such vast intimate knowledge?

"There is one person who knows my entire life," Monalisa tells Dayanita. "I've told Suketu every little detail." She reveals it to me, in large and small chunks, till her life is transferred from Monalisa to me. What will the consequences of this transfer be, on her and on me?

At some point the Monalisa that I'm writing in these pages will become more real, more alluring, than the Monalisa that is flesh and blood. One more ulloo, Monalisa will think. But imagine her surprise when she sees that what I am adoring, what I am obsessed with, is a girl beyond herself, larger than herself in the mirror beyond her, and it is her that I'm blowing all my money on, it is her that I'm getting to spin and twirl under the confetti of my words. The more I write, the faster my Monalisa dances.

Golpitha

Madan, a street photographer, asks me to walk with him through Golpitha, the collective name for the red-light district. So much of Bombay is a red-light district that the Dalit poets call the entire city Golpitha. At the end of our walk, Madan and I are sitting in a bar full of men, open to the street. It is the bowels of the earth. The whole area has an unclean aura to it. The rooms are advertised on first-floor windows: WELCOME 55. AC" Men, singly or in twos and threes, walk past the women standing outside the bar in the yellow light of the streetlamp, mustering up the courage to talk to them, sizing them up: age, complexion, and breast size. The older women sit down on the nearest stoop, tired, as the night wears on.

Madan is making sport of a boy of around twenty who has come into the bar and is sitting across the table from us. Shezan is a bright-eyed Mallu on his way to work in a hotel in Dubai; this is the suspended time for him, a night in Bombay, in transit. "I think we should get a babe and all three of us should screw her," Madan suggests. He points to me. "This guy is so horny. He just wants to screw."

Shezan Babu has just "had a shag from an Andhra babe" for 150 rupees. He likes it when the babes give him some caring. In Dubai there will be Russian babes for a thousand a night, and he's heard they're very caring. There are also Tajik babes and—what's that short race?—Filipinas. Filipina babes are very good. It's not like Saudi, where there's nothing. In Mangalore he has been having a fine time with African students who come for the universities there. "The Negro babes were very caring. With them, you have to be really decent. Maximum decent. You have to be decent for three–four months and then they'll let you do anything." And then you can have one, and then you can have so many.

A short pimp had taken him to a room where there were five–six babes, and he chose the Andhra one. They went into the room and she said I'll take off all my clothes and he said no (he was afraid of the diseases he could get, VD is all right but this AIDS is really bad), and he took off all his clothes and just lay down in the dark and she shagged him. She had offered him a condom; he always wears double condoms when fucking. Madan is aghast. "I hate condoms. Your dick becomes an alien object."

Madan is having him on, telling him to go to the whores outside and ask them if they'll have all three of us. Three hundred rupees for the three of us, one says, and then brings it down to eighty each. The room is extra. Drinks are extra. In his last encounter Shezan was given a pellet of some drug, he thinks it was grass but Madan says it was hashish, for 20 rupees. "When you have grass and screw it'll never come out," Shezan observes.

In the middle of his whoring, he takes time out to phone his mother in Mangalore. "Where are you?" she asks, anxious. "I'm in the hotel. I haven't gone out." "Have you eaten?" she asks. "No, I haven't gone out of the hotel."

The women are like any others in central Bombay, except there are more of them with East Asian features, the Nepalis. The others are Maharashtrians or Andhras, dark hued. They are not dressed provocatively. They just have flowers in their hair and might be dressed for going out to a movie or to a hotel for dinner. There are children all around them. The streetwalkers tell us to buzz off when Shezan inquires if they'll give him anal sex. "Then what *will* you do?" he asks. One of them points to her groin. "Put the dick in the cunt, that's all." Another makes him an offer: If he gives her 100 rupees, she'll lubricate a piece of wood and put it up *his* ass. The streetwalkers seem very much in control, both of the kinds of men they'll take on and what they will or won't do with them. But then a pimp comes up to two women standing by the streetlamp. He pulls out an account book, makes notations in it. The women give him some bills; he takes them, notes them down, and walks on. I start walking away too. Shezan is puzzled; the night is still young, the endless Bombay night. There are 8 million stories in the naked girl.

Bombay is a city humming, throbbing, with sexual energy. A city of migrant men without women; a city in heat. The womanless rickshaw wallahs, the Bollywood wannabes, the fashion models, and the sailors from many countries—all in search of some heat, a hurried furtive fuck in whatever hidden corner the world will permit them. They do it in trains, railway stations, the backs of taxis, parks, urinals. The rocks by the sea are a favorite. Along Carter Road in Bandra, at Scandal Point in Malabar Hill, rows of couples are wrapped in each other on the rocks, all facing the sea. It is no matter that the thousands of people walking by can see them, because they can see only their backs, not their faces, and the lovers to the left and the right of them are all busy with each other, kissing, feeling. Anonymity is erotic. That woman hanging out clothes on her balcony, with the hair long and wet around her shoulders from her bath. The crowds of girls in short skirts outside the Catholic colleges. "The whole city is a bedroom," says my maid. She knows about the memsahibs who come to meet their drivers at Haji Ali. The man who comes to fix the cable approaches her when she is alone in the house. "Is there anything to eat?" he asks. "There are some chapatis," she replies. "Can I get something to eat?" he repeats.

But the sexual hunger isn't confined to the lower classes. In the China Garden, at the Oberoi, groups of society women discuss their lovers over lunch. The young blades of Walkeshwar watch the painted women of the

West gyrate on the music videos and download hard-core pornography on the Internet and can't get a peck on the cheek from the good girls of their social circle. In the five-star hotels, young male models pray to their gods before beauty contests, while aging Parsi queens cruise them in the toilets, trying to look at their dicks. An industrialist's wife, the organizer of one of those male pageants, is caught on tape with one of her contestants. The pornographic cassette ends up in the hands of a rival business family, and they convene an emergency family meeting. What are they to do with this material? It could be a gold mine or it could be disaster. They decide to hold it for a rainy day. Women are held and held back: in the streets, in the skyscrapers, in the beer bars, in the chawls. It is the sexual frenzy of a closed society, and the women of Golpitha are the gutters for these men's emissions.

GIRISH, THE PROGRAMMER, takes me one evening to meet one such man, a college friend of his named Srinivas. We descend to a basement, where Srinivas works in a brokerage firm. A bespectacled, cheerful young man, he is a dedicated downloader of pornography on his computer, right next to the Reuters wire. Srinivas grew up in Kamathipura, where sixth-standard schoolboys take money given to them by their parents for toffee, pool it together, and buy blow jobs. Until a year ago, he would get together with his friends and buy 500-rupee whores, take them to empty apartments or hotel rooms, and share them. He tells us what passes for postcoital conversation with the prostitutes. Nine out of ten of the girls under Srinivas will tell him, You're from a good family. You shouldn't be doing all these things. But Srinivas likes to have sex. "It's the simplest thing you can do, as a human being."

A few months ago, he got ill with jaundice and lost twenty-two pounds, so he gave up whoring and drinking. But he's all right now, so he's planning to start again in a month or so. Until then, he gets his pleasure from the computer. He has acquired a new CD, which features a woman on the screen. The viewer can do things to her via the mouse, and she responds appropriately; moving the arrow into her vagina elicits tinny moans of programmed pleasure from the computer speaker. He walks me over to where he will go once he gets better.

The biggest whorehouse in Bombay is called Congress House. It is named for the headquarters of the Congress Party across the street. The eighty-six-year old watchman will tell you that Mahatma Gandhi set up camp here during the freedom struggle. The chaste leader, whose most epic battle in his life was not against the British Empire but against his own sexuality, would not be gratified at what independence has brought, because directly across the street is a music academy, as the signboard above it tells you; inside, it is a fortress of whores. Hundreds of whores, bar dancers, and their inebriated customers, young men in well-tailored clothes and good shoes, are standing, cooking, flirting, spitting tobacco in the midst of the most incredible filth: open gutters, moisture everywhere, spoiling food, organic matter. On Holi the girls of Congress House go wild. They get drunk and mix gutter water and mud with used menstrual pads, catch other girls and throw them into the mixture, or fling the bloody pads at each other.

All around us are open windows and doorways through which we can see the women washing clothes, washing themselves, stirring pots over stoves, and generally going about their domestic chores. This is where they live; their customers, if they are regulars, come here to pick them up and then take them to the hotels and guesthouses to do their business. I have to step carefully around the garbage, but it doesn't bother Srinivas. "The garbage is more than covered up by the beautiful sights," he says, looking around appreciatively at the galaxy of choices, from every corner of India and Nepal. The rates of the prostitutes begin at 50 rupees in the nearby Pila House, he says, to 1,000 rupees for the ones he is partial to, to 50,000 for a Bollywood starlet.

Monalisa's friend Ranjita lives in Congress House, as do many of the other bar dancers. Ranjita moved from a lavish flat in Lokhandwala to a filthy room in Congress House—which rents for 15,000 rupees a month plus a deposit of several lakhs—even though she owns a nicer flat in Jogeshwari. "There is security in Congress House," Monalisa explained. Everybody knows what most of the tenants do, and it is all right. No housing society will raise objections, as they are starting to with Monalisa in Juhu.

Pila House is where the Nepali whores live. It is the area around a nineteenth-century theater, a playhouse. Around Pila House are buildings with hundreds of whores lining the stairs, and as you walk up, "they grab you by your luggage and take you inside the room," explains the cabbie who is escorting us. I ask how long 30 rupees would buy you. "Five minutes, ten minutes, fifteen minutes. It depends on you." I can see men walking back from Pila House in lungis, looking relaxed, smoking cigarettes. The men that go there are laborers, cart pullers, coolies: men who work with their bodies all day long and, in the night, buy another working body.

Bachu-ni-wadi, where we go to next, is a series of streets behind a small doorway. The first few shops sell seekh kababs, and at all hours of the night there are men eating kababs with onions. Slabs of ice in front are adorned with fresh green mint to be sprinkled on the meat. Inside, the impression is that of an open dollhouse; inside each of the hundred-odd rooms are male musicians and female singers and dancers performing the mujra, a North Indian courtesan's dance. The sounds of different mujra-walis, of tabla and harmonium, float out into the alley. I send the cabbie to negotiate in one house that sports an air conditioner. He comes back with a price: 300 rupees for three songs, and we take off our shoes at the door and sit inside on mattresses on the floor. The room has a fridge where liquor is kept, a TV above it, a small stereo player, and a paper Indian flag protruding from a showcase above. The singer, unnaturally fair, asks us in Urdu-accented Hindi what we would like to hear, ghazals or songs, old songs or new songs? She begins with a ghazal, accompanied by another female singer in chorus, and a tabla player and a harmonium player behind her. The singing is unremarkable. What is distinctive is when she brings her hands together to clap out the beat; it is the loudest sound I have ever heard a pair of human hands make. It has a metallic quality to it, but there are no rings or instruments hidden between her fingers. She has crooked a finger of one hand in a particular way, cupped her palms just so, and the sound is a thunderclap in the small room. Presently a dancer is summoned, a very pretty girl in an expensive silk dress; but when she dances it is so bad we have to laugh. She throws her arms about and twirls in a bad imitation of the countless mujra scenes in Hindi films. Most of these dancers work in the bar line until closing time, 12:30 a.m., and then they finish out the night dancing in Bachu-ni-wadi. Here, in this alley, there are no closing hours; it seems to exist in a jurisdiction all its own.

There is a picture of the singer, much younger, hanging in the room; it is a concert she has given in some hall. She and the rest of the musicians are from Benares. She tells us about the nawabs of old who sent their sons to be sexually educated by the tawaifs, the courtesans; it is not like that anymore, and the true mujras are not like the filmi ones. "Dawood used to come here and stay all night. He would take any girl he pleased, and he gave any amount that was asked." It is a matter of great pride that the don frequented these houses; a film star or politician could not do them greater honor by coming here.

We walk back out through the lane, which is stunningly filthy. While sitting down on a cot outside the room to tie my shoes, my left hand has touched something; I bring it up to my nose and it smells of vomit. Inside the rooms there is light and music and Urdu poetry; outside is a dumping area for the wastes of the body.

The cabbie tells me about a club where the women take off all their clothes but it is forbidden to drink alcohol; and another that is popular among foreigners and Arabs, where four hundred girls dance in front of you and you can select one and take her to the adjoining hotel right away. In the city of night, there are all kinds of girls in all kinds of price brackets; no one need be lonely or frustrated. One group of men rents a flat and brings in lactating women, blindfolded. Then the men take turns suckling at the women's breasts.

Toward morning, I am in a solitary taxi speeding from the city toward the suburbs; not even airport traffic is coming the other way. It is the suspended time before the first train comes in from Virar with the fisherwomen. All cities are alike in their stillness, after the bars have closed. All those who have been loved during the night must go home now.

Two Lives: Honey/Manoj

I had mentioned Honey, the man who dances dressed as a woman, to Monalisa. "Honey is a woman who was born as a man by mistake," Monalisa promptly volunteered. "She's a very good friend of mine." One night, I make plans to meet Monalisa after work in the all-night coffee shop at the Marine Plaza. Presently she appears and whispers in my ear, "There was a party at Dilbar. Honey still has her work clothes on, and a robe over them. Is it okay?" Monalisa has told Honey how much she trusts me and has convinced her to join us. She brings her friend to the plush, quiet coffee shop on the first floor of the hotel. For the first time I see Honey in proper lighting. She is very fair and has no hair on her face whatsoever. She is

Sindhi, born in Bombay, and is now twenty-five. Her name—his name—is Manoj. Over iced coffee and French fries, she tells us about her life in the bars.

Manoj was first drawn into the bar line through a neighbor, Sarita Royce, a dancer who has traveled all over the world. "Honey was my protégé," Sarita told me later. Her mother used to mind Manoj and his brother Dinesh during their parents' frequent absences. "You know about them, don't you? Their background is not too rosy." Manoj's mother made a living smuggling appliances from Singapore. Manoj made thirty-four round trips to Singapore with his mother on these smuggling expeditions, starting at the age of nine.

Sarita used to ask the boy, whose gestures were feminine, to dance for her to movie songs. She also organized private parties. Some of the parties were in her home, and the young Manoj used to go there and watch everyone dance. He thought to himself, I could do better. One day, Sarita had organized a private show in a hotel, and one of the girls who was supposed to dance called and said she couldn't come. Sarita looked around, and her gaze settled on the young boy. She asked his mother to send him to the hotel. There, Sarita took a plait and attached it to the boy's head with scores of pins. As soon as Manoj went onto the stage, the plait fell off. The audience responded favorably: "What a girl! Sweet as honey!" Sarita's mother started calling Manoj "Honey." Some of the men in the audience asked Honey if she would be willing to dance in a bar for money. Thus began Honey's career in the dance bars and the bifurcation of Manoj/Honey. "First there was the feeling that people were waiting for me," says Honey. "People were waiting for a heroine."

Manoj was attending an English-language boarding school in Khandala, from which he was thrown out in the eighth standard. He was caught in a toilet with another student, who was about to rape him. When Honey first started dancing, her contract was for 100 rupees a day. This was good money for her mother, who had been caught and fined for smuggling ball bearings on one of her trips back from Singapore. In one day she lost what she had earned in three years and was left with 50,000 rupees in debts. She tore up her wedding saris to make women's clothes for her thirteen-year-old son and sent him out to dance.

One of the customers in Honey's first bar left a note for her, saying she was being cheated and her mother should call him. He was Punjabi and had a hotel in Vashi, the Maya Bar. Honey became so popular there that the owner offered to pay her one lakh if he would undergo a sex change operation. There was one caveat: After the operation, she would have to have sex with him. Honey left that bar for another, the Indraprashta in Saki Naka. There she started making a name, working there for three years. The owner of the bar fell in love and cut his wrists for her. The bar staff would refer to Honey as "sister-in-law."

Honey's father collected receipts from theaters for a producer, G. P. Sippy, but would not take any of his wife's illegal earnings. He must have been uneasy watching his son put on a dress and dance in front of strangers, and he grew estranged from Honey, but his wife kept driving the child on, glad of the extra income. The first time a customer took Honey shopping, she asked the customer to buy some gifts for her father: Bermuda shorts, shirts, and two-liter bottles of Fanta. Then Honey went home and deposited the gifts in front of her father. It was the son's first earning. Honey's father accepted the gifts, and they shared a glass of Fanta. The mother came in and was pleasantly surprised: "What is this, father and son are drinking together?" And the father replied, "If my son earns, I have to drink with her." Then he blessed his son. Honey remembers his words: "He put his hand on my head and said, 'You will earn such a name in your life!' " In Honey's recounting of those words, her father uses the feminine pronoun to refer to Honey. He had accepted his son's strange manner of earning a living. That night, as he stepped off a bus in Dadar, a truck speeding in the opposite direction struck him and flung him in front of another bus, which finished him.

One day, a dancer who lived in Congress House asked Honey to go with her to a new bar named Sapphire. Honey was hesitant; she had heard that pimps from Congress House went to Sapphire looking for girls for their stable. But her doubts disappeared as soon as she made her entry. Honey started dancing on the Sapphire stage and the place went wild. "Once more, once more!" the customers yelled. She was supposed to do only one dance, but neither the customers nor Pervez, the owner, were willing to let her go. Pervez had no idea about Honey's identity. By the time Sarita enlightened him, he didn't care. "Honey made Sapphire," BK told me.

When she first came in, Honey was, at sixteen, the youngest of the dancers and the most inventive. When planning a dance, she would think to herself, How is it in films? And she would wear different costumes for each number, changing from Indian to western clothes as the song demanded. For a song with an Arabic theme she would wear gauzy Arab-style dresses; for a song with a folk beat, she would wear ghungroos, little bells, on her ankles; in the song about a hatted hero, "Tirchi Topiwale," she would come to the stage with a bunch of hats and throw them on her favored customers' heads. It was Honey who started the call-and-response game in the dance bars. "Oye, oye!" she would shout, and the customers would shout back, "Oye-o-oooaah!" She jumped up on the tables and danced; she thought of herself as a second Helen, the incomparable cabaret vamp of Hindi films during the sixties and seventies. Her oriental-style dresses left her waxed legs bare; she would dance up to a customer and lift her whole leg and put it on his shoulder, as he sat below her, "and they went mad."

Then she started another trend. "I shot an arrow in the dark and it hit the target." She started picking up the customers and making them dance: "I'm requesting you. Just for a second, please." Then she would blow *her* money over their heads. They were delighted; the whole bar was witnessing their stardom. If Honey threw 50 rupees at them, they would throw 500 back at her. Honey was inverting the whole equation of performer and audience in the bar line. "I don't want that the girls dance and the men just sit there." On one of the girls' birthdays her main customer decorated the entire hall with fruit—hanging pineapples, mangoes, apples, and oranges all around the hall on strings—while the birthday girl danced in the orchard. Honey started taking the fruits off the walls and sticking them on the older customers, gluing bananas on their pants, oranges on their chests, so the old men walked around festooned with fruit and dancers and customers were united in uproarious laughter. The fivers changed into 100-rupee notes, till 5-rupee notes were banned altogether from the bar. She would throw some money at a customer; he would respond by hitting her with entire bundles of 100-rupee notes. She got so many currency notes pelted at her that she couldn't hold all of them. There were people waiting in line to give her money. "I used to throw and run, throw and run." BK scolded her. "Don't leave your money lying around." So important was Honey to Sapphire that the bar gave her the greatest honor available in a city that has among the world's most expensive commercial real estate: her own makeup room.

The other dancers stopped talking to her. They wished upon her the ultimate revenge: that a customer would fall in love with her and stop her from dancing altogether. But Honey wasn't so much interested in the money as she was in the performance itself, in hearing the customers clap and shout, "Once more, once more!" When she danced a full shift, sweating heavily, "I felt like I'd eaten a full meal." Honey has since performed for celebrities as diverse as Steven Seagal and Chotta Shakeel. She has been to Nairobi for two months. She has customers from Africa, Jakarta, Mauritius, and Singapore. Honey was profiled in *Savvy* magazine and featured on the Priya Tendulkar show, but as a woman, a bar dancer. Her secret was safe.

Honey tells us about her breast operation. At the time, her daily collection was 35,000 rupees. But she thought that if she had breasts, her tips would increase, and she could get a break in the movies. "I wanted cleavage." She used to tape the skin on her chest with bandages, to simulate breasts, and would get whistles. But when she took off the tape, bits of skin came with it. Manoj would change into Honey in the taxi going to the dance bars. She would put on her bra and stuff the cups with a handkerchief or a sponge. Sometimes she had to fill the bra with scrunched-up balls of newspaper, which scratched like hell. So she sought surgical intervention, going to the best cosmetic surgeon in India for silicone implants. When she woke up after the operation, she started screaming. It felt like there were two great weights on her. Now Honey had what she'd dreamt of: a pair of size 32 breasts. "Take them out!" she shouted. The doctor said she should be patient for a month; she'd get used to them. She left the hospital and got into a taxi.

Then the cab hit a speed bump.

"They bounced with such force, I had to grab on to them." Honey directed the taxi to take her to another hospital right away; she was in pain and wanted her brand-new mammaries removed. When the doctors at the second hospital heard the name of the prestigious doctor who had put them in, they sent Honey packing. That night, the girls at Sapphire clustered around and poked at the sudden protrusions on her chest. "Honey didi, what is this? Tun, tun." After weeks of searching, she found a doctor who agreed to remove them. Honey lifts her shirt and shows me the scars on her chest. His chest.

What Honey did had consequences for her family's image in the community. At one point early in her career, Honey was dancing in a bar in Ulhasnagar, stronghold of the Sindhis and a suburb where many of Honey's relatives lived. Her uncle had a shop there. Customers of the bar told her uncle, Your nephew dresses up as a girl and dances in a bar. Her uncle spoke to Honey's father. "Don't bring your son by this lane in front of my shop. People will laugh at me." Honey felt terrible about this, but she respected her uncle's wishes and avoided that street. When Honey got famous and successful, this same uncle came to her to ask her for a loan of three lakhs, for another shop, and Honey gave him the money. Honey has also bought flats for her family and a phone shop for her brother Dinesh.

The bodyguard at Dilbar, a rather scrawny fellow, is in love with Honey and gives her 100 rupees a night. He calls her regularly and is very shy and polite. If Honey's voice is a little deep, he'll quickly apologize for having disturbed her sleep. "Did you eat?" he says, making conversation. "Did you sleep well?" He knows about her. That's how Honey puts it: "He knows about me," as if there is only one thing to know, as if someone who knows that Honey is a man who dresses as a woman has grasped the totality of her existence. That is the thing about secrets, and that is why we are so eager to know them. They give us, once revealed, a false impression of wider knowledge.

Some of the people who come to the bar think they know what is to be known about Honey: that she is a eunuch. Chotta Shakeel, the man who runs the D-Company, is one of these people. He came twice or thrice to Sapphire. Honey remembers a very short man, very respectful; he would never throw money with his own hands but instructed his boys to, a lot of money, after which Shakeel would ask Honey to pray for his soul. God has a special connection with eunuchs and hears their prayers. "Salaam," the don would say to Honey. "Please do my dua." But he would never publicly refer to Honey as a eunuch, because that would be insulting her credentials as a dancing girl.

Honey shows us a "portfolio" that she hired a photographer to shoot. First there are several dozen pictures of her as a woman, garish dresses and garish prints. Then there are smaller photos, of her as a boy. The difference is startling. The boy, Manoj, has a goatee and is dressed in jeans or a suit and tie. He is not overly feminine. "Two lives," explains Honey. By day a man, by night a woman. What did this conflict do to Honey? It drove her to drink, drugs, and marriage.

Sarita Royce got the young Honey started on vodka. Drinking did not come naturally to her; she would shout at her father when he drank beer. But the vodka led to other kinds of spirits, till it became a need. Then one night, during one of the frequent dry days in the state, three customers came into Sapphire high. Honey asked them what they'd been drinking, and they came out with liquor bottles filled with Corex, a powerful codeine-based cough syrup. Honey took a swig; it made her pleasantly numb. That was the day she started on her habit. She was soon drinking eight or nine bottles a day. The bottles normally cost 30 rupees each; the couriers Honey sent out from the bar would see her drugged condition and charge 100. Customers saw this, and those who wanted to win her favor started buying bottles of Corex as gifts. This cough syrup is a favorite narcotic of the bar-line dancers; there are certain pharmacies in central Bombay outside which you can see a crowd of beautiful young women after one in the morning, all woozy from the medicine.

The drug screwed up her system. Long after she quit it, Honey had stones in her gallbladder and needed an operation to take them out. Midway through the operation, she started coming to. The anesthetic was ineffective on her system, trained on heavy sedatives like Corex, and the doctors quickly had to administer a more powerful one. The addiction undid Honey. She would, while dancing, lift the liquor glasses of customers and gulp down the contents. Meanwhile, her jealous mentor, Sarita, noticed that customers were deserting her own private shows to go watch Honey dance and were throwing money on her. So Sarita started spreading the story of Honey's real identity. The relationship with her neighbor cooled; even now, Honey barely says hello to the woman who got her into the bar line. But the customers started making remarks, calling her a eunuch, a homosexual. They would shout out, "Hey, Chakka!" "Hijda!" "Gaandu!"

On Honey's last night at Sapphire she was high on Corex and a customer began cursing her. "You don't belong here, get out, you motherfucker." She told the bouncer, who told BK, but the customer was not thrown out. That night she couldn't take it anymore. She picked up a bottle and smashed it over the head of her tormentor, gashing his eye. Then she left the dance floor and packed her makeup. She had been working at Sapphire for nine years; she started working at White Horse the following week.

After Sapphire, Honey hit the Corex even harder. Every day, Honey bought 400 rupees' worth of the cough syrup. Her mother and brother, alarmed, stopped giving her money, so she cut her wrist with a razor blade. But, she recalls, she did it below her building, among a crowd of people, so someone would notice and alert her family. "If I cut myself somewhere I was alone, no one would notice." She laughs. The cut was so minor that when she was taken to the doctor, no stitches were required.

The personal history of bar dancers is written on their arms. Honey shows me another mark and tells me the story behind it. There was an Irani man in the bar, a loyal customer who professed to be in love with Honey and would blow as much as 40,000 rupees a night on her. One night, he was also spending on another girl, Sonali. Sonali was trying her best to woo the free-spending Irani away from Honey; she whispered into his ear that Honey loved him only for his money. So he asked Honey if this was true. Honey grabbed a glass, smashed it, and slashed her arm with the jagged edge. She said she would write "I love you" in blood on her arm to prove it. The Irani begged her not to further injure herself and asked what he could do to atone for doubting her love. "Go to Sonali and tell her to tie a rakhi on you," Honey demanded. The Irani beckoned to Sonali and gave her 5,000 rupees to tear off a piece of her dupatta and tie it around his wrist, in front of the whole bar, forever making her his sister. The bleeding Honey had to listen to Sonali's abuses, but the Irani has treasured that piece of glass that Honey cut herself with for three years now.

"So he won't give money to Sonali now?" I ask.

"He will give, but not that much. A man won't give as much to his sister as he gives to his lover."

One day, at the height of her addiction, Honey's mother and Dinesh asked her to come with them to Pune. They offered an incentive: two bottles of Corex. So Honey went and found herself, by the end of the trip, engaged to be married, to a Sindhi girl named Jyoti. It was all done in a Corex daze. "I was like a cow." Her head lolls, slack, bovine. Honey has been married for four years. "There is no love with my wife. I know what is love, when you know what the lover is thinking, when the lover knows what you're feeling." Though Manoj is not in love with his wife, he does want children, two boys. "Because boys care for their mother more, so they will care for me." Then she realizes what she's said and corrects herself. "They care for their father more."

I ask Honey if she has sex with her customers.

"The time I'm in my sex mode, I've got my wife. I'm satisfied with her." But she will allow her customers, especially the good-looking young guys, some liberties. "I do smooching." Then she reflects. "How strange it is, one tongue searching around for another tongue. It cleans out my teeth. I tell my customers, I won't have to brush my teeth in the morning."

"Do the men realize you're not a woman when they get close to you?" I ask.

"The men are not in their senses. When a person is hungry he doesn't care what he eats, even if it's stale." Honey explains the excuses she uses when she doesn't want to talk on the phone with a new customer. She'll pick up the phone, pretend to be her sister, and say to the eager caller, "Honey can't come to the phone right now. She's gone to the shithouse." This image destroys a certain delicacy essential to romance, and the customer rings off.

Honey had no idea about how to kiss till she met the dancing girls. "One of these bitches taught me. But then I didn't like it. She was drunk, and I felt like vomiting." But she has to give at least this to her customers, so she allows the customers to kiss her. Parked in a car, they put her on their laps, put a hand up her T-shirt, and try to remove her brassiere. She protests, just like a woman: "Not today, I'm not feeling well." Not all of them stop at this point. Some men try to unzip her skirt from the back; Honey grabs their hand at that crucial point, just before discovery. They take her hand and put it on their erections, or they grab her by her hair and thrust her face in their crotches. "Some of these assholes, they are just dirty assholes. They just would rag themselves on me and discharge on me. You can make out a person coming desperately on sex and then stopping. Then they are satisfied." Honey says she doesn't let the customers penetrate her; but some of them boast to the other customers, "I've taken Honey." Honey doesn't mind. "This is good for me. Then four more people say, Take me around in your car." It is the life of a man constantly teasing other men, constantly fending them off at the last moment.

Monalisa and Honey have no sweet men, no protectors. This has put Honey, especially, in some very dangerous situations. The most notorious customer of the bars, the sabertooth tiger of the dancers' nightmares, is a man named Mehmood. All the girls know about him. Honey says, "He would have sex with them and then burn them with cigarettes on that par-

ticular place. He put needles inside. He was a maniac type, a sex maniac."
There was a girl in Congress House that he loved; he would piss in her
mouth to show his love. He had a daughter with this girl, and the mother
ran off to Dubai. When the daughter came of age, he took her to Congress
House in revenge.

One day Mehmood asked Honey to come out to Chembur for a private
party. "He was a Muslim," begins Honey. "You know how these Muslims
are." Among Honey's customers, Gujaratis and Marwaris are the most
free-spending, because they come from rich families. "Muslims are the
most rough. They are the real motherfuckers. Assholes." I remember that
her family is Sindhi, partition refugees from Pakistan. When she got to
Mehmood's residence, his men were beating up someone they had kidnapped. They broke his legs with hockey sticks; there was blood all over
the floor. After they had finished, Mehmood turned to Honey. "So you're a
dancer. Show us. Dance." She felt threatened and didn't want to. They
insisted. She was in a chowk, surrounded by buildings. So Honey danced
among the buildings, and all the people leaned out of their windows to look
and threw coins—25 paise, 50 paise—at her. Then Mehmood took her into
a hut and locked the door. He was going to have sex with her, he told her.
Honey tried to fob him off. "I said, I've sworn on the Koran that I won't do
all these things." So had he sworn on the Koran, responded Mehmood: that
he would have sex with Honey. "He said, either have sex with me or with
ten of my friends." There followed an encounter that Honey variously
describes as either a rape or a providential escape. Tonight, she says that
she escaped by telling Mehmood she had to go back to Sapphire for just one
dance, and then she would return to him. He let her out, and the next day
she ran away from Bombay to a village.

But I later read the *Savvy* magazine article on Honey that claims that
she was raped by Mehmood and then tried to kill herself by swallowing
Baygon. I ask her if it's true. "He came on me," Honey says. "He would
smooch me. He fell off the bed."

"Did you try to kill yourself after the rape?" I ask, citing the magazine
article. It features vivid descriptions of Honey trying to do herself in with
a bottle of insecticide, cutting her wrists, and dancing in a frenzy on her
knees till they bled. Honey laughs raucously. "Why should I try to kill
myself, only girls do that. The day after the magazine came out, my mother
and Sarita and I burst out laughing. 'Whore! Rape! Rape!' "

One day his victims got back at Mehmood. He had gone into Congress House to pick up a girl and was identified. The girls of Congress House covered their faces and surrounded him. Gathering strength in their numbers, they beat him up and made him drink from the gutter. At one point they even pooled their money and put out a contract on Mehmood's life. The hit man fired on him; the bullet missed and struck his friend, making Mehmood even angrier. Then Mehmood did something that finally brought the police down on him: He raped a girl from a rich family. This was beyond the pale for the police; they arrested him, beat him up, and put him in prison. "Now he's become a little cold," says Honey.

"Everyone should have two brains," Honey announces suddenly. "One to keep in the freezer when it gets hot from thinking too much. Then you work with the spare brain till the other one cools down."

MONALISA AND I HAVE BEEN TALKING to Honey in the coffee shop all night. We walk out, say good-bye to Honey, and Monalisa and I sit on the parapet overlooking the sea at Marine Drive. The city is just coming to life. The early morning joggers trot by. A beggar ambles along, and Monalisa gives him money. She gives every beggar who asks money. For the first time, I see the lights of the Queen's Necklace being switched off, in sections, all along the bay. Monalisa looks at the waves under her feet and points out the crabs crawling on the rocks. She asks me, "Do you believe that this is Kalyug? That Kalkiavatar will come? That Shiva's third eye will open?"

She believes the world still has another couple of hundred years before Kalkiavatar arrives and it ends "because there are still many good people left." She doesn't want to leave the sea face. She is happy sitting there and talking about the good people in the world and how the others can be pacified, and about how many hours we can talk; she counts them each time we meet, like I used to once upon a time with a girl in a faraway country. Each time she is amazed that we find new things to talk about. She is sitting close to me and the top of her bra is visible from her loose top. But she's a kid. She wants to go to Essel World, romp with me in the waterslides. She sits on the seawall with the morning tide coming in, in jeans and a kid's zippered top, swinging her legs over the edge, while I perch gingerly next to her, looking nervously at the steep drop below. "I wanted to die," she says. "But then I changed my mind. Now I want to live."

"What changed your mind?"

"Nothing. My brain was not working."

And then I understand why older men fall in love with younger women. It is not because of their bodies; that is enough for lust but not for love. It is because of their minds—new, clean, still not cynical, still not hard. They drink their newness.

HONEY HAS ASKED DAYANITA to take pictures of her in Sapphire too, but BK doesn't want Honey in the bar even as a spectator. BK will help his girls out when they're in trouble, but he will not forgive Honey. Honey is heartbroken. She swears she's off the Corex and the chewing tobacco. She won't drink the customer's pegs anymore. She's apologized for her past mistakes; why won't BK take her back? But I get the feeling that none of this has anything to do with why she can't go back to Sapphire. "You should have seen her five years ago," BK says to me. "Nobody could have guessed she wasn't a woman."

So Honey invites us home one afternoon, Monalisa, Dayanita, and me, to meet her wife, and have Dayanita take pictures. Honey's apartment building is next to the zoo. At 4 a.m., she can hear lions roar and owls hoot. It is a handsome old building, built by the inventor of Afghan Snow, a face cream reputed to turn dark complexions into fair ones. Honey owns a row of rooms in the building. One is for her mother, one for her brother, one for herself and her wife, and one for her grandmother. The rooms are connected by doors that are always kept shut, so traffic between the rooms is through the long lobby outside. Honey spends the days in her room, which is dark and cool, eating lunch, receiving visitors, watching television. The suite has a bathroom, a living room with a daybed on which Manoj and his wife sleep, and a balcony that is half kitchen and half prayer room. There are posters of two fat white babies on one wall.

Manoj sits on the bed now in a black buttoned T-shirt and jeans. The only trace of Honey is long hair tied behind the neck, and nail polish, and bad skin around the face where the hair has been tweezed. Even the voice has come down, an octave or two. Manoj shows me an album of his brother's wedding in 1995. There is Honey, being hugged by Pervez, the owner of Sapphire; and there, he points out, are many of the bar's customers. They paid for the wedding, so Honey came to the ceremony, not Manoj.

I ask him, "Did you also go to your own wedding as Honey?"

"No, as Manoj. Does Honey want to die, getting married?"

His wife, Jyoti, comes into the room, a tall, fair, good-looking Sindhi woman in her early twenties. She doesn't say much; she is not so much shy as quiet. Manoj and Jyoti are not an entirely harmonious couple; there is a distance between them. "If she gives me a suggestion, and my friend gives me the same suggestion, I'll listen to my friend's suggestion," Manoj had told me earlier.

There was somebody in Manoj's life whom he has alluded to only once: "There was a girl long ago." She was beautiful, he says, and lived on Foras Road. Manoj met her before he got married. He and the girl would go for long drives, as far away as Khandala. After a full night's dancing, the girl and Manoj would go back to his flat and stay over. "She was the only girl I told about my whole life, all that has happened." They had some sort of a physical relationship: "Smooching and this and that we had, but no sex." It went on for a couple of years, and then they broke off, because both families were pressuring them. Now she has two or three children and still lives on Foras Road.

Around five o'clock, Manoj is in front of the mirror, in his undershirt; his chest is still flat. Every day at twilight, Manoj puts on a padded bra and three corsets. But he has broken out. He raises his shirt to show me the rash, and I feel I should turn my eyes away. Then, for the first time in my life, I hear a husband say to his wife, "Hand me my brassiere." Jyoti helps Manoj turn into Honey with patience and skill and what looks to me like love. She pins her husband's blouse, ties his sari. She knows exactly what points on the wig to press while Manoj attaches the pins that will keep it on his head. Says Manoj, "Sometimes I'll be talking and my glance falls on a mirror and I think, 'Who's this?'" So skilled is the makeup. So adept is his deception.

I am fascinated by how Honey and Manoj mark their boundaries in the self; how the dancer keeps the two personas separate. Among the customers who are aware that Honey is not a woman, half think she is gay, half think she's a eunuch. But she is neither of these. Not a transvestite, or a homosexual, or a eunuch, or a cross-dresser, but a man who dresses as a woman out of economic necessity. Her closest equivalents are the jatra or tamasha artists, the men who make their living playing female characters in folk theater, who spend their entire lives playing one female character, till the character takes over the life.

The people who know Honey's secret make the necessary distinctions between her and Manoj. I am standing early one morning with Minesh on Marine Drive, watching Dayanita take pictures of Honey and Monalisa together. Monalisa leans over on the divider on Marine Drive and hugs Honey from behind, kisses her on the cheek.

"Are you jealous?" I ask Minesh, watching this exhibition.

"Not with Honey. Maybe with Manoj."

Even Manoj's family seems confused about his identity. I once ask for Honey on the phone, and her mother says, "She's sleeping. Fast asleep." At home during the day, Manoj generally dresses like other men of his class, in shorts and a T-shirt. When Manoj speaks to his wife in Sindhi, he never, even accidentally, refers to himself in the feminine person. In the bar, when Honey speaks to her customers or the other girls, she never, even accidentally, refers to herself in the masculine person. How are they kept apart, compartmentalized?

"Because I've never fallen in love. Neither with a woman nor with a man." Manoj elaborates. "If love or even the hint of it had entered my life, my whole life would have changed." If he had really been in love, he would not have been able to talk to his girlfriend as Honey. "I would have slipped into a man's tone." He would be talking to her all the time, even from the bar, and love would make it impossible to lie, to pretend to be a woman with his lover. Love exposes you, makes you vulnerable, and kills all the personas built on top of the true self. If Manoj falls in love, Honey will have to depart, killed off by Manoj's lover. Jyoti poses no such threat, because Manoj is not in love with his wife. Jyoti actually helps Manoj turn into Honey every evening. I have a feeling that Jyoti might actually be closer to Honey.

The bar girls' involvement with love is total. It is their bread and butter, their dharma. They often fall in love themselves, which Manoj can't fathom. "Now Monalisa's mind is half in love, half in business. I don't understand these people. Love is the blade that cuts down the ladder toward your goal in life. I am not falling in love," Manoj repeats. "In this line we have lost our identity." And a sense of your identity is essential to being able to truly love.

We go up to the terrace of Honey's building, where the evening light is perfect for Dayanita's camera. Monalisa looks stunning, in her simple black dress. Her hair is up in a loose bun behind her head, and Dayanita points out to her that she has an exceptionally fine neck. She glows, unfurls, under the gaze of the camera. After the shoot, she is ravenous and eats everything that Jyoti gives her. Jyoti is amused by her. "She's mad," she declares, "but the world needs a little madness." I feel very happy in this little room, with its whole spectrum of gender and marital status, from me, the married man with two children; to Dayanita, who claims to be having a love affair with Monalisa and Honey; to Honey, straddling the territory between all of us, in no-man's-land; to his wife, who wants to get pregnant; to the exuberantly feminine, unmarriageable Monalisa.

Monalisa and Honey are putting makeup on each other for the evening, and they are clearly enjoying the ritual.

"Is my face too white? Do I look like a ghost?" asks Monalisa.

"Put some brown on your nose," Manoj responds. They are only going to work, but if you listen to their laughter and their jokes you would think they were going to a party. I feel a longing, watching them. Men never have this, this time among their own sex, this mutual boosting of self-esteem in the hours before a party. "Oh, you look lovely." "Wow, look at that dress! Watch out, Bombay!" This time that is so often more fun than the actual party.

As it indeed is for Honey. Business has been very bad for her at Dilbar. "Yesterday I only had four hundred rupees," says the former Queen of Sapphire, who in her heyday would take home a hundred times that amount. Honey attributes her poor earnings to the fact that she can't, or won't, have sex with the customers. "Other girls go for night problem, they'll get." BK is not returning her calls begging to be taken back, and she feels it deeply. The dancer that made Sapphire an institution is not welcome there anymore. "The main thing isn't even money." Honey sighs. "The main thing is: The way I used to dance at Sapphire I can hardly dance half at Dilbar." An artist scorned, unable to find a fitting audience for her art.

Sapphire strings her along—or maybe she strings herself along on the expectation of returning to the scene of her glory. Honey is desperate, ready to do anything, even dance in the daytime among the faltus, the government clerks on their lunch hour, the idlers, the men with lots of time and little money. When she speaks to BK or Pervez, they never say no outright to her. It is always: Wait. Wait till after the elections. Wait till after the third hall opens. Wait till the hours are extended. Wait till this inconvenient DCP is transferred. It is the established strategy of avoidance in the Country of the No, and by this time in Bombay I am well familiar with it. So Honey sits at home in the afternoon watching television and dances at night in the sorry nightclub, waiting for the call from Sapphire.

Surely all those men in the audience at Dilbar, at Sapphire, can't have failed to notice Manoj's sex. Is it this very fact that attracted so many of them and made Sapphire an institution? Has Honey unknowingly tapped some tremendous current of homosexual desire in the metropolis that needs to lie to itself about its origins, that can only pay to watch a man dance when he is disguised as an exaggeratedly feminine woman?

I had mentioned Sapphire to Sunil, the Sena man. "That's where the eunuch works," he said promptly. He had gone there and seen the eunuch do a dance to a song he still remembers. The great secret about Honey, I am gradually beginning to realize, is that her identity is not really a secret. Men will bring their friends to the bar knowing about her, and watch their friends swoon over her, and then kid them about falling for a man. Lots of people know about Honey: models, gangsters, taxi drivers, journalists. And they all think they're the only one, or one of a select few, to know the secret.

Honey shows me a picture of herself at fifteen, in a short skirt with a fetching jacket over it. I would have gone out with such a girl. She is slim and attractive. She fits the accepted definition of pretty. But as Honey ages, she is outgrowing pretty. Her tread is heavier. There is a solid line to her jaw. She has put on weight, and there has entered an unsettling sexual attraction to her body: the way her belly button presents itself, a prominent gash in the center of the pudgy white flesh of her stomach. Most women are in a race against time: As they get older, they lose their looks. But Honey is in a different, altogether more desperate race. As Honey gets older, she is losing her very sex.

Honey and Manoj are at war over their body. Manoj wants to grow biceps, a beard, a gut. Honey wants breasts, smooth skin, an admirable ass. Honey is constantly trying to outsmart Manoj, aided by a retinue of surgeons in Bombay. She has started popping diet pills, three capsules at a time, to become slim. "After having sex, after marriage, the stomach starts to come out," she avers. But occasionally the desire to change runs the other way. Once, Honey ate sindhoor, the red powder put on a woman's forehead, in the belief that it would make her voice deeper, more like what would be expected of Manoj's. Honey cut her hair short about a year ago, when she decided she was going to get out of the bars for good and try to find work as a male model. She got a photographer to make up a portfolio, a set of pictures of Manoj. Then he went around the advertising companies to find work. But in the waiting rooms he saw the other male models: hunks with bulging biceps, aggressively masculine. He soon realized he had no chance in this world. Manoj could not earn a living. So he came back to the dance bars, put on his wig and brassiere, and called Honey back into his life.

I get the impression that, along with her gender, Honey's sexual life is also bifurcated. Manoj attempts to impregnate his wife in the day; at night, Honey goes with men in cars, smooches with them, and they rub against her till they discharge. Manoj/Honey is like one of those earthworms that are simultaneously male and female, at opposite ends. This makes her tremendously lonely. "I have been searching for a friend who does it for the stomach." Honey is aware of others who want to be like her. There are two or three boys who put on ladies' makeup—but still wear men's clothes—and dance in smaller bars, going from one to the next, as a curiosity item. But they are gay boys.

I notice that Manoj is wearing a thread around his wrist. Eunuchs had recently come to his building, to bless his brother's child, and tied the red string around his wrist to ward off nazar, the evil eye. The eunuch community has also heard about Honey and sought her out. One day the famously beautiful eunuch Sonam, from Kamathipura, came to see Honey dance in Sapphire. "She thought I'm like them." Sonam asked Honey why she was wasting her life and suggested that Manoj should have a sex change. Honey wanted to know how Sonam had had her breasts enlarged, and Sonam gave her the name of a drug that induces lactation in nursing mothers. Sonam told Honey to inject herself with 250 milliliters of the drug; Honey doubled the dosage. After a couple of weeks two knots the size of lemons appeared on Honey's chest; when she wore a tight bra it hurt. "I wanted to be in the picture line. I was possessed." Manoj was afraid of what the hormones would do to his sex drive. His family doctor gave him another set of injections to get rid of the breasts.

Honey has even traveled on a woman's passport, which she obtained by bribing the passport officials. The passport photo was taken when she had no facial hair. But for some years now, she has been tweezing her hair for two to three hours every evening, which has left her face a mess of pimples and blotchy skin. She has a problem with ingrown hairs; the skin forms over the hair and has to be broken. "It is hard, like an eggshell," she says, and every second day it bleeds. Her customers are beginning to notice. Honey has been getting advice from her eunuch friends to start shaving instead of tweezing. The eunuchs maintain that they have been shaving for years without getting a bluish shadow. So Manoj sends Jyoti out to buy a Gillette razor. Manoj says, "They told me not to shave upside down. What does that mean?" I tell the twenty-five-year-old boy the correct way to hold a blade, as my father did when I was sixteen, and always to use downward strokes on the face.

The assumption that Honey is a eunuch leads to some strange propositions. Once, a customer was giving her money every day for fifteen days. Then finally he said he wanted to talk to her in private. Oh, no, thought Honey. But the customer explained. "I want you to get twenty of your brothers and sisters and go to this man who owes me thirty-five lakhs. I need to recover that money." Honey realized what he wanted. He thought Honey was a eunuch. If she went with her eunuch "brothers and sisters" to the debtor's office, to sing and dance and curse and raise their skirts, the businessman, shamed in front of the world, would pay up.

Honey got very angry that she was being taken for a eunuch, but the customer was on to something. Shortly afterward, I notice the following advertisement in the SERVICES section of the classified ads in a Bombay paper:

Outstanding Dues???
Take It Easy!!
Now Available with
UNIQUE RECOVERIES:
A Trained Group of Educated
Eunuchs Who Ensure Speedy

Recovery from Defaulters
Enquiries Invited from Individuals, Banks, Corporate Sector

A Matunga East address is given, and a phone number. By the time I call, it has been disconnected.

New Year's Eve

In December of 1999, Honey is finally allowed back into Sapphire. The new Congress government has a freer hand upon the city. The bars close later. Some don't close at all, and Sapphire needs more dancers to fill the extra hours. Honey had made a promise at the nearby Hanuman temple that if she got back into Sapphire she would feed the hungry. A couple of weeks go by after the god delivers, and one night her brother Dinesh has a dream in which he sees fifty-one coconuts. So Honey and Dinesh go to the temple, offer fifty-one coconuts, buy 11,000 rupees' worth of food, and drive around the city distributing it to the hungry. Thus does the money thrown on the dancers circulate around the city.

As soon as she gets back to Sapphire, Honey starts earning a minimum of 2,500 rupees a night, ten times what she used to earn at Dilbar. Since her return to Sapphire, Honey has been attracting new customers, not all of whom know about her. She has been threading the hair on her eyebrows, rather than tweezing them, and she attributes her new luck to this. For Honey, facial hair is destiny.

"Are you a new girl here?" the customers ask.

"Yes. I'm a virgin," Honey replies.

I have acquired a reputation in Bombay society as the best guide to Sapphire. People pester me to take them there, and sometimes I oblige. Some are fascinated, some repulsed, others underwhelmed. An author asks me to bring Monalisa with me to parties in haute Bombay. I am to tell her what to wear, how to behave, what to talk about. My friends want to open worlds for her, guide her, protect her. There are others who would not be so careful. "She's the Tendulkar of the dance bars," a sports agent remarks. "Lips like pillows," salivates a music channel executive. "You could drown yourself in the pools of her eyes," rhapsodizes a crime journalist. They will not have so much self-control if I ever introduce her to them. "She'll be eaten up," I am warned by a society woman. Monalisa can deal with the men who come up in the bar and give her money and tell her they'd like to fuck her; but she is easy prey for the South Bombay charmers, the ones she would give her heart to. Afterward, there would be another notch on Monalisa's wrist, and this time it might be the last one. Her wrist has no more space to mark the ending of yet another love.

Monalisa gives me a pass to come to Sapphire for New Year's Eve 1999: a small blue card with a white border. It doesn't mention the name of the bar, only the address. A leprechaun straddles the lower border. "Entry strictly by invitation only." Only the most favored, the best-paying customers will get these passes.

On New Year's Eve, Sapphire is packed with lovers. Most of the songs being played tonight are maudlin, weepy songs from old films, songs that the men and their true loves think proper to express their feelings for each other, songs they have held each other to, songs that are not urgently throbbing with need but are about what the great poet Faiz identified as the true subject of poetry: the loss of the beloved. All the lovers here in this bar tonight will break up, in a month or a year or five, every single one. It is a palace of impossible love.

"We string along the ulloos till that night," explains Monalisa. "We tell them, come on the thirty-first, and then we'll go out with you." If a customer wants to think he is special to his girl, he'd better be there on this night and prove it to the world, otherwise her attention will greatly diminish in the new year. The previous New Year's Eve, Soni, another dancer at Sapphire, was publicly celebrated by Sajid, her main customer. He spent 900,000 rupees on her that one night.

Monalisa leads the way into the packed mujra hall, parting the waters. Space is made for me. Two cushions are moved, and the man to my left moves several piles of 10-rupee notes closer to him, some falling between the cracks of the cushions, some under the bolsters, and his hand is shuffling the stacks of currency closer so I don't have to sit on them. For the first time in a long time I see Honey dance and understand what the big deal is about. It is not his looks; for the first time I think of him, in the evening, as a man. His belly is out and has a four-leaf henna design on it. He is wearing a wig and a veil over it, and his legs are bare up to just below his knees. But then I get to see his "knee dance," and the illusion reappears.

When her song comes on, Honey gets down on the floor on his knees and swings rapidly around, from one end of the dance floor to another, three quick turns on the knees, so fast you find yourself catching your breath. The whole room breaks out in spontaneous applause. Honey is by far the most energetic of the dancers. She is exhausted by one-thirty. She leans over and tells me, "I've been dancing since seven o'clock." But she is getting garlanded with hundreds. That night, Honey makes 110,000 rupees, more than several months' earnings at Dilbar. She says we must have lunch, and this time it's on her. "I have a reason." There is a pause, and her eyebrows go up; she is holding herself back from smiling. "Can you guess?"

"You're going to be a father!"

"Yes." His wife is pregnant. If all goes well this time around, Manoj will become a father before the year's out. Honey will become a mother.

For New Year's Eve, the girls wear outfits that cost them up to 100,000 rupees. One small dancer, Kavita, has a lot of jewelry on her head, 35,000 rupees' worth. "Don't you think it is a little over?" Honey asks me disapprovingly. I find it difficult to agree with her, since Honey's own head is covered with a blue scarf fringed with gold balls weighing several pounds. And she has bought colored contact lenses with the outline of a flower on each one: "It's soooo sexy." Everything that night is "a little over." Nobody minds.

Muskan is there too, taller than Monalisa, fairer than Monalisa, younger than Monalisa. Muskan has just turned fifteen. Should Muskan lose her virginity to love or money? There is Mohammed the Arab, and there is a teenage boy that Muskan is sweet on. Monalisa advises her that her first time should be with someone she loves—"but Raju is determined to break her seal." Raju is a man living in America who has given her a lakh as a down payment on her virginity. He is fifty years old. Monalisa advises her to chill out for a year or a year and a half. To not go down that path at all. But Muskan is thinking. The man from America has offered her a lot of money.

In the VIP room there is a party of men from Gujarat with their whores. One of the whores is all over the men, indiscriminately. She is on their laps; two of them are touching her at the same time. She is dressed in a black sari. After a while I notice she is on the floor; she has fallen down. One of the men, in jest or anger, has shoved her and she fell forward, hit her head against the table, and passed out. A whole gaggle of the men take her away. She might be unconscious; what will they do to her now? She would be around twenty. They will defile her.

Monalisa, too, is attending to the men from Gujarat, big thick men with cops' mustaches. One of them is on the floor, dancing with her. "I'm earning well from them," she tells me in my ear. But it is a delicate art; she has to dance with them and keep the money flowing without stimulating them to the point of madness. So her dance is inviting without being provocative; she is not rotating her buttocks in their direction. Every time they try to touch her, she fends them off with a smile. They follow her from room to room.

Monalisa has not made as much money as she could have. She is helping the other dancers with their saris and dresses and only comes out of the dressing room at eleven-thirty, missing out on two lucrative hours in the room with the group from Gujarat. Her collection at Sapphire is "not so good" nowadays; most of the customers know she is faithful to Minesh and there is no chance of anything beyond coffee. There are many other dancers with whom the horizon of sexual or romantic possibility is unlimited. So Monalisa tries to move up in other areas of the world. To get into modeling, everyone tells her, she has to learn English. She has hired a tutor to come to her home and give her English lessons. Her phone message is now in English. "You have reached Patel residence. Sorry we can't attend to your call right now." Minesh coached her, including the inflections of voice and the pauses. She sounds like a scheduled-caste receptionist now.

What is Monalisa's future? What can she do after the bar line? I finally ask Rustom bluntly if she could ever get work in advertising. "I don't think so," he replies. "The face and everything. . . ." Monalisa is not going to be a high-fashion model. This face can stop traffic, but it cannot be in a Pond's Face Cream ad. She has no college degree. Her English is weak. She could be a dancer in films or music videos; she would make in a year what she now makes in a week. This is where she shines: on the floor at Sapphire. But here she has three, maybe four years left before she's too old or the bar line changes.

When Monalisa shows the pictures Rustom and Dayanita took of her to the girls at Sapphire, the reaction is less than enthusiastic. They are in black-and-white, which the bar girls do not consider an attractive set of colors. In the villages most of them come from, black-and-white was what you got because you didn't have enough money to pay for color. Monalisa tries explaining to them that these are art pictures. But she is increasingly alone in the bar.

I take Monalisa one evening for cocktails at my friend Manjeet's, a large flat overlooking the Oval. Manjeet is a journalist for an American magazine, and the guests are diplomats and a lawyer. They interact with her with the manners of the well bred. Monalisa is struck by the fact that even though the people at the party know what she does, they treat her "as family." This is going too far; Manjeet has only offered her a glass of orange juice and made light conversation with her, avoiding difficult topics such as her work. But for Monalisa, any kind of acceptance into these unapproachable Bombay circles is a huge gesture, and she is grateful to me for showing her this world. Here nobody is pawing her, scattering currency over her head, speaking to her with overt sexual intent. She has to go from this party to work at Sapphire, where immediately another dancer accuses her of wanting to steal a client the previous night—she had given him her phone number—and curses her in the most foul language in front of the other dancers. Monalisa gives it back, full-throated, and the screaming match almost turns physical—the bar girls occasionally bite, scratch, punch, and pull each other's hair—before BK restrains her. Monalisa is caught between these two worlds, the one she aspires to but can never be accepted in and the other, which she wishes to leave but which keeps pulling her back. She is in transit between these worlds, and it is a damned lonely journey.

She dreams about her kid brother's wedding. "I'll give him a great wedding. I'll dance a lot. Really, I'll dance so much."

"What about your own wedding? When will you get married?"

"I'll never get married."

Minesh is fading as a romantic possibility. He was not present at the bar on New Year's. His business partner ratted on him; he told Minesh's father that his son was seriously involved with a bar-line dancer. The father promptly demanded that he move back home, put the Juhu flat off limits to him, imposed a curfew, and monitored his mobile phone bills. Now he can't even call Monalisa except from a public phone. She hardly ever sees him.

The last year has been bad for Minesh. He lost a huge amount in his software business. He has pledged 25,000 rupees for Monalisa's account at Sapphire but hasn't paid the money yet. He has begged her to wait for him.

He has two unmarried sisters, one older, one younger, and their chances of finding a suitable match would be blighted if the world knew their brother was associated with a bar dancer. As soon as his sisters get married he will rebel against his family and come out with her in the open. But his older sister is in her thirties. If she hasn't found a man in all this time, she is unlikely to find anyone soon. Monalisa is bored, sitting at home waiting for Minesh to give her time. So she has resumed going out with her clients, "for coffee"—young Gujarati and Marwari boys.

Monalisa has not seen her father again. He keeps planning trips to Bombay but doesn't come. "He has his own family. I don't want to disturb him." She has accepted the distance, internalized it. Monalisa now has no friends. She has only her clients; Minesh, sometimes; her mother and brother; and me. She makes plans with me: to go to the new restaurants, to go dancing at Fire & Ice, the new disco. One rainy day after my wife and children have left for America, she comes to my apartment at one in the afternoon and stays till eight in the evening, eating, sleeping, watching a movie on TV, talking. She calls Minesh from my place and tells him she is relaxed here. In this friendless time of her life, I am someone who is neither customer nor lover.

I finally tell Monalisa about my family. I show her pictures of Sunita and the children, and I explain to her why I kept my family isolated from most of the people in the book, and how I regret now that she wasn't able to meet my children, at least. But it is fine. She's used to deceit; to the "jooth ki duniya." She is not angry with me, nor does she say "I wish I had met them." All the people she has ever known have had a hidden life, a locked room that is off limits to her, like her father's second wife and Minesh's family. The twenty-one-year-old girl gives me advice about marriage: "It's like a rubber band," she says, pulling the two ends in the air and letting them pull back. "You're not one of those boys who eat, drink, and wash your hands. If you take such good care of me, I can imagine how much care you must take of someone that you have chosen."

MANOJ IS VERY EXCITED. He has just seen the sonograph of his child. "I could make out a little face and two little dots that were the hands." But the pregnancy brings with it a host of problems. Through the night, he has to keep waking up to satisfy Jyoti's cravings for food and drink. She is getting irritable in her first trimester, and Manoj is thinking of dropping her off at her mother's place in Pune for a month. Honey's collection has diminished at Sapphire, which keeps going back and forth between a 12:30 a.m. closing and a later one, depending on the whims of the police. Honey has just had a gallbladder operation. It is becoming increasingly difficult for her to dance.

The bar line, in its current form, is ending. "It's like what it was when it started," reflects Honey. "People are throwing five-rupee notes." The stock market boom is over. No longer are men content to see girls dancing in full saris and for the wilder ones to gyrate erotically; they are not satisfied with a smile or a quick caress on the face. "Pressing and kissing goes on nowadays!" she exclaims in disgust. "The bar line has become nightlife, it's all sex." And this is one area where Honey can't compete with the girls.

Honey has one great wish in her life. "My heart wants one thing so much: that once in my life I should come in front of people as Manoj. Hide nothing." Make Manoj an important name too, maybe as a makeup man, maybe as a wardrobe supplier to the fashion or movie industries. He might save Honey's earnings and open a transport agency like his brother's, with a few cars and trucks he can rent out. Or he might go to America with me, where Manoj can work in his aunt's store or Honey can dance in a gay bar. After the child is a year old, he says, Honey will leave the bar line. One way or another, Honey will die in a year or two. In the end Manoj will win; it was decided from the beginning. But it was beautiful to watch her while she was alive.

Monalisa, too, is thinking of getting out of the bar line in two or three years. Maybe she'll do a course in fashion design or work in a beauty parlor. If she saves fifty lakhs she can open a clothes boutique. The problem with the bar line, she says, is that "it's all going western." It is becoming just like the discos, just like the colleges. Soon, the bar-line girls won't be wearing these full saris and dresses; "it will be short short." The customers know what they want. In the early days, they used to come to the bar for fifteen days before asking for a girl's name; now they ask point-blank: "Are you coming or not?"

So Monalisa tells me her dream. It is to make a speech when she wins the Miss India title.

She speculates about what a sensation it would cause, the country discovering that the newly appointed paragon of Indian womanhood is a dancer in a bar; that this representative of the demimonde has bested all the convent-educated girls from Malabar Hill and Friends Colony. "What a headline it would make! It would be like a bomb falling." She is serious about making this speech. She has started working out, taking speech lessons, and going to the dentist to get her teeth fixed. But, almost twenty-two, she is getting old for the pageant.

Her dream is not to win the title; it is to make the speech, with millions of people watching. "I'll tell everyone that I am a girl from the bar line. Now you can take back all your prizes, all your money, but I wanted to prove that I could get to this point. That we in the bar line are also part of society. I went into the bar line because of need. I'm not being forced to do anything." Monalisa tells me the rest of the speech in English, the English she has been learning all these months so that when the time comes she can get onto the glittering stage in the vast auditorium and tell the whole country, "I'm in the bar line, but I am not doing anything wrong. I'm just dancing here."

Distilleries of Pleasure

ALL MADANPURA IS AGOG. The movies have come home. The stars have stepped off the big screen and here they are, so close you can almost touch them. Which star is it? Karishma Kapoor or Shahrukh Khan, depending on which rumor you believe.

The film is called *Sangharsh,* and it is directed by a slight, confident young woman named Tanuja Chandra. Her last movie did not do well but this one will be different, because, she explains to me, "In this story the hero is integrated into the plot." It is a Hindi version of *Silence of the Lambs*—with songs. Preity Zinta is the Jodie Foster character, a trainee CID inspector who falls in love with a gangster. And I have introduced Tanuja and her famous producer, Mahesh Bhatt, to Madanpura in darkest Bombay and found real gangsters to protect the making of this gangster movie.

Anees has rounded up forty of his boys for crowd control. They are controlling the crowd by thrashing it. In front of me, a tall man named Farid slaps a gawking bhaiyya back and forth across his face, four times. The small bhaiyya looks up at him, wondering if his rage and his pain will give him the strength to say something to Farid. A policeman has seen what's happening, witnessed the assault. He rushes in and drives his iron-tipped bamboo stick at the bhaiyya—and at everybody else. The lathi makes contact on soft bodies, and the whole crowd flees helter-skelter down the lane, screaming. There are small children inside that crowd, fleeing before the swinging stick.

It's a great day for Madanpura.

"In five minutes they'll all be back," says Anees.

In five minutes they're all back.

The karkhanas, the workshops, of Madanpura are shut; the meat shops and tailors aren't doing much business; the man making rotis directly in front of the house we are shooting in has never kneaded his dough with such energy. People linger in front of the pan shop and, when challenged by the cops or by Anees's boys, say they're waiting for their pan to be made. They're given a shove to go on. Over us there is a tin roof, which must be sizzling in the sun. On it are dozens of people, almost on the edge of the overhang, many with bare feet frying on the roof. Through a crack in the karkhana next to the house I spot three faces, like cherubs glimpsed in the woodland. Small boys have clambered onto the roofs overlooking the small courtyard of the house and have to be shooed out of the frame. A jocular policeman is sitting on a motorcycle in front of the house's entrance, dispensing witticisms. "There's nothing to see. Go, go and feed your mothers and fathers. Go, Shilpa Shetty and Amitabh Bacchan are coming at four o'clock. Line up now!"

Tanuja, the only woman to have made it in the commercial film industry as a director, is thrilled to have begun her film in Madanpura. All the men in the unit are scared of the mob; only Tanuja, Preity, and her female assistant brave the crowd. When Preity gets out of her van, her mobile phone at her ear, and moves fast within a cordon of locked hands through the roaring crowd, I understand for the first time what the word "mobbed" means. The assistant, a diminutive figure, pushes back at people with vigor. The mob retreats in front of this sprite as they had not in front of the police or Anees's thugs. "Woman power," the assistant observes.

The scene being shot is Preity Zinta coming into the inner city to meet the gang lord. She sits down next to me, and I introduce myself. She asks about Anees's boys. "Have they killed anyone?" I respond that many of them probably have. Her eyes widen. "Can you point out someone who's killed?" She is as fascinated by the gangsters as they are by her. All the crowd wants is a glimpse of her face or her body, clad in a white Old Navy sweatshirt and white platform sneakers. What she wants is to catch a glimpse of a killer.

Gangsters and whores all over the world have always been fascinated by the movies and vice versa; the movies are fundamentally transgressive. They are our eye into the forbidden. Most people will never see a human being murder another human being, except on the screen. Most people will never see a human being have sex with another human being, except on the screen. Cinema is an outlaw medium, our flashlight into the darkest part of ourselves. For the criminals and prostitutes who live these outlaw lives, the movies are close to realistic; they are for Monalisa and the hit man Mohsin what a Cheever story might be for a businessman living in Westchester: a sympathetic depiction, only slightly exaggerated, of his work and life.

Anees says, "Look at my feet." They are unnaturally brown and wrinkled. All day long the public has been trampling on them as he attempts to push it back from the action. Anees's boys will have lots to answer for after today; they have beaten back the crowd with fists and lathis. But today they are with the unit; they are part of the film world, aiding in its realization of their dreams.

A squad of policemen arrives. The inspector demands that the film crew pack up. They have not obtained the necessary permissions. The unit's negotiator speaks to him in soft tones. The local member of the legislature, who looks like a powerfully built thug himself, appears, swinging a stick. "Shut all this down! Pack up, pack up! The public is getting inconvenienced." But Tanuja is not finished with her takes, which involve filming a gangster who is eating biryani. There is an enormous plate of greasy rice in front of him, and we can hear Tanuja screaming at him, "Khate raho! Keep eating!" It is money the inspector really wants, but Tanuja doesn't realize this. She has to pack up before lunch. She ultimately ends up throwing away the street scenes because there are so many people looking at the camera that she has to constantly keep narrowing the frame. In Bombay, of all places, she's trying to shut out the crowd.

It barely made it into the movie, but that one morning in Madanpura now has outsize significance: for Anees, for Ishaq the STD shopowner and his cousin Dr. Shahbuddin, and for everybody who helped Tanuja with the shoot. Ishaq is now besieged by people wanting a meeting with the stars or small roles in the movie. The shooting changes the status of Ishaq and Shahbuddin in the community. The doctor's barber refuses to take money for shaving Shahbuddin every morning. He wants Shahbuddin to do him a favor next time the stars come visiting: He wants a picture of himself with one of them. Shahbuddin's wife, who is in Malaysia, refuses to believe he met all these stars; she thinks he is lying. It is something they will talk about till they are old, and it is something their children will talk about. "My father met Preity Zinta. Mahesh Bhatt came to our shop, right here. He sat down and had a Coke."

Whether they're making art films or masala films solidly in the mainstream, the people in the movie industry are all the same: big dreamers. In India, their dreams have to be bigger than everybody else's. In India they're making collective dreams; when they go to sleep at night they have to dream for a billion people. This distorts their personalities. It also accounts for their egos: the demands of scale. The Bombay moviemakers are afflicted by megalomania. "This is the beginning of a shift in orbit of Planet India, the ultimate revenge where the Indians are going to take over the Western mind. Welcome to the cultural aggression of the 21st century," writes the producer Amit Khanna in a newspaper column. The Indian entertainment industry at the beginning of the twenty-first century is worth $3.5 billion, a minor part of the global $300-billion entertainment industry. But it is the world's biggest movie industry when it comes to production and viewership. The 1,000 feature films and 40,000 hours of TV programming and 5,000 music titles that the country produces are exported to seventy countries. Every day, 14 million Indians see a movie in one of 13,000 theaters; worldwide, a billion more people a year buy tickets to Indian movies than to Hollywood ones. Television is galloping in; the country has 60 million homes with TV, of which 28 million are cabled, bringing to city and hamlet alike a choice of around a hundred channels. "There now are more television channels available in Mumbai than in most U.S. cities," Bill Clinton noted on a trip to the city in 1999.

India is one of the few territories in which Hollywood has been unable to make more than a dent; Hollywood films make up barely 5 percent of the country's market. Resourceful saboteurs, the Hindi moviemakers. When every other country's cinema had fallen before Hollywood, India met Hollywood the Hindu way. It welcomed it, swallowed it whole, and regurgitated it. What went in blended with everything that had existed before and came back out with ten new heads.

Hindi film directors detest the term Bollywood: They point out that the film industry in Bombay is older than the one in Hollywood, because American filmmaking started out on the East Coast before moving to California in the early twentieth century. The Lumiere Brothers brought their *cinématographe* to Bombay in 1896, only a few months after the wondrous invention debuted in Paris. A Maharashtrian named Bhatvadekar started making short films on wrestling matches and circus monkeys in Bombay in 1897. Through the movies, Indians have been living in Bombay all their lives, even those who have never actually been there. The wide sweep of Marine Drive, the beach at Juhu, the gateway to the West that is Andheri airport—all these are instantly recognizable in Kanpur and Kerala. And Bombay is mythic in a way that Los Angeles is not, because Hollywood has the budgets to create entire cities on its studio lots; the Indian film industry has to rely on existing streets, beaches, tall buildings.

Most commercial Hindi films are musicals, with anywhere from five to fifteen song sequences. Western moviemakers abandoned musicals when they abandoned the movies themselves, in favor of television. Musicals demand sweep, scale; they do not fit on a pinched nineteen-inch screen. There was another unreasonable demand that reviewers and audiences imposed on Hollywood musicals: that the song fit the plot. Hindi movies face no such fascist guidelines. The suspension of disbelief in India is prompt and generous, beginning before the audience enters the theater itself. Disbelief is easy to suspend in a land where belief is so rampant and vigorous. And not just in India; audiences in the Middle East, Russia, and Central Asia are also pre-cynical. They still believe in motherhood, patriotism, and true love; Hollywood and the West have moved on. So the Russian families in my apartment building in Jackson Heights, New York, sang the same Raj Kapoor songs that we Indians did. "They are clean movies," an Egyptian taxi driver in New York once explained to me. "You can see them with your family. You're not embarrassed by them."

Toward the end of the twentieth century, Hindi films started getting segmented. A gulf opened up for the first time: What the computer engineer in San Jose likes is not what the farmer in Bilaspur wants. So filmmakers like Yash Chopra, Subhash Ghai, Mani Ratnam, and Karan Johar changed their movies to fit the overseas taste, where, in the long run, the money is. Tanuja paraphrases what such filmmakers believe: "We don't want any poor people in our films, we only want beauty."

Before coming to India this time, I have watched an average of one Hindi film a year. The plots can't hold me past the beginning. Increasingly, the overseas market demands plotless musicals: movies with a dozen elaborate song sequences and minimal conflict, such as *Hum Aapke Hain Kaun*, a film that is essentially an extended wedding video with fourteen songs. The movies replaced the ancient traditions of Hindu weddings in my extended family in England and America. The costumes, the sets, and many of the ceremonies are taken from the movies the community watches every night on the VCR. The bride and the bridesmaids now dance, not to the parting-lament songs of the villages but to sprightly Bollywood numbers.

The diaspora wants to see an urban, affluent, glossy India, the India they imagine they grew up in and wish they could live in now. They want love stories with minimal conflict, even between rivals. Back home, the movies play on the newest insecurity of the children of the Indian middle class. Their parents won't arrange a marriage for them, as parents have for generations. Now everybody is expected to find love by themselves, in college, at work. Women are expected to know how to flirt, to play games. The movies show them how.

Overseas Indians want a film they can take their kids to on a Saturday afternoon, to show them an example of "Indian values." The wedding-and-romance extravaganzas fit the bill. Violence doesn't work for them. The lust for story is in Bihar, UP, places where villagers listen to the Ramlila, the staged version of the Ramayana, driven by the same hunger for narrative. So another class of filmmakers makes movies just for the interior of the country, filled with more violence, more earthy sex, and more goddesses, following the B-movie trail. The Hindi movies can unify Bihar and Delhi, even Bihar and Karachi, but not, in the end, Bihar and London.

I grew up in a Bombay before television, and my dreams were bigger than the dreams of children growing up in the city today because they were played out on a vast screen, hundreds of times bigger. The movies gave me the raw material for my fantasy life, in which I rescued the girl I loved from villains and saved her from dishonor in the nick of time. My plots closely followed those of the movies, which in those days closely followed those of the epics. Growing up in the cities, we did not have the benefit of the temple priest reciting the Harikatha at dusk. We had to go to the movies for our story fix. Few stars lived on Nepean Sea Road; they were mostly those who had retired from the industry. I knew nobody connected to the film industry in my childhood. But then, I knew nobody connected to crime or prostitution or politics, either. The movies were safely unreal; the players distant enough not to interfere with what my imagination made of them.

When I moved to America I would watch Hindi movies for nostalgia's sake; it was the cheapest round-trip ticket home, four bucks at the Eagle

Cinema in Jackson Heights. Then, in college and beyond, I stopped, finding them increasingly absurd and pointless. Coming back to Bombay this
time, I realized I would have to undergo a crash course in Hindi films if I
wanted to talk intelligently to the people who make them. It was not something I looked forward to.

One day in the summer of 1998 I found myself in distant Arunachal
Pradesh, which even Indians need a permit to enter. There, a woman at a
tea shop on the highway told me about the sacred geography of the area.
"And here, near the water tank in this village, the shooting for *Koyla* happened. Shahrukh Khan was here." This is where the new myths come
from. The old tribal gods have been replaced by the Bombay gods. In the
neighboring country of Bhutan, in a mountain town that has only one
street, I saw Tanuja's name on a film poster. This most isolated country on
earth knows the Bombay movie stars, their food habits, and who they're
romancing, as if they were their neighbors.

What is a South Asian? Someone who watches Hindi movies. Someone whose being fills up with pleasure when he or she hears "Mere Sapnon
ki rani" or "Kuch Kuch Hota Hai." Here is our national language; here is
our common song.

Vidhu Vinod Chopra: Mission Kashmir

One afternoon soon after I move to Bombay I am to meet the writer
Vikram Chandra for tea at the Sea Lounge, but when I call him on his
mobile I discover that he is in Bandra. I am supposed to be in that suburb
later that evening, so I suggest we meet somewhere in Bandra instead. He
asks if I would like to come along to a story session he is participating in
with his brother-in-law, a director named Vidhu Vinod Chopra.

The house is a six-story bungalow in a small winding lane near the sea,
in the Catholic part of Bandra, with its little villages. A private elevator
takes me up to the fourth floor, to a cheerful well-appointed living room
with a view of palms and the sea from floor-to-ceiling windows. It is luxurious, but not in the Bombay filmi sense. There are no wall-sized mirrors,
no chandeliers. I shake hands with Vinod, a trim, intensely forceful man,
who is pushing fifty but looks younger. His trademark in publicity photos is
a baseball cap over thinning hair, but he is not wearing this at home. In collaboration with Vikram and a young Gujarati playwright named Abhijat

Joshi, he is writing a film about the conflict in Kashmir. Amitabh Bacchan, hero and god of my adolescent dreams, has agreed to star in the project. Bacchan is to play Khan, a police officer, and Shahrukh Khan will play Altaaf, a militant. By the end, the militant will have seen the error of his ways and had a patriotic conversion. Vinod is a Punjabi Hindu who grew up in Srinagar; his ancestral house was burnt down by the militants. His last film was a love story, *Kareeb,* which flopped.

The next day I phone Anu, Vinod's wife (and Vikram and Tanuja's sister), who ably covers Bollywood for *India Today,* to speak to her about the industry. I hear Vinod's voice on the speakerphone instead. "We miss you, yaar! Why don't you come here for the story session?" And so I go again that day to the house in Bandra, sit with Vinod, Vikram, and Abhijat, and discuss plot, character, motivation. Over the next two years, without ever formally signing anything or even making a verbal commitment, I find myself becoming part of the scriptwriting team on *Mission Kashmir.* I am now doing what millions of Indians dream of doing: working on a Bollywood movie.

A Hindi movie script is not so much written as talked out, and the director has to display enormous enthusiasm for his own ideas. Although Vinod comes truly alive when he's speaking in Punjabi, most of our conversation about the script, including the dialogues, is in English. The industry is dominated by the middle and upper-middle classes, and a newcomer who doesn't speak English well is at a distinct disadvantage and has to learn fast. In the Hindi films I've seen being made, most of the directing—the development of the story, the instructions to the actors, the barked commands to the crew—is done in English. A couple of years previously, I sat with the actors Shahrukh Khan and Madhuri Dixit over lunch as they talked about the American films and TV shows they loved— *Sleepers, Jack, The X-Files*—and complained about an interview they had just done for Doordarshan, the government TV channel, and being forced to speak in Hindi. They didn't even know some of the words in Hindi, they said.

Vinod's study is full of English books, screenplays by foreign directors. Vinod says this will be his last Hindi film; if it does well, he wants to use the profits to make a Hollywood film. His entire career is at stake. After *Kareeb,* he is about a crore in debt. If the next film he produces doesn't make money, his time in the movie business is essentially finished. "If this film fails, my house will be put up for sale." The audience should come into the theater already educated in the narrative—the newspapers would be the silent partners of such a topical movie—but nothing should be allowed to provoke or challenge the state's position on the conflict or, for that matter, that of the militants, who could bomb his house if displeased. Most of the political complexity of the Kashmir issue—the alienation that the majority of the people in Kashmir are feeling, the economic and administrative reasons for the long slide into rebellion—has to be rigorously eliminated during the scripting. Again and again Vinod says, "I don't want this to be a controversial film. I don't want death threats and I don't want it to be banned. The Censor Board is made up of little shits. They will watch my film and get up and say, 'Chopra saab, great film.' Then half of them will vote not to give me the U certificate." This would restrict the audience to those over eighteen, killing the film's commercial prospects. For Indians, going to the movies is a family enterprise.

Every afternoon, we sit around the study with the nice view, drink tea, and throw ideas at one another. I learn about the construction of a script. Every single scene has to have dramatic value, not merely convey information. Vinod says, "I shouldn't have to be doing this. I would love nothing more than if the three of you went away somewhere and came back and gave me a bound script. I should be directing." He has two fatal comments about an idea he doesn't like: "too filmi" (offending his senses as an artist) and "the Hindi film audience won't accept it" (causing him financial concern). Although they might be generated by the writers, the ideas that make it into the script are the ones Vinod can somehow make his own, as if they had come from him all along.

Vikram writes a series of changes that make the script much more complex. Vinod has his doubts. "Let's not forget that we're making a Hindi movie. If the movie was to be in English it would be completely different."

Vikram is a fan of *L.A. Confidential,* and he uses the thriller's structure to argue for his version of the script. "I've seen it seven times and I could see it seven more times."

"If *L.A. Confidential* was a Hindi movie, it wouldn't run for a single day," says Vinod. "It's too brainy."

I point out to Vinod that the Indian audience is fully capable of understanding complexity; after all, it is schooled in the most complex narrative myths in the world, the Ramayana and the Mahabharata. Each character in the epics is multidimensional, the plots multilayered, and the message morally ambiguous, demanding a high degree of thought. There is nothing easy about the epics and they both end unhappily, with the death of the leads. But it is not my movie or Vikram's or Abhijat's; it is Vinod's. And he is certainly possessed by it. At one point both he and Abhijat, while illustrating the kind of song they want in a scene, start singing Kishore Kumar's "Aa chal ke tujhe." They continue singing, their faces shining, till they've sung the entire song. It has nothing to do with the work at hand; it is a detour into pleasure. When Vinod demonstrates a violent scene, he becomes violent. He thrusts his face in yours, grabs your shirt, and screams out the lines: "Madharchod, I'll fucking kill you!" I am energized by Vinod's violence. I come home one night, and Sunita tells me someone has been ringing the doorbell and running away. "I'll kill them, motherfuckers. I'll fuck them," I tell her, and then bend down to say my nightly prayers.

What is fascinating to me is not so much the scriptwriting process as hearing Vinod explain what is politically acceptable and what's not. Infinite care has to be taken, as the papers put it, to avoid "hurting the sentiments of a particular community." Vinod goes back and forth and back again over what religion the female leads should profess, what might cause offense, what would play well with the audience. Finally, he splits the difference: Mrs. Khan, the cop's wife, is Hindu, and Sufi, the militant's girlfriend, is Muslim. The constraints we operate under are peculiar to the country. Vinod can't have fade-to-black in his movies. He had five of them in one of his early films, after he came out of the Film Institute, and the audience started jeering and whistling. They thought the arc light was going. In the interiors the projectionists cut fade-outs out of the reels to keep the audience from wrecking the theater.

One early draft ends with the heroine waiting for the hero to come down from a helicopter, dead or alive. When she sees him alive, she starts laughing. "You're alive!" are the final words. But then Vinod runs through the end again and shakes his head. "Too late. The lights will come on and the doors open before they even get into the helicopter." In theaters all across India, audiences have a built-in sense about when a movie is ending. This sense is aided by the doors opening and the dimmer lights coming on, five minutes before the actual ending. People with small children need to leave early, to get a taxi or rickshaw outside. So the last five minutes of any Hindi film are inevitably lost even if you stay in the theater, because most people in front of you are standing up. This is why most movies end with a song or a rapid reprise of the film's highlights, like the life of a dying man flashing before his eyes. It stretches out the end. Thus, *Mission Kashmir* ends with a pointless dream sequence of playing cricket in the snow and a reprise of a song.

The influence of the epics is strong. An incident in which Mrs. Khan asks the boy to lay down his arms for the sake of her husband is referred to, naturally and always, as the "Kunti scene," after the mother in the Mahabharata. Like most Bollywood films, the film is a paean to motherhood, the one thing you can never be cynical about in a Hindi movie. Most Indian movies are about the joint family splitting up and coming back together again. For two and a half hours, they depict and overcome the dissolution of the country's urban families into nuclear, single-parent, and divorced households. This film category is called the "social" movie. Housewives come to the matinee showing and weep copiously into little white cotton handkerchiefs embroidered with small colored flowers. Vinod himself is devoted, like a good Hindi movie son, to his mother. He cancels dinner plans with us once because his mother says you can't eat food cooked during an eclipse.

The narrative principles that propel the plot are alien to those of, say, the Iowa Writers' Workshop, where I spent two years. I entertain myself by imagining what would happen if the script were put up in workshop. My contribution to the script is minimal at best. I propose an idea that departs from the standard Hindi film formula. Vinod thinks about it. "We can't do it because if we put it in the film the audience will burn down the theater. They will rip out the seats and burn down the theater."

I withdraw the suggestion.

He is not exaggerating. Indians take their films as seriously as Italians take opera. When they feel their heroes are diverging radically from what they ought to be doing, the audience can get physical. As we are scripting, we read that in Ludhiana, after the first showing of the film *Fiza*, in which the hero also plays a terrorist, the audience was disappointed by the way their idol was portrayed. They expressed their disappointment by getting up and ransacking the theater. I feel an enormous responsibility now as a scriptwriter. We construct the film with one anxious eye on the rickshaw wallah in the lower stalls with the can of petrol.

I ask Vinod his opinion of the art films made in India. It is not high. "I think the art film in India is like speaking Greek or Latin to an average Indian. This is our colonial hang-up. The art cinema is made for the West, except Ghatak, who made films in Bengali for Bengalis. Ray's power came from the West, after *Pather Panchali*, not from Bengal."

Vinod can speak with authority about art films. As you learn in the course of a first meeting with him, he has been nominated for an Oscar. Fresh out of film school, he made a short film about homeless children in Bombay, *An Encounter with Faces*, which was nominated in the short non-fiction category for the Academy Awards. The two movies he made later were critically praised but barely broke even. After that, he started making flat-out commercial films: thrillers, romances, starting with *Parinda*, his first mainstream film. The underworld loved *Parinda;* it was the first time in Hindi movies they had been shown as they really are. I remembered Mohsin the hit man watching a scene from *Parinda* on the hotel room TV and telling me, "This is a correct scene."

Since then, Vinod has made only two films, *1942: A Love Story* and *Kareeb*, for a total of five feature films in his entire career of two decades. Why does it take him such a long time, when other Bollywood directors are turning out one or two every year?

"Primarily because of the writing. I'm not a writer." He resents having to make movies with hackneyed plots for what he calls the ulloo audience. "I'm constantly saddled with a viewer who's cinema illiterate. It's like trying to talk Shakespeare with Khem Bahadur"—Vinod's Nepalese cook. "My fear is that through constant simplification and trying to talk Shakespeare with Khem Bahadur, I've lost the ability to discuss Shakespeare with people who know Shakespeare."

This is something I gradually find out about Bollywood: The people working in it are far smarter than the product they turn out. "We are dwarfing our intellectual selves in order to make films for a Hindi film audience. You're writing this great novel in the English language. Try doing it in Hindi; then you'll know my tragedy. You'll get fucked. You'll have no fucking money to pay your children's school fees."

He allows himself to think, sometimes, of how it would be if his earlier art films had been a success, of if he had chosen to live in the United States after his Oscar nomination. He is sometimes burdened by the sense of a life not lived, the feeling that he took the wrong fork in the road a while back. "I want to make international films for the world market. I want to grow.

Where will I go from here? I can sit here in my wooden study with my Jacuzzi and stagnate for the rest of my life."

There are two Vinods fighting "eyeball to eyeball," as he is fond of saying about Khan and Altaaf, our lead characters. One is the avant-garde filmmaker from the Film Institute at Pune, student of Ghatak and Mani Kaul, worshiper of Kurosawa. The other is the big-budget Bombay producer, with something to prove to his commercially successful stepbrother, who cannot afford subtlety in his films lest it go over the heads of the ulloo audience. If he pledged his troth to either of these two personas—became wholly Vinod the committed art filmmaker or Vinod the Bollywood hack—he would be less tortured. As it is, the conflict is apparent in his films; it keeps him from winning an Oscar or having a megahit at the box office.

Vinod is attached to his home but not to the city. "Bombay's never thrilled me. If I could take all my friends from here and live in Florida, that wouldn't be a bad idea. Bombay has become like a goon city since the Sena and Bal Thackeray have taken over. There's just one man who's fucked up Bombay, and that's Thackeray." He was told by a government bureaucrat that if he wanted tax exemption for *Kareeb*, he would have to go to Thackeray. The most effective method of government control over popular cinema isn't the censor's office, it's the tax office. Granting tax exemption to a film lowers the price of a ticket by half and could mean the difference between life or death for a film. But Vinod will not kowtow in front of Thackeray. If the Supremo causes trouble for him, he says, he will move out of the country.

Vinod tells me about the New Quit India Movement. It is a group of some fifty Bombay luminaries: dancers, actors, diplomats, and so on, loosely coordinated by a Parsi hairdresser who is in charge of some of the city's most famous heads, and she has invited Vinod and Anu to join the exodus. They have resolved to emigrate en masse to Canada: to Vancouver. To this end, they have meetings, where they bring in experts to conduct lectures on how to get abroad and how to live there. They are all rich and can afford the $200,000 it costs to get Canadian papers. It is a uniquely Bombay dream of exile: You want to get out of Bombay, but you want to take your Bombay with you. The New Quit India Movement dreams of traveling in a social bubble halfway across the world, where it can re-create Malabar Hill and Pali Hill in a more salubrious environment.

* * *

YEARS FROM NOW they will be asking me, "And what did he look like? And how did he walk?"

We are in Amitabh Bacchan's bungalow, and I am shaking his hand. Not his waxwork in Madame Tussaud's, the real thing. I have grown up with this man—or, rather, with his image. Now, for the second time, I am seeing him live. The first time was in 1979, at the old Deluxe Cinema in Woodside, Queens, where he'd come to launch *Kala Patthar*. He gave a speech onstage; I worshiped from afar. Bacchan was, then, the biggest star in Hindi films; the man who, when he was injured in the filming of a movie stunt, had the entire country praying for his recovery and tens of thousands of people lining up outside Breach Candy Hospital to give him blood.

The man himself is surprisingly bigger than his screen persona. He wears a loose white silk Pathan suit. When he shakes my hand, a smile comes on; I have never seen so many teeth in my life. It is not a smile of pleasure, or even of greeting. It is as if a switch has been flicked; there is a flash of light. A moment later, the switch is flicked off and the face resumes its stillness, sinks back into its slight daze.

Outside his bungalow, at all hours, groups of people wait to get his darshan, an auspicious viewing. Inside, he reigns in his office, which is just this side of showy, all beige leather and black wood. A large figurative painting of an old bioscope-wallah with a cluster of kids peering into it dominates one wall. On his desk are stacks of videocassettes and a couple of books, one of his father's poems and, on top of it, Paul Reiser's *Couplehood*.

Vinod asks me later, "Do you think he weaves his hair? It looked strange, in the front." From the back, too, it looks strange, unnaturally elongated over his neck. It is not just his hair that he has lost. Bacchan is desperate; his last few movies have flopped badly and the future of his production company, ABCL Ltd., is in doubt. When Bacchan first called Vinod from Mauritius, the director was so revved up about Vikram's plot for a film about Kashmir that he started swearing. "Motherfucker. It's a fucking brilliant idea." Bacchan listened politely and agreed that it was brilliant. Later that night, Vinod felt bad that he had been so coarse around Bacchan, who is senior to him. But that was also a subtle indication of the new position of the star—that a director could swear like a sailor around him and he would have to take it, to hang on the line from Mauritius. After the failure of his last couple of films, it was Bacchan who now had to call about roles.

Unlike many Hindi directors, Vinod shoots from a written and bound script, but no such product is necessary—or sufficient—to sign up the talent for the film. We have to go physically and "narrate" the script to the stars. This is the reason we are in Bacchan's bungalow. We are going to tell him a story.

Bacchan tells us what effect our film should have on the audience. "You need to catch them by the crotch and shake them up." He wants to make a truly breakthrough film, one in a different paradigm. As examples, he cites *Bombay* and *Bandit Queen*. And he has a keen sense of the primacy of his role as hero, the only hero. He wants something in the plot by which Khan can show his "smartness—supreme smartness."

After we narrate the story to him, the superstar has a suggestion. "Can we make the system the villain?" asks Bacchan. "The common man is disinformed," he begins. He saw Oliver Stone's *JFK*, and it changed the way he looked at the world. In India, although the common man is intelligent, he has been lied to by the politicians and by the movies. But now the common man is waking up and realizing that the system is responsible for his travails. So now the common man will not accept a cliché ending in which the hero wins and everybody can go home.

Bacchan wants us to make a movie with an ending that will awaken the common man to what the system is doing to him. He wants the two protagonists, the cop and the militant, as they clasp in embrace at the end, to be shot dead by a single bullet. "Let's really give the audience something to think about," the star proposes. "They'll sit in the theater for fifteen minutes after the lights have come on, thinking about who could have shot them. Then they'll say, 'Shit . . . it's the system!' "

"What about the censors?" I ask, remembering Vinod's concerns about making a controversial film.

"Don't worry about the censors," Bacchan swats them away in the air, like houseflies. He relates what happened at the National Defense Academy, where his latest film, *Major Saab*, is set, in which he plays the academy commander. When he showed the film to some army officers, they had complained that certain scenes were not true to life and implied that they could make trouble with the censors. "Ban it, I said to them, and I'll make a film about what *really* goes on in the army: the gunrunning in the forward posts, the senior officers sleeping with the junior officers' wives." The officers backed down and said, Let's talk about this over some drinks. Amitabh Bacchan had won a true hero's victory; he took on the army single-handed, and the army gave in. I feel a glow within.

Vinod paces about his terrace after the meeting with Bacchan. He asks me what I think of Bacchan's suggestions. I tell him I'm not sure the public will accept a movie in which both leads die. The basic difference between an art film and a commercial film is that in an art film the hero dies at the end. Vinod wants the militant to be reunited with his girlfriend and with his father at the conclusion of the film. So he rehearses the appeal he will make to Bacchan: "Sir, the system may be screwing the common man. But if I kill both my stars at the end of the picture, the system will surely screw me."

What accounts for the star's paranoia? Bacchan's foray into politics came to a humiliating end; he was forced to resign his parliamentary seat in 1988, after his name was linked to the Bofors arms scandals. His entertainment conglomerate, ABCL, is on the front pages of the newspapers; his bank wants to sell his house to recover money loaned to the company. His movies are failing left and right. The whole country had loved him; the whole country had been ready to give its blood for him. It couldn't be the people who had withdrawn their love. It couldn't be that they were faithless. No, it had to be something else. It had to be the system.

WE GO BACK to Bacchan's house late one night with the latest draft of the script. Jaya Bacchan, his wife, is there, along with his actor son, Abhishek, and the family accountant. Jaya is a dignified, gracious lady. I can still see the actress that delighted me in *Guddi* and *Mili*. Some snacks are offered to us in the living room. We talk about the Starr report, which is just out. The recent bombings of American embassies in East Africa, Bacchan now sees, were a plot to distract attention from Clinton's troubles with Miss Lewinsky. I sense the dread hand of the system again.

We are discussing all this at three in the morning. Then we say good night to Jaya and go upstairs with the star to his study. Bacchan watches the location shots Vinod has taken in Kashmir. They show a gorgeous, peaceful country, with old bungalows and cascading fountains in well-laid-out gardens. He makes approving noises about the revised script; I sense he is dog-tired and just wants to get the meeting over with. When we come down, it is about 4 a.m. Jaya is still there, at the foot of the stairs, in the low lights, gliding silently over the carpeted floor. Abhishek and the accountant also appear out of the shadows. We tell Jaya we thought she was turning in. "I'm always up till at least four-thirty," she responds.

"We're a family of insomniacs," Abhishek explains, with no little pride.

Bacchan sits down again in front of the ever-present salted snacks, this time complemented by a dish of Rajasthani sweets. They all seem quite prepared to talk for another hour. We take our leave. The ghosts stay on.

SHAHRUKH KHAN, OUR FIRST CHOICE to play Altaaf the militant, comes to Vinod's house one day to talk about the script. He is not good-looking in the conventional way but is bright, focused, and energetic. He comes wearing a black shirt with all the buttons undone down his hairless chest, blue jeans of which the too-long cuffs are not folded but ripped at the seams, and sneakers. I've met Shahrukh before; the first time was on the set of *Dil To Pagal Hai*. A shot was being filmed when the hero is meeting the heroine. She is shopping for vegetables, haggling over the price of a water-melon. Shahrukh comes to her aid; he puts his arm around the vegetable seller, a dark fellow with a huge mustache, and talks to him in a low voice. The vegetable seller looks chastened and puts the watermelon into a plastic bag. In the films I grew up with, heroes saved heroines from brigands; now they negotiate better prices on vegetables.

As Shahrukh enters Vinod's living room, we are talking to Ajay, who has dropped in for lunch. The star is highly deferential toward the cop; Ajay once saved him from the gangs when he was targeted for extortion. Vinod's servant, Khem, is not in the kitchen, and Anu says she will make tea. Shahrukh sees that we are not finished talking to Ajay. He gets up— "I'll make tea; I make very good tea"—and disappears into the kitchen.

Then the servant comes up the stairs. "If Khem goes into the kitchen he'll have a heart attack," notes Vinod. Khem goes in and sees somebody pounding cardamom for tea. He is irritated, we find out later, that some interloper, maybe another servant, is doing his job. It is not until Shahrukh comes out with the tea on a tray and Khem notices our attitude to him that he realizes who the man in his kitchen was. Stardom is not intrinsic; stars acquire their light through reflection, on the faces of their fans. At the moment, Shahrukh is the biggest star, in the country and in the region. Two Pakistani boys were recently caught by Indian soldiers as they illegally crossed the border in Kashmir. It turned out that they hadn't crossed to join the jihad; they had braved death at the border in order to see their idol in the flesh. They had planned to travel to Bombay to see Shahrukh Khan.

Next on the list of Vinod's decisions is the choice of the heroine. But it's not very important. In an action film, the heroine is only slightly more important than the scenery. Vinod has already spoken to Tabu, who is a fine actress but, as a distributor advises him, "you should go for the glamour." Preity Zinta, the actress I had met in Madanpura for Tanuja's shoot, has a bubbly smile. Plus she's from Himachal Pradesh. She is a pahari, a mountain girl. She gets the role of Sufi, the love interest.

Vinod chooses an old friend of his, Jackie Shroff, for the role of the villain. I knew about him and his friends when I came back for visits to Bombay. They hung around Wonderworld, the video-game parlor on Nepean Sea Road, and got the girls. Jackie, unlike most other Hindi film stars, makes eye contact with you when he talks. He is a big man, running to fat; when he eats Vinod's biscuits, his assistant reprimands him. Vinod and Jackie—Jaggu to his friends—have an easy, affectionate, joking relationship. They've been through some times together. At one point, Vinod says, Jackie owed him five lakhs. He gave him twenty-two checks. All of them bounced.

Unlike the Hindi movies I grew up watching, in our film there is no vamp playing opposite the villain. Why aren't there any vamps in Bollywood anymore? I ask Tanuja. "The heroine became the vamp," she explains. In the glory days of Bindu and Helen, the vamps were the only screen women who were allowed to wear shocking costumes, gyrate erotically, drink whiskey. All that can now be done by the heroine; at least one song number where the woman who is later the dutiful wife seduces the hero by flashing her thighs is obligatory in today's movies. Another role to be swallowed up by the lead is the comedy routine: Asrani, Paintal, Johnny Walker, the sidekick or fool who used to throw in a few accidental punches in the climactic fight sequence. Bacchan destroyed the comedy roles; he incorporated them into his own. He was the only actor with enough stature to be able to do that and still look heroic.

THE PROPORTION of popular movies that deal with political issues, with terrorists, has been steadily growing. I can hardly recall any when I lived here as a child. India now deals with threats to its integrity through the movies. Many of the Hindi films of recent days are about a vast international conspiracy against the country, headed by a villain of vague ethnic outlines. There are scenes of bombings, terrorists, usually in league with Gandhi cap–wearing politicians. It is a simple explanation for the million mutinies: It's all coming from outside, what governments since independence have called the Foreign Hand. If we could only get to the one man who wants to destroy our country, everything would be all right. Somewhere in Pakistan, in Switzerland, sits Mogambo in his fabulous mansion, plotting with his minions ways to break up Hindustan.

I feel distanced from many of the scenes in *Mission Kashmir*. In writing them, I am a lawyer, putting words I do not believe in the mouths of my characters. Politically, I am at left angles to the film. I argue that we need to insert something about the social and economic conditions that go into the making of a terrorist, especially in Kashmir. I talk about visiting Kashmir in 1987 and seeing perhaps the most corrupt state government in India; about the wishes of most of the locals I had spoken to not to be part of the Indian Union; about the double standard in India's keeping Muslim-majority Kashmir on the grounds that the maharajah had acceded to us at independence, and refusing to let the Muslim princes of Hyderabad and Junagadh accede to Pakistan because they ruled over Hindu-majority states. But I don't push the point. I do not have the necessary weight on the script-writing team.

Vinod wants the film to reinforce in the popular imagination the syncretic idea of Kashmiryat, the age-old ideology that allows Muslims at the Hazratbal mosque and Hindus at the Shankaracharya temple to worship in the same country. He is not blind to the recent history of his troubled homeland. At one point, he says, "The Indians have fucked Kashmir. I'm a Kashmiri, I know. They've been fucking Kashmir for fifty years." The script presents a full panoply of the political views of the country's Muslims, represented by Khan, the pro–Indian state Muslim, to Altaaf the duped Muslim terrorist, to Hilal the troublemaking fanatic from Afghanistan. At one point, a Hindu bureaucrat questions Khan's loyalty. Khan responds angrily. "Mr. Deshpande, it is not the misfortune only of the Muslims but that of the entire country that a soldier who has braved bullets for twenty-one years must prove his loyalty repeatedly because his name is not Deshpande but Inayat Khan. . . . My love for this country needs no certificates from a bureaucrat."

The script also keeps making halfhearted attempts to balance the view of the Indian state with that of the Kashmiris. But it is always tempered, always compromised. In one of the scenes, a terrorist explains his reasons for joining the movement. "First they shamed my mother. I picked up a gun and came here." This brave statement is quickly balanced by his next sentence, which he says while holding a letter from home. "Now across the border they have done the same with my sister." In all things, equivalence. Equivalence can freeze the censor's scissor in mid snip. Equivalence can stop the terrorist's bullet half an inch from your chest.

All along, drafts of the script are shown to police officers and army officers, to check the fictional world against the real one. In Kashmir, Vinod shows the script to a top Intelligence Bureau officer. The officer wonders about the scene where Khan shoots two of the militants right away, during an interrogation. "You've just blown him away!" he points out to the filmmakers. "With me, I won't cut a finger off, because it's that much less of the body for me to work with. If I cut an arm off, that's even more lost; if I kill the person, I can't work with anything." To the IB officer, the body is a precious resource, to be conserved for its value as a source of pain; every organ, every digit, is valuable.

WITHOUT MUCH WARNING, Amitabh Bacchan backs out of the film. He sends Vinod a fax. Since they have not discussed "many aspects" of the project, the star concludes, "regretfully, I'll have to give this one a miss." Vinod scrutinizes the handwritten fax with distaste. "Is this 'money aspects' or 'many aspects'?" He goes to Bacchan's house with a hundred white roses to persuade the star to sign for his film. The star says he is committed to another movie with himself and Shahrukh in it. We now have to think of the Kashmir film without Bacchan. But there is a dearth of dignified older actors. Indian male movie stars don't age gracefully. They grow fat and lose their hair but they still insist on acting opposite heroines in their twenties—as their lovers, not their fathers.

One day Vinod tells me that Shahrukh, too, will not do the Kashmir project. His fees are too high. Vinod is now considering spending the rest of the year making advertising films. The real money is in TV spots. Shahrukh was initially offered thirty lakhs for appearing in Vinod's film, for which he would have had to travel and work for months. For three days' work in a Pepsi ad, he'll get ten times that money. But without the films, Shahrukh's face in commercials would be unrecognizable. The advertising industry subsidizes the movies by funding the lifestyles of the stars. In return, the movies move product. Product placement in films reaches territories unknown in Hollywood; an entire song might be paid for by Coke, for example, and the hero and heroine dance around giant Coke cans for five to seven minutes of screen time. Nobody minds; there is no division between the sacred and the profane in Indian films.

I finally get a chance to see one of Vinod's films, *Kareeb,* in a theater in the hill resort of Lonavla.

An Indian cinema hall is never the chamber of mass unconsciousness it is in the West. For one thing, you can never tell anyone to shut up. Everyone talks at will, often keeping up a running dialogue with the characters. If a god appears onscreen, people might throw coins or prostrate themselves in the aisles. Babies howl; during a song, a quarter of the audience might get up and procure refreshment in the lobby. Complex dialogue doesn't work, because most of the time the audience doesn't hear it. The sound is so bad in most Indian theaters that, as in a play, there can be no whispering in a Hindi film and the score always has to be played at top volume. It wasn't always so. To ask directions to the theater in Lonavla, you ask where the "talkies" are.

The audience is indifferent to *Kareeb.* They are jeering at the screen, hooting when the heroine shows any signs of getting close to the hero. I go out to get an ice cream during a tender scene between the heroine and her mother. "They're being really disgusting," Sunita tells me when I come back. "Making comments about mother-daughter intimacy." But the audience doesn't like the parody to be on the screen. In a scene where the mother is kidding the daughter about having a lost twin sister—which is meant to be comic, to play with the conventions of the formula—the audience is absolutely silent. Dangerously silent.

Kareeb is not a good film. The script moves along with the aid of contrivances. The acting, especially by the first-time heroine, is so bad it borders on parody—she wanders through the movie looking stoned. Vinod blames her for his losses on *Kareeb*, because he had to waste so many takes on an untrained actress. Once, on the set, she was supposed to lift her right hand to her head. She kept flubbing it by raising her left hand. After it happened one too many times, Vinod went over to her, grabbed her right hand, and bit it. "The pain will remind you which hand to use." He is the Werner Herzog of Indian cinema, a little bit mad.

After Amitabh and Sharukh back out, Vinod decides to work on another script with me. It is set partly in London, with its theme the reconciliation possible between Indians and Pakistanis overseas. The film deals with Partition and is called *Mitti*, Soil. Vinod has a vision of two soldiers, one Indian, one Pakistani, growing up in similar homes in Bombay and Lahore. They grievously injure each other in a battle fight and find themselves in the same hospital in England. There, they gradually realize that their hatred is recent and shallow. They belong to the same "mitti."

It is a hokey plot, but it has a kind of benevolence; it is on the side of the angels. And it is in keeping with the headlines in the newspapers. Friendship is in the air; it is the spring of possibilities. The idea for the movie has its genesis in a journey from Delhi to Lahore through Wagah in 1999, when Prime Minister Vajpayee got on a bus—not a plane, not a limousine—to make peace with his enemy, Nawaz Sharif, in Lahore. Bollywood senses keenly that it marks a "moment" in the subcontinent's history. I get calls simultaneously from the director Mahesh Bhatt and from Vinod to help them with projects based around the cataclysm that happened here fifty years ago. Partition affected them both: Vinod because he is a Punjabi Hindu from Kashmir and Mahesh because his mother was Muslim. Bollywood has long grappled with the vivisection of the motherland. Part of the reason is that this is one of the few industries in which Muslims and Hindus are equally represented. Muslim writers often write Hindu mythological epics; the ten-headed gods spout Urdu poetry.

Bollywood is essentially a Punjabi- and Sindhi-dominated industry, founded by Partition refugees who took up a business that the established

Bombay elites of the forties looked down on. In this, it parallels the story of Hollywood and the Jews. The saga of Partition fits with the great love stories of this part of the world, of Laila Majnooh, Heer Ranjha, and thousands of Hindi movies: two people who love each other against all odds against the tyrant father of the state, or twin brothers separated at birth in an accident of history. Partition, with all its heightened emotion, its sweep and tragedy, is a ready-made plot for Bollywood. It fits within the formula. Perhaps, deep in the scarred psyches of the refugees who made Bollywood what it is today, Partition *created* the formula.

But in 1999, the Kargil war breaks out between the two countries and *Mitti* is abandoned, left in the dust. From Pakistanis as brothers we go back to the theme of the Kashmir film: Pakistanis as archfiends. A whole slew of movies about the conflict is released. Movies that have nothing to do with the war in the mountains but feature an army man or even a policeman fighting cross-border terrorism are being advertised as prophetic about Kargil. The script for *Mission Kashmir* struggles to catch up with the changing headlines. It is impossible to predict what the mood of the public might be when the film is finally released, whether it will want to see Pakistanis as a brother people or as murderous fanatics. Vinod's worst nightmare now is that the developments in Kargil will run out of control and the unimaginable will happen: One country will drop an atom bomb on the other. "Then our film would be so outdated!" Without an atom bomb in it, the movie would bomb at the box office.

VINOD STILL HAS TO CHOOSE new leads for *Mission Kashmir*. Amitabh Bacchan is replaced by Sanjay Dutt, the troubled star out on bail for his involvement in the bomb blasts of 1993. Sanjay's career is in bad shape at the moment; he seems to be on a gradual slope downhill from his summit. To replace Shahrukh, Vinod has picked someone completely new. This twenty-five-year-old son of a sporadically successful star of the seventies has made exactly one movie, which has been directed by his father and is several months away from release. His name is Hrithik Roshan.

One morning Hrithik comes to Vinod's house to have the script narrated to him. The first thing I notice about the newcomer is how startlingly, even uncomfortably, handsome he is: green eyes, a strong nose and jaw, arms like Popeye's, and a thin body that has been worked out with zeal till it bulges in all the right places. He is polite and humble, listening closely to the story. But Vinod is taking a huge risk. If *Kaho Na Pyaar Hai*, Hrithik's debut film, flops when it is released, so, in all probability, will *Mission Kashmir*. His role as Altaaf is central. But Vinod has seen the rushes of the movie and has made his choice, compelled perhaps by financial exigency. Hrithik comes cheap.

There's a reason Hollywood is unable to produce Indian films: Negotiating contracts in Bollywood would make any Wall Street entertainment lawyer jump out of his twenty-sixth-floor suite at the Oberoi.

Vinod contacts several music directors and asks for their ideas for scores and songs. Anu Malik, the composer he has been working with on *Kareeb*, gets very emotional when he hears that Vinod is shopping around. He has a two-hour conversation with Vinod one Sunday morning in which he declares he is ready to work for free. He weeps and wails; he will not ask for one single paisa. The money is nothing compared to their friendship, he declares through his sobs. Vinod hears a crunching sound on the other end of the line. "What's that?" asks Vinod. "I'm eating a radish," answers the composer. "Just a minute, I'll finish it." Vinod hears him furiously crunching away; then he comes back to the phone, ready to weep afresh. "Not one single paisa! Not one single paisa will I take from you, if it's about the money."

There are five territories in India where a film is sold and one territory that comprises all the overseas markets. A distributor comes to Vinod wanting the Central India territory. He hands Vinod a blank check. "You write the figure, sir. You know that scene in *Parinda* when he looks into the rearview mirror? I have it by heart. By heart!" Negotiating in the Hindi film industry is always an emotional business. Shameless flattery is a must.

A distributor from Calcutta, Mr. Bagadia, comes in, and Vinod immediately greets him with an effusive hug. It is, I learn later, the first time the two have ever met. "Congratulations on the new issue," says Mr. Bagadia. He might be referring to Vinod's newborn son or to the Kashmir project or both. We talk with Mr. Bagadia about casting. He urges us to go for the glamour, for stars who are currently fashionable and, that most important quality, lucky. He has analyzed hundreds of films and has come up with certain lucky pairs, actors and actresses who, whenever they appear together in a film, it so happens that that film has been a hit. The film may not be a hit *because* of the pair; it is just a lucky omen. "Raakhee and Suresh

Oberoi. No film in which they have both appeared has ever failed. Put them in your film, even if it is a small part. They don't even have to be opposite each other." Mr. Bagadia has spent a lifetime pondering why some films do well and others don't. It is crucial to catch a star while he is still in vogue. Because, he says thoughtfully—and here I sense he is offering us the nub or gem of his accumulated experience, that single aphorism on which men base their lives—"A star is like a lipstick. When it fades, it fades."

The distributor is here to talk about money. For the entire Bengal and Bihar circuit, the distributor claims to have made less than fifteen lakhs in revenues for *Kareeb*. There is great bonhomie during the meeting, with only the slightest undercurrent of tension. The distributor allows as to how *Kareeb* flopped miserably and lost him lots of money, but he declares to Vinod that he distributes films for prestige, not money. Even if he knows in advance that it won't make him money, if it is a prestige project like any film of Vinod's, he will take it on at once. "We are not stalwarts of the industry like Vidhu Vinod Chopra," he says, turning to me.

As soon as he is out the door, Vinod asks me what I thought of Mr. Bagadia. I say I thought something sounded fishy. "That bastard swindled me," says Vinod. The movie has done at least thirty to forty lakhs of business in Mr. Bagadia's territory; the distributor gets 10 percent of whatever he reports. It is mostly a cash business; there are no mechanisms Vinod has at his disposal to check the real ticket sales. "There's nothing I can do," he says. He trusted him, on the director Yash Chopra's advice. The distributor left saying he was going on to Yash Chopra's house because he had a meeting scheduled with the director. Vinod asks his assistant to call Yash Chopra's house. Yash Chopra is out of town.

Vinod draws up agreements but normally doesn't put his signature to them. "Legal agreements mean nothing," he points out. The contract that the star and the director sign means nothing; the payment all depends on whether the star's most recent film is a hit or a flop. To hedge their bets, the stars often work on three or four films at the same time, morphing from the role of a policeman in the morning to a terrorist in the afternoon to a demon lover at night. Vinod reaches over and shows me a piece of paper. It is that most closely guarded of Bollywood secrets, a written contract. It spells out the stars' payment terms in language that would be a curiosity in a court of law, but is only a written form of the melodrama that Vinod puts into all his oral negotiations.

Dear Sanjay,

SUBJECT: *Mission Kashmir*

1. I believe what has been happening over the last few weeks in the context of *Mission Kashmir* is astounding in terms of the shape that the project is taking, whether it is the script or the music or most of all the interest and the commitment being shown by you. I truly believe that the project is taking on staggering proportions.

2. I appreciate this commitment but I want to let you know that I value your friendship and our relationship even more. I don't ever want any misunderstanding specially on the more mundane issues of remuneration etc. to come in the way of this relationship. This is why I have discussed this issue with you quite frankly and candidly. I just want to put down here as a memory jogger what you and I have agreed on this issue.

3. Much as I would like to pay you what you would be getting outside, but keeping in view that I do not take recourse to the normal ugly channels of finances, I would be paying you Rs. *25 lakhs*. However, please bear in mind that if the film does not do well, I would only pay you a token sum of Rs. *0*. I hope this finds your approval.

With best wishes,

Yours truly,

VIDHU VINOD CHOPRA

And underneath, a handwritten line: *Bonus 25 lakhs if film is a success*.

The contracts for the three leads are identical in their language. The figures in the case of the second male lead, Hrithik, are 11 lakhs if the film breaks even, 1 lakh if it doesn't, and a bonus of 10 lakhs if the film is a hit. For the female lead, Preity, the payment is 15 lakhs if the film makes money, 1 lakh if not, and a bonus of 10 lakhs for a hit. Although the figures change later as the budget and Hrithik's popularity swell, Vinod has covered his bets well; if *Mission Kashmir* goes the way of *Kareeb*, the total payment he will be out for to his stars is a piffling 2 lakhs. Similar terms have been arranged with the music directors, the cameraman, and others in the crew. Nobody gets any advances. Sometimes, nobody gets anything after they work either. "When *Kareeb* flopped, my art director didn't get any money," Vinod says. But he made it up later. When he made an advertising film, he hired the same art director and paid him three times the normal rate. "It's very un-American. This can't happen in America," notes Vinod.

WE NEED AT LEAST FOUR SONGS for *Mission Kashmir*. Ideally, the record companies would like a movie to have eight songs, so they can fill both sides of a cassette. But recognizing that strife-torn Kashmir, with two bloodthirsty antagonists, does not make an ideal locale for a Bollywood number, Vinod originally thinks of settling for four songs, which is enough for one side of a cassette. "The other side can be filled with background music." By the time the movie is finished, the number of songs has almost doubled, to seven. This is another creative decision forced by economics; the earliest revenue a Hindi film producer will see comes from advance sales of the music to record companies. Vinod's films have traditionally done well overseas, as have the soundtracks of his previous films. His films are known, above all, for the excellence of their music; even people who have never seen *1942* will instantly recognize the tune of "Ek Ladki ko Dekha" and start humming along. He sells the music up front for three crores before he's shot a single frame, getting two crores in advance, which partly finances the production of the film.

Vinod reads out the lyrics composed for the songs by Rahat Indori. They have to do with flowers, with homeland, with destruction, with bombs. I ask Vinod if the lyrics are always in Urdu. "It's difficult to know which is Hindi and which is Urdu," he says. Since this is a film about Kashmir, the language used will tilt toward Urdu. This nationalist filmmaker, like all the rest of them, makes his films in Hindustani, not Hindi.

The musicians are three hip young guys from the ad world: Shankar, Ehsaan, and Loy; a Hindu, a Muslim, and a Christian. I call them Amar Akbar Anthony. They play three songs for us in their music studio. They've overlaid the tracks with samples from all over the world. "Give me the Burundi drums," says Ehsaan. Then he overdubs a Senegalese call to prayer from the album *Passion Sources,* itself a compilation of world music sources for the Martin Scorsese–Peter Gabriel collaboration *The Last Temptation of Christ.* The talk in the studio is of Nino Rota, Vangelis, John Coltrane. Into the mix are thrown tablas, guitars, piano, water bells, and the sound of an oar dipping into lake water. Hindi film music was world beat before Peter Gabriel or Paul Simon ever heard a talking drum. "For centuries people have been taking rhythms from all around the world, not instruments," Loy points out. For example, music from the coastal regions of the world often shares the same basic rhythms. He drums them out with his mouth.

Bombay music now is different from the Bombay music I grew up with. For one thing, it relies more on electronic instruments and on African rhythms and voices. Many of the dance numbers feature a deep black voice popping up in the middle of the Hindi, declaring his laughing love for the very female Hindi voice. Indians like their male voices deep and their female voices high. But these days not that many people know the names of the playback singers; the Mangeshkar sisters no longer hold a monopoly. With the advent of electronic music, background music now competes with voice in a Hindi film song; the synthesizer is often more important and noticeable than the singer. And the masses love it; the great panwallah audience dances to it. Old-timers wince and complain, as old-timers are wont to do. They get especially incensed when the new boys set their elec-tronics on the old songs and remix them with thumping disco beats and reggae voices and samples of rap. Suddenly a slow song, a lament, or a ten-der ballad becomes an urgent call to congress.

Electronics opened up a whole new world to the Hindi film composers. They went a little crazy. Now they do not have to look for instrumentalists who know what a samba or a merengue beat is. They can steal it right off the synthesizer, off the sample compilation CDs. The digital readouts on Loy's synthesizers announce the instruments they are mimicking: SWEET VIOLINS, AFRO DRUMS. I can make out ZOUK, and SENEGALESE CHANTING, and ZYDECO. Anything with a beat. This includes European classical music; the Indian musicians have not forgotten Mozart and have dressed up the Viennese lad in bongos and congas. Hindi film music is like Hinduism. All who come to invade it are themselves absorbed, digested, and regurgi-tated. Nothing musical is alien to it.

One evening I take my family to see *Kuch Kuch Hota Hai,* a wonderfully entertaining film even though it falls apart in the home stretch. There are no villains in it. It is a big Punjabi puppy-love film about college romance, the middle-class Indian's halcyon days. I have seen this school campus before somewhere. I know these characters. I try to think where. Then two words in a newspaper report about the set designer bring it back to me: Riverdale High. It was the American comic book resurrected in Hindi: Betty and Veronica fighting over Archie. The filmmakers grew up on Archie comics, which I too read, for a peep into America. When you want to escape India, you go to suburban America.

My son Gautama sings "Kuch Kuch Hota Hai" and "Chal Mra Ghoda," in addition to "I'm a Barbie Girl" and "Twinkle Twinkle Little Star." He is gathering his sources of pleasure from East and West. He is building his own vocabulary of Hindi film music that I have carried around all my life. When he is asked what he will miss when he goes back to America, he says straightaway, "Hindi movies." When he misses Bombay in New York, he will sing "Kuch Kuch Hota Hai" on the sidewalks of the far city. An Indian boy in America, singing a Hindi song from an Indian movie imitation of an American comic book; a Ping-Pong game of kitsch. Along with the Bhagavad Gita and Thoreau's essay on civil disobedience, this too has wings.

OVER THE MONTHS we work on *Mission Kashmir,* Vinod opens his home and his heart to me. He has been married three times, "and none of them knows how to make an omelet," he complains. But both ex-wives visit his house regularly. When he has a backache, I walk into his house to witness the filmmaker lying on the floor, each of his three women—his harem, Anu calls it—massaging a different segment of his body. When he married Anu, he took her to the house of his first mother-in-law, who put the tilak on her forehead and blessed her, saying, "You are a daughter of this house." He sees no reason to stop loving his ex-wives because he's not married to them; more important, he sees no reason why they should stop loving him.

I'm not sure why Vinod has taken me on. Then, slowly, I realize that what he wants is not so much a writer as a friend. I start getting invited to intimate functions at the Chopra household: birthdays, anniversaries, celebrations. No film folk are invited; often it is just Anu and Vinod's immediate families, my family, and Ajay Lal and his family. Vinod has a way of sucking up other people's lives and making them his own. He calls me every single morning and demands to know when I am getting to his house for the script session; when I make signs of wanting to leave in the evening, his face falls like that of one who is doomed to a long, lonely night. In the beginning I would accede to Vinod's request to show up at eleven in the morning; gradually, as I realize I am getting to the director's house before he has risen from his bed, I start stretching it.

When my family leaves for America and I am alone for two months, Vinod summons me to his house one day and then calls for his cook. "From now on," he instructs Khem, "lunch and dinner will be sent to Suketu from our house." I protest, but Vinod will hear none of it. Every evening, Vinod's driver arrives with an insulated tiffin full of Punjabi or Chinese or Italian vegetarian food; every morning another driver takes away the empty tiffin. In a poor country with a bad public health system, food takes on heightened meaning. In this filmi family, improbably, I have found a species of home.

I invite people to my house for my birthday, and it is a tense party, with people who don't like one another and not enough of them. Vinod changes his shooting schedule to make it. He arrives late, when almost everybody has left, but he fills up the room. He has just been to a filmi party and is full of entertaining stories and three beers. All of a sudden my party is happening, and I feel a rush of affection for him. In my two years in Bombay, he has been the one man who has always been generous with his time and his hospitality. It is done in a Punjabi way, not without taking something back and not without calling this fact to my attention. But there is an exuberance to him, a gregariousness, that puts a smile on the faces of people around him, people in the late stages of a lukewarm party. Being around Vinod, I get a sense that anything is possible: to marry and divorce women, make a lot of money, own a big house in Bandra, live a large life. Vinod carries his own power source within him, like an alkaline battery, like a nuclear submarine.

Mahesh Bhatt's Wound

Mahesh Bhatt is in a bad mood. We are on a set for *Mumbai Meri Jaan*, a story about a middle-class immigrant to Bombay who makes good while retaining his small-town values. Tanuja Chandra is assisting him, and it is not going well. "I'm angry," he rumbles ominously through the microphone. "There's no enthusiasm."

The set is supposed to be Chunky Pandey's bedroom—"my open-air Taj Mahal," as one of his lines reads. There are the accoutrements of middle-class success: a bar stocked with Chivas Regal, a TV, a kitchen, and "a western-foreign-German-style toilet," as another of Chunky's lines describes it, continuing, "I stole the seat cover from a five-star hotel." This visual extravaganza is being staged on the roof of the Happy Home and School for the Blind in Worli. A giant CEAT tire sign above us comes alive in red, gradually extinguishes itself, and reappears. There are about a hundred and fifty people on the set: light boys, sound people, actors, assorted assistants, and a sizable group of people who are doing absolutely nothing. "Only two or three people here know their job," says Mahesh disgustedly. "That's why our films have rough edges. It's not like Hollywood, where everyone's trained. I'm running a giant employment agency. They work with the whip." The Indian film industry, like every other industry in the country, employs far more people than it needs to. The actors, especially Chunky, flub their lines repeatedly and the whole shot has to be done again. "Bhatt saab, please come here," pleads Chunky after a rehearsal. Mahesh stays where he is. "You don't need me to come there. You need to learn your lines. *Learn* your *lines!*"

Mumbai meri Jaan, like so many other movies, offers a generic Bombay for sale to the provinces: rich people, fast women in fast cars, gangsters, policemen, consumer goods. To the Bihari immigrant walking around South Bombay, this part of the city is unreal, a film set. So astronomical are the prices for the flats here that the outsider does not say to himself, walking around Malabar Hill, "One day I shall live here." He is walking in a dreamscape. Like this ridiculous set. If it were real, it would be washed away—the bed, bar, toilet, red phone booth "stolen from MTNL," the phone company—everything, with the first rain.

I don't know what I had expected when I met Mahesh: a good artist who had sold out? a philanderer? He has a reputation as a gasbag, losing no opportunity to be quoted in the papers on all manner of issues, including those entirely unrelated to cinema. I find an overweight, balding, rumpled man who looks older than his forty-nine years but is charming and likable and most at ease with the young.

He is now writing a film set during the time of the riots, about his mother. She is a woman of two secrets. One is that she is his father's mistress; he and his siblings are illegitimate. The other is that she is a Shia Muslim. One day his mother stopped outside a wedding hall and asked his elder sister to go inside. When the girl returned, his mother interrogated her about the wedding—how did the bride look? how was the groom?—and wept all night. It was the wedding of her lover, Mahesh's father, to a more respectable woman.

The relationship continued after the marriage, all his mother's life. When his father, a Gujarati Brahmin producer of B movies, would visit their home, "there was never any completion," says the producer son about his producer father. "He never once took his shoes off. He would never take off his shirt like other fathers and put on a singlet and sit down and read the newspaper." Mahesh adores his mother, now in her eighties. "I used to bring glowworms in a bottle to put in my mother's hair," he says, with an easy laugh.

The film about his mother and the riots—*Zakhm*, Wound—is the last film Mahesh will direct. He has sworn this. He has averaged more than one movie a year, some twenty-seven films in his quarter-century career. Mahesh is bored by the whole exercise of direction. It is concentrated hard work, seven days a week, toward a pointless exercise. He is now at the stage where he "phone-directs" some of his movies. He hates driving to the film shoots, hates having to appear enthusiastic. So he issues instructions to the actors on the set over the phone, as he's driving or from home.

"My earliest memories of the movies are sitting inside a preview theater on someone's lap—my mother or my aunt or the maid—and seeing this black-and-white screen. I went toward it to try to touch it"—he mimes a child's hand slowly touching a huge screen—"but as I got nearer it was just black and white dots and I lost the picture. Then I was pulled back. My life has become like that; I don't see the magic anymore. It's just the making of the film, and there are no arms to pull me back so I can see the whole picture."

He tells me the plot of *Zakhm*, in which the secret of the hero's mother's religion comes out only at the end, when he has to decide what type of funeral to give her. The film is in the form of a flashback during the Bombay riots, when the hero is at the hospital at his mother's bedside with

Thackeray's mobs loose outside. He would not, however, name Thackeray in the movie. "I don't want to make a film about politics."

The Hindi film industry has always had the secularism of a brothel. All are welcome as long as they carry or make money. The financier might be a hard-core Hindu nationalist. The lyricist can be a fundamentalist Sunni. A star who plays a Hindu will actually be Muslim, and his heroine, playing a Muslim, will be Hindu, and none of that matters to the public. But the 1993 riots toppled the pyramids of power in the film industry. The lower-level technicians became newly bold and demanded favors, questioned authority. The Sena men were making the rounds of the studios to check for Muslim employees. Hindus higher up in the industry, not knowing that Mahesh's mother was a Muslim, would abuse Muslims in front of him. One of Mahesh's light men was trapped in Behrampada, one of the worst-hit areas. His family was surrounded by a Hindu mob and his wife was screaming on the phone to Mahesh, "They're coming to get us!" Mahesh was trying to get food sent to the light man's house when one of his Hindu spot boys came up and told him their union was asking Bhatt Saheb not to take up the case of the Muslims. Mahesh responded angrily, "He's not a Muslim, he's an employee!"

We discuss how all this might enter into *Zakhm*. He sees the hero as a man in love with his mother, deeply hating the man who would come to fuck her. "It's a triangle," he explains. At his mother's funeral, as he is walking, sacred verses from Hinduism, Islam, and Christianity ring through his head. "I have the soundtrack in my head," he says. He tells me about how his mother would take him to a church, where he would be asked to "kiss the blood of Christ, kiss the blood of Jesus." Then she would take him to a Muslim shrine and make him recite, "Lahilla Allah Lahilla." While bathing him, she would recite his caste origins, "You are a Nagar. Your gotra is Bhargava." Because she considered herself married to her Hindu lover, she kept the Muslim part of herself secret. As a boy, Mahesh hated her for being Muslim, so he would try to disturb her namaaz. As an adult, he has decided to celebrate her and her religious identity through this movie. But his mother is fearful. During the riots, she asked whether it was safe for him to give his two daughters Muslim names. *Zakhm* will borrow from Mahesh's life in more ways than one. His mother will be played by her own granddaughter, Mahesh's daughter Pooja.

Like Vinod, Mahesh hates the business that has been so good to him. "This is a sick industry. There's no fucking money here—it's a victim of its own hype." When he makes a film now, there is a fear it won't work, right at the outset, because nine out of eleven films don't make back their investment. He has lost his feel for the formula. "I can analyze it but the flow is missing." But he knows exactly what his purpose in life is, as a man who makes movies. "We are distilleries of pleasure."

TANUJA ARRANGES A PREVIEW of *Sangharsh* just for my friends, in gratitude for having helped her in the making of it in Madanpura. It is a strange meeting of worlds, my book come alive. There is Monalisa and Girish and Sunil and Kamal and Rustom and Ishaq, and a whole host from Madanpura. After the show, they all stand in two lines along the corridor, resting against the walls, shy, awkward, as Mahesh and Tanuja stand at the head of the line and talk to me. They have just been to the Novelty cinema and have seen a full house, hundreds of people, rapt in their creation. *Sangharsh* is getting blasted by the critics. "But when I saw all those people at Novelty," Tanuja says, "I felt they were a more important audience than the intellectuals."

"That is your *only* audience!" booms Mahesh. "Never forget that."

We all go to the Gallops restaurant at the racetrack. The maker of the film about the riots sits across the table from the rioter. Sunil patiently feeds his daughter, whom he has brought along to see the big people. But conversation flags. The class boundary is too high.

The preview for my friends turns out to be unexpectedly profitable for Tanuja. A couple of days later, she calls me, frantic. She has just seen her film, not three days old in the theaters, on her TV screen. It is being aired illegally by the cable operators in Bandra and Borivali. The overseas distributors, who don't have a stake in the Indian market, sell prints of new films to the local cable operators. The first week is crucial for a Hindi film; most of the money it makes in its lifetime will be made during that week, and if people can already watch it on their TV screens, why should they pay to see it in a theater? Tanuja wants me to ask Sunil, the cable operator, not to screen it in his area. Sunil tells me there is one cable "distributor" for the suburbs whom she should speak to. A deal is struck. As a favor to

Tanuja, because she is a friend of Sunil's and has done him the honor of inviting him to her premiere, the cable operators of Bombay and Thane will desist from screening it for their subscribers for one month on the distributor's orders. And for a payment of 50,000 rupees.

"But this is blackmail!" I protest.

"It's a good deal," she responds.

Filmmakers go to great lengths to protect their films from getting into the hands of the pirates, who sell DVDs even before the film is released. With *Kareeb,* Vinod traveled around India, personally appealing to police departments to protect his films from cable piracy. In Ahmadabad, he told me, a senior police officer lined up the leading cable operators of the city after Vinod complained that it was being shown illegally on TV there. "What shall I do with them?" the policeman asked Vinod.

"Break their legs," he suggested.

"No problem," responded the officer.

I OPEN THE PAPER one Monday morning and see a large photograph of an old woman under the name SHIRIN, a Muslim name—but she is wearing the Hindu tilak on her forehead. Mahesh's mother has died. But her celluloid version is about to be born on the big screen.

As the film's release date approaches, a controversy arises over whether or not Mahesh is really a bastard. Mahesh's film—and much of his life—is built on the premise that he is. His father says he isn't and places an advertisement in the papers to that effect, claiming he legally married Mahesh's mother. Ugly insults fly between the family members. "My mother was supposed to be his mistress," Mahesh insists to me. "Though they repeatedly claimed they were married, they had no documents to prove it." Mahesh's illegitimacy is very important to his sense of who he is. And now Mahesh is a big man. The bastard has become a star and can fight his demons in 70mm, with 1 billion people as his audience. His mother, who always had to hide her love, for her God and her man, has been reincarnated as her granddaughter and is now the goddess, the object of veneration, of celebration. Her son has made her legitimate again. By celebrating his illegitimacy, Mahesh is also vanquishing it. Art is where you fight your demons.

Mahesh takes me to the all-important Censor Board preview of *Zakhm*. We wait outside on the terrace of the Liberty Cinema until the board is finished viewing and debating the film. As we go in, the chairwoman of the committee says, "We want to commend you for a very sensitive film."

Mahesh, Tanuja, and I stand in one of the front rows, with our backs to the screen, facing the censors: four Hindu women and one Hindu man, all middle-class types, doctors, accountants.

The chairwoman starts asking why the Muslim policeman is shown as the good guy. The policeman is Hindu, Tanuja insists. "What's his name?" the chairwoman asks. Mahesh and Tanuja look at each other. He's a Hindu policeman, they say, but he is just called Sharad, which is the actor's name. The censors want that to be made explicit, so it won't look as if the police are divided along communal lines. "Although we all know that the force is communalized," the chairwoman adds. Also, the line spoken by the bad Hindu cop, "This Mussulman boy—" should be changed to "This boy—"

Mahesh agrees with the woman before she finishes her sentence. This is his last film, and he has been to dozens of such bargaining sessions. In the elevator going up, he had told me about how, at his first censor screening when he was twenty-one, he argued with the censors and refused to make the cuts they demanded and walked from Liberty to Mahim because he was so angry. He thought that twenty-five years later things would have changed for the better, but they haven't. All that's changed is that he is much less confrontational.

The chairwoman commends Mahesh for the fact that his film has no nudity, no onscreen violence, no profanity, and for the sensitive handling of the illegitimacy issue. However, she says that because the film deals with issues of communalism, the board has decided on the A, for Adult, certificate.

This is a death blow to the film's revenues; people will not be able to bring their children under eighteen to the movie, eliminating a substantial part of the audience.

Mahesh makes a very low-key plea for them to change their minds. "I don't want to get into an argument, but I feel this film should be seen by younger children." If fourteen- and fifteen-year-olds could see it and be swayed by its ideas of tolerance and for the ideal of a united country, it would benefit the country, he says. But he leaves it up to them. The chairwoman says they will think about their decision and let him know tomorrow. If they stick with their A decision, it will also affect the television sales of the film. So there is an economic incentive for filmmakers not to deal with political issues. Reality is not for children—or for teenagers either.

THE CENSORS FINALLY INSIST on an A certificate. The chairwoman of the committee argued strenuously for a U/A certificate, but the others on the committee wanted to go even further, showing it to the police force for their approval, lest it incite communal hatred. If the film caused trouble, the committee would shoulder the blame for having passed it without any cuts.

As it turns out, getting an A certificate is the least of Mahesh's troubles. Without having seen the film but on the basis of a written synopsis, the chairperson of the overall Censor Board, a faded actress, refers the film to the state Home Department for clearance. One of the functionaries on the Censor Board—made up mostly of housewives and men with time on their hands—has been unable to sleep all night after watching the film, and this is one of the reasons the chairperson gives for needing it to be cleared by the government. The film should properly have been referred to the Union Government, since it is an India-wide release. Taking a film about the riots for approval to the very government that was implicated in the riots is asking for certain trouble. And the state government can really make things tough for Mahesh if it has a yen to; it can shut down all his projects, including his television serials. He tells me this is his last film, and he's not prepared to lose his dignity; like other filmmakers, he won't go to Bal Thackeray, cap in hand.

Mahesh's daughter Pooja comes along to our meeting with the chief secretary of the Maharashtra government, Mr. Subrahmanyam. I am traveling with them as one of their writers. It is in the bureaucrat's office; through its two large bay windows, all I can see is the sky and the Air India building. It is one of the rare views in Bombay uncontaminated by human beings. The secretary himself is a fat man with a face scarred by a skin disorder that has turned it white and red, as if it were strobe-lit. Pooja is there essentially as ornamentation, as star dazzle. The chief secretary isn't dazzled. He is a big man in his chair, a god in his frog pond. And he lets us know it.

The secretary recounts how he had cleared the film *Bombay,* on which he says he was alone against the government in holding that an artist had the right to his opinions. The police had opposed him. But clearance was possible only after the film's director had appealed to Thackeray; Amitabh Bacchan had personally gone to the Sena leader and begged for his permission to release it. The film was about the riots, and Hindus and Muslims were shown as being equally to blame for the events. When the film was shown to the Saheb for his imprimatur, he wanted just one scene cut: the one at the end where his alter ego is shown apologizing for the massacres and the burning. He had no wish to forgo responsibility for his valiant acts.

"He bought his peace," the secretary recalls, suggesting that Mahesh should do likewise. Mahesh refuses. "I am not prepared to do that." The secretary's assistant then says he will have to get a letter from the chairperson saying that the Censor Board would not release the film, but the letter wouldn't be forthcoming. She would say the film would be judged by a higher tribunal, and the matter was being looked into by the state government. "Since they have not made any decision, you can't appeal it," the secretary points out. Mahesh's timing is bad, he adds. The Srikrishna Commission Report has just come out. "If your film is anti-Hindu—and if you are saying the truth about the riots it *has* to be anti-Hindu—it won't see the light of day."

Mahesh says that it does take a position against the Hindus.

In that case, declares the secretary, "It will remain in the cans. We will ban it." He does it all the time; that very morning, the secretary says, he banned a play. He makes it very clear that he thinks the Hindus started the riots; nevertheless "the present government is pro-Hindu. You would not have had this problem under the Congress government."

Mahesh and Tanuja try to explain that the riots figure only peripherally in the film, and scenes of rioting are never actually shown. The chief secretary says he hasn't seen the film but, he repeats, it will still "never see the light of day" if it said the truth and took a position against the Hindus. "Hindus like to think they are secular, when they aren't." He laughs. "Muslims aren't secular at all." Recalling the emotional power of Mahesh's earlier films, such as *Saaransh* and *Arth*, the secretary adds, "If it's emotionally very strong you're in trouble." Mahesh's movies are innocent of subtlety or restraint. A Sikh always carries a sword; a Muslim always has on a skullcap and Ali Baba–style shoes. He doesn't believe in holding back the tears; he gets his actors to cry as often as possible. Tanuja, who had co-written *Zakhm*, had defined for me the secret of success in a Hindi movie: "It has to make people's insides churn." The Indian public thinks with its heart. This passion can topple governments, empires. The government can stomach a documentary film about the riots but not an emotional, main-stream one. The Enlightenment hasn't reached these shores; it carries no weight. Democracy here is a balancing of opposing passions.

Mahesh responds that he will go to Delhi and meet the prime minister, who had recently told him he admired his work. The chief secretary laughs. "He has a hawk as home minister. The film will be shown to him" and it will be banned.

MAHESH AND TANUJA WORK right through Diwali, frantically trying to get the film through the various political and bureaucratic hurdles, tak-ing the issue to the media. The film is screened for a committee of govern-ment officials, including the Bombay Police Commissioner, who then asks for a police nominee on the Censor Board, to screen every film to filter out negative portrayals of policemen. "It generates more heat—the fact that a bad cop is there—than the neutral effect generated by a good cop," the commissioner explains.

Mahesh gives in and makes some cuts and reshoots some scenes to please the censors. The saffron headbands that the rioters wear, which "represent a certain political party" according to the written report from the Censor Board, are replaced with black ones. A scene "where Muslim char-acter is pointing out his frustrations is not necessary." A staged encounter where the police shoot a man running away from them is deleted. A speech made by the Thackeray stand-in—"We have tolerated these people long enough and now the time has come for a national cleansing"—is cut. Mahesh wants it both ways. He wants to be a hero to the press, for holding the torch of defiance against a fascist establishment; but he also wants his film released. Crores are riding on it.

After the political cuts are made, *Zakhm* is released and goes on to win an award from the President of India: Best Feature Film on National Integration.

The Struggler and the Goddess

I am at a table outside the Sun 'n' Sand Hotel in Juhu in the late afternoon, watching the sun begin its decline and fall into the sea. This is the hotel where movie stars and gang lords used to come to see and be seen, the hotel where Monalisa lost her virginity to the movie producer Hari Virani.

Ali Peter John likes lounging by the poolside of the Sun 'n' Sand hotel, especially when his vodka and chicken sandwich are paid for by someone else. But he is no sponger; he pays for his meal in stories, many times over. For Ali Peter John is, as his former drinking buddy Mahesh Bhatt describes him, "God of the strugglers." His perch as a columnist for *Screen* magazine gives him license to roam the highways and bylanes of Bollywood.

Ali is a fixer, a messenger between worlds, a conduit between high and low Bombay. In appearance he is a low, shambling, suspicious sort of figure, with what is called in the marriage market "disunited vision," so he can look at you without looking at you. He sports a short beard that makes him look like a smuggler's henchman and generally fails to button the top half of his shirt. But his articles in *Screen* read almost like sermons, so full of moral purpose are they.

Ali is an authority on B and C movies, the sudras and untouchables— and sure-fire moneymakers—of the industry. The film trade magazines are filled with full-page color ads for them, in the sex-and-horror category. Such films are shot very quickly, start to finish in a week, in rented bungalows on Madh Island. Then they are shown to the Censor Board in Madras, where the censors are more lenient than in Bombay. They often do better than the big-budget films in the interiors, places like UP and MP, and the small theaters in Old Delhi, and they have names like *The Devil and Death*, *Thirsty Soul*, and *Vampire*. "They're a mix of horror, sex, and loud music," explains Ali. Often, in the late shows, hard-core porn is inserted at random within the film by the individual theater owners, footage that has nothing to do with the advertised film but is the real draw for the almost entirely male audience.

Listening to Ali, you get the impression of a man who is haunted by the struggling actors who have come to Bombay and failed; he retains special solicitude for women. Ali says that of every hundred girls who come to the city to become actresses, "ten are lucky, ninety are doomed." The auditions are often held in places like the Hotel Seaside in Juhu, which Ali has renamed the Hotel Suicide, because of what it drives some of the female strugglers to after an audition in one of its rooms.

The movies will always be linked with sex and death for Ali; both signify opportunity. "Whenever anyone died we got a holiday in school and saw films." He grew up in Andheri East, home of poor Christians and Warli tribals. When the junior artistes started renting flats there, "it was like the invasion of a certain culture." The Warli women were very beautiful, and the struggling actors would pick them up, telling them, "we are from the world of the movies." The boy Ali was very impressed by the flamboyant actors, and it was a shock for him to learn, when he grew up, that "they were working as peons in offices." He now sees them in the speakeasies on Yaari Road in Andheri, in the Urvashi beer bar, in Leo's Country Liquor Bar, behind the dirty curtain, sitting over their 9-rupee bottle of desi liquor and planning the ways they will conquer the world, telling the other strugglers, "Tomorrow I have a shoot with Amitabh Bacchan."

"Being in this line for so many years, I am very shocked at their level of hiding reality," says Ali. "They will never show you they are frustrated." The better-off strugglers live in certain hotels and guesthouses that are associated with luck. The Marina Guest House in Bandra, for example; Rajendra Kumar used to live there. Ali tells me what the strugglers survive on: the Rice Plate. "Eight rupees. Rice, six puris or two chapatis, one dal. If the hotel is very large-hearted, then a small container of very watery curd and two vegetables. Eaten in the right place, it is the most balanced diet. Sometimes if they are in a good mood they give you sweet also." For the struggler who is getting small roles, there are the Muslim-owned hotels, where for 20 rupees he can get a very good biryani.

Ali and I take a rickshaw to Yaari Road, which is buzzing in the evening, with lots of little eateries along the sides. Ali points out a waiter at one shack: "That guy has eight stories in his pocket. He is ready to narrate. There must be lakhs of film stories in Bombay." Just as there are struggling actors, there are also struggling scriptwriters. They seek an audience with a producer or director and narrate their story in real time and with real acting. In the emotional scenes, they weep affectingly. In the action scenes, they jump and flail around in the director's office. They will usually have saved the director the trouble of casting; the star is already picked out. "And Vinod Khanna is running, running . . . he falls on the ground, rolls on the ground . . . and then he gets caught." Ali mimics the narration. "Meanwhile, Vinod Khanna is nowhere, he is away drinking somewhere."

The long-distance telephone booths of Yaari Road are full of young people phoning home, telling their parents, their siblings, that the big break is just around the corner. Many of them belong to the junior artistes guild and have a precise caste system, Ali explains. If an actor in a party scene is wearing a suit, he is considered A-Class and gets paid double the amount that goes to another actor, relegated to C-Class because he is standing behind the A-Class actor. The strugglers whom nature has blessed with a resemblance to Amitabh Bacchan or Shahrukh Khan find work as professional doubles. Some female equivalents work in brothels. The hick from out of town is shown a photo album of the house's inventory. He picks a film-heroine look-alike, pays an exorbitant sum for her favors, and due to the low light and his nervousness goes back home convinced that he has spent a night with a Bombay actress. Every time he sees her onscreen he flushes with secret pride.

Ali promises to introduce me to a "genuine struggler," a man named Eishaan.

A few days later, we are sitting in the canteen of Filmalaya Studios. It is a shack, but a five-star shack according to Ali, because it has five fans. Across from me at the table—which is fashioned from a giant Coca-Cola billboard—is a clear-faced, bright-eyed young man, wearing an earring in one ear and a gold teddy bear dangling from a chain around his neck. His brother Hitesh sits next to him, so different in looks he must have come from another gene pool. This is one of Ali's acolytes, Eishaan the struggler. "If he wasn't struggling he'd never be sitting in this canteen," declares Ali. For Eishaan did not run away from a village in Bihar to come to the film world to try his luck; he managed a flourishing cloth business in Dubai for five years before he came to Bombay. He is a Sindhi, a nonresident Indian struggler, who has seen both feast and famine in his twenty-five years. He has traveled in a Mercedes, in a Rolls-Royce, and in the Bombay local trains. He stayed with thirteen people in a one-bedroom flat in Andheri before his family moved to a house in Jaipur, which his mother sold her jewelry to buy. He's been dreaming about being a hero since he was sixteen and poring over the centerfolds in *Screen* magazine. At that time one of his uncles, working for a production company in Bombay, got him work as a model in a photo shoot, and he pocketed 800 rupees. For a teenager in Jaipur, it must have been a big deal, signifying much more than its purchasing power.

The teenager finished school up to the twelfth standard and then his family moved to Dubai, where he managed a textile shop for an Arab man, making 70,000 rupees a month. Then in the Gulf War business went down. He kept visiting Bombay. He felt he should do something else, something closer to his heart. Back in Dubai, a supermarket manager named Starson—"he knew about stars"—wandered into the cloth shop. "He used to tell me, You are not an ordinary person. I see something in you." The young man was in this cloth shop at this time, Starson said, but it was only a rest stop, to drink some water. "This is not the end. You'll be ruling."

This boy felt he could tell Starson his dream. "He said do it. There will be a lot of trouble, but never give up."

So the cloth shop manager left Dubai and went to Bombay to be a movie star. When he came to the city, it had changed its name to Mumbai, so he changed his name too. When he was born, his parents, with their middle-class lack of imagination, had named him Mahesh, the sheer ordinariness of which he had been laboring under all these years. In the fifties and sixties, Muslim actors changed their names to Hindu ones—such as Dilip Kumar—to be accepted. In the nineties, there was no such need. Even as the BJP and the Sena were ascendant, the biggest movie stars in the country were a trio of Muslim stars, the Khans: Shahrukh, Aamir, and Salman. Mahesh changed his name to Eishaan, which has an Urdu ring, a filmi ring, to it.

Eishaan started out taking a multitude of classes: action classes, acting classes, dance classes. The dance class cost 1,000 rupees a month, the action class 5,000 rupees for three months, and the acting class cost 15,000 rupees. In the action classes they were taught Tae Kwon Do. Then they would be taken to the beach to learn filmi action—diving and rolling and throwing punches. He demonstrates. "They should pass by just a little bit," just barely missing the body, just as the audience hears the satisfying *dhishoom!* He thought the acting teacher saw something special in him. "My sir Roshan Taneja kept me on as an assistant for a year and a half," he says proudly. Then he adds, "Unpaid. It was my honor."

He got offered roles in C films and in television serials, but he had set his sights on the A films. Eishaan is very clear about what kind of roles he will accept. "I came here with an intention of becoming a hero. It was not to become an actor." He then met a producer who promised him a role in a film he was doing. Every two or three months he would inquire of the producer about the status of the film and would be told, "We're looking for a director." The director was never found. Meanwhile, Eishaan had stopped making his rounds of the producers' offices, believing that his launch was imminent. He kept waiting for a year and a half, and in that period he lost his other contacts.

He started afresh, and after four or five months he met Chetan Anand at a fashion studio and gave the director his portfolio. Chetan Anand was a legendary film director who had come over from Pakistan after Partition and was part of a film dynasty. He was doing a film about Partition, a Muslim girl falling in love with a Hindu boy. Eishaan was at a friend's place when he got the call from Chetan Anand. "You're on," said the director. "I was out of the world," recalls the struggler. "I started dreaming, when they say 'Action!' how I would react." He spent nine months with the director, recording seven songs. Then the eighty-seven-year old Anand fell sick. "He had some liver problem; he lost both livers," says Eishaan. Anand died, and so did the movie.

Eishaan's family and friends demanded that he come back to the cloth business. "But people don't understand the importance of a Chetan Anand sitting with me discussing a scene for hours on end. That was pleasing to the actor in me. But a mother and father sitting in Jaipur don't know who Chetan Anand *is*. My parents were praying to God: 'Give him some intelligence and make him come back.' "

Eishaan decided to stay in the city, because if he left he could never return. "Now here came the truth: However much you bend, the world will make you bend more." The struggler was now having trouble even getting into television, at which he had turned up his nose earlier. Now even film actors were ready to do television, in the economic slump of the mid-nineties. And the TV producers wanted known faces even on the small screen. Eishaan made his daily rounds of the producers' offices, carrying his two pictures of himself. "I know what happens to those pictures, when there are more than ten thousand people coming to your office."

I have seen such pictures in a thick photo album in Vinod's office, for the director to consult when he is casting minor roles. The album has young people, old people, children, mothers, grandfathers. It has attractive, even stunning, people; it has repulsive and villainous people. It has demure Hindustani naris; it has tarty vamps with breasts spilling out of tight blouses. All of humanity that is useful to the screen is represented here. They start out in the pages of this album on the first stage of their long journey to the screen, where the pictures come alive with a jerk.

Every morning Eishaan goes to the gym or for a jog, to keep fit and, more important, to look fit. He has to spend on clothes, to keep up his presentation, until he proves himself as an actor; then, as with the older, established Hindi film actors, he can safely run to fat and dress like a slob. His car is in an advanced state of melancholy. The white Maruti has a large brown rust spot on the front, and when you close the door it rattles shut. But he keeps it anyway, at considerable expense. "To get entry inside a studio you need a car, so the doorman will salute you. In a taxi he'll let you go; in a rickshaw he'll ask you questions; and if you're walking he won't allow you in. When I was working in Dubai I was the boss; now I have to say 'sir, sir.' For a struggler, this is the rule of life: You have be very buttery."

His is the eternal quandary of the novice job seeker. "I don't understand when they ask you 'What have you done? Have you done anything before?' If everyone asks the same question, when do I get the chance to do something?" He envies the female strugglers. "Girls have it easy; there is the couch." Eishaan avoids modeling because of the homosexuals in the fashion business. He sometimes resents the hundreds of thousands of people who want to be stars and compete with him at the lower end of the chain, who are willing to work for free. "Every Tom, Dick, and Harry brushing his teeth in the mirror thinks, If Nana Patekar can do it why not me? But they make it tough for people who are actually talented."

When Eishaan came to Bombay, he was inspired by the stories of stars who had come up the rough way, such as Mithun Chakraborty. "He was my idol, the way he struggled, the way he came up in life. He used to sleep in footpaths, he was eager to get his bread." So worshipful of Mithun was Eishaan that he once had a big fight with his father over him. In his house in Jaipur, he had installed a huge laminated portrait of the star in the living room. When Eishaan's father came down from Dubai and saw the picture, he removed it without his son's knowledge. Eishaan went on a hunger fast.

His family, faced with a choice between living with the dark actor's massive likeness and their son's starving to death, yielded. They put the picture back up.

Eishaan is on the lookout for One Good Role. He knows that people aren't taking chances on newcomers—the costs of movies these days don't allow for risk-taking—but One Good Role can make it all happen, like it did for Manoj Bajpai, who struggled for years before he got the role of the villain in *Satya*. It will happen for Eishaan too, he says. "I know my caliber."

"These struggle stories are the biggest enemies of the younger generation," says Ali mournfully. "One success story destroys one thousand lives." He could write about Anupam Kher, who came from Simla to Bombay to make it as a star. He used to walk from Bandra to the Prithvi Theater, says Ali; he had only two pairs of khadi kurta-pajamas, which he would wash in the night and walk dry in the morning. He lived on vada-pav and tutored slum children for 50 rupees a month. Then Mahesh Bhatt discovered him and cast him in *Saaransh*, and now he is a star as well as a director. "These stories drive mad the people sitting in the village," notes Ali.

I tell Eishaan that I'd stopped over in Dubai for a day on my way to America. He had loved living there. "The traffic was so disciplined, everyone drove in their lanes."

His family there is wealthy. I ask whether he would return to Dubai.

"I love my India," he says, in the manner of a man confessing to adultery.

He does think sometimes about what it might be like if he returned to his life in Dubai, with all its comforts. But Bombay has a unique advantage for an actor. "In Bombay you watch everything. For an actor you need to observe so many things." It begins when he flies into the city, observes the people in the slums by the airport, and sees a city of strugglers. "They are fighting with their lives. It's raining, pouring, but still they're fighting. Probably we people are addicted to this life, we need news every moment of every day." If he leaves Bombay, after two days he wants to come back, Eishaan declares.

Ali goes him one better. "It takes me *one* day. I want to come back after one day away." Ali is not at home outside Bombay. He tells us about a recent trip to the small town of Khambhat, where he was watching a movie. Midway through the film, a message flashed on the screen: "Chandulal Shah is dead." Chandulal Shah was somebody who lived in the town. The movie had to end and everybody had to go home.

When Eishaan came to Bombay to make it in the movies, he knew it would be a struggle. "But I never thought it would be harder every time." He had enough savings for two or three years and supportive family and friends. In the beginning, he had rented a flat, paying 5,000 rupees a month. But his expenses averaged 35,000 a month. Once every three days he would go out to dinner, buying meals for a multitude of cousins who were always coming and going, taking out-of-town visitors to the beer bars.

Over the years, as his star dipped, so did his budget, which is now down to 11,000 rupees a month. He has had the great good fortune of being able to stay rent-free in a flat owned by one of his best friends, who has given it to him for two years. Eishaan doesn't go out to the discos anymore, doesn't even go out for dinner. "Today, to pay three hundred fifty for a prawn dish—it's horrible, a criminal wastage." He has learnt to cook and clean for himself.

The cousins have by now withdrawn their financial support, Hitesh tells me, but he still sends his brother money and keeps trying to persuade him to come back to the soft life in Dubai. "I speak to him for twenty minutes on the phone—"

"That costs him around five thousand rupees," interjects Eishaan, quantifying his brother's love.

"—and I tell him you can live a better life somewhere else. He has gone through such a bad phase. Every second of these four years huge tension." Hitesh recalls Eishaan's excuses for not getting roles: It was the monsoon, so there were no shoots; then it was Ganapati, so there was a holiday, then Diwali; then it was the sradh time, so no filming. After a while, Hitesh got angry with him. It wasn't because he wasn't earning money but because of "the psychological point: He suffers. That is more important, for me at least." He was worried that Eishaan would do something dangerous, something wrong, "when people bang you on every part of your body."

It has gotten so Eishaan doesn't go home to Jaipur anymore. "They all ask, 'Is nothing happening?' A friend who doesn't know me much in Dubai calls me up and asks, 'Nothing is happening?' My parents, relatives, well-wishers are saying, 'All these people are coming in, why not you?' I have no answer to this question, 'Why not me?' Sometimes I blame it on God, sometimes I don't answer."

Eishaan is a devout follower of Goddess Durga in all her many avatars. "I . . . I have a small temple at home. When I feel like breaking down I break down in front of God. I always feel that God is trying my patience. Every ten to fifteen days I have a tendency to crack." So Eishaan, in his depths, weeps and wails in front of the statue of his Ma. Why is she being so cruel to him? She has given a chance to all the others, why is she denying a chance to him, her most devoted son?

A FEW MONTHS LATER, Ali gives me the glad news that Eishaan has signed a B film, in which he is the star. Ali thinks I have something to do with this. "He met you, and within two meetings he became a hero; otherwise he has been waiting for last four years."

I meet Ali and Eishaan at the Sun 'n' Sand and the struggler tells me how it happened. On Durga Asthami, he prayed to Durga, and finally the goddess responded. A well-wisher, the secretary to an actress, called him. There was a director looking for a lead. Eishaan met the director in a hotel, he met the photographers, and it was finalized in less than an hour. It is a mythological film about Shakumbhari Devi, the Vegetable Goddess, one of the nine avatars of Durga. In times of great hunger, the goddess appears and distributes food. Once, when there was a famine, she wept, and her tears irrigated the land. There is currently a vegetable shortage all over the country—onions are at 30 rupees a pound—and it is bringing down governments. There is a temple dedicated to this devi in the north, but it has no idol; now this film is going to give her a celluloid one. The goddess has incarnated herself expressly for Eishaan, so that he could get work.

The project is a low-budget film; it will be shot in 16mm and transferred to 35mm for projecting. Nobody's getting paid much, and the filmmakers will release it themselves, since Eishaan is sure "no one will want to buy it." But there is a consolation, as far as Eishaan is concerned: "They're sure they want to complete it." The producers have decided to capitalize on their assets. Mr. Agarwal, the financier, owns a lodge in the foothills of the Himalayas where the cast and crew will stay. The producers have also funded an ashram in Hardwar featuring a 108-foot statue of the Goddess Vaishno Devi, another of Durga's incarnations, which will be prominently featured in the movie, along with sermons from the guru of the ashram, to whom the producers are devoted. Religious merit and financial profit will be accumulated simultaneously.

"This would play in the villages. The devi would be hyped." The producers might give the film different names for the big centers and the interiors; for the villages, *Jai Mata Shakumbhari Devi* would be appropriate; for the urban areas, they might go with *Vilayati Saas, Desi Bahu* (Foreign Mother-in-law, Domestic Wife) or *Kudrat ka Kamaal* (Heavenly Miracle). They've already recorded five songs with top singers; Eishaan is featured in a duet and in a sad song. The film's trump card: Two of the songs are full-scale aartis; it would be incumbent on the devout Hindu audience to get to its feet in the theater, clasp their palms in worship, and throw coins at the screen when the goddess is glimpsed. Some might even bring their own lamps to the theater and wave them around the screen during the songs. "The director—Shiv Kumar—is getting a kind of rebirth," says Eishaan.

Shiv Kumar is a big name in Bhojpur. He has made three sex films, guiltily. He is actually a very religious person, associated with the Radhaswami group, and has taken an oath that he won't drink alcohol or eat meat. Shiv Kumar's previous directorial ventures were titled *Be-Abroo* (Shameless), *Badnasib* (Unlucky), and *Badkar* (Worse Than Bad). The producer made back his money in all three.

"He was a struggler who I put into college as a student," declares Ali. He worked as a production assistant and thus got into the industry. Then he started *Be-Abroo.* "The story was about women being used. Men selling them and women being sold. Every third scene was a sex scene. The girl is about to take off her clothes, the man is about to take off his clothes, the bed is shown, and *cut!*" All the songs had double meanings. But the film had a message, explains Ali. " 'No, such things should not happen. This is very bad!' The censors were saying, 'What a message! This is fantastic!' " It became a huge hit for its circuit.

Kumar's fourth film will be shot in Dehra Dun, Hardwar, and Mussoorie, over forty-five days. The heroine, Raashee, is slim and tall and has an "Indian look," explains Eishaan. She's dark. The role came just in time for him. "Since I saw you last I have gone through a lot of mental torture with my family," Eishaan tells me. An astrologer had come to his home and, in the presence of his brother and his cousin, told him he was wasting his time. "It's a criminal waste. Go back." His family members seized on the astrologer's prophecy. "They took me left-right. 'See, see what he said? Now you leave this.' "

But then Eishaan brought out his trump card: his starring role in *Jai Shakumbhari Maa*.

And what was their reaction?

"They are excited. I know. They have to be." His brother didn't believe it till he showed him the train tickets given to him to travel north for the shoot. Eishaan hasn't seen the script yet. The director has narrated the story to him. "I didn't want to ask the director for a script," Eishaan says.

Ali approves of his decision. "If you ask for a script, you're almost asking for disqualification, even if you're an established star. 'Who are you? You think we are making shit?' "

Eishaan is prepared to go in complete humility. "People won't have much of an ego problem under this banner. I told the director, Even if your cook is missing, I'll be there." Ali advises the star that he should not put on weight during the shoot, as will happen if they look after him well. Eishaan responds that he is carrying his jogging shoes, and will live on jaggery and peanuts. Ever generous, Eishaan is lending his flat—which is itself on loan to him from a friend—to his Muslim neighbors, in whose family there is a wedding, for the time he's gone. Property is always communal in Bombay; there is a constant circulation of sleeping space.

THE STAR COMES to my office in Elco Arcade, fresh from the first segment of his shoot. He looks good; he has just been jogging on the beach. He has thrown himself into the film. "I want to sleep and breathe the role." Eventually he would like to work with a renowned director, he tells me, like Vinod Chopra. But I don't think he's asking me for an introduction to Vinod. Eishaan is not that pushy. It's part of his problem: He's not that pushy.

The shooting of *Jai Shakumbhari Maa* has come to a hopefully temporary halt, because the director suddenly got a spate of TV work. He was asked to submit two serials to Doordarshan. He has offered Eishaan the role of the heroine's second husband in the serial. Eishaan has now actually been paid for his work—a first installment of 10,000 rupees, for what was supposed to be three days' work. It grew into twenty-two days. There's just one small problem: "The check hasn't cleared yet."

The producers had put their star up in the hotel they owned, in a leaking room with another actor who smoked like a chimney and snored. Eishaan can't take cigarette smoke. He recorded his roommate's snores and played them for the producers, who agreed to transfer him to another room.

The budget was one notch below shoestring; it was the plastic tip of the shoestring. The producers were too cheap to give Eishaan a tape of the songs, so he stole it from the sound studio. They were too cheap to give him a photo to show his brother that he was working; so he stole it from the stills album. The inexperienced producers didn't arrange for enough security on the sets. "When I was not shooting I used to assist the director. I used to shout, *Silence!* and give the clap." This led to altercations with the public. One Saturday, Eishaan was trying extra hard to keep control of his temper, because he realized the hot-headed influence of Shani Maharaj, the god to whom Saturday is dedicated. But a tapori kept interfering with the shot. The star–cum–security guard asked him to keep quiet. It escalated into fisticuffs. Eishaan pulls out a newspaper clipping. HERO THRASHED BY PUBLIC, reads the headline, from a Hardwar paper. Actually, insists Eishaan, it was the other way: "I bashed him straightaway." But he is grateful that the newspaper wrote it the way it did; if he had been portrayed as a hero that beats up the public, the local toughs would have been hunting for him.

The shooting ratio was roughly 1:1. "Usually the first take was the last, except when a person in the public was passing by and got caught in the background of the shot." Then, grudgingly, there was a second take. The costume department in the film depended on what was available daily in the market, like vegetables. Every morning the woman in charge of costumes went shopping in the local market for clothes; until they arrived, the entire set was in a state of tension. The hotel where they were staying had an "exhibition-cum-sale" of garments on the premises. The producer spotted this and instantly saw an opportunity. He asked his star to select the clothes he needed for the day's shoot from the sale, wear them for the filming, and then return them at the end of the day, telling the merchants they didn't fit.

On the set of the film about the vegetable goddess, there was a severe shortage of vegetables. The cast and crew were fed a diet of potatoes. "Not a single dish excluding potatoes. Even the yogurt had potatoes." Eishaan began losing his patience with the tuberous diet. He tried hinting subtly at his discomfort; he composed and recited aloud satirical verse on the potato. The producers simply said, Eishaan complains too much. Shooting on the set alternated with an unseemly scramble for nutrition. The technicians were hardened veterans of many a B movie. "When the food was served the technicians would take four or five rotis and a lot of vegetables and disappear. We would have to wait in line with our plates till they got more food."

It got worse. One day Eishaan was eating his meal, which turned out to be kadhi with pakodas, yogurt soup with dumplings. He has a habit of picking and turning over his food before putting it into his mouth, which served him well on this occasion. A pakoda broke open under his fingers, and he found a whole cockroach nestled in it. The next day he found a worm in the rice. So the star took on yet another role: that of maid. He got a broom and mop and went into the kitchen and started in. He didn't stop till he had cleaned out the whole kitchen.

Eishaan carried his statue of Durga with him to the shoot and made a small temple in his hotel room. He believed that as a result of bad karma, she was punishing him with bad food. "I never dreamed of this kind of khana. My goddess was showing me that this is also part of life."

In the middle of all this a hero of my childhood days appeared on the set. Eishaan shows me a photo of a man dressed in saffron swami's robes. "Dara Singh," he says, and the name takes me back. Dara Singh versus King Kong. He was India's greatest pro wrestler, and his name became a synonym for a strong man, a fighter. He used his wrestling success to become a god of the B films and was even nominated to the Rajya Sabha, the upper house of parliament. The director knew the wrestler well; he had launched his son in another film. In *Jai Shakumbhari Maa*, Dara Singh plays a saint who worships the goddess. The wrestler is known all over India. Buses pulled off the highway near the town when the drivers heard that Dara Singh was in a shoot there, and everyone got off and came running toward him to touch his feet. "Daraji! Daraji!"

The wrestler stayed on the set for a day. Dara Singh was still supple in his old age; he never ate rice and his fingers were still very strong. Then came mealtime. "They gave him potatoes." Eishaan had a conversation with him about food, which was predominant on the minds of the starved crew, especially after they were forced to watch but not touch the red and green baskets full of vegetables in the scenes. The wrestler agreed with Eishaan about the necessity of eating well. "He said, Whatever a man does, he does for his stomach. If the stomach doesn't have good food, what use is anything?" So Eishaan bought fruits and sent them to him.

The potatoes kept coming. Eishaan started going to the market and buying his own provisions. He laid out a breakfast spread in his room every morning: cheese, jam, bread, butter, fruits. The crew began their mornings in his room and loaded up for the day. Sometimes, the star would also buy the crew dinner. All this was not cheap. Of the 21,000 rupees that Eishaan is to get as his total fee, his personal expenses ran to 13,000. I ask him if he was reimbursed by the producer, and he laughs. While returning to Delhi, the bus with the crew broke down for a couple of hours. It was dinnertime, and the bus would not reach Delhi till 2 a.m. The producer distributed 400 rupees for twenty people, to buy dinner. "He's a Muslim but he has a PhD in Bania," the merchant caste. It was obviously going to fall short, so the struggler from Dubai brought out his wallet and bought dinner for everyone, paying 1,200 rupees. He did not ask his fellow artistes to split the check. "I can't tell people, 'Give me twenty rupees each.' " For his pains, the woman who plays his mother called him a fool.

The whole experience with *Jai Shakumbhari Maa* has driven home at least one truth for Eishaan. "In films, I know I can never be a star unless something clicks." No Subhash Ghai or Yash Chopra will spend crores of rupees on him, he now knows. He thinks he trusts people too much—such as the producers who were supposed to launch him early in his career and never did, or died on him. He thinks he gets too emotional with people, and he should save his emotion for the camera.

But then his natural optimism reasserts itself. "Nana Patekar became a star at forty-two," the twenty-five-year-old remembers.

Eishaan turns over the pictures of the photo album and stops at one picture, which shows him wearing a U.S. Cavalry hat and writing something, surrounded by a crowd of people. "This was the moment of my life," he recalls. He is signing autographs. At last, Eishaan the cloth merchant is signing autographs. When he went for his morning jog, the crowd used to jog with him. They would come to the hotel and ask at reception, We hear there's a hero staying here, we want to meet the hero. "They used to come in fives to my room. They used to come to shake my hand. Then I said, I wish my brother was here to see all these things." The aunty whose house Eishaan used to go to sometimes for food had three daughters, and all three developed a crush on him. They still call him in Bombay and send him cards. A girl in the film sent him a message through another girl, to tell him that she was in love with him. And the go-between herself fell in love with him. He turned both of them away: "I said, I've just had a major breakup a year and a half ago, I don't want to get into any mess." The late-afternoon light falls on his face from the window, illuminating it. "I was very popular among the girls."

THE WORLD WAS TO END on May 8, 1999. The papers were full of it: a particularly malevolent arrangement of the constellations. Tens of thousands of people fled Alang, the shipbreaking yards in Gujarat, for their villages. Hundreds of thousands fled Bombay, especially the Gujaratis; Sunil, the Sena man, opened a travel agency to take advantage of the phenomenon and made a killing by scalping bus tickets out of the city. When I call up Ali one day that summer and ask him why I haven't heard from Eishaan for a while, he laughs pretty hard. "He's very stupid," says Ali. Eishaan is back in Jaipur. Things had been going well for Eishaan; besides *Shakumbhari Maa* and the TV serial, he was just about to sign another film. Then he got a call from his father in Dubai. "Son, the world is going to end, so let us die together! Come to Jaipur." The father flew in from Dubai, and on May 6 Eishaan fled Bombay and got on the train to Jaipur. There, the whole family awaited the apocalypse. Meanwhile, Eishaan missed out on the second film. "I really thought it was a joke," says Ali. "He doesn't know what to do; he's trapped between extreme orthodoxy and extreme modernism. That's his problem."

WHEN THE WORLD SURVIVES, Eishaan goes back north for the second shoot of *Shakumbhari Maa*. When he returns to Bombay, he comes over with Ali and my friend Anuradha Tandon, a woman-about-town, to my office one night for a fine evening of drink and story. The presence of a pretty woman in the room adds to Ali and Eishaan's volubility; they are refreshed, as if by a fresh breeze from over the sea. Eishaan is talking to Anuradha about his film, searching for a parallel. "Have you ever heard of a film called *Jai Santoshi Ma*?"

"Shakumbhari Maa is her aunty," Ali mumbles into his vodka.

Eishaan has brought a small video camera, on which he shows us scenes from the second shoot of his film. "This is *The Making of Shakumbhari Maa*." There he is, in a disco, with a bottle of liquor in front of him. A troop of dancers in western clothes are singing, in English, "She made me crazy."

"Here I have this misunderstanding that my wife is carrying on with my cousin. So I am drinking."

"Social message," explains Ali.

Normally, the liquor bottles in Hindi films—they were all Vat 69 in the seventies—are filled with Coke. But *Shakumbhari Maa* did not have the lavish budgets of those films, to throw away on Coke. "They mixed the Coke with water. They got one Coke between six liquor bottles." So Eishaan had to take swigs from bottles of highly diluted Coca-Cola and act like a drunk. After he gets drunk, he throws the bottles around, demonstrating his distress. When he did, there were two assistants standing behind the camera holding a sheet spread to catch the bottles, so they could be used again. Another scene takes place in dense fog. The production ran out of the powder used for the fog effect, so they burnt cow dung. It stung the stars' eyes, which led to a further happy economy: "I didn't need glycerine for the scenes."

The schedule of the second shoot was packed, from noon to midnight every day. This time, to avoid the problems of technicians stealing food ahead of more genteel members of the cast, the producer had an inspiration: He parceled out individual portions in plastic bags for each person. The food came from a Sardar's hotel and was very good and copious, with costly ingredients—"paneer was like bloody flowing"—but the producer did not believe in the added expense of plates. The crew was expected to eat straight from the bags, four in each parcel, for rice, roti, dal, and vegetables. They had to tear open each bag with their teeth to get at the nourishment within. Eishaan remarked to the producers that when the autopsy was done on their dead bodies, they would find a hundred yards of plastic in each corpse. "Out of shame the producers called up friends in an ashram, and they sent a hundred plates."

After a while, the plastic-enhanced diet took its toll on the star. "I got stomach problems. I got loose motions." The whistle of the cooker in the house of the people who owned the hotel tormented Eishaan; here was good homemade food being cooked every day. The daughter of the owner had a crush on him. He took advantage of this to ask her to get him some dal and khichdi for his unsettled intestines, and she obliged.

We see another scene on the camcorder, of the young heroine in a river, drowning. She is flailing her arms around and screaming; she has really thrown herself into the scene. Then the hero saves her. We remark to Eishaan that she acted well.

"She wasn't acting. She can't swim. She really was drowning."

Acting the scenes on the banks of the Ganges posed special problems. Eishaan recalls the time when he had to sing a tender love song to the heroine. "On the shores of the sea"—he sings the song for us, clicking his fingers—while, just out of the frame, dead bodies floated by in the river.

At one point, a bald head appears in the frame. "Who's that?" I ask. It belongs to a sadhu; this being Hardwar "there were always thirty or forty sadhus around, all of them potheads." They were taking a break from their religious austerities, crowding around the sets of the mythological film, creating a traffic jam. All of them wanted bit parts in the film, and their requests could not be taken lightly, since many of them were dangerous. "All the dacoits from Bihar and UP, whoever has a criminal record, runs up there and shaves his head," explains Eishaan.

I ask him when the film will be released.

There is a pause.

"They have to find buyers first."

Jai Shakumbhari Maa is competing with another mythological, *Devi*, which has, reel for reel, many more miracles. Eishaan is thinking of buying the rights to release his film in Rajasthan, where he is confident he can double his money. He would need two to three lakhs for publicity, which with this sort of movie mostly involves hiring auto-rickshaws with loudspeakers roaming through the villages, alerting the citizenry to the fabulous entertainment soon to set up tent in their midst. Since filming began, the producers have discovered that a new temple to Shakumbhari Maa is about to be installed somewhere in the northern suburbs of Bombay. The director instructed his cast and crew that henceforth everybody was to pray to this goddess.

Eishaan is much more confident now than when I first met him. He doesn't answer all my questions unless I repeat them three or four times, and even then he doesn't answer some of them. He has started to stand me up; he is not returning some of my calls. There is no disrespect involved, it is just that his status has changed. In my office, he automatically takes the armchair. But even so, he mixes the drinks and serves all of us, refreshing our glasses periodically.

At last I see *Jai Shakumbhari Maa*, in a plush preview theater in Bandra. The audience is mostly Eishaan's friends and family and a couple of distributors. It is the kind of movie where most of the people in the titles have only one name. My friend doesn't seem to be very high up on the totem pole of this movie, judging by the misspelling of the star's name in the titles. It is now "Eisshan."

It is not just an out-and-out mythological film. As Eishaan tells me, "It has romance, action, everything." Since the big stars are charging a crore and up for their films, even mainstream producers are getting into the quickie B and C movies, Ali had explained. There were three ways to survive. One was to make a horror film that didn't need to show any famous faces, another was to make a sex film, and the third was to make a religious film. "Or a combination: horror, sex, and tantric religion." *Shakumbhari Maa* possesses all three ingredients.

The film deals with a contest between the forces of evil, summoned by a tantric, and the forces of good, marshaled by the vegetable goddess. In the beginning, there is an extended family in a village, including two brothers, one with a virtuous wife, the other married to a harridan. The second brother wishes to go to America. A wandering singer sings the praises of Shakumbhari Maa, and the entire village turns out to pray to her. The brother sings and prays, and immediately a telegram arrives, summoning him to an American job. His noble sister-in-law sells her jewelry so the family can pay for the tickets. When they come back from living abroad (established through two shots of an Air India plane, one taking off, the other landing), they are "Americanized." They have brought a suitcase full of money (ten lakhs) to save the older brother's business, but alas! they checked it through and, as per Air India custom, their baggage has been lost in transit.

When we first see Eishaan, he is wearing a denim shirt, jeans, and a hat such as was favored by the U.S. Cavalry. The mother and daughter wear

T-shirts, pants, and skirts; they are NRIs and therefore sluts. Through the film, the producers seem to have utilized the exhibition-cum-sale of garments well. The costumes range from high-slit long skirts to a polka-dotted vest and bright red cravat for Eishaan to a raggedy dress with patches that the bad mother and daughter are forced to wear when they become poor.

But Eishaan is finally a hero, not just an actor. He goes through every single heroic action. He sings love songs while thrusting his crotch forward and rotating it in a circle, he takes on three armed thugs single-handedly and vanquishes them—so powerful is his punch that it creates a reverse sonic boom; you hear the sound *dishoom!* of fist connecting with villain even before it has actually done so on the screen—he drinks whiskey when he loses his girl, and he makes money in business.

The plot, like the Lord, moves in mysterious ways. The storytelling style of the movie follows a kind of jump-cutting of the script. A character proceeds from one momentous event in his life to another—marriage, expulsion from the family, heartbreak—without the tedious intermediary details of motivation or purpose explained to the audience. You see them going from point A to point Z; the intervening alphabet actions have occurred offscreen. As a result, each succeeding scene is a happy surprise, because you never know what to expect next. My attention is seized in a way that it never is in mainstream Hindi films.

The film knows the issues and prejudices that press most heavily on the rural Indian's mind. On the shoot, when Eishaan was subjected to the potato-heavy diet, he had told the producers, "You are treating us like a new bride who's come without a dowry." Meanwhile, in the film, the goddess was rescuing Eishaan's bride, who had indeed come without one. The evil mother interrupts her son's wedding to demand a dowry from the bride's poor father. The father is humiliated—this is the ultimate nightmare of a village father with an unmarried daughter—but the bride prays to Shakumbhari Maa and, in contravention of the Indian Penal Code, the goddess is incarnated as an old woman bearing an impressive dowry: stacks of rupees, jewels, and saris. All this later turns into ashes when the mother and her evil brother, Mr. Bob, try to steal it.

The periodic interventions of the goddess knit the film together. When all seems lost, she appears, a young maiden of a startling shade of blue, adorned with ornaments in an equally alarming shade of gold. In one scene, her powers transport a series of plates of food through the air from the dining table to the shrine room; when the hungry villains follow, her clay idol smacks them about the head and shoulders while flying through midair.

Shakumbhari Maa is sometimes preceded by her singing dhoot, or agent, the singing wrestler. Dara Singh is the "fakir baba" and wears saffron. "Is he meant to be Muslim?" I ask Eishaan. "No, he is a pir. We don't know what religion it is." A holy man, maybe Muslim, maybe Hindu, wandering the countryside, singing the praises of a Hindu goddess. The villages will have no problem with this. The music composer and lyricist responsible for writing the Hindu devotional songs is a Jain. The executive producer and villain (Mr. Bob), Shaheed Khan, is Muslim. He too is a follower of Vaishno Devi.

As soon as the heroine gets married, she stops flouncing around in a miniskirt and ankle boots and appears in a sari. As Eishaan reposes on their flower-bedecked nuptial bed during their wedding night, his new bride blows a conch and pauses to sing a devotional hymn while he drifts off to sleep. A little later, she saves her sister-in-law from premarital sex. "Old-fashioned!" complains the interrupted male, abusing the heroine. Does she realize that abroad this kind of behavior is common? "This is India," the virtuous wife responds, and delivers the following peroration in furious Bengali-accented English: "What do you think to play with the chastity belt? Is it the culture of any country? Show me one of the university which educates and encourages to this type of vulgar and sinful deed!"

I laugh very hard at this, till I notice that none of the old ladies sitting in the theater are amused and I have to put my hand over my mouth and bite hard. The audience for this movie is not cynical; they have no notion of irony or camp. I am still laughing, a few days later, as I tell Monalisa about it. "It's a hilarious film."

The bar dancer doesn't laugh either. She immediately corrects me. "It's not funny. It's a movie about God."

The deep roots most Indian movies have in the epics are evident in this film. The evil mother is called Kaikeyi, the evil uncle Shakuni, the loyal cousin compares Eishaan to Ram, his wife to Sita, and himself to Lakshman. These names function as a shorthand for the village viewer, readily slotting each character into an established mythological role: the bad stepmother, the good brother. The Indian viewer doesn't like surprises. And there is an added bonus for the audience. A note at the end of the press release at the preview screening promises that Shakumbhari Maa will surely grant the desires of anyone who sees this film, hears its story, or preaches its message. These words preface the Mahabharata and many other Hindu narratives. The very act of listening will confer spiritual benefit upon the listener.

DURING THE INTERMISSION, Shiv Kumar, the director, tells me he has tried to send a message to the youth, in a format that would be pleasing to them. This may explain why the heroine, wearing six-inch heels, gyrates her butt in one of the shortest skirts I have seen onscreen, shortly before she dons a sari and prostrates herself in front of the goddess. There are quite a few such scenes pleasing to the youth: plenty of short skirts, transparent blouses, on-screen kisses, and raucous innuendo in the dialogue, interspersed between scenes of devout fervor. The director reminds me that he has been making very different types of films for many years, sex comedies mostly. Here now is a completely new genre: the mythological sex comedy.

Kumar claims the budget of the film was eighty lakhs; Eishaan tells me it was closer to forty. In the film industry, every person has a "discount level," a percentage by which what he says should be disbelieved. Kumar's discount level, therefore, is 50 percent. Whatever the budget, unlike many bigger films it has a good chance of making money. One of the reasons is that the Uttar Pradesh government, bowing before the goddess, has exempted it from entertainment tax.

THE FILM INITIALLY RECEIVES favorable publicity. The trade magazine *Super Cinema* reports, "The price that a devotional film fetched in North recently left many gaping. Once in a while comes a devotional film that really sweeps the market like hurricane." Unfortunately, the hurricane turns into a light sprinkle and then dries up altogether. *Shakumbhari Maa* was never incarnated on a Bombay theater screen for paying customers. In Bombay nobody dies of famine; the city needs not a Vegetable Goddess but a Housing Goddess, a Traffic Goddess, a Good Government Goddess.

But the goddess in her many avatars continues intervening in the course of Eishaan's life. One night he is at a cousin's house in Worli. They keep insisting that he stay for the night; three times he is about to leave and three times they pull him back, even getting out shorts and a toothbrush for him. But something compels him to drive back to his place in Andheri. At around 2 a.m., near Mahim Church, he sees a mob on the street. He had been thinking about his forthcoming pilgrimage to Vaishno Devi, eagerly anticipating the eight-mile trek up to her shrine. When he sees the mob, his first thought is that riots have broken out; it is a heavily Muslim area. The mob stops his car and demands that he open the door. Then he sees a body on the road, of a woman who has been knocked down by a cab. Her head and thigh are bleeding profusely. The cab has fled, and she needs to be taken to the hospital. The crowd puts her in the backseat and he drives to Leelavati Hospital, where he discovers that she has no money for treatment. So the struggler takes out his wallet and gives 2,000 rupees to the doctor for the stranger's treatment and stays by the woman's hospital bed all night. The next day he searches out her relatives, puts them and the woman into a cab, and gives the cabbie money to drive them to a less expensive hospital in Malad.

Eishaan is of the opinion that the goddess was testing him. "When I was driving I was thinking about Vaishno Devi, and how it would be the best place to celebrate my birthday." If the goddess had not moved him out of his cousin's house in the middle of the night and placed him at that exact spot where the woman had just been knocked over, she might not be alive today. So he will go to Vaishno Devi with his parents, celebrate his twenty-seventh birthday, and know that he has been faithful to her dictates.

After *Shakumbhari Maa,* the heroine, Raashee, goes on to star in *Club Dancer No. 1.* From playing the chaste devotee of the goddess, she goes back to playing with the chastity belt. Eishaan disappears from Bombay, perhaps to Jaipur, perhaps back to his family business in Dubai.

Accused: Sanjay Dutt

When Vinod first told Ajay Lal that Sanjay Dutt had been finalized for the role of Khan in *Mission Kashmir,* the policeman commented, "It's going to be a TADA movie." He was referring to the Terrorist and Disruptive Activities Prevention Act, under which the actor had been jailed for two years for his involvement in the bomb blasts. One of Ajay's best friends has cast as his lead a man that Ajay himself has interrogated. Sanjay is not the only one involved in the film who has been indicted for murder and conspiracy. Ramesh Taurani, out on bail for the murder of the music producer Gulshan Kumar, has bought rights to the music for *Mission Kashmir*.

I first meet Sanjay Dutt when he comes to Vinod's house to hear the Kashmir script. It will be quite a challenge for him, as he is stepping into a role written for Amitabh Bacchan. He sits on the terrace with Vinod, Anu, and me. "You guys must feel small sitting next to him," comments Anu. Sanjay is built like a brontosaurus.

I mention my photographer friend Dayanita Singh in Delhi, and he says, "That's my sister. She stays with us whenever she comes to Bombay." Dayanita went to school with Sanjay; he considers her his rakhi sister. In boarding school, he was always the one who got beaten most by the teachers. He is the son of two of the country's greatest stars, the powerful member of parliament and actor Sunil Dutt and the Muslim actress Nargis. The teachers had to demonstrate to the world that they were not awed by this. They had the power to beat this Bombay film-world brat; who does he think he is? Once, for some minor infraction, a teacher asked him to crawl up a gravel slope on his hands and knees. The skin came off his forearms and knees. The next day the teacher ripped off the bandages and asked him to crawl back up the same slope. Another time he was beaten so badly that gangrene set in. His parents had to put him in hospital in Delhi. He was a skinny boy in a British-style boarding school. So he sought out the tough boys, the Sardars, and made Dayanita tie rakhis on them, making them, by extension, his brothers too. He grew up fascinated by guns and muscles.

I have been told by Mahesh that Sanjay will not talk about his jail experiences. Dayanita has said the same thing. But sitting on Vinod's terrace, Sanjay is extraordinarily friendly. Maybe it's because of who has introduced me to him. "Those were dark days," says Sanjay. Almost all of the film industry turned their backs on him when he was arrested. "This man"—indicating Vinod—"was the only guy that stood by me." His case will take years more to get through this level of the courts. If the verdict goes against him he can appeal, and so it will go on well into the twenty-first century. He invites me to go to court with him the next day, where he is to sign his bail register.

* * *

When we step outside the car at the TADA court on Arthur Road, one of the passersby in the crowded street sees Sanjay and yells out *Kartoos!* It is the name of his latest film, Hindi for a bullet cartridge. The whole street is staring at us. One of Sanjay's fellow undertrials in the blasts case whispers with him. A man has been shot in Chowpatty by the Rajan gang. Sanjay is well acquainted with the man who was shot; he too is one of their mates in the trial. I get the sense that Sanjay considers these outlaws his real kin. Among them, he has found the friends he never had in boarding school, the tough guys who will protect him from the class bullies and sadistic teachers.

We drive back to his apartment, which has a nice view of the Bandra seafront. He moved into this flat just two weeks ago. We sit in his study, which is furnished in blond wood. Tea is brought in, and he pours me a cup, adds sugar to my taste, and stirs it before giving it to me. He talks about growing up troubled. He started taking drugs in the way a boy from a good Bombay family might, "Just to be in the scene. Smoking a little grass, meeting the women." But the grass wasn't enough. "One out of every ten people is an addict. I was the one." So he got onto the stronger stuff: quaaludes, cocaine, heroin. "I've done everything," he says, a couple of times. "I was all the time in the loo, fixing a shot, sleeping." He allows himself an excuse. "I've had a hard life. My mother died when I was twenty." He lost his mother to cancer in 1981 and then his wife, in the same hospital, Sloan-Kettering in Manhattan. He used to walk wintry New York streets alone, weeping.

Sanjay used to get his supply from Do Tanki in Null Bazaar. I remember Mohsin the hit man telling me about Sanjay coming to that part of the city "to smoke charas with Muslims." They were proud of him, proud of his Muslim mother. Gradually he realized that he was addicted and traveled to Jackson, Mississippi, to seek treatment. Sanjay is fascinated by a certain Marlboro Man idea of America. One of his friends in the treatment center raised longhorn cattle in Texas. Sanjay had money saved up in Bombay and decided to put it into a cattle ranch with him. He stayed with the rancher for a month before his father came to retrieve him. It took his father two hard days of pleading and arguing to persuade his son to come back to Bombay.

As we are talking, Sanjay's mobile phone rings and he lies to someone, probably a director trying to find out why he isn't on the set. "I'm in Alibag," he says. He makes another call, speaks in a low tender voice to someone else.

He was always extremely protective of the women in the family, Dayanita told me. When she would stay at the Dutts' house in Bombay, on the nights she was out late in the city she would come home to find Sanjay waiting up, no matter what hour of the night it was. He would look at his watch, look at her, and then go off to his room without saying a word.

He took this concept of protection to extreme lengths. "I love guns," the star declares. During the riots, he became possessed by the idea that his family was in danger. He had been fearing for their lives: that the Hindus were out to get the Dutts during the riots because of his Muslim mother and his father's public stance against the Sena. So, according to Ajay Lal, he called Anees, the brother of Dawood Ibrahim, and Abu Salem and asked them to send down some "guitars," AK-56s. Ajay told me what they extracted from Sanjay in return for the guitars. "The guys who did the blasts brought a Maruti laden with AK-56s and grenades in a special hidden cavity from Pakistan to Bombay. They needed a place to open the cavity—they couldn't just do it on the roadside—so the natural place was Sanju's garage. Sanju, like a lot of other people, had a fascination with the underworld." The cop did not think well of the star.

Sanjay was at the peak of his career in 1993, when the blasts occurred. His film *Khalnayak* (Villain) was that year's highest-grossing film. He played an assassin hired by the underworld. AN AMAZING PORTRAIT OF A SENSITIVE VILLAIN, the posters announced. He was shooting in Mauritius when Ajay detected the blasts case and started arresting the conspirators. The guns were taken from Sanjay's house by his friends and destroyed in a foundry. In the foundry, the police found a spring and a rod belonging to one of the rifles, on the basis of which he was arrested.

Sanjay blames his troubles on Sharad Pawar, the powerful leader of the Nationalist Congress Party, one of whose main rivals is Sanjay's extraordinarily popular father, Sunil Dutt. I tell him about my meeting with a Muslim government clerk in Jogeshwari, who, when I asked him what party he votes for, had said, "Whatever party Sunil Dutt is in."

Pawar had told his father that he could get Sanjay released in fifteen days if he turned approver in the case. "If I had turned approver that would mean admitting that I was part of the conspiracy. How would that look? How would it reflect on my family?"

His father told him to come back from Mauritius. Pawar had assured Sunil Dutt that his son would be picked up for half an hour and then released. But when Sanjay came down the escalator from the arrival gate, he saw two hundred commandos waiting for him with drawn guns. Among them was Ajay Lal, who whisked Sanjay away and interrogated him. Then he was put in the Arthur Road jail. In the middle of his first night there, men came into his cell. They were prisoners, and they belonged to the Ashwin Naik gang. The men took Sanjay to their leader, an engineer, educated in London, who had to come back home to join his brother the gang lord. (Vinod's gangster film *Parinda* was based on the relationship of these brothers.) The don asked him how he was faring. Sanjay said he missed his father. So the don got out his cell phone and gave it to Sanjay. His father was astonished to receive a call from his jailed son at 11 p.m.

Shortly after he was put in prison, his father came to visit him. "Now I can do nothing for you," he admitted to his only son, and went away. "I cried and cried," Sanjay recalls. He could not be released on bail; the government wouldn't grant it. The first judge, Patel, had become fixated on getting Sanjay. According to Sanjay, the trouble began when his lawyer asked the judge to recuse himself. The judge rejected the petition and turned on Sanjay with new hatred.

In the jail he was removed from the general population. "They said they had information that I would be killed. For my safety they put me in solitary confinement, which was a fucking joke." For three months he hardly saw daylight. It was an eight-by-eight-foot room with a toilet in it, in which the star had to bathe, shit, and brush his teeth. His family sent food to him from home, but it was eaten by other convicts before it got to him, and he had to eat the barely edible jail food. The solitude could drive a man out of his mind.

Sanjay made friends with the natural world. Through the tiny air vent, four sparrows would come into his cell every evening, and Sanjay would put his massive hand out with crumbs in it. He was starved for touch, and they would let him touch them, so he would caress the little birds. He made friends with the ants, too, that came out of the sewage pipe. "Amazing things, these ants. There is some kind of language between them. If one is going the wrong way, another ant will tell him." He would lie flat on the floor and watch them for hours on end, as they struggled with their crumbs of food, carrying them over the sewer line. "If the crumbs were too big for them, I would hold the crumb and lift it over the sewer line. It was like a helicopter ride for them." There were no clocks, of course, in the cell, but Sanjay knew the time because of a rat, an enormous bandicoot. "I named him General Saab because in the night he used to enter the cell exactly at twelve, and at one o'clock he used to leave. He was like a general, walking around the barracks."

But the attractions of the vermin paled. He hadn't seen his family in three months. One day he went berserk and banged his head against the bars till it bled. His head required ten stitches. Frightened, the jail authorities removed him and put him in another cell with twenty-one hard-core terrorists from Punjab, who looked after him very well. "They were highly emotional, lovable Sardars." They cooked for him. They took stones, made a hearth, took the jail food, and transformed it into something else altogether, tastier, more nutritious.

Gunmen of all the gangs mixed freely in the jail. Sanjay met a lot of shooters, studied how the recruiting was done, starting from the children's barracks, where the sharp boys were picked up, their bail arranged, their families taken care of. After he was released, he shared this knowledge with directors of gangster movies, who made films based on the characters he'd met. And his own ability to play gangsters was unsurpassed in the industry. Jail was good for his acting skills. "People say I've matured and there's a lot of pain in my eyes."

But none of the real shooters looks remotely like Sanjay. I remark to him that the shooters I've met tend to be small and skinny and he nods. He has noted the same thing. "Their eyes are absolutely cold." He has noticed another quality of the gangsters and terrorists. "People who are connected with crime are very godfearing. They used to pray a lot, they used to hate the fucking government." Once he became involved with crime, he followed suit. In jail, he prayed for four hours a day.

What was the worst thing about jail? I ask him.

"It was, Why have you done this to me? Why have you put me in jail? I saw shooters who have killed thirty people come and go in front of me. I started thinking, I'll fucking kill people when I get out. I was two hundred pounds of muscle weight when I went into jail. In three months, I lost seventy-five pounds." And he was threatened with torture. "They showed me the third degree to break me."

So Sanjay Dutt is an angry man. "They talk about this country being the biggest democracy. It's a fucking piece of shit," says the man who will play a patriotic Muslim cop saving India in our movie. The star has a historical analysis of what's wrong. "When the British left India, they left behind the law and they left behind all that shit. Ambedkar changed the constitution of the country, but he didn't change the law. For the British, all those freedom fighters—Tilak, et cetera—were terrorists. When the constitution and the law don't match, you're talking about deep shit out here."

On the wall of Sanjay's study is a caricature of him, lifting weights and smoking a cigarette at the same time. The cartoonist is Raj Thackeray, the Saheb's nephew. The only politician about whom he is careful not to say a negative word is Bal Thackeray, leader of the political party that started the riots that made him so fearful he asked for guns to protect his family from them. Because Bal Thackeray is the same man who, having demonstrated to all Bombay that he could put the Muslims in their place, also demonstrated his power, his magnanimity, and his love of the film industry by ordering his government to furnish bail for Sanjay Dutt, son of the Muslim Nargis Dutt.

Mahesh Bhatt is clear about what he feels for Sanjay: "He's a criminal. He has the heart of a criminal." It hasn't stopped Mahesh from having just released a movie starring Sanjay. In 2000, Sanjay is on his third comeback in films, with *Vastav* and *Mission Kashmir*. Sanjay's encounters with the underworld convinced him that they were superior to people in the film world. "They are honest about what they do. They don't hide what they do. Film line is a piece of crap, bhenchod. Here it is how to fuck each other. If he's coming up, send people to the movie theater to boo him, write bad things about him in the press." His hatred for the family business is almost a physical object on the table between us.

I ask him what he would like to do if he were free of the case. He responds that he wants to make $3 million and then move to New York and live off the interest. He maintains a small apartment opposite Macy's in Manhattan. He wants to open a steakhouse, and he knows all the famous ones: Peter Luger's in Williamsburg, Morton's of Chicago, Sparks' on 43rd

Street. In any case, he wants to get out of Bombay. "I used to love this place. It's fucking too dangerous now." His daughter by his first wife goes to public school in Bayside. He is happy for her. "Education is fun for them. I don't see that here. Here you're studying some shit: When did Aurangzeb invade India? Who the fuck cares?"

He asks me to stay for lunch. For Sanjay it consists solely of sautéed spinach, which he eats without rice or bread, in big spoonfuls. I am surprised, after all his talk about steakhouses. He explains that his high-protein diet caused kidney problems, so he now has to eat a mostly vegetarian diet. Sanjay's personal trainer has just had a heart attack from the overuse of anabolic steroids and had to retreat, back to Venice Beach. Sanjay eats seven small meals a day, of stuff liked the boiled spinach.

A FEW DAYS LATER, on a Monday, I go to the TADA court again with Sanjay. This time there is to be an actual hearing of the blasts case. We pick up a man named Hanif Kadawala, not too far from my office.

"Are you also one of the accused?" I ask him.

"We are all innocent," declares Sanjay.

Hanif, a small-time film producer and restaurateur, is one of the people alleged to have given Sanjay an AK-56 rifle after the riots. I did not know it then, but I was sitting with a man in the last months of his life. In February 2001, he was shot dead by the Rajan gang very near where we picked him up. Chotta Rajan had decided to take upon himself the determination of Hanif's guilt or innocence. By that year, the gang lord or the police had killed 7 of the 136 accused in the case.

Sanjay spends the car ride juggling shooting schedules. He touches his eyes and lips and prays on sight of each temple en route.

I spend most of the morning trying in vain to get into the TADA court. While I wait, a succession of people come and go through the police post outside the jail: lawyers; the accused out on bail, come for their weekly registration; a mother and her two young children, a boy and a girl dressed in their Friday best, come to see the father inside; a stunningly beautiful young woman in a black burka, come to give comfort to her man in jail.

Finally, in the afternoon, I get an audience with Judge Kode, because, he explains, "It is my duty to help a young man." He then embarks on a soliloquy about, among other things, my dharma as a writer, the nature of the city of Bombay, and the role of the judiciary. All the while he talks, he chews pan; there is a largish lump inside his left cheek, like the tumor it foreshadows. The judge tells me I must give a good impression of my country to the foreigners. "They think we are primitives." He wants me to show them that India has the greatest judicial system in the world. He has personally recorded 8,000 pages of evidence, the total number of pages runs to 13,000. "I have not even taken a single day's leave. Not one day casual leave, not one day—by the grace of God—sick leave." Kode has twenty-three men guarding him. He met Ajay and asked for fifteen more.

Judge Kode's court commences. Sanjay tells me, "It's like a family." And sure enough, the police and the court officers are chatting familiarly with the accused, asking after their families. Once we are inside the court-room, Sanjay directs me to the front. "You sit here." He smiles, turning to the rear. "We are the accused."

The judge enters and the roll call is read, 124 names in all. "Hanif Kadawala!" and he stands up. "Salim Durrani! Yakub Memon!" I look back and there is a ragged army of hardened toughs sitting on rows of wooden benches, along with about five women sitting to the side. "Sanjay Dutt!" and the movie star half stands, and then sits back down, just one of the bomb-blasts suspects.

The judge takes his place. Behind him are wood-paneled walls without the usual picture of the Father of the Nation. Various administrative mat-ters are dealt with, various petitions put forward by the lawyers. They want their clients to be exempted from court appearances because they are being hunted and killed by the Chotta Rajan gang. Nobody is using the mikes provided. I am seated right up front, one row behind the lawyers and directly in front of the judge, but I can't make out what's being said. The accused behind me cannot hear a single word. There is a constant murmur among them as they discuss the World Cup and their various careers in crime. An officer of the court periodically gestures toward them: "Shhhh! Shhhhhh!" And the hubbub quiets for a moment, then rises up again to its former volume. The fans overhead beat the air coming in through the open windows, through which I can see a palm tree and blue skies. It is overall a pleasant, restful atmosphere, and the man next to me, carrying a cell phone in defiance of the strict orders posted in the court, nods off. When he wakes up, he slyly reads a newspaper. I look at the clock on the wall, willing it to move faster, thinking of my lunch and of women, exactly as I did in school during a slow period. The fans, the constant murmur of the backbenchers, the drone of the lawyers and the judge: collectively they bring back those dead afternoons in class. The court is adjourning for summer vacation for two weeks. For the TADA boys, it is the last day of school and there is a holiday mood. With this difference: When it comes time to graduate, a decade hence, the ones who don't do well will be hanged.

The judge gives them two weeks off. They can go anywhere in India. "But there should be no complaint against you," the judge admonishes, ever the headmaster. Afterward Sanjay says, "It's a joke. We can flee to Nepal and nobody would know."

We leave the court in his car. At a traffic light, the usual street children run up. One of them presses his face against the darkened window and sees Sanjay. At once, we are surrounded by street children carrying newspapers and magazines. "Sanjay Dutt, you did good work in *Border*," one of the kids says. "Sanjay Dutt, Sanjay Dutt, buy a magazine." The star is half amused, half annoyed. "Ma ki chud! Gimme a *Mid-Day*." The window is opened to get the afternoon paper and the kids crowd around. Sanjay reads the newspaper, paying no attention to them. "Look at what our man is doing," he says, pointing to a headline about Sharad Pawar splitting from the Congress. The kids are entranced, but only for a moment; the red light at the opposite intersection has come on and there is business to be done. They leave the star and run off across the road, skinny bodies balancing heads stuffed with practical dreams.

I drive with the bomb-blasts suspect back from court, through Bombay roads plastered with giant blowups of his face.

Dreamworld/Underworld

Mission Kashmir has finally started shooting. Vinod is fond of quoting Fellini: "The only place where you can be a dictator and still be loved is on the movie set."

The vast set for *Mission Kashmir* in Film City booms with Vinod's amplified voice. *"Silence!"* The whole set is fiercely air-conditioned; everyone is wearing a sweater and people are catching colds. There is an army of people, men everywhere, even on top, on the catwalks. I ask Vinod what all these people are doing, if they're all needed. "Everything is labor-intensive," he replies. Each piece of equipment carries its own crew; a light will travel with three humans. Then there are other people, stragglers, visitors, gawkers, who just appear and are generally ignored, unless they get in the way. Dignitaries visit the set every day. The education secretary's family comes one day, and Vinod's child's admission to a good school is assured.

Vinod is among the hardest-working people I have ever known. Right now, he is speaking on the phone, reading an article for research on the film, and answering my questions simultaneously. He has a motto: "The harder I work, the luckier I get." He is obsessed with every little detail of the production. "Who do you delegate to?" he asks me. "The standards of mediocrity are so deeply rooted here." Vinod comes home around midnight from a day of shooting; his voice is hoarse and I ask him why. "I shouted, I cursed, I hit." He has physically struck his assistant director.

Part of the shoot is in Kashmir, in Srinagar, where Vinod moves around in bulletproof cars under armed protection. In the middle of shooting a scene, the crew hears a series of loud pops. "They're fireworks; they're celebrating Dussehra," Vinod explains to the crew, and asks the cameraman to hurry up with the shot. After it's finished, he shouts out to his unit to pack up fast and clear the area. The crew now realizes there is no Dussehra in Muslim Kashmir; that was real shooting going on around them. Rocket-propelled grenades were fired at the Government Secretariat, two hundred yards away from the set, and four people died. But the shot got taken.

At another point, an actor playing an escaped militant is running along a canal when policemen on the other side of the canal, on the lookout for terrorists, see him running and raise their guns to shoot him. At the last minute they realize he is an actor. While there are real bombs going off in the city, Vinod is blowing up boats in Dal Lake in the service of entertainment. The line between the battles going on in the city and those staged for the film is so thin it almost disappears.

Vinod has decided to eliminate any mention of Pakistan as the villain. In the final version of the film, the conspirators announce, to the camera and to any interested terrorists, gang lords, governments, or academics, "We owe no allegiance to any government. We're an independent group." Vinod's movies have a large following in Pakistan. There is, however, a shadowy figure in the foreground, seen only in silhouette, whom everyone answers to; he is the Mr. Big. Vinod directs the dialogue writer, Atul Tiwari, to put on a beard. "Osama," he says, anointing him.

In the second half, all of a sudden, amid the bombing and the killing, the terrorist and his lady love are magically transported to childhood, to a lush cinematic valley of waterfalls and flowers, through a song of fantasy. Since Vinod can't take the crew back to Kashmir—it is too dangerous by this time in Srinagar—the song is shot in Bombay, which is fitting. It is a Bombay re-creation of Kashmir, a studio set of Kashmir with carpets of flowers, cotton-wool blizzards of snow. Nobody need take war all that seriously. There will always be a break in the fighting for love and song.

I GO TO VINOD'S HOME shortly after Vikram says with satisfaction, "The climax is solid." Hrithik Roshan, the boy newcomer we substituted for Shahrukh Khan, is now the biggest star in the country with just one picture, *Kaho Na Pyaar Hai,* made by his father, Rakesh Roshan. A phenomenon has been observed in theaters where Hrithik's first film, a love story, has been showing: Young women faint when he comes into the frame. They have been fainting all over India and abroad too; there is a report of a mass fainting that his image occasioned in a theater in Mauritius.

Near riots are breaking out over Hrithik. A theater owner from Raipur calls his father, frantic. He needs two hundred thousand pictures of Hrithik with his signature printed across them; a mob of women is besieging the theater for them. When Hrithik visits the Taj coffee shop, another invasion of his female fans forces the staff to smuggle him out through the kitchen. In the suburbs, he is enjoying a quiet dinner at an Italian restaurant with his girlfriend when he is spotted. A crowd gathers and a passing double-decker bus stops and empties out, as its passengers rush in to get a look at his face.

His film has experienced the fastest climb to the top in the history of Hindi cinema; 99 percent collection for the Bombay circuit in the first week. Week by week, the receipts for *Kaho Na Pyaar Hai* actually grow, instead of diminishing as with other films. Hrithik, who was number three in the star list of *Mission Kashmir* (his contractual salary was eleven lakhs, four less than Preity's), is suddenly elevated to the top. He is now asking for and getting two crores per picture from other directors. "I can't sleep,

I'm delirious," the boy confesses to Vinod. The directors and producers are lining up outside his house with money in their hands.

Part of the reason for this fevered worship of the boy is that the traditional gods of the country, the cricketers, have just taken a bad fall. Most of them have been implicated in the match-fixing scandals; they have taken money to sell their country's honor. When Sachin Tendulkar and Hrithik appear in a stadium together at a celebrity cricket match, the crowd's long sustained applause is for the Bollywood star, not the sportsman. And all that Hrithik has completed so far is one movie. He is, in the age of television, an instant god.

So the "solid" climax melts. "There's no way we can let Hilal Kohistani be killed by the ISI," says Vinod. The villain can't just be bumped off by unseen enemies. The hero of the box office has to be the hero of the movie. He asks me to write a truly heroic climax for Hrithik, in which he, not Sanjay, takes center stage. I come up with the idea of his killing Hilal in a climactic confrontation with his two fathers; his killing Hilal would mean that he kills what is worst in himself. "He becomes a hero," says Vinod, nodding. Policeman Khan's starring role gives way before the invincible might of the box office. Sanjay goes from main hero to one of two leads.

For the new climax, Vinod constructs a series of burnt-out houses around a man-made lake in Film City. Vast amounts of water are trucked to the set and dumped in a hole in the ground. Multiple fog machines wreath the set in a Kashmiri mist. The brochure for the film tells what happened next:

> In the intense heat of the Bombay summer, the organic matter in the water rotted and liquefied and sent up a fierce stink. The director and crew and actors worked for more than a month in this miasma, struggling to control water and fog and wind, until they themselves absorbed a reeking odor that no amount of showering could fully banish.

I take my son to Film City to see the climax: two hundred gallons of petrol and a mighty blast. It is a tradition in Vinod's action films to demolish his work at the end. For *1942*, Vinod built a set that cost eighty lakhs and blew it up for the climax. The houses erected for *Mission Kashmir* meet the same fate: They go up in a ten-story-high column of fire, and everybody flees from the debris and ash raining down from the sky as the wind blows it toward us. Vinod is knocked backward by the force of the explosion. The loudspeakers on the set ring out, demanding, "Ice for Vinod Saab's backside!" I grab Gautama and run up the hill adjoining the lake. We keep hearing explosions as the gas pipes inside the set burst and jets of multicolored flame shoot up. As flaming pieces of the set fall down from the sky, they ignite small fires on the ground; the crew runs around putting them out. A group of sightseeing bureaucrats and their wives pause in their flight up the hill, turn around, and come back to watch, responding to the inner pyromaniac in all of us.

Vinod recovers his costs through sales of the music and some of the distribution rights, long before he has completed the film. It will do well, it might even be a hit, due to Hrithik's phenomenal stardom. Because of all the women who fainted over him in *Kaho Na Pyaar Hai*, there is an automatic audience of many millions, never mind the merits or flaws of script, music, direction, or any other element in the movie. My work, I'm amused to realize, is irrelevant to the film's commercial prospects.

Vinod appraises Hrithik like a prize heifer. On his set, he dresses his star in a tank top. "I want something that shows the most skin. They thought there was skin in *Kaho Na Pyaar Hai;* we'll have much more." He has Hrithik demonstrate, putting his shirt on and taking it off many times. The star's biceps seem permanently flexed, even when he's at rest. They feature prominently in many gratuitous scenes, as soon as the star drops into the picture, from the roof of a house, heaven-sent.

Hrithik is on the cover of the biggest newsmagazine in the country that week. The newspapers run several dozen articles on him each day. But he is modest as always; when we are watching the replay of a scene on a monitor, he sits on the floor on his knees while Vinod and I are on chairs. When Hrithik shakes my hand, I notice he has two thumbs on his right hand, a regular one and a smaller vestigial thumb growing out of it. It was not removed at birth because it is reputed to bring luck—and it certainly has, on a Cinemascope scale. The boy slaved for five years as an assistant director, eating bad food, sleeping in tents on location, and then in one week he became the biggest star in a country of 1 billion people. At the end of the year, Hrithik is to get married to his longtime sweetheart.

"It's going good!" my friend Rustom, who has shot the stills for the movie, observes to him.

"It's going too good."

It *is* going too good. The balance of good and bad fortune in the universe is dangerously tilted toward this young man; it has to right itself. And so it is that, one day in January, as the man Hrithik most loves on the earth—his father, Rakesh Roshan—is getting into his Mercedes, two young men walk up and fire six bullets at him with a .32 pistol. One of the bullets lodges in his breastbone, saving his heart. It is four days after the release of the film Roshan has directed and produced. He had the foresight to keep distribution rights for most of the territories, so overnight he has become one of the wealthiest men in the industry. All the movie industry congregates around his hospital bedside, sympathizing, fearing, asking, "Why?"

Vinod tells me why. "They want Hrithik to do a film for them."

So popular is Hrithik that the gang lord Abu Salem, who has branched off from the D-Company, wants him to act in his film. They—that is, a frontman for Salem, another Bollywood director—went to Rakesh Roshan a few days ago and asked him to get his son to sign on to a film they were producing. Roshan refused. Smita Thackeray, the Saheb's daughter-in-law, had also asked; she could be safely refused now since the Shiv Sena was out of power. Roshan had been getting calls from Abu Salem and had told his son, "Drive carefully." But not much else. Two days after the meeting, the hit men shot him. The Roshans are considering settling with the gangs. It would be quite a twist on the Hindi film formula: A father gets shot, and the son, instead of taking revenge, becomes the star of the killers' film. He may not be able to summon the requisite level of enthusiasm needed for a great performance, but his face alone will cause women to faint, and the gang will make its money. Here was the casting couch turned on its head with a vengeance.

So now both our lead stars are under the shadow of the underworld: The older one is out on bail for his connections to them and the younger one has seen his father shot because of his success. Underworld and dreamworld—in Bombay they are reflections of each other.

Some of this has to do with the nature of film financing in the 1990s. Most Bollywood productions do not get bank loans; they are funded privately. The banks do not understand or trust Bollywood. The funds required for a production are huge, and a family in the industry may be working on several projects at once. The time between investment and return can be years if the film doesn't do well. Who would have that amount of cash lying around? Only the underworld. The gangs are very happy to see black money turn into Technicolor dreams. A hit film can bring in a fourfold return on investment within the first four weeks of its release. So for the underworld, investing in films is one of the quickest ways to get a return on illegal investment. Without underworld financing, the Hindi film industry would collapse overnight. It would have to rely on financing from banks and stockbrokers, who do not share the cinematic taste of the dons. Their dreams would be nowhere near as extravagant, as violent, as passionate.

The gangs have an advantage when it comes to casting. Their preferred way of doing business is to take an unknown but pliable director and producer with a couple of B films to their credit, and then call around to the leading stars of the moment, demanding that they cancel their other commitments and act in their film. With a prominent star, the producer is at least guaranteed recovery of costs. The gangsters are particularly keen to acquire overseas rights for the films and have a near lock on the Bollywood roadshows, those hybrid assemblages of actors, musicians, and vaudeville comedians that roam the globe from Barcelona to Boston, wherever Indians and those who love Indian movies reside.

There is a curious symbiosis between the underworld and the movies, as I had seen with Tanuja in Madanpura. Hindi filmmakers are fascinated by the lives of the gangsters and draw upon them for material. The gangsters, from the shooter on the ground to the don-in-exile at the top, watch Hindi movies keenly and model themselves—their dialogue, the way they carry themselves—on their screen equivalents. Like everybody else in Bombay, the gangsters are starstruck. They delight in their power over the industry's biggest names. In their conversations, they make it a point to denigrate them. Chotta Shakeel, talking with one of his producers, calls Rakesh Roshan Takla, baldy; Hrithik Chikna, dandy; and Shahrukh Khan Hakla, stutterer. It is the easiest way of demonstrating to fellow Indians who is boss: Bring a movie star who can vanquish a thousand brawny villains on the screen down to his knees with just one phone call, begging for his life in front of a puny tapori. Some of the gangsters frown upon the immorality of the movie folk. In between religious discussions, the men sitting in Kamal's office often talk about the sex lives of people in the film industry, what the producers and directors make their female stars do. "It's a very cheap line," says the mob financier with disgust, and the others repeat, "Very cheap line." It's a complex relationship between the gangsters and the stars, part adoration, part self-hatred. In the end, it's not about the money.

A CLOSE FRIEND of Vinod's, Manmohan Shetty, who owns the leading film processing facility in the country, gets a threatening call from Abu Salem, demanding money. (It was Abu Salem who ordered music magnate Gulshan Kumar killed for not paying up.) At Vinod's suggestion, Manmohan goes to Ajay Lal for protection, just before Ajay is to go on leave, and asks if he should just pay the extortion demand. Ajay tells him that if he does he will have to pay all the gangs. The producer won't accept an armed police escort because he is too embarrassed to be seen with a gun-toting bodyguard, so he mostly stays in his house. One day he is walking from his car to his office. A man in his early twenties fires at him from five feet. The gun locks; Manmohan hears the *click-click* and runs into the office before the shooter can fire again. Manmohan was under the impression that there was an understanding and he had until January to pay.

Abu Salem calls him after the encounter. "This is just the trailer. The main picture is about to start." He wants to make an example out of Manmohan. The public is now thinking that the extortionists are not serious but have been wiped out in encounters. The public needs to read the name Abu Salem in the papers, so that if he calls on their phones they will know who he is and be frightened.

There is to be a meeting of film producers with Chaggan Bhujbal, the state's home minister, about the extortion issue. Vinod has been advised by Ajay not to attend, because half of the producers who will show up are themselves connected in some way to the underworld. Their identities are common knowledge. But Vinod cannot come out like a hero and demand stern action against the gangs, since he has been advised by Ajay that the gangsters will be getting a full update on who says what at the meeting immediately after it ends, from their front men in the industry. Besides, even the government officials at the meeting have ties to the gangs.

Vinod and Tanuja Chandra take me along to the meeting on Saturday evening, in an enormous conference room of the State Guest House, Sahyadri. No one asks me for identification as I walk in. In Bombay, you get past doormen if you look like you're not going to tolerate questions. The room is filled with producers, a couple of mid-level stars, Chaggan Bhujbal, and the entire police leadership of the city. As we enter the room, there are dozens of TV cameras and journalists; the meeting seems more of a photo opportunity than anything else. Then the TV cameras are told to leave, so we can talk. The chief of the Crime Branch, Sivanandan, starts on the offensive. In reply to a question about why the filmmakers in the south are not being targeted by the gangs, he replies that maybe the southern film producers do not get their financing from the underworld.

The minister and the police complain that most filmmakers targeted for extortion never come to the police for help; when they do, they claim, they are never touched. At this, Manmohan Shetty points out that he had asked both Ajay and Sivanandan for protection when he got calls from Abu Salem, and both of them told him that the Abu Salem gang was a "negligible force" in Bombay. "Thanks to the underworld's inefficient equipment I was saved," Shetty concludes.

Then begins a parade of film producers suggesting to the minister what he should do. One of them says, "These people are not criminals. They are traitors and should be treated as traitors. Everybody knows that when they enter the police station they are treated as VIPs." His voice rises a couple of decibel levels. "Bring their whole families and put them against a wall and shoot their entire families!"

Sivanandan reads out statistics demonstrating that the number of alleged gangsters killed in encounters has increased every year; in 1999 there were 89, "an all-time record," he points out, with no little pride. Nobody comments that the crime charts also rose correspondingly. The encounters have not stopped the necessity of this very meeting. One producer says he was provided police protection but the gangs shot his watchman right at his gate. "The protection was provided to you, not to the watchman," the police commissioner retorts. "You were not touched." The watchman, of course, was expendable.

Vinod speaks up. He wants to know why the government isn't making serious efforts to ask for the extradition of the gang lords from the countries they are hiding in. Instead, the state government has recently made public a list of people in the movie industry who have huge outstanding dues for police security provided to them. The directors and stars shouldn't have to pay for security, notes Vinod, since as taxpaying citizens it is their right to have the state protect their physical safety. If things continue this way, the industry may move to Hyderabad to the super-efficient domain of Chandrababu Naidu. Lakhs of people work for the film industry in Bombay, one of the producers notes. Bombay's economic livelihood depends on the movie business.

But it is an empty threat. Vinod spoke to me about it earlier. "All said and done, it is the best city in India in terms of living. The Hindi film industry doesn't have an option." It is no accident that the Hindi film industry is based in Marathi-dominated Bombay rather than Hindi-dominated Delhi, because film is not about language. It is fundamentally a mass dream of the audience, and Bombay is a mass dream of the peoples of India.

Bhujbal, the home minister, promises to act. "Since this is a democracy, I can't say it openly. But let me tell you, I have decided to impose the strictest penalty on the extortionists. The ultimate penalty. I can't say it publicly, but it is the ultimate penalty."

On our way out we meet a senior policeman from the territory where most of the movie folk live. "I don't have much to do with these higher-ups," the new commissioner reassures Vinod. "But I want you to know that I am fully committed to my job. In the last five days I have killed two people."

On the way home from the meeting, Vinod and I are driving past a garbage-infested lot in Juhu, over which is a sign, THIS LAND IS THE PROPERTY OF THE COMMISSIONER OF POLICE.

"Look at that," Vinod points out. "That's the state of our police. This country is fucked."

IT HAPPENS EARLIER than expected. The first call comes to Vinod's production office before he's even finished shooting the movie. His accountant picks up. The caller asks for Vinod; the accountant says he is on the set. "Tell him to call Abu Salem." And a phone number is left. By evening, another phone call comes. "Why hasn't he called? We'll blow his head off."

Vinod's production manager arrives on the set in the middle of shooting the climax. Vinod knows instantly from his face, which has gone white, that something is seriously wrong. Within five minutes, Vinod starts making his calls. He goes all the way to the top and speaks to the country's home minister, L. K. Advani. Advani tells him not to worry; all the security agencies of the country are with him. In short order, Vinod has a commando sitting in his car, a jeepful of armed policemen following him, and fifteen guards around his house, his office, and the sets.

By the next day, he tells me the matter has been sorted out; he received another call saying, "You are like our brother." Some string was pulled somewhere, and some puppet's hand jerked up and dropped the gun pointed at Vinod. I go that night to Vinod's. He is in a good mood, dancing around his son. We sit on the ledge outside the living room, looking at the almost full moon, drinking scotch. It isn't Advani who has fixed it with Salem, it is Sanjay Dutt. It was Salem who had taken the Maruti to Sanjay's garage; Salem was a batchmate of Sanjay's in the bomb-blasts case, Number 87 in the Bombay Blasts Conspiracy. Salem had been treated as a servant by Dawood and his court. He had always wanted to be in the movies, so now he was a specialist in extorting the film industry. Sanjay had called up his old colleague and reminded him, "I've spent two years in jail for you. Vinod is like my brother," he said. "He stood by me when I was in jail."

Vinod has been extraordinarily lucky in his casting choices. Signing Sanjay Dutt has turned out to be even more fortuitous than signing Hrithik. Bacchan could never have called off Abu Salem's killers. But Anu is petrified.

Her husband's grandiose talk does not help either. "My brother owns an interest in a resort in the Maldives. We will go there and raise a private army and spend six years going after these guys." He will call Farrokh Abdullah to send Kashmiri commandos to protect him. "I'm a Kashmiri citizen." He will take Hrithik to Delhi and hold a press conference, during which he and the star will publicly ask for political asylum from another country, because India has become a "banana republic." The union government will thus be shamed into seriously going after the extortionists. Vinod is going to buy a revolver! He is on his third scotch now and feels personally affronted, unmanned, by having to hide out in his house behind a wall of armed guards. His Punjabi machismo is threatened. He recites what he would like to say to Salem: "Come to Carter Road, motherfucker, and let's have it out."

The calls stop for the moment. But just in case, Vinod plans to leave the country well before the film's release.

* * *

A GOLD MINE OPENS UP in the sky: Sony/TriStar decides to buy the rights to distribute *Mission Kashmir* overseas. It will open in Times Square, the first Hindi movie ever to do so. As the October 2000 release date approaches, there is an enormous buzz about our movie. Representatives from the gluemaker Fevicol come to Vinod before the film is even finished. They want to be "associated" with the film. The company's ad slogan is Bharat Jodo; they will glue the splintering country back together. *Mission Kashmir,* they feel, is a film about national integration, the glue of secularism that holds the country together, and is a fit enterprise for Fevicol to be associated with. For this privilege they offer one crore. Vinod rejects it, and chastises his assistant for even entertaining the offer. Not because it is cheesy, but because the price is too low.

For the premiere, Sony flies forty-nine people around the world, in first and business class, and puts us up in first-class hotels in London and New York. But Hrithik and Preity Zinta are absent at both the London and the New York premieres, which takes the wind out of the events. Why? I ask Anu.

"Abu," she replies.

The actors can leave the country only at the pleasure of the exiled gang lord. Hrithik has signed up to do a touring show for the man who shot his father. This is to be his first stage show, but it is not till next year; with the star's popularity among overseas Indians, it is guaranteed to bring in unprecedented revenues. Salem does not want Hrithik leaving the country to promote anybody else's venture first, even if it is just a movie. So he had demanded of Rakesh Roshan, not long after Salem's bullets had come out of his body, that his son stay home. He called Preity and told her not to go either. Sanjay was also similarly instructed, but because he had spent two years in jail for Salem, he got a special dispensation. The bhai has now become an emigration officer, issuing or denying exit permits as it suits him.

MISSION KASHMIR OPENS to mixed reviews. They praise the performances and the music but find holes in the script. They point out, justly, that the script doesn't mention the everyday sufferings endured by the

Kashmiris that drove their young men into militancy. Some of the criticism is unfair; it originates from a powerful critic–turned–movie director whom Vinod once hit in public for insulting Anu. He had slapped the critic in the balcony of a movie theater, regretting only that he hadn't toppled him over the balcony into the stalls below.

But there are pleasures in the finished film. Vinod's technical prowess, his natural feel for cinema, is obvious in scenes such as the one where the boy Altaaf waits in the darkness for Khan with a gun. Khan and his wife come home and move through a series of rooms, switching lights on; the camera moves between light and dark, light and shadow. Sanjay gives one of his best performances: the sense of a man overwhelmed by tragedy but somehow struggling on. For the first week of its release, it is the number-one film in the vast country. One million people a day are watching the characters we have been living with for the past two years.

At a screening at Rashtrapati Bhavan for the President of India, both Sanjay Dutt and Ramesh Taurani, who is releasing the music for the film, are present; both are officially out on bail and are being tried for murder.

The columnist Ali Peter John interviews the actor in *Screen:*

ALI: Just some years ago, you were lying alone desperate in a dark dungeon in Arthur Road Jail. What were the thoughts that crossed your mind while you climbed the steps of Rashtrapati Bhavan?

SANJAY: I just couldn't believe what was happening around me. I was in a haze. I was in a state of delirium. I couldn't for the life of me believe that I who was considered and is still considered a criminal by the court was invited by the President of India himself. I also started believing that the high powers in the land were aware that I was innocent, caught in a trap, built by my enemies whom I couldn't visualise or recognise. It was my greatest moment when the President, Mr. Narayan, shook my hands and patted me. I slept that night like I have never slept before. India loved me. The people of India wanted all the best things to happen to me. They were willing to give me all the love I asked for.

Success had sanitized everything.

When the film is released in Kashmir, the audience in the Jammu theater is split, the Hindus cheering for Sanjay and the Muslims for Hrithik. Something that I haven't foreseen happens: The militants claim Hrithik for their own, delighted that this most handsome star, the country's most recognizable face, is playing one of their own, never mind the ending. This movie will not give Vinod trouble with the terrorists. It will bring more young men into the movement, so that they too may sing and dance with Preity and imagine themselves as godlike, Hrithik-like. Other Kashmiris like it because at least it demonstrates that their young men have a reason to turn to militancy; Hrithik becomes a terrorist only after his family is wiped out by the security forces. So little do the Kashmiris expect from the mainstream Indian media.

In Pakistan, which has gone to battle with India three times over Kashmir and even now is training subversives to send over the border, the "Bumbro" song from the film becomes obligatory at every wedding. The people of the enemy country ignore the message and dance to the music, blocking out the topicality of the story and focusing on the eternal themes at its core: a boy who wants a girl, a father who is in conflict with his son. Opposition, in fact, comes from the right. Members of the Indian security forces complain that the film is too soft on terrorists. The sentiments of a particular community are hurt, but it is not the community we expected. Shortly after the film's release, a Sikh organization demands that Vinod issue a public apology and delete a scene in the film where a Sikh policeman is shown pissing his pants from fear as a bomb is about to go off on a boat he's standing on. The Sikhs claim that this reflects poorly on the martial prowess of their people.

When his third film comes out, Hrithik's fame approaches maniacal proportions. Schoolgirls scratch his initials on their arms with their geometry compasses. When Pepsi makes a commercial with Shahrukh and a Hrithik clone who is made gentle fun of, many of the country's youth boycott Pepsi. Calcutta police stop more than a dozen teenagers from boarding trains and planes to Bombay to get a glimpse of Hrithik. Schoolteachers try to confiscate the wave of Hrithik posters and souvenirs that are swamping the classroom, but there is no end to it. His face starts appearing on the covers of school notebooks, along with such inspirational phrases from the star as: "To dream of the person you would like to be is a waste of the person you are." Some authorities propose using the star for educational purposes. One school principal feels students would appreciate their subjects better if Hrithik's appeal were employed imaginatively. "For instance, students could be told that the capital of Maharashtra was Bombay, from where Hrithik hails, or the longest bone in Hrithik Roshan's body was the femur."

Once again, things are going too well for the superstar. A month after the film is released, a rumor sweeps Kathmandu that Hrithik said, in a television interview, that he hated Nepal and its people. I think of the gentle, courteous actor I met and find it impossible to believe he said anything of the sort. But the rumor has currency. The leftist student unions in Nepal send their followers into the streets. They ransack the theater in which *Mission Kashmir* is playing, burn down posters and cutouts of Hrithik, and are about to do the same to the Indian embassy when the police intercept the march. They shoot two teenagers dead. Three more people die that night; 150 are injured. The government bans all of Hrithik's films from playing anywhere in the kingdom. Hrithik goes on the radio, denies making the alleged remarks, and says he loves Nepal and its people. As evidence, he cites the fact that his family has had a faithful Nepalese cook for decades. This fails to mollify the students. Mobs go out and target Indian-owned businesses, setting them on fire. The city of Kathmandu is effectively shut down for several days. The incident almost brings down the Nepali government. Sixty of the ruling party's 113 members of parliament ask the prime minister to resign over the episode, even after Hrithik's denial. The same face that inspired mass fainting among young girls is now inspiring mass hatred. In both cases the reaction is hysterical. I understand again Vinod's concern that the script might give offense. In this part of the world, people are ready to die for a lie.

Over the next few weeks, the origins of the Nepalese rumor become apparent. It first appeared in a Kathmandu newspaper owned by the country's biggest cable network and was then taken up by Maoist students. Pakistani intelligence services have long used Nepal as a base for incursions into India, and the D-Company's Pakistani hosts would be only too happy to stir up trouble over films in a country friendly to India. According to Indian intelligence, the D-Company instructed the newspaper owner to print the fabrication, and then the cable network pulled all Indian films off the air and did not carry Hrithik's denial for several crucial days. This time it was not Hrithik's father that was targeted for assassination. It was his own character.

* * *

VINOD MAKES A LOT of money off *Mission Kashmir;* it is the biggest hit of his career. Although the film tapers off at the box office after the first week, the film's distributors and exhibitors in India all eat well. Now Vinod has been having meetings with Columbia-TriStar about the possibility of making an English-language film for an international audience. It's a way of hedging his bets, getting out of the country. "In ten years I don't know if the politicians we are electing will make life worth living." After I'm back in New York, I get a package, overnight mail from Bombay. It is a poster for Vinod's new film, *Chess,* which doesn't have a script, cast, or budget but does have this poster, which shows a chessboard rising out of someone's nightmare and the tagline TWO PLAYERS. ONE ALIVE, ONE DEAD. A GAME UNFINISHED. And, of course, the obligatory *A Vidhu Vinod Chopra film.* For Vinod, step one in the creation of a film is its publicity.

He wants me to work with him on the script. "Forget about your book," he says. "How many people read books? *Millions* watch cinema." And he is right. There is something about the movies, about a big commercial blockbuster, that no book can compete with. I have never felt more truly accepted back into the country I was born in than when I was asked to write Hindi films, to construct the dream lives of my countrymen. No outsider, no firang would be allowed near our dreams. Everything about Bollywood—the numbers, the personalities—is huge, but after all is said and done, it is an intimate passion.

PART III * PASSAGES

Memory Mines

THE ONLY EVENT in the Bombay weather is the monsoon. The first rain comes early this year, in the middle of May. I can smell it coming, over the sea. I say to the workmen in my flat, "It's going to rain."

"Now?" they ask, surprised.

Now. I know that smell.

It used to be like this, when I was a child: For four days there was thunder. All of us looked at the pale gray sky. Animals and men drew long breaths, felt dry and humid at the same time. Winds came up suddenly, stirred the sleeping dust, and carried it away in little whirlpools. The summer had been hotter, longer than anyone could remember, although they said the same thing at the end of last summer and every summer before that. It's what you say at the cusp.

It was the time of the year at which the season of cricket, that game of hot long summer days, was poised to give way to soccer, hopscotch, and marbles. We swatted the bat desultorily, bored of the waiting.

Day by day the tension grew in the sky. At times everything would be covered in the false black. Birds would fly rapidly; we would think they were flying in advance of the storm, so we came out in old clothes to the compound. As we waited, we grew irritable and hit each other, fooled around, played tricks on the weak and the stupid. We let the air out of tires, wrote obscene doggerel on the walls of the girls' school. The grandmothers said, "It is coming for sure."

And yet it would not.

Farmers and governments grew alarmed. The papers were full of dire predictions. Grass wilted in the playing fields of the girls' school, forbidden to us, so we made it a point to sneak in and play hockey and trample the carefully tended flower bushes.

The sea lay supine, exhausted, needing rain to lubricate, replenish herself. We went to the shallows and fished with our palms, catching the minute sea creatures left behind in the suddenly created lakes when the sea retreated from the rocks.

The city and the building ran out of water.

There was nothing with which to wash bodies or the clothes the bodies had made dirty. There was barely enough to drink; tankers came from the interior, and all the servants lined up with buckets, paying exorbitant rates for the brackish water and then splashing half of it into the thirsty ground, earning them outraged shouts from their mistresses.

At night the exhausted people dreamt of rivers and waterfalls; in the cinemas they watched the song sequences for the shots of snow in Kashmir and saris wet in manufactured rain, watching the falling, flowing water, silently, greedily. They bought and fell asleep to the recorded sounds of oceans and running brooks, clear water over mountain rocks.

Then one day you knew. You saw it coming over the sea. There was a powerful wind and at first just a shower of dust, a huge hell of a lot of dust, all the dust of the world up and in through the open windows of the buildings. If you were downstairs you had to stop your games and cover your mouth and your eyes. It entered your hair and your nose and you were sick of summer, you had been sweating all day and you could not stand summer for one more second.

The clouds passed by overhead at great speed, carrying urgent dispatches from someone unknown to us to somebody whom we could never talk to. The sky was blue-black, like the poison-filled neck of Shiva.

Then the first drop, so light you might have imagined it. It might have been an air conditioner leaking.

The leaves and branches were in a fine frenzy. Windows slammed open and shut, and there was the sound of breaking glass. The birds knew. They were gyrating wildly in the sky, desperate to get to their nests, to the crannies and crevices of the buildings.

All at once, the next few drops, and everybody knew. Servants and wives rushed to the windows to take in the laundry.

A massive crack in the sky and then another huge roar from the earth, from hundreds of thousands of children all over the city as the torrent fell upon them. All day long you have been sweating, all day long your body has been ready to receive it and has sensed it like the cows and the crows, and now the first rain is upon you. Your parents have warned you about it, screamed at you about it: Never bathe in the first rain! It is black with the dust and pollution of the atmosphere and you will get sick but you don't care. All the children of the world are out dancing in the streets and the parking lots and the gullies, and for once the cars are stilled by the mighty juvenile throng, with the invincible force of the monsoon at their backs. Big drops of water are coming down very close together, walls of water, worlds of water. And you are in the middle of it and nothing can be seen except the water. There is lightning and all is daylight again, but only for an instant. You raise your face to the water and wash the summer off. It enters your eyes and nose and mouth and carries away all sin and sorrow with it.

When the rain stops, the air is suddenly sweetened. The trees and the shrubs and the weeds have dispensed fragrance into the air. Hundreds of long brown earthworms are crawling out of the softened ground. Bombay will open its windows and the rain-sweetened air will come in and Bombay will sleep well tonight. And if the first rain is early, you will sleep especially well tonight, because you still have fifteen days left till the beginning of school.

Mayur Mahal Multipurpose

The bell is still there. I am sitting in the principal's office when a peon comes in, reaches out the window, and yanks at a thick white rope. There is a peal; I know that sound well. The rope leads across the yard to the other school building, to a thick brass bell whose ringing could be a glad sound, signifying release from a day of torment, or a dread sound, bringing on Mrs. Qureshi's period. Period means "class," but so cranky was the Hindi teacher that it could equally well have meant the other thing.

"We would like to felicitate you." Cheroot, as we called the man who was my science teacher and is now the principal, is smiling. "On November fourteenth, we will be holding a function for you. Also for Salil Ankola, cricketer, Shweta Shetty, singing sensation, and Krishna Mehta, designer. All Mayur Mahal students," he informs me happily. He has cut out a newspaper article about me and put it up on the notice board. I am now a "distinguished alumnus." The invitation that came in the mail said *We are proud of your outstanding performance in the field of Literature.* At last the institution that displayed no signs of pride in me while I was enrolled in it, that first beat me for having bad handwriting and then for not taking notes in class, wants to honor me for being a writer.

Mayur Mahal Multipurpose. Its full name is Mayur Mahal's Shreemati Nandkunvar Ramniklal J. Parikh Multipurpose High School, and it is principally known for having its own street named after it. It imposed the title on one of the lanes that connect the sea with the top of Malabar Hill. The original name can still be seen on a faded BEST electricity box: Wilderness Road. When the wilderness disappeared, so, appropriately, did the name.

We lived in Bombay and we lived in Mumbai and sometimes we lived in both of them at the same time. Mayur Mahal was where the Gujarati and Marwari traders sent their offspring. Not for us the sophistication of the convent schools, Cathedral or Campion. Our parents were more likely to discuss grain prices than Gershwin; we ate fafda rather than foie gras. Mayur Mahal dispensed instruction in two languages, Gujarati and English, but the English medium tended to be nominal. The administration strove mightily to get us to speak in English at all times, but we jabbered away in Hindi and Gujarati. "Gadherao, English ma bolo ne!" a teacher famously screamed at us. "Donkeys, speak English!"

Mr. Maskawala, the gym teacher, had been standing by the gate when I returned to Mayur Mahal. He had clasped my hand with his sweaty one. He is still a buffoon, with his split lip; he's probably still trying to romance the Catholic teachers. He led me past the stone elephant and past the little shrine to Saraswati. Past the cold-water taps under which we cupped our palms and drank and in the trough of which you could always discover, from the chewed debris that had slipped out of the mouths of previous drinkers, what everyone had been having for lunch. Past the little compound in the back where we made pav bhaji in our scouting class, up two flights, and into the principal's office. Here, the same old scene is being played out. Two boys are standing by Cheroot's desk. He calls in Verma Sir (the biology teacher, who scandalized the Jain trustees by bringing in a fish to dissect). "There have been three written complaints against these boys. Take them away, and tell them that they will have to leave school, and they won't be able to continue SSC or anything." The boys are led away to their fate, the threat of not matriculating hanging over them. It comes back to me, how when I was fourteen, another teacher had slapped me hard on my face for shutting a classroom door during recess, then dragged me to this same principal's office, and the vice principal had written out a leaving certificate, and I cried, thinking I would never be able to get into a school in the country I was about to move to. He let me sweat for a couple of days and then, after repeated apologies on my part, he rescinded the certificate. He was just having his sadistic little bit of fun.

All the teachers are old now, and they look not much different from the peons. Cheroot explains why the school has deteriorated. The school administration had embarked on a policy of deliberately taking in poor students, the residents of the slum colonies all around Malabar Hill that I had seen when I went campaigning with Jayawantiben Mehta, the "lower strata," as Cheroot calls them. "We are a trust, after all." It is a huge school now: eighteen hundred students in two shifts, tended to by some sixty teachers and staff. A blanket of melancholy, of sadness, of decay, hangs over the entire place. The children streaming from school in the late afternoon are now darker and worse dressed, their haircuts more unfashionable, than when I studied here. "It's a school for the children of dhobis and drivers," my cousin had told me. When I went there, "the aristocracy sent their children to Mayur Mahal. But now you wouldn't send your son to this school. You sent him to New Era," Cheroot points out. "You wouldn't want your son and your driver's son studying in the same class," he concludes. He is presiding over the systematic deterioration and democratization of an institution.

I ask him what kinds of methods the school uses these days to discipline its students. "We have to use 'threatening.' " He pronounces the word like a thunderclap—*"threatening!"*—shaking his hands as he does so. "Of course now we don't do it so much. But we give a couple of slaps now and then," he admits, chortling. "You know that I and Verma Sir were known as disciplinarians. We even slapped the students!" Yes, as you did me.

I have been reading reports in the newspaper, on two successive days, of children being brutalized in Bombay schools. Yesterday's article was about an eighth-grader in J. B. Khot High School who didn't hand in an assignment. The teacher stripped off his shirt in front of the class; then she wanted him to take off his shorts. She pulled at his zipper to take them off, yanked it, and his penis got caught. When he got home, he went to bed. He can't piss properly now. "His mind is disturbed," his father stated. In the same school, a kindergartener was asked to produce his calendar. Some other children were playing with it. So the teacher stood him in front of an adjoining class and stripped him, amid a jeering chorus of his schoolmates yelling, "Shame, shame!" A counselor, interviewed in the paper, condemned the incidents and suggested that when teachers need to discipline students, "the whole class should participate in framing a punishment." I think of a Mayur Mahal class collectively framing a punishment. What pleasant hours we would have passed! We would have come up with some good ones.

Then in today's paper: A seven-year-old girl in Jogeshwari forgot to paste the picture of a train in her notebook for homework in her art class. To teach the little girl a lesson, her art teacher went at her hands, legs, and back with a wooden ruler and then slapped her hard on her face and arm. After the thrashing, the girl quietly walked to her grandmother's house. The next day she started vomiting blood. Then bruises showed up on her arm and patches of blood coagulated on her face. Her liver is badly injured, and the doctors say the veins in her forehead may burst at any time. If she lives, her parents, who have three other children in the school, say they may send her back. Her art teacher was arrested and released on bail the next day. He teaches at, and the little girl attends, Mahatma Gandhi School.

The name is not an accident. What Gandhiji knew was that if the country were allowed to go, it would have been the most savage independence movement in world history. The violence begins early in life. When an adult Indian is hit, he is instantly reminded of his schooldays. The teachers at Mayur Mahal felt very free with their hands around the students; they assumed a familiarity with our bodies. "Do you know, to beat a child is actually against the law," we whispered to each other. When a noise was heard in the back of the class, the entire class was punished, girls and boys both, with two thwacks of the foot ruler on the open palm. A good way to reduce the pain was to rub our hands on our oiled heads, and then hold the palm at an angle, so that the wood lightly glanced off the skin. The teachers often broke rulers across our hands in their fury.

The days I would be sure of getting a beating were those on which our notebooks were checked. We were supposed to write down every word of what the teachers said in class, which was mostly what they read out aloud from the state textbooks, and write it back for them in the examinations, so that education became an exercise in repetition, "learning by heart." The notebooks accounted for 20 percent of the marks. Something in me rebelled against the idea of taking notes to perpetuate this cycle of government-written facts. The previous day, the other students would have gone frantic copying each others' notes. I would be woken up by my mother, and my first thought would be, I am going to get beaten today. I washed, put on a clean uniform, was given a glass of milk by my mother, and left home bright and shining so I could walk to the building where I would be beaten.

In class I would watch the clock on the wall as if it were my greatest friend, as if it were a lover, and will the hands to speed toward the close of the period. Sometimes the teacher would forget to check the notes that day; when the bell rang, ending the period, there would be the relief of the condemned spared his execution. The next few hours were happy; then slowly, toward evening, the dread would descend once again like a heavy fog. The punishment had not been evaded; it had only been postponed.

There was one ingenious punishment in which the teachers excelled. It was a simple piece of white cardboard, with a string around it, bearing the inscription, in large letters readable across a room, I HAVE NOT DONE MY HOMEWORK. When this was the case, you had to wear it for public display. One day I did not do my homework, and the teacher garlanded me with the board. As she did so, I wondered why there were black streaks running down the white cardboard. I soon found out. Wearing the sign, I was instructed to stand not only in front of my own class but also all the other classrooms on the floor. The door of the next room would be opened and I would walk in unsteadily and go to the head of the class. There I would turn, face forty of my fellow students, and stand silently. Children love nothing so much as to see other children in pain, especially at Mayur Mahal, where pain was so prevalent it formed part of the masonry. My humiliation was a relief from their own, so the room erupted in a chorus of mocking laughter, hooting, and jokes. In the beginning I tried smiling—as if I got the joke too and wasn't it hilarious—but I quickly discovered what the black streaks were. They were the tears of all previous wearers of the board, and I added my own to them. When I had finished my performance in one classroom I would have to go the next, and the next, and after I'd finished all of them, I would have to stand in the passage outside the classrooms, standing and shifting against the wall, desperately trying to keep my advertised shame from the eyes of those who passed by.

The way we dealt with all this was through laughter. Not kind laughter, indulgent laughter, but mocking, profane, evil laughter. We laughed at the teachers and reduced the female teachers to sex objects; big-titted Miss Easo got dubbed—what else?—Petrol Pump. We laughed at other children when they got beaten, and after a while they laughed about it too. When I meet people from Mayur Mahal now, we recall the stinging slaps we were given and laugh about them; we remember the beatings we got in the way that children in other schools remember the school plays or the prizes they won.

ON CHILDREN'S DAY, I go with my wife and son to be honored by the school that tormented me for nine years.

"This is Suketu Mehta." Cheroot introduces me to the other felicitees as soon as I walk onstage. "He was given a literary award by Bill Clinton."

"No, I wasn't."

"By President Bill Clinton."

"No, I wasn't," I say, more emphatically this time and shaking my head as well.

"You were not given an award by Bill Clinton?" he asks, a trifle suspiciously.

"No."

"Then *who* gave you the award?" asks Cheroot, a darkness coming over his face as if he's caught me cheating on an exam.

I think. What would the name Mrs. Giles Whiting mean to him? "A . . . literary academy."

Fifteen minutes later, I hear the emcee, a boy in jeans, a white shirt, and tie, introducing me to the audience. "And we are proud to have Suketu Mehta, the laureate of literature, who was given an award by Bill Clinton."

The poetic license of the introductions is not restricted only to me. Another outstanding ex-student is a karate instructor, whom the announcer introduces as a "sixteenth-degree black belt in karate." There are titters in the audience, many of whom have sent their sons to this instructor to learn survival in the Bombay streets, and a teacher rushes up to the boy. He corrects himself. "Sorry, sixth-degree." The school, which grudged a single complimentary word when we were its students, is now exaggerating our achievements beyond credibility, as if in compensation. It is not enough to have gone to Cornell for an MBA, as one of my fellow felicitees did; he was "a topper of all the Cornell MBAs." There is a lawn-tennis champion who has accumulated twenty-one points in the lawn-tennis contests. "After one hundred points he will reach Wimbledon." There is a "ball-bearing tycoon" and assorted diamond merchants, builders, and doctors, all lords of their profession. There is only one lady, "the Best Designer in Asia," whom I sit next to and trade memories with while the speakers go on at length about the ills of modern education. The craft teacher comes in late, her hair glowing red with henna, in a semitransparent sari. She had us build tanks out of matchboxes glued together and plant shrubs in pots; mine all died. "She told me I can't stitch and sew," the Best Designer in Asia whispers to me. "I feel like telling her that's what I do for a living now."

The Cornell MBA's brother was in my class. He reminds me of this fact. "When I told him yesterday who was being felicitated, he remembered you. 'Terrible handwriting,' he said." This was my singular distinction in that school. My handwriting had been screwed up when I entered Mayur Mahal, in the second standard. My previous school, in Calcutta, had taught me to write in "joint handwriting," cursive script, but at Mayur Mahal the standard was separate letters. My hands resisted the new script and got hit with a foot ruler for doing so. So my handwriting stayed stuck in the transition stage, between joint and separate, between Calcutta and Bombay: a font, a code of its own, decipherable only by myself. It gave the teachers migraines; samples of it were sent far and wide to demonstrate the hardships of a teacher's life. It was variously compared to modern art and to ants dipped in ink crawling across the page. On the other hand, a teacher fond of me pointed out, "Gandhiji also had bad handwriting." I took considerable solace in that observation and eagerly sought out all samples of the Mahatma's scrawl, until I was convinced that bad handwriting was not only compensated for by greatness later on in life but a prerequisite for it. My English teacher failed to share this theory and refused to read my English essay. I would fail English, my best subject. My father got fed up and hired a handwriting tutor.

The tutor was a mousy little man with a mustache and thick black glasses who was a drawing teacher in a Gujarati school. He was also, I discovered after our first session, a devoted Communist. He declared that he would first teach me the fundamentals of drawing in order to improve my calligraphy. To that end, he directed me to sketch out two hands clasped in a handshake, demonstrating Indo-Soviet friendship. In later lessons, he had me write lengthy essays on Indo-Soviet friendship, so that I could practice my handwriting. My father the diamond merchant realized that my writing wasn't showing any signs of being any more legible. While he was out every day trying to expand his capital through oppression of the diamond workers, his only son was being systematically indoctrinated in class conflict in his own home, at his own expense. He kicked the handwriting teacher out. My handwriting stayed as tortured as ever, but I knew a lot more about the Soviet Union.

Onstage now, Kanubhai, the eighty-two-year-old managing trustee of the school, with a white Gandhi cap on his skull, is forced repeatedly to get up and receive the salutations of the endless felicitees. After each name is announced, someone prods his back, and, startled from slumber, he darts forward and up from his chair, deposits the valedictory shawl around the honoree, and sinks back gratefully into his chair and his stupor. The doctor on my left leans close to me. "I examined him only last week. He's not in good health at all. I'm worried." It would not look good if Kanubhai breathed his last on Children's Day; on the other hand, it would be somehow appropriate.

After the ceremony, we walk off the stage, looking for the way out. I have an overpowering urge to leave. But we are shepherded into a back room from which there is no exit; I have to be there with my wife and child, while plates of samosas and sandwiches are thrust at us. I am tense. I do not want to look at the past, not here, not with these people.

"Hi, Suketu," someone says. I turn around to see a short dark man with an unfortunate face, which at this moment is all smiles, standing in front of me. "You don't remember me."

I do, instantly. "Urvesh?"

He shakes my hand. I should have gone down on my knees and begged forgiveness. A quarter of a century ago, I had hurt him in the worst possible way; and the memory of that shame still lingers.

Urvesh was a little squeak in our playground at Dariya Mahal who delighted in pitting the bigger boys against each other, which he did with great success. He would carry tales, first in the ear of one dada, then the other tough, and get them fighting. Urvesh was small and pockmarked, and he had been the subject of many beatings before he learnt this survival tactic. One day his mother died. His head was shaved. I got in a fight with him very soon after, and I was searching for a way to truly hurt him. I had beaten him up many times before, but he never cried; he had learnt to never cry, as small boys do. So I shouted at him, "I know your mother's croaked!" There was an awful stillness in the small playground. Then my best friend, who until that moment had also wanted to give Urvesh a good kicking, slapped the back of my head—hard. Urvesh had said nothing, nothing at all. Out of all my ghosts, why should he be standing in front of me, right here, now?

But Urvesh remembers none of this; he is eagerly talking to me. He tells me he still lives in the neighborhood and is in the diamond market. He has a wife and children. How could he forget what I did to him when he was most vulnerable? After all, *I* haven't. I don't know who else might come up to greet me, and I am also afraid of the converse—that I will be left alone, ignored. The room is closing in on me and I look desperately for the exit. My son has finished his sweets and asks for a samosa. I grab his hand and lead him and my wife from the room, out to the street to look for a taxi. I am more nervous than in my meetings with the gangsters. There is real danger here. I know I should stay, should try to see who still remembers me, has stories for me. But it is too close. Even outside, I'm not safe. A woman comes up to me smiling. She lives in my building; she is the sister-in-law of the man who had parked his car in my space. She says she didn't know I was a student at Mayur Mahal. I smile, mumble something, and herd my family into a taxi.

BUT I MUST GO BACK to the school. It contains nine years of my ghost time; I must come to terms with it. I go when I can't avoid it any longer.

As I ascend the stairs on my second visit, my heart is already thumping. I have to stop for a moment, in front of the display *Lincoln's letter to his son's teacher*, on the mezzanine floor. They still have my old mark sheets, my records. I will look at them. I am brave enough now. In the administrative office, the peon reluctantly digs out my record of leaving from a 1977 register. I see my name, with the entries. CASTE: *Hindu Bania*. Under the column titled PROGRESS, all the students down the page are awarded *Good* except for one *Not Good* and mine: *Satisfactory*. Another entry is under CONDUCT, in which mine was deemed *Good*.

My academic career in this school peaked in the fifth standard, when I came in first, then tanked steeply, so that by the time I left my class rank was comfortably in the double digits. Shortly after the state examination results were out, the photos of the toppers would appear in the newspapers, in ads for the coaching classes where they had toiled night and day. They wore thick glasses and looked enervated from frequent masturbation. BHAVESH SADASYACHARI, ALL-INDIA NUMBER 6. None of them were smiling at their triumph. They didn't look like they'd smiled in a month. And they were almost all of them destined to be parked on bureaucrats' chairs, in government and in corporations, to make life hell for all the rest of us who goofed off in school, went out dancing, and generally had been arousing their envy from kindergarten.

The peon calls me into the supervisor's room. Verma Sir is getting a large bundle of notes from two girls. I remember his teaching geometry in his south Indian accent: "Ven yex meets vuy. . . ." After greeting me, he explains the notes. "They're to pay the staff. The parents contribute, because all our money is going to Surendranagar, where we have a school for destitute girls. Other than four or five teachers like me, who are rich through tutorials, we don't have money for the rest of the staff according to the scales of the Fifth Pay Commission. So the parents give whatever they can. . . ." He is not suggesting anything, but I guess the purpose of his long explanation of the school's finances, and I say, "Perhaps I can make a donation."

"It is enough that you have come!" he responds at once. "Your very presence is itself a donation!" He walks me around the school. The first floor is now all entirely staff rooms, except for one where a group of girls are singing a patriotic song, led by a teacher sitting on the floor with a harmonium. We walk into different classes, and the students stand up abruptly at our entrance, in a body. They remain standing till Verma Sir tells them to sit down. "This is Suketu Mehta," he introduces me. "He is a full-time writer. He was given a medal by the U.S. President." I correct him again. "Who gave you that award?" he asks. I give up. The presidential origin of my award will forever stick to me in this school, like an irreversible computer error. "It was . . . the U.S. government." This satisfies him. "He was given a scholarship by the U.S. government." The class bursts into spontaneous applause. Embarrassed, I walk out. This approval is as unendurable as the school's earlier punishments.

In another class, he asks the students if they have any questions for me.

"He has published many novels," he informs them. I ask if there is something I can teach them. "Geometry!" they shout. "Geometry!"

I ask to see an English class, and we go into one and sit in the back. The teacher is leading the class through a poem from the "Balbharti" state textbook: Tennyson's "A Farewell." On the board are two words: *Somersby* and *Lincolnshire*. The girl next to me has her book open to the poem. "Flow down, cold rivulet, to the sea, . . ." The crevices and crannies of the letters are filled in with blue ink. Above the title she has written *Terminal*—her knowledge of the poem will be tested in the terminal exams—and has drawn a smiley face next to it. The illustration on the page is a rushing stream, and the girl has written *Varsha* on the English body of water, thus Indianizing its name, explaining it to herself, making it less forbidding.

"The poet is speaking to the river," the teacher explains to the class. "This is a figure of speech. It is called an apostrophe." I did not know this. I will have to look it up in the dictionary later. I am still learning new things at Mayur Mahal. The classroom is almost exactly the same as when I used to sit in it. The same badly painted walls, the same speaker above the same blackboard, which boomed out patriotic and religious songs and admonitions from the principal each morning. A calendar on one wall marks the passage of time for the children of abstemious Jain and Hindu parents, compliments of Standard Wine Stores. The same scarred and pitted wooden benches, like the one I am sitting on, with its gutter for writing implements, ballpoints now acceptable. Out of the windows on one side of the building, a view of the leafy compounds of the mansions of Malabar Hill. "Flow down, cold rivulet, to the sea, . . ." The teacher is explaining what the poem is about. "If you change your residence, if you leave the memories of your school life, of childhood, how it would be to have to adjust to a new school, a new life." A poet is bidding good-bye to his country, the country of childhood.

> *A thousand suns will stream on thee,*
> *A thousand moons will quiver;*
> *But not by thee my steps shall be,*
> *For ever and for ever.*

Outside, in the passage, I dare not turn around, because a boy might come running up to me out of those classrooms, anxious to get outside for recess, bump into me, and say, "Sorry, sir," and look up at me and see himself.

A World of Children

On Sundays we go to Hanging Gardens with the children. I like seeing my children among the visitors from the suburbs. I have a basic trust in these families of clerks, these grandmothers who put food in the picnic baskets, these children dressed in Indian imitations of western clothes. I trust what they want for their children: to have a home, a wife, and a little more comfort than they have had.

On my older son Gautama's birthday we take him to the Mahalakshmi temple. Outside the temple lane, a woman sits with a cow and a basket filled with bundles of grass. I give 5 rupees to the woman, she gives Gautama a sheaf of grass, and he feeds it to the cow, accumulating merit and wonder. The animals my children saw in storybooks in the West—elephants, camels, peacocks—are out walking in the streets of India. Gautama's best friend has recently been bitten by a monkey, on the lawn of his plush building on Ridge Road. It is an unusual urban hazard in other countries.

As we walk toward the temple we see a bookshop: Motilal Banarsidas, Indological Book Publishers. I have been to branches of this bookstore in Varanasi, Delhi, and Madras, and my shelves are stacked with the harvest, so we decide to walk into this anteroom of the temple for a while. The manager, noticing the birthday cap on Gautama's head, asks the peon to get a fistful of chocolates for him. We browse happily for a long time and select some books to buy; we will pick them up on our way back. Then we walk toward the temple, to witness the present-day enactment of the philosophy preserved in the books here.

As we go up the stairs leading to the temple, we pass under a huge banner welcoming the chief minister of Maharashtra, Narayan Rane, who earlier in his career was tried for murder and acquitted on a technicality. Sunita and Gautama get in the women's line for the darshan, and I stand in the men's line. When they reach the idol, Gautama folds his palms and begins talking to the goddess—"Thank you for giving me a nice birthday"—but he and his mother are pushed from behind; move on, move on, others want their audience. They rejoin me, and we stand behind the rear latticed wall as the aarti begins. We don't know the rituals; we don't know all the words to the songs. The worshipers chant vigorously, and there is a great sound of bells and drums. We are just beyond the boundary, and the priest does not bring his oil lamp near us, over which the others cup their hands and gather them to their forehead, seeking blessing. I always came to this temple with my grandparents, but they are no longer here to tell me what to do, how to get the coconut prasad, where to buy the flowers for the deities. So we leave, my foreign wife and foreign son and myself, and on our way out purchase for Gautama a lotus flower, Lakshmi's flower, paying too much. Back at the bookstore, we pick up our books: a translation of devotional poems to Vishnu by the ninth-century Tamil poetess Antal; a one-volume version of the Bhagvata Purana; and an illustrated comic book of the life of Ambedkar for our son. I first learnt my Hinduism through my grandmother, and it was unanalytical, mystical. Then I learnt it again, in American universities. The stories that those people in the temple know by heart we needed to have explained to us by American academics.

MY YOUNGER SON, AKASH, IS a serene baby, a baby who basically likes being happy. When he smiles, I see the white line of his teeth ready to break out of the confinement of his gums, like eggs. The other life, the one just worn, is still with him, but it is going fast. One morning Akash is standing, holding the sofa. All morning he has been giving us signs. He has a fever, and a cough that sounds like a bark. He has been up all night, and this morning I found him on our bed. He had climbed up by himself. I put him down on the floor and he repeated the feat. Then there was the second sign: He stood up on the bed, up from a sitting position. Now, standing by the sofa, the plastic water bottle he is teething on falls out of his hand and rolls away. He watches it go away from him, then turns from the sofa and puts one leg in front of the other, then brings the other leg forward, and then the first leg again, till he is close to the bottle. Without realizing what he has done—a defeat of gravity so casual, so flawless, so roundabout, that it looks accidental—and without pausing to celebrate his mastery, he bends down and then sits down and resumes gnawing on the bottle. We see this, I and my first son both. For many days now I had been resenting working at home; my children were disturbing me as I worked. But now I am here to watch my baby take his first steps; I am not away in my office, and it is a vision that will remain with me for the rest of my life.

After having my own children, I have become conscious that the world is full of children. They were not there when I was twenty-five.

I have promised my sons I will be home by afternoon, and it is now 10 p.m. and I am still in my office in Elco Arcade. I see a taxicab parked right outside and am walking to it when I see a group of very young children on the road. They are being chased away by the owner of the milk booth—"Haddi!"—a sound you use to chase away a stray dog. I stop. There are four of them: a girl, maybe six, another girl and boy a couple of years younger, and the youngest, a boy certainly no older than two. Only the girls are wearing clothes, dirty oversized frocks. The boys don't have a stitch on, except for some white beads around their necks. They are gathered around the older girl, who is examining something she has retrieved from the detritus of the snack stalls; it is a sandwich, two slices of bread smeared with green chutney. As the other three look on hungrily, she eats the sandwich intently. The others play with straws found in the garbage of the coconut stand, threading the white pipes into each other. The smallest child breaks away; it's obvious he isn't going to get anything, and he lies indolently down on the road and rolls over one and a half times, leisurely—a movement of the body I know so well from watching Akash—rolling on the road, gathering up the filthy water, the dog shit, the juice pulp, the betel spit, and the ordinary dust from the road all over his naked brown body, his little arms, his plump pouty belly. Then he gets up and wanders out on the road, dreamily, as children do. Taxis, buses, and rickshaws are zooming by at great speed and he is one-fourth of his way into the middle of the road and nobody is saying anything, not the girl, not the passersby, not me. He is too close to the ground to be noticed by the automobile drivers. There is no mother in sight. My heart jumps up in my mouth, but then the boy stops, grins, and walks back to the side of the road. The children have sat down around the sandwich right in the middle of the driveway to my building, and the milk-booth man is halfheartedly shouting at them to get out of the road, cars are coming. "Where is their mother?" I ask the milk-booth man, and he says he doesn't know. He has asked the coconut-stall vendor to mind the children, and the coconut man has responded angrily that they aren't his. I cannot walk to my taxi. I am paralyzed, I am choking, and a desperate sadness rises up in me. I can't just give them money. The little boy's head is shaved, just like Akash's. Will somebody please do something? I can't leave this child here, abandoned, but I want to get away. I can't take him home. I think of getting a cop, but the child will just be picked up and sent to the remand home. A three-year-old in a Bhiwandi children's "observation" home recently died from prolonged beatings. A three-year-old! Who would beat a three-year-old baby to death? How great an anger could he cause?

Then the older girl's eyes meet mine, and she knows immediately. She comes over and says, "Saab, something to eat," and holds out her palm. I ask where her mother is and she says she's not here. I ask if they've eaten and of course she says no. At this moment a peanut vendor passes by and I gesture at him. "We won't eat that," the girl says. Then what will you eat? "Milk."

I go over to the milk booth and the vendor sees them following me. "Not too close to the shop!" he barks at them. "Four milks," I order. His assistant comes over with a large stick, the kind used to chase away monkeys, and waves it at the children. "I'm getting milk for them!" I exclaim. Four bottles of Energee, pistachio-flavored, are put on the counter, and the four children sit on the road and start sipping at the bottles through straws. I look at the smallest boy; his face is whole delight and he can't wait to get at the milk as he puts the straw in his mouth. I walk toward the taxi, anxious to get home and kiss my children.

Sone ki Chidiya

"BAMBAI TO SONE KI CHIDIYA HAI," a Muslim man in the Jogeshwari slum, whose brother was shot dead by the police in the riots, tells me. A Golden Songbird; try to catch it if you can. It flies quick and sly, and you'll have to work hard and brave many perils to catch it, but once it's in your hand, a fabulous fortune will open up for you. This is the reason why anyone would still want to come here, leaving the pleasant trees and open spaces of the village, braving the riots and the bad air and water. From the village to the city, to found villages in the city. The slums and sidewalks of Bombay are filled with little lives, unnoticed in the throng, uncelebrated in the Bollywood movies. But to each one of them, the scale they are living in is mythic. It involves battles of good versus evil, survival or death, love and desolation, and the ceaseless, life-affirming pursuit of the Golden Songbird. What they have in common with each other—what they have in common, in fact, with me—is restlessness, the inability or disinclination to stay still. Like me, they are happiest in transit.

Girish: A Tourist in His City

"You need a sherpa," an editor told me when I was researching my article on the riots. Then I found Girish Thakkar, working as a programmer in a friend's office. He turns out to be the right person; Girish lives as a tourist in his own city.

Our journeys generally begin at Churchgate, where Girish takes the train home. Many of the signs in the station are of escape: ASSIGNMENTS

ABROAD, for a newspaper, and another—enclosed in glass, next to a sleeping dog that has found a niche—for those who want to go the other way:

ENCORE FARMS (Farm House Plot)
only Rupees 20/ square foot
40 Fruit Trees * 20 Mango * 10 Cashew * 10 Others
Tukashi Village

As the people come hurrying into the city in the morning, as they trudge home in the evening, they might glance at the sign, and they might take with them a small vision with them through the day at the office, through the long cramped train ride: a little village, a little house, surrounded on all sides by a wealth of trees, their branches heavy with fruit waiting to be picked, a silence resting easy over the orchard. A vision of a childhood spent on grandmother's farm.

We take the train to Jogeshwari and trudge through the lanes of the slum till we get to the alley off which Girish's shanty sits; you would not be able to find it unless you were led to it. The room is filled with people. Visitors stream in and out all day long; as new people come in, the earlier occupants move and make room for them on the cot, like a continuous game of musical chairs. They are asked to stay for lunch and they know to refuse. The room contains one metal folding chair, reserved for honored guests, on which I am sitting, a stool for people who come a little too often, one metal cot, a metal wardrobe, a counter for the gas, a TV, a table, and some shelves. This is the entire furniture of the lives of seven people: two parents and five children in their twenties. The father sits on the ground shelling peas. There is laundry drying on plastic lines overhead. The door is open till late; you will find few closed doors in the slum. All the windows are on one side, the side facing the little lanes that the doors open onto. A salesman comes by, asking in all the doorways "Vicks Ayurvedic Balm?" and holding an open bottle. They all laugh at him. There is a good deal of laughter today. It's a holiday, and everyone's relaxed and enjoying the novelty of the whole family being at home together. The boys take turns sleeping on one side of the cot as others sit along its edge. In all Girish's life, he has never had a whole bed to himself to sleep in at home.

The Thakkars' home is a sanctuary. During the riots, the women of three families were staying in this room. It was considered a safe place, and it had a phone, which people would come in to use, to inquire anxiously about their relatives. Then there was the Bulgarian sailor. He had been robbed of all his money and his bags at the airport. Paresh, Girish's younger brother, who teaches disco dance classes, ran into him at a hotel, found him crying, and brought him home. He had no money to travel to the Gujarat coast, where his ship was berthed. The family gave him some money for the train ticket. Then they thought, This man can't speak the language, he will be robbed again. So they sent Paresh with him, all the way to the coast, several days' journey, to make sure he got there safely. Their fears were well founded. During a check by police on the train in Gujarat, which is a dry state, they found a bottle of cooking wine and a set of threatening-looking knives, which the sailor, a cook, had kept in his handbag. Those were his tools, he said, but the policemen asked for a fine of 2,000 rupees, which Paresh bargained down to 200 and the bottle of wine. The family still talks about this incident. They show me a photo album, with a picture of the tall white sailor, his arms around his Indian friends. He never wrote them after going back.

The room had bamboo walls and a mud roof when the Thakkars moved in. Over the years they've improved it, put on a tin roof, plastered the walls. "What could we get on a salary of a hundred and fifty rupees a month?" his mother reminisces. "Girish's father wanted all his children to do well. The eldest is doing well; all this is from his salary. Girish can't give anything. When he lost that money in the share bazaar he got sick. Now his condition is bad, he can't give anything. His father was saying, Look, my second son can't contribute anything."

Girish has his ever-present smile on. Perhaps this is the reason he's never at home. He is twenty-five; he should be bringing in money and he's not. At this point, Girish is a drain on the household.

For the vast majority of families in Bombay—73 percent, according to the 1990 census—home consists of only one room, for living: sleeping, cooking, eating. The average is 4.7 persons to a room; Girish's family exceeds this by 2.3 persons. The furniture of the room changes roles continuously, through the day; the bed of the night is the sofa of the morning; the dining table is the study table between meals. The residents, too, are quick-change artists, changing from nightclothes to day clothes under a towel, behind a curtain, so quickly you would think they are invisible. But invisibility is actually bestowed upon them, as the other inhabitants of the room avert their eyes during the moment of transformation. How on earth did the parents conceive five children in this slum room? There must have been a good deal seen and not watched, heard and not listened to.

Girish spends as little time in Jogeshwari as possible, leaving by the seven o'clock train and getting back at midnight. If it is a Sunday, instead of taking a nap at home, he will go to Kandivili to a friend's computer class to teach for two hours. There are all manner of implicit understandings about how the family members will divide up their time in the room. There isn't enough space for everybody to be there at once, except when they're all sleeping, when body movements are kept to a minimum. It's the only way they can be stacked, when they're sleeping or dead. Home, in the slum, is a time-share.

I ask how Girish sleeps with his family in the room. He looks at me, then takes out a pen. "See, we are seven people." I give him my notebook to sketch the plan of the sleeping arrangements. He pushes it away and takes a paper napkin. "Me and my older brother on the cot," and he sketches two circles on a rectangle. "Then my two younger brothers on the floor." Two more balloons below the rectangle. "My parents in the kitchen," only notionally separated from the front half of the room. Then he draws a line, writes on it TABLE. "My sister under the table."

After this explanation, he takes the paper napkin, folds it once, folds it over again, scrunches it into a ball, presses it very hard in his fingers, presses it with all his might, and when it has become small, so small that it is insignificant, he throws it away. Then he looks up and smiles at me.

WE WALK OUT into the lanes of the slum. There is a diversity of occupations here not found in the richer precincts. Girish shows me a room filled with seashells; a man is making gift items from them, some with an electric bulb implanted inside. Near the station, Girish runs into an acquaintance, a struggler in the film industry, who describes his new movie: "Love story plus a little bit mafia." Next Girish pays his respects to a local mafia dada, Ramswamy, who lives above the Sai Betting Parlor and runs an extensive bootlegging operation. In his living room are several pictures of himself, lushly mustached, in none of which is he smiling. The dada is lying on his side, bare-chested. "A man needs to feed his stomach," he says, and pats his belly, which has a life and shape of its own, spilling out like a seal over the bed, two deep knife marks etched into its sides like a mother of twelve's stretch marks. Ramswamy has three official wives and ten or twelve unofficial ones; he usually begins every sentence with "Bhenchod . . . ," but with Girish he doesn't. "He gives me respect." I ask Girish why Ramswamy hasn't bought himself a better flat, out of the slum. "He will only live where he can rule," Girish explains.

Walking on, we pass a sign over a shack: BRIGHT COMPUTER CLASSES. "Every Tom, Dick, and Harry has started computer classes here," says Girish. The slums of Bombay are filled with programmers learning Visual Basic, C++, Oracle, Windows NT. It is a hospitable new world for the bright young slum children of Bombay, people like Girish, showing them the way out, like boxing or basketball in Harlem. The papers are filled with notices from companies near and far wanting our children, for honest work, well-paid work, with an air-conditioned office and a chance to see the world. Girish's young sister, Raju, works at getting those children from here to there. She runs an exam-coaching class from the second floor of a shack. Dharmendra, eldest of the Thakkar siblings, pitches in with history lessons when he can.

A first-standard girl gets up on Raju's command to recite the pledge:

> "*India is my country.*
> *All Indians are my brothers and sisters*
> [Hence we are all bhenchods, I remember from my schooldays]
> *I am proud of my country.*
> *I . . .*"

She looks down. She has forgotten the rest. She sits back on the floor.

A good part of Raju's job involves counseling children from troubled homes. She transforms her students from repeaters to successes who score more than 80 percent on their exams. But it's a nonprofit enterprise for her; she's not making any money this year from the classes, after the expenses of rent and salaries for the other teachers. When she goes home from the coaching class, she immediately sets to work helping her mother make lunch. Her father looks at me and nods his head. "Very hardworking." She is good to her father and her brothers and her mother. She will be good to her husband and children when they come into her life. I see her walking along the lanes of the slum, somehow staying fresh and pretty among the open gutters.

The high point of the year for the Thakkars is their annual trip to their village, Padga Gam, near Navsari, for two or three blissful weeks. There they own a little farm that grows sugar cane, eggplant, and this year rice. For several miles around the house the land is clear. It is a big house, Girish says. It has more than one room. In his village he gets up in the morning and immediately starts eating. His mother cooks on a clay wood-fired stove, in earthen pots, food fresh from the farm. Girish idles on the bed. He sleeps some more. He eats some more. There is a little black-and-white portable TV that they all watch in the evenings. He hates coming back to Bombay. "I feel depressed when I come into Virar," says Girish. "I feel really depressed. If someone pulls my leg I may even hit him."

GIRISH AND I STROLL outside his office in central Bombay one afternoon for some bhelpuri. At Bora Bazaar, we come up to the Shree Krishna Bhelpuri House—"We exchange old and torn notes"—a cart in the middle of some mounds of onion and potato peels. Girish points to a stack of old or torn notes behind the bhaiyya. Yesterday he gave him 24 rupees in soiled notes and got back 20 in clean ones. Bombay has a service for every human need.

Near Girish's office, opposite the General Post Office, are a group of letter writers. They sit in front of the kabutarkhana, where thousands of fluttering pigeons gather to eat grain left by Jains, around a nonfunctional fountain. They prepare packages for foreigners, serve as a mailbox for those living on the streets, fill out forms and money orders for those literate but unskilled at bureaucratic writing, and write letters for the illiterate back to their villages. The letter writers are a bridge between the city and the village. "Household matters," a letter writer named Ahmed explains to me. News of a son born, questions to a wife about domestic matters. Letters from workers in the city instructing their wives to send the children to school, to take care of the old folk. In the village, the letters will be read out to the recipients by the postman, who is thus an encyclopedia of the overt and secret life of the community. A subject that comes up often is an inquiry to people in the village about a wife's behavior. The migrant men working in the city might see their wives for less than a month every year. There is a commonly told story in Bombay: "My gardener's wife in his village had a son. But he hadn't seen his wife for three years. My gardener was so happy. I pointed out that the child couldn't possibly be his. But he said the son was in his name. It didn't matter who planted the seed, the fruit would belong to him. And then he gave me some sweets."

The news they communicate is a mixture of good and bad, but mostly good, Ahmed tells me, because people feel it necessary to deliver really bad news in person. "And if someone is having an affair. Letters of love," Ahmed says.

"Love letters?"

"Yes, if a young man is writing to a woman he comes to us. We throw in our own wordings."

"What types of wordings?"

"Oh, the usual. *You wait for me.*" If a boy is far from his girl, he writes to her, *Don't get married without me. I'll come very soon. I'm building a house here. Wait for me.* Girls have love letters written on their behalf to Arabs in the Gulf.

"Is there any one of you who is an expert in love letters?"

"Him," they say, and point to the drunk I have been ignoring. The drunk's face lights up, his mutterings in English get louder. "Anil," they say. "Ashok Sinha." Perhaps Anil is a nom de plume. "The Holi effect still hasn't come down," the others explain, referring to the bacchanalia of the previous day.

Initially, the largest single group of their clients were prostitutes. They would dictate letters to their parents: *I have a good job in the city. Your daughter is doing well as a secretary. Here is some money. Please get brother educated, please get sister married. I will be sending you more every month.* The letter writers provide the facility of a return address, as they do for street kids and runaways. Occasionally the parents will decide to visit their daughter in the big city, see how she is doing, take in the sights. They turn up at V.T. Station, right behind the GPO, and trudge with their bags and boxes and baskets of choicest fruit from the village to the address given. Seeing the puzzlement on the faces of the old folks, the letter writers guess immediately, ask them to sit down on the stools, and force upon them a glass of tea, while a messenger is dispatched to the prostitute: Come quickly, your parents are here. "We never give away their address," the letter writers tell me.

The letter writers also help the prostitutes craft piteous appeals to clients in other cities. *Send money, come quickly, send ten thousand, I am in big problems.* Many of the working girls have children, and they use guilt to manipulate the purported fathers: *I need money to run the house, take care of the kids, oh, please send money, the last thing you gave me got spent or I gave it away on credit.* As the letter writers recite the stock phrases, it is clear that their opinion of their clients' veracity is not high. They are most often written in Bombay street language, a mix of Hindi, Marathi, and English, with snatches of Tamil and Gujarati thrown in.

If you go to speak to the letter writers, you will be given a stool under the blue tarpaulin roof. When there is a gust of wind the tarp shakes and lets loose a hailstorm of pigeon shit on your head. While I speak to Ahmed, four or five of the other letter writers are busy picking pigeon droppings out of my hair. "Doesn't it bother you?" I ask Ahmed. All their heads are covered with small white feathers, grainy pellets of dung. "We shake it off only when we go home; we don't keep cleaning each time it happens." It's very picturesque, though, the men sitting with sealing wax and stamps all in a row in front of the little square, with thousands of pigeons perpetually in flight, ascending and descending, crapping on them all day while they're trying to write love letters.

But they won't be around much longer. "Business is half what it used to be," they complain. "The number of illiterates must be a tenth of what it used to be." The availability of cheap telephone calls to the village has also cut into their business, and telegrams have almost ceased. Most of the time, these days, the letter writers are mere postal clerks, wrapping parcels, affixing stamps.

As I'm leaving, Anil, the love-letter expert, is gesticulating, grinning. I had introduced myself as being from America. "Saddam," he says. "I like Saddam."

FOR THE FIRST TIME in a generation, the Thakkars are about to move out of the slum. They have scraped together the money to buy a one-bedroom flat in the new city of Mira Road, just outside the municipal limits of Bombay. The family is thinking about the move with exultation and dread. They will find it difficult leaving Jogeshwari, they say, because of the "community" here. But for the first time in Girish's life, he will be living under a roof not made of tin and tarp.

Coming out of the train at Mira Road, we hear three office girls conversing in English. They attract a sound from a group of idle men, not a whistle but a sucking of the lips, somewhat like the chirruping of birds. It is a startlingly obscene sound, air being sucked in, suggestive of great sexual menace. As we walk across the skeleton of an overpass spanning the tracks, we can see a huge sign on a school near the station: ENRICH ACADEMY. The people who've flocked to the new city know the true purpose of education: not to lift the spirit toward a higher god but to enrich yourself. The shops outside the station are all real estate offices; Mira Road is a city whose sole business is selling itself. There is still possibility here. It is a city inventing itself, separate from Bombay.

We walk toward Girish's house, through a vast half-empty city of kitsch. A freestanding pair of columns supporting a huge Greek pediment adorns the side of the road, rising out of the mud and leading to no other structure. It is so incongruous it looks like a movie prop, something so bizarrely out of place in the northern suburbs of Bombay that I have to look at it again to make sure I'm not dreaming. The buildings are postmodern on the cheap: randomly placed pediments, Chippendale tops, finials, and facades done up in various pastels, at least until the first rain, which washes away the thin paint and leaves everything looking the same dull yellow shade of streaked mud. The buildings of Mira Road want to be in Europe. Accordingly, they are given misspelt European names: TANWAR HIGHTS, CHANDRESH REVEARA. Hundreds of them are placed anyhow all around the landscape, and others lie half constructed, waiting for real estate prices to go up. At the moment they are low; Girish's family bought the flat for three and a half lakhs and now it is worth two-thirds of that. A slum room in Jogeshwari fetches more.

The reason for the ornate facades is that the builders want to give the owners the impression of luxury, which is defined as living in a foreign country: another time, another place. A Bombaywallah will do without functioning appliances or running water, he will do without good roads, but he won't do without style, shaan. The Mira Road residential blocks are mostly facade; the rooms behind the Palladian columns, under the Chippendale tops, have no substance. The walls, newly built, already leak. Many of the multistory buildings have only a shaft for a lift, no machinery inside. This is all that the slum dweller can afford in his first move. He can't afford practicality, so he might as well have the glitz and the flash, because that is cheaper than to build something solid. The bombastic entrances also fit with the Bombay idea of shaan: The outside should lead you to believe that the inside is bigger than it is. Even in central Bombay, a chawl might have several imposing arches leading to its matchboxes.

Young couples stroll up and down the one main street, enjoying the evening breeze. It feels cooler here than in the city, and when you get off the train there is a pleasant impression of green space to the west, where there are no buildings, only salt pans and marshes. The suburb is being built to the east, a reversal of the pattern farther down the line toward Bombay, where the western side, the one near the sea, is more desirable. The nights here, though mosquito-infested, are quiet; most of the people living here are taking their first step out of the slums and cannot afford cars. Besides, there are no roads worth driving on; they are all rutted. As we get closer to Girish's building, there is a large undrained swamp from which issue clouds of mosquitoes that attack all of us. I see a street vendor bang a dark streetlight. It responds to his blow and flickers on.

The buildings are all grouped in enormous complexes named after the builder or one of his dearly departed relatives. All the buildings around Girish have the first name Chandresh, Chandresh Darshan, Chandresh Mandir, Chandresh Heights, Chandresh Accord. Girish lives in Chandresh Chhaya—the Shade of Chandresh. "Who built this place?" I ask Girish.

"Mangal Prabhat Lodha."

During the elections, I had been trekking around Malabar Hill with this same Mangal Prabhat Lodha, a BJP member of the legislative assembly, watching the campaigning. Chandresh was his father. And I myself had lived in Mangal Chhaya, since Mangal Prabhat Lodha turns out, much to Girish's amazement, to be living two floors above the flat I rented in Dariya Mahal.

On the Thakkars' front door is this sticker, U R NOBODY IF YOU AIN'T AN INDIAN, sponsored by Proline, an importer of foreign sports equipment. Whenever Mr. Thakkar hears the national anthem played on the

TV, he makes everybody in the household stand. "If we are sleeping, he wakes us up and makes us stand up. If we are sick, we can sit up," says Dharmendra.

His faith in the nation has at last been realized. Years ago, in the Jogeshwari slum, Girish's mother saw a vision of the future in the pages of a Gujarati magazine. It showed the window of a house, fringed by curtains and with a lamp hanging from the ceiling next to the window. She asked of her God, When will I have something like this? Now the family point to the window of the living room of the flat. It has curtains, and a lamp hangs from the ceiling.

There is a nonstop party in the Thakkar household. People will be coming and going for weeks, mostly their former neighbors from Jogeshwari, but also relatives, Dharmendra's and Girish's coworkers, Raju's students, Paresh's dancer friends. The Thakkars, after two generations, have just stepped into a pukka house, into the middle class. The progress of the Thakkar family is the story of the growth of Bombay. They moved from Fort, where Girish's father lived in a large house with his extended family, to the Jogeshwari shanty and now to the Mira Road flat. Girish wants to move on to America, the peak of that trajectory.

For the first time in their lives, the children don't have to sleep with their parents. The luxurious sleeping arrangements were chalked out when they moved in. In the bedroom: Dharmendra (the man on whose salary the family runs and the flat was bought) and Paresh, Girish's younger brother, on the bed. The other brother, Sailesh, is working as a salesman in interior Maharashtra but visits often. In the living room: the mother on the divan, the father on the lower daybed, Girish near him, separated by a small gap, and Raju on the mattress by the kitchen. The two rooms, small to my eyes, are cavernous to the Thakkars. "One day it was actually uncomfortable for me," Dharmendra says. "I couldn't sleep." So most nights they all sleep in the living room, watching the new TV, whose sleep timer shuts it off after thirty minutes. They like being lulled to sleep by the sound of familiar human voices. Having grown up in one room, they don't know what to do with the extra room when at long last they get it.

The living room has hand-painted flower vases. There is nice light coming from the plant-fringed window but also a lot of mosquitoes, to which the family seems immune. Paresh's drawings—one of the Eiffel Tower, another of the Statue of Liberty, and a third of a man shrugging off his clothes and what appears to be his skin too—prominently adorn the showcase. One whole wall of the Thakkars' living room is covered with dark brown stone tiles. It is vastly out of place with the other three white-washed walls. Two spotlights on the top, near the ceiling, struggle to bring some light to the hard stone surface. "People think the stone is for decoration," explains Dharmendra. "It is actually there because there is leakage in that wall." In the brand-new building, water invades the structure from all sides and seeps through the walls. However, when visitors to his flat comment on how nice the stone looks, Dharmendra doesn't correct them.

He shows me the brochure that enticed him and his family and all the other occupants to Chandresh Chhaya. It is extravagantly colored in a 1950s style—all bright reds, yellows, blues—and the kind of broad gaudy typefaces that American land companies used to attract migrants to sunny California. The misspelt text reads:

In 1980, a group of dynamic young entrepreneurs had a dream. A dream of creating an oasis of beauty and peace amidst the barren monotony of city apartments. Under guidance of Founder Late Sh. Chandresh Lodha Group has a dream to bring a lush green environment of the harrassed house-hunters of Bombay. . . . Today, Lodha Group symbolize home radiant with beauty, warm with comfort, bright with happiness and shining with prosperity. Today, a Lodha home means happiness forever.

The illustrations in the brochure show a silhouetted skyline of sky-scrapers and a pair of drawings of low buildings surrounded by palm trees, strolling couples, limousines gliding by on uncluttered roads, a children's playground, and a blue sea wave about to break. A host of "special amenities" ranging from a bus service to the station to a tennis court, clubhouse, and library are promised, none of which have materialized. But if you were sitting in your shack in Jogeshwari, with the open gutter flowing outside, the shouts of the drunks and taporis at battle coming in with the giant mosquitoes through your one window, and examining this brightly colored brochure, your heart too would strain to believe it, would lend its promises the necessary credence. Perhaps your sleep that night would be illuminated with a dream of your children playing in that lush green playground, your wife preparing food on that marble kitchen counter, and yourself walking back from the station toward your own flat on a Saturday night on the hundred-foot road, breathing the country air.

Chandresh Chayya is in terrible condition. The walls are uneven, gaping holes in the wall exist where electric fittings are meant to be placed, and as usual there is no lift in the elevator shaft. The stairs are also unfinished. The builder had promised amenities such as a garden, and an "ISI Mark geyser" for hot water. The garden became another building next door, and there was no geyser in Chandresh Chayya. So Dharmendra complained and a geyser was installed. It is a ridiculous little thing. "It won't heat up water to wash a rat." But it is, within the definition of the agreement, a geyser, and it has a good sense about how much water is available for it to heat up. Water for bathing comes into the taps here only every alternate day. The Thakkars have built water tanks in the loft to store it.

Municipal drinking water comes only once a week, in tanker trucks, and only if the drivers are bribed 100 rupees per tanker. But it's still not enough, so the housing society pays for three tankers of water every day from private suppliers, at 325 rupees a tanker. The tanker operators are the most powerful political lobby in Mira Road. They have divided up the tanker routes among themselves and prevent the municipality from laying new pipes, which would eliminate their business. Getting rid of water is as much of a problem as getting it in. Since the drainage systems are badly built, the society has to pay another 400 rupees a month to drain the ground of water. Periodically, when the water supply fails altogether, housewives and accountants emerge from their buildings and riot, sitting down on the train tracks to force the rest of the city to pay attention.

The residents also have to pay for a private sweeper to collect the garbage and take it away to God knows where. If they use the municipal bin, it gets picked up once a fortnight. There are no public bus routes in the suburb. At one point, the Thakkars' housing society had started a service, paying a man with an eight-seater minicab to ferry the people of the complex back and forth to the station for 2 rupees each. The Mira Road rickshaw wallahs, who charge 20 rupees for the same service, surrounded the minicab and prevented him from operating. The police and the local assemblyman were called in; both took the side of the rickshaw wallahs. So the residents of Mira Road spend a major portion of their income paying for the most basic of municipal services: water, sewage, and transportation. Mira Road is just outside the limits of the Bombay Municipal Corporation.

That explains its attraction and its deficiencies: It is a border township. But on the whole, the Thakkars are happier here. In Jogeshwari, better-off relatives would visit, look around, and ask them why they didn't move. "It got irritating," says Dharmendra. "Who doesn't want to shift? But Father had done some wrong investment. Money was blocked." In Jogeshwari, "I never used to give my address or anything to friends. I could not call my office colleagues. I would not go to their place. Now we are free to invite them. Relatives can stay overnight. Anybody can come anytime."

Girish's father spends his days finding out where the shops are, where the freshest vegetables can be bought. Girish says of his father, "He might never have thought that he would be in such a place in his life. Today we have a mixer, washing machine, TV. What don't we have? A car. We don't need it. Maybe we might have it after a couple of years." The building abuts the train tracks; the suburban locals go by in a cacophony of diesel horns and the clackity-clack of wheels against the steel tracks. It takes two hours for Dharmendra to reach his workplace. "But we are in sales, so we can make up," he explains, with a twinkle in his eye. Hours can be fudged.

The father compares Mira Road favorably to the slum he has just left. "There is silence now. In Jogeshwari there would be a fight somewhere, some noise." (In Jogeshwari, I think, Sunil and Amol would burn down the municipal office to focus their attention on the water problem.) As people leave, the family shuts the door behind them. I have never seen the door in Jogeshwari shut during waking hours, and I ask about this. "It's the system here," explains Dharmendra. "It's the flat system." You are supposed to maintain your privacy when you move up to the middle class, into a flat. In the slum there is no such delusion.

Raju is twenty-five and unmarried, almost a spinster by the standards of their community. The Thakkars were waiting to move into this flat before they looked for a boy for her or a bride for Dharmendra, who just turned thirty. What kind of family would marry into a slum? Girish doesn't revisit his old home in Jogeshwari, and neither does Paresh. It's had three break-ins since they've moved, and the family doesn't seem to mind very much. Raju goes back every day for her coaching classes, but their parents don't go. Sitting in a third-story flat of his very own, Dharmendra, the perfume company executive, dismisses the place in which he was born and brought up: "Jogeshwari was a chawl."

"What kinds of people live here?" I ask Dharmendra. "Gujaratis, Maharashtrians, Muslims?"

"Cosmopolitan," he responds. It is a fellowship of the upwardly mobile. The social networks of Mira Road, while not as cohesive as those of Jogeshwari, are still stronger than those of Nepean Sea Road. After Girish comes home to Mira Road, at ten in the evening, he goes to the neighboring building and brings over the two-year-old daughter of an acquaintance, to play with. He has about half an hour of this, which relaxes him. Then he drops off the toddler and comes back home to sleep. On a Sunday, Girish will go to Naigaon with his upstairs neighbor and buy the fermented sap and the fruit of the toddy tree. Then he will come back to his neighbor's room and drink a liter and a half of toddy and eat a couple dozen tadgolas. He recommends it to me. "If you drink toddy it will clean out your system. You will be able to shit really well. Everything will come out easily."

WALKING PAST THE LOVERS on the parapet of Marine Drive, Girish says wistfully, "One day I'll also come here. With someone." Girish and his brothers were role models in the Jogeshwari slums. Parents pointed them out to their children and asked them why they couldn't be like the Gujaratis.

Girish has never had a girlfriend. He offers as his excuse the fact that from his first year in college, which is when middle-class Indians traditionally discover the opposite sex, he started tutoring to bring in money. As soon as his classes were over, at one-thirty, he would go to his students' homes to give tutorials, until nine in the evening. "I never got time to run behind these females." He thinks he can start something with a girl, if he stands at the same bus stop where a girl waits, for ten days. "Basically you have to pamper her." There was a girl in a friend's office, and Girish had once asked her to have coffee. She refused. "I said, Be off, who has time to run after you? I don't have time for you. Sorry."

Girish once had an Internet chat companion, a young Gujarati woman living in Japan. "I used to chat in a different style. I used to try and reach her heart. What do you think about life, philosophical, this, that. Then she came to India. Her father bought an apartment in Walkeshwar. She didn't contact me in Bombay." There is no disappointment in his voice; or it is well hidden. After all, she is a posh Walkeshwar girl now, more inaccessible to him than when she was Japanese.

Kamal, the mob comptroller, like Girish's other friends, is greatly exercised by Girish's continuing virginity: "He has great need of some oiling-greasing." Kamal advises Girish, "Sex is connected to the brain; when you release, you can think better. That's why your thinking is confused. You need to get laid. You say you have all these big contacts but you can't utilize them. People don't trust you because you are yourself confused. Get an item and get lightened." He suggests a place where Girish can do so: Tip-Top Hairdressers in Goregaon, where the female hairdressers start with a head massage and work their way south.

Srinivas, his whoring friend, tells me he admires Girish's contacts, his knowledge of people from every world, but is dismissive about his business prospects. "He has not been able to build a future," unlike the rest of their group from college. "He is too honest." He has been trying to persuade Girish to join the Landmark Forum, an organization that runs encounter groups and motivational classes. There are five levels, and Srinivas has reached the fourth one. It teaches him how to succeed in business. He has successfully motivated Girish into not feeling sad when he comes back from Navsari and first glimpses the outskirts of Bombay, at Virar. Girish went to a guest session of the Forum, but decided against taking the full three-day class because it cost 3,000 rupees.

Bombay has raised and nurtured Girish, but now he has reached the end of something. "I'm not getting back what I'm putting into struggling," says the programmer. "There are times when I don't even have ten bucks." Girish realizes that what he does is not essential to human happiness. "I'm in the service industry. A person can manage without my service." Dharmendra's perfume company, meanwhile, is feeling the pinch of the recession. Nobody's getting fired, but nobody's getting any raises, and the company's not filling in posts that are vacant. Girish is their only winning horse now. The next move—to Borivali, where they've set their eyes on a thousand-square-foot flat—is contingent on a steadily increasing flow of money, and the only possibility of that happening is with Girish, with computers.

Girish has now ended up in the front room of his business partner's flat on Pedder Road. He likes working in the fancy address. "I never thought in my life that I'll reach Pedder Road. I only knew Jogeshwari." The address is just about the only reason Girish is in the business, with a man he met in the stock market. "My partner is no help to me in my business. He won't even open the yellow pages and make calls from it." Instead, he stays up till three in the morning downloading pornographic pictures. But his partner is from Bombay high; Girish is from Bombay low. "I am with him because I'm hoping he will pick me up." He makes a spider with his palm and fingers and lifts it high in the air. "He will pick me up."

I had told Girish about a friend of mine at the U.S. Consulate, in the visa section, and this set him thinking. Perhaps he could use my influence to secure a green card. "I haven't asked you to take me," he lets me know. "I just said I'd like to go, and I'm learning these computer languages. I'll strike when the iron is hot." If he can send $1,000 a month home to his father after he meets his expenses in America, that's all he wants.

"Then you can buy the flat next to you in Mira Road," I say.

"Dariya Mahal. Think big," he immediately corrects me. "If one man goes, six people will be blessed. My entire family." And not just his family. "If I go, I want to bring up one or two guys." He would like to get Srinivas out of the country too. Srinivas's father has just died; he has three sisters and a mother. Girish has another friend who is working in his uncle's cloth shop. "I want to bring him up. I know he's a good guy. He struggles too." If Girish has a sum of money, he will give his friend money to rent a shop for a year. I am enchanted by this invisible network of assistance, a man going abroad and sending small sums of money back to seed cloth shops, college degrees, and weddings. It is not a Mercedes or an Armani suit that Girish craves; it is the opportunity to "bring up" others like him.

I ask him about his idea of America.

"I only know one thing for sure: If you struggle there the same amount you struggle here, the success rate is two hundred times."

What else besides money?

He recalls a recent accident we were both witness to: An auto-rickshaw had knocked down a woman selling balloons on the street. She looked terribly wounded and clutched her head. The brightly colored balloons, which had been aloft over her, were now all bunched up on the pavement. I was alarmed, but Girish predicted, "Watch, she'll get up and ask for money." A rain shower suddenly drenched us, and the stricken woman got up quickly and ran for shelter under a shop. Another woman selling balloons approached the rickshaw and abused the driver, demanding money for her colleague.

"That balloon lady had a power," Girish notes. "She could enter the rickshaw and stand there. In America it would be different. You saw the female went into the rickshaw and asked for money. There it would be analyzed, whose mistake it is. She can't just enter your rickshaw and say give money or I won't get off your rickshaw." Here is an interesting take on class: Girish, who is poor, thinks the people even poorer than him have too much power. I ask him what he thinks of them, of the very poor.

"I don't like them, I hate them." He thinks that the beggars of the Bombay streets spend all their money on liquor and other vices. Many of them make more than the salary of a government official, he says. He will help a friend in need but almost never gives money to beggars. He is repulsed. "They hold your feet. Little children hold your feet and touch their foreheads to your feet." He speaks of them with a vehemence I have not seen in him before. They are uncomfortably close. There is a complex relationship between the poor and the very poor. A distance has to be maintained, always in battle with a natural sympathy. A mix of "There but for the grace of God go I" and "They have nothing to do with me."

I ask him if he will go back to Jogeshwari to live.

"Why are you sending me to Jogeshwari again? I have a higher vision. From Mira Road I want to go to Vile Parle, and from Vile Parle I want to go to Bandra, and from Bandra to Pedder Road." It is a train catcher's dream of upward mobility; switching from the local to the express till he gets to his destination, in South Bombay. He wants at least to get to Vile Parle in three or four years. He can only reach even this middle-class suburb if he takes a shortcut; if he gets on the fast train to America. "Being in Bombay I can't go to Parle. I need twenty lakhs, which in Bombay I'll need twenty years to earn. I can spend four thousand a month all my life. But I can't buy a ten-foot-by-ten-foot house in Bombay. I cannot do that."

He does not think such a move—from Mira Road to South Bombay—would even be possible in a town like Navsari, where his family is from. "The reason is, the society there is small. You know what background a man comes from. In Bombay, you will never know I stayed in slums. My business partner never knows I stayed in slums. I only told him I stayed in 'chawl type.' "

I ask him if he thinks he had a happy childhood in the chawl in Jogeshwari. It is of some interest to me, because I don't think of my childhood in Bombay as having been particularly happy.

"At this time I can't tell you whether I was happy or not because it is gone now. I never knew what a football was. I had a red rubber ball." He holds out his palm, very small.

DHARMENDRA COMES to my house one day to invite me to his wedding, which is in his village in Gujarat. I ask him if he is enjoying the days of his engagement, if he is going around the city with his fiancée. He looks baffled. "I have not met her."

He means he has not seen her after he went with his parents to her house, where not one word was exchanged between them. Her name is Mayuri. He asked his sister to talk to her. The second time in Dharmendra's life he sees his bride will be when she lifts her red sari–covered head to accept him as her swami. They are getting married four weeks after seeing each other for the first and only time.

"Is she good looking?" I ask about his wife-to-be.

"Average."

"What was it about her that you liked over the other girls you saw?" I ask Dharmendra.

He shrugs. "It was mostly the timing." Dharmendra has seen five or six other girls, but he wasn't ready to get married before. But now the family's moved into the Mira Road flat, and he's over thirty, and there are four siblings in line behind him, notably his sister. It's getting rather late for Raju to marry. But she can't until her elder brother does. So Mayuri arrived at the right time, and without really looking at her or talking to her he agreed to marry her.

"How do you know you'll get along? That you won't fight?"

"We will be adjusting. We have to adjust for some things; she also has to adjust for some things." I notice that he doesn't say *I* have to adjust. His whole family will have to adjust. Dharmendra, like most of the people in Bombay, lives all his life under the shelter and protection and tyranny of the We. But chances are that Mayuri won't have to do much adjusting. The Thakkars don't believe in dowry, to begin with. It is the custom to give the groom a new suit and a ring. Mayuri's parents asked him to choose material for a suit to be tailored. Dharmendra, conscious that a suit would cost more than 6,000 rupees, asked for a blazer, which would be considerably cheaper.

ALL DAY LONG the women of Padga Gam are singing wedding songs. Loudspeakers spread their atonal, tuneless voices all over the village. I am sitting in the Thakkars' country home, talking to a yellow man. All the women of the family and the wives of the guests have molested Dharmendra, spreading yellow tamarind paste over every part of his body that can be touched in public: his hair, his thighs, his chest. A pair of shorts covers up the only part of his body that is not yellow. There is, says Dharmendra, a "hat trick" of marriages in the village. There are no more auspicious days after tomorrow till Diwali, five months away, which also explains the haste. Dharmendra's marriage was decided first, so he took one of the three auspicious days. The others couldn't take the same day, he says.

"Why not? Are they related to you?"

"No. But they are from the same village." All the cooking, the arrangements for beds to put up visitors, is done by village people. In Padga Gam, marriages are not of individuals or even families. They are of villages. Most of Padga Gam has been invited to Dharmendra's wedding, as it was to the wedding yesterday and as it will be to the wedding tomorrow. All the neighboring houses are thrown open to the out-of-town guests of the Thakkars. The owners of the houses will come back specially from Bombay, to attend the wedding and also to make sure their neighbors' guests are comfortable. The village headman is coming back from New Zealand. The sense of community that the Thakkars and people in the slum areas abound in is brought to Bombay from the village.

A wide assortment of cousins and uncles attends the marriage. One works on an oil rig in Abu Dhabi ("forty-five days on, thirty days off"); another is a property dealer in Bombay who spent six years in Nigeria getting rich off the currency scam in the eighties. In the evening, the men sit on a sheet behind the house and drink warm beer, which tastes good because it is illicit; Gujarat is supposed to be a dry state.

I walk around the village with Girish. We go into one of the older houses, a cool, quiet sanctuary with thatched roofs and a mud-and-dung floor. I want to stay in here, there is such a serenity about it. But houses like these are not the future of the village. People are now building structures like the brick-and-cement bungalow of the Thakkars' next-door neighbor: hot in the summer, cold in the winter. Girish takes me out into the cane and rice fields, past the mango groves, and shows me a concrete ledge, site of the greatest pleasure he derives from his village: shitting in the open. He squats on this ledge and, with a view of open fields as far as the eye can see, he shits at leisure. "Thirty minutes?" I ask. "Forty-five," he replies. I laugh, but then I think about Girish's bathroom in the Jogeshwari slum, the one he used every day till last year. I compare the cramped, dark crevice above the communal open pit, with someone always banging at the door telling him to hurry up, to this pastoral idyll, where a man can take his time doing his business, ruminating on the beauties of God's green earth, with the air fresh in the nostrils and the field slowly getting fertilized behind him. "I like to feel the grasses tickling my bottom," he adds. It's as good a reason as any to come here.

But for me, the night before the wedding is stupendously uncomfortable. The mosquito repellent I spread on my skin functions as an attractant. The rented mattress is infested with fleas, which have direct access to my body, since it lacks a sheet. I put a bath towel over my head to shut out the whine of the mosquitoes, but the wedding band is playing till early morning. None of the other people sleeping next to me on the terrace seem to be much disturbed. But then, around four, a boy wakes up and says to his father, "The mosquitoes here are small and poisonous." This does not help me sleep either. These mosquitoes are used to getting their blood supply through the thick hides of cattle; they are biting me through my clothes. In the morning, as I groggily edge my way around the turds in the field, looking for a spot to piss, a vision of a book appears in my mind, an illuminated manuscript I saw once in Chantilly, and I have to say the title aloud: *"Les très riches heures du Duc de Berry."*

I flee the village before the wedding. So does Girish's business partner from Bombay and the property dealer from Nigeria. As the train enters the suburbs and the red buses and multistory buildings come into view, we feel excited, happy, metropolitan.

BEFORE I MOVE BACK to America, I meet Girish one last time. We go to the new Shiv Sagar on Hill Road and get idlis, a grilled vegetable sandwich, and fresh custard apple with ice cream. He is under more financial pressure than ever. Girish's sister-in-law is pregnant and the family is looking at Girish for money to buy the flat next door; he needs to bring in 15,000 rupees a month. He is now working with Kamal, the mob controller, in Phone-in Services. But the new business is not earning either, and the phone bills alone are killing Phone-in Services. Girish sees no way out, but he resists taking up a job. "There is no charm in a job." It is a Gujarati's natural inclination toward entrepreneurship.

Girish fills me in on what's happening with his family. The new bride has taken her place in the household, and Girish is approving because "she doesn't talk much." When he comes out of his bath in the morning, she silently has breakfast ready for him—chapatis with butter, a vegetable, and three-fourths of a cup of coffee. "My mother really missed her when she went back to visit her parents for three days. When my father found out she likes fish he's been buying only fish."

In the little two-room flat, the newlyweds have been allotted the bedroom. The Thakkars have also invested in a 950-square-foot flat in Borivali, through a housing scheme for the poor initiated by a socialist politician; a flat in Bangalore; and three well-built shanties in Borivali. The three slum rooms will probably be sold to buy another flat. None of the flats have been built yet, but they are waiting there, all these rooms, comfortably in the future, so that all five children, or at least the four sons, will have houses of their own someday.

Why do people still live in Bombay? Every day is an assault on the individual's senses, from the time you get up, to the transport you take to go to work, to the offices you work in, to the forms of entertainment you are subjected to. The exhaust is so thick the air boils like a soup. There are too many people touching you: in the trains, in the elevators, when you go home to sleep. You live in a seaside city, but the only time most people get anywhere near the sea is for an hour on Sunday evening on a filthy beach. It doesn't stop when you're asleep either, for nighttime brings the mosquitoes out of the malarial swamps, the thugs of the underworld to your door, and the booming loudspeakers of the parties of the rich and the festivals of the poor. Why would you want to leave your brick house in the village with its two mango trees and its view of small hills in the east to come here?

So that someday, like the Thakkars, your eldest son can buy two rooms on Mira Road. And the younger one can move beyond that, to New Jersey.

Your discomfort is an investment. Like insect colonies, people here will sacrifice their individual pleasures for the greater progress of the family. One brother will work and support all the others, and he will gain a deep satisfaction from the fact that his younger brother is taking an interest in computers and will probably go on to America. His brother's progress will make him think that his life has meaning, that it is being well spent working in the perfume company, trudging in the heat every day to peddle Drakkar Noir knockoffs to shopowners who don't really want them.

In families like the Thakkars', there is no individual, only the organism. Everything—Girish's desire to go abroad and make and send back money, Dharmendra's taking a wife, Raju's staying at home—is for the greater good of the whole. There are circles of fealty and duty within the organism, but the smallest circle is the family. There is no circle around the self.

In inquiring about Girish's family, I ask if they've found a match for his sister yet. She will be married by Diwali, he says. He does not look happy about it.

"There's a problem?" I ask.

He nods.

"Love marriage?"

She has chosen for herself—a Marwari boy, a fashion designer with two or three of his own shops. He is relatively wealthy and comes from a good family. Girish and the other brothers—all four of them—have not been on speaking terms with Raju for two or three months now, even though they live in the same house.

"Everyone in our society comes to my father for advice. Now how will he be able to advise them?" asks Girish. At first I think he is referring to his building society in Mira Road. Then I realize he is talking about his caste. The brothers are angry at their only sister for wanting to marry outside the caste. The parents, on the other hand, have reconciled themselves to it. I tell Girish he is being silly. He should accept her choice and be happy about it, since there is nothing wrong with the boy. But he doesn't like the manner in which she told him. She had asked Girish to come downstairs for a moment; there was something she wanted to say to him. He left the flat downcast. He thought he would have to explain why he wasn't contributing to the family income, why his businesses kept failing. But instead she told him about this boy. Girish heard her out, then told her that in six months he was going to be earning a lot of money through his Internet business, and then he himself would go out with his father and look for a suitable boy from the caste for her. Somehow Raju's finding a boy on her own, and a Marwari boy at that, became linked in Girish's mind with his not earning and therefore not contributing to the prosperity of the family, a prosperity that would have attracted many eligible boys for its sole daughter. But Raju was adamant; she would marry the Marwari boy. And Girish stopped speaking to her.

I tell him his sister needs him, needs his support in all that she is going through. He shakes his head. She has stained the reputation of their father in his society. I persist, asking him what is wrong with the boy and isn't it a good thing that she has chosen on her own? I tell him to make peace with her. I tell him I myself had entered into a love marriage.

He stops arguing and says, "You're not from here. It is different for you."

He cuts off his words, but the implication is clear: I am a foreigner. I cannot understand the Indian customs. Here is the difference between us, out at last in the sunlight.

Babbanji: Runaway Poet

One day, my friend the poet Adil Jussawala was browsing among the books on the sidewalk opposite the Central Telegraph Office. The boy who was behind the stall got into conversation with him about a book of French short stories, and Adil saw something different about him. So he invited him to a writers' salon at an open-air courtyard behind the Tata Theater, not far from there. He is a runaway from Bihar, Adil tells me. The boy told his employer, the stall owner, that he would be going; a time of five o'clock had been given. The employer said, If you go, you're fired. He went to the salon. He got fired.

The boy is interested in poetry, a slender youth with a thin mustache and wispy sideburns creeping into a beard. He appears very self-confident, even stubborn. He may have come to the group lured by the possibility of meeting poets, but he may also find a proper job through connections with English-speaking people. Through most of the evening, he is quiet, looking down at the table. He can't join in our conversation, which is in English. When people want tea or chairs, he gets up and fetches it for us without being asked. It is his station.

An architect-poet asks him to recite some of his poetry. And so he does, a metrical piece about destinations, in Hindi. I like the sound of it. At the end, nobody says, "Wah, wah," as they might have in Bihar. There is, instead, an embarrassed silence. The architect asks him if he has any more. He reads another, one he wrote just the previous night—on the footpath, under the streetlamp—to the same reaction. Then I ask him if he's written any on Bombay. He brings out a sheaf of papers, all written over, every inch of every sheet. But by this time the people around the table have lost interest in his poetry. He brings out a calendar, and that too is all written over. "More poetry?" I ask.

"No, it's my diary. Every day I write it."

I write down my name and phone number for him. In my notebook, in a fine script, he writes his name, "Babbanji." He pauses. "What else?" There is nothing else. He has no phone number. Tonight, he is going to try to find a patch of footpath to sleep on. He'll try Churchgate. He has a tote bag with him that contains all his belongings. He is to call me the day after. I will try to find him a job.

I enlist Girish, who finds many people jobs while losing money at his own. I watch him listening to Babbanji. "How much money do you have? Do you have any relations in Bombay? Anybody who knows you, who can give you a recommendation?" Then Girish asks for my mobile and phones his friend Ishaq. Ishaq's cousin Dr. Shahbuddin is starting a dispensary and could use an assistant, to work from 9 a.m. to 1:30 and then 6 p.m. to 9:30. That would leave plenty of time for Babbanji's writing, the whole afternoon. Plus he could stay in the dispensary, get off the footpath.

Babbanji is not enthusiastic. "I'll do anything that involves writing or reading. In some magazine, some newspaper." But Girish has tried; he has reached out to a boy he has met half an hour ago and tried to make his life better.

Ishaq's immediate reaction to the possibility of hiring Babbanji: "All Biharis are thieves." This from a man himself from Azamgarh, crime capital of Uttar Pradesh, the state next to Bihar. But Bihar has an even worse reputation than UP. Bihar and Bombay are the two polarities of modern India, the success story and the disaster. If Bombay were only rid of its

Bihari migrants, I have heard society people argue, it could be a booming city-state like Singapore, like Hong Kong. Biharis come to Bombay with hat in hand. Babbanji carries his state's reputation like the mark of Cain wherever he goes: All Biharis are thieves. It was recently stated in those exact words by the captain of the Indian cricket team Azharuddin when he found his cap missing after playing a match in the state.

BABBANJI COMES to my uncle's apartment and looks for several minutes at the sea from the eighteenth-floor window. He has with him his blue cloth travel bag, bearing the Marlboro logo. He is wearing the same plaid shirt I have seen him in before, with metal buttons. It is not dirty; he must find a way to wash it during his bath. Without saying anything, he sits down, takes out a piece of paper, and begins composing a poem. Periodically he peers at the view for fresh inspiration. When he is finished, he reads it out to me. It is about the sea, and how all the rivers of the world can flow into it; it will refuse nobody. He will not leave the sea, the poet promises.

He asks me why everyone in Bombay speaks English. He had been to Matunga earlier today and heard a chaiwala's son speak to his father in English: "Hey, Dad." The tea vendor gamely struggled to respond. The boy's mother insisted that he speak in English. Babbanji is perturbed about this; in Japan, he points out, it is all right to speak in Japanese but in India it's a liability to speak Hindi.

Babbanji's friends at the writers' salon have also been making calls, trying to find him work. Madan, the photographer I had gone to the red-light district with, took Babbanji to meet the film writer Javed Akhtar and his wife, the actress Shabana Azmi. Babbanji was struck by the fact that Javed and Shabana have a simple home—"They have a simple way of talking"—and that the great actress was actually writing. She is a member of parliament and an activist. She is his father's favorite heroine.

But Akhtar made fun of him for his Bihari origins. He declared his certificates must be fake since he's heard these things are manufactured in Bihar. He doubted Babbanji's ability to read and write. Akhtar was joking, but it is part of a now-familiar suspicion that the citizens of this city share against his home state. Adil has approached friends at the *Navbharat Times*, the country's leading Hindi-language paper. "We are looking for people who can write Allahabadi Hindi. We don't care for Bihari Hindi." This is

the state of Pataliputra, capital of the Sun King, Vikramaditya. This is the
state where the Buddha was born and where he achieved enlightenment.
This is the state of the great Buddhist university of Nalanda, one of the
world's foremost centers of learning from the fifth to the eleventh centuries. But that was all in the past. Bihar is now the state of the buffoon
Laloo Prasad Yadav, who stoops to the extent of stealing animal feed. Babbanji cannot escape the historical tragedy of his homeland. He has come to
Bombay to steal. He brings nothing with him but a sheaf of poems.

I tell him what Ishaq said about why he couldn't get Babbanji a job:
"All Biharis are thieves."

"Absolutely true!" the young man responds, with the bitterness of
someone who recognizes his tag and has almost lost the will to fight it. The
bookstore owner he had worked for, a Rajasthani, had told him the same
thing to his face: "Bihari bastards are thieves." Then he fired him. "In
Bihar people are not literate," Babbanji explains to me. "The rate is 39.51
literacy data. It is twenty-one percent lower than the Indian data. A simple
villager, who is illiterate, comes to the city to work. He is innocent. But he
can't find work in the city; he wanders about. If someone takes pity on him,
that villager will take him to be as a god. But if anyone gives two rotis
nowadays, he doesn't give it without a reason; his charity has a motive to it.
Now if the patron turns out to be a bad man, a smuggler, he will take the
villager into the bad business. The Bihari will take roti from anyone. But if
he gets out from the net, runs away, he will be called a thief." Hence their
reputation all over.

Babbanji is not yet seventeen. He is confused about why I want to write
about him and advises me of the arduousness of the task if I'm really interested: friendly advice from one writer to another. "A story is written about
those who have a destination in mind. I have come here to start my story. If
you are interested you will have to wait. The road is very long, and I have
to walk on it. I have to let the story develop. What can you write about sixteen years?"

His bag is filled almost entirely with papers: certificates, poems, a notebook. He picks up odd pieces of paper to write on. He shows me one such:
a dust jacket he found on the road. "Angela Lansbury's Positive Moves: My
Personal Plan for Fitness and Well-Being." The copy on the back of the
jacket reads, "I believe it's never too late to take certain measures to maintain our mobility and engage life more fully. . . . By being involved in a

positive way, you reward yourself, and you can then move forward with enthusiasm for life and its multitude of possibilities."

Inside, on the blank space, there is a poem Babbanji has written on Bombay:

> *What could be sold in this carnival?*
> *What intoxication could there be in this earth*
> *that the naive and innocent*
> *come to this crossroads of rushing and thieving? . . .*
> *They are in search of dreams*
> *that will clash with their dreams.*

After reading out the poem, he looks at the picture of Angela Lansbury for a moment. "I had a need to come to Bombay," he says, beginning something. Then he looks up at me. "Will you keep this to yourself?"

"Yes."

Babbanji's father is a college lecturer in geology, in an intermediate college in the small Bihari town of Sitamarhi; he dreamt of his son becoming a scientist. Babbanji did well in chemistry and participated in a school science competition, devising an apparatus that could make petroleum from waste plastic. He came in third. The girl who came in second, Aparna Suman, came to congratulate him. He smiles, recalling the moment. "Maybe she came to tease me. I normally came in first."

"Was she beautiful?" I ask.

"No. She was of medium class."

Babbanji enrolled in the college where his father taught and found that Aparna was in the same college. She asked to borrow a geology textbook. When she returned it, she had enclosed a love poem, which began, "From my loneliness I am speaking to you. . . ." She borrowed a second book. This time it came back with a photograph of her and lyrics from film songs. Word got around in the small town that they were having some sort of affair, which attracted the attention of some thuggish students his father had expelled from the college. Prodded by a jealous rival—a boarder in Aparna's house—they walked into the college classroom and beat up Babbanji in front of the professor. "Bihar is such a place that if you are beaten in front of the professor, he won't do anything," he says bitterly. If the professor interferes, he himself will get beaten. The goons threatened the

young poet with their knives and commanded him, in front of the whole
laughing crowd of his classmates—in front of Aparna—to get up on the
bench, cross his arms, hold his ears, and do fifteen sit-ups, double-quick.

The next day, he felt like killing himself. He couldn't show his whipped
face to his parents. He went to meet Aparna's parents, to complain about
the boarder. When the boarder was summoned, he claimed Babbanji was
harassing Aparna. Babbanji presented her parents with the love letters she
had written him.

In front of them all, her mother asked Aparna, "Do you love him?"
She replied, "No."

They read out loud a poem he had written to Aparna, which she had
shared with the boarder:

> "Why are you seeking for your loneliness one who could go away
>   tomorrow?
> I am a breeze of wind; here now, gone later . . .
> Forget me, flower of my garden."

They were mocking him. "I had tears in my eyes but I wouldn't let
them out. That moment I decided that science was not for me; the reason I
was going to kill myself, this poem, would be my destination, my reason to
live. I decided I wanted to write."

He went home and wrote a letter to his parents, who were at work.
*When I come back to Sitamarhi I will be something. For all the people whom I
am leaving, I will come back with an answer.* Then he got on the bus to the
nearest train station. "All I had was this bag"—he pulls out a yellow plastic
bag such as you go vegetable shopping with—"in which I had this file [with
all his poems], a sheet, and this." He searches deep in the recesses of the
yellow bag and pulls out a garment, a crumpled and slightly soiled undershirt, maybe white originally but turned light blue through washing and
use, heavy with a man's wearing. He holds it in the air in front of me, and
for the first time in his story his eyes are full of tears. "I love my papa. I
took my papa's undershirt. For remembrance. From childhood he has been
both mother and father to me." His voice breaks, and he quickly puts the
undershirt back in the bag.

He took a train going to Lucknow, in the north. Babbanji woke up as
the train was pulling in to Lucknow, in the morning. He looked at his wrist;

his watch, which his father had given him when he stood first in his class, was gone. He got out at the station and pondered his next step. At the station he saw two trains waiting: one going to Delhi, one going to Bombay. The Delhi train was sparsely filled, with some politician types, some journalists. The Bombay train had a vast mass of people waiting to board it. The police were holding them back. Mingling with the mass, Babbanji found that the crowd was composed of all types of people: rich, poor, those who had reservations, and some who looked to be runaways like himself. He had never been to Bombay or Delhi, but he had relatives in Delhi. He had heard that Delhi was not as congested as Bombay, that the hardships of daily life for the poor were not as great there. Babbanji did not know Bombay through the world of the Hindi film; he knew only, from his father, that the city was home to the Tata Institute of Fundamental Research and the Bhabha Atomic Research Center.

All this ran through Babbanji's head as he was waiting on the platform in Lucknow between the two trains. On the one platform there was the Delhi train, half empty, promising a quick trip to a city where he had uncles who would let him stay with them or, if not, lots of space on the broad sidewalks to sleep on. On the other platform was the Bombay train, waiting to be overrun with bodies, taking him a much longer distance to a city where there were unimaginable stresses of living, where he knew not a soul. "I thought, Why are all these people going to Bombay? What is there in Bombay that from all directions there is the cry, 'Bombay! Bombay!' " Waiting on the platform between the two trains, the young man made his decision. If all these people were going to Bombay, it must be for a reason. These people must know something. And so Babbanji forced his destiny. He took his place in the vast throng waiting to get on the train to Bombay.

The journey took two days. He spent a day standing and the rest holding on to his little clutch of ground on the floor of the unreserved compartment. At the stations the police would hold back people from the unreserved bogies and let in people who had bribed them. But to the young poet, the physical discomfort was outweighed by the thrill of direct observation of the masses, the fuel it gave his work. "This was a great experience for me—how people come to Bombay. There were one hundred ten seats and about two thousand people. They were poor people, laborers; they were fitted like animals, people on top of people."

Finally, the Bombay–Lucknow Express pulled in to Victoria Terminus and Babbanji slowly descended onto the platform. "I touched the ground and did pranaam to it," he says, lifting his hand to his forehead. "I took its blessings. I thought, This is my karmabhoomi," the land of his destiny.

At V.T. Station, he was accosted by some officials who asked him for his ticket. They took him to a room and, since he had no ticket, told him he would have to pay 300 rupees or go to jail for fifteen days. They searched his pockets; he had 130 rupees left, and they relieved him of 100. Then Babbanji fled from V.T., took a local train as far as Bandra, and wandered around Carter Road, by the sea. He now had only 22 rupees; 8 rupees had gone for the local train ticket. He stayed hungry for three days, living on water. Then he ran across a watchman in a marble shop, who noticed his condition and sent him back to South Bombay, to someone in Horniman Circle, who gave Babbanji no help. As he was walking around the area, he ran across a bookstall owner, Ram Babu Joshi. He hired Babbanji. "He sold books at outrageous prices after sizing up the customer." His language was also most foul; after a while Babbanji could not stand his curses, so when Joshi fired Babbanji for attending the writers' salon, he was not unhappy.

He came back to Flora Fountain and found a more amiable bookseller, Vijay. Vijay pays Babbanji 50 rupees a day. The money starts going first thing in the morning, when he has to pay 1 rupee to go to the toilet in a nearby facility and 5 rupees to bathe. The owner had suggested a nearby dhaba that serves lunch for 17 rupees, but Babbanji can fill his stomach with some rotis, for 6.5 rupees, and 2 rupees for bananas. Dinner is 14 rupees in a nearby "hotel," rotis and some vegetables. "I'm lucky I'm vegetarian, otherwise it would cost forty rupees or more." So, miraculously, Babbanji manages to save from his salary; he has disposable income. He uses it to buy books, from pavement stalls all over the city. He shows me a recent acquisition, *History and Problems of Indian Education*, for 30 rupees, because he is interested in Muslim education.

Near the bookstall is a little stand that sells sandals. In the night, after business closes, the owner folds down his stall, spreads a piece of plastic on the planks, and it becomes a bedroom for four or five people, who sleep in the open air: himself, Vijay of the bookstall, a cobbler, Babbanji, and another man who lies down next to Babbanji after he is asleep and goes away before he wakes up, so that he has never spoken to him or seen his face, only slept next to him every night.

Babbanji takes me around to the dhabas and the toilets he uses: where he eats, and where he lets it out. In the maidan behind Churchgate is a tent, under which vast pots of food are constantly being stirred by sweating men. This is where you can get a meal of rice and dal for under 10 rupees and live another day. You would not know there was such a site in the heart of Bombay unless you looked for it; it is well hidden from the commuters rushing to the station. There are two toilets nearby; the Sulabh Sauchalaya, set up by a private charity, is much the worse of the two. There is a line of people even now, in the heat of the afternoon, in front of each of the three toilet stalls. In the mornings the line snakes out of the door, down the steps, and onto the footpath. Babbanji has made a calculation. A human being needs eight minutes to go to the toilet. "But by the time you take your clothes off, people are banging on the door; they start banging in two minutes, fifty people banging on the toilet while you sit." Babbanji has taken to getting up before six-thirty in the morning, so he can go to the toilet in peace.

On his first day in Bombay, Babbanji also figured out another survival skill of living on the streets: Never close your eyes when you bathe. There is a hose attached to the sink of the Sulabh Sauchalaya that lets out into a bucket. Babbanji waited his turn, squatted in front of the bucket, filled it up, and started soaping himself. He heard a sound, opened his eyes, and saw the man behind him grab Babbanji's entire bucket and pour it over himself. He had stolen his water. Babbanji wanted to take issue, but the man was big and menacing. He started washing his head from the trickle issuing from the hose. But the man behind him had grabbed his place in the bathing queue, and Babbanji was forced to sit to one side and watch, the soap drying on his skin. Then the man behind the interloper took pity on him and gave his turn at the bucket to Babbanji. "Here, finish your bath." All this is in full view of, and just in front of, the line waiting for the toilets. There is no privacy while you bathe; you have to bathe in your underwear and have a hundred eyes watching you. Frequently brawls break out between the bathers. The Nepali who manages the place charges 5 rupees for the bath and 1 rupee for the toilet, when the rates are clearly posted: 3 rupees for a bath, half a rupee to use the toilet. Still, the rush is so great that the road in front of the toilet is rutted and the paving broken from the stream of soapy bathwater that runs out past the feet of the line and into the road.

How does he like the footpath life? I ask him.

"I like it very much. I have no problems. I don't want a home; I am more free on the footpath."

"How do you find Bombay?" I ask him, as others have asked me. "The flats, the cars?"

"These things don't attract me. I don't want to live in these flats; they imprison people. On the footpaths you can establish relationships, friendships. If I become rich, these relations will be spoiled; if my poor friends come to visit me the security guards won't let them in. The footpath is the friend of the poor. How many people it accommodates to sleep on!"

A recent survey showed that two-thirds of the city's footpaths are unusable for pedestrians, in large part because of people like Babbanji. The battle over the footpath is a battle over rights: of the pedestrians to walk on it (the original purpose); of the homeless to sleep on it; of the hawkers to make a living on it; of the vehicle owners to park on it. The city is in a continuous agonized debate over whose need is the greatest.

I ask Babbanji what he remembers of Bihar.

Two things. First, his father and his admonition to him: "Son, make something of yourself. Do something with your own hands. If you are a thief, be the best thief." Second, "the Bihari heart, their hospitality, the readiness with which they accept outsiders. This I don't find here." In Bombay, Babbanji points out, even a drink of water costs money; to fill a water bottle with water fit to drink costs a rupee or two. "In Bombay people don't have heart, this I have found out in one month." But he knows exactly what he wants to do now. "I want to be among writers. I want to keep writing." He has titled his collection *And the Candle Burns On.*

When most people hear that Babbanji is a poet, they ask him to recite a shayri, a recited form of rhyme that infests modern India. "I don't like shayris. I write poetry. Shayris are for entertainment; poetry tells the truth. People start clapping when they hear shayri, not when they hear poetry," he points out. He likes the circle of poets he met at the writers' salon in the courtyard. "It is a meeting of intellectuals, of society people. There is an exchange of thoughts." He is learning to see things their way, to speak in the language of a critic. He quotes a visiting poet from London. "He said it correctly: Poetry is dead in India today." Writers have been helping him. Babbanji sometimes wonders why, what we stand to gain. "Maybe they want to foster talent, and when I am recognized I will mention them. If people ask me, 'How did you rise up from the footpaths?' I can acknowledge all of you—Adil, you, Madan."

Babbanji tells me I can use his life story for my book and asks if he can suggest a title for it. I nod, and he says, *Untold Life*. "It's the life about which nothing is told. There is plenty of discussion about the lives of the rich, but nothing is spoken about the lives of the poor." Alternatively, he suggests *Secrets of Arrival*. I tell him I like his first title. The world outside—and that includes the people in Bombay I grew up with—know nothing about these lives because nothing has been told about them.

Babbanji's main hunger is for time: time to write. "If I get time I can write a book in a day. I write minimum five–six poems a day." The bookshop is open from eight to eight. After work, he walks the short distance to the sea, near Marine Drive, sits below the block of flats that cost $3 million each for the people who live in them, looks at the same view for free, and writes. He had never seen a sunset in Bihar, he is convinced, after seeing the sun set on the Arabian Sea. "It was very beautiful, very beautiful. I bent down to write and lifted my head after two or three seconds and the sun had set." I too, as a child, had gone to the rocks behind Dariya Mahal at dusk, pen and paper in hand, witness to this intersection of great beauty and great sadness, eyes straining to see where fire ended and water took over.

Among his favorite poets is Atal Bihari Vajpayee. In his notebook, he has copied out one of the prime minister's poems, "Seam in the Hot Milk," about two brothers fighting, an allegory about Partition. "Who am I writing for?" he asks himself. "I want my poems to reach the public of Bombay; I don't want them to stay within myself. These poems should be read by poor people. I don't want them to be in five-hundred-rupee books. I want to write for a publication put out by the Bihar Welfare Association." He wants to tell them what Bombay is, what the footpath is.

In his free time, Babbanji travels around the city, looking at sunsets and destitution. He goes to disaster areas, such as the site of a recently collapsed building, and writes a poem titled "Builders' Hands Stained Red." Babbanji takes me to the winding lanes behind Flora Fountain. There is a group of African drug peddlers and addicts who sleep and conduct business here. One morning Babbanji was passing by this spot when he saw a crowd had gathered. The police had raided the addicts, who line the roads here in the morning. The cops jumped out of their trucks and went after them. Those who could ran away, but one of them had both his feet amputated and was hobbling along on his crutches. The police caught up with him easily, broke his crutches, and felled him with a blow of their lathis. Then, in full view of the crowd, they assaulted the crippled addict with their sticks, raining blows on him as he attempted to slither away on the ground. Babbanji felt greatly moved and composed a poem about the incident from the addict's point of view.

He has also been going to Santacruz, to a shantytown where people live over an open sewer. He heard a group of people singing on the trains and took 3 rupees out of his pocket and asked one of them to sing "Zindagi ka Safar." When they got off the train, he followed them home. Babbanji looked at the sewer; it was overflowing with all kinds of plastic—plastic bags, plastic bottles, plastic odds and ends separated from their original entities—and Babbanji thought of his school science project, which could turn plastic into petrol. "And I thought, This is a treasury!"

Another place he recommends to me is a two-hundred-foot-long ditch between Bandra and Mahim, filled with sewage, totally black. He tells me how to get there: "There is a little jungle, some flats, and below it, for hundreds of meters on the banks, slums. For two to three hundred meters you have to cover your face because of the stench." There is a colony of people living there, migrants like himself. It is empty from eight in the morning to seven-thirty in the evening; the migrants are not beggars. He wanted to see how people could live there in such conditions and wrote poetry about them. "The ditch water is used to grow spinach," he tells me. He finds this remarkable. So do I.

AFTER MONTHS OF LOOKING, Babbanji is unable to find a proper job in Bombay. He has many reasons for avoiding steady employment. "I want to be free. If I take a job I will be bound. This poetry is something that can't be done without seeing. If I can't see Bombay how will I write?" So, forced by the demands of his craft, he has left the bookstall and is seeking a part-time job that will give him time to write. He drifts in and out of favor with the bookstall owner, who won't let him sit there in the day. Babbanji now passes the day sitting on the steps outside the high court.

"Suketuji," he begins, one day, "there is a need of some money."

"How much?" I ask, suddenly wary.

"One hundred fifty."

It is nothing, really—just $4—but by giving him money at this juncture, I am directly influencing the course of his life, the course of the story. Instead, I buy him 500 rupees' worth of meals at the Samovar restaurant in the Jehangir Art Gallery. That entitles him to fifteen good lunches of rice and vegetable curry. I won't give him cash. "I won't take pity," he had said to me. Babbanji often goes to the Jehangir Art Gallery and wanders about the paintings. He says he likes the Sabhavala exhibition, although I suspect he's been taught to, by his illustrious friends in the poets' salon. At the Samovar, I watch the way he eats his cheese sandwich. First he lets it lie on the plate in front of him. Then he eats one quarter at a time, slowly. As long as a little bit of the sandwich is left on the plate in front of him he won't be hassled by the waiters to leave. So he balances his hunger with the need to stay in a shaded place in the afternoon. It is a precise calculation: how much of the sandwich will he allow himself to eat, at what pace.

Babbanji is torn between science and poetry and between Bihar and Bombay. He had researched the plastics-into-petrol phenomenon for three years and then presented it on the national level. He feels the burden of his discovery. "If I pursued this and brought it in front of the world, I would have to go again into the research line. But I want to be a poet. I will transfer this research to my father." Science and poetry can coexist in his life, he thinks. "I will become a poet but somehow science will be in my poems." He says he might have to travel back to Bihar to receive a science award. I suspect he's ready to go back home, but he denies this, saying, "Bombay is my karmabhoomi. If I die it will be in Bombay. I have forgotten my previous life, in Sitamarhi."

But his parents probably have not forgotten about him, I point out. At my urging, he writes a postcard to them:

Dear Papa and Mummy,

I touch your feet.
I have broken your dreams and come here. Please forgive me. But I am trying to mend your broken dreams. I have left the career of science and entered a career of literature and I am starting my career on the footpaths of Bombay, and I am trying to do something through my poems.

If they want to search for him, he tells me, he has written his address—
Flora Fountain, Churchgate—and they can find him in a second. He is
close to tears as he considers the possibility.

"SUKETUJI!" Babbanji phones me early on a Sunday morning. "My papa
has come!"

"Where is he?"

"He is here with me now. I have to go back to Bihar at eleven o'clock.
Some important work has come up. Some very important work."

At nine-thirty, we are at the Café Mondegar, a short walk from Babbanji's home on the sidewalk. The Café Mondegar, open to the traffic of
Colaba, is conducive to gaiety. The beer is cold and arrives in inventively
shaped pitchers; one looks like a fishbowl. The tables are close together,
and a sort of beery bonhomie links the young men, the backpackers, the
dating couples in the bar. But the waiter is smarmy with the two Biharis;
they don't know what to order. The waiter insists on speaking to them in
English. I order breakfast for them.

The father hasn't shaved during the three days it took the train to get
here. He is a balding, bespectacled man of forty-five who looks older, in
the way college lecturers do, and has a nice smile. Today he talks and talks,
nothing can stop him. And it is a pleasure listening to him speak in Hindi,
for he has a nice touch with a phrase. At least some of Babbanji's poetry fire
seems to be inherited.

Babbanji's father had arrived at Victoria Terminus with his father-in-
law at five-thirty this morning and had walked from V.T. to Churchgate,
looking for bookstalls along the way. Near one of them, he saw a group of
sleepers on the footpath; one of the figures stirred and lifted the thin cotton
sheet over his head for a moment, and the professor exclaimed, "Son!"
Babbanji was wearing the same shirt he saw him in last. "Father and son
clasped each other and were weeping," the professor tells me. He recalls
that Babbanji was always a delicate child; he was born in great difficulty. At
this point he almost breaks down. "He couldn't drink mother's milk—his
jaw wouldn't latch on. I've kept him since he was four. He has never asked
anything from me."

Babbanji's eyes water.

"How did he treat his body," the professor wonders, holding up his son's thin hand, "that his parents worked so hard to bring to this stage. Didn't take a sweater, didn't take money from home." They noticed that he had taken a khadi sheet with him, not a more expensive woolen one. "I feel that my house was of glass and has shattered. He was the support of this old man, and he did a very bad thing." But he's also trying to explain his son's behavior to me, as if apologizing, letting me know it's not Babbanji's fault. "The reason is that at an early age he got more knowledge than necessary. He should have told his father about his troubles, but he didn't want to trouble his father. The students beat him because of me."

When Babbanji disappeared, his mother started having dreams about her son, visions. In one, the boy was holding his head and was kneeling on the road. He had a fever, and some kind man was helping him. If she saw a boy with a headache, she would say, "That's my son." They thought about who they could call on for help in locating Babbanji. As is done in times of crisis, times of insufficient knowledge, they went to an astrologer. The astrologer consulted the stars and told them that he was living in Varanasi, with a man whose first name began with the syllable "Ra." Further, the astrologer said, Babbanji was living in a house colored yellow and white.

So the father's wanderings had begun, through the town and cities of North India, searching for his lost son. He had gone from house to house in Varanasi, looking at the walls to see if they were yellow and white, asking groups of students if they knew of a boy with such a name. He went to Deoband, Saharanpur, Aligarh. In the lanes his heart would quicken whenever he would see a group of boys, and he would scan each one's face to see if it matched that of his boy. Nobody could tell him anything.

On the second of April the college lecturer had a dream. His son came to him in the college campus and walked across the campus toward him, in silence. No words were exchanged between them in the dream. On that same day Babbanji wrote to his father at last. "The peon gave his mummy a letter. Daily she waited for the peon. The address was in English. She ran to me. I was afraid that it might be a self-addressed letter for a competition." The letter was signed *Babbanji of Flora Fountain*. He read it twice, thrice. Only two words in the letter made him angry. He pulls it out now and reads out what Babbanji wrote above his name: "Your worthless and vagabond son."

"These two words hurt my heart. My beta is not worthless or vagabond."

Babbanji says, "The world will call me a vagabond, no?" His eyes are full of tears.

"No son is a vagabond for his mother and father."

The jukebox behind us is playing the Bee Gees song "It's Only Words."

After receiving the letter, the professor and Babbanji's grandfather set out immediately for Bombay, to find the boy lying in front of a wall colored yellow and white. Later, Babbanji's father found out that the first man to have given his son shelter was the bookseller Ram Babu Joshi.

Babbanji's father is also angry that his son did not reveal his troubles in the college. "I won't keep my son in Sitamarhi. I'll try to get a transfer."

His son objects. "I will stay in Sitamarhi. When I go back to Sitamarhi I won't be a local man." He will be Bombay-returned. The college bullies will look upon him differently now.

His father, too, can see the positive side of Babbanji's adventure in the huge city. "He has not been derailed. He got an education. Now you have to help him." The lecturer appeals to me. "We are only his parents."

"You tell me as a friend what I should do," Babbanji asks. Should he go back or not?

I point out that Bihar is in pretty bad shape.

They forget their differences and both jump to the defense of their home state. "Bihar has many scientists. There is a ten-year-old boy who has a BSc degree. Each one is brilliant."

"Our earth is very fertile," says Babbanji. The best Hindi poets are Biharis, he says.

The father wants Babbanji to return to Bihar and to science. "A scientist is a very great litterateur," he avers.

"I will do in Bombay; my karmabhoomi is in Bombay," Babbanji repeats, trying to convince both his father and himself. "Look at how fate works. If I weren't working at a bookstall I wouldn't have met Adil."

"But the way you lived?" I ask him.

"I have no fear of the footpath. Now that I'm on the road, I'm on the road."

He reads out a poem he has just written, on a Bombay train "which carries thousands on its shoulders and brings them back." No one understands the train's pain, the poet feels.

"How did he learn all this?" his father asks in wonderment. "How did he enter the world of literature? I find it strange, these additional qualities, how did they come? Maybe it has come down to him through my grandfather, who had many books of literature." While searching for clues about why his son had run away, he had come across a notebook in which his son's secret was revealed: a long poem he had written. "I was surprised—when did he start writing poetry? I couldn't write like that. In Bihar's present condition even an MA pass boy couldn't write like that." But he should get a degree. The professor had one great regret in his life; he had been unable to do his doctorate. "Last year I took a vow that I would get my PhD through my son. My son should be two degrees ahead of me, not less."

Now he would like his son to be a teacher or doctor, "but not a doctor for money." His father is trying to convince me to tell Babbanji to reenroll in college. "This work won't stop," he says of Babbanji's poetry, gingerly stepping around the word. "If you get the inspiration you can write it immediately, half an hour a day. It can't be stopped." And besides, "When will the world recognize him? How many people will like his poetry? There are many poets, writers. The only ones who do well are in the film world. Who reads literature, who reads the truth?" He recites a shloka in Sanskrit: "You should say the truth, but not if it's bitter." All sound, practical arguments against the world of literature. I hear the voice of my father using almost these exact words in New York with me, many worlds away. Babbanji's father isn't directly prohibiting him from entering into a career as a writer. He's using love and fear instead, projecting the anxiety of his middle forties onto the young man of seventeen. Babbanji conceives of himself as a poet; and as he walks the city that gives him rich layers of experience for his poetry, this idea of himself exalts him way above the billionaires on the twenty-third floor.

His father now wants to leave Bombay at once, a few hours after he stepped into the city. When he arrived this morning, he said to Babbanji, "Come, son, let's leave at once. This is a maya ki nagri"—city of illusion. "All these big buildings, they aren't made with truth; they have been built by snatching someone else's wealth." He tells me, "This is a town of money, and I don't give much importance to money." It is a hierarchical city; you are always comparing yourself to others. "There is someone on top of you, and someone on top of them."

Babbanji suggests to his father that he go to his grandfather, whom they have left waiting at the train station, while Babbanji gets his belongings. His father emphatically refuses. He won't let his son out of his sight. That morning when Babbanji went to the public toilet, his father went with him and stood just outside the door. All the footpath people were very happy that the two were reunited, "but they didn't want him to go," recalls his father. His son had found a community among them. His father paid back all the debts his son had incurred and prayed God to bless the man who had sheltered him. Babbanji has also written down a precise accounting of the number of meals he's had at the Samovar and the dates of each. There is still money left over from my 500 rupees.

So the three of us walk to the bookstall to get Babbanji's belongings. What does a man take back to his village after living in the big city? For Babbanji, it is four books, an assortment of the treasures he found on the racks of the bookstalls:

Noise: The Unwanted Sounds
History and Problems of Indian Education
The History of Wilde Sapte (a firm of London solicitors)
Water: The Nature, Uses, and Future of Our Most Precious and
Abused Resource

Then we walk to V.T., where we find Babbanji's grandfather sitting on his bag, placidly chewing his pan. The grandfather is an old man in a dhoti. He doesn't want to talk about his grandson. He wants me to come to Bihar. "There is a lot to see in Bihar," he says with pride: Buddha's birthplace, Patna, many places of great natural beauty. I ask the father if he wouldn't care to take the night train and see a bit of Bombay, now that he's come here from across the subcontinent. "If I see my son I see the whole world," Babbanji's father points out. "My light is here. I see the world through him. I will see you through him, I will see America through him. He is my screen." And looking at the seventeen-year-old beaming at me, his eyes and his heart eager to discover, to react, to live, and the father next to him, now also smiling, I believe it. There will be many long evenings now, after all the explanations have been made, perhaps after a thrashing from his mother, after a sense of disturbance has passed, that Babbanji will sit on the cot in front of the lecturer's house in the stifling small town in Bihar and tell him about the Queen's necklace, about the screen goddess he had seen weaving a garland of jasmine into her hair, about the big cars and the people living on the sewer, about the English poets with their drink, about the building that fell down and the people it fell upon, about the fight for water in the public toilet and the small kindnesses of the footpath dwellers. Isn't that why we have children, after all: to see the world a second time, on their screen?

Standing in V.T. under the big clock, where the commuters come and go, Babbanji says good-bye to me. "I feel like I'm leaving home. In Bihar I will meet people from Bombay, people who have come back for the summer holidays, and I will ask them about Bombay, get news of Bombay. This is just a break for me, not a stop."

I ask him why he has come to feel this way about the city. "Bombay is in my mind because it has given me something to write." The simple truth of this statement comes home to me.

We embrace in parting. He takes my hand, bows, and touches it to his forehead. And so I leave him there, in the gigantic terminus, with the train announcements booming overhead.

"I'll go to the Patna branch of *Time* magazine and write for them!" he yells out to my departing back.

Adjust

Bombay is a fast-paced, even hectic city, but it is not, in the end, a *competitive* city.

Anyone who has a "reservation" on an Indian train is familiar with this word: Adjust. You might be sitting there on your seat, the prescribed three people along it, and a fourth and a fifth person will loom over you and say, "Psst. . . . Adjust." You move over. You adjust.

It is a crowded city, used to living with crowds. In our building in Manhattan, people found it strange when Sunita's parents came to live with us for six months in our one-bedroom apartment. Our landlady withheld part of our security deposit for "excess wear and tear" caused by the presence of two more adults. Nobody in Bombay asked us how many people were going to live with us in our apartment; it was taken for granted that we would have relatives, friends, and friends of friends coming to stay with us, and how we would put them up was our problem.

A recent magazine advertisement for an Ambassador car, the sturdy workhorse of the Indian roads, illustrates what I mean. The car, an unadorned version of a 1950s Morris Oxford, is trundling along a rain-drenched street. The ad copy doesn't devote the usual lascivious attention to leather seat covers, digital dashboards, electronic fuel injection, or the trim lines of the car's design. The Ambassador is actively ugly but lovable in the way elephants are, with a jaunty visor and a wide grin. Instead, there is a snatch of dialogue from within the car. Three people can be seen squashed together in the front bench seat. A man crosses in front of the ungainly pachyderm, holding a briefcase over his head to ward off the downpour.

"Arre . . . isn't that Joshi?"

"Yes. Let's take him also."

"But we are so many."

"Have a heart, we can always adjust."

Car ads in most countries usually focus on the luxurious cocoon that awaits you, the driver, once you step inside. At most, there might be space for the attractive woman you'll pick up once you're spotted driving the flash set of wheels. The Ambassador ad isn't really touting the virtues of space. It's not saying, like a station wagon ad, that it has lots of spare room. It's saying that the kind of people likely to drive an Ambassador will always *make* more room. It is really advocating a *reduction* of personal physical space and an expansion of the collective space. In a crowded city, the citizens of Bombay have no option but to adjust.

I am on the Virar fast train during the evening rush hour, possibly the most crowded of the locals. I am clutching the strip at the top of the open door with both hands, my only other connection the front half of my feet. Most of my body is hanging substantially outside the speeding train. There is a crush of passengers. I am afraid I may be pushed out by their pressure, but I am reassured. "Don't worry, if they push you out they also pull you in."

Someone says, "This is a cattle shed."

Girish once drew for me on a piece of paper a diagram of the dance, the choreography of the commuter trains. The Bombay Central contingent stands in the center of the compartment from Borivali to Churchgate. The people surrounding them move clockwise around the BC contingent like this: first are the Jogeshwari batch, then Bandra, then Dadar. If you are new to the Bombay trains, when you get on and are planning to get off at, let's say, Dadar, you must ask, "Dadar? Dadar?" And you will be directed to the precise spot where you must stand to be able to disembark successfully at your station. The platforms are on different sides of the train. There are no doors, just two enormous openings on either side of the compartment. So when the station arrives, you must be in position to spring off, well before the train has come to a complete stop, because if you wait till it's stopped, you will be swept back inside by the people rushing in. In the mornings, by the time the train gets to Borivali, the first stop, it is always chockful. "To get a seat?" I ask. Girish looks at me, wondering if I'm stupid. "No. To get in." This is because the train in from Dadar has started filling up from Malad, two stops ahead, with people willing to loop back.

It doesn't help to travel in first class, which is only marginally less crowded during rush hours. Girish's brother Dharmendra has a first-class season pass. But when the train is really crowded, he'll go for the second-class coaches. "In second class they are more flexible. First class, you'll have some Nepean Sea Road type. He won't move, he'll stand where he is."

I mention to Girish a statistic I'd read, about the "super-dense crush load" of the trains being ten people per square yard. He stretches out his arm, says, "One yard," and makes a calculation. "More," he says. "More. In peak time, if I lower my arm like this, I won't be able to raise it." Many movements in the trains are involuntary. You just get carried along; if you're light, you might not even have to move your legs. In 1990, according to the government, the number of passengers carried in a nine-car train during rush hour in Bombay was 3,408. By the end of the century, it had gone up to 4,500. According to a letter to the *Times* by G. D. Patwardhan:

> This is a mockery of our statutes, which lay down the precise number of live animals—cows, buffaloes, goats, donkeys, and so forth—that can be carried in a wagon of specified dimensions. Any breach of such rules is an offence punishable under the railways' own disciplinary action procedures and also under the Prevention of Cruelty to Animals legislation. But no such rules and legislation govern the transportation of human beings.

When I ask people how they can bear to travel in such conditions, they shrug. You get "habituated." You get "used to."

The commuters travel in groups. Girish travels with a group of some fifteen people that take the same train from stations farther down the line. When he gets on, they make space on their laps for him and have a potluck breakfast together; each of them brings some delicacy from home—the Gujaratis batatapauua, the Telugus upma, the bhaiyyas alu-poori—and they unwrap their contribution in the cramped space of the compartment. They pass the hour agreeably, telling jokes, playing cards, or singing, sometimes with castanets on their fingers. Girish knows where the best singers are on each train. There is a group on the eight-fifteen that sings nationalistic and anti-Muslim songs very well. There are others who specialize in bhajans, and in call-and-response chanting. Thus the journey is made bearable for those who get a seat, and diverting for those standing. When Girish worked for Kamal right at home in Mira Road, he continued taking the train to Bombay Central once a week, just for the pleasure of breakfast with his train group.

The trains are a hive of industry. Women sell underwear in the ladies' compartment, huge abdomen-high panties that are passed around and inspected, the money passed back through many hands for those bought. Other women chop vegetables for the family dinner they are going to cook immediately on reaching home. The ads on the Bombay locals are the same as the ads in the New York subway, dealing with indescribably private subjects: hemorrhoids, impotence, foot odor. In this safely anonymous mass, these ads can be perused; there is comfort in knowing that these afflictions of the body are universal, shared by the flesh pressing all around. They too need these pills and potions, this minor surgery.

THE WESTERN BRANCH of the train terminates in beauty, the eastern branch in horror. On the Churchgate train, past Charni Road station as it sees the sea, past the gymkhanas—Islam, Catholic, Hindu, Parsi—as the shacks fade away, Bombay becomes a different city, an earlier city, a beautiful city. All of a sudden there is the blue sky and the clear water of Marine Drive, and everybody looks toward the bay and starts breathing.

The eastern branch, the Harbour Line, toward its end passes slowly through people's bedrooms: in stretches the shacks of the poor are less than a yard away from the tracks. They can roll out of bed and into the path of the train. Their little children come out and go wandering over the tracks. Trains kill more than a thousand slum dwellers a year. Others, who are on the train, are killed by electricity poles placed too close to the tracks, as they hang on to the train from the outside by the windows. One such pole kills about ten commuters a month as the train comes rushing around a curve. One of Girish's friends on the 9:05 from Jogeshwari was killed when he was hanging from the window and a pole loomed up, too close, too fast. Just the previous year another of that group, playing the daredevil by riding on top of the moving train, was hit by an arch and survived. Girish muses on the injustice of the two accidents. The showoff survived and the shy window hanger, to whom Girish had only minutes before offered a place inside the train, died.

Paresh Nathvani, a kite dealer from Kandivili, performs a singular social service: He provides free shrouds for those killed by train accidents. About a decade ago, the kite merchant saw a man run over by a train at Grant Road. The railway workers tore down an advertising banner to cover the body. "Every religion dictates that the dead be covered with a piece of fresh white cloth," he realized. So every Thursday, Nathvani visits four railway stations and supplies them with fresh shrouds, two yards each. The biggest station, Andheri, gets ten shrouds a week. The stationmaster initials a ledger that Nathvani maintains and stamps it with his seal. He runs through 650 yards of cloth a year. But it's not enough; it's a long way from enough. The trains of Bombay kill four thousand people yearly.

THE MANAGER of Bombay's suburban railway system was recently asked when the system would improve to a point where it could carry its 6 million daily passengers in comfort. "Not in my lifetime," he answered. Certainly, if you commute into Bombay, you are made aware of the precise temperature of the human body as it curls around you on all sides, adjusting itself to every curve of your own. A lover's embrace was never so close.

Asad bin Saif works in an institute for secularism, moving tirelessly among the slums, cataloging numberless communal flare-ups and riots, seeing firsthand the slow destruction of the social fabric of the city. Asad is from Bhagalpur, in Bihar, site not only of some of the worst communal rioting in the nation but also of a gory incident where the police blinded a group of petty criminals with knitting needles and acid. Asad, of all people, has seen humanity at its worst. I asked him if he feels pessimistic about the human race.

"Not at all," he responded. "Look at the hands from the trains."

If you are late for work in the morning in Bombay, and you reach the station just as the train is leaving the platform, you can run up to the packed compartments and find many hands stretching out to grab you on board, unfolding outward from the train like petals. As you run alongside the train, you will be picked up and some tiny space will be made for your feet on the edge of the open doorway. The rest is up to you. You will probably have to hang on to the door frame with your fingertips, being careful not to lean out too far lest you get decapitated by a pole placed too close to the tracks. But consider what has happened. Your fellow passengers, already packed tighter than cattle are legally allowed to be, their shirts already drenched in sweat in the badly ventilated compartment, having stood like this for hours, retain an empathy for you, know that your boss might yell at you or cut your pay if you miss this train, and will make space where none exists to take one more person with them. And at the moment of contact, they do not know if the hand that is reaching for theirs belongs to a Hindu or Muslim or Christian or Brahmin or untouchable or whether you were born in this city or arrived only this morning or whether you live in Malabar Hill or New York or Jogeshwari; whether you're from Bombay or Mumbai or New York. All they know is that you're trying to get to the city of gold, and that's enough. Come on board, they say. We'll adjust.

Good-bye World

I AM SICK OF MEETING MURDERERS. For some years now, I have been actively seeking them out, in Varanasi, Punjab, Assam, and Bombay, to ask them this one question: "What does it feel like to take a human life?" This unbroken catalog of murder is beginning to wear on me. So when my uncle phones me one day and tells me about a family in the diamond market that is about to renounce the world—take diksha—I put aside everything else and go to meet them. They are the other extreme from Sunil, Salaskar, Satish, and their ilk; they are Jains. They are becoming monks in a religion which for 2,500 years has been built on the extreme abjuration of violence. They are preparing to enter an order that has a different conception of life and its value, where they will stay indoors all four months of the rainy season because if they inadvertently step into a puddle of water they will be taking life—not only killing minute water organisms but also killing the unity of the water. From men who sleep tranquilly after taking human life, I want to go to a family that thinks it sinful to end the life of a puddle of water.

I grew up with Jains. Many of my best friends in India and in America are Jains, and when the marriage broker came to my uncle with proposals for me, he brought them both from Gujarati Hindu and Jain families, since there is so little difference. My uncle is married to a Jain. In Sripal Nagar, in Bombay, we lived above a Jain temple; every day I saw monks sitting in the lobby of our building working on each other's hair. I did not know what they were doing; it looked like they were picking lice. Later I learnt that it was how they kept their hair short, by pulling it out by the roots. Some days they sang hymns about renunciation set to Hindi film tunes. On a particular day, the Jains paid the men with birdcages sitting outside the temple to release the birds; every soul they freed aided in the account book of their personal salvation. The small birds flew out and settled on the rooftops of the city, there to be devoured by crows, kites, and eagles. And the bird sellers went back to the forests and trapped more birds to bring next year to the city.

My family never thought of the Jains as members of a separate religion; we just regarded them as especially, sometimes nuttily, orthodox Hindus. In the diamond market, Hindus are in the minority; most of the merchants are Jains. In America, I found almost nobody who knew about Jainism. It is the least accessible religion. Nobody drops out of Berkeley to become a Jain monk. No Hollywood actors or rock stars make public declarations of their devotion to Jain gurus.

THE FAMILY'S FLAT IS HIGH UP in a good building near Haji Ali, with a Jain temple in the compound. When the door opens, I step into a space that could be a village hut or an Indian restaurant abroad straining for the native ambience. The space is lit only by oil lanterns encased in glass, suspended from the ceiling. The walls are hung with religious tapestries. On one wall is an exhortation, written in chalk: *Samsara* [worldly life] *is as worth leaving as Moksha* [salvation] *is worth reaching.* The floor of one room is lined in a mud-and-cowdung mixture, the same flooring I have seen in village houses all over India. A village abode has been re-created in this flat. I have seen this sort of design before in Bombay, in the flats of other rich people, but for different reasons. It was in style a few years ago, the "ethnic" look.

My escort, another diamond merchant, leads me to a divan at the far side of the room by the window—there is no fan—on which reposes a dark, slender man in his forties with a thin mustache, wearing a gold-braided silk kurta and diamonds on his ears and fingers. This is Sevantibhai Ladhani, the patriarch of the family that is going to give up everything. He is one of several brothers in an extended family that has done very well in the metal business and then expanded into diamonds. He looks like a minor princeling. My escort goes up to him and touches the much younger man's feet; the figure on the divan blesses him.

In one month, this family of five—a father and mother in their early forties, their nineteen-year-old son, and seventeen-year-old twins, a son and a daughter—are going to leave this flat, this city, and everything they own. They will spend the rest of their lives wandering on the rural highways of the country, the men and the women separated, never to be a family again. Sevantibhai says, of his wife of twenty-two years—he refers to her as shravika, laywoman—and the three children she has given him, "Now we are only united by selfishness. Hundred percent." In a month, they will go to a small town in the northernmost part of Gujarat, and there Sevantibhai will say good-bye to all of them. And they will say good-bye to each other. From then on, the sons are to travel with the father, and the daughter with her mother, but as their disciples, not as their children. His sons will stop calling him pappa and refer to him as gurudev; his daughter will call him gurubhagvan. But male and female members will be forever separated: The mother can never again meet her sons or her husband, unless they happen to be passing by on the road. Sevantibhai will never meet his daughter, except by accident, and then only in the presence of the guru maharaj of his order, lest his vow of celibacy get contaminated. The bonds of family, formed over a lifetime, will be voluntarily broken in one massive public ceremony.

They are doing this in order to sever all ties with samsara and attain moksha. In the simplest sense, moksha means not having to be born again. Sevantibhai is looking for moksha to end not just his life or his children's lives, but his entire lineage. But before doing this, they will show everybody that they aren't leaving the world because they have failed in it; they will go out in the full noonday light of worldly success. In one month, they will go to the Gujarat town and give away, physically throw away, everything they have earned up to this point: between $2 million and $3 million. It will be a dramatic rejection of Bombay, of the sole reason why anybody would want to live here. Once your desire to make money stops, you should leave by the next train.

Sevantibhai had originally been a most unobservant Jain. He didn't even go to pray in the Jain temple below his own building. He lived like any well-off Bombayite, enjoying the city and its pleasures. One evening at 11 p.m., Sevantibhai was reading a book written by a Jain swami titled *I Should at Least Be Human*. In the book, Sevantibhai came across a sentence that electrified him. "Are you going to be dismissed or will you resign?" He thought about it and then woke up his wife and told her he had decided to take diksha. He had decided to resign before he could be dismissed.

It was a momentous decision, but it was not sudden. Several years ago, he had chanced to hear a speech at Chowpatty by a Jain guru, Chandrashekhar Maharaj, which had set him thinking. For the last few years, Sevantibhai had been progressively renouncing modernity. He had already ceased using allopathic medicine eighteen years ago, well before his interest in his religion had been awakened. After the twins were born, they were in some pain. Sevantibhai went to an ayurvedic doctor in Khetwadi, who gave him the urine of a cow. He made the babies drink it twenty-one times a day, and they got better.

Next to go was diesel and petrol. He gave up using automobiles. Sevantibhai impresses upon me the great sins committed during the extraction of fossil fuels: the drilling through the layers of the earth, the killing of snakes and other subterranean life forms while doing so. It is bad for the country too: "You have to import the petrol from Saudi Arabia and send them things like laboratory mice and human blood in exchange." The use of the automobile also takes life. "If you use a bullock cart, a man doesn't die if he collides with it. And then the bullock is also employed." For the actual diksha ceremony, he wanted to go from Bombay to Dhanera, the diksha site, in a convoy of bullock carts, a journey that would take several days. His extended family objected vehemently, so he has reluctantly agreed to take a train.

Then went electricity. For the last seven years, Sevantibhai has been living in his Bombay high-rise flat without electric lights or appliances. He enumerates the sins racked up in its production. In the case of electricity generated through a dam, he explains, the great force of the water falling onto the turbines kills so many fish and crocodiles that every half hour the dam builders have to clean out the turbines. The disaster at Chernobyl, he points out, was a direct result of the desire of people to have electricity. Even the oil lamps that burn in the apartment kill germs. Sevantibhai admits with some shame that for the last year and a half, because of a back problem, he has had to use the electric elevator in his building instead of the stairs. He asks me to think of all the electrical connections in the city of Bombay, the immense accumulation of sin in the bright lights of the city.

I ask Sevantibhai if it is all right to use my computer to write down what he is saying. I assure him that it is battery-powered and won't use the electricity in the flat. He looks doubtful but then assents, on the grounds that what I am writing may spread the Jain message in the wider world. This, as he puts it, is "using sin to combat sin." So we continue the conversation, the light of the screen illuminating my face in the lamplit apartment as I write.

Sevantibhai began a course of study in Gujarat with Chandrashekhar Maharaj, the senior Jain guru he had heard speak at Chowpatty, and started taking his family along. The children had been studying in English elementary schools in Bombay—his older son at the Tinkerbell School—but Sevantibhai had pulled them out seven years ago to study the dharma, first at home and then with Chandrashekhar Maharaj. When the children were first taken out of school, there was no talk of diksha. Sevantibhai had simply felt that something was lacking in the education provided by their schools. Now the children have been studying the Jain scriptures in the languages they were written in, Sanskrit and Prakrit. They are more advanced in the study of these languages than Sevantibhai, because the children's minds are younger, sharper. "They are reading the Tilakmanjari, the hardest book in Sanskrit," he says with pride.

He followed the tenets of the religion as a layperson, from his comfortable flat in Bombay. Underlying the guru's lectures was always this theme: The only way to reach moksha is to renounce the world, to take diksha. Sevantibhai says it was not he, but his older son and his wife, who first felt the strong urge to take diksha. The teacher had said that the family should start with his older son, Snehal. But Sevantibhai's brothers objected; they said they would give their consent only if he, Sevantibhai, took diksha along with his son. Sevantibhai wasn't quite ready, and the family stayed in Bombay.

In the summer of 1997, Sevantibhai heard about a group of seventy people who were going to take diksha together. He asked his teacher's permission to join them with his family. The maharaj saheb asked Sevantibhai to get his brothers' permission first; there should be no bad blood in the extended family. All five of them packed their clothes and asked the brothers to give their approval. But a sister was getting married, and his brothers asked him to wait for another year. If he still felt like it at that time, they would allow him to go. Sevantibhai postponed it for six months. The extended family was hoping that Sevantibhai would come to his senses, and they were trying to delay his departure till he did. But his determination to go was stronger than their will to hold him back in the world. And now, finally, in a month's time, all five of them will say good-bye: to samsara, to Bombay, to modernity.

Sevantibhai constantly refers to the India of the past and its fall in the present. "Before, in India, we used to have families of twenty-five or thirty people. If someone dropped by for dinner, there were twelve women to cook. Now we have families of three people, and if someone comes unexpectedly for a meal, our faces get all twisted up. Before, we used to know who was who in the whole village. Nowadays, we don't even know who lives in the next flat." The staple grain was millet, which grew side by side with grass that cattle could also eat. Now it is wheat, which does not flourish amid grass, and the cattle have to be kept out of the wheat fields. Money was never used; it all ran on barter. "Milk was never sold before; it was considered a sin." And the line of authority was clear: "When the mahajan came out, nobody had the courage to look him in the face." It was a functioning system, the India of the villages, the India of the old times. It had vyavastha, order. "All our vyavastha was there, and now it has been broken. We want to make that vyavastha again."

There is a battle in the making between city and countryside. Political earthquakes have been set off by the insecurity of the city dweller who doesn't grow his own food; when prices of onions shot up dramatically in 1998, the national government almost fell. The outrage is principally from the cities; the rural areas actually benefit from a rise in vegetable prices. The biggest battles between urban and rural India are being fought over water. Cities need dams, which destroy villages; they need them for water and for electricity. Sevantibhai intends to desert the city's side and go over to the village.

But there are cities and there are cities. There is a big difference between Bombay and a city like Ahmadabad, he maintains. In the half-mile stretch below his building, he has seen all the fleshpots of the world. Nothing is forbidden: There is a bar, there are eateries serving nonvegetarian food, there is a shop selling whiskey. Bombay is "paap ni bhoomi"—a city of sin—a visitor sitting at Sevantibhai's feet agrees.

New sadhus such as he will be cannot stay in Bombay, Sevantibhai explains. When they go around the high-rise flats for their daily round of gathering food, the doors are usually shut. Sevantibhai never refers to food-gathering as begging—a man from a business community like the Jains is never a beggar—but as gocari, the grazing of a cow, which only takes some grass, never the whole clump. They have to walk around with a layperson to ring the bell (the use of electric appliances is forbidden). "If the door is opened, the television is usually on, and if the sadhu's glance happens to fall on the TV just once, it is enough to send him straight to hell." The layman has to make sure, after pressing the bell, that the TV is switched off before the monk walks straight into the kitchen to gather the food. "Dharma Labh," says the monk, inviting the householder to gain religious merit, and inspects all the pots, and takes from each only enough so that the family does not have to cook again, in which case the sin of the second fire would accumulate to the monk. The monk will graze in several different houses, once a day, mixing everything he finds into one or two pots: vegetables, rice, dal, and chapatis from different kitchens, mixed together and eaten cold, strictly for sustenance. Here, too, Bombay makes a monk's grazing difficult. In towns like Ahmadabad, a monk can tell in advance if the television is on in a particular house, because the doors are never closed during the day.

Sevantibhai's older son, Snehal, is sprawled sleeping across the divan, in a sweater, the windows closed against the January chill. Utkarsh, the younger son, enters, along with his mother, Rakshaben. They too wear gold and diamond ornaments. All the family is bedecked with jewelry; it is their way of showing how much of the world they are leaving behind, how rich they are, the extent of their contempt for the attractions of samsara. They all are also resplendent in silk clothes. At my wedding, which was in the South Indian style, I was not allowed to wear silk, because for the Brahmin community I was marrying into, the destruction of silkworms to make silk was a sin. But the Jains believe that silk is less sinful than mill cloth, since the production of silk destroys only two-sensed beings, whereas the occupational hazards of making fabric in a mill destroy five-sensed beings, in addition to incurring the sin of using electricity. In every activity of life—eating, drinking, wearing clothes, traveling—there is a conscious balancing of harm, a series of decisions constantly being made so as to incur the least amount of karmic matter possible.

When I ask the mother questions, the younger son speaks in a low, irritated voice; he is berating her for inaccuracies in her responses. She has a lovely smile. He is a bit peremptory with her.

"We will live a life completely without sin," Rakshaben tell me, her face shining. "We leave in happiness."

Utkarsh explains further. They will be walking constantly, observing the five vows: no violence, no untruth, no stealing, no sex, no attachments. They will be wearing two white unstitched pieces of cloth, nothing else; every six months, their hair will be pulled; and they will have no shoes, no vehicles, no telephone, no electricity. On the day they take diksha, they will bathe; it will be the last bath they take in their lives. They will not put their foot into a puddle; they will stay in the same place during the months of the rainy season; they will not bathe in ponds or rivers or seas; and they will stay indoors while it's raining. Occasionally, if they feel very hot, a light wipe of the skin with a wet cloth is allowed. They can wash their clothes only once a month, and rinse out their gocari bowl after eating. "I, my father, and my brother will live together," Utkarsh explains. "Mummy and Sister will stay with their sadhvin. If we happen to be in the same village we can meet; otherwise we can't." He seems almost eager about the coming separation.

I ask the mother why she isn't allowed to see any relatives after she takes diksha.

"Because we want to break the attachment, the affection. Only then will we get moksha." Rakshaben is not from one of the more orthodox Jain families; she was raised in Ulhasnagar and educated in a Catholic convent school. "My husband felt we should all take diksha together," she explains. Women who aren't getting along with their husbands sometimes take diksha instead of divorce. For a traditional Gujarati woman, society understands diksha, but divorce will mark her. But Rakshaben is taking diksha for the opposite reason: to keep the weird unity of the family. I get the sense that she loves and follows her husband and that this love will lead her to follow him even into permanent separation.

After they become nuns, Rakshaben and her daughter will be free to wander anywhere they choose—except Bombay. The sadhvin of the order they are to join has decreed that the territory south of Virar, where the local trains terminate, is forbidden to them forever. "The environment is not good. The thinking is good in the villages, not in the city." But the prohibition doesn't apply to all cities. "Only Bombay. Delhi, Calcutta, and other cities are okay," explains Rakshaben. Bombay is the Sodom and Gomorrah of the Jain religion, "Paap ni bhoomi."

The phone rings and the daughter, Karishma, comes to answer it. It is the only powered appliance in the whole place, and it feels odd to see her so comfortable using it. She is a slight dark girl who seems the least articulate of the five. She sits shyly behind her twin brother and her mother.

Downstairs, as I get into a taxi, I look around the street landscape of the paap ni bhoomi at night. On the ground floor of their building is a Fiat showroom; opposite is a bank, urging its loan money upon the public; and next to it is a bar, the Gold Coins. The murderers I have been meeting recently live only a short walk away.

I come home from Sevantibhai's house to find my friend Jaiman waiting for me, the half-Marwari, half-American man who has just been made editor of the Russian edition of *Playboy*. We go to a party in the Casbah Room at the top of the Khyber restaurant; three rooms of people drinking, dancing, flirting, feasting. Women stroll by in abbreviated skirts. Jaiman is immediately pounced upon by Bombayites wanting to know what it is like being editor of *Playboy*, whether he selects the models himself. Beautiful women come to his office every day, he says, and he asks them to take off their clothes to shoot a couple of test rolls and they unbutton their shirts, unzip their skirts. He has just been on a family trip to Bhilwara, in Rajasthan, where he couldn't quite tell his Marwari relatives what he did in Moscow. They are fantastically orthodox, very much like the Jains. A tall, big-boned Punjabi woman hugs and kisses the men in the room. "I can't wear this dress because my mother says I'm popping out all over," she says, pointing to her breasts. She sits down on a man's lap, their arms around each other, one long leg emerging from a slit in the skirt. Rivers of liquor flow from the bar; there is no closing hour here. When someone puts a cigarette in his mouth, passing waiters stoop and light it. Large tables are stacked with Punjabi and Italian food: racks of meat, hundreds of birds and animals and fishes, dressed and cooked and adorned so they look nothing like the living beings they once were. A steady electronic pulse comes out of a darkened room, where people are writhing on the dance floor. Jaiman has his eye out for someone he can take to bed during his three nights in Bombay. He is like a pointer dog when he sees a pretty girl. His hair bristles, and his whole body turns reflexively in her direction. Until he possesses the girl, or at least makes a pass at her, he is in a state of acute unease, a profound anxiety. He has come to India prepared; from his bag, he pulls out a small white pill: Viagra. The magazine's head office in Chicago has sounded out Jaiman about launching an Indian edition of *Playboy*. They think it would do very well here.

WHEN I GET to the Diamond Merchants' Association Hall a few days later, there is a large banner on the wall: HEARTY WELCOME TO THE MOKSHA-STRIVING JEWELS. The renunciates—diksharthis—are to be felicitated by the wealthy community of diamond merchants. Tikkas are applied to our foreheads, with glitter instead of the traditional rice. We are all given little plastic packets of dry fruits—almonds, cashews, raisins, pistachios—that must be worth, at a minimum, 50 rupees each. The Hindu chairman of the industry association, who is one of the felicitators, takes me into a corner and asks me what I think of the whole thing. He is more than a little disapproving. The children are so young; he wonders if they have received enough of an education to be able to make an informed choice. Seventeen is too early, he says. He comes from a family of BJP leaders. "You and me are getting associated with these rituals." This is a premodern religion, not the kind the Hindu nationalists would like to be associated with. "What a religion," the chairman observes of Jainism, "which can have both": the billionaires on the dais, with their extreme love of money, and the diksharthis, with their extreme abnegation of it.

The program begins. A religious singer produces the sounds of traditional Indian instruments—the oboelike shehnai, the tabla—from a Casio synthesizer and sings bhajans, all set to the tune of Hindi film songs. The crowd swells. It is the middle of the trading day, but by now hundreds of men and a few women are here, the men dressed in simple light-colored cotton-blend shirts and dark pants. You would not know the wealth of these men from their clothes. I see friends of my uncle, people I have known since childhood in Calcutta, merchants from Dariya Mahal, and many other faces I recognize but can't put a name to. The talk as we wait for the Ladhanis is of sizes and weights, of the glittery stones they trade in. "I need some half-caraters, natts, browns. . . ." I have grown up amid such conversations; it has been a constant in my shifting life, and it soothes me like a song I have been listening to since birth.

The family comes into the hall. Sevantibhai is dressed in silk robes and turban like a peshwa, Rakshaben in a green gold-braided sari, everyone laden down with fabulous diamond jewelry all over their visible bodies: fingers, ears, noses. Jewelry is ultimately useless ornament, and their casting away of these baubles is going to make no difference in their lives, as it made little difference while they were wearing them. They sit on the white mattress and bolsters on the dais, the men and the women very separate. Not once during the ceremony does Sevantibhai cast so much as a glance toward his wife and daughter, but he occasionally smiles and converses with his sons.

As the compere, a bearded man dressed in a khadi kurta, acquaints us with the bare facts of the family's renunciation, a merchant seated next to me starts sobbing uncontrollably. I see he keeps his eyes open as his face shakes, so as not to miss anything happening onstage.

The speeches begin. The diamond merchants talk about wanting to do this; every year a few of them renounce the world. "We have gathered here to get the idea," one says. "We need the idea before we do the deed. We all will have to do this sooner or later, if not in this life then in the third or fifth birth from now on." And another: "His understanding is two steps ahead of ours." The steps are, first, be born in India. "If we were born in America this wouldn't even be possible." Then, observe the regimen of a Jain layperson, which the Ladhani family has been doing for the past several years. A giant pilgrimage was recently undertaken, on which my aunt and uncle went. They walked from temple to temple in Gujarat for ten days, doing without electricity, following the Jain dharma more or less strictly for the duration. Thousands of diamond merchants had participated. The final step is to take diksha. In a subsequent birth, if your karma has been erased, your soul may be reborn as the prophet Mahavir, and only at the end of that life will you reach moksha. It is comfortably in the future.

The compere talks about the time three of them from a Jain organization went to a place where dogs and other stray animals were slaughtered. They had tape recorders and small video cameras, and they asked the manager of the establishment what they did with the carcasses. They melted down the animal fat, the manager said, and sold it as tallow, 16 rupees a kilo for the lower quality, 22 rupees for the better quality. Who would buy such a product? the Jains asked. "His answer was such that even now when I think about it I break out into a sweat," the compere recalls. The manager told him he had advance orders from the leading snack-food merchants of the city. The fried snacks that Gujaratis are especially fond of were cooked in dog fat. With such sin within us, the compere thunders, how can we even hope to improve ourselves? It is the same with ice cream, he continues. Do we know what happens with the bones, the hooves, and the horns of old cows? He had asked the owner of an ice-cream factory how come the ice cream didn't melt. It was because those bovine byproducts were melted down and put into the product, as gelatin. This brings murmurs and expressions of disgust from the crowd. "Let us vow from this moment on not to eat ice cream!" the compere shouts.

The speeches very rarely mention God. They also don't talk about helping the poor. The principal thing you can do for others, they suggest, is to lead them away from samsara. There is no mention of heaven or the delights of moksha. It is a phenomenally pessimistic ideology. The compere describes the present state of the community. There are 10 million Jains. Of them, only about 20,000 are monks. "The Jain community is like a man who has swallowed poison, has poison in his belly, and is being attacked by a man with a knife. As he steps back from the attacker, he is one step away from the edge of the open terrace, beyond which is the abyss."

We are sitting on the floor. All around the vast hall, very close to the building we are in, are the windows and balconies of other buildings in the densely packed quarter. A woman comes out on the balcony just outside the window in front of me. She leans over the parapet and meditatively throws up, controlled release of a thin stream of white mucus, somewhere between spitting and puking. Perhaps she is pregnant; she isn't retching. A merchant in front of me nurses his chapped lips with a tube of Vicks lip balm.

Then the most riveting speaker of the afternoon comes up to the mike. He is the brother of Atulbhai, an extremely rich merchant who had taken diksha in Ahmadabad; farewell processions for him were taken out not just all over India but also in Antwerp and New York. Sevantibhai took advice from Atulbhai about his decision.

The brother asks us to consider what we are doing with our lives. He paints a picture of the Ladhanis after the thirtieth, wandering from village to village in the blazing heat of Kutch, not knowing if they will get food in the next village, mixing five different types of vegetables and six different types of dal in the same pot and swallowing it. "We have to think about what we listen to now, and what we will do this evening in our offices. We get distressed even if the air conditioner doesn't work for a little while. We complain if the air-conditioning in the first-class compartment of the Ahmadabad train fails. And think of this family, in the extreme Celsius heat of Kutch! This little Karishmaben!" He asks us to consider how impatient we have become with time, how we complain if we can't get a train reservation, and how time will stop having meaning for this family, and how much they will have to walk. "This has now become our culture: Have more! Have more!" In rapid, vigorous Gujarati he describes the crazed world that the diamond merchants live in, a world of mobile phones, of global plans made for office expansion in Bangkok, New York, Antwerp, of billions of rupees' worth of dealings every day, of waiting lists for airplane tickets, of constant accumulation—"Have more! Have more!"—and contrasts this with the lifestyle this family is about to adopt, which is one of "de-attachment." The crowd is overflowing past the entrance now, there are hundreds of people in this vast room, and it is hot with breath and sweat even on a winter afternoon.

An elderly merchant is brought to the stage, one of the leaders of the industry, a former diamond smuggler from Antwerp who knew my grandfather well. He does not speak, and with great difficulty gets up to bless Sevantibhai. His family owns a mansion on Malabar Hill and a Manhattan apartment above a Rolls-Royce showroom. Another merchant, Arunbhai, dressed simply in a white half-sleeved shirt but a billionaire in any currency, tells us that a few years ago his mother had also wanted to take diksha. He convinced her against it. But he speaks of the monk's life with yearning, as something he will have to do sooner or later.

One speaker is frank about Sevantibhai's past: "There is no sin which he has left undone. One of his friends told me, 'Whenever he was on the plane with me, he was always tight.' " There are dark hints of other sins, of a life enjoyed to the full before he turned to the religious way. A merchant tells me that Sevantibhai's first engagement was broken when the girl's family found out about his reputation. A broker in my uncle's office had said he was once with Sevantibhai for three days running in the police station; he had been accused of stealing goods. The police recognized him; they salaamed him. The broker speculated that there must have been something huge, some fraud or financial disaster, that made the diamond merchant decide suddenly to take diksha. All around, Sevantibhai's reputation is of one who has committed more than his fair share of sin.

But now, Sevantibhai Chimanlal Ladhani, the dark little man with the easy smile, is not just a moderately successful diamond merchant. He has become a figure of power, a leader on the path that even the billionaire Arunbhai will have to tread sooner or later. At one bound, he has surpassed people far more successful in business than he. He is now, in this hall, in this afternoon, the subject of their admiration, even of their envy.

The diksharthis are now felicitated by the leading merchants, with plaque, tilak, shawl, and garland. The wives of the merchants felicitate the women; it is the first time they are really noticed. The girl, Karishma, has barely been mentioned in the speeches. There is little glory in this for her; almost all the speeches mention only the father's sacrifice. This is a Bombay girl who now will never go to a movie, put on makeup, go on a date, or go to college. She will never return to the city she grew up in.

The woman on the balcony opposite reappears, this time with a kite. She flies it out into the little bit of sky visible between the buildings, and she is grinning.

THE MODERN METROPOLIS is a collection of transients, on their way from somewhere to somewhere else. New York is a collection of migrants from other cities; Bombay is a collection of people from villages, who come into the city and seek to re-create the village. The anxiety of the city dweller is the anxiety of transience; he does not know where he will be next year or where his children will be. He cannot form lasting friendships, because sooner or later his friends will be scattered. In the village, his grandfather knew where he was going to die, the funeral ground he would be burnt on, and the river his ashes would be scattered into; he knew that the friends and cousins he grew up with would be a short walk away till he died. The city dweller has no such trust in the permanency of relationships. Satish could not go about his deadly missions in a village, where there is no protective anonymity. Monalisa would not be needed in a village; her sympathetic ear, her status as an object of public consumption, is relevant only in a city. The human spirit has not caught up to the speed at which things change in cities. We began as a village species; we have not readjusted to city life. That is why Sevantibhai seeks to escape the city; he is renouncing the city as much as he is renouncing anything else, wealth or family.

SEVANTIBHAI SMILES as soon as he sees me through the throng in his ancestral home in Dhanera. We have all gathered here to see the Ladhanis off. "Have you eaten?" is the first question he asks me. Outside, one of his brothers is chanting, "My dear brother has taken diksha!" to be met by the answering chorus, "Wah bhai wah!" A woman shouts out the first line, and the whole extended family roars the chorus, the force of their voices perhaps convincing them that this is an occasion for celebration. There is to be a grand parade around Dhanera on this, the last day that the Ladhanis will spend in samsara.

As Sevantibhai is carried out of his home on the shoulders of his family, the din is enormous. All the traditional musicians for miles around the small town have been called for this procession. I take a place atop the terrace of a house overlooking the route of the procession and settle down to watch. There are a lot of people on this terrace, all leaning over the brick parapet. The owner warns us, "Don't press against the parapet! It might break!" Below us, all the wonders of rural Gujarat are passing by. White-clad Jain sadhus glide by seated on dolis, little platforms slung on the shoulders of their followers, heralding the coming of the procession. First come the drummers of the small dhol, cymbalists, men playing elongated trumpets, and a man on the hump of a camel playing two enormous turmeric-smeared drums. Then come the dancing horses, decorated with rich embroidery. Two little turbaned boys ride two snow-white dray horses. A bevy of village girls comes by, each holding a brass pot on her head, each brass pot topped by a coconut. Then the members of the extended Ladhani family ride past on floats pulled by camels—each one a little straw-covered village hut. Now the actual diksharthis arrive, preceded by men in tribal costume playing, of all things, bagpipes. The three Ladhani children are seated in the middle of enormous sculpted birds: one a peacock, another a swan. Each bird sits on a cart pulled by an elephant. Behind them are Sevantibhai and Rakshaben, seated high on twin thrones, on another elephant-pulled cart. A man holding two swords follows them, as does an enormous mob, for Sevantibhai and Rakshaben are literally throwing money away. They fling out their arms, scattering rice mixed with gold and silver coins and currency notes. In front of them are baskets full of this lucrative mixture. By this stage of the procession, their movements have become practiced, automatic: They dip, gather up an armful of their wealth, and straighten out, throwing out their arms as they do so, the glistening white rice and the gold and silver traveling outward from their bodies in a wide arc to the frenzied mob below. On the street, I am kept at a distance by the throng jostling to grab their discarded wealth, but even from afar I can make out the couple's exhilaration. Rakshaben's white teeth gleam in her dark face. They are unburdened. I am reminded of the customers unburdening themselves in Sapphire, the beer bar, blowing their money over the heads of the dancing girls. It's the same flinging out of your wealth, with both hands, getting rid of it as fast as possible.

Following the diksharthis, two human horses (men walking with life-sized cloth horses attached to their bodies) do a dance; others blow conch shells; a man beats a metal plate; a monk continuously pours water on the ground through the spout of a jug. The last float features an idol of the prophet Mahavir himself, a golden cobra hooding him as he sits in meditation. It is a surprisingly tiny image. The floats are followed by a cart heaped with cardboard boxes, out of which men are distributing clumps of dates and cylinders of jaggery to the poor. The throng is intense around this cart too. As the men give out the gifts they are also swinging sticks at the crowd to keep them back.

All the tribals of Dhanera and the surrounding villages are dressed up for this event, men and women both, in extravagantly colorful cottons and silks. The procession passes by under the statue of Ambedkar. The diksharthis fling out extra amounts to the mostly Dalit mob, who surround them like pigeons flocking around someone scattering grain in a park. The great liberator of the Dalits has an arm out, holding his finger up in censure or prohibition.

As the diksharthis approach the eating ground, a carnival has sprung up outside the tent of giving, where peasants have been lined up for hours, to get gifts of grain and cloth from Sevantibhai's fortune. I can see a man walking on a tightrope above the crowd. Sevantibhai and Rakshaben come down the road on their float, a king and queen on their thrones. Men shout from a cart preceding them, urging the crowd, "Abandon the world!" Something catches Sevantibhai's eye, and he gestures to the woman whom he will call his wife only for the next twenty-four hours: Look. And she looks. The tightrope walker is balanced on the end of a very tall pole, high, high above the crowd, silhouetted against the clear January sky. The couple salute him with folded hands, but he is the only one in the crowd who doesn't notice. He is facing away from them and is now suspended upside down on his tightrope. Sevantibhai and Rakshaben behold the carnival performer, and there is delight on their faces.

Sevantibhai's guests have been fed for seven days. Today, on the eighth and final day, every single person in the fifty-seven villages of the district of Dhanera has been invited for a grand feast. Thirty-five thousand people sit side by side for the meal—men and women in separate tents—which has been bought from those same villages. The village leaders have been instructed to prepare the ingredients using the old ways: the water is from wells, not taps; the oil is pressed by bullocks; the vessels are handmade brass; the ghee is from the local cows, not buffaloes; the sugar and the jaggery are organic; the grain and vegetables have all been grown locally. The flour is hand-ground, not mill-ground, which would be inevitably contaminated with dead insects. It is all as Sevantibhai has specified. On the eve of the twenty-first century, it is still possible to prepare a strictly Jain meal, grown and cooked locally, and feed thirty-five thousand people with minimum harm to the planet. It is good, wholesome Gujarati food: two sweets, two farsaan savories, puri, two vegetables, two dals, pappadams, rice, a stuffed chili, chutney. There are no onions, garlic, or potatoes in the food; nothing that the earth has to be dug up for to harvest. But the water, when it is poured into my glass, is muddy with sand.

Back where I am staying, with old friends of my grandfather, the doctor who owns the house sits down on the veranda to educate me about Jainism. He only came out once to glance at the procession when it passed by his hospital. He is of the opinion that what the Ladhanis are doing is a travesty. He is from the Sthanakvasi fold of the Svetambara Jain sect, which doesn't worship idols—"like in Islam"—and considers a temple only a hall of prayer. Sevantibhai belongs to the Deravasi sect, or, as the doctor calls it, the murtipujak—idol-worshiping—sect. There are eighty-four Jain sects now, he says, and only 10 percent of the sadhus are authentic. The rest steal money meant for the poor; the diksharthis keep money saved up in case they decide to go back to samsara, and while they might themselves walk from place to place, they make sure their followers and relatives accompany them in cars, catering to their every need, bringing modern medicines, arranging the itineraries of their travels in advance. Each leader of a sect is preoccupied with how many diksharthis he can attract to his order. The Ladhani children are just doing it because their father told them to. Everybody knows this, but he can't say these things in public, the doctor says, because there would be fisticuffs.

Dhanera is a town of thirty thousand people, from which most of the Jain population has emigrated; only about a hundred families remain. Even so, fifty Jains from families originating in Dhanera have taken diksha in the last ten years, a point of considerable local pride. But Sevantibhai's ceremony is unique. "Nothing like this has been seen in Dhanera," the doctor says. About Sevantibhai's reasons for taking diksha, the doctor opines: "Blind faith." I ask him about the rituals of the renunciation. He gives me a parable. A long time ago, a man was conducting a wedding. A cat was running around the marriage hall, disturbing things. So he tied it to a pillar. Afterward, generations of the man's family, whenever they had a wedding, found a cat and tied it to one pillar of the hall, believing it to be a required wedding custom. The goings-on around this diksha, the doctor says, are like that cat tied to the pillar: The original meaning has been lost, and people are just doing it because that is how it has always been done. The leaving of institutions has become institutionalized.

When I get back to Sevantibhai's house in the evening, I am introduced to the extended Ladhani family, milling about in the courtyard, as one of the fold. "One hundred years in the business," a merchant who grew up with my grandfather says about my family. Most of the people around here know my grandfather, my uncle, my father. I am introduced to a large dark man wearing glasses, speaking English with a Gujarati-American accent, an enforced drawl. Hasmukh lives in Los Angeles and is a diamond merchant and nephew of Sevantibhai, though he is only a year and a half younger. He is also the renunciate's best friend. He is eager to tell me how close they are. He has known his uncle since he was five years old. People refer to them as a pair of bullocks yoked together, inseparable. When Sevantibhai and Rakshaben went on their honeymoon to Srinagar, he went along. They set up the diamond business together. Every Sunday they used to go with their wives to the Copper Chimney restaurant and eat and drink. "We've done everything. We used to drink every Saturday and Sunday; we *needed* to drink whiskey. We would be watching the other's glass, say, There's more in yours, and fill ours higher. After prayers, we would go and eat pav bhaji [which is chockful of the forbidden onions and potatoes and garlic]. After prayers, we *needed* to eat pav bhaji. We've done everything: drinking, drama, movies . . . everything." Sevanti is a sensualist, Hasmukh informs me. He loves getting massages; at home there were always two people massaging him. In Dhanera, Hasmukh has been fighting with his best friend, swearing at him. "I told him last night, bhenchod, chutiya, don't do this. What is this chodu thing you're doing? I am totally frank. He said if I were to take diksha with him, I would reach moksha first."

After Sevantibhai started walking on the religious path, their friendship was put under some strain. On his regular trips back to India, Hasmukh began to avoid meeting him. Not because he felt uncomfortable with his friend's penances, but because he was afraid he was retarding his friend on his path toward moksha. When Hasmukh came, Sevanti would temporarily stop his daily prayers, and then he would have to fast the whole of the next day to atone for the sin. Their conversations took on an increasingly didactic tone. One day, Sevanti talked to Hasmukh for four hours on the nature of a drop of water, of the lives in it, of the cosmic significance of that one drop. On that day too, Hasmukh found out that the whole family would be leaving the world.

Suddenly, in the midst of the jubilation, we hear a loud wail. Laxmichand, Sevantibhai's eldest brother and King of Metal Business, is crying. He wails, and everybody rushes to console him: the women of the household (who have also been wailing), the men, and, not to be outdone, the Jain swamis standing around. (Later, Laxmichand comments acidly about the senior gurus who keep harassing him with instructions about the ceremony. "Have they no other business?") Suddenly, the atmosphere in the Ladhani household changes from one of a wedding to that of a funeral. An older man is remonstrating with him that this is a joyous occasion. Hasmukh, weeping, says, "Look at that. That man is Raksha's father; he is losing his own daughter, and he is consoling Laxmichand! That takes guts!" Even now, says Hasmukh, Laxmichand would rather that his brother stop the whole show and stay in samsara. There have been fierce fights among the brothers—some of the merchants say to stop the diksharthis from leaving their fold, others say over distribution of their property.

Utkarsh, the younger boy, is sitting outside. Here, in the midst of the huge clan, I learn the family's nicknames for them: Utkarsh is called Chiku, his older brother, Vicky. "Tomorrow I'll have to say maharajsaheb to you and fold my hands in front of you, but today you're still Chiku to me," Hasmukh says, and laughs with the boy. During the last meal, the entire extended family—a hundred strong—feed them, one last time, with their hands. One of the children asks for bhelpuri. After today there can be no pleasure permissible in food, and that will rule out bhelpuri forever for the kids from Bombay. The meal ends, the women begin singing, and a man comes to the courtyard with a flame at the end of a long wick and begins lighting hundreds of oil lamps. Then someone reads out a document that has the tone of a will. Sevantibhai is disposing of the remains of his wealth among his relatives. All of them will get something, from a few lakhs to 2,100 rupees. Then Sevantibhai folds his hands and says to his relatives, "I have made many mistakes. Forgive me if I've hurt anyone."

Later, Hasmukh takes me inside the room where Sevantibhai is being massaged by his relatives. The diksharthi confesses to me that he is in some turmoil. "I've been trying to think, but I keep getting disturbed. I'm thinking, What will I do after tomorrow? Where will I be? I've been sick, I have a temperature, and right now I have all the facilities, they're pressing my arms and my legs, but I think, How will I tolerate this sickness after tomorrow?" Of all his family, he is the only one that admits publicly to some doubt or uncertainty. Perhaps he is the only one allowed to. I ask him what he intends to do now. "I want to study Sanskrit for ten years. Only after ten years of study will I speak."

I ask him how he will bear the separation from his family, if he is thinking about not seeing his wife and his daughter again. He replies that he feels confident at the moment. "But I will only know the real test the day after tomorrow, or the day after that, when I'm really separated from them." Would he come back to Bombay? "The desire to return to Bombay is less, both mine and my guru's." Hundreds of people are waiting to see him, so I give him my salutations and leave the dark room.

I speak to the rest of the diksharthis, first to Rakshaben. "I only feel ulhas," says the woman from Ulhasnagar. So much happiness, she says, that she won't miss her husband or her sons. Snehal, too, says he is giving up samsara "for real happiness." Moksha is real happiness, and you can get moksha only after you take diksha. It is a circular definition: happiness is moksha, and moksha is happiness. Then Karishma is summoned for an "interview" with me, by Laxmichand, who is sitting stubbornly under a fluorescent light. Someone is kidding her about her power to demand, on the next day, the day of the diksha, any boon from her family. Will she ask Laxmichand to give up smoking? "I can't give such a rule," the girl says. "He'll only give it up if it comes from within." When her uncle was weeping, the others asked her to go and comfort her Laxmi Kaka. "Why is he crying, on such a happy occasion?" she demanded to know. In Bombay, when she left, she didn't look back once at the building she grew up in. Of all the diksharthis, the youngest is the one who has the least doubt, the least hesitation in her answers. Perhaps she has never asked the questions.

That night, which is his last in the world before his diksha, Sevantibhai goes to bed at 3:15 a.m. "He couldn't sleep till then," Hasmukh tells me afterward. "I saw that he was really thinking, How will I begin my life tomorrow?" Forty-five minues later, he rises, goes to the temple, and prays to the god, does his puja. It will be the last time. After becoming a monk of his sect, he will never be able to do a puja. The senior maharajsahebs are forbidden from even folding their hands and bowing to the gods in the temple; Jainism is, at its purest, an atheistic religion. Not the least of the worldly comforts Sevantibhai will be renouncing is faith in God.

THE LADHANIS' FINAL MORNING in samsara is so cold that my diesel car won't start. When I leave the doctor's house at six, the sky over the arid country is crowded with stars. There are very few people on the roads, and all of them are going toward the Ladhani household. Inside the house, there are even more people than the night before. This is, after all, the moment the five diksharthis will be saying good-bye to their families. The women lament and celebrate:

> *"What kind of day is it?"*
> [Chorus:] *"It's more valuable than gold."*
> *"What's more valuable than gold?"*
> *"Self-restraint, Self-restraint."*

> *"One more heave!*
> *Samsara you leave."*

The Ladhanis are praying in the storehouse, and then a cordon is formed outside it. Big steel plates are put down in a line outside their room, filled with rice, coins, precious stones, and the keys to their various houses. I am standing near the first plate. Sevantibhai emerges at great speed, clad in his most extravagant costume, and kicks aside the plate full of his wealth. Then his wife and children do the same thing, all in a line; by the time Karishma comes out of the storehouse there is hardly any money left on the trays to kick aside. Outside, there are men with crossed swords blocking their path; the renunciates push aside the swords and march on. As they leave their ancestral house, it is very important that they never turn back, even for a second, to look at what they are leaving behind.

All along the route from the house to the diksha site, which is lined with more plates heaped with the Ladhani fortune, village children with their sharp eyes scan the ground for the money the Ladhanis have kicked away. The entrance to the diksha-mandap is flanked by five elephants. Inside is a vast tented enclosure and thousands of people seated in separate groups on the floor. I take my place in the diamond merchant section. The audience is handed out packets of a pearl-and-rice mixture and invited to shower the diksharthis with the fabulous confetti. On the stage above us, first the parting, like the bidai at a wedding (when the bride's family says good-bye to her), is done in full public view, by the blood relatives and the business partners. Another will is read out. Over two crores has been given away to charitable institutions, including money to animal shelters, and another crore to religious bodies. The compere, the same one from the diamond merchant meeting, reads out a good omen: The previous day, the Bombay Municipal Corporation lost a Supreme Court appeal against a lower-court verdict that forbade the killing of stray dogs. A Jain family's petition will now save the lives of fifty thousand stray dogs a year. There is a resounding cheer from the audience.

The moment has come. In front of thirty-five thousand people, Sevantibhai seeks permission to take diksha from his guru. A flare of trumpets announces the guru's assent, and the diksharthi dances madly around the stage, clutching a large white duster. The rest of the family follows, and then they leave to get their heads shaved, except for seven hairs, which will be plucked out by the maharajsaheb. Meanwhile, the charitable auction starts, for the right to buy the vestments that are to be presented to the diksharthis for their monastic life. The first item, a cloth for Sevantibhai, is sold for 151,000 rupees. A string of white prayer beads for Snehal goes for 68,000. All around me, there is a tremendous din of figures, as the auctioneers shout out the competing bids, standing amid the seated audience and egging them on to invest in spiritual gain, like a hot stock tip. "This kind of opportunity for labh won't come again! Only thirty-one thousand, you lucky people!" There is wealth on the stage, and wealth in this audience, as the assembled millionaires and billionaires compete for public demonstration of their piety.

Then the name auction commences. First, the name-page is opened. The gurumaharaj has given each of the men the names they will be called henceforth; and the head sadhvin has done the same for the women. Now the entire audience waits to hear the new names of the diksharthis. The bidding begins for the right to reveal Sevantibhai's name; a layman will announce it to the audience. That right is purchased for 361,000 rupees, and the winner turns to the crowd and pronounces it: "Raj Ratna Vijayji!" The huge space rings out with applause. Then the right to say Snehal's—Vicky's—new name is bought: "Raj Darshan Vijayji!" Then Utkarsh, or Chiku's: "Ratna Bodhi Vijayji!" Then Rakshaben's: "Divya Ruchita Sreeji!" Finally, when the bidding starts over Karishma's name, the three sisters of her father, who had the right to name her when she was born and had given her a name that most Indians associate with a sexy movie heroine, outbid all others to give her this new name and pay 150,000 rupees—one and a half lakhs—to face the audience and shout out, through their sadness, the three words: "Darshan Ruchita Sreeji!"

When the Ladhanis come back onto the stage, the change is startling. They have replaced their uniform cream-colored silk robes and saris with uniform white sheets; almost all of their hair is gone. After Rakshaben comes out with her head shorn, Hasmukh tells me later, "I marked that Sevanti didn't look at Raksha. Raksha didn't look at Sevanti. The children looked, but the couple didn't look at anybody." It was Hasmukh's wife who wept when she saw what had been done to Raksha. "When her head was being shaved, Raksha put her face in her hands and didn't look for one second at anybody as her hair, the mark of beauty for an Indian woman, was taken off."

Hasmukh also tells me that during the hair-cutting ceremony, all the family members had to pour water—in the January morning, this meant freezing water—on the diksharthis as their final bath. They poured the frigid water on the feverish Sevantibhai, and they poured it on the other four. After this, Rakshaben and Karishma started running temperatures as well. "They had to first bathe with cold water. I don't understand why," says Hasmukh, shaking his head, like a child trying to understand an adult custom or rule that he is told has some sense behind it but the logic of which he is unable to grasp. Then Hasmukh said farewell to his best friend and uncle. "When I come back to India, I will visit you." But his friend didn't answer him. "He had his stick in his hand, he had his belongings around his neck. He didn't look in my eyes, he just shook his head." When Hasmukh said good-bye to the other four, they didn't respond either.

Sevanti and Raksha have been married for twenty-two years. The last time they touch each other is when Raksha puts the tilak on Sevanti's face, as she did the first time she touched him—when she married him. The little woman reaches up with her thumb, anointing his fevered brow with the saffron paste, and they smile at each other and laugh. His hot forehead feels the cooling impress of that last touch from his wife.

Finally, the five diksharthis sit on the front of the stage, and all the extended family honors them. The maharajsaheb says to Laxmichand, "Look, Laxmichand bhai, they were yours, and they are yours, but now they belong to all of us." Laxmichand keeps weeping; the maharaj has ever so gently reminded him that the five of them have now gone beyond the Ladhanis' orbit, beyond the extended family and out into the world. They have left behind everything from their former world; all traces of Sevanti-bhai the diamond merchant, Rakshaben the housewife, and their Bombay-bred teenagers, Vicky and Chiku and Karishma. At long last, they have abandoned all their possessions. Except their spectacles. The two boys keep their spectacles. They will need them to see the path ahead.

They sleep the night in the upasara, or rest house. At four-thirty the next morning, the first day of their lives as renunciates, they will set out to gather their first meal—they have fasted all the previous day—and the first house they will go to is the Ladhanis'. It is a fitting metaphor for renuncia-tion: The first house you beg in should be the one you've left as its owner. Then, with the two adults and Karishma still in the grip of fever, they will set out on the road away from Dhanera. They will not be able to come back to their ancestral town for at least five years. After Bombay, it is the next forbidden place.

* * *

DRIVING AWAY from the house, my driver, a tough taciturn Rajput, wonders, "Why did all five of them take diksha? They're billionaires."

"They're diamond merchants," I say.

"The Dawood gang must have been after them," he speculates.

We drive from Dhanera to Ahmadabad, from where I have to take a train back to Bombay. I have relatives in Ahmadabad and stop to see them. These are the poorest relatives I have, and when I go to their house most of the family members are walking around in clothes I recognize: They belonged, when new, to my father, my mother, my sisters, myself. There is a new baby in the house, but her father, my cousin, is absent. He is at work in a diamond factory, where he is a cutter. Most days he does not see his first child, who is only a couple of months old; he has to leave as soon as the sun is up and comes back home well into the night. He works most Sundays as well; even during Diwali, traditionally a holiday time for the industry, he may be asked to work if the demand is high. He gets paid per diamond he cuts, and for all that work, for all that sacrifice, he makes less than my driver in Bombay. All day he cuts stones, denying himself to his new daughter, so that the merchants of Sevantibhai's class can throw into the air the profits he earns for them.

I catch up with Hasmukh in Bombay the following week, in his brother's flat in Tardeo. Hasmukh is fairly religious himself. On his trips to Bombay, he always prays first at the Sankeshwar temple, and only then does he go to Opera House to buy his diamonds. In Los Angeles, he is a devotee of the Swaminarayan sect, which, though Hindu, he finds similar to Jainism. But he has married outside the religion; in fact, outside the Gujarati nation. His wife is a Mangalorean whose family owns sixteen restaurants in Bombay; it was a love marriage. A restaurant is a breeding ground of sin for Jains. And this fact, I sense, has put him at variance with the community into which he was born. They don't shun him or his family, but there will always be the sense that he has crossed the threshold, and an awkwardness around his wife.

At this point a boy comes in, wearing a green T-shirt with the Nike swoosh on it. He is Hasmukh's son and has just been to see a Hindi movie with Hasmukh's brother, his uncle. The boy is disagreeing, in an American accent, with his uncle about the message of the movie, a melodrama about an Indian taxidriver in New York torn between a westernized Indian woman and a traditional Indian woman. "All I'm saying," says the boy, who is in the sixth grade in Diamond Bar, California, "is India has love but America also has love."

The uncle disagrees. "America has less love than India." He points to America's high divorce rate as proof.

The boy responds, "They take divorce for a reason." He tells me he was asked by Sevantibhai to come back to India to live. "I said I would like to but my everything is over there."

It is in this flat that I learn there is an insurance policy for the Ladhanis in case the path to moksha gets too steep, as has happened with other renunciates. A trust has been set up with four family members as trustees, endowed with a sizable fund—in the crores. It will disburse money on Sevantibhai's instructions. In his wanderings, when he meets needy people or deserving institutions, the trustees will send money to them. "In case the children want to come back, they don't have to stretch out their hand to anybody. They can get a car, a house," explains Hasmukh. For Sevantibhai, there is this security. If he changes his mind, all of samsara will not be lost to him. He has given away a good deal of his fortune, but there is enough left to provide him or his family with a reasonable standard of comfort in Bombay. It is a strange concept: a wandering monk able to fund a temple or change the fortunes of an entire village with one phone call. Is the life of a renunciate made easier or harder when he knows that if he returns to samsara, he can immediately have the goods of life back? Sevantibhai and his family will always have a choice. Each step of their wanderings will be taken out of free will. Whenever they are tired from walking in the hot sun, something at the back of their minds will always be telling them that they can afford to travel in a Rolls-Royce, even now. All they have to do is to admit defeat.

SEVEN MONTHS after the diksha ceremony, I go to see how Sevantibhai is doing in his life as a monk. He and the two boys are spending the monsoons in Patan, in northernmost Gujarat, where my grandfather studied as a boy. The Jain temple and its attendant institutions are in a quiet quarter of the town, with old painted wooden houses all around.

After Dhanera, Sevantibhai walked from town to town in Gujarat, to Tharad, then Deesa, Patan, Bhabhar, Ahmadabad, then Patan again, to a private house in the city. And now, seven months later to the day of his diksha (by the lunar calendar), I find Sevantibhai, or Raj Ratna Vijayji Maharajsaheb, sitting in an enormous room in Patan. He has been here for two months and will continue to stay a further two months, till the rains end. There is a large painting on the entrance to the hall, which is the temporary home for the entire order of twenty-one monks. It is entitled *A Compassionate View of Worldly Life* and depicts a man hanging on a tree above a well filled with snakes and crocodiles, with rats gnawing at the vine the man hangs on, and an elephant shaking the trunk of the tree.

As soon as I enter the hall I see him and he sees me. He makes an indication, touching his fingers to his head; it is a comment that my hair has grown. Sevantibhai, on the other hand, has just had his first lochan after becoming a monk: all the hair on his head, face, and lips had been pulled out, hair by hair, tuft by tuft, over a period of several hours, by his superior. His scalp was bleeding. "It is just a sample of the tortures of hell for my sins. The hair is pulled out by hand to make the body strong, and so that you can understand others' suffering." He got through the ordeal by remembering the tortures inflicted on the Jain gurus of old. When the enemies of their faith would pull off not just the hair but the very skin on their bodies, the response of the gurus was to ask their tormentors, "In what way would you like me to stand so that you are put to the least inconvenience while peeling off my skin?" The courage of those martyrs redoubled his own.

The retreat hall, the paushadhshala, is an enormous room open on two sides. It does not belong to the monks. They are guests of the sangha, the community, which has built it for the monks to rest in. The monks sit at a series of low tables, reading from ancient manuscripts and writing commentaries on them in their notebooks. Laypeople come to visit them and are instructed in the proper conduct of quotidian life; those with special promise are encouraged to take up diksha. There are a number of laypeople sitting in the hall getting a taste of the monastic life. They can choose to observe the life of a sadhu for one day or, for the merest sample, for exactly forty-eight minutes. During those forty-eight minutes, their thoughts and deeds should be pure of violence. There are no fans in the hall; as I sit cross-legged talking to Sevantibhai in the August afternoon, I sweat and wave away the flies. If the ceiling were not so high it would be intolerable. At night, the monks sleep where they are sitting, but with a caveat: They can't sleep in the path of the fresh breeze coming in, because that will kill the lives in that breeze. It would also mean that they desire the bodily pleasure of the cooling breeze. If a window is closed, they are forbidden to open it for the same reasons. Sevantibhai has to bleach his life of all comfort or pleasure. It is only then that moksha can be attractive. His life has to be so bereft of luxury, so continuously tormenting, that it will be easy to slip into the dark waters of nonexistence.

Sevantibhai has taken five vows. The first is that he can't do violence to life, make someone else do violence, or approve of someone else doing violence. This means, for example, that he can never compliment a householder on the taste of the dal that he gives to Sevantibhai during gocari—to say "What a fine dish!" would mean that Sevantibhai approves of the multiple killing the householder had to perform in order to make it. The second vow is that he can't tell a lie, tell others to tell a lie, or approve of a lie being uttered. The third is that he can't steal, cause others to steal, or approve of stealing. For example, he says, if I were to drop my pen on the floor, and if he borrowed it for a minute without asking my permission, that would be considered stealing. The fourth is that he cannot be uncelibate, cause others to be uncelibate, or approve of uncelibacy. Thus, he can never praise a wedding ceremony or suggest that a particular girl might be a good match for a particular boy. The ascetics keep wandering to avoid breaking the vow of celibacy. They should not get to know any female during their travels. If a monk were to visit the house of a devout laywoman regularly during the process of gocari, and if she were to think, How noble is this monk! or if the monk were to think, How devout is this sister! it would be a sin, and he would be breaking his vow. A nomadic life prevents any possibility of intimacy between the sexes. The fifth is a vow of poverty. He can't own anything, not even the single cotton sheet he wears on his body. It has to be gifted by a layman.

The head of the order, Chandrashekhar Maharaj, sits at the head of the hall, ever on the alert for any slippage into samsara among his monks. His entire family of six had taken diksha together when he was eleven. A mother with a boy in his lay clothes, who looks to be under ten years old, is sitting in front of Chandrashekhar Maharaj. The boy is sulking; his mother is smiling, tenderly persuading him about something. The boy keeps worrying his foot. After a while the maharajsaheb takes over, again speaking to him in a low, gentle voice but not letting up, not fazed by the fact that the boy isn't saying a single word to his mother or to the maharaj, isn't looking at either of them. Sevantibhai enlightens me. The boy and his mother are from Bombay, and he has been staying here for three months studying with the maharaj in his preparation for taking diksha. But now the boy misses Bombay and misses his family and wants to go to the metropolis for four days with his mother. The maharaj instead advances his preferred alternative: The mother should stay with the boy for four days. If he were to go to Bombay now, he would fall much farther behind in his studies than four days. The boy, a bright child, has not been concentrating on his studies. He wants to play. He sees other children outside, children of visitors, and wants to watch television. The mother, her love for her child writ all over her face, is gently but insistently telling him to stay here—so that, in the fullness of time, all connections might be severed between them.

The boy comes over to where I am sitting with Sevantibhai. "I wish I had taken diksha thirty years ago," Sevantibhai says to me. Then his body would have been better able to stand the demands he is putting on it. As it is, he sometimes feels weak and can't stretch his body as much as he'd like to. "I wish I had taken diksha thirty years ago," he says again, in the presence of the wavering boy.

His own sons, or ex-sons, have not become as single-minded as he has or as he would like them to be. "Out of the twenty-four hours, they still want to play for an hour with the other young monks," he says. "It's not desirable, but it's understandable." I ask him what kind of playing they do. He points to some colorful labels stuck on a couple of shelves. "They'll stick these labels, they'll draw, they'll gather all the books and arrange them in a row, they'll want to wash their clothes once a week instead of once a month as we do. They want to play, they're still young. Not cricket, of course—the ball hitting the bat is himsa"—violence—"but this kind of playing, sticking labels, washing clothes."

Before Sevantibhai sits down in the hall, he sweeps the ground with his duster to move away any lives. The sweeping of the hall is constant, and the tiled surface is very clean. I watch him sweep a large patch of the hall, gather up the dust in a small plastic dustpan, take the dust to a window of the hall, and scrupulously deposit it on the windowsill just outside, being careful not to drop it. Then he sifts the dust, spreading it out. If it is dropped from a distance greater than the breadth of the palm it will kill the lives in the air. For this reason, he explains, the monks are forbidden to use a toilet to urinate or defecate. It is one of the stories non-Jains spread about the monks: that they are filthy and throw their shit on the roads. Sevantibhai now explains it for me. Their urine and feces have to dry within forty-eight minutes of coming out of their bodies. Otherwise, lives will be created in the liquid or the moist mass, lives that are invisible to us but which the Universal Soul can see. This is why, when Sevantibhai finds himself stopping in a place without a sandpit in the back (such as the one in Patan), he has to walk outside the city limits or to a stretch of railroad tracks, or the rocks by the sea, and carefully spread out his feces so that they dry fast; if they are just dropped in piles or mounds they won't dry within the required forty-eight minutes. This is difficult in the rains. "That's why we can't go to America or Antwerp. It stays wet there all year." The West is forbidden to Jain monks because of its lack of appropriate toilet facilities.

Sevantibhai does not miss anything about Bombay and has no wish to return. He will go only if his teacher, his acharya, commands him to. The city is filled with sin and temptation. "Bombay is only for those who are very firm. It will take me at least ten years, I think." The problems of the city are a direct result of the impoverishment of the countryside. He gives me an example. "Everybody uses peanut oil now. But much better for you is sesame oil. At the diksha only sesame oil was used. The seeds would be pressed in a mill turned by bullocks, we would get the oil, and the bullocks would eat the crushed seed pulp. Forty years ago there were six lakh [600,000] bullock oil presses. Each employed two bullocks, so there were twelve lakh [1.2 million] bullocks in these presses. Now there are about sixty. Where did all those bullocks go? To the slaughterhouse. What happened to all those bullock drivers? What happened to their families? They went to the cities, in search of employment. Have you seen Dharavi [one of Bombay's biggest slums]? It is full of people like those bullock drivers. But there, too, they don't find work, leading to crime and corruption." It is a remarkably accurate description of the causes of migration from the village to the city, brought down to the difference between a peanut and a sesame seed.

There was no competition in the village, he says. A potter would make only enough pots and cups as could be bought by the villagers, and he would barter them with the farmers for food. There would only need to be one potter, and he would work on a hand-powered wheel. But now, with electricity powering up his wheel, he can make many more pots than the village needs. "What is he to do with all these pots? He has to go elsewhere to try to sell them, and that creates competition." It is the same with diamonds. Electric cutting machines have made possible the cutting of diamonds on a mass scale. "A diamond doesn't degrade, it doesn't get old with use. So with more and more diamonds being cut, people have to use more and more of them. What do you do after you have rings on all ten of your fingers?" Technology leads to surplus production, which leads to competition, to the death of the village and its barter economy, and to consumption for its own sake. It is a Jain version of Marxism.

Throughout the day, I keep returning to the hall whenever the monks have time for me in between their meditation and their lectures. Sevantibhai keeps directing me to one of the senior acharyas, saying I should pose my questions to him. But the guru has the habit of launching into a discourse without being asked, and it is difficult to interrupt him. Sevantibhai is yet questionable, not practiced. I ask him what was the hardest to give up: his family, his wealth, or his house and its comforts? After a long pause, he answers. "Family. The hardest thing to leave was family." His extended family or his wife and children? "Not the extended family. They are not religious. But my own family. We learnt together." He hasn't seen the woman who was his wife for four months now. For a month and a half after the diksha they traveled side by side—but not together, he is at pains to point out. He doesn't know when he will see her or the girl who used to be his daughter again. Neither do the boys who used to be his sons. "If I say something that upsets them, there is no mother now to soothe them. But they have Chandrashekhar Maharaj," he adds quickly, pointing to the guru. "He is more than a mother."

What was the hardest thing for Sevantibhai to get used to after taking diksha? He considers, then says, "There are twenty-one sadhus in this group. They come from different backgrounds, different homes, some rich, some poor. They have different ways of thinking, different tempers. That took getting used to. For a month and a half there was a tough time." He heard harsh words from them; he saw how their faces turned sour during gocari when the food was not to their liking. He has had to deal with this: this strained fellowship. He attributes these personality conflicts within the group to the demise of the extended family. "I have known families of up to a hundred people, following one patriarch. They would grow up obeying him. Before, the sadhus used to come from these extended families, and they would all obey the acharya. But now they come from small families, and they are not used to living in big groups. If there are forty people, all of them think differently. Their capacity for work is different. It will take me a few years to adjust." All the sadhus give up their worldly possessions to enter this life, but Sevantibhai and his family gave up more of this world's goods than most of the rest of this order put together. This knowledge, I get the feeling, persists with him past the diksha and into monkhood. Perhaps class has carried over into the classless society of the sadhus. It is like the army: The man who was a millionaire in civilian life finds himself taking orders from one who used to be a clerk.

Modernity has been hard on the sadhus. For instance, they can drink only boiled water, and few people boil water nowadays; most houses of Jain laymen have water filters. In the old days, every house in the village would boil water for later use in boiling feed for the cattle, and the monks would come early enough in the day to get some. But householders also cannot be commanded to boil water for the exclusive use of the monks. The monks are willing to allow the laymen to sin by boiling water for general use, but it is *their* sin; if the water were to be boiled just for the monks, then the sin would accrue to the monks. Roads are another problem. In their wanderings, the monks try to look for unpaved roads, which are getting rarer and rarer. Paved tar roads are hard on the feet and especially on the eyes; the heat glinting off the tarmac is very bad for their eyesight, which they need to keep sharp for prolonged study of ancient texts, as well as to scan the path ahead to avoid stepping on lives.

The most difficult time physically for Sevantibhai was a journey from Bhabhar to Ahmadabad, where he was to attend another diksha ceremony. Every day they walked eighteen miles, five hours in the morning after sunrise and more in the evening. On one stretch, after walking six miles, his feet started to hurt, so they rested in some fields. But by nightfall they had to reach a particular village where there was a Jain house. The last half hour was excruciating. When he looked at his feet he saw that huge boils and blisters had developed on them. So he took a thorn and burst the blisters, which were filled with water and pus. Since he doesn't believe in allopathic medicine, he doused the wounds with castor oil and turmeric, as an antiseptic. He shows me the soles of his feet. These are abused feet: cracked, callused, split, and blackened, with layers of skin overlapping each other, cratered like the surface of the moon. But "we can't hold it in our minds that our feet hurt." There is greater peril in his traveling on paved roads than sore feet: "All the violence of road building accumulates on us." Many sadhus these days die in accidents on the highway, which have no space for pedestrian traffic.

But the present state of the world is almost rosy compared to what is to come. Time for the Jains is divided into a continuously repeating cycle of six eras, the first being the most ideal. In this, the fifth era of Jain cosmology, men live to a maximum of 130 years. In the sixth era, the bottom of the cycle, men will be able to live only for 20 years. There will be no vegetable life, no religions—not even the non-Jain ones—and men will have to live in caves in the bottom of rivers, to avoid the fierce heat all around. The height of human beings at the start of the era will be no more than twice the distance between the elbow and the palm and will gradually decline to no more than that span. Therefore, in the Jain worldview, *this* is the gloomiest historical time to live in, not the next one. For at least in the sixth era, people will have the hope that things will get better in the time after that (the cycle starts again; it goes back up to the fifth). In our time, we don't even have that comfort. Bad as this time is, it's only going to get worse.

Sevantibhai is sure he will not reach moksha from this birth. All he can do is to take a dramatic step forward on the path, by concentrating on moksha wholeheartedly. But he will still incur negative karma, merely by living on the planet in its present state. Then why doesn't Sevantibhai end his life? There are other orders of Jain monks, such as the Sthanakvasis, who make a voluntary exit from the sinful world. They simply stop eating and invite laypeople to their retreat hall to watch them slowly starve to death. But Sevantibhai's order is more rigorous. "We don't have the freedom of suicide. There are no shortcuts to the next birth." There is one exception, however. If Sevantibhai were to find the pull of samsara too great, if he were unable to follow the rules of the order, suicide is preferable to going back to the world.

Permission is sought from Chandrashekhar Maharajsaheb for me to talk to the two younger maharajsahebs. Sevantibhai explains that I have come back to India after twenty-one years abroad. "You have made an excellent decision," the guruji says, nodding his head at me.

Sevantibhai admits to still feeling the vestiges of fatherhood. He points to a boy monk sitting against a pillar. "I can't scold him like I can my own sons. I still call them mine. They listen to me. If the guruji is asking everyone to come eat, I can command them to come at once to eat. If they are not studying, I will scold them, as I won't the other maharajsahebs of their age. Why? Do I feel I have a right with those two and not with the others?" When we are talking about them, he doesn't use any names for them— perhaps not yet comfortable with calling his boys, so lately Vicky and Chiku, Raj Darshan Vijayji and Ratna Bodhi Vijayji.

The older boy is sitting in a specific type of mediation, with everything he owns touching him: his eight pieces of cloth, his staff, and his bowls for gocari. Around him the other swamis are eating, and there is a stench of sweat, urine, and food. The monks have bad breath—they are forbidden to brush their teeth, as the very purpose of brushing is to kill bacteria—and it is an effort to talk to them at close quarters. All day for a month Vicky has to sit like this. His hair has been freshly pulled. He feels peace and joy in his new life, he says, "not running around like before." He wakes up at four every morning and spends the day in studying and prayer. At nine-thirty he stretches out in the same hall and goes to sleep. "Four or five times a day I think, when will moksha come? When will I be free?"

The younger boy is still studying while the others are eating. There is something tender about him, and I have the impression that he is keeping up a brave front. Sevantibhai tells me, "He was always more attached to his mother." So when he is scolded by the father, he writes complaints about Sevantibhai to the nun who used to be his mother. And she writes back. There is a weekly exchange of letters between the two of them. Chandrashekhar Maharaj doesn't object. When I ask the son about this, he will not admit it, in the manner of a teenager pretending to be indifferent to a girl he's heartsick about. "If she writes to me, I reply."

Neither of the boys refers to her as Mummy. Instead, they call her Divya Ruchita Sreeji, her post-diksha name. They don't talk about their sister. As twins, Utkarsh and Karishma had a bond that went far beyond normal sibling ties. Not once does he mention his renounced sister. The older boy points out that if they were to meet the women, they couldn't sit close to each other. "Far," he says, indicating with one arm the necessary distance between them, now no longer mother and son, or brother and sister, but only male and female, susceptible to temptation if not restrained by monastic rules. They can come together to discuss points of doctrine, if permitted by both their gurus, but neither of them should look directly at the other, and they have to be holding a cloth over their mouths. The mother can never, ever, again touch the boy who came out of her womb. "Where I sit a lady can't sit for one hundred forty-four minutes, and where a lady sits I can't sit for forty-eight minutes, because the aura of the body lingers on."

Sevantibhai and the two boys used to eat only once a day. But then the younger boy developed jaundice and now is allowed to eat twice a day. The rules about eating can be waived during illness, since the body, the vehicle of sadhana, needs to be kept alive. But not comfortable. While the boy was stricken with jaundice, the gurumaharaj decided he had to have his lochan. His hair had grown too long. So, yellowed and weakened by jaundice, he sat down before the guru, the guru smeared coal ash on his head, gathered fistfuls of hair one at a time, and yanked it all out by the roots. It was the most difficult time for him in the last few months, the boy tells me.

The younger boy doesn't remember much about his past, about Bombay. I ask him about his future. "I'll do as the guru maharajsaheb says." I ask him why he took diksha. And then the boy, sitting in front of his notebook in which he is revising his Sanskrit lessons, says to me—admits to me—"They say if you take diksha, you'll get moksha. Right now I have no knowledge of that." He trusted his father. What choice did he have?

Sevantibhai had defined moksha for me: "In the bliss of moksha there is no desire." It is a simple straightforward definition: salvation is absence of desire.

On the way back from Patan, I decide to stop in at the great eleventh-century Sun Temple at Modhera. My driver says the temple is well worth seeing, and he drives into the little village and parks outside a spanking new temple, all pastel walls and large-print lettering of the various donors associated with its construction. I tell him there is an older one also.

The Sun Temple is exquisite. The central idol was stationed in such a way that the first rays of the equinox illuminated it directly. There is no idol anymore, but as I walk around the walls of the ancient stone structure, I see that they are filled with lovemakers. A woman is bent over, taking one man in her mouth while her rear is serviced by another. In another figure, a man is kissing a woman with tender passion, holding up her left leg to his waist; under her, another woman is kneeling, fellating the man. They are surrounded by stone plants, stone elephants, and attendants, in full view of God; there is nothing secret or shameful about this. Sex in a Hindu temple is intended for glorious public display. Tourists come in, groups of villagers and tribals and middle-class families from the towns, and children scamper amid the lovers. The figures throb with eroticism; the faces have been hacked off or have been erased by time or the acids in the droppings of the hundreds of pigeons that roost in the crevices of the temple, but their very postures reveal the delight they are taking in the body and its possibilities. This also is holy. This too is sacred.

It is not easy to talk about the Jains without ridiculing them. The Jain beliefs are favorite sport for intelligent Westerners, from Gore Vidal's jaundiced portrait of the prophet Mahavir in *Creation* to Philip Roth's pathetic Jain convert Merry in *American Pastoral*. I find it difficult to explain to people even in Bombay why I do not consider the family insane, or idiots, or fanatics. The stark details of their lives—their fantastic privations—terrify the city people; they shudder even more when hearing about them than when I talk about the hit men. "This is true violence," says Mahesh, the director of dozens of films filled with blood and murder. "I'm traumatized." Sevantibhai's search is rigorous; there is absolutely no room for compromise. Its purity, its singleness, is incomprehensible to people in the city of a thousand distractions.

Wandering through the villages of Gujarat, Sevantibhai is thinking about the great questions, about the purpose and order of the universe, about the stupidity of nationalism, about the atomic nature of reality. More than anybody else I know, he lives with a daily and nagging realization of the amount of violence our species perpetrates, each hour, each minute, not only on our fellow humans but on all life and upon creation itself. The diamond merchants I have met throughout my life are not, by and large, given to this kind of questioning. Their trade has done well. These questions tend to occur more frequently to people in financial hardship. The Jain diamond merchants of Bombay are pretty happy with their lavish homes and offices, their occasional trips to Antwerp for business, to Disneyworld with their children, and to the hill resort of Lonavla on the weekends. They are almost to a man BJP supporters, and they think the proposed Narmada dam—a huge project strongly opposed by environmentalists—will be a blessing for Gujarat.

Sevantibhai's decision puts him in another sphere of thought altogether. He is against the dam, because it will lead to development of the fishing industry; he has heard about the Kashmir conflict but, to him, an Indian and a Pakistani and an American life are equally valuable; nations have no meaning for him. The Jain monks are mostly apolitical, unlike many present-day Hindu gurus, who dabble in right-wing politics. Sevantibhai has decisively rejected every value held dear by the middle classes: western education, consumerism, nationalism, and, most important, family. But the people he rejected come to him now with reverence; merchants with firms considerably larger than his, who would not have socialized with him in the life he has left, now travel great distances to bow before him and touch his feet and those of his teenage sons. His children are studying Sanskrit when other teenagers in their building in Bombay have not grown out of Archie comics. They had not been good students in the city schools, but now they spend several hours a day in study of some of the most sophisticated epistemology that human beings have ever produced. Where Aristotelian logic admits only two possible states of being for a proposition, that it is true or false—there is no middle ground—Jain logic expands these to no fewer than seven possibilities. The name given to this predicated conception of truth is syadvada, "the doctrine of maybeness." The Ladhanis are free to study. Within the rigid structures of the monk's day there is a freedom to live the life of the mind.

And what was that joy I saw on his face, that frequent smile? His children I am less sure about. He had a huge loss once in his business. Was that the real reason he quit the world? What did he get tired of? Did he quarrel with his wife? "My past was very bad," Sevantibhai said to me. "All of Dhanera knew this." Sevantibhai admitted that his head had been full of worries for the seven years before he took diksha, worries about money, worries about his family. He had shown me his two red vessels, made out of a gourd, that he now uses for gocari. "I eat, I wash. I don't worry about whether the servant will come today to wash the dishes. There is no tension. I don't worry about what to do tomorrow." His mind is completely free to concentrate on moksha. Whether his family survives or not, whether his business thrives or not, is no longer an issue.

For a long time afterward, in my life in the cities, I think of Sevanti-

bhai, of the utter final simplicity of his life. In New York I am beset with
financial worry. How will I educate my children? Will I be able to buy a
home? Approaching the middle of my life, I feel poorer every day compared to my friends who went to school with me, who are making money in
technology and on the stock market, and who are buying up apartments
and cars and raising their prices beyond my reach. I am earning more than
I ever have before, and I am also feeling poorer than ever before. Each time
it feels like I almost have it within reach at last—financial security (if
not wealth), a working family, a career—it slips out of my grasp like the
frogs in the pond of Walshingham House School. We would catch these
frogs with our hands and clutch them so tight it seemed impossible or
miraculous when they jumped out of our fists. Sevantibhai has just
bypassed all this. He has taken a leap over his worries, outdistancing them,
outfoxing them. In response to the possibility of a loss in his business, his
answer is: I have nothing, so I can lose nothing. When faced with losing his
loved ones through death or illness, his attitude is: They mean nothing to
me, so their illness or death doesn't affect me. Before anything can be taken
from him, he has given it away himself. And I continue on my way, always
accumulating the things I will eventually lose and always anxious either
about not having enough of them or, when I have them, about losing them.
Anxious, too, about death.

The greatest violence is your own death—that is, if you fight it. Sevantibhai has even triumphed over death. He has divested himself of
everything—family, possessions, pleasure—that is death's due. All that
remains is his body, to which he has renounced title in advance and treats as
a borrowed, soiled shirt. He can't wait to take it off. Sevantibhai has beat
death to the end. He has resigned before he could be dismissed.

A Self in the Crowd

DURING UTRAN I take the children to my cousin's in-laws' place in Prarthana Samaj, in the central city. I remember this festival well and with pleasure. On this day we flew kites, very simple contraptions made of tissue paper and twigs, and as they rose in the sky we guided them, adjusting them minutely by letting the string run free or taut, feeling the flight far, far above the concrete city. My heart ran free in the sky. When the kites ripped, we repaired the tears with a paste made with mushed leftover boiled rice and water. We got on the roof and dueled with kites from surrounding buildings. The string was studded with glass to cut through the rival's string; many a boy lost a digit when it ran free and sliced clean through his finger. When we won a kite fight, a mighty shout went up, "Kaaayyypooo che!" The boys these days install powerful loudspeakers on the terraces of their buildings during Utran. When a duel is won, the speakers boom out all over the victorious skies the voice of that lost Bombay boy Freddie Mercury: "We are the champions!"

There are many of my cousin's relatives on the roof, and they adore his new son. They are nice to my kids too, but it is not the same: We are not immediate family. Holding my boys' hands, I feel the difference keenly. They watch the kite fliers, again from the outside.

"Why do you want to go back to America?" I ask Gautama, as we're walking back one day from our snack on Pali Hill, after he's picked up a yellow-and-white champak flower and I've shown him how—by folding the petals back and threading them through the stem—he can make a brooch for his mother; after I've shown him the seed pod that makes a good rattle for Akash if you shake it.

He doesn't answer for a while. I ask him again. I bend down to his level and ask him seriously.

"Because my family there misses me. They say it every time on the phone."

It's a good enough reason to go back: because your family misses you. It's the reason I've gone back, been pulled back, again and again. Family is there—not just parents but grandparents, aunts, cousins—and family is what little children need, more than culture, more than country. So just when we finally get comfortable in Bombay, we prepare to move again— back to New York. But it's all right, because, after two and a half years, my question has been answered. You can go home again, and you can also leave again. Once more, with confidence, into the world.

My last day in Bombay is a Sunday, the beginning or the end of the week. I have a big lunch at Khichdi Samrat, a dive in Madhavbagh. They serve khichdi of several kinds out of vast vats, and bring it to your table with a little kadhi and pickle. Along with cauliflower parathas, sev tamatar ki sabzi, pappadams, and some cold buttermilk that comes to your table in a beer bottle, it makes for a fine meal. Then I wander around CP Tank buying incense, drinking a masala Coke, and looking for cast-iron vessels to take to New York. Cast-iron vessels aren't in fashion these days; people prefer stainless steel or aluminum or nonstick. The few people I meet on the road profess not to know about any shop that sells them and tell me that if by some miracle I were to find one, it would be shut anyway. It is a Sunday afternoon, when Bombay exhales. In these parts, they have had their mango pulp and puris and are supine under the fan. Then I inquire at a used-paper seller, and he sends a boy to rouse a man living above a shop with its shutters down. The man comes out in a lungi, and I tell him what I am looking for. He disappears behind the shutters and comes out again with a set of four little cast-iron bowls for tempering. They are 15 rupees each, really nothing, and I buy all four. He has risen from his Sunday-afternoon slumber to sell something that makes him very little profit. I don't know why he would make an exception to his business hours for me; maybe he appreciates the fact that I am out on this quest in the July heat. But he has done something important, on my last day, for my sense of my place in the city I have grown up in.

The Country of the No has become, in that one small gesture, the Country of the Yes. I now realize that if you refuse to understand the No, pretend it doesn't exist, was never said, then, slain by your incomprehension, it will transform itself abruptly into its opposite. Or it might never become a Yes but will turn into a wagging of the head, which can mean either No or Yes, depending on your interpretation. You will interpret the wagging generously, charitably, and proceed.

We fought with Bombay, fought hard, and it made a place for us. I went home and they opened the door and took me in, and they took in my wife and foreign children and made them feel it could be their home too. They gave me the food I liked to eat, and played for me the music I liked to hear, though I had forgotten how much I liked that music. They asked me to write for them—for their movies, for their newspapers. "As a concerned citizen, we want to know what you feel about Kargil," the editor of a book of essays on the war asked me. I was given a place here that I've never had in the country I'm going back to, a voice in the national debate. "How are you going to go back to New York after this?" actresses, accountants, whores, and murderers ask me. "New York will be boring."

After two and a half years, I have learnt to see beyond the wreck of the physical city to the incandescent life force of its inhabitants. People associate Bombay with death too easily. When five hundred new people come in every day to live, Bombay is certainly not a dying city. A killing city, maybe; but not a dying city. When I first came here I thought I was here in the city's final stages. Then I moved to a nicer apartment. A city is only as thriving or sickly as your place in it. Each Bombayite inhabits his own Bombay.

BECAUSE I HAD BEEN AWAY and then returned, I was alert to what had changed: the way the colors of the buildings had faded, the extent to which the banyan tree shading the bus stop had grown. If it had been cut down altogether, I remembered that there had been one there. I had left as a teenager, spent twenty-one years wandering around the cold countries of the world, and returned to resume an interrupted adolescence. I had the freedom—indeed, the mission—to follow everything that made me curious as a child: cops, gangsters, painted women, movie stars, people who give up the world. Why did I choose to follow these particular people and not others? They were, for the most part, morally compromised people, each one shaped by the exigencies of city living. What I found in most of my Bombay characters was freedom. The pursuit of a life unencumbered by minutiae. Most of them don't pay taxes, don't fill out forms. They don't stay in one place or in one relationship long enough to build up assets. When I get back I will have to deal with minutiae: send out invoices on time, balance my checkbook, worry about insurance. Surviving in a modern country involves dealing with an immense amount of paper. He who can stay on top of the paper wins.

Each of us has an inner extremity. Most of us live guarded lives and resist any pull that takes us too far toward this extremity. We watch other people push the limits, follow them up to a point, but are then pulled back, by fear, by family. In Bombay I met people who lived closer to their seductive extremities than anyone I had ever known. Shouted lives. Ajay and Satish and Sunil live on the extreme of violence; Monalisa and Vinod live on the extreme of spectacle; Honey is on the extreme of gender; the Jains go beyond the extreme of abandonment. These are not normal people. They live out the fantasies of normal people. And the kind of work they do affects all other spheres of their lives, till there is no separation between the work and the life. They can never leave behind the work at the bar or the police station or the political party office; in this sense they have all become artists. The attraction, the immense relief, of total breakdown, a renunciation of order in one's life, of all the effort required to keep it together! Since I couldn't do it in my own life, I followed others who did and who invited me to watch. I sat right at the edge of the stage, scattering these pieces of paper over them as payment. And in watching them I followed them closer to my own extremity, closer than I had ever been.

Bombay itself is reaching its own extremity: 23 million people by 2015. The city's population, which should halve, actually doubles. Walking alongside every person in the throng on the streets today will be one more person tomorrow. With every year Bombay is a city growing more and more public, the world outside gradually crowding the world inside. In the mad rush of a Bombay train, each one of the herd needs, as a survival mechanism, to focus on what is most powerfully himself and to hold on to it for dear life. A solitary human being here has two choices: He can be subsumed within the crowd, reduce himself to a cell of a larger organism (which is essential to the makeup of a riot), or he can retain a stubborn, almost obdurate sense of his own individuality. Each person in that train has a sense of style: the way he combs his hair, the talent he has for making sculptures out of seashells, an ability to blow up a hot-water bottle till it bursts. A character quirk or eccentricity, extrapolated into a whole theory of selfhood. I always found it easy to talk to people in a crowd in Bombay because each one had distinct, even eccentric, opinions. They had not yet been programmed.

The Battle of Bombay is the battle of the self against the crowd. In a city of 14 million people, how much value is associated with the number one? The battle is Man against the Metropolis, which is only the infinite extension of Man and the demon against which he must constantly strive to establish himself or be annihilated. A city is an agglomeration of individual dreams, a mass dream of the crowd. In order for the dream life of a city to stay vital, each individual dream has to stay vital. Monalisa needs to believe she will be Miss India. Ajay needs to believe he will escape the police force. Girish needs to believe he will be a computer magnate. The reason a human being can live in a Bombay slum and not lose his sanity is that his dream life is bigger than his squalid quarters. It occupies a palace.

But what every Indian also desires, secretly or openly, is to devote his life to a collective larger than himself. The Muslim hit men of the D-Company think of themselves as warriors for the qaum, the universal nation of Islam. Girish wants to bring money home to his family. Sunil claims, when he is not thinking about business, to be working for the nation. For in this country, which of all civilizations has been devoted to the most exquisite consideration of the interior life—of the form, structure, and purpose of the self—we are individually multiple, severally alone.

One blue-bright Bombay morning, in the middle of the masses on the street, I have a vision: that all these individuals, each with his or her own favorite song and hairstyle, each tormented by an exclusive demon, form but the discrete cells of one gigantic organism, one vast but singular intelligence, one sensibility, one consciousness. Each person is the end product of an exquisitely refined specialization and has a particular task to perform, no less and no more important than that of any other of the 6 billion components of the organism. It is a terrifying image. It makes me feel crushed, it eliminates my sense of myself, but it is ultimately comforting because it is such a lovely vision of belonging. All these ill-assorted people walking toward the giant clock on Churchgate: They are me; they are my body and my flesh. The crowd *is* the self, 14 million avatars of it, 14 million celebrations. I will not merge into them; I have elaborated myself into them. And if I understand them well, they will all merge back into me, and the crowd will become the self, one, many-splendored.

AFTERWORD

I woke up in Brooklyn one September morning to find a thick gray cloud outside my window: the debris blowing over the East River from the burning World Trade Center. That morning, in the city I had moved back to, set off a chain of events that decisively changed the nature of the gang-war in the city I had recently left.

In December 2001, Kashmiri separatists attacked the parliament in Delhi, and war almost broke out between India and Pakistan, hampering the movement of men and matériel across the border. President Pervez Musharraf has always publicly denied that Dawood Ibrahim lives in Pakistan. The country's image was not good after it emerged that its intelligence service had fostered the Taliban, and after the murder of Danny Pearl; it would make the country look even worse to be harboring gangsters. In October 2003, the U.S. Treasury Department officially designated Dawood Ibrahim a "global terrorist," saying that the don "has found common cause with Al Qaida, sharing his smuggling routes with the terror syndicate and funding attacks by Islamic extremists aimed at destabilizing the Indian government." It listed him as living in Karachi and published his Pakistani passport number.

The D-Company leaders now live in a constant state of anxiety: They fear being killed or handed over to India as part of a goodwill gesture on the part of their Pakistani hosts; they fear being assassinated by Rajan's men; and, most of all, they fear one another. The fear they use to make their livelihoods, to convince an extortion target to part with millions of rupees without a shot being fired, has come home to stalk them. But the terror in Bombay hasn't stopped. In August 2003, two car bombs went off, at the Gateway of India and in the diamond market, killing 52 and maiming 150 people. It was a form of revenge, again: for the riots in the neighboring state of Gujarat, in which hundreds of Muslims had been burnt alive by Hindu mobs earlier that year. His city again needed Ajay Lal, who was brought in from the railways to take over the investigation.

In September 2000, a squad of Chotta Shakeel's men stormed into a house in Bangkok, where Chotta Rajan was attending a dinner, and blazed away. While the assassins were firing, they kept their cell phones on; Shakeel, sitting in Karachi, had the pleasure of hearing the screams of the traitor as the bullets penetrated his body. Then, as a don in a Hindi film might, Rajan jumped over the balcony and escaped, hobbling away on broken legs. He was last reputed to be in Luxembourg, still controlling, by telephone, what was left of his gang in Bombay. Abu Salem, the man who had ordered the hit on Rakesh Roshan and had threatened Vinod, was arrested in Lisbon in 2003, in the company of a Hindi movie starlet, and is being held pending extradition to India.

Meanwhile, on the ground, the Bombay cops had embarked on a wholesale campaign of encounter killings. In 1998, forty-eight men that the police had labeled "gangsters" were killed in encounters. In 1999, the number shot up to eighty-three and declined slightly to seventy-four in 2000. In 2001, more than a hundred men were shot dead by the Mumbai Police. As the gangwar diminished, the crime columns of the city papers began filling up with unorganized crimes: servants murdering their employers, spurned lovers extracting revenge.

And then, in 2003, came Abdul Karim Telgi. He was a former peanut vendor who had printed 320 billion rupees' worth of forged revenue-stamp forms, one of the biggest corruption scandals in the nation's history. He got away with the forgeries by bribing Bombay's politicians and cops wholesale. The scandal affected all ranks of the police, including the commissioner, who was arrested. So were encounter specialists like Pradeep Sawant, who was packed off to jail, as he never had been for killing human beings. Telgi, it emerged, had been taking his stacks of rupees and blowing them over the dancers at a beer bar called Sapphire, which Honey had just quit after fathering a child, a beautiful, bright-eyed little boy named Love.

ACKNOWLEDGMENTS

GRATEFUL ACKNOWLEDGMENTS TO THE FOLLOWING:

In Bombay: Vasant and Naina Mehta, Anupama and Vidhu Vinod Chopra, Farrokh Chothia, Manjeet Kripalani, Dayanita Singh, Mahesh Bhatt, Tanuja Chandra, Rahul Mehrotra, Naresh Fernandes, Meenakshi Ganguly, Anuradha Tandon, Ali Peter John, Eishaan, Asad bin Saif, Kabir and Sharmistha Mohanty, Adil Jussawala, Rashid Irani, Kumar Ketkar, Foy Nissen, Sameera Khan.

In New York: Ramesh and Usha Mehta, Sejal Mehta, Monica and Anand Mehta, Ashish Shah, Amitav Ghosh, Akhil Sharma, Zia Jaffrey, Somini Sengupta.

In London: Viswanath and Saraswati Bulusu, Ian Jack.

My gurus: James Alan McPherson and U. R. Ananthamurthy, and my agent, Faith Childs.

My editors: David Davidar, Sonny Mehta, Deborah Garrison, Geraldine Cook, Ravi Singh, Vrinda Condillac, Janice Brent.

The Whiting Foundation, the New York Foundation for the Arts, and the MacDowell Colony.

Many of the names in this book have been changed, as has that of the city. Much of this book was made possible through the generous help of people I cannot name. They have my profound thanks.

And most of all, to Sunita, Gautama, Akash. Thanks for bringing me back to the present tense. I owe you.